the portable
petswelcome.com

The Complete Guide to Traveling with Your Pet

the **portable**
petswelcome.com

The Complete Guide to Traveling with Your Pet

 An Imprint of
Hungry Minds, Inc.

HOWELL
BOOK
HOUSE

New York, NY 🌐 Cleveland, OH 🌐 Indianapolis, IN

We'd like to dedicate this book to our pets, who made this book necessary, to our wives, who permitted us to pursue this project, and to our kids, who still have no idea what we do. We bow the petswelcome.com "Not Worthy" bow to Scott Prentzas for finding us—and especially to Mike Singer and Kristi Hart for their hard work and professionalism beyond the call of duty.

Fred N. Grayson
Chris Kingsley

Howell Book House

published by
Hungry Minds, Inc.
909 Third Avenue
New York, NY 10022

www.hungryminds.com

For general information on Hungry Minds' products and services please contact our Customer Care Department within the U.S. at 800-762-2974, outside the U.S. at 317-572-3993 or fax 317-572-4002.

For sales inquiries and reseller information, including discounts, premium and bulk quantity sales, and foreign-language translations, please contact our Customer Care Department at 800-434-3422, fax 317-572-4002, or write to Hungry Minds, Inc., Attn: Customer Care Department, 10475 Crosspoint Boulevard, Indianapolis, IN 46256.

Library of Congress Cataloging-in-Publication Data

The portable petswelcome.com : the complete guide to traveling with your pet / Petswelcome.com with Fred N. Grayson & Chris Kingsley.
   p. cm.
   ISBN 0-7645-6426-9
   1. Pets and travel. 2. Hotels—Pet accommodations—United States—Directories. 3. Hotels—Pet accommodations—Canada—Directories. I. Grayson, Fred N. II.Kingsley, Chris, 1957- III. Petswelcome.com (Firm) IV. Title.
   SF415.45 .P67 2001
   647.9473'01—dc21   2001016661

Manufactured in the United States of America

10 9 8 7 6 5 4 3 2 1

Book and cover design by **Edwin Kuo**

Illustrations by **Zenon Slawinski**

Table of Contents

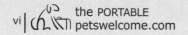
The petswelcome.com Pet-Friendly Seal of Approval

At petswelcome.com, we list thousands of establishments that are pet-accessible, but we pride ourselves in encouraging those establishments that are truly "pet friendly." To further that aim, we have devised a petswelcome.com Pet-friendly Seal of Approval. To receive the seal, a lodging must be nominated by a traveling pet-owner who has stayed at the establishment with his or her pet and had a good experience. The lodging must also adhere to the basic tenants of a charter we established that enumerates the criteria we believe are essential to designating a venue "pet friendly." Look for this Seal of Approval whenever you are traveling with your pet. It ensures that the venue will be happy to welcome your whole family.

a pet-friendly ESTABLISHMENT

petswelcome.com's Pet-Friendly Charter

The following are the minimum criteria for an establishment receiving the Pet Friendly Seal of Approval:

1. **That the establishment accepts pets.**

2. **That persons traveling with a pet are not charged an exorbitant fee for having a pet. And that, if a fee is charged, it is a reasonable amount, reflecting the extra cleaning costs or maintenance expenses the lodging incurs for accepting pets. The fee should not represent a penalty to the pet owner for simply bringing an animal to the premises. The pet owner should not otherwise be financially penalized in any way for having a pet.**

3. **That persons traveling with a pet are not relegated to a smoking room or any other substandard accommodation in that establishment.**

4. **That pets are not forced to be kenneled in substandard facilities while owners are away.**

You will find a book version of the Pet-friendly Seal of Approval in the lodgings sections of The Portable petswelcome.com, as well. It will appear to the left of the name of the establishment:

Majestic Valley Wilderness Lodge
HC03 Box 8514
Palmir, AK 99645
907-746-2930
RATES: Single $60, Double $80
PET POLICY: Fee $20, nonre-fundable, all sizes welcome
AMENITIES: Dog houses, run.
POI: Hiking trails, skiing trails.

Obviously we'd like a pet-friendly establishment to provide amenities that benefit pets, such as a walking area and fresh drinking water. Finally, though, we're more concerned that travelers with pets are at least treated equally and do not feel like second-class citizens upon arriving with their pets.

Once an establishment is nominated for the Pet Friendly Seal of Approval by a traveling pet owner, we will verify that the previously listed conditions are met, place the seal next to its listing, and assist the establishment in becoming even more pet-friendly by providing it with a list of local pet sitters, veterinarians and other pet services to provide to its customers if requested.

If you see the petswelcome.com logo before a listing in this book, you will know that is has been nominated by a traveling pet-owner like yourself. Due to the constraints of space, however, you will not be able read what was said about the establishment but will know that it was extremely pet friendly. If you want to see what was said, you can visit our website, call up the listing, and click on the logo to read the comments.

This charter, then, serves to promote consistent standards of pet-friendliness, as well as the recognition of those standards, through the joint efforts of petswelcome.com and traveling pet owners everywhere.

Introduction

Traveling with a Pet

Why travel with a pet? The answer to this question is as individual and diverse as the personalities of pet owners themselves. Some people want to take their pets every place they go, while others might consider taking them occasionally if the circumstances warrant it. And there are those who would never take their pets anywhere.

Whatever your inclination, it isn't a reflection on your affection for your animal. At petswelcome.com, we don't believe that people who take their pets on trips care about them more than those who don't. It's simply a matter of personal choice. And doggone it, as the television character Stuart Smalley would say, that's okay.

Over the past four years, petswelcome.com (http://www.petswelcome.com) has heard from the gamut of pet owners. Recently we received an e-mail from one man who complained that we were "an embarrassing by-product of a booming economy" and questioned why people would want to treat their dogs like "dress-up dolls" and take them on vacation. "The last thing I want to do is take my animal on vacation," wrote the indignant pet owner.

Okay. That's a legitimate opinion—as are those we receive from other pet owners who won't step out of their homes without taking their "fur babies" with them. We've found that most people, however, aren't so strident. Their attitude falls somewhere in the middle. For the majority of pet owners, taking a pet on vacation is not so much a cause as it is a good idea, once in a while, if it doesn't prove too difficult.

If you'd like to take your pet with you when you travel, you should consider whether the particular trip is compatible with taking along an animal. This requires you to understand your pet's limitations, as well as the limitations of the places and people you'll be visiting.

For example, you may enjoy fine dining and plan to visit a city with a lot of outdoor cafes that allow pets (knowing that most health codes do not permit pets in restaurants). If you own a Yorkie or a Tabby, you should be able to indulge in your passion while satisfying your pet with an occasional mouthful of foie gras or a saucer of milk. However, if you own two Bernese Mountain Dogs, you probably will have a difficult time convincing the cafe owners, not to mention the other patrons, that your dogs won't knock down the overhead canopy or pilfer the steak au poivre from the next table. Of course, *you know* that your two dogs represent the height of sophistication and civility; other people just don't see it.

At the other extreme, if you are headed for the great outdoors, it's not a good idea to bring a cat. But if you own an energetic dog that is usually confined to your house or yard, such a trip could be a unique and wonderful opportunity to take him for a walk and watch him come alive with the sounds, scents and sensory stimulation of a scenic woodland trail.

Obviously, there are no hard and fast rules when it comes to matching pets to places and activities (hey, Bernese Mountain Dogs might love deviled eggs as much as Yorkies—and may actually be a lot calmer in a crowded cafe setting), but you should give extra consideration to the reactions of people who will inevitably be around you.

Taking into account other people is one of the most important considerations you can make when traveling with a pet. They are the x-factor, the great unknown, the missing variable.

You could plan your trip with the thoroughness of a tour director—covering every detail, including the number of water stops you'll be taking and the availability of dog runs, emergency vets and pet sitters at your final destination—only to have your trip ruined because a person in the room next to yours complains to management that your dog barked. And though the hotel billed itself as "pet-friendly," you suddenly are faced with the ultimatum of getting "that animal" under control or leaving the premises for good. It's an unfortunate, but not uncommon, scenario, and one we hear about constantly at petswelcome.com.

It isn't that the public is a rude, intolerant bunch of louts who have no sympathy for pets and that pet owners are always well-meaning victims, but it does point out the extra care that pet owners need to take when bringing their animals out into the real world.

So what's the answer? Again, it's a matter of common sense. As traveling pet owners, you shouldn't constantly cower in fear that your pets are going to offend the public, but you should realize that, fairly or unfairly, the onus is largely on you to prevent unpleasant episodes from occurring. Obviously you can't stop your dog from barking at all times, but you can assess whether your dog barks unduly in unfamiliar settings and, if so, try to find a way to quickly make him feel at home and comfortable upon arriving at your destination.

The good news is that most pet owners are very adept in these situations. Why? Because to own a pet is to be responsible. This dictum does not lose its validity when people take their pets on the road.

At petswelcome.com, we know that pet owners, on the whole, possess an abundance of common sense and are extremely responsible. Still, there is no doubt that there is a prejudice against people who travel with pets. Many inns, B&Bs, hotels and motels, if they accept pets at all, still charge exorbitant nonrefundable fees or relegate pets and their owners to smoking rooms.

However, a change is taking place. More lodgings are beginning to realize that people who show up with pets are extremely considerate and turn out to be ideal guests. We are now finding that many lodgings are not only dispensing with unreasonable, nonrefundable fees, but they are also including various pet amenities, including biscuits upon arrival, water bowls and dog runs. In short, they are beginning to understand that treating pet owners well is not just the right thing to do, it's good business.

So, if you have the inclination, if your trip and pet seem compatible and if you're up for being extra responsible, there should be nothing stopping you, right? Wrong.

What stops most people from bringing along their pets is the certainty of not being allowed in most extra-lodging venues, including restaurants, museums, historic landmarks, theme parks—the list goes on and on. Even if you make a noble effort to stay in the company of your pet for most of the trip, you will certainly find yourself in situations where you can't take your pet with you. And, if your hotel does not allow unattended animals in the room, what do you do?

That's where *The Portable petswelcome.com* comes in. We understand that traveling with a pet is not a novelty; it's a very real challenge.

We started our website back in 1997 because we sensed a need for a common-sense approach to traveling with your pet,

one that considered all the realities and offered the most useful information and practical solutions. While there were guides on the market that touted the fun and novelty of taking along your pet, they usually provided only minimal information with regard to pet-friendly venues—hotel name, address and phone number—as though all pet-friendly lodgings were the same.

As pet owners ourselves, we realized that people needed much more information and support. That's why we've included detailed pet policies and room rates, as well as pet amenities and points of interest, if applicable. Equally important, we understand that you can't take your pet everywhere and that you need other options, like pet sitters or kennels in the vicinity of your vacation destination.

With the advent of the Internet, our mission—to expand the network of pet services that can assist owners who travel with their pets—became possible. Though

the Internet has been overly hyped in the past few years, we realized that its main strength is that it enables people to network and gather information. In a very real way, the Internet erodes the traditional barriers of physical distance with regard to accessing information.

In the past, even if you had the idea to find a pet sitter at your vacation destination, you would have had to call information and blindly search for one or thumb through the Yellow Pages for that area—if you could find one. Now, if you are connected to the Internet, most information is in effect "local," in that you can search for it, punch it up and see it in your own home almost instantly.

In subtle ways, the access to remote information has changed our thinking. That's why *The Portable petswelcome.com* doesn't adhere to the conventional notion that pet sitters are only used at home, but that they can also be used *on the road*. We realized that a pet sitter in Juneau, Alaska, can now be as local as a pet sitter in your own neighborhood.

Why think of pet sitters as professionals who enable you to leave your pet at home? Why not enlist their talents to make it easier to take your pet with you? We believe they can make your trip extremely enjoyable by allowing you peace of mind when you do leave your pet behind, either on day trips or on excursions that will not be pet-friendly. Instead of worrying about whether your pet is coping, alone, in a new and foreign environment, you can feel good that she's in the hands of a professional who will take extra-special care and deliver her back to you, good as new.

The same holds true for kennels and emergency veterinarians. And the networking continues: On our site we are constantly adding more pet-friendly venues, including pet-friendly stores, cafes and bars. Our goal is to let you travel everywhere with your pet. (But remember, if you don't want to—it's *okay*—you're still a good person.)

Beyond making disparate and far-flung services local, the Internet also enables the information to stay current. If a hotel changes its pet policy or is no longer pet-friendly, we can update the listing online immediately. This is critical because the lodging industry has a large turnover rate due to closings, name changes and new ownership. Policies are constantly changing, and the Internet allows us, for the most part, to keep up with them. It also gives pet-friendly venues the ability to contact us quickly and easily.

Within hours of the time that a lodging notifies us of their services and/or pet-friendly amenities, we can post them on our site for all our visitors to see. In short, the instantaneous communication and networking capabilities of the Internet have enabled us to create a reliable safety network that didn't exist previously, one that affords pet owners greater freedom to roam with their pets far from their own locales.

So, why take a pet? The last thing we want is to be called gushy (after all, we run a website and take pride in hip, ironic posturing), but we honestly do believe that, in the right circumstance, a pet can significantly enhance the pleasure of travel. Whatever the reasons you have for taking your pet, it's *The Portable petswelcome.com*'s job to ensure just one: Because you can.

How to Use This Book

The Portable petswelcome.com offers pet owners the best of two worlds. It takes advantage of the virtues of the Internet in that it presents much of the comprehensive, up-to-date information we have on our website, and it offers you the prime virtue of a printed format (or book, if you must be old-fashioned): You can take it with you.

At petswelcome.com, we still believe in the merits of books over gadgets and are confident that this guide will serve pet owners in practical ways that the Internet cannot.

Most of the lodgings listed in this book have contacted us and have filled out a very detailed form to convince us of their pet-friendliness. That's why you can be assured of the reliability of the listings. However, since policies are constantly changing, you can also double-check that the listings are still current by going to our website and searching the city or lodging you are considering.

With regard to our book and website, we always stress the petswelcome.com Golden Rule: always call ahead. In certain sections of this book we elevate the petswelcome.com Golden Rule to the Platinum Rule (*always* call ahead), meaning it's especially important that you call first before utilizing one of our listings. It becomes especially important with businesses that are individually owned and therefore have a greater chance of turnover or changing addresses, etc. The last thing we want is for you to get stuck without any place to turn to. We apply the Platinum rule to many of our Cool Spots, as well as Emergency Vets, Kennels and Pet Sitters. When possible, we will supply the numbers/websites of related professional associations you can call if a listing you have tried in our book cannot be reached.

We have arranged the book for ease of use. In chapter 1, we present our special "best of petswelcome.com" selections. The rest of the book contains separate chapters on lodgings and campgrounds, kennels and pet sitters, and emergency veterinarians. Within each category, the establishments are listed alphabetically by state (with the exception of Canadian lodgings, which have their own section) and then by city within each state.

When you decide on an establishment, we encourage you to visit petswelcome.com for updates. Or, if you can't decide which of several lodging choices is best for your trip, you can use our on-line route planner to help you determine which hotel is closest to your travel route. In fact, on the next page, you can take a peek at how the route planner works. Hey, we want to help make traveling with your pet go as smoothly as possible. Have a nice trip!

THE PETSWELCOME.COM ROUTE PLANNER

Enter the address you'll be leaving from:

Address _____

City _____

State _____

Zip / Postal Code _____

Enter your destination (at least city and state must be filled in):

Address _____

City _____

State _____

Zip / Postal Code _____

Choose the maximum number of miles to search for a pet-friendly lodging off your main route:

❏ 2 miles

❏ 5 miles

❏ 10 miles

❏ 20 miles

Choose the result you'd like to see:

❏ Text Only

❏ Overview Map with Text

❏ Turn-by-Turn Maps with Text

If you'd like to avoid any of the following, please check it:

❏ Avoid Major Highways

❏ Avoid Toll Roads

❏ Avoid Ferry Lanes

Choose the type of directions you want:

❏ Detailed Directions

❏ Summarized Directions

THE PROPOSED ROUTE

From 46th St., Sunnyside, NY 11104, to Mystic Ct., W. Palm Beach, FL 33414.

Directions and Distances

1: Start out going South on 46th St. towards 43rd Ave. by turning left; 0.2 miles (0.3 km).

2: Turn Right onto Queens Blvd.; 0.8 miles (1.2 km).

3: Turn slight Left; 0.0 miles (0.0 km).

4: Turn slight Left onto Van Dam St.; 0.4 miles (0.7 km).

5: Turn Left to take the I-495 W ramp towards Midtown Tunnel/Manhattan; 0.1 miles (0.2 km).

6: Merge onto Long Island Exwy.; 0.8 miles (1.3 km).

7: Long Island Exwy. becomes I-495 W.; 1.5 miles (2.3 km).

. . .

24: Take I-395 S.; 13.4 miles (21.6 km).

25: I-395 S becomes I-95 S.; 916.9 miles (1475.4 km). Following are some of the places to stay

Days Inn; 818 Radford Blvd.; Dillon, SC 29536 US

Days Inn South; I-95 & US 76; Florence, SC 29502 US

Comfort Inn; 249 Britain Street; Santee, SC 29142 US

Holiday Inn; I-95 & US 78; St. George, SC 29477 US

St. George Economy Motel; 125 Motel Drive; St. George, SC 29477 US

Days Inn Stateline; I-95 & US 17, PO Box 1150; Hardeeville, SC 29927 US

Econo Lodge Gateway; 7 Gateway Blvd. W.; Savannah, GA 31419 US

Days Inn; I-95 & US 17; Richmond Hill, GA 31324 US

Townsend Days Inn; P.O. Box 156; Townsend, GA 31331 US

Embassy Suites Brunswick - Golden Isles; 500 Mall Boulevard; Brunswick, GA 31525 US

Baymont Inn & Suites - Brunswick; 105 Tourist Drive; Brunswick, GA 31520 US

Days Inn Kingsland; 1050 E. King Avenue; Kingsland, GA 31548 US

26: Take the SR-70/Okeechobee Blvd. exit, exit 65; 0.3 miles (0.4 km).

27: Merge onto FL-70 W.; 0.6 miles (0.9 km).

28: Turn Left to take the Florida's Turnpike ramp; 0.6 miles (1.0 km).

29: Merge onto Florida's Turnpike S (Portions toll); 52.5 miles (84.4 km).

30: Take the SR-704/Okeechobee Blvd. exit, exit 99, towards W. Palm Bch.; 0.6 miles (1.0 km).

. . .

37: Turn Left onto Stratford St.; 0.2 miles (0.3 km).

38: Turn Right onto Mystic Ct.; 0.0 miles (0.0 km).

Total Distance: 1227.1 miles (1974.5 km), **Estimated Time:** 21 hours, 4 minutes.

1

The Best of petswelcome.com:

Truly Cool Spots to Go with Your Pet

At petswelcome.com, it's always been our philosophy that taking a pet on a trip requires more than just finding a pet-friendly lodging. Beyond securing a pet sitter (if necessary) and taking your pet for walks around the lodging grounds, we highly recommend stepping out with your four-legged friend to explore the area and to visit cool places that might not ordinarily be thought of as pet-friendly. After all, you don't want to drag your German Shepherd halfway across the country in your car just to walk her on a different street.

We encourage you to visit bars, restaurants, museums or anyplace that is fun and that allows your pet to share the experience with you. Wouldn't it be great to sit in a bar in Key West with your Golden Retriever, nursing a beer, as both of you watch the sun go down? Accordingly, at petswelcome.com, we strive to enhance our listings of accommodations, pet sitters, kennels and veterinarians with unique, perhaps offbeat, places you can go with your pet once you get there—wherever there is.

Whatever you like to do, whether it's going for a swim, watching a baseball game, shopping or just hanging out at a bar, there are places for you and your pet, and you can search our website to determine if that activity is available at your destination. For *The Portable petswelcome.com,* we thought it best to give you our "best of" selections to give you a start and an idea of the panoply of activities awaiting you, and that's what this chapter is all about.

The great thing about these pet-friendly establishments and events is that you can finally drop your defenses. As we mentioned in the introduction to this book, one of the most trying aspects of traveling with a pet is worrying about the non-pet-owning public you'll inevitably be in contact with. However, that's not a problem when you step into one of these pet-friendly places: You'll be among your own—hobnobbing with other pet owners who are happy to see you *and* your pet. So, who cares if your Rottweiler rips the taco out of the mouth of the woman sitting next to you? Instead of a lawsuit, you'll probably have a friend for life. Well, that might be an exaggeration, but it's our experience that when two people meet with pets, they usually greet each other with smiles and exhibit infinite patience with the other person's pet. This usually leads to a laugh or two and a friendly conversation as their respective pets get to know each other in the way pets get to know each other.

While we'd like to take the credit for finding all these places ourselves, a sense of appreciation (as well as various plagiarism and libel statutes) compel us to share the kudos with many of our visitors at petswelcome.com. Every week we get e-mail from travelers who have found offbeat places to take their pets. One of the great enjoyments we get at petswelcome.com is passing that information on to other pet-owners who can then enjoy the find for themselves.

That is also what this chapter is about: sharing discoveries. The diversity of these venues always startles us and keeps us looking for more. (We've even found a few community colleges that accept pets. Unfortunately, our legal counsel, a much-decorated Water Spaniel named Ch. Whatsinitforme, has advised us not to publish the institutions' names because of a threat of legal action from various human alumni now holding high public office.) No matter—it's our mission to keep discovering new, offbeat pet-friendly venues so pet owners will have a wide variety of options to choose from when they're on the road.

To this end, we've even started a pets-welcome.com Watchdog Club to encourage pet owners to tell us about neat pet-friendly places that they've found on their own. Every week we award a Watchdog T-shirt to the best entry. So if you find any places we don't list in the book—or on our site—please join the club. You might even win a cheesy T-shirt. More importantly, though, you'll be helping out traveling pet owners everywhere who would love to take their pets to these unique and interesting places.

The Golden Rule at petswelcome.com is *always call ahead* before you take your pet with you. With regard to these "Truly Cool Spots" it becomes the Platinum Rule—that is to say, it's even more important that you call. Since many of these places are not traditional pet-friendly venues or territories, we don't want you getting in trouble when you show up with your dog. The last thing we want is for you to discover a pet-friendly jail because the manager or owner of one of these places called the police when you arrived with your Irish Setter. We're sure that won't happen, but we still highly recommend calling first. Then, once you are confident in your plans, you will find that by going to one of these cool and unique spots with your pet you will be doing much more than just dragging along your animal on vacation—you will be reveling in the experience of discovering new and fun places together.

Amusement Parks

Canobie Lake Park
85 N. Policy St. (Rte. 93, Exit 2)
Salem, NH 03079
603-893-3506

Very small, quaint and beautiful, this park has been around since 1902. It's not big and flashy, and doesn't have a lot of extreme rides like many of the newer parks, but there are very beautiful gardens and a picnic area right on the shore of Canobie Lake and fireworks on the weekends. It's a great place to spend the day with your pet (though animals are not allowed on the rides). Please note that they do discriminate against Pit Bulls and Rottweilers.

Dollywood
1020 Dollywood Ln.
Pigeon Forge, TN 37863
865-428-9488

While lots of amusement parks have kennel facilities for dogs, Dollywood allows you to take your pet into the park and theaters, as well as on a 5-mile train ride through the surrounding park. Dogs must be leashed and aren't permitted on most rides or in restaurants.

Bakeries/Food Service

Doggie Drive-Thru
2639 S. 3rd Street
Niles, MI 49120
616-683-7511

This drive-through restaurant for dogs also has a bakery with fresh treats, one-on-one pet nanny services, a U-Wash pet wash and natural chew toys.

Three Dog Bakery
16 Eureka St.
Sutter Creek, CA 95685
209-274-6305

This is a great place to take your dog for birthday parties, treats or just a special day out.

(There are approximately 30 Three Dog Bakeries throughout the US. You can visit their website at www.threedogs.com or call 1-800-487-3287 for more information.)

Bars/Restaurants

Archie's on the Beach (Archie's Seabreeze)
401 So. Ocean Drive
Ft. Pierce, FL 34949
561-461-3352

Bring your dog or another favorite pet to this indoor-outdoor bar and restaurant on the beach. Their motto is "No shirt, No shoes ... No problem!" You can get great burgers, and hear great blues music on Sunday afternoons.

Barking Dog Luncheonette
1678 Third Ave.
New York, NY 10128
212-831-1800

NYC's upper east side is the home of this nice, casual dog-themed restaurant. They allow pets in their out-door cafe, and even have a "dog bar" water trough in case your best friend gets thirsty.

Cafe Giardinetto
250 E. 40th St.
New York, NY 10016
212-599-2992

Outdoor cafes are the perfect place to watch the world go by with your furry companion. At Café Giardinetto, you and your dog can feast on grilled chicken, grilled ham and, of course, dog biscuits (if she still finds them palatable after munching on Chilled Asparagus Tips).

Empire Diner
210 Tenth Ave. at 22nd St.
New York, NY 10011
212-243-2736

Your pet's "order" is served in a special bowl. They seem to anticipate visits and always have treats available.

Schooner Wharf Bar
202 William St.
Key West, FL 33040
305-292-9520

All the local dogs hang out at this waterfront, open-air bar to watch the sunset.

Beaches/Parks

Please note that with regard to many beaches and some parks, it is nearly impossible to give an address or phone number. We get a huge amount of requests—and reports—about pet-friendly beaches and parks and have decided to list them with the city name and state if we can get no further information. In such cases we leave it to you and your dog to sniff out the exact location once you're there. Think of it as a voyage of discovery. Besides, it's usually pretty easy—just ask somebody else walking their dog, and you and your wave-surfin' pup will be in the foam in no time.

Bay of Fundy
New Brunswick/Nova Scotia, Canada

This is where the world's highest tides come in and go out to the delight of visitors from all over the world. When the tide goes out, the depressed among us look at the empty ocean bottom puddled with sea water and think of a vast, empty wasteland; the hungry among us think of it as a huge opportunity for some very fresh clam chowder—but those of us with dogs think "FRISBEE!" and "ROMP, ROMP, ROMP!" Spend an afternoon with your dog in the bay (before the tide comes in!) and then relax and watch the water come back to tickle your toes—and your dog's paws.

Dog Beach
San Diego, CA

Located in Ocean Beach (part of San Diego), this is a great open stretch of beach where the dogs are free to run with no leash or other restriction. Dogs are also welcome in the water. The beach is open year-round. The local authorities only ask that pet owners come with plastic bags and clean up after their pets.

Henry's Beach
Santa Barbara, CA

Henry's is a favorite—though many of Santa Barbara's beaches are very dog friendly. You can't miss having a good time with your pet at any one of them.

Hilton Head Island
Hilton Head, SC

Labor Day through Memorial Day is the prime time to take your pooch to the beach on Hilton Head Island. Dogs are also welcome on the island's numerous bike paths. In the summer they're allowed on the beaches only before 10 A.M. and after 5 P.M.

McCormick Park
Tucson, AZ

The coolest park in town has a section set aside for pets, which has pet exercise equipment and was created to let pet lovers gather and schmooze. It's also a great place for singles to meet (but that wasn't the real intention).

Point Isabelle Park
Richmond, CA

This is a large open area where pets of all shapes and sizes can be off-leash and enjoy seaside romps (in the water and out) with other pets, free of charge. Free dog waste pickup bags and receptacles are also available, as well as a full-service dog-washing hut (for a small fee) to wash your dirty dog after a romp (for a small fee). A coffee house and information kiosks are provided for the human companions.

Whitefish Dunes State Park
3701 Clark Lake Rd.
Sturgeon Bay, WI 54235
920-823-2400

In this tourist hot spot, you and your pet—who must always be leashed—can enjoy over a mile of beautiful, sandy Lake Michigan beach, 14 or so miles of hiking trails and some rocky limestone shoreline and cliffs. This is one of the few state parks where pets are allowed on the entire beach. The only place pets aren't permitted are the picnic area and interpretive loop. You must always clean up after your pet. In the winter, pets are allowed on any trails not groomed for cross-country skiing. *Note:* the dunes are protected as a State Natural Area (many endangered and threatened resources), so no dune climbing for you or your pet. Located in Door County, it is about 13 miles north of Sturgeon Bay off Hwy. 57 on Cty. Hwy. WD.

Dog Camps

Camp Gone-to-the-Dogs
PO Box 600
Putney, VT 05346
802-387-5673

Owners and their dogs spend a week here enjoying all aspects about dogs: training, obedience, agility, tracking, flyball, hunting, herding, handling, swimming lessons and lectures—about 50 activities a day. Daily attendance is 7 A.M. to 9 P.M. for 120 people during June, July, August and September.

Camp Winnaribbun
PO Box 50300
Reno, NV 89513
702-747-1561

Owners and their dogs spend a week here enjoying all types of activities, competitions, herding, tracking, obedience, flyball, crafts for the owners, talent shows, evening programs, photo sessions and so on.

Dog Days of Wisconsin—Summer Camp
1879 Haymarket #24
Waukesha, WI 53189
800-226-7436
Three-day seminars include obedience training, agility, grooming animal behavior. Lodging/camping on premises.

Dog Scouts of America
5068 Nestel Road
St. Helen, MI 48656
517-389-2000
In the summer there's a series of 5-day camp vacations with pets and their owners that promote responsible pet ownership, including training, leadership, sports and other activities.

Events

Annual Reindog Parade (December)
Charleston, WV
304-348-6419
304-346-6792
Music, costumes, contests and a whole lot of fun as a holiday parade of pooches take to the streets decked-out in their holiday finery. Proceeds to help Animal Aid

Best Costumed Pet Competition (October)
Rehoboth Beach, DE
800-441-1329
Dress up your pet on the last October weekend each year at The Sea Witch Festival.

Boston Pops Fourth of July Concert
See the entry under "Fine Arts" later in this chapter for details.

Bernese Mountain Dog Walk (October)
Ridgefield, CT
203-438-1616
More than 250 Bernese Mountain Dogs parade with their owners along Main Street, from the Fountain to town at this annual event.

Dog Day at Comiskey Park
Chicago, IL
312-674-1000
Home of the Chicago White Sox, Comiskey Park lets you bring your dog with you to watch the game—and get treats, too!

Dog Days Contest (end of August)
Smithfield, VA
757-357-3288
Competitions for different classes of dogs of all sorts are held behind the old courthouse on Main Street. Prizes and gift certificates are awarded.

Dogs Walk Against Cancer (May)
American Cancer Society
Riverside Park
New York, NY
212-586-8700
A great time is had by all when thousands show up to raise money for cancer research (10% for animals, 90% for humans). Music, contests, gifts—a great way to spend an afternoon.

St. Hubert's Dog Walk and Fair (May)
Madison, NJ
973-514-5888
This annual festival for dogs benefits a major animal shelter. Take your dog on a two-mile fun walk—all breeds welcome—around the beautiful gardens of Giralda Farms, and enjoy canine-related activities and games.

Trailside Nature & Science Center Pet Fair (1st Sunday in May)
Mountainside, NJ
908-789-3670
Enjoy presentations, photos, contests, displays, adoptions and more with your pet.

Wiener Dog Race/Oktoberfest (October)
Savannah, GA
912-234-0295
As part of the annual Oktoberfest celebration, the Wiener Dog Race features all types of dogs, but primarily dachshunds, and is held along the Savannah River over two days.

Fine Arts

Boston Pops Fourth of July Concert
Hatch Memorial Shell
Charles River esplanade
Boston, MA
1-888-4TH-POPS
If you don't plan on sitting to close to the Hatch Shell, just bring a blanket and other essentials (water, Frisbee, chew toys) and park yourself near the Charles River. The show starts at 8 P.M., but get there a lot earlier because a quarter of a million other people have the same idea. Also, there are fireworks after the concert, so make sure your pooch can handle the noise.

National Bird Dog Museum/ Field Trial Hall of Fame
Grand Junction, TN 38008
901-764-2058
Over 40 breeds of bird dog portraits, art, displays, various exhibits and a gift shop are presented for you and your dog to enjoy. Dogs eat this stuff up. Curiously, Abstract Expressionism leaves them cold.

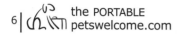
Stephen Huneck Gallery

49 Central St.
Woodstock, VT 05091
802-457-3206

What could be better than an art gallery where your dog is actually welcomed with oohs, coos and biscuits? Watch as your pet walks over to the slightly-larger-than-life-size statue of Huneck's infamous black dog and sniffs its, well . . . tail. Also for sale are framed prints and unique furniture, such as tables and benches.

Historic Places

Colonial Williamsburg

Williamsburg, VA

History is for the dogs, some might say, and it has never been truer than at this re-creation of an eighteenth-century village where pets can stroll through Market Square and Duke of Gloucester Street, and ride with you on the shuttle buses. Dogs are not allowed in the historic buildings, but they really don't seem to mind.

Historic Concord Walking Tour

Concord, MA

Your dog can enjoy a history lesson as you both explore Hawthorne's and Emerson's old stomping grounds. There's also a ton of fascinating Revolutionary War sites as well. Your dog can't go into the buildings, but he'll probably be more interested in the historic fire hydrants (if there are any) than Louisa May Alcott's house anyway. Maps are available at the North Bridge Visitor Center.

Magnolia Plantation and Gardens

Charleston, SC

Pets are permitted to roam the grounds—and especially enjoy the large labyrinth made out of shrubbery.

Mt. Vernon

PO Box 110
Mt. Vernon, VA 22121
703-780-2000

Many people don't realize that pets are allowed on the grounds of Mt. Vernon, George Washington's estate just outside of Washington, DC. Even Martha didn't know it. Pets are not, however, allowed in the buildings.

Old Sturbridge Village

Sturbridge, MA
800-SEE-1830 (733-1830)

Bring your pets to Old Sturbridge Village and enjoy a day exploring these historic households and shops with your "best friend." There are plenty of pet-friendly hotels in Sturbridge, as well as nearby antiquing, walking and hiking trails and outlet stores.

The Mall

Washington, DC

Your dog might not be able to run for office, but he can run his tail off on the Mall—from the Capitol to the Washington Monument. Dogs are officially restricted to leashes, but we see an awful lot of dogs off-leash playing Frisbee with their owners. Hey, if you're going to rebel and break a stupid little rule by letting your dog run free, you might as well do it right under the nose of "The Man." It's very American and can be explained in court as "exercising my patriotic birthright, Your Honor, Your Reverence, Sir."

Religious

Stephen Huneck Dog Chapel

Spaulding Rd.
St. Johnsbury, VT
802-748-2700

As you traverse these 150 acres, you'll encounter wonderful vistas, outdoor sculptures and a chapel with stained glass windows. About this most personal piece of artwork, Artist Stephen Huneck writes that it celebrates "the spiritual bond we have with our dogs" and is "open to dogs and people of any faith or belief system." Amen.

Resorts

Marsh Harbor

Grand Bahama Island, Bahamas

The islands of Abacoa off Grand Bahama Island in the Bahamas. These islands are very dog friendly. All outdoor restaurants welcome pets, as do the beaches. The people of these islands love dogs.

Marriott Laguna Cliffs Resort

25135 Street of the Park Lantern
Dana Point, CA
949-661-5000

If you call ahead with reservations, they have a little "doggy" gift for your pet. They charge an additional $50 per visit (not per night) so that they can clean the room properly afterwards—not necessarily for damage but for clients with allergies. There are loads of green areas and walking trails, and it's very close to the beach and Dana Point harbor.

Retail

Chinook Bookstore
210 N. Tejon St.
Colorado Springs, CO 80903
719-635-1195

This independently owned bookstore keeps treats behind the counter, and the clerks fight over who gets to give them out while you browse their bookshelves. There are chairs to sit on while you peruse your next purchase.

Home Depot
325 120th Ave. NE
Bellevue, WA 9800
425-451-7351

Employees at this particular Home Depot are always very friendly and stop to admire dogs of all kinds. Just put a blanket down in a shopping cart and head for the lumber section (to build a dog house, of course).

Paragon Sports
867 Broadway (at 18th St.)
New York, NY 10003
212-255-8036

There are always some doggies roaming around with their masters here—or sitting patiently while the two-leggers try on 18 different pairs of hiking boots. It'll all be worth it in the end, however; the better the boot, the less they'll have to wait around looking "engaged" on the next nature hike while their eco-challenged owners huff-and-puff to catch up with them.

Stanford Shopping Center
680 Stanford Shopping Center
Palo Alto, CA 94301
650-617-8230

This is an outdoor mall with many cafes and eating places. You can eat outside and enjoy the great weather while in the company of your pet.

2 Before You Leave Home

You've given it a lot of thought, and you're ready to take your pet with you. What's the game plan? Success largely depends on thorough preparation and a basic knowledge of what your pet will need while you are on the road. You should also be aware of the rules, regulations and pet policies not only at your destination, but at all the stops in between. If you are leaving the country or the continental United States, it is especially important to plan well ahead of time. Canada, for example, requires that cats or dogs entering the country from the United States have certification signed by a licensed veterinarian stating that the animal was vaccinated against rabies during the preceding 36-month period. Hawaii requires a 120-day quarantine even if you are traveling from the mainland United States. Some countries, such as the United Kingdom, have much lengthier quarantines that make it virtually impossible to take your pet on vacation. Taking the time to do a little research before your trip will save you a lot of trouble and make it much more enjoyable for both you and your pet.

Before leaving, you should always have your veterinarian examine your pet to make sure that he is in good health and that vaccinations are up to date. Schedule an appointment well ahead of the departure date so that your pet can receive any required inoculations. If your animal is on medication, make sure your vet prescribes enough medicine to cover the whole trip. Also, if your pet is excitable or has a history of difficulty when traveling, ask your vet about prescribing sedatives or tranquilizers. (Do not use sedatives if your pet is flying—

they do not mix well with high altitudes.) If you do give your pet tranquilizers, observe him closely after administering the first dose to make sure that the proper effect is achieved.

It is a good idea to take along a health certificate when traveling with your pet. A health certificate is a document you can obtain from your vet certifying that your pet is in good health. It should contain a description of your pet, his vaccination history and a statement that he is free from infectious diseases. Make sure the health certificate is up to date and meets the requirements of the locale you are visiting. Do not assume that the certificate you used last year will work again this year.

Preparing Your Pet

Most likely, your animal will be thrilled to be traveling with you. But happiness can be fleeting if your pet is not prepared for the realities he will face when he finally leaves your home. What are the realities?

First, your pet will be subjected to a radical change of schedule. Many pets are extreme creatures of habit. Milo, the resident Vizsla at petswelcome.com, likes to lay on the porch in the sun at exactly 11 A.M. everyday and then move inside to a couch at about 1 P.M. Around 3:25 P.M., he gets up and readies to bark at the beagle who is always walked by the offices at 3:30 P.M. He only starts showing real signs of life at about 5 P.M., when he expects to be let loose in a field down the road for a run before dinner. You get the idea.

If you pop your pet in a car and take him to a hotel room for a few days where he

Traveling with a Ferret

No matter what type of animal you take with you on a trip, certain general commonsense rules always apply. Make sure your pet has ample food, water, room, exercise and a portable carrier or cage to keep her contained. Other items to pack when bringing along a ferret are

- Proof of current rabies vaccination and a health certificate issued by a vet

- A harness and leash

- Litter box and litter

- A change of bedding

- *Lots* of toys

With a ferret, you need to be aware of existing prejudices and make sure you don't take him where he's not appreciated—or not legally allowed (called ferret-free zones). While the United States Department of Agriculture designates ferrets as domesticated animals, there are some state agencies that classify ferrets as wild or exotic animals. This means that special rules apply and that they are not allowed in certain designated places. While Hawaii and California are the only states that still outlaw ferrets, don't assume that you can take your ferret anywhere else in the United States. Many cities have their own rules regarding ferrets and may not allow your pet to visit. The best method of finding out whether your ferret will be welcome is to call the local Fish and Game Department, Wildlife Department or Department of Conservation of the place you'll be visiting.

If you are flying, the same basic rules apply as with dogs and cats (see the section below, "Traveling by Plane"), but make sure the airline has no special restrictions against ferrets. If you are going international, always find out the particular country's pet and quarantine policies.

can't enjoy any of his customary pleasures, there's a real possibility he's going to start acting a little restless and uncomfortable. So we suggest that before you leave on your trip, you get your pet out of the house on drives or visits to friends. This will disrupt the usual schedule and let you know how amenable your animal will be to new circumstances and environments. We also advise that you take along your pet's favorite blanket or toy, something that will make him feel at home while in unfamiliar surroundings.

During any trip, there's a good chance your pet will be spending a lot of time in a carrier or portable kennel. That's why it's one of the most useful items you can take on your trip. It will become your pet's home while he's away from your home, so it's a good idea to acclimate him to it weeks ahead of time. If you are traveling by air, make sure you put food and water dishes into the carrier. If you are traveling by car, make sure the carrier is well secured. Take your pet out for short drives before the trip so he will feel comfortable in the carrier by the time you leave. If your dog has been crate-trained, you should have no problem making the transition to a portable kennel. If it's not too big, you can even bring along the dog's crate.

In addition to taking a portable kennel or carrier, a blanket and a toy, other essentials include a supply of your pet's regular food, his food and water bowls, a leash, grooming supplies, a first-aid kit, room deodorizer or freshener, and a pooper scooper and/or plastic bags. If you are going camping or if you will be in a rural area, make sure your pet's flea collar has not expired, and bring along extra spray or liquid flea and tick repellent. Always carry a supply of drinking water. In addition, make sure that your pet's identification and rabies tags are firmly attached to his collar. If you are staying at one destination for a long time, it's a good idea to include the address of that destination on an ID tag, along with your permanent address.

Finally, do not feed your pet immediately before leaving on your trip. Feed him a light meal and some water about four hours before you leave. This holds true regardless of the type of transportation being taken. Traveling can upset an animal's stomach, so it's preferable to keep feeding to a minimum while on the road.

Traveling by Car

MacDuff and Lola, two Gordon Setters at petswelcome.com, love to travel in the car. Whenever they sense that we're going somewhere, they both bound down the stairs, race out the door and wait impatiently for the back of the SUV to pop open so they can jump in. If you listen closely under their panting, you can hear them say, "Take me. Take me. Take me." They've gone on a lot of trips and know that even a long car ride can be an enjoyable experience.

If you are driving and want to make it an enjoyable experience, make sure your pet is comfortable traveling in your car. Unless he is very young, he probably has taken a few rides with you to the vet or other places, so you should have a pretty good idea of how he will behave in the car. Of course, if you are taking your pet on vacation, he will be spending a lot more time in the car than he usually does. If your pet is not generally comfortable when you're driving, it's a good idea to take some longer rides in the weeks before you leave to help him settle down and become resigned to the reality of the world passing by at 55 or more miles per hour.

You should confine your pet to a portable kennel or carrier while he's in the car. If you don't want to do this, there are a number of other options. If you own a station wagon, SUV, or any vehicle with back seats that fold down, you can use a pet gate or divider that keeps your dog in the back section of the vehicle. There are also dog "seatbelts" and restraint harnesses available on the market. They will allow your family more contact with your pet while driving. The main consideration, however, should be to prevent your animal from having access to the driver and from being tossed around while your vehicle is in motion.

Once you're on the road, never let your animal stick his head out of the window, even though he might thoroughly enjoy it. Your pet's eyes and nose are extremely sensitive and can be harmed by flying insects or other debris. Also, make sure to schedule stops at regular intervals to allow for a small drink and a short walk. Always exercise your animal on a leash, and always attach the leash before you open the car door. Even if your animal is well-behaved off the leash at home, highway rest stops are extremely dangerous places because of the high volume of traffic, not to mention the dangerous distractions of unfamiliar people and animals.

Never leave your pet unattended in a car at any time. In warm climates, heat can be a real danger. Beyond that, however, there is also the very real possibility of animal theft. While you are parked, at least one family member should stay with the pet. Also, whether you are parked or moving, think about running a small, portable solar-powered fan; this is a nice travel amenity to help keep air moving in the car.

What About Birds?

Just as there are many people who can't bear to leave their furry friends behind, there are a lot who feel the same way about their feathered counterparts. Since birds are more easily frightened and much more susceptible to drafts and changes of temperature, it's important to take extra-special care when traveling with them. Here are some general travel tips for birds:

- Have your bird checked by a vet before leaving.

- If you have a large cage, use a smaller one or a travel carrier.

- Keep his cage or carrier covered when on the road.

- Remove water and any swinging toys from the cage.

- Avoid weather extremes.

- Take along a spray water bottle for cooling and cleaning.

- Let airlines and hotels know that you are traveling with a bird.

- Bring enough food and water, and keep to your bird's normal feeding and sleeping schedule.

Traveling by Plane

Traveling with your pet on a commercial airliner can be risky and, in most instances, should be avoided unless there is absolutely no alternative. Of the three primary ways your pet can travel on a commercial plane—as carry-on luggage, as checked baggage or as cargo—the preferable way is as carry-on luggage. This method is obviously the safest because your pet is in your presence for the entire flight. The problem is that only very small pets are permitted in the cabin. The standard rule is that they need to be in a portable carrier that must fit under the seat directly in front of you. Such a situation will work fine for most cats and small dogs, but anybody traveling with a medium to large size dog will be forced to check their animals as baggage or put them on a separate flight as cargo.

Recently many airlines announced that they would no longer accept pets as checked baggage during the summer months or on travel routes to extreme climates. Some major airlines have extended these embargoes indefinitely because of the very real liability involved with having unattended pets traveling as baggage.

Even though the baggage compartments are climate controlled and ventilated, there are often wait-periods between the time when your animal leaves you and when he actually gets on—and off—the plane. If the temperatures are extreme, your animal will suffer. Accordingly, most airlines have temperature restrictions that will not allow your pet to travel if the temperature is below 45°F or above 85°F. If your animal must fly as baggage in the summer months, it's generally a good idea to book a flight during the cooler hours: early in the morning or toward the evening. Similarly, if your pet flies in the winter, it's best to travel in the midafternoon when it is warmer.

If you ship your animal as cargo, which means as baggage on a separate flight, the same temperature rules apply. Many airlines operate cargo divisions, apart from their standard commercial airliners, that handle pets as cargo. For example, Continental's Cargo service is called QUICKPAK; Alaska Air's is Goldstreak; Delta's is called Delta Air Logistics. Within Delta Air Logistics, there are two options for shipping pets, including DASH (Delta Airlines Special Handling) and Priority First Freight. The bottom line is that if you are going to ship your pet as cargo, there will be a lot of acronyms and choices thrown at you, and it's a good idea to do some research before you make any commitments.

What about shipping your pet with a professional pet shipper? Most professional pet

Airline Phone Numbers and Websites

Air Canada
RESERVATIONS: 800-776-3000
CUSTOMER RELATIONS: 800-272-4088
CENTRAL BAGGAGE OFFICE: 888-689-2247
WEBSITE: http://www.aircanada.ca/services/
  luggage/ pets.html

Alaska Airlines
RESERVATIONS: 800-252-7522
WEBSITE: http://www2.alaskaair.com/Help/
  FAQs/PetsCarryOn.asp

America West Airlines
PET RESERVATIONS: 800-2-FLY-AWA (235-9292)
WEBSITE: http://www.americawest.com/
  productservices/services/ps_pets.htm

American Airlines
RESERVATIONS: 800-433-7300
AIR CARGO: 800-277-4622
WEBSITE: http://www.americanair.com
GO TO: Programs & Services
GO TO: Customer Service & Travel Assistance
GO TO: Traveling with Pets

ATA
RESERVATIONS: 800-I-FLY-ATA
WEBSITE: http://www.ata.com/flifo/
  beforeyoufly.html#animals

Continental Airlines
RESERVATIONS: 800-525-0280
LIVE ANIMAL HELP DESK: 800-575-3335
WEBSITE: http://www.continental.com/dash/
  build_dash.asp?service_12

Delta Airlines
ADVANCE PET ARRANGEMENTS: 888-SEND-PET
  (736-3738)
CARRY-ON PET: 800-221-1212
WEBSITE: http://www.delta-air.com/travel/
  trav_serv/pet_travel/index.jsp

Northwest Airlines
RESERVATIONS: 800-225-2525
HEARING IMPAIRED: 800-323-2298
VIP OR CARGO: 800-NWCARGO [692-2746]
WEBSITE: http://www.nwa.com/travel/
  tips/pets.shtml

United Airlines
RESERVATIONS: 800-241-6522
UNITED CARGO: 800-UA-CARGO (822-2746)
WEBSITE: http://www.united.com/site/
  primary/0,10017,1047,00.html

US Air
RESERVATIONS: 800-428-4322
WEBSITE: http://www.usairways.com/
  customers/baggagepolicy.htm#Pets

Cats and Flying

While many cat owners complain to petswelcome.com that cats are not as accepted as dogs in many places, one great advantage cats do have is that they're usually small enough to be brought on a plane as carry-on luggage (though many European and foreign countries will *not* allow animals to arrive in the cabin). This leads to two obvious questions.

How Do I Get My Cat Through Security?

In the United States, you usually have to take your cat out of the carrier to get through the metal detector, so make sure she's wearing a collar and leash or harness (but not too many metal tags). If you have a soft carrier and they let you leave your cat in the carrier, try to hold her in front of you so she passes through the detectors by herself and doesn't have to be rummaged through because something you were wearing set the alarm off. The less stress for your cat the better.

How Do I Handle a Litter Box on the Plane?

Bring a disposable litter box and enough litter in your carry-on luggage (approximately 4 to 5 pounds will cover most trips). If you sense that your cat has to go, you can bring everything (cat, litter and box) to the restroom and set everything up. But since this is a highly unusual setting, your cat might not be inclined to use the box, so always bring along an emergency kit consisting of an absorbent towel or paper towels, a plastic bag for disposal and some antibacterial soap and/or baking soda for the odor.

shippers focus on relocation—if you're actually relocating your household from one part of the country or world to another—and usually do not handle vacations. In general, they can handle all aspects of the move, from pickup and delivery to airports, reservations, health certificates, import and export arrangements and so on. If you are shipping your pet as cargo, some airlines will not let you take a pet unless you are a "known shipper," which usually means that you're a professional transporter or pet professional who has met the FAA requirements to ship. When planning your trip, it's worth visiting the website of the Independent Pet and Animal Transportation Association (www.ipata.com) to see what your options are.

No matter how you fly your pet, there are some basic rules you should follow. You should feed your pet four to six hours before departure; a full stomach could make him uncomfortable during the flight. On the other hand, you should give your pet water right up until the flight, but make sure to empty the water dish at check-in so it doesn't spill during travel. It's also a good idea to put a blanket at the bottom of the carrier or kennel for comfort and as an absorbing agent.

Most importantly, *do not sedate your pet.* According to the American Veterinary Medical Association, air transport of sedated animals can be fatal and is one the most common causes of animal deaths during air travel—accounting for almost half the fatalities. Little is known about the effects of sedatives on animals at high altitudes—they should be avoided in all air travel situations.

A portable kennel or carrier is required for all methods of air travel. Many airlines sell kennels, but since the standard for kennels at most airlines is generally universal, it's probably not a good idea to wait to buy one until you get to the airport. First, you'll probably be in a rush and, second, it's better to have your pet acclimated to the kennel ahead of time, rather than throwing her into a new environment before she endures the further stresses of the flight.

Most airlines require that the carrier adhere to United States Department of Agriculture standards, but you should check with your airline to make sure your kennel meets any specific requirements the airline imposes. According to USDA regulations, your carrier must be hard-sided and made of hard plastic, wood or metal. (Soft-sided carriers are permitted by some airlines for in-cabin flight only.) It should be ventilated on two sides and be large enough for your animal to stand, sit, turn around and lie down comfortably during the flight. It should have secured dishes for food and water.

Whatever type of carrier you choose, make sure that no part of your pet can protrude from it, as this may cause injury. For pets checked as baggage or cargo, it is also a good idea to label the kennel with a "LIVE ANIMAL" label and have arrows indicating the kennel's correct position. Most airlines require the kennel to have a latch so it can be closed securely, but *do not lock the carrier!* This can be dangerous during an emergency.

In general, we do not recommend air travel for pets—especially as checked baggage or cargo. However, if you have a larger animal

and are an avid traveler, you are most likely going to find yourself confronting the reality of flying with your pet. Amtrak and virtually all cruise lines do not accept pets, so if you're traveling any distance and not driving, air travel is your only option. For those occasions, we suggest you do a lot of research and then adopt an attitude of cautious resignation. After all, how many times have you stuffed yourself into a tiny cabin, eating things at 35,000 feet you wouldn't feed the squirrels on the ground? The bottom line is that you got through it. So will your pet.

Emergencies on the Road

There are many emergencies you may encounter on the road. Before you leave on your trip, ask your vet if she knows of a veterinarian or animal hospital she could recommend in the place you'll be visiting. Nothing can replace the peace of mind you'll enjoy from a recommendation by a trusted professional, especially when you're venturing out with your pet into the unknown. Even so, the reality is that most of the time you'll be on your own when it comes to finding emergency medical care for your pet. Hopefully, you'll never have to use it but, just in case, we're supplying a list of emergency vets around the country so that you'll have a minimum safety network in case you need it.

After health issues, the most common emergency is losing your pet. Obviously, the fear—and possibility—of losing your pet increases while you are away from home. It's one of the risks you take when you bring an animal on a trip. We don't believe that it should scare you to the point that you never

Pet Registry and ID Resources

AKC Companion Animal Recovery
5580 Centerview Dr., Ste. 250
Raleigh, NC 27606
800-252-7894
E-MAIL: found@akc.org
WEBSITE: www.akc.org/love/car

AVID's PETtrac
3179 Hamner Ave.
Norco, CA 91760
800-336-AVID (336-2843)
E-MAIL: Pettrac@aol.com
WEBSITE: www.avidid.oom

AWOLPET.com
888-743-6465
WEBSITE: www.AWOLPET.com

I.D. Pet
74 Hoyt St.
Darrien, CT 06820
888-283-8343

National Dog Registry
PO Box 116
Woodstock, NY 12498
800-NDR-DOGS (637-3647)
E-MAIL: info@natldogregistry.com
WEBSITE: www.natldogregistry.com

Petfinders
661 High St.
Athol, NY 12810
800-666-LOST (666-5678)
E-MAIL: petclub@capital.net
WEBSITE: www.petclub.org

Pets 911
888-PETS-911 (738-7911)
WEBSITE: www.1888Pets911.org

Tatoo-A-Pet
6571 S.W. 20th Ct.
Fort Lauderdale, FL 33317
800-828-8667
WEBSITE: www.tattoo-a-pet.com

take your pet with you, but you need to be on extra-alert status, know your options and take a few commonsense precautions.

Proper Identification

Always check to make sure that your pet's ID tags are securely fastened to the collar. If you are going to be staying at one place for more than a day or two, attach a temporary ID tag (in addition to the standard tag) with the address and phone number of the place you are staying.

If you're not satisfied with a standard ID tag on your pet's collar, there are a growing number of sophisticated ID options to choose from, including microchips that will immediately identify your dog. These can be painlessly embedded in your pet's shoulder area or the scruff of its neck. A scanner is needed to detect the chip, however, and the person who finds your pet would need to know where to take your pet to have it scanned. Another option is a tattoo ID that is painlessly imprinted on the pet's belly or inner thigh. If you choose either of these options, they should be used *in addition* to standard ID tags. The reality is that most people who find your dog will look for the tags first. If the tags are missing, they might not know to check for other identifying marks or even realize that there are additional methods to determine the animal's owner.

No matter which ID option you choose, be sure to register your pet with an established and reliable lost-and-found registry. This will ensure that once your pet is found, a mechanism will be in place to contact you immediately. While the telephone is still the surest and most common way of contacting the owner of a lost animal, it makes sense to have back-up resources. A host of lost-and-found registries, such as www.awolpet.com, have sprung up on the Internet and are a good place to register your pet. Most of them charge a minimal fee (under $10) to have your pet listed. Once a pet is lost or found, the owner or finder can get on the Internet and announce the situation so that others can be alerted to the animal's status.

Pet Insurance

Interest in pet insurance has grown over the last several years, primarily because of the ever-rising cost of veterinary bills. A number of providers, such as www.petinsurancenow.com, offer practical options for many pet owners, who have discovered that insurance can spare them the agonizing choice of whether to move forward with care or not. Like any insurance, you should know what you're purchasing before you commit. You should assess how affordable it is. A good rule of thumb is to choose a plan that costs no more than $.50 to $1 a day.

Also, make sure you know what's being covered. At the very least, accident and illness should be covered. Diagnostic tests, prescriptions and hospital stay coverage are also important. In addition, we recommend that you purchase a plan that allows you to visit any vet you choose and not just those designated by the insurance company. Finally, make sure that the plan benefits are determined by vet costs—not arbitrary insurance tables. Read the fine print.

It's important to understand that, generally, pet insurance policies do not cover the loss of a pet, though some do include coverage

to pay for advertisements and rewards if a pet is lost or stolen. However, insurance still might be worth considering before you take your pet on a trip. There is always a greater risk for an accident when you take your animal out of his usual environs. Just check to make sure that the policy would cover you in the area where you'll be traveling.

Lost Pet Scam

Beware of this heartbreaking scam, reported to us by the Pet Club of America (www.petclub.org), a nonprofit organization that helps members find lost pets. Since we ran this notice on our site, we've had numerous people e-mail us to report that it had happened to them. Here's how the scam works.

A man claiming to be from Canada calls the pet owner and says he has found their missing pet while vacationing in the United States with his wife and family. Allegedly, the pet was injured and needed medical treatment, which he paid for. Because he is leaving the country on a plane in the next few hours, he asks the pet owner to wire him money to cover part of the vet's bills and the pet's air transportation back to the owner. He's even able to provide flight information and lots of other details that would seduce the pet owner into believing him. Obviously, once the money is wired, the pet is not returned.

Don't let these people get away with it. Tell your friends and family about this scam. Another way to combat this scam, and others like it, is to contact a lost-and-found registry such as the Pet Club of America who will—for a nominal fee—register your pet in their database, where it is immediately available if the animal becomes lost. You will also receive special identification tags with the Club's toll-free number.

3

Where to Stay

When it comes to finding a place to stay, remember this: All "pet-friendly" lodgings are not the same. There's a wide disparity in the pet policies among the hotels, motels, inns and b&bs that accept pets. When we first started petswelcome.com, we only listed the pet-friendly lodgings' addresses and phone numbers, like other guides did. Soon enough, however, we began hearing from pet owners complaining that a particular inn charged a fee for the pet which, the pet owner felt, made it not so pet-friendly, after all. Others complained of being put in smoking rooms, not because they smoked, but simply because they had their pet with them.

It became clear to us very early on that all lodgings that accept pets are not necessarily pet-*friendly*. While some lodgings truly welcomed pets, there were others that simply tolerated them, and a few that actually seemed to dislike pets. Why, we wondered, would someone accept pets if they really didn't like them? Why wouldn't they just have a no-pet policy? The answer is simple: so they could get away with charging a high, nonrefundable fee to pet owners who don't know any better.

It was at that point that we decided to list as many pet policies on our site as possible so owners can know what they are getting into. Overall, we take a nonjudgmental approach to lodgings that accept pets. If they accept them, we list them on our site. However, if they put you in a smoking room and charge a nonrefundable $150 fee per night, we list that information as well. We think it's best to let pet owners make the call themselves. Our general feeling is that there's nothing wrong with a lodging charging a small fee for a pet as long as it's reasonable and used to cover extra costs (for example, the additional cleaning and maintenance that may be required). The fee should not be punitive. The main consideration should be that the pet owner actually feels welcome and is not treated like a second class citizen.

Pet policies can range from "No fees. All pets accepted" to policies with a host of different restrictions. The most common restrictions are size: no pets over 25 pounds, for example. There are also restrictions on the type of animal: only cats and dogs, being the most common. Then there is the issue of fees and deposits. As alluded to above, many lodgings require pet owners to put down a refundable deposit to cover possible damages, which is returned if everything is okay.

Some lodgings charge nonrefundable fees to cover extra expenses or simply to keep pet owners away. Another common practice is to put pet owners in smoking rooms. Though this practice seems bizarre to us, the skewed logic probably is that both smokers and pets will require extra cleaning and deodorizing, so they should be put in the same rooms. While pet owners who smoke may have no problem with this, many nonsmokers find it extremely offensive. Our advice? Avoid lodgings with this type of policy. Or, if you find you have no choice, request an ionizer in your room. We've had many nonsmoking pet owners tell us that when the hotel used an ionizer in their room, they could not tell

Hotel Chains

Though most hotel chains are made up of franchises involving different owners/management groups who decide for themselves whether to be pet-friendly or not, there are a few that accept pets across the board (the only exception being where local ordinances forbid it):

Drury Inns: Over 80 inns in 14 states, with a large percentage in Missouri and Texas, Drury Inns allow one pet per room. 800-DRURY-INN (378-7946); www.drury-inn.com

E-Z 8 Motels: E-Z 8 has motels in California and Arizona. All the EZ8's accept pets, though the management of each motel can exercise their discretion to not accept a particular pet if it seems too aggressive. The motel will ask for a credit card impression as insurance against possible damage. (Number TK);

Four Seasons Hotels and Resorts: Over 20 hotels in major cities in the U.S. Four Seasons hotels have a weight restriction of 15 pounds or under. 800-819-5053; www.fourseasons.com

Motel 6: Over 800 properties located throughout the contiguous U.S. and Canada. They charge no fee for pets and prefer dogs less than 25 pounds, but our experience is that they will accept larger if you call in advance. 800-4-MOTEL-6; www.motel6.com

Red Roof Inn: There are more than 350 Red Roof Inns located throughout the country. They accept dogs up to 80 pounds. 800-RED-ROOF; www.redroof.com

Shilo Inns: Shilo Inns has approximately 39 pet-friendly hotels in nine western states, including California and Oregon. They charge a $10 fee per pet per night and have no size or weight restrictions. 800-222-2244; www.shilohinns.com

that it was a smoking room. We haven't tested the validity of the claim ourselves, but it's worth a try as a last resort.

We always recommend that you research the lodging—starting with petswelcome.com, of course. Our golden rule? Call ahead. Make sure they still accept pets. As mentioned earlier, the lodging industry has a large turnover rate. Even though we can immediately post information on our website to reflect any changes, we still need to be told of the changes—and that doesn't always happen as fast as we'd like. That's why we always recommend that you call. In addition, if you have the time, talk to the owners or managers to find out if they own pets themselves. A quick conversation will reveal whether they just tolerate pets or actually welcome them. Beyond the restrictions and fees, many lodgings actually provide pet amenities such as fresh water or biscuits, a running/walking area, trails, or pet cushions and/or beds. If a lodging does provide any pet amenities—or knows of places nearby that do, such as pet-friendly beaches or parks—we list them as well.

Look for the special icon that indicates a lodging has received our seal of approval: 🐾

To receive the seal, a lodging must be nominated by a traveling pet-owner who has stayed at the establishment with his or her pet and had a good experience. It must also adhere to the basic tenets of our pet-friendly charter (see page vi).

If your itinerary does not allow you to book reservations ahead of time (for example, if it will take a few days to drive to your destination, and you don't know where you'll be stopping each night), consider using a hotel chain on your route that has a consistent pet-friendly policy, like Motel 6 and Shilo Inns. But be aware that because many hotel chains are franchised or are owned by different corporate entities, many of them do not have a consistent, across-the-board pet policy. For example, a Holiday Inn in one city might accept pets for a small fee while a Holiday Inn in another city might not accept pets at all. In *The Portable petswelcome.com,* we have broken out information on the few pet-friendly chains with consistent pet policies (see "Hotel Chains" on page 20) and listed many of their individual properties within the state each is located. In addition, we've also listed individual chain hotels if they accept pets, even though the chain they belong to has no consistent policy.

The bottom line is that we want you to have as wide a choice as possible. So, even if your trip does not allow you the luxury of knowing exactly where you're going to be each night, and the section on lodgings does not give you enough flexibility, you can still check out our website, which has a new route-based search capability that will show you all the pet-friendly lodgings between your point of departure and destination.

HOTELS, MOTELS, BED & BREAKFASTS

United States

ALABAMA

Andalusia Days Inn
1604 E. Bypass Hwy. 84
Andalusia, AL 36420
334-427-0050
PET POLICY: Fee $6.

Best Western
Hwy. 78 & AL 21 S.
Anniston, AL 36203
256-831-3410
RATES: Single $67, double $69.
PET POLICY: No fee, pets under
25 lbs.

Athens Days Inn
1322 Hwy. 72
Athens, AL 35611
256-233-7500
PET POLICY: Fee $5.

Bomar Inn
1101 Hwy. 31 S.
Athens, AL 35611
256-232-6944
RATES: Single $30, double $35,
suite $45.
PET POLICY: Fee $10, small pets
only.

**Auburn Univ. Hotel
& Conference Center**
371 N. College St.
Auburn, AL 36830
334-821-8200
RATES: $79–$149 (seasonal).
PET POLICY: No fee, all sizes,
restrictions.

Bay Minette Days Inn
1819 Hwy. 31 S.
Bay Minette, AL 36507
334-580-8111
PET POLICY: No fee.

Birmingham Days Inn
1121 9th Ave. SW
Bessemer, AL 35022
205-424-6078
PET POLICY: No fee.

Motel 6
1000 Shiloh Ln.
Bessemer, AL 35020
205-426-9646

PET POLICY: No fee. Dogs under
25 lbs. preferred (larger animals by advance approval).
Do not leave animals in room
unattended.

**Baymont Inn & Suites—
Birmingham**
513 Cahaba Park Cir.
Birmingham, AL 35242
205-995-9990
PET POLICY: No fee.

Best Suites of America
140 State Farm Pkwy.
Birmingham, AL 35209
205-940-9990
RATES: Single $79, double $89.
PET POLICY: No fee, pets under
10 lbs.

Best Western
3510 Grandview Pkwy.
Birmingham, AL 35243
205-967-2450
RATES: $59–$79.
PET POLICY: No fee, pets under
30 lbs.

Birmingham Super 8 Motel
1813 Crestwood Blvd.
Birmingham, AL 35210
205-956-3650
RATES: Single $42.95, double
$47.95.
PET POLICY: Fee $10, all size pets
accepted. Pets in special rooms.

Drury Inn & Suites
3510 Grandview Pkwy.
Birmingham, AL 35243
205-967-2450
RATES: $59–$79.
PET POLICY: No fee, pets under
30 lbs.

Holiday Inn
260 Oxmoor Rd.
Birmingham, AL 35209
205-942-2041
PET POLICY: Small pets.

Howard Johnson Inn
275 Oxmoor Rd.
Birmingham, AL 35209
205-942-0919
RATES: Single $45, double $50.
PET POLICY: No fee, deposit $25,
refundable. All size pets accepted.

La Quinta Birmingham
905 11th Ct. W
Birmingham, AL 35204
205-324-4510
RATES: Single $49, double $75.
PET POLICY: No fee, pets under
40 lbs.

Motel Birmingham
7905 Crestwood Blvd.
Birmingham, AL 35210
205-956-4440
RATES: Average of $54.
PET POLICY: Fee $15, all size
pets accepted.

Red Roof Inn
151 Vulcan Rd.
Birmingham, AL 35209
205-942-9414
PET POLICY: No fee, pets under
80 lbs. Must be leashed to and
from rooms. Do not leave in
room unattended.

The Mountainbrook Inn
2800 Us Hwy. 280
Birmingham, AL 35223
205-870-3100
RATES: 80–$105.
PET POLICY: Fee $20, non-
refundable, pets under 20 lbs.

The Tutwiler Hotel
Park Pl. at 21st St. N.
Birmingham, AL 35203
205-322-2100
RATES: Single 121, double
$131–$151.
PET POLICY: Fee $25, pets under
25 lbs.

Key West Inn
410 E. Mill Ave.
Boaz, AL 35957
256-593-0800
RATES: Single $55, double $65.
PET POLICY: Fee $5, nonrefund-
able. Up to 50 lbs., all pets
welcome.
POI: Across from outlet centers.

Calera Days Inn
11691 Hwy. 25 and I-65
Calera, AL 35040
205-668-0560
PET POLICY: No fee.

U.S. Lodgings > ALABAMA

Camden Days Inn
39 Camden Bypass
Camden, AL 36726
334-682-4555
PET POLICY: No fee.

Lighthouse Restaurant & Motel
Hwy. 68
Cedar Bluff, AL 35959
256-779-8400
RATES: Single $40, double $45.
PET POLICY: Fee $5, nonrefundable, all size pets welcome. Do not leave unattended.
POI: National Park, 32,000-acre lake.

Childersburg Days Inn
33669 Us Hwy. 280
Childersburg, AL 35044
205-378-6007
PET POLICY: No fee.

Clanton Days Inn
2000 Holiday Inn Dr.
Clanton, AL 35046
205-755-0510
PET POLICY: Fee $5.

Days Inn
4th St., SW
Cullman, AL 35055
205-739-3800
PET POLICY: Fee $4.

Decatur Knights Inn
3429 Hwy. 31 S.
Decatur, AL 35603
256-355-0190
RATES: Single $36, double $42.
PET POLICY: Fee $2, nonrefundable; up to 50 lbs., pets must not be left unattended in room except in crate.
POI: Point Mallan Park-4 miles away, Joe Wheeler Park 18 miles, Pineville Racing Horse Arena 6 miles.

Decatur Days Inn Conference Center
810 6th Ave. NE
Decatur, AL 35602
205-355-3520
PET POLICY: Fee $10, nonrefundable.

Dothan Days Inn
2841 Ross Clark Cir.
Dothan, AL 36301
334-793-2550
PET POLICY: Fee $5.

Motel 6
2907 Ross Clark Cir SW
Dothan, AL 36301
334-793-6013
PET POLICY: No fee. Dogs under 25 lbs. preferred (larger animals by advance approval). Do not leave animals in room unattended.

Eufaula Days Inn
1521 S. Eufaula Ave.
Eufaula, AL 36027
334-687-1000
PET POLICY: No fee.

Evergreen Days Inn
901 Liberty Hill Dr.
Evergreen, AL 36401
205-578-2100
PET POLICY: Fee $5.

Florence Days Inn
1915 Florence Blvd.
Florence, AL 35630
256-766-2620
PET POLICY: No fee.

Birmingham Days Inn
616 Decatur Hwy.
Fultondale, AL 35068
205-849-0111
PET POLICY: Fee $5.

Gadsden Days Inn
1612 W. Grand Ave.
Gadsden, AL 35904
256-442-7913
PET POLICY: No fee.

Red Roof Inn
1600 Rainbow Dr.
Gadsden, AL 35901
256-543-1105
PET POLICY: No fee, pets under 80 lbs. Must be leashed to and from rooms. Do not leave in room unattended.

Bon Secour Lodge
16730 Oyster Bay Pl.
Gulf Shores, AL 36542
334-968-7814
RATES: Single $60–$70.
PET POLICY: Fee $6, one-time. All sizes welcome. Dogs must behave when left alone.
AMENITIES: Flea program. Dog walking. Swimming.
POI: Gulf Shore beaches, Ft. Morgan, fishing guide, boat launch, boat slips.

Gulf Pines Motel
245 E. 22nd Ave.
Gulf Shores, AL 36542
334-948-7911
RATES: Single, double $54.41.
PET POLICY: No fee, all sizes welcome.
POI: Gulf State Park, Bellingrath Gardens, Nat'l Museum of Naval Aviation, Riviera Centre, USS Alabama, Waterville USA, factory stores.

Hamilton Days Inn
1849 Military St. S.
Hamilton, AL 35570
205-921-1790
PET POLICY: Fee $5.

Shoney's Inn & Suites
226 Summitt Pkwy.
Homewood, AL 35209
205-916-0464
RATES: Single $55–$75, double $65–$85.
PET POLICY: Fee $25, refundable. All size dogs and cats.

Days Inn South
1535 Montgomery Hwy.
Hoover, AL 35216
205-822-6030
PET POLICY: No fee.

Baymont Inn & Suites— Huntsville
4890 University Drive NW
Huntsville, AL 35816
256-830-8999
PET POLICY: No fee.

Holiday Inn
3810 University Dr.
Huntsville, AL 35816
256-837-7171
PET POLICY: Fee $1, $50 deposit.

Holiday Inn Express
3808 University Dr.
Huntsville, AL 35816
256-721-1000
PET POLICY: $50 deposit.

U.S. Lodgings > ALABAMA

Motel 6
8995 Madison Blvd
PO Box 6123
Huntsville, AL 35824
256-772-7479
PET POLICY: No fee. Dogs under 25 lbs. preferred (larger animals by advance approval). Do not leave animals in room unattended.

Leeds Days Inn
1835 Ashville Rd.
Leeds, AL 35094
205-699-9833
PET POLICY: Fee $5.

Days Inn of Mobile
5480 Inn Dr.
Mobile, AL 36619
334-661-8181
PET POLICY: Fee $8.

Drury Inn Mobile
824 S. Beltline Rd.
Mobile, AL 36609
334 344-7700
PET POLICY: No fee, pets under 30 lbs.

Howard Johnson Express Inn
370 W. Lee St.
Mobile, AL 36611
334-457-4005
PET POLICY: Fee $10, nonrefundable. Up to 50 lbs. Must call ahead.

Motel 6
400 S. Beltline Hwy.
Mobile, AL 36608
334-343-8448
PET POLICY: No fee. Dogs under 25 lbs. preferred (larger animals by advance approval). Do not leave animals in room unattended.

Motel 6
5488 Inn Rd/I-10 Service Rd.
Mobile, AL 36619
334-660-1483
PET POLICY: No fee. Dogs under 25 lbs. preferred (larger animals by advance approval). Do not leave animals in room unattended.

Red Roof Inn
5450 Cola Cola Rd.
Mobile, AL 36619
334-666-1044
PET POLICY: No fee, pets under 80 lbs. Must be leashed to and from rooms. Do not leave in room unattended.

Red Roof Inn
33 S. Beltline Hwy.
Mobile, AL 36606
334-476-2004
PET POLICY: No fee, pets under 80 lbs. Must be leashed to and from rooms. Do not leave in room unattended.

Shoneys Inn Mobile
5472 A Inn Rd.
Mobile, AL 36619
334-660-1520
RATES: Single $49, double $54.
PET POLICY: Fee $25, refundable. All sizes welcome.
POI: Dauphin Island, Bellingrath Gardens, Downtown Historic Area.

Baymont Inn & Suites— Montgomery
5225 Carmichael Rd.
Montgomery, AL 35242
334-277-6000
PET POLICY: No fee.

Holiday Inn
1185 Eastern Bypass
Montgomery, AL 36117
334-272-0370
PET POLICY: Small Pets.

Montgomery Days Inn Airport
1150 W. South Blvd.
Montgomery, AL 36105
334-281-8000
PET POLICY: Fee $5.

Montgomery Days Inn Midtown
2625 Zelda Rd.
Montgomery, AL 36107
334-269-9611
PET POLICY: Fee $5.

Motel 6
1051 Eastern Bypass
Montgomery, AL 36117
334-277-6748
PET POLICY: No fee. Dogs under 25 lbs. preferred (larger animals by advance approval). Do not leave animals in room unattended.

Howard Johnson Express Inn
370 W. Lee St.
North Mobile, AL 36611
334-457-4006
RATES: Single $50, double $55.
PET POLICY: Fee $10. Call for restrictions.
POI: Gulf Shores, beaches, Pensacola.

Opelika Days Inn
1014 Anand Ave.
Opelika, AL 36801
205-749-5080
PET POLICY: Fee $5.

Motel 6
1015 Columbus Pkwy.
Opelika, AL 36801
334-745-0988
PET POLICY: No fee. Dogs under 25 lbs. preferred (larger animals by advance approval). Do not leave animals in room unattended.

Anniston Days Inn
One Recreation Dr.
Oxford, AL 36203
205-835-0300
PET POLICY: Fee $5.

Best Western
Hwy. 78 & AL 21 S.
Oxford, AL 36203
256-831-3410
RATES: Single $67, double $69.
PET POLICY: No fee, pets under 25 lbs.

Motel 6
202 Grace St.
Oxford, AL 36203
256-831-5463
PET POLICY: No fee. Dogs under 25 lbs. preferred (larger animals by advance approval). Do not leave animals in room unattended.

U.S. Lodgings > ALASKA

Montgomery Days Inn North/Prattville
I-65 & Us 31 N. Exit 186
Prattville, AL 36067
334-365-3311
PET POLICY: Fee $6.

Scottsboro Days Inn
23945 John T. Reid Pkwy.
Scottsboro, AL 35768
205-574-1212
PET POLICY: No fee.

Travelers Inn of Selma
2006 W. Highland Ave.
Selma, AL 36701
334-875-1200
PET POLICY: No fee, all sizes accepted. Pets must be housebroken.

Shorter Days Inn
I-85 Ex 22 I-85 & Shorter Depot Rd.
Shorter, AL 36075
205-727-6034
PET POLICY: No fee.

Thomasville Days Inn
424, Hwy. 43 N
Thomasville, AL 36784
334-636-5467
PET POLICY: No fee.

Thomasville Inn
1200 Mosley Dr.
Thomasville, AL 36784
334-636-0614
PET POLICY: No fee. All size dogs accepted.

Troy Days Inn Troy State University
1260 Us Hwy. 231 S.
Troy, AL 36081
334-566-1630
PET POLICY: Fee $5.

Motel 6
4700 McFarland Blvd. E.
(Hwy. 82E)
Tuscaloosa, AL 35405
205-759-4942
PET POLICY: No fee. Dogs under 25 lbs. preferred (larger animals by advance approval). Do not leave animals in room unattended.

Days Inn
17700 Hwy. 17
York, AL 36925
205-392-5485
PET POLICY: Fee $10.

ALASKA

Anchorage Days Inn Downtown
321 E. Fifth Ave.
Anchorage, AK 99501
907-276-7226
RATES: Single, double $79–$159. Summer rates always higher.
PET POLICY: Fee $25 deposit, refundable. All sizes accepted.

Anchorage Super 8 Motel
3501 Minnesota Dr.
Anchorage, AK 99503
907-276-8884
RATES: Single $49.88–$129.88, double $10–$20 additional, depending on season.
PET POLICY: Fee $25, refundable. All sizes accepted.

Best Western Barratt Inn
4616 Spenard Rd.
Anchorage, AK 99517
907-243-3131
RATES: Single $59–$209, double $10–$20 additional, depending on season.
PET POLICY: Fee $5 per night. All sizes accepted.

Hillside on Gambell
2150 Gambell St.
Anchorage, AK 99503
907-258-6006
RATES: Single $60, double $70.
PET POLICY: Fee $5, nonrefundable.
AMENITIES: Scenic dog walk.
POI: Shopping, movies, bike trails, Sullivan arena, Downtown.

Parkwood Inn
4455 Juneau St.
Anchorage, AK 99503
907-563-3590
RATES: Single, double $65–$115 (seasonal).
PET POLICY: Fee $5 per pet, plus $50 refundable deposit.

Bald Eagle Ranch Bed & Breakfast
PO Box 568
Delta Junction, AK 99737
907-895-5270
RATES: Single $85, double $125.
PET POLICY: No fee, all sizes and all pets welcome (dogs, cats, birds, ferrets, rabbits, reptiles). Must be friendly to pets and people.
AMENITIES: Very warm hospitality for guests and their pets! Lodging and horseback riding guest ranch.
POI: Hiking trails, Quartz Lake, Clearwater Lake, Alyeska Pipeline Bridge, Majestic Mountain Range, Rika's Roadhouse, Official end-of-Alaska Highway.

Regency Fairbanks Hotel
95 Tenth Ave.
Fairbanks, AK 99701
907-452-3200
RATES: Single $99–$165, double $99–$165.
PET POLICY: Fee $50, refundable. Up to 50 lbs. Do not leave in room unattended, unless in crate.

Majestic Valley Wilderness Lodge
HC03 Box 8514
Palmer, AK 99645
907-746-2930
RATES: Single $60, double $80.
PET POLICY: Fee $20, nonrefundable, all sizes welcome.
AMENITIES: Dog houses, run.
POI: Hiking trails, skiing trails.

Kenai Peninsula Condos
Box 3416A
Soldotna, AK 99669
800-362-1383
RATES: Single $119, double $119.
PET POLICY: No fee, all sizes welcome.
AMENITIES: Large yards. End of road with no traffic.
POI: Kenai River, ocean beaches, parks.

Westmark Valdez
100 Fidalgo Dr.
Valdez, AK 99686
907-835-4391
RATES: Single, double $99.
PET POLICY: No fee, all sizes and pets welcome. Pet-friendly rooms are smoking rooms also.

ARIZONA

Tal-Wi-Wi Lodge
PO Box 169
Alpine, AZ 85920
520-339-4319
RATES: Single $65, double $65.
PET POLICY: Fee $5, nonrefundable, per day per dog, 2-dog maximum.

Motel 6
637 S. Whetstone Commerce Dr.
Benson, AZ 85602
520-586-0066
PET POLICY: No fee. Dogs under 25 lbs. preferred (larger animals by advance approval). Do not leave animals in room unattended.

Hotel La More—
The Bisbee Inn
45 OK St.
Bisbee, AZ 85603
520-432-5131
RATES: Single $50–$155, double $55–$160.
PET POLICY: Fee $40, refundable. All sizes welcome but cannot be left in room unattended.

Buckeye Days Inn
25205 W. Yuma Rd.
Buckeye, AZ 85326
623-386-5400
PET POLICY: Fee $25.

Days Inn
2200 Karis Dr.
Bullhead City, AZ 86442
520-758-1711
PET POLICY: Fee $20.

Red Roof Inn
7400 W. Boston Ave.
Chandler, AZ 85226
480-857-4969
PET POLICY: No fee, pets under 80 lbs. Must be leashed to and from rooms. Do not leave in room unattended.

Arizona Mountain Inn
4200 Lake Mary Rd.
Flagstaff, AZ 86001
520-774-8959
PET POLICY: Fee $5 per dog per night, 2 dogs per cabin, $50 refundable deposit for cleaning, keep on leash, do not leave unattended.

Days Inn—Highway 66
1000 W. Route 66
Flagstaff, AZ 86001
520-774-5221
PET POLICY: No fee.

Econo Lodge
2355 S. Beulah Blvd.
Flagstaff, AZ 86001
520-774-2225
RATES: Single $49–$59, double $79–$89.
PET POLICY: Fee $5 per night per pet. All sizes welcome everywhere.

Hilltop Bed & Breakfast
01 N. Curling Smoke Rd.
Flagstaff, AZ 86001
520-779-9633
RATES: Cottage $125.
PET POLICY: Fee $5, all sizes and pets welcome. (Charge for long-haired animals only.)
AMENITIES: Five acres for pets, cottage has doggie door.
POI: Grand Canyon (72 miles), Navajo and Hopi reservations, Museum of North Arizona, downtown Flagstaff, Wapatki Indian ruins, Meteor Crater.

InnSuites of Flagstaff
1008 E. Route 66
Flagstaff, AZ 86001
520-774-7356
RATES: Single $69, double $69.
PET POLICY: Fee $25, refundable. All sizes welcome.
POI: Grand Canyon.

La Quinta Inn & Suites
2015 S. Beulah Blvd.
Flagstaff, AZ 86001
520-556-8666
RATES: Single, double $49.99–$59.99, suites $79.99.
PET POLICY: No fee. Pets under 20 lbs.

Motel 6
2745 S. Woodlands Village
Flagstaff, AZ 86001
520-779-3757
PET POLICY: No fee. Dogs under 25 lbs. preferred (larger animals by advance approval). Do not leave animals in room unattended.

Motel 6
2440 E. Lucky Ln.
Flagstaff, AZ 86004
520-774-8756
PET POLICY: No fee. Dogs under 25 lbs. preferred (larger animals by advance approval). Do not leave animals in room unattended.

Red Roof Inn
2520 E. Lucky Ln.
Flagstaff, AZ 86004
520-779-5121
PET POLICY: No fee, pets under 80 lbs. Must be leashed to and from rooms. Do not leave in room unattended.

Residence Inn by Marriott
3440 N. Country Club Dr.
Flagstaff, AZ 86004
520-526-5555
RATES: $99–$170.
PET POLICY: Fee $10 per day, nonrefundable. All sizes welcome.
POI: Grand Canyon, Bark Park (dog park), pet-friendly hiking trails.

Arizona Trails
Bed & Breakfast
PO Box 18998
Fountain Hills, AZ 85269
480-837-4284
RATES: Double $95–$125.
PET POLICY: No fee, up to 50 lbs.

Hampton Inn
2000 N. Litchfield Rd.
Goodyear, AZ 85338
623-536-1313
RATES: Single $99, double $109.
PET POLICY: Fee $25, refundable.

Red Feather Lodge
Box 1460, Hwy. 64
Grand Canyon Nat'l Park, AZ 86023
520-638-2414
PET POLICY: Fee $5 one-time, $45 deposit.

U.S. Lodgings > ARIZONA

Holiday Inn Express
1308 E. Navajo Blvd.
Holbrook, AZ 86025
520-524-1466
RATES: Single $59, double $64.
PET POLICY: No fee, all sizes welcome.

Motel 6
2514 Navajo Blvd.
Holbrook, AZ 86025
520-524-6101
PET POLICY: No fee. Dogs under 25 lbs. preferred (larger animals by advance approval). Do not leave animals in room unattended.

Days Inn East
3381 E. Andy Devine
Kingman, AZ 86401
520-757-7337
PET POLICY: Fee $10.

Hill Top Motel
1901 E. Andy Devine
Kingman, AZ 86401
520-753-2198
RATES: Single $28, double $36.
PET POLICY: No fee, all size dogs, only. Do not leave in room unattended for more than 30 minutes.

Motel 6
424 W. Beale St.
Kingman, AZ 86401
520-753-9222
PET POLICY: No fee. Dogs under 25 lbs. preferred (larger animals by advance approval). Do not leave animals in room unattended.

Holiday Inn
245 London Bridge Rd.
Lake Havasu City, AZ 86403
520-855-4071
RATES: Single, double $62.95.
PET POLICY: Fee $10 per night, nonrefundable. All sizes and pets welcome. Do not leave pets unattended in room.

Island Inn Hotel
1300 W. McCulloch Blvd.
Lake Havasu City, AZ 86403
520-680-0606
RATES: Single, double $49–$125.
PET POLICY: Fee $10. No size restrictions.

Motel 6
111 London Bridge Rd.
Lake Havasu City, AZ 86403
520-855-3200
PET POLICY: No fee. Dogs under 25 lbs. preferred (larger animals by advance approval). Do not leave animals in room unattended.

8 Phoenix Days Inn
333 W. Juanita Ave.
Mesa, AZ 65210
480-844-8900
PET POLICY: No fee.

Arizona Golf Resort & Conference Center
425 S. Power Rd.
Mesa, AZ 85206
800-528-8282
RATES: Single, double $109–$149 (seasonal).
PET POLICY: No fee, all sizes welcome.

Best Western Mesa Inn
1625 E. Main St.
Mesa, AZ 85203
480-964-8000
RATES: Single $69, double $89.
PET POLICY: Fee $5, nonrefundable, up to 50 lbs.

Motel 6
336 W. Hampton Ave.
Mesa, AZ 85210
480-844-8899
PET POLICY: No fee. Dogs under 25 lbs. preferred (larger animals by advance approval). Do not leave animals in room unattended.

Motel 6
141 W. Mariposa Rd.
Nogales, AZ 85621
520-281-2951
PET POLICY: No fee. Dogs under 25 lbs. preferred (larger animals by advance approval). Do not leave animals in room unattended.

Kohls Ranch Lodge
E. Highway 260
Payson, AZ 85541
800-331-5645
RATES: Single, double $75–$95, cabins $200–$270.

PET POLICY: Fee $10 per day. Dogs stay in lodge's kennel and are not permitted in rooms.

Payson Days Inn & Suites
301 A S. Beeline Hwy.
Payson, AZ 85541
520-474-9800
PET POLICY: Fee $6.

Comfort Inn Turf Paradise
1711 W. Bell Rd.
Phoenix, AZ 85023
602-866-2089
RATES: Single $60–$85, double $65–$90.
PET POLICY: Fee $10, $25 refundable deposit, all sizes welcome.
AMENITIES: Water/food dishware free, PetSmart delivery to room on request, dog walking service free of charge 24 hours daily.
POI: Large grassy park 1 block from hotel, great environment for pets, "pet-friendly" staff.

Crowne Plaza
2532 W. Peoria Ave.
Phoenix, AZ 85029
602-943-2341
PET POLICY: No fee.

Days Inn Phoenix Airport
3333 E. Van Buren St.
Phoenix, AZ 85008
602-244-8244
PET POLICY: No fee.

Holiday Inn
1500 N. 51st Ave.
Phoenix, AZ 85043
602-484-9009
PET POLICY: $25 deposit, nonrefundable.

Homewood Suites Hotel
2536 W. Beryl Ave.
Phoenix , AZ 85021
602-674-8900
PET POLICY: Fee $50, $200 cash or credit-card deposit.

Homewood Suites Hotel
2001 E. Highland Ave.
Phoenix, AZ 85016
602-508-0937
PET POLICY: Fee $100.

U.S. Lodgings > ARIZONA

Hotel San Carlos
202 N. Central Ave.
Phoenix, AZ 85004
602-243-4121
PET POLICY: Fee $25, refundable, all sizes.
AMENITIES: PetSmart delivery to room on request, free dog walking, water/food dishware free.

InnSuites Hotel Phoenix
1615 E. Northern Ave.
Phoenix, AZ 85020
800-752-2204
RATES: Suites $129.99.
PET POLICY: Fee $25, nonrefundable. No restrictions, all pets and sizes accepted.

Phoenix Days Inn
3333 E. Van Buren
Phoenix, AZ 85008
602-244-8244
PET POLICY: No fee.

Motel 6
2330 W. Bell Rd.
Phoenix, AZ 85023
602-993-2353
PET POLICY: No fee. Dogs under 25 lbs. preferred (larger animals by advance approval). Do not leave animals in room unattended.

Motel 6
5315 E. Van Buren St.
Phoenix, AZ 85008
602-267-8555
PET POLICY: No fee. Dogs under 25 lbs. preferred (larger animals by advance approval). Do not leave animals in room unattended.

Quality Hotel & Resort
3600 N. 2nd Ave.
Phoenix, AZ 85013
602-248-0222
RATES: Single $99, double $109.
PET POLICY: Fee $25, nonrefundable; must have cages for some types.
AMENITIES: Very friendly resort.
POI: Bank One ball park, America West arena, Phoenix Civic Plaza, Arizona Center.

Red Roof Inn
17222 N. Black Canyon Freeway
Phoenix, AZ 85023
602-866-1049
PET POLICY: No fee, pets under 80 lbs. Must be leashed to and from rooms. Do not leave in room unattended.

Red Roof Inn
5215 W. Willetta
Phoenix, AZ 85043
602-233-8004
PET POLICY: No fee, pets under 80 lbs. Must be leashed to and from rooms. Do not leave in room unattended.

South Mountain Village Retreat
113 E. la Mirada Dr.
Phoenix, AZ 85040
602-243-3452
RATES: Single, double $300 per week (seasonal).
PET POLICY: Fee $100, nonrefundable. All sizes accepted (dogs, cats, ferrets, birds). Must provide proof of vaccinations. Maximum of 2 pets (3 on prior approval). Minimum stay of 1 week.
POI: Completely fenced-in 1/8-acre yard. Veterinarian and grooming nearby. Ample mountain paths for walking.

Best Western Prescottonian Motel
1317 E. Gurley St.
Prescott, AZ 86301
520-445-2096
PET POLICY: Pets in smoking rooms only.

Cascade Motel
805 White Spar Rd.
Prescott, AZ 86303
520-445-1232
RATES: Single $32, double $35.
PET POLICY: Fee $5–$10, nonrefundable. All sizes welcome. No reptiles.
AMENITIES: Nice neighborhood for walks. Close to downtown parks.

Days Inn
7875 E. Hwy. 69
Prescott, AZ 86314
520-772-8600
PET POLICY: No fee.

Motel 6
1111 E. Sheldon St.
Prescott, AZ 86301
520-776-0160
PET POLICY: No fee. Dogs under 25 lbs. preferred (larger animals by advance approval). Do not leave animals in room unattended.

Motel 6
8383 E. US 69
Prescott Valley, AZ 86314
520-772-2200
PET POLICY: No fee. Dogs under 25 lbs. preferred (larger animals by advance approval). Do not leave animals in room unattended.

Safford Days Inn
520 E. Hwy. 70
Safford, AZ 85546
520-428-5000
PET POLICY: Fee $20.

Abode Apartment Hotel
3635 N. 68th St.
Scottsdale, AZ 85251
480-945-3544
PET POLICY: Fee $100 refundable, all sizes, all pets (dogs, cats, birds, reptiles, etc.).
AMENITIES: Single/double $121–$195.

Hampton Inn "Old Town" Plaza
4415 N. Civic Center Pl.
Scottsdale, AZ 85251
480-941-9400
PET POLICY: Fee $50, nonrefundable.

Holiday Inn Hotel and Suites
7515 E. Butherus Dr.
Scottsdale, AZ 85260
480-951-4000
RATES: Single, double $49–$189.
PET POLICY: No fee, $50 refundable deposit. Pets under 50 lbs.
POI: 11 miles to historic district, 2–5 miles to golf course, 3 miles to shopping center.

U.S. Lodgings > ARIZONA

Homewood Suites Hotel
9880 N. Scottsdale Rd.
Scottsdale, AZ 85253
480-368-8705
PET POLICY: Pets allowed under
15 lbs.

InnSuites Hotel Scottsdale
7707 E. McDowell Rd.
Scottsdale, AZ 85257
480-941-1202
RATES: Single, double $89.99.
PET POLICY: Fee $25, nonre-
fundable. All sizes and pets
welcome.
AMENITIES: Grass lawns to walk
pets.
POI: Phoenix Zoo, Desert
Botanical Gardens, golf,
Scottsdale shopping.

**Marriott's Camelback Inn
Resort**
5402 E. Lincoln Dr.
Scottsdale, AZ 85253
480-948-1700
RATES: Single $419, double
$419.
PET POLICY: No fee, up to 50 lbs.
All pets welcome (dogs, cats,
birds, ferrets, rabbits, reptiles).
Inform front desk of pet, and
use "pet inside" sign on door.

**Marriott's Mountain
Shadows Resort and
Golf Club**
5641 E. Lincoln Dr.
Scottsdale, AZ 85253
480-948-7111
RATES: Single $249, double $249.
PET POLICY: No fee, up to 50 lbs.
All pets welcome (dogs, cats,
birds, ferrets, rabbits, reptiles).
Inform front desk of pet.

Motel 6
6848 E. Camelback Rd.
Scottsdale, AZ 85251
480-946-2280
PET POLICY: No fee. Dogs under
25 lbs. preferred (larger animals by advance approval).
Do not leave animals in room
unattended.

**Ramada Hotel Valley Ho
Resort**
6850 Main St.
Scottsdale, AZ 85251
480-945-6321
RATES: Single $59–$119, double
$69–$129.
PET POLICY: Fee $25 nonre-
fundable. One pet per room,
all sizes welcome.
AMENITIES: 14 acres to walk
your dog.
POI: Papago Park, Phoenix,
zoo, Botanical Gardens, shops,
galleries, restaurants.

**Renaissance Scottsdale
Resort**
6160 N. Scottsdale Rd.
Scottsdale, AZ 85253
480-991-1414
RATES: Single $150, double $150.
PET POLICY: Fee $50, refund-
able. Up to 25 lbs. dogs, cats,
ferrets, birds and rabbits. Will
charge for any damages.

Residence Inn by Marriott
6040 N. Scottsdale Rd.
Scottsdale, AZ 85253
480-948-8666
RATES: Single $79–$289, double
$99–$289.
PET POLICY: Fee $50, nonre-
fundable, plus $6 per day per
pet. Up to 50 lbs.

Rodeway Inn
7110 E. Indian School Rd.
Scottsdale, AZ 85251
480-946-3456
RATES: Single $79, double $79.
PET POLICY: Fee $10, nonre-
fundable. All pets and sizes
welcome.
AMENITIES: Large grassy area for
pets.

**Scottsdale Pima Inn
& Suites**
7330 N. Pima Rd.
Scottsdale, AZ 85258
480-948-3800
RATES: Single $89, double $99.
PET POLICY: Fee $10, nonre-
fundable. All size dogs and
cats. Do not leave pets in
room unattended.
AMENITIES: Pet exercise area and
welcome goodies.

Scottsdale Siesta Suites
7601 E. 2nd St.
Scottsdale, AZ 85251
480-947-7244
RATES: Single $49, double $69.
PET POLICY: Fee $10, nonre-
fundable. All sizes and pets
welcome. Leash laws enforced.
Must sign liability form.
AMENITIES: Several parks in
walking distance.
POI: Walking distance to Old
Town Scottsdale; Scottsdale
Memorial Stadium; 10 min-
utes to A.S.U.; 15 minutes to
Sky Harbor Airport.

Sleep Inn
16630 N. Scottsdale Rd.
Scottsdale, AZ 85254
480-998-9211
PET POLICY: Fee $50, refundable
(deposit). All pets welcome up
to 50 lbs.

Bell Rock Inn & Suites
6246 Hwy. 179
Sedona, AZ 86351
520-282-4161
RATES: Single $99.95, double
$139.95.
PET POLICY: Fee $20, nonre-
fundable, all sizes.
POI: Bell Roch Pathways, Oak
Creek Canyon, Oak Creek,
Cathedral Rock, Grand
Canyon, Telaquepaque
Shopping Village.

Holiday Inn Express
6175 Hwy. 179
Sedona, AZ 86351
520-284-0711
PET POLICY: $25 nonrefundable
deposit.

Oak Creek Terrace Resort
4548 N. Hwy. 89 A
Sedona, AZ 86336
520-282-3562
RATES: Single $72, double $165.
PET POLICY: Fee $25, nonre-
fundable. Only dogs, up to
25 lbs., must be leashed.
POI: 2½ miles south of Slide
Rock State Park, 4 miles
north of Sedona, near hiking,
Indian ruins and Grand
Canyon.

U.S. Lodgings > ARIZONA

White House Inn
2986 W. Hwy. 89A
Sedona, AZ 86336
520-282-6680
RATES: Single $42, double $46.
PET POLICY: No fee, all sizes welcome. Call first, sometimes there's a fee.

Days Inn
480 W. Deuce of Clubs Ave.
Show Low, AZ 85901
520-537-4356
RATES: Single $57, double $70.
PET POLICY: Fee $5, up to 50 lbs.

Motel 6
1941 E. Duece of Clubs
Show Low, AZ 85901
520-537-7694
PET POLICY: No fee. Dogs under 25 lbs. preferred (larger animals by advance approval). Do not leave animals in room unattended.

Days Inn
125 E. Commercial St.
St. Johns, AZ 85936
520-337-4422
PET POLICY: No fee.

Windmill Inn at Sun City West
12545 W. Bell Rd.
Sun City West, AZ, 85374
602-583-0133
PET POLICY: No fee.

Windmill Inn Suites
12545 W. Bell Rd.
Surprise, AZ, 85374
623-583-0133
RATES: Vary by month.
PET POLICY: No fee, all sizes accepted.

Silver Creek Inn
825 N. Main
Taylor, AZ 85939
520-536-2600
RATES: Single $55.95, double $75.95.
PET POLICY: Fee $10–$20 depending on size, nonrefundable. Up to 50 lbs.
POI: Petrified Forest, Painted Desert.

Hampton Inn
1429 N. Scottsdale Rd.
Tempe, AZ 85281
480-675-9799
PET POLICY: Fee $50, nonrefundable. All size dogs and cats accepted.

Innsuites Tempe Airport
1651 W. Baseline Rd.
Tempe, AZ 85283
480-897-7900
RATES: Single $105+, double $129+.
PET POLICY: Fee $25, nonrefundable. All size pets accepted.

Motel 6
513 W. Broadway Rd.
Tempe, AZ 85282
480-967-8696
PET POLICY: No fee. Dogs under 25 lbs. preferred (larger animals by advance approval). Do not leave animals in room unattended.

Red Roof Inn
2135 W. 15th St.
Tempe, AZ 85281
480-449-3205
PET POLICY: No fee, pets under 80 lbs. Must be leashed to and from rooms. Do not leave in room unattended.

Red Roof Inn
1701 W. Baseline Rd.
Tempe, AZ 85283
480-413-1188
PET POLICY: No fee, pets under 80 lbs. Must be leashed to and from rooms. Do not leave in room unattended.

Baymont Inn & Suites
2548 E. Medina
Tucson, AZ 85706
520-889-6600
PET POLICY: No fee.

Candlelight Suites
1440 S. Craycroft Rd.
Tucson, AZ 85711
520-747-1440
RATES: Suites $44.95–$79.
PET POLICY: No fee, but call before coming. Short stays preferable.

Four Points Hotel by Sheraton
350 S. Freeway
Tucson, AZ 85745
520-622-6611
RATES: Single, double $79.
PET POLICY: Fee $50, nonrefundable. All sizes and pets welcome.

Ghost Ranch Lodge
801 Miracle Mile
Tucson, AZ 85705
520-791-7565
PET POLICY: No fee, all sizes welcome.

Innsuites Hotel & Suites Resort
475 N. Granada Ave.
Tucson, AZ 85701
520-622-3000
RATES: Single, double $89.99–$149.
PET POLICY: Fee $25, all size pets accepted. No restrictions.

InnSuites Hotel Tucson Oracle
6201 N. Oracle Rd.
Tucson, AZ 85704
800-554-4535
RATES: Single, double $89–$169.
PET POLICY: Deposit $25, refundable. Dogs only, under 20 lbs.

Motel 6
755 E. Benson Hwy.
Tucson, AZ 85713
520-622-4614
PET POLICY: No fee. Dogs under 25 lbs. preferred (larger animals by advance approval). Do not leave animals in room unattended.

Motel 6
1031 E. Benson Hwy.
Tucson, AZ 85713
520-628-1264
PET POLICY: No fee. Dogs under 25 lbs. preferred (larger animals by advance approval). Do not leave animals in room unattended.

U.S. Lodgings > ARKANSAS

Motel 6
4630 W. Ina Rd.
Tucson, AZ 85741
520-744-9300
PET POLICY: No fee. Dogs under 25 lbs. preferred (larger animals by advance approval). Do not leave animals in room unattended.

Red Roof Inn
4940 W. Ina Rd.
Tucson, AZ 85743
520-744-8199
PET POLICY: No fee, pets under 80 lbs. Must be leashed to and from rooms. Do not leave in room unattended.

Red Roof Inn
3700 E. Irvington Rd.
Tucson, AZ 85714
520-571-1400
PET POLICY: No fee, pets under 80 lbs. Must be leashed to and from rooms. Do not leave in room unattended.

Rodeway Inn
1365 W. Grant Rd.
Tucson, AZ 85745
520-622-7791
RATES: Single $59, double $69.
PET POLICY: Fee $10, nonrefundable. All sizes and pets welcome (dogs, cats, ferrets, rabbits, birds, reptiles).

Tucson Days Inn
222 S. Freeway
Tucson, AZ 85745
520-791-7511
RATES: Single $44.95.
PET POLICY: Fee $10, refundable. Pets up to 25 lbs.

Motel 6
921 N. Bisbee Ave.
Willcox, AZ 85643
520-384-2201
PET POLICY: No fee. Dogs under 25 lbs. preferred (larger animals by advance approval). Do not leave animals in room unattended.

Holiday Inn
950 N. Grand Canyon Blvd.
Williams, AZ 86046
520-635-4114
RATES: Single $79, double $79.
PET POLICY: No fee, all sizes welcome.
POI: Grand Canyon.

Motel 6
710 W. Bill Williams Ave.
Williams, AZ 86046
520-635-4464
PET POLICY: No fee. Dogs under 25 lbs. preferred (larger animals by advance approval). Do not leave animals in room unattended.

New Canyon Motel
1900 Rodeo Rd.
Williams, AZ 86046
520-635-9371
RATES: Single, double $49.95–$79.95.
PET POLICY: No fee, all sizes and pets welcome.
POI: Near mountains, national park, airport.

Motel 6
520 Desmond St.
Winslow, AZ 86047
520-289-9581
PET POLICY: No fee. Dogs under 25 lbs. preferred (larger animals by advance approval). Do not leave animals in room unattended.

Winslow Days Inn
2035 W. 3rd St.
Winslow, AZ 86047
520-289-1010
PET POLICY: No fee.

InnSuites Hotel Yuma
1450 Castle Dome Ave.
Yuma, AZ 85365
800-922-2034
RATES: Single, double $99–$149.
PET POLICY: Fee $25, pets under 25 lbs. Call for bigger pets.

Motel 6
1640 S. Arizona Ave.
Yuma, AZ 85364
520-782-6561
PET POLICY: No fee. Dogs under 25 lbs. preferred (larger animals by advance approval). Do not leave animals in room unattended.

Oak Tree Inn
1731 Sunridge Dr.
Yuma, AZ 85364
520-539-9000
RATES: Single $59, double $69.
PET POLICY: Fee $10, nonrefundable. All sizes and pets welcome.
AMENITIES: Grass and sand.
POI: Cocopah Casino, Yuma Proving ground, Marine Corps Air Station, Cocopah Indian Reservation, Historic Downtown Yuma, Imperial Sand Dunes.

Radisson Suites Inn Yuma
2600 S. 4th Ave.
Yuma, AZ 85364
520-726-4830
RATES: Single $69–$139, double $69–$139.
PET POLICY: No fee, all sizes and pets welcome (dogs, cats, ferrets, birds, and rabbits).

Shilo Inn
1550 S. Castle Dome Ave.
Yuma, AZ 85365
520-782-9511
RATES: Single $99, double $109.
PET POLICY: Fee $10, nonrefundable. All sizes, all pets welcome.

ARKANSAS

Holiday Inn Express
150 Valley St.
Arkadelphia, AR 71923
870-230-1506
PET POLICY: Fee $10.

Benton Days Inn
17701 Interstate Hwy. 30
Benton, AR 72015
501-776-3200
PET POLICY: No fee.

U.S. Lodgings > ARKANSAS

Days Inn & Suite Bentonville
3408 S. Moberly Ln.
Bentonville, AR 72712
501-271-7900
PET POLICY: Fee $25.

Drury Inn Blytheville
201 N. Access Rd.
Blytheville, AR 72315
870 763-2300
PET POLICY: No fee, pets under 30 lbs.

Brinkley Days Inn
Interstate 40 and Hwy. 49N
Brinkley, AR 72021
870-734-1052
PET POLICY: No fee.

Super 8 Motel
PO Box 828
Brinkley, AR 72021
870-734-4680
RATES: Single $45, double $49.
PET POLICY: No fee, up to 50 lbs.

Cabot Days Inn
1114 W. Main
Cabot, AR 72023
501-843-0145
PET POLICY: Fee $5.

Clarksville Days Inn
2600 W. Main St.
Clarksville, AR 72830
501-754-8555
PET POLICY: No fee.

Comfort Inn Clarksville
1167 S. Rogers Ave.
Clarksville, AR 72830
501-754-3000
RATES: Single $47–$80 (w/jacuzzi).
PET POLICY: Fee $5. All sizes accepted.

Motel 6
1105 Hwy. 65 N
Conway, AR 72032
501-327-6623
PET POLICY: No fee. Dogs under 25 lbs. preferred (larger animals by advance approval). Do not leave animals in room unattended.

Alpen Dorf Motel
6554 Hwy. 62
Eureka Springs, AR 72632
501-253-9475
RATES: Single, double $24–$125.
PET POLICY: Fee $5, nonrefundable. All sizes welcome.
POI: Passion Play, Historic Eureka Springs.

Best Western Inn of the Ozarks
PO Box 431
Eureka Springs, AR 72632
501-253-9768
RATES: Single $55, double $65.
PET POLICY: Fee $5, nonrefundable. All sizes welcome. Must be in crate if left alone in room.
POI: Resort area.

Carriage Inn at Busch Mountain
20856 Hwy. 62 W.
Eureka Springs, AR 72631
501-253-8828
RATES: Double $129.
PET POLICY: Fee $50, refundable, dogs up to 50 lbs., all pets welcome. May not be left alone.
AMENITIES: Lots of room to roam.
POI: Near water for those who like to swim.

Days Inn
102 Kings Hwy.
Eureka Springs, AR 72632
501-253-8863
PET POLICY: Fee $12.

Howard Johnson Express
Rt. 4, Box 309A
Eureka Springs, AR 72632
501-253-6665
RATES: Single, double $32–$99.
PET POLICY: Dogs must be crated if left unattended.

Motel 6
3169 E. Van Buren
Eureka Springs, AR 72632
501-253-5600
PET POLICY: No fee. Dogs under 25 lbs. preferred (larger animals by advance approval). Do not leave animals in room unattended.

Road Runner Inn
3034 Mundell Rd.
Eureka Springs, AR 72632
501-253-8166
RATES: Single $37, double $47.
PET POLICY: No fee, all size dogs, birds accepted. Pets not left unattended in room without crate.
AMENITIES: Several acres of lawns and woods.
POI: 1 mile to Starkey Park on Beaver Lake, 10 miles to historic Eureka Springs.

White Dove Manor Bed & Breakfast
8 Washington St.
Eureka Springs, AR 72632
501-253-6151
RATES: Double $115.
PET POLICY: No fee, do not leave pet unattended, or keep in crate.

Fayetteville Days Inn
2402 N. College Ave.
Fayetteville, AR 72703
501-443-4323
PET POLICY: Fee $15.

Motel 6
2980 N. College Ave.
Fayetteville, AR 72703
501-443-4351
PET POLICY: No fee. Dogs under 25 lbs. preferred (larger animals by advance approval). Do not leave animals in room unattended.

Red Roof Inn
1000 S. Futrall Dr.
Fayetteville, AR 72701
501-442-3041
PET POLICY: No fee, pets under 80 lbs. Must be leashed to and from rooms. Do not leave in room unattended.

Motel 6
6001 Rogers Ave.
Fort Smith, AR 72903
501-484-0576
PET POLICY: No fee. Dogs under 25 lbs. preferred (larger animals by advance approval). Do not leave animals in room unattended.

U.S. Lodgings > ARKANSAS

Holiday Inn
PO Box 790
Forrest City, AR 72335
870-633-6300
PET POLICY: Pets under 10 lbs.

**Baymont Inn & Suites—
Ft. Smith**
2123 Burnham Rd.
Fort Smith, AR 72903
501-484-5570
PET POLICY: No fee.

Days Inn
1021 Garrison
Fort Smith, AR 72901
501-783-0548
PET POLICY: Fee $5.

Driftwood Resort
242 Driftwood Ln.
Gamaliel, AR 72537
870-467-5330
RATES: Single $57, double $67.
PET POLICY: Fee $10, nonrefund-
able. All size dogs and cats.
Keep on leash and clean up.

Scenic Seven Motel
4057 HWY 7 S.
Harrison, AR 72601
870-741-1800
RATES: Single $30, double $35.
PET POLICY: No fee.
POI: National Park, mountains,
rural.

Best Western Inn of Hope
I-30 & State Rd. 4
Hope, AR 71801
870-777-9222
RATES: Single $50, double $60.
PET POLICY: No fee, all sizes
welcome.
POI: Home of President Bill
Clinton. Bill Clinton birth-
place and museum. Shopping
center 2 blocks away.

**Box Hound Marina Resort
& RV Park**
1313 E. Tri-Lake Dr.
Horseshoe Bend, AR 72512
870-670-4496
RATES: Single $55, double $65.
PET POLICY: No fee, all sizes
welcome, Dogs and cats only.
POI: Beach on premises.

All Seasons Lodge
1127 Central Ave.
Hot Springs Nat'l Park, AR
71901
501-624-7131
RATES: Single $39–$55.
PET POLICY: Fee $5, medium-
size pets welcome.

Avanelle Motor Lodge
1204 Central Ave.
Hot Springs Nat'l Park, AR
71901
501-321-1332
RATES: Single, double $40–$45.
PET POLICY: No fee, all sizes
accepted.

Historic Park Hotel
211 Fountain
Hot Springs Nat'l Park, AR
71901
501-624-5323
RATES: Single $70, double $70.
PET POLICY: No fee, all sizes
and pets welcome (dogs, cats,
ferrets, birds, rabbits, reptiles,
etc.).
POI: Located in the middle of
Hot Springs National Park.

Lake Hamilton Resort
2803 Albert Pike Rd.
Hot Springs Nat'l Park, AR
71913
501-767-5511
RATES: Single $89–$100, double
$99–$110.
PET POLICY: Fee $10, nonrefund-
able. Pets under 40 lbs., only.
POI: On lake.

Margarete Motel
217 Fountain St.
Hot Springs Nat'l Park, AR
71901
501-623-1192
PET POLICY: Deposit, $40, all
pets accepted.

Park Hotel
211 Fountain
Hot Springs Nat'l Park, AR
71901
501-624-5323
RATES: Single $70, double $95.
PET POLICY: No fee, all sizes
accepted.

Royal Vista Inn
2204 Central Ave.
Hot Springs Nat'l Park, AR
71901
501-624-5551
RATES: Single $39, double $45.
PET POLICY: No fee, small pets
only.

Vagabond Motel
4708 Central Ave.
Hot Springs Nat'l Park, AR
71913
501-525-2769
RATES: Single $30, double $39.
PET POLICY: No fee, all pets
welcome, up to 50 lbs. Owner
responsible for any damages.
AMENITIES: 1.5 acres for pet
exercise.
POI: Near Lake Hamilton.

Jacksonville Days Inn
1414 John Harding Dr.
Jacksonville, AR 72076
501-982-1543
PET POLICY: Fee $5.

Little Switzerland Cabins
PO Box 502
Jasper, AR 72641
870-446-2643
RATES: Cabin-single $60.
PET POLICY: No fee, all sizes,
dogs and cats, only.

Motel 6
2300 S. Caraway Rd.
Jonesboro, AR 72401
870-932-1050
PET POLICY: No fee. Dogs under
25 lbs. preferred (larger animals by advance approval).
Do not leave animals in room
unattended.

**Gaston's White River
Resort**
1 River Rd.
Lakeview, AR 72642
501-431-5202
RATES: Single $65, double $65.
PET POLICY: No fee, all sizes
welcome.
AMENITIES: Nature trails for pets.
POI: White River, trout fishing.
float trips.

U.S. Lodgings > ARKANSAS

**Baymont Inn & Suites—
Little Rock West**
1010 Breckenridge
Little Rock, AR 72205
501-225-7007
PET POLICY: No fee.

Days Inn
5800 Pritchard Drive N.
Little Rock, AR 72117
501-945-4100
PET POLICY: Fee $10.

Days Inn
7200 Bicentennial Rd.
Little Rock, AR 72118
501-851-3297
PET POLICY: Fee $10.

Holiday Inn Select
201 S. Shackleford Rd.
Little Rock, AR 72211
501-223-3000
PET POLICY: Small pets allowed
under 30 lbs.

Little Rock Days Inn
2600 W. 65th St.
Little Rock, AR 72209
501-562-1122
PET POLICY: No fee.

Motel 6
7501 Interstate 30
Little Rock, AR 72209
501-568-8888
PET POLICY: No fee. Dogs under
25 lbs. preferred (larger animals by advance approval).
Do not leave animals in room
unattended.

Morrilton Days Inn
1506 N. Hwy. 95
Morrilton, AR 72110
501-354-5101
PET POLICY: No fee.

Red Roof Inn
7900 Scott Hamilton Dr.
Little Rock, AR 72209
501-562-2694
PET POLICY: No fee, pets under
80 lbs. Must be leashed to and
from rooms. Do not leave in
room unattended.

Sunrise Point Resort
88 Sunrise Point Ln.
Mountain Home, AR 72653
501-491-5188
RATES: Single $63, double $87.
PET POLICY: Fee charged, all
sizes, dogs only.
POI: Blanchard Springs
Caverns, Mountain Village.

Mountain View Days Inn
Junction of Hwys 5,9,14
Mountain View, AR 72560
501-269-3287
PET POLICY: Fee $5.

**Holiday Inn Express Hotel
& Suites**
4301 McCain Blvd.
N. Little Rock, AR 72117
501-945-4800
PET POLICY: No fee.

Motel 6
400 W. 29th St.
N. Little Rock, AR 72114
501-758-5100
PET POLICY: No fee. Dogs under
25 lbs. preferred (larger animals by advance approval).
Do not leave animals in room
unattended.

Newport Days Inn
101 Olivia Dr., Hwy. 67N.
Newport, AR 72112
501-523-6411
PET POLICY: No fee.

Newport Days Inn
101 Olivia Dr.
Newport, AR 72112
501-523-6411
PET POLICY: No fee.

Baymont Inn and Suites
4311 Warden Rd.
North Little Rock, AR 72116
501-758-8888
PET POLICY: No fee.

Red Roof Inn
5711 Pritchard Dr.
North Little Rock, AR 72117
501-945-0080
PET POLICY: No fee, pets under
80 lbs. Must be leashed to and
from rooms. Do not leave in
room unattended.

Southern Comfort Resort
75 CR 129
Oakland, AR 72661
870-431-8470
RATES: Single $48, double
$56–$65.
PET POLICY: Fee $3, per night,
nonrefundable. All sizes
welcome.

Days Inn
8006 Sheridan Rd.
Pine Bluff, AR 71602
870-247-1339
PET POLICY: Fee $5.50.

Rogers Days Inn
2102 S. 8th St.
Rogers, AR 72756
501-636-3820
PET POLICY: No fee.

Russellville Days Inn
204 Lakefront Dr.
Russellville, AR 72802
501-966-5511
PET POLICY: Fee $5.

Motel 6
215 W. Birch St.
Russellville, AR 72802
501-968-3666
PET POLICY: No fee. Dogs under
25 lbs. preferred (larger animals by advance approval).
Do not leave animals in room
unattended.

**Baymont Inn & Suites—
Springdale**
1300 S. 48th St.
Springdale, AR 72764
501-751-2626
PET POLICY: No fee.

Baymont Inn & Suites
5102 N. Stateline Ave.
Texarkana, AR 71854
870-773-1000
RATES: Single $49, double $59.
PET POLICY: No fee, 50-lb. size
restriction.

**Baymont Inn & Suites—
Texarkana**
5102 N. Stateline Rd.
Texarkana, AR 71854
870-773-1000
PET POLICY: No fee.

U.S. Lodgings > CALIFORNIA

Motel 6
1716 Fayetteville Rd.
Van Buren, AR 72956
501-474-8001
PET POLICY: No fee. Dogs under 25 lbs. preferred (larger animals by advance approval). Do not leave animals in room unattended.

Motel 6
2501 S. Service Rd.
W. Memphis, AR 72301
870-735-0100
PET POLICY: No fee. Dogs under 25 lbs. preferred (larger animals by advance approval). Do not leave animals in room unattended.

Red Roof Inn
1401 N. Ingram Blvd.
West Memphis, AR 72301
970-735-7100
PET POLICY: No fee, pets under 80 lbs. Must be leashed to and from rooms. Do not leave in room unattended.

CALIFORNIA

Adelanto Days Inn Casino Area
11628 Bartlett Ave.
Adelanto, CA 92301
619-246-8777
PET POLICY: No fee.

🅰 **Anaheim Marriott**
700 W. Convention Way
Anaheim, CA 92802
714-750-8000
RATES: Weekdays $219, weekends $159 (rates vary).
PET POLICY: No fee. No restrictions. All sizes welcome.

Best Western Anaheim Stardust
1057 W. Ball Rd.
Anaheim, CA 92802
714-774-7600
PET POLICY: No fee. Dogs under 120 lbs. accepted. Do not leave unattended in room.

Motel 6
1440 N. State College
Anaheim, CA 92806
714-956-9690
PET POLICY: No fee. Dogs under 25 lbs. preferred (larger animals by advance approval). Do not leave animals in room unattended.

Motel 6
100 Disney Way
Anaheim, CA 92802
714-520-9696
PET POLICY: No fee. Dogs under 25 lbs. preferred (larger animals by advance approval). Do not leave animals in room unattended.

Motel 6
225 Colorado Pl
Arcadia, CA 91007
626-446-2660
PET POLICY: No fee. Dogs under 25 lbs. preferred (larger animals by advance approval). Do not leave animals in room unattended.

Quality Hotel Maingate
616 Convention Way
Anaheim, CA 92802
714-750-3131
PET POLICY: Fee $10 per night, plus $25 cleaning fee, nonrefundable. All sizes accepted.

Red Roof Inn
1251 N. Harbor Blvd.
Anaheim, CA 92801
714-635-6461
PET POLICY: No fee, pets under 80 lbs. Must be leashed to and from rooms. Do not leave in room unattended.

Pelican's Nest
408 Trout Gultch Rd.
Aptos, CA 95003
831-685-3500
RATES: Average $250–$300.
PET POLICY: No fee, all pets, up to 50 lbs. Do not leave unattended in room without approval.
AMENITIES: Miles of sandy beaches and hiking trails in Sunset Beach State Park. Near doggie day spa. Many pet-friendly restaurants nearby.

POI: Between Monterey and Santa Cruz in Sunset Beach State Park.

Hotel Arcata
708 9th St.
Arcata, CA 95521
707-826-0217
RATES: Single $66–$72, double $72–$77.
PET POLICY: Fee $5, nonrefundable, damage deposit $50, refundable.
POI: Redwood parks, beaches, bird marshes, six rivers.

Motel 6
1819 Auburn Ravine Rd.
Auburn, CA 95603
530-888-7829
PET POLICY: No fee. Dogs under 25 lbs. preferred (larger animals by advance approval). Do not leave animals in room unattended.

Bakersfield Days Inn
2700 White Ln.
Bakersfield, CA 93304
661-396-8417
PET POLICY: Fee $5.

Comfort Inn Central
830 Wible Rd.
Bakersfield, CA 93304
661-831-1922
RATES: Single $40, double $50.
PET POLICY: Fee $5, nonrefundable. Pets up to 50 lbs.

Motel 6
5241 Olive Tree Ct
Bakersfield, CA 93308
651-392-9700
PET POLICY: No fee. Dogs under 25 lbs. preferred (larger animals by advance approval). Do not leave animals in room unattended.

Motel 6
2727 White Ln.
Bakersfield, CA 93304
651-834-2828
PET POLICY: No fee. Dogs under 25 lbs. preferred (larger animals by advance approval). Do not leave animals in room unattended.

U.S. Lodgings > CALIFORNIA

Oxford Inn & Suites
4500 Buck Owens Blvd.
Bakersfield, CA 93308
661-324-5555
RATES: Single $50, double $55.
PET POLICY: Fee $20, nonrefundable. Dogs, cats, and birds, only.
POI: Buck Owens Night Club, Kern River, 25 miles of bike paths.

Banning Days Inn
2320 W. Ramsey St.
Banning, CA 92220
909-849-0092
PET POLICY: No fee.

Barstow Days Inn
1590 Coolwater Ln.
Barstow, CA 92311
760-256-1737
PET POLICY: Fee $10.

Barstow Super 8 Motel
170 Coolwater Ln.
Barstow, CA 92311
760-256-8443
RATES: Single $52, double $52.
PET POLICY: Fee $5, nonrefundable. All sizes and all pets welcome.
POI: Factory Merchants Mall, Calico Ghost Town.

Budget Inn
1111 E. Main St.
Barstow, CA 92311
760-256-1063
RATES: Single $28.99, double $36.99.
PET POLICY: No fee, small pets up to 25 lbs.
POI: Lake Delores, 15 miles; Calico Ghost Town, 6 miles; Factory Outlet, 6 miles.

Executive Inn
1261 E. Main St.
Barstow, CA 92311
760-256-7581
RATES: Single $30, double $38.
PET POLICY: No fee, small pets only.

Gateway Motel
1630 E. Main St.
Barstow, CA 92311
760-256-8931
RATES: Single $30, double $38.
PET POLICY: No fee, small pets only.

Motel 6
150 N. Yucca Ave.
Barstow, CA 92311
760-256-1752
PET POLICY: No fee. Dogs under 25 lbs. preferred (larger animals by advance approval). Do not leave animals in room unattended.

Raffles L'Ermitage Beverly Hills
9291 Burton Way
Beverly Hills, CA 90210
310-278-3344
RATES: Single $418, double $448.
PET POLICY: Fee $150, refundable. Dogs and cats only, up to 50 lbs. Pets must be quiet.
AMENITIES: Special "pet menu" with appetizers and entrees ($12–$20).

Red Lion Hotel Pendleton
9336 Civic Center Dr.
Beverly Hills, CA 90201
310-278-4321
RATES: Single, double $59.
PET POLICY: Fee $20, refundable. All sizes and pets welcome.
AMENITIES: Large back lawn area to walk pets.

Motel 6
42899 Big Bear Blvd.
Big Bear, CA 92315
909-585-6666
PET POLICY: No fee. Dogs under 25 lbs. preferred (larger animals by advance approval). Do not leave animals in room unattended.

Alpine Village Suites Resort Rentals
546 Pine Knot Ave.
Big Bear Lake, CA, 92315
909-866-5460
PET POLICY: Deposit, $100, refundable. Pets up to 60 lbs.

Bear's Den Vacation Rental
42636 Falcon Ave.
Big Bear Lake, CA 92315
760-961-8779
RATES: Cabins $129–$750.
PET POLICY: No fee, all sizes, no restrictions.
POI: Approximately 1 mile to lake or ski slopes.

Black Forest Lodge
PO Box 156
Big Bear Lake, CA 92315
909-866-2166
RATES: Cabins $165–$205 weekends.
PET POLICY: No fee, no size restrictions.

Frontier Lodge & Motel
40472 Big Bear Blvd.
Big Bear Lake, CA 92315
909-866-5888
RATES: Cabins $70–$335.
PET POLICY: Fee $10 per pet per night. No size restrictions.

Bishop Days Inn
724 W. Line St.
Bishop, CA 93514
760-872-1095
PET POLICY: No fee.

Motel 6
1005 N. Main St.
Bishop, CA 93514
760-873-8426
PET POLICY: No fee. Dogs under 25 lbs. preferred (larger animals by advance approval). Do not leave animals in room unattended.

Vagabond Inn—Bishop
1030 N. Main St.
Bishop, CA 93514
760-873-6351
RATES: Single $80, double $90.
PET POLICY: Fee $5, medium pets up to 50 lbs. All pets welcome. Must keep pets on leash. Do not leave pets unattended. Not allowed in pool area.

Woodfin Suites Hotel—Brea
3100 E. Imperial Hwy.
Brea, CA, 92621
714-579-3200
PET POLICY: Fee $5 per pet per day, deposit $150, refundable.

Motel 6
500 W. Donion St.
Blythe, CA 92225
760-922-6666
PET POLICY: No fee. Dogs under 25 lbs. preferred (larger animals by advance approval). Do not leave animals in room unattended.

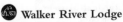

U.S. Lodgings > CALIFORNIA

Walker River Lodge
1 Main St.
Bridgeport, CA 93517
760-932-7021
RATES: Winter $50–$100,
in-season $70–$100.
PET POLICY: No fees, no restrictions. All size pets accepted.

Days Inn Buena Park
7640 Beach Blvd.
Buena Park, CA 90620
714-522-8461
PET POLICY: Fee $7.

InnSuites Hotel Buena Park
7555 Beach Blvd.
Buena Park, CA 90620
800-842-4242
RATES: Single $55.99, double
$79.99.
PET POLICY: Fee $25, refund-
able. Small pets only.

Red Roof Inn
7121 Beach Boulevard
Buena Park, CA 90620
714-670-9000
PET POLICY: No fee, pets under
80 lbs. Must be leashed to and
from rooms. Do not leave in
room unattended.

Red Roof Inn
777 Airport Boulevard
Burlingame, CA 94010
650-342-7772
PET POLICY: No fee, pets under
80 lbs. Must be leashed to and
from rooms. Do not leave in
room unattended.

**Vagabond Inn—San
Francisco Airport**
1640 Bayshore Hwy.
Burlingame, CA 94010
650-692-4040
RATES: Single $99, double $104.
PET POLICY: Fee $10 per night,
small dogs and cats under
25 lbs. Do not leave in room
unattended.
AMENITIES: Bayside path behind
hotel for dog walking.

Meadowlark Country House
601 Petrified Forest Rd.
Calistoga, CA 94515
707-942-5651
RATES: Single, double $165–$230.
PET POLICY: No fee, all size dogs,
only. Must have prior approval.
AMENITIES: 20-acre country
estate with space to play with
your dog.

**Washington Street
Lodging**
1605 Washington St.
Calistoga, CA 94515
877-214-3869
RATES: Weekdays $90–$140,
weekends $125.
PET POLICY: Fee $15 per visit.
Do not leave pets in rooms
unattended, unless crated.

Cambria Shores Inn
6276 Moonstone Beach Dr.
Cambria, CA, 93428
805-927-8644
RATES: Single, double $95–$150.
PET POLICY: Fee $10. All size
dogs accepted. Do not leave
pets unaccompanied on property. Must be on leash. Please
clean up. Must have vaccination record.
AMENITIES: Pet-welcome basket
with pet beach towel, canine
bedspread, dog treats, "Bark"
magazine, placemat for food/
water bowls, special dog
breakfast treat delivered to
door. Lots of lawn to run.
Include dogs in VIP Photo
Book.
POI: Hearst Castle, wine country, elephant seals, artist community, bird sanctuary, golf,
whale watching, near Big Sur,
some off-leash beaches, all
outdoor activities.

Motel 6
750 Raintree Dr.
Carlsbad, CA 92009
760-431-0745
PET POLICY: No fee. Dogs under
25 lbs. preferred (larger animals by advance approval).
Do not leave animals in room
unattended.

Residence Inn by Marriott
2000 Faraday Ave.
Carlsbad, CA 92008
760-431-9999
RATES: Single, double $109–$149.
PET POLICY: Fee $!0 per day per
pet. All sizes and pets welcome.
$150 deposit, refundable; $100
nonrefundable cleaning fee.

Blue Sky Lodge
Flight Rd.
Carmel Valley, CA 93924
831-659-2256
PET POLICY: No fee, pets on
leash and not left alone in
room.

Carmel Valley Lodge
Carmel Valley Rd. at Ford Rd.
PO Box 93
Carmel Valley, CA 93924
831-659-2261
RATES: Single $129,
double $169–$199,
cottages $219–$299.
PET POLICY: Fee $10 per night.
All sizes accepted.

Motel 6
4200 Via Real
Carpinteria, CA 93013
805-684-6921
PET POLICY: No fee. Dogs under
25 lbs. preferred (larger animals by advance approval).
Do not leave animals in room
unattended.

Cayucos Beach Inn
333 S. Ocean Ave, Box 227
Cayucos, CA 93430
805-995-2828
PET POLICY: Fee $10, nonre-
fundable, all sizes and pets
welcome (dogs, cats, ferrets,
birds, rabbits, reptiles, etc.). Pet
blankets, potty area, dog bones
available. Do not leave pets
unattended.

Dolphin Inn
399 S. Ocean Ave.
Cayucos, CA 93430
805-995-3810
RATES: Single $59, double $69.
PET POLICY: Fee $10, nonre-
fundable.

U.S. Lodgings > CALIFORNIA

Chowchilla Days Inn Gateway to Yosemite
220 E. Robertson Blvd.
Chowchilla, CA 93610
559-665-4821
PET POLICY: No fee.

Motel 6
745 E. St.
Chula Vista, CA 91910
619-422-4200
PET POLICY: No fee. Dogs under 25 lbs. preferred (larger animals by advance approval). Do not leave animals in room unattended.

The Inn at Harris Ranch
Route 1, Box 777
Coalinga, CA 93210
559-935-0717
PET POLICY: Fee $10. All sizes accepted.

Riverside Days Inn
2830 Iowa Ave.
Colton, CA 92324
909-788-9900
PET POLICY: Deposit required.

Corning Days Inn
3475 Hwy. 99 W.
Corning, CA 96021
530-824-2735
PET POLICY: Fee $5.

Shilo Inn
3350 Sunrise Way
Corning, CA 96021
530-824-2940
RATES: Single $69, double $79.
PET POLICY: Fee $10, nonrefundable. All sizes, all pets welcome.

Crown City Inn
520 Orange Ave.
Coronado, CA 92118
619-435-3116
PET POLICY: Fee $8, nonrefundable. Pets accepted up to 50 lbs. Do not leave pets unattended in room.

Motel 6
1441 Gisler Ave.
Costa Mesa, CA 92626
714-957-3063
PET POLICY: No fee. Dogs under 25 lbs. preferred (larger animals by advance approval). Do not leave animals in room unattended.

Vagabond Inn—Costa Mesa
3205 Harbor Blvd.
Costa Mesa, CA 92626
714-557-8360
RATES: Single $54, double $63.
PET POLICY: Fee $5, all sizes and pets welcome (dogs, cats, ferrets, birds, rabbits, reptiles). Do not leave pets unattended for long periods. Pets other than dogs and cats must be caged at all times.

Marriott Laguna Cliffs Resort
25135 St. of the Park Lantern
Dana Point, CA 92629
949-661-5000
RATES: Single, double $119–$1200.
PET POLICY: Fee $50, nonrefundable. Dogs must have proof of current shots. Cats allowed also. Pets must be quiet and are not allowed in restaurant or lounge.
AMENITIES: Doggy treats on check-in.

Motel 6
4835 Chiles Rd.
Davis, CA 95616
530-753-3777
PET POLICY: No fee. Dogs under 25 lbs. preferred (larger animals by advance approval). Do not leave animals in room unattended.

Shilo Inn
2231 Girard St.
Delano, CA 93215
661-725-7551
RATES: Single $69, double $79.
PET POLICY: Fee $10, nonrefundable. All sizes, all pets welcome.

GCL Properties—Cabins
PO Box 801
Del Mar, CA 92014
619-246-0678
RATES: Double $135.
PET POLICY: No fee, all sizes and pets welcome.

GCL Properties—Cambria
PO Box 801
Del Mar, CA 92014
619-246-0678
RATES: Double $125–$175.
PET POLICY: No fee.
AMENITIES: Beach, open space to hike and run.

Stardust Motel
66634 5th St.
Desert Hot Springs, CA 92240
760-329-5443
RATES: Single, double $55–$75.
PET POLICY: Fee $7, one-time fee for month, $30 for more than month. Dogs must be kept on leash.

Tamarix Spa
66185 Acoma Ave.
Desert Hot Springs, CA 92240
760-329-6615
RATES: Single $40, double $55.
PET POLICY: No fee, all sizes welcome. No puppies or Pit Bulls.

Downieville River Inn & Resort
PO Box 412
Downieville, CA 95939
530-289-3308
RATES: Single $75, double $84.
PET POLICY: Fee $10, nonrefundable. All size dogs, cats, birds welcome. Pets must be friendly toward other pets and people.
AMENITIES: Great Dog Walks. Pet beds available.
POI: North Yuba River, Lakes Basin area—over 45 Alpine lakes.

Cedar Lodge Motel
4201 Dunsmuir Ave.
Dunsmuir, CA 96025
530-235-4331
RATES: Single $42, double $47.
PET POLICY: Fee $5, nonrefundable; all size pets welcome, including dogs, birds and rabbits. Keep on leash on property; do not leave unattended.
AMENITIES: Lots of trees!

Motel 6
550 Montrose Ct.
El Cajon, CA 92020
619-588-6100
PET POLICY: No fee. Dogs under 25 lbs. preferred (larger animals by advance approval). Do not leave animals in room unattended.

U.S. Lodgings > CALIFORNIA

**San Diego Thriftlodge—
El Cajon**
1220 W. Main St.
El Cajon, CA 92020
619-442-2576
PET POLICY: Fee $10 per pet, non-refundable. All sizes welcome.

**Summerfield Suites Hotel
El Segundo**
810 S. Douglas
El Segundo, CA 90245
310-725-0100
PET POLICY: Fee $10 per night per pet, up to 50 lbs., plus $200 nonrefundable cleaning fee.

Greenwood Pier Inn
5928 S. Hwy. 1
Elk, CA 95432
707-877-9997
RATES: Single $150, double $150.
PET POLICY: Fee $15, nonrefundable. All sizes welcome.
POI: State park with beach next door.

Encinitas Days Inn
133 Encinitas Blvd.
Encinitas, CA 92024
760-944-0260
PET POLICY: No fee.

Motel 6
900 N. Quince St.
Escondido, CA 92025
760-745-9252
PET POLICY: No fee. Dogs under 25 lbs. preferred (larger animals by advance approval). Do not leave animals in room unattended.

Motel 6
1934 Broadway
Eureka, CA 95501
707-445-9631
PET POLICY: No fee. Dogs under 25 lbs. preferred (larger animals by advance approval). Do not leave animals in room unattended.

Shilo Inn
46290 W. Panoche Rd.
Firebaugh, CA 93622
559-659-1444
PET POLICY: Fee $3, nonrefundable. All sizes, all pets welcome.

Tenaya Lodge at Yosemite
1122 Hwy. 41
Fish Camp, CA 95338
209 683-6555
PET POLICY: Fee $50, nonrefundable. All size dogs and cats only. Dogs must be leashed, and are not allowed in public areas. No room service with pets in room. Do not leave unattended in rooms for extended periods of time. Additional fees for damages.

Old Town Inn
300 Reading St.
Folsom, CA 95630
916-985-3482
RATES: Single $125, double $135.
PET POLICY: Fee $100, refundable. All sizes, dogs only. $20 per night cleaning fee; keep created if left unattended.
AMENITIES: Open private park with surrounding forest land.
POI: Historic Sutter Street. American Bike Trail. Golf, tennis, factory outlets, Folsom Dam, Amador Wine country, The Lakes Specialty Center, Apple Hill.

Motel 6
10195 Sierra Ave.
Fontana, CA 92335
909-823-8686
PET POLICY: No fee. Dogs under 25 lbs. preferred (larger animals by advance approval). Do not leave animals in room unattended.

**Rendezvous Inn &
Restaurant**
647 N. Main St.
Fort Bragg, CA 95437
800-491-8142
RATES: Double $85.
PET POLICY: No fee, all sizes and pets welcome. Must be well-behaved.

Best Western Country Inn
2025 Riverwalk Dr.
Fortuna, CA 95540
707-725-6822
RATES: Single $75, double $75.
PET POLICY: Fee $100, refundable. All sizes welcome.
POI: Victorian Ferndale. Avenue of the Giants. Centerville Beach.

Motel 6
34047 Fremont Blvd.
Fremont, CA 94536
510-793-4848
PET POLICY: No fee. Dogs under 25 lbs. preferred (larger animals by advance approval). Do not leave animals in room unattended.

Fresno Days Inn
1101 N. Pkwy. Dr.
Fresno, CA 93728
209-268-6211
PET POLICY: Fee $5.

Motel 6
4080 N. Blackstone Ave.
Fresno, CA 93726
559-222-2431
PET POLICY: No fee. Dogs under 25 lbs. preferred (larger animals by advance approval). Do not leave animals in room unattended.

Motel 6
1240 Crystal Ave.
Fresno, CA 93728
559-237-0855
PET POLICY: No fee. Dogs under 25 lbs. preferred (larger animals by advance approval). Do not leave animals in room unattended.

Red Roof Inn
6730 N. Blackstone
Fresno, CA 93710
559-431-3557
PET POLICY: No fee, pets under 80 lbs. Must be leashed to and from rooms. Do not leave in room unattended.

Red Roof Inn
5021 N. Barcus Ave.
Fresno, CA 93722
559-276-1910
PET POLICY: No fee, pets under 80 lbs. Must be leashed to and from rooms. Do not leave in room unattended.

U.S. Lodgings > CALIFORNIA

Travelodge
3876 Blackstone Ave.
Fresno, CA 93726
559-229-9840
RATES: Double $45.95.
PET POLICY: Fee $5, nonrefundable, up to 50 lbs.
POI: Yosemite National Park. Sequoia and King Canyon National Parks.

Los Angeles—
Days Inn Glendale
600 N. Pacific
Glendale, CA 91203
818-956-0202
PET POLICY: No fee.

Vagabond Inn—Glendale
120 W. Colorado St.
Glendale, CA 91204
818-240-1700
RATES: Single $79+, double $89+.
PET POLICY: Fee $5. Small dogs and cats under 25 lbs. Also birds and rabbits. All pets must be crated. Do not leave in room unattended.

Coach & Four Motel
628 S. Auburn St.
Grass Valley, CA 95945
530-273-8009
RATES: Single $54, double $75, family suites up to $110.
PET POLICY: Fee $10, nonrefundable, all sizes welcome. $50 security deposit.
POI: Empire Mine.

Mar Vista Cottages
35101 S. Highway 1
Gualala, CA 95445
877-855-3522
RATES: 12 cottages: $100–$120.
PET POLICY: No fee. All sizes accepted. No more than 3 per cottage.
AMENITIES: Plenty of land to run free.

Highlands Resort
14000 Woodland Dr.
Guerneville, CA 95446
707-869-0333
RATES: Single, double $85–$125.
PET POLICY: Fee $25, nonrefundable. All sizes and all pets welcome. Pets allowed in 3 cabins, must be on leash, not allowed in pool or hot tub.

POI: This is a gay-friendly resort. Near Russian River, Pacific Ocean beaches (dogs on leash), Armstrong Woods (redwood forests), River Wofe pet specialty shop.

Russian River Getaways
14075 Mill St.
Guerneville, CA 95446
800-433-6673
RATES: Double $200.
PET POLICY: Fee $75, refundable. All size dogs. Not allowed on furniture and cannot be left alone unless crated.
AMENITIES: Bag of treats on check-in.
POI: Many of our beaches are leash-free running, and there are swimming areas for dogs.

Motel 6
1154 S. Seventh Ave.
Hacienda Heights, CA 91745
626-968-9462
PET POLICY: No fee. Dogs under 25 lbs. preferred (larger animals by advance approval). Do not leave animals in room unattended.

Motel 6
820 W. Sepulveda Blvd.
Harbor City, CA 90710
310-549-9560
PET POLICY: No fee. Dogs under 25 lbs. preferred (larger animals by advance approval). Do not leave animals in room unattended.

Motel 6
30155 Industrial Pkwy SW
Hayward, CA 94544
510-489-8333
PET POLICY: No fee. Dogs under 25 lbs. preferred (larger animals by advance approval). Do not leave animals in room unattended.

Vagabond Inn
20455 Hesperian Blvd.
Hayward, CA 94541
510-785-5480
RATES: Single $79, double: $89.
PET POLICY: Fee $10, dogs and cats up to 50 lbs. Do not leave in rooms unattended.

Days Inn Suites
14865 Bear Valley Rd.
Hesperia, CA 92345
619-948-0600
PET POLICY: No fee.

Motel 6
1738 N. Whitley Ave.
Hollywood, CA 90028
323-464-6006
PET POLICY: No fee. Dogs under 25 lbs. preferred (larger animals by advance approval). Do not leave animals in room unattended.

Tahquitz Inn
25840 Hwy. 243
Idyllwild, CA 92549
877-659-4554
RATES: Single $63–$68, double $68–$85.
PET POLICY: Fee $5, nonrefundable. All size dogs.
AMENITIES: Miles of hiking trails and pet-friendly restaurants with outdoor dining nearby.

Super 8 Motel
81-753 Hwy. 111
Indio, CA 92201
760-342-0264
RATES: Single $45–$85.
PET POLICY: Fee $5 per pet and $25 deposit. Up to 25 lbs.
POI: Western Pet Show. PGA Golf.

Crowne Plaza
17941 Von Karman Ave.
Irvine, CA 92614
949-863-1999
PET POLICY: No fee.

Residence Inn Irvine
10 Morgan St.
Irvine, CA 92718
949-380-3000
RATES: Single $99–$134, double $129–$199.
PET POLICY: Fee $40–$60 cleaning fee, nonrefundable, all sizes and all pets welcome. Deposit of $200, refundable. Additional charge of $6 day.
POI: Disneyland. Laguna Beach. Irvine Spectrum Center. Equidistant between L.A. and San Diego.

U.S. Lodgings > CALIFORNIA

Mojave Rock Ranch Lodge
PO Box 552
Joshua Tree, CA 92252
760-366-8455
RATES: Single, double
$275–$325 up to 4 people.
PET POLICY: Fee $10 per day
per pet. All sizes welcome.
Must clean up after dogs.
AMENITIES: Enclosed areas with
doghouses, blankets, bowls and
biscuits.
POI: Joshua Tree National Park.
Mojave Scenic Preserve. Big
Bear Lake. Palm Springs.

Gull Lake Lodge
PO Box 25
June Lake, CA 93529
760-648-7516
PET POLICY: Fee $6 per night,
nonrefundable. All sizes welcome. Downstairs rooms only.

Best Western Inn
33410 Powers Dr.
Kettleman City, CA 93239
559-386-0804
RATES: Single $63.50+, double
$72.50+.
PET POLICY: Fee $2 per pet,
nonrefundable. Pets accepted
up to 50 lbs.
AMENITIES: Pet treats in lobby.
POI: 2 hours to Sequoia,
1½ hours to Hearst Castle.

King City Days Inn
1130 Broadway St.
King City, CA 93930
831-385-5921
PET POLICY: Fee $10.

Motel 6
3 Broadway Cir.
King City, CA 93930
831-385-5000
PET POLICY: No fee. Dogs under
25 lbs. preferred (larger animals by advance approval).
Do not leave animals in room
unattended.

North Lake Lodge
8716 N. Lake Blvd.
Kings Beach, CA 96143
530-546-2731
RATES: Single $70–$85, double
$80–$90.

PET POLICY: Fee $5 per night,
all size dogs acceptable, also
ferrets, birds, rabbits, reptiles.
AMENITIES: 3-minute walk to
"dog-friendly" beach.

Casa Laguna Inn
2501 S. Coast Hwy.
Laguna Beach, CA 92651
949-494-2996
RATES: Single, double
$120–$295.
PET POLICY: Fee $10 per pet per
night. All sizes accepted.

Tahoe Valley Lodge
2241 Lake Tahoe Blvd.
Lake Tahoe, CA 96150
530-541-0353
PET POLICY: Fee $10, small dogs
only, up to 25 lbs.

**Prophet's Paradise
Bed & Breakfast**
26845 Modoc Ln.
Lake Arrowhead, CA 92352
909-336-1969
RATES: Single $100–$165,
double $100–$165.
PET POLICY: No fee, all sizes
welcome.
POI: Ice skating. Hiking. Snow
Skiing.

North Lake Lodge
8716 N. Lake Blvd.
Lake Tahoe, CA 96143
530-546-2731
PET POLICY: Fee $5 per night,
all size dogs acceptable, also
ferrets, birds, rabbits.

**Spruce Grove Cabins
& Cottages**
PO Box 13197
Lake Tahoe, CA 96150
800-777-0914
RATES: Cabins $150 for 2 people,
$185–$195 for 4.
PET POLICY: Fee $10 per day
per dog. Do not leave pets
unattended for prolonged
amount of time. Sitter avail-
able if necessary.
AMENITIES: Fenced acre of
wooded pine where pets can
run freely.
POI: South shore of Lake Tahoe,
Heavenly Ski Resort, Stateline
Casinos.

Tahoe Valley Lodge
2241 Lake Tahoe Blvd.
Lake Tahoe, CA 96150
530-541-0353
RATES: Single $95, double $145.
PET POLICY: Fee $10. Small dogs
only, 25 lbs. maximum.

Motel 6
7621 Alvarado Rd.
La Mesa, CA 91941
619-464-7151
PET POLICY: No fee. Dogs under
25 lbs. preferred (larger animals by advance approval).
Do not leave animals in room
unattended.

Lathrop Days Inn
14750 S. Harlan Rd.
Lathrop, CA 95330
209-982-1959
PET POLICY: Fee $10.

The Inn at Lee Vining
2nd and Mono St.
Lee Vining, CA 93546
760-647-6300
RATES: Single $65, double $70.
PET POLICY: Fee $35, refundable.
All size dogs and cats, only.

SS Seafoam Lodge
6751 N. Highway 1
Little River, CA 95456
707-937-1827
RATES: Single, double $95–$175,
winter rates lower by 30%.
PET POLICY: Fee $10, per dog
per visit. All sizes accepted.

Dow Villa Motel
310 S. Main St.
Lone Pine, CA 93545
760-876-5521
RATES: Single $75–$105, double
$85–$105.
PET POLICY: No fee, all sizes and
all pets welcome (dogs, cats,
birds, ferrets, rabbits, reptiles).
Do not leave pets unattended
in rooms.

**Los Angeles—Days Inn
Long Beach City Center**
1500 E. Pacific Coast Hwy.
Long Beach, CA 90806
562-591-0088
PET POLICY: Fee $10.

U.S. Lodgings > CALIFORNIA

Motel 6
5665 E. 7th St.
Long Beach, CA 90804
562-597-1311
PET POLICY: No fee. Dogs under 25 lbs. preferred (larger animals by advance approval). Do not leave animals in room unattended.

Best Western Hollywood Hills Inn
6140 Franklin Ave.
Los Angeles, CA 90028
323-464-5181
RATES: Average $89.
PET POLICY: Fee $25 per pet per night.

Beverly Hills Plaza Hotel
10300 Wilshire Blvd.
Los Angeles, CA 90024
310-275-5575
RATES: Suites $165–$215.
PET POLICY: Fee $100, nonrefundable, plus $500 deposit, refundable. Small pets under 25 lbs.

Beverly Laurel Motor Hotel
8018 Beverly Blvd.
Los Angeles, CA 90048
323-651-2441
RATES: Single $75, double $79.
PET POLICY: Fee $10 per day, all sizes accepted.

Century Wilshire Hotel
10776 Wilshire Blvd.
Los Angeles, CA 90029
800-421-7223
RATES: Single, double $95+.
PET POLICY: Fee $200, nonrefundable. Pets under 20 lbs.

Four Seasons Los Angeles
300 S. Doheny Dr.
Los Angeles, CA 90048
310-273-2222
RATES: Single $340+, double $370+.
PET POLICY: No fee, small pets only (under 13 lbs.).

Hilton Los Angeles Airport and Towers
5711 W. Century Blvd.
Los Angeles, CA 90045
310-410-4000
RATES: Single $165, double $168.
PET POLICY: Fee $15, all size pets accepted.

Le Meridien at Beverly Hills
465 S. La Cienega Blvd.
Los Angeles, CA 90048
310-247-0400
RATES: Single, double $252.
PET POLICY: Fee $100 first 4 nights, $25 each additional night. All sizes and pets accepted.
POI: Beverly Center, Rodeo Drive, Pacific Design Center, LA County Museum of Art.

Los Angeles USC Vagabond
3101 S. Figueroa St.
Los Angeles, CA 90007
213-746-1531
RATES: Single $85, double $95.
PET POLICY: Fee $10, all sizes accepted.

Marriott Los Angeles Airport
5855 W. Century Blvd.
Los Angeles, CA 90045
310-641-5700
RATES: Single $85, double $95.
PET POLICY: No fee, pet rooms on first floor. All sizes.

Los Banos Days Inn
2169 E. Pacheco Blvd.
Los Banos, CA 93635
209-826-9690
PET POLICY: Fee $5.

Regency Inn
349 W. Pacheco Blvd.
Los Banos, CA 93635
209-826-3871
RATES: Single $45, double $55.
PET POLICY: Fee $4, nonrefundable. Small pets only, up to 25 lbs.

Lost Hills Days Inn
14684 Aloma St.
PO Box 295
Lost Hills, CA 93249
805-797-2371
PET POLICY: No fee.

Madera Days Inn
5327 Ave. 16
Madera, CA 93637
209-674-8817
PET POLICY: No fee.

Motel 6
3372 Main St.
Mammoth Lakes, CA 93546
760-934-6660
PET POLICY: No fee. Dogs under 25 lbs. preferred (larger animals by advance approval). Do not leave animals in room unattended.

Shilo Inn
2963 Main St.
Mammoth Lakes, CA 93546
760-934-4500
RATES: Single $99, double $109.
PET POLICY: Fee $10, nonrefundable. All sizes, all pets welcome.

Residence Inn by Marriott
1700 N. Sepulveda Blvd.
Manhattan Beach, CA 90266
310-546-7627
RATES: Single $169, double $179.
PET POLICY: Fee $75–$100, nonrefundable. All pets up to 50 lbs. welcome (dogs, cats, ferrets, birds, rabbits, reptiles).
POI: Pet Walk—Manhattan Parkway. One mile from beach. Numerous restaurants.

Motel 6
100 Reservation Rd.
Marina, CA 93933
831-384-1000
PET POLICY: No fee. Dogs under 25 lbs. preferred (larger animals by advance approval). Do not leave animals in room unattended.

Mariposa Lodge
5052 Hwy. 140
Mariposa, CA 95338
209-966-3607
RATES: Single $50, double $76.
PET POLICY: Fee $8, nonrefundable. Pets accepted up to 50 lbs.
POI: Yosemite National Park.

Stanford Inn by the Sea
Hwy. 1 & Comptche Ukiah Rd.
Mendocino, CA 95460
707-937-5615
RATES: Single $242–$309, double $242–$342.
PET POLICY: Fee $25, nonrefundable. All sizes and pets welcome (dogs, cats, birds, rabbits, reptiles).

U.S. Lodgings > CALIFORNIA

AMENITIES: Pet dishes, furniture covers, dog bones and treats, pickup bags.
POI: Big River Beach adjacent to Headlands State Park (dogs can run leash-free).

Motel 6
1215 "R" St.
Merced, CA 95340
209-722-2737
PET POLICY: No fee. Dogs under 25 lbs. preferred (larger animals by advance approval). Do not leave animals in room unattended.

Inns Of America— San Jose North
270 S. Abbott Ave.
Milpitas, CA 95035
408-946-8889
RATES: Single, double $169.
PET POLICY: No fee, pets accepted up to 30 lbs.

Best Western Victorian Inn
487 Foam St.
Monterey, CA 93940
831-373-8000
PET POLICY: Room service for 4-legged guests.

Monterey Beach Hotel
2600 Sand Dunes Dr.
Monterey, CA 93940
831-394-3321
PET POLICY: Fee $30, nonrefundable. Pets up to 25 lbs.

Motel 6
2124 N. Fremont St.
Monterey, CA 93940
831-646-8585
PET POLICY: No fee. Dogs under 25 lbs. preferred (larger animals by advance approval). Do not leave animals in room unattended.

The Beach Resort
2600 Sand Dunes Dr.
Monterey, CA 93940
831-394-3321
RATES: Double $89–$299.
PET POLICY: Fee $25, nonrefundable. Dogs and cats accepted up to 50 lbs. Rooms are first floor gardenside.
AMENITIES: Doggie Welcome.

Days Inn & Suites Hotel
434 Potrero Grande Dr.
Monterey Park, CA 91755
213-728-8444
PET POLICY: No fee.

Adventure Inn on the Sea
1150 Embarcadero
Morro Bay, CA 93442
805-772-5607
RATES: Single $39–$99, double $49–$119.
PET POLICY: Fee $10, nonrefundable. All sizes welcome.
POI: Hearst Castle. Montana de Oro State Park.

Best Western El Rancho Motel
2460 N. Main St.
Morro Bay, CA 93442
805-772-2212
RATES: Single $69, double $109.
PET POLICY: Fee $10 per pet, nonrefundable. All sizes welcome.
AMENITIES: Park on premises.

Morro Bay Days Inn
1095 Main St.
Morro Bay, CA 93442
805-772-2711
PET POLICY: Fee $5.

Motel 6
1420 "J" St.
Needles, CA 92363
760-326-3399
PET POLICY: No fee. Dogs under 25 lbs. preferred (larger animals by advance approval). Do not leave animals in room unattended.

Motel 6
63950 20th Ave
PO Box 942
North Palm Springs, CA 92258
760-251-1425
PET POLICY: No fee. Dogs under 25 lbs. preferred (larger animals by advance approval). Do not leave animals in room unattended.

Motel 6
10646 E. Rosecrans Ave.
Norwalk, CA 90650
562-864-2567
PET POLICY: No fee. Dogs under 25 lbs. preferred (larger animals by advance approval). Do not leave animals in room unattended.

Motel 6
8480 Edes Ave.
Oakland, CA 94621
510-638-1180
PET POLICY: No fee. Dogs under 25 lbs. preferred (larger animals by advance approval). Do not leave animals in room unattended.

Motel 6
1801 Embarcadero
Oakland, CA 94606
510-436-0103
PET POLICY: No fee. Dogs under 25 lbs. preferred (larger animals by advance approval). Do not leave animals in room unattended.

Motel 6
3708 Plaza Dr.
Oceanside, CA 92056
760-941-1011
PET POLICY: No fee. Dogs under 25 lbs. preferred (larger animals by advance approval). Do not leave animals in room unattended.

Oceanside Days Inn at the Coast
1501 Carmelo Dr.
Oceanside, CA 92054
760-722-7661
PET POLICY: Fee $20.

Three Buck Inn
PO Box 2048
Olympic Valley, CA 96146
530-550-8600
RATES: Single, double $105–$195 (seasonal).
PET POLICY: No fee, all pets welcome. No restrictions.
AMENITIES: Dogs receive gourmet cookies, squeaky toy, dog bed, Le Bistro water feeder, sheet for comforter, *Bark* magazine, and "vacation" dog tags. Lots of hiking trails.
POI: Alpine Meadows, Squaw Valley, hiking, swimming, skiing and more.

U.S. Lodgings > CALIFORNIA

Red Roof Inn
1818 E. Holt Boulevard
Ontario, CA 91761
909-988-8466
PET POLICY: No fee, pets under
80 lbs. Must be leashed to and
from rooms. Do not leave in
room unattended.

Motel 6
2920 W. Chapman Ave.
Orange, CA 92868
714-634-2441
PET POLICY: No fee. Dogs under
25 lbs. preferred (larger animals by advance approval).
Do not leave animals in room
unattended.

Oroville Days Inn
1745 Feather River Blvd.
Oroville, CA 95965
916-533-3297
PET POLICY: Fee $7.

Travelodge
580 Oroville Dam Blvd.
Oroville, CA 95966
530 533-7070
RATES: Single $55, double $65.
PET POLICY: Fee $25, nonre-
fundable. All sizes welcome.
POI: Lake Oroville.

**Casa Sirena Hotel
& Marina**
3605 Peninsula Rd.
Oxnard, CA 93035
805-985-6311
PET POLICY: Fee $50, nonre-
fundable.

Oxnard Vagabond
1245 N. Oxnard Blvd.
Oxnard, CA 93030
805-983-0251
RATES: Single $60, double $75.
PET POLICY: Fee $5, all sizes and
pets welcome.

Radisson Suite Hotel
2101 Vineyard Ave.
Oxnard, CA 93030
805-485-9666
PET POLICY: Fee $50, nonre-
fundable.

**Bid-A-Wee Motel
& Cottage**
221 Asilomar Blvd.
Pacific Grove, CA 93950
831-372-2330
RATES: Single $59, double $69.
PET POLICY: Fee $10, nonre-
fundable. All sizes welcome.

Inn at Deep Canyon
74470 Abronia Trail
Palm Desert, CA 92260
760-346-8061
RATES: Single $59–$149, double
$79–$179.
PET POLICY: No fee.
AMENITIES: Nearby dog park.
POI: Pet-friendly patio at
local restaurant, McCallum
Theatre, Living Desert,
El Paseo shopping.

Residence Inn by Marriott
38-305 Cook St.
Palm Desert, CA 92211
760-776-0050
RATES: Single $89, double $329.
PET POLICY: Fee $5 per day.
$100–$200 Deposit. Small
pets under 25 lbs. No pets in
Gatehouse. Do not keep pets
in room unattended.

Motel 6
660 S. Palm Canyon Dr.
Palm Springs, CA 92264
760-327-4200
PET POLICY: No fee. Dogs under
25 lbs. preferred (larger animals by advance approval).
Do not leave animals in room
unattended.

Motel 6
595 E. Palm Canyon Dr.
Palm Springs, CA 92264
760-325-6129
PET POLICY: No fee. Dogs under
25 lbs. preferred (larger animals by advance approval).
Do not leave animals in room
unattended.

Crowne Plaza
4290 El Camino Real
Palo Alto , CA 94306
650-857-0787
PET POLICY: No fee.

Motel 6
4301 El Camino Real
Palo Alto, CA 94306
650-949-0833
PET POLICY: No fee. Dogs under
25 lbs. preferred (larger animals by advance approval).
Do not leave animals in room
unattended.

Sheraton Suites Fairplex
601 W. McKinley Ave.
Pomona, CA 91768
909-622-2220
RATES: Single, double
$135–$229.
PET POLICY: Fee $25, all sizes
and pets accepted.
POI: Historic district, on-site
attractions, mountains, skiing,
golf course, lake, all nearby.

**Shilo Inn Pomona—
Diamondbar**
3200 Temple Ave.
Pomona, CA 91768
909-598-0073
RATES: Single $69, double $79.
PET POLICY: Fee $10, nonrefund-
able. All sizes, all pets welcome.

Paradise Inn
5423 Skyway
Paradise, CA 95967
530-877-2127
RATES: Single $45, double $55.
PET POLICY: Fee $7 per day, non-
refundable. All sizes welcome.

Oxford Suites Resort
651 Five Cities Dr.
Pismo Beach, CA 93449
805-773-3773
RATES: Single $90, double $109.
PET POLICY: Fee $5 per day, non-
refundable. Up to 50 lbs. Do
not leave in room unattended.
AMENITIES: Cookie at check-in.
Food available in gift shop.

**Hilton Pleasanton at
the Club**
7050 Johnson Dr.
Pleasanton, CA 94588
510-463-8000
PET POLICY: Fee $25, nonre-
fundable. All sizes and all pets
welcome.

U.S. Lodgings > CALIFORNIA

Motel 6
10694 Olson Dr.
Rancho Cordova, CA 95670
916-635-8784
PET POLICY: No fee. Dogs under 25 lbs. preferred (larger animals by advance approval). Do not leave animals in room unattended.

Motel 6
69-570 Hwy. 111
Rancho Mirage, CA 92270
760-324-8475
PET POLICY: No fee. Dogs under 25 lbs. preferred (larger animals by advance approval). Do not leave animals in room unattended.

Red Bluff Days Inn & Suites
5 John Sutter St.
Red Bluff, CA 96080
530-527-6130
PET POLICY: Fee $5.

Holiday Inn Express
1080 Twin View Blvd.
Redding, CA 96003
530-241-5500
PET POLICY: Fee.

Motel 6
1640 Hilltop Dr.
Redding, CA 96002
530-221-1800
PET POLICY: No fee. Dogs under 25 lbs. preferred (larger animals by advance approval). Do not leave animals in room unattended.

Vagabond Inn— Redondo Beach
6226 Pacific Coast Hwy.
Redondo Beach, CA 90277
310-378-8555
RATES: Single $74, double $89.
PET POLICY: Fee $5, small dogs and cats under 25 lbs. Also ferrets, birds, rabbits accepted. Do not leave pets unattended.

Motel 6
1260 University Ave.
Riverside, CA 92507
909-784-2131
PET POLICY: No fee. Dogs under 25 lbs. preferred (larger animals by advance approval). Do not leave animals in room unattended.

Motel 6
7780 Stockton Blvd.
Sacramento, CA 95823
916-689-9141
PET POLICY: No fee. Dogs under 25 lbs. preferred (larger animals by advance approval). Do not leave animals in room unattended.

Motel 6
1415 30th St.
Sacramento, CA 95816
916-457-0777
PET POLICY: No fee. Dogs under 25 lbs. preferred (larger animals by advance approval). Do not leave animals in room unattended.

Red Roof Inn
3796 Northgate Boulevard
Sacramento, CA 95834
916-927-7117
PET POLICY: No fee, pets under 80 lbs. Must be leashed to and from rooms. Do not leave in room unattended.

Residence Inn— Sacramento-South Natomas
2410 W. El Camino Ave.
Sacramento, CA 95833
916-649-1300
RATES: Single, double $139–$169.
PET POLICY: Fee $50, nonrefundable, pets under 35 lbs.

Residence Inn Sacramento
1530 Howe Ave.
Sacramento, CA 95825
916-920-9111
RATES: Single, double $134–$155.
PET POLICY: Fee $100, nonrefundable. Small pets only.

Vagabond Inn—Sacramento
909 3rd Ave.
Sacramento, CA 95814
916-446-1481
RATES: Single $85, double $100.
PET POLICY: Fee $10, nonrefundable. Small dogs and cats only, under 25 lbs. Do not leave in room unattended.

Barlocker's Rustling Oaks Bed & Breakfast
25252 Limekiln Rd.
Salinas, CA 93908
831-675-3225
PET POLICY: Fee $25, nonrefundable. Pets accepted up to 50 lbs.

Doublearlocker's Rustling Oaks B&B
25252 Limekiln Rd.
Salinas, CA 93908
831-675-3225
PET POLICY: Fee $25, nonrefundable. Pets accepted up to 50 lbs.

Motel 6
140 Kern St.
Salinas, CA 93905
831-753-1711
PET POLICY: No fee. Dogs under 25 lbs. preferred (larger animals by advance approval). Do not leave animals in room unattended.

Motel 6
1257 De La Torre Blvd.
Salinas, CA 93905
831-757-3077
PET POLICY: No fee. Dogs under 25 lbs. preferred (larger animals by advance approval). Do not leave animals in room unattended.

Samoa Airport Bed & Breakfast
900 New Navy Base Rd.
Samoa, CA 95501
707-445-0765
RATES: Double $85.
PET POLICY: Fee $15, nonrefundable. All sizes and pets welcome.
AMENITIES: On the beach, with plenty of room to run and exercise pets.

Motel 6
111 Redlands Blvd.
San Bernardino, CA 92408
909-825-6666
PET POLICY: No fee. Dogs under 25 lbs. preferred (larger animals by advance approval). Do not leave animals in room unattended.

U.S. Lodgings > CALIFORNIA

San Bernardino Days Inn
1386 E. Highland Ave.
San Bernardino, CA 92404
909-881-1702
PET POLICY: Fee $20.

Beach Haven Inn
4740 Mission Blvd.
San Diego, CA 92109
619-272-3812
RATES: Single $75–$110, double
$75–$140.
PET POLICY: Fee $10 per pet per
night. Small pets. Do not leave
in room unattended. Limited
number of pet-designated
rooms.
AMENITIES: Dog Beach at
Ocean Beach (5 miles).

Blom House
Bed & Breakfast
4600 Kensington Dr.
San Diego, CA 92116
858-467-0890
RATES: Single $89, double $139.
PET POLICY: Fee $5 per night,
nonrefundable. Do not leave
alone on premises. Must be
with owners at all times.
POI: Sea World, Zoo, Balboa
Park, Museums, Organ pavil-
ion, Del mar Race Track, Old
Town, Qualcom Stadium,
Mexico border.

Crown Point View Suite
Hotel
4088 Crown Point Dr.
San Diego, CA 92109
619-272-0676
PET POLICY: Fee $50 one-time.

Doubletree Hotels—
San Diego-Mission Valley
7450 Hazard Center Dr.
San Diego, CA 92108
619-297-5466
PET POLICY: No fee.

Four Points Hotel
San Diego
8110 Aero Dr.
San Diego, CA 92123
858-277-8888
PET POLICY: No fee, small pets.

Good Nite Inn
Sea World Area
3880 Greenwood St.
San Diego, CA 92110
619-543-9944
PET POLICY: No fee, small pets.

Hanalei Hotel
2270 Hotel Cir. N.
San Diego, CA 92108
619-297-1101
PET POLICY: Fee $50 one-time.

Harbor View Inn & Suites
550 W. Grape St.
San Diego, CA 92101
619-233-7799
PET POLICY: Fee $10 per pet, non-
refundable. All sizes welcome.

Hilton San Diego Resort
1775 E. Mission Bay Dr.
San Diego, CA 92109
619-276-4010
PET POLICY: Fee $50 one-time.

Horton Grand Hotel
311 Island Ave.
San Diego, CA 92101
619-544-1886
PET POLICY: Fee $50 one-time.

InnSuites San Diego
2223 El Cajon
San Diego, CA 92104
877-343-4648
RATES: Studios: $79.99–$99.99
($30 higher in summer).
PET POLICY: Deposit $50,
refundable. Pets under 50 lbs.

Lamplighter Inn & Suites
6474 El Cajon Blvd.
San Diego, CA 92115
619-582-3088
PET POLICY: Fee $5 daily, up to
25 lbs.

Marriott San Diego Hotel
and Marina
333 W. Harbor Dr.
San Diego, CA 92101
619-234-1500
PET POLICY: No fee.

Marriott San Diego
Mission Valley
8757 Rio San Diego Dr.
San Diego, CA 92108
619-692-3800
PET POLICY: No fee, up to 50 lbs.

Marriott Suites San Diego
Downtown
701 A St.
San Diego, CA 92101
619-696-9800
PET POLICY: $50 one-time fee.

Motel 6
1546 2nd Ave.
San Diego, CA 92101
619-236-9292
PET POLICY: No fee. Dogs under
25 lbs. preferred (larger animals by advance approval).
Do not leave animals in room
unattended.

Motel 6
5592 Clairemont Mesa Blvd.
San Diego, CA 92117
858-268-9758
PET POLICY: No fee. Dogs under
25 lbs. preferred (larger animals by advance approval).
Do not leave animals in room
unattended.

Motel 6
2424 Hotel Circle North
San Diego, CA 92108
619-296-1612
PET POLICY: No fee. Dogs under
25 lbs. preferred (larger animals by advance approval).
Do not leave animals in room
unattended.

Old Town Inn
4444 Pacific Hwy.
San Diego, CA 92110
619-260-8024
PET POLICY: Fee $5 daily, up to
50 lbs.

Pacific Inn
1655 Pacific Hwy.
San Diego, CA 92101
619-232-6391
PET POLICY: Fee $10 per pet, non-
refundable. All sizes welcome.

Pacific Inn Hotel & Suites
1655 Pacific Hwy.
San Diego, CA 92101
619-232-6391
PET POLICY: Fee $10 per pet, non-
refundable. All sizes welcome.

U.S. Lodgings > CALIFORNIA

Residence Inn San Diego
5400 Kearny Mesa Rd.
San Diego, CA 92111
858-278-2100
PET POLICY: Fee $6 daily or $50 one-time, up to 25 lbs.

Sun Beach Vacations
3243 Ocean Front Walk
San Diego, CA 92109
619-543-1212
RATES: Single $90, double $120.
PET POLICY: Fee varies.
POI: Mission Bay Park. Giant Dipper Roller Coaster. Sea World. San Diego Zoo.

Vagabond Inn—Mission Bay
4540 Mission Bay Dr.
San Diego, CA 92109
858-274-7888
RATES: Single $62, double $73.
PET POLICY: Fee $10, all sizes and pets welcome. Pets must be supervised at all times.

Vagabond Inn— Mission Valley
625 Hotel Circle South
San Diego, CA 92108
619-297-1691
RATES: Single $70, double $80.
PET POLICY: Fee $10, all size dogs and cats. Do not leave in room unattended.

Vagabond Inn— Point Loma
1325 Scott St.
San Diego, CA 92106
619-224-3371
RATES: Single $61, double $71.
PET POLICY: Fee $10, all size dogs and cats. Pets must be caged or removed for room cleaning. Do not leave in rooms unattended. Must be on leash, and owners must clean up afterwards.

Red Roof Inn
204 N. Village Ct.
San Dimas, CA 91773
909-599-2362
PET POLICY: No fee, pets under 80 lbs. Must be leashed to and from rooms. Do not leave in room unattended.

Crowne Plaza
400 Sutter St.
San Francisco, CA 94108
415-398-8900
PET POLICY: No fee.

Laurel Inn
444 Presidio Ave.
San Francisco, CA 94115
415-567-8467
RATES: Single $145, double $145.
PET POLICY: No fee, all sizes welcome. Do not leave pets in room unattended.
AMENITIES: Peanut butter dog biscuits.
POI: Golden Gate Park. Golden Gate Bridge. Alta Park. Presidio of San Francisco.

Marina Motel
2576 Lombard St.
San Francisco, CA 94123
415-921-9406
PET POLICY: Fee $10, per night. All size dogs, only. Selected rooms only.
AMENITIES: Off-leash beach and park nearby.

San Francisco Days Inn
2358 Lombard St.
San Francisco, CA 94123
415-922-2010
PET POLICY: Deposit required.

The Westin St. Francis
335 Powell St.
San Francisco, CA 94102
415-397-7000
RATES: Single $219, double $279.
PET POLICY: Fee $30, nonrefundable, pets up to 30 lbs. Need to have own crate.
POI: Union Square shopping. Chinatown within walking distance. Cable Car outside door.

Doubletree Hotels San Jose, CA
2050 Gateway Pl.
San Jose, CA 95110
408-453-4000
PET POLICY: Fee $100 deposit, designated rooms.

Hilton San Jose and Towers
300 Alamaden Blvd.
San Jose, CA 95110
408-287-2100
PET POLICY: Fee none.

Homestead Guest Studios
1560 N. First St.
San Jose, CA 95112
408-573-0648
PET POLICY: Fee $75 deposit, up to 25 lbs., designated rooms.

Hyatt Regency Monterey
One Golf Course Dr.
San Jose, CA 93940
831-372-1234
RATES: Single $205, double $230.
PET POLICY: Fee $50, nonrefundable.

Motel 6
2560 Fontaine Rd.
San Jose, CA 95121
408-270-3131
PET POLICY: No fee. Dogs under 25 lbs. preferred (larger animals by advance approval). Do not leave animals in room unattended.

Summerfield Suites Hotel San Jose
1602 Crane Court
San Jose, CA 95112
408-436-1600
PET POLICY: Fee $75 deposit, $75 one-time fee, up to 25 lbs.

Best Western Royal Oak Motel
214 Madonna Rd.
San Luis Obispo, CA 93405
805-544-4410
PET POLICY: Fee $10, nonrefundable. Pets up to 50 lbs.

Motel 6
1625 Calle Joaquin
San Luis Obispo, CA 93401
805-541-6992
PET POLICY: No fee. Dogs under 25 lbs. preferred (larger animals by advance approval). Do not leave animals in room unattended.

U.S. Lodgings > CALIFORNIA

Rose Garden Inn
1585 Calle Joaquin St.
San Luis Obispo, CA 39407
805-544-5300
PET POLICY: Fee $10 per night,
3-4 dedicated rooms (smoking).

Sands Suites & Motel
1930 Monterey St.
San Luis Obispo, CA 93401
805-544-0500
RATES: Single $69, double $99.
PET POLICY: Fee $5 per pet, non-
refundable. All sizes welcome.

Motel 6
9070 Castillo Dr.
San Simeon, CA 93452
805-927-8691
PET POLICY: No fee. Dogs under
25 lbs. preferred (larger animals by advance approval).
Do not leave animals in room
unattended.

Red Roof Inn
2600 N. Main St.
Santa Ana, CA 92705
714-542-0311
PET POLICY: No fee, pets under
80 lbs. Must be leashed to and
from rooms. Do not leave in
room unattended.

Marina Beach Motel
21 Bath St.
Santa Barbara, CA 93101
805-963-9311
RATES: Single $84–$139, double
$109–$169.
PET POLICY: Fee $10. Dogs and
cats only. Pets up to 50 lbs.
Must be pre-approved at
reservation time. Do not leave
unattended on premises.

Motel 6
3505 State St.
Santa Barbara, CA 93105
805-687-5400
PET POLICY: No fee. Dogs under
25 lbs. preferred (larger animals by advance approval).
Do not leave animals in room
unattended.

Vagabond Inn—Santa Clara
3580 El Camino Real
Santa Clara, CA 95051
408-241-0771
RATES: Single $109, double $129.
PET POLICY: Fee $5. Small dogs
and cats under 25 lbs. Also,
birds. Do not leave in room
unattended.

Guesthouse Inn
330 Ocean St.
Santa Cruz, CA 95060
831-425-3722
RATES: Single $69, double $98.
PET POLICY: Fee $10, nonre-
fundable. All sizes welcome.

Holiday Inn
120 Colorado Ave.
Santa Monica, CA 90401
310-451-0676
PET POLICY: Fee $50 nonre-
fundable, up to 20 lbs.

**Loews Santa Monica
Beach Hotel**
1700 Ocean Ave.
Santa Monica, CA, 90401
310 458 6700
RATES: Single, double $305-345
(partial ocean view)
PET POLICY: No fee. All sizes
and pets accepted.

Motel 6
12733 S. Hwy. 33
Santa Nella, CA 95322
209-826-6644
PET POLICY: No fee. Dogs under
25 lbs. preferred (larger animals by advance approval).
Do not leave animals in room
unattended.

Motel 6
2760 Cleveland Ave.
Santa Rosa, CA 95403
707-546-1500
PET POLICY: No fee. Dogs under
25 lbs. preferred (larger animals by advance approval).
Do not leave animals in room
unattended.

Motel 6
3145 Cleveland Ave.
Santa Rosa, CA 95403
707-525-9010
PET POLICY: No fee. Dogs under
25 lbs. preferred (larger animals by advance approval).
Do not leave animals in room
unattended.

**Thompson Creek Lodge
Cabins**
52431 Hwy. 96
Seiad Valley, CA 96086
530-496-3657
RATES: Single, double $65.
PET POLICY: Fee $5.50, nonre-
fundable. All size dogs, only.
Must be on leash, river front
property and hiking.
POI: Pacific crest trail access, Marble
mountain wilderness area.

**Mountain View
Bed & Breakfast**
12980 Mountain View Rd.
Sonora, CA 95370
209-533-0628
RATES: Single $75, double $100.
PET POLICY: Fee $10, per night,
nonrefundable. Dogs only, up
to 50 lbs.
POI: Mountains, National Park.

Sonora Days Inn
160 S. Washington St.
Sonora, CA 95370
209-532-2400
PET POLICY: Fee $20.

Alder Inn
1072 Ski Run Blvd.
South Lake Tahoe, CA 96150
530-544-4485
RATES: Single, double
$38.50–$95.50.
PET POLICY: Fee $10 per pet per
night. All sizes. Do not leave
pets unattended in rooms.

Cedar Lodge
4069 Cedar Ave.
South Lake Tahoe, CA 96150
530-544-6453
RATES: Single $40–$85, double
$50–$95.
PET POLICY: Fee $10, nonre-
fundable. Up to 50 lbs.
Do not walk on property.
POI: Casinos. Lake. Ski Resort.

U.S. Lodgings > CALIFORNIA

**Inn at Heavenly
Bed & Breakfast Lodge**
1261 Ski Run Blvd.
South Lake Tahoe, CA 96150
800-692-2246
RATES: Single $125–$175,
double $125–$185 (seasonal).
PET POLICY: Fee $100 refundable,
all sizes, dogs only. Must be
kenneled if owner not in room.
AMENITIES: 2-acre park and forest gives pets a place to play.
Dog on premises.

**Lake Tahoe Days Inn
Casino Area**
968 Park Ave.
South Lake Tahoe, CA 96157
916-541-4800
PET POLICY: Fee $5.

Motel 6
2375 Lake Tahoe Blvd.
South Lake Tahoe, CA 96150
530-542-1400
PET POLICY: No fee. Dogs under
25 lbs. preferred (larger animals by advance approval).
Do not leave animals in room
unattended.

Red Carpet Inn
3794 Montreal Rd.
South Lake Tahoe, CA 96150
530-544-2261
RATES: Single $50–$65, double
$50–$65.
PET POLICY: No fee, all sizes welcome. Must have credit card
on file in case of damages.
POI: Casinos.

Salsa's Chalet
1288 Peninsula
South Lake Tahoe, CA 96150
707-795-5292
RATES: Cabins, $125–$175 per
night.
PET POLICY: Fee $100, refund-
able (deposit). All size dogs
and cats, only.
AMENITIES: Cabin equipped
with two dog beds and bowls.

Super 8 Motel
3600 Lake Tahoe Blvd.
South Lake Tahoe, CA 96150
530-544-3476
RATES: Single $45–$275, double
$45–$275.

PET POLICY: Fee $10 per day,
nonrefundable. Dogs and cats
only, up to 50 lbs.

Tahoe Colony Inn
3794 Montreal Rd.
South Lake Tahoe, CA 96150
530-544-6481
RATES: Single $50, double $65.
PET POLICY: No fee, all sizes
welcome. Credit card must be
on file for security.
AMENITIES: Property backs up
to the mountain with lots of
room to run.
POI: Casinos.

Tahoe Keys Resort
599 Tahoe Keys Blvd.
South Lake Tahoe, CA 96150
530-544-5397
PET POLICY: Fee $25 nonrefund-
able, $100 security deposit
(refundable). Call for specific
properties that accept pets.

Howard Johnson Express
222 S. Airport Blvd.
South San Francisco, CA 94080
650-589-9055
PET POLICY: Fee $10 per pet, non-
refundable. All sizes welcome.

Motel 6
817 Navy Dr.
Stockton, CA 95206
209-946-0923
PET POLICY: No fee. Dogs under
25 lbs. preferred (larger animals by advance approval).
Do not leave animals in room
unattended.

Red Roof Inn
2654 W. March Ln.
Stockton, CA 95207
209-478-4300
PET POLICY: No fee, pets under
80 lbs. Must be leashed to and
from rooms. Do not leave in
room unattended.

Stockton Days Inn
33 N. Center St.
Stockton, CA 95202
209-948-6151
PET POLICY: Fee $5.

Motel 6
806 Ahwanee Ave.
Sunnyvale, CA 94086
408-720-1222
PET POLICY: No fee. Dogs under
25 lbs. preferred (larger animals by advance approval).
Do not leave animals in room
unattended.

Sunnyvale Vagabond
816 Ahwanee Ave.
Sunnyvale, CA 94086
408-734-4607
RATES: Single $89, double $179.
Weekday rates generally
higher.
PET POLICY: Fee $10, nonre-
fundable. Dogs and cats under
50 lbs.
POI: San Jose Airport, near
Intel, Sun Microsystems,
Boeing.

Holiday House
7276 N. Lake Blvd.
Tahoe Vista, CA 96148
530-546-2369
RATES: Single $95–$175, double
$95–$175.
PET POLICY: Fee $25 per pet
(up to 5 days), nonrefundable.
All sizes welcome. Do not
leave in room unattended.
AMENITIES: Private Beach.
Snowpark in winter close by.
POI: Tahoe Regional Park.
Squaw Valley Tram: Summer
and Winter.

Three Buck Inn
135 Alpine Meadows Rd. #34
Tahoe City, CA 96145
530-550-8600
PET POLICY: $10, nonrefundable,
all sizes, cookies, dog bed,
water bowl, hiking tails, swimming, doggie shower, and
more.
AMENITIES: Dog beds available,
water, food bowls, cookies,
hiking trail nearby, dogs can
run off-leash and swim in
river, doggie shower with soap
and towels, doggie day camp,
sitter numbers, two Goldens
on premises.

U.S. Lodgings > CALIFORNIA

Golden Hills Motel
22561 Woodford-Tehachapi Rd.
Tehachapi, CA 93561
661-822-4488
RATES: Single $29.95, double
$34.95.
PET POLICY: No fee, all sizes wel-
come. House-trained pets only.
POI: Tehachapi Railroad (Walong)
Loop. Mourning Cloak Ranch.
Indian Hill Ranch. Tehachapi
Mountain Park.

Motel 6
1516 Newbury Rd.
Thousand Oaks, CA 91320
805-499-0711
PET POLICY: No fee. Dogs under
25 lbs. preferred (larger animals by advance approval).
Do not leave animals in room
unattended.

Thousand Oaks Inn
75 W. Thousand Oaks Blvd.
Thousand Oaks, CA 91360
805-497-3701
RATES: Single $95, double $105.
PET POLICY: Fee $75, nonre-
fundable. Small dogs and cats
only. No more than 2 pets per
room, additional Fee $25.

Red Roof Inn
72-215 Varner Rd.
Thousand Palms, CA 92276
760-343-1381
PET POLICY: No fee, pets under
80 lbs. Must be leashed to and
from rooms. Do not leave in
room unattended.

Bishop Pine Lodge
1481 Patricks Point Dr.
Trinidad, CA 95570
707-677-3314
RATES: Single $80, double $80.
PET POLICY: Fee $10 per day, non-
refundable. All sizes welcome.
POI: Clam Beach, Moonstone
Beach, Trinidad on leash.

The Inn at Truckee
11506 Deerfield Dr.
Truckee, CA 96161
530-587-8888
RATES: Single $84, double $94.
PET POLICY: Fee $11 per night,
nonrefundable, do not leave
pets unattended in room.
AMENITIES: Welcome snack.

POI: Lake Tahoe. Donner Lake.
Squaw Valley. Alpine Meadows.
Historic downtown Truckee.
Northstar at Tahoe.

Tulare Days Inn
1183 N. Blackstone St.
Tulare, CA 93274
559-686-0985
PET POLICY: Fee $10.

Motel 6
72562 Twentynine Palms Hwy.
Twentynine Palms, CA 92277
760-367-2833
PET POLICY: No fee. Dogs under
25 lbs. preferred (larger animals by advance approval).
Do not leave animals in room
unattended.

Motel 6
1208 S. State St.
Ukiah, CA 95482
707-468-5404
PET POLICY: No fee. Dogs under
25 lbs. preferred (larger animals by advance approval).
Do not leave animals in room
unattended.

**Blue Lakes Lodge
& Restaurant**
5135 W. Hwy. 20
Upper Lake, CA 95485
707-275-2181
RATES: Single $60–$80, double
$60–$80.
PET POLICY: No fee, all sizes,
only dogs and cats, must be
on leash and must clean up
after dogs.
AMENITIES: 1/2-acre grassy area.
Lake for swimming.

Holiday Inn
1000 Fairgrounds Dr.
Vallejo, CA 94589
707-644-1200
PET POLICY: Small pets (25 lbs.
or less) $25 Wkly fee.

Motel 6
2145 E. Harbor Blvd.
Ventura, CA 93003
805-643-5100
PET POLICY: No fee. Dogs under
25 lbs. preferred (larger animals by advance approval).
Do not leave animals in room
unattended.

Vagabond Inn—Ventura
756 E. Thompson
Ventura, CA 93001
805-648-5371
RATES: Single $50, double $70.
PET POLICY: Fee $5. All sizes and
pets welcome. Call for more
information.

Red Roof Inn
13409 Mariposa Rd.
Victorville, CA 92392
760-241-1577
PET POLICY: No fee, pets under
80 lbs. Must be leashed to and
from rooms. Do not leave in
room unattended.

Motel 6
125 Silver Leaf Dr.
Watsonville, CA 95076
831-728-4144
PET POLICY: No fee. Dogs under
25 lbs. preferred (larger animals by advance approval).
Do not leave animals in room
unattended.

**Pelican's Nest at
Sunset Beach**
93 Sunset Dr.
Watsonville, CA 95076
831-722-0202
RATES: Double $250–$300.
PET POLICY: Fee $50–$100,
nonrefundable. All sizes and
pets welcome.
AMENITIES: walking trails. Miles
of beaches.

Westley Days Inn
7144 McCracken Rd.
Westley, CA 95387
209-894-5500
PET POLICY: No fee.

Motel 6
8221 S. Pioneer Blvd.
Whittier, CA 90606
562-692-9101
PET POLICY: No fee. Dogs under
25 lbs. preferred (larger animals by advance approval).
Do not leave animals in room
unattended.

U.S. Lodgings > COLORADO

Pepperwood Motel
352 S. Main St.
Willits, CA 95490
707-459-2231
RATES: call or e-mail.
PET POLICY: Fee $5, nonrefundable.
POI: World famous Skunk Train. 30 minutes to Giant Redwoods. Mendocino County Museum.

Days Inn
475 N. Humboldt Ave.
Willows, CA 95988
916-934-4444
PET POLICY: Fee $5.

Motel 6
1564 Main St.
Woodland, CA 95776
530-666-6777
PET POLICY: No fee. Dogs under 25 lbs. preferred (larger animals by advance approval). Do not leave animals in room unattended.

Sheep Dung Estates
PO Box 49
Yorkville, CA, 95494
707-894-5322
RATES: Cottages: $95–225 (mid-week and week rates)
PET POLICY: No fee unless 2 dogs or more. Then $20 per pet per night. No restrictions.

The Redwoods In Yosemite
2085 Wawona Station
PO Box 2085
Yosemite Nat'l Park, CA 95389
209-375-6666
PET POLICY: Fee $10 per day, nonrefundable. All sizes welcome.

Motel 6
1785 S. Main St.
Yreka, CA 96097
530-842-4111
PET POLICY: No fee. Dogs under 25 lbs. preferred (larger animals by advance approval). Do not leave animals in room unattended.

Yuba City Days Inn
700 N. Palora Ave.
Yuba City, CA 95991
530-674-1711
PET POLICY: Fee $5.

Yucca Valley Super 8 Motel
57096 Twentynine Palms Hwy.
Yucca Valley, CA 92284
760-228-1773
RATES: Single $47, double $54.
PET POLICY: Fee $10, nonrefundable. Dogs and cats, only, up to 50 lbs. Selected pet rooms only, on first floor.
POI: Joshua Tree Nat'l Park, 29 Palms Marine Combat Center, Desert Christ Park, Hi-Desert nature museum, Giant Rock, Gubler orchid Farm.

COLORADO

Hotel Jerome
330 E. Main St.
Aspen, CO 81611
970-920-1000
PET POLICY: Fee $75, nonrefundable. All sizes welcome.

Motel 6
14031 E. Iliff Ave.
Aurora, CO 80014
303-873-0286
PET POLICY: No fee. Dogs under 25 lbs. preferred (larger animals by advance approval). Do not leave animals in room unattended.

Boulder Broker Inn
555 30th St.
Boulder, CO 80303
303-444-3330
RATES: Single $108, double $108.
PET POLICY: No fee, all sizes, dogs and cats, only.

Boulder Days Inn
5397 S. Boulder Rd.
Boulder, CO 80303
303-499-4422
PET POLICY: No fee.

Canon Inn
3075 E. Hwy. 50
Canon City, CO 81212
719-275-8676
RATES: Single $60, double $90.
PET POLICY: Fee $20–$50, refundable. All sizes welcome.
POI: Royal Gorge Bridge. Arkansas River.

Colorado Springs Days Inn
2850 S. Cir. Dr.
Colorado Springs, CO 80906
719-527-0800
PET POLICY: Fee $25.

Hampton Inn
1410 Harrison Rd.
Colorado Springs, CO 80906
719-579-6900
PET POLICY: Deposit required.

Motel 6
3228 N. Chestnut St.
Colorado Springs, CO 80907
719-520-5400
PET POLICY: No fee. Dogs under 25 lbs. preferred (larger animals by advance approval). Do not leave animals in room unattended.

Red Roof Inn
8280 Highway 83
Colorado Springs, CO 80920
719-598-6700
PET POLICY: No fee, pets under 80 lbs. Must be leashed to and from rooms. Do not leave in room unattended.

Days Inn
PO Box 1048
Cortez, CO 81321
970-565-8577
PET POLICY: No fee.

Denver Days Inn
620 Federal Blvd.
Denver, CO 80204
303-571-1715
PET POLICY: No fee

Drury Inn Denver
4400 Peoria St.
Denver, CO 80239
303 373-1983
PET POLICY: No fee, pets under 30 lbs.

Econolodge
2020 E. Main St.
Cortez, CO 81321
970-565-3474
PET POLICY: No fee, special pet rooms (nonsmoking).

U.S. Lodgings > COLORADO

**Embassy Suites
Denver Airport**
4444 N. Havana
Denver, CO 80239
303-375-0400
RATES: Suites $99.
PET POLICY: No fee, all size dogs
and cats. Ferrets, rabbits, birds,
and reptiles must be kept in
cages.

Motel 6
12020 E. 39th Ave.
Denver, CO 80239
303-371-1980
PET POLICY: No fee. Dogs under
25 lbs. preferred (larger animals by advance approval).
Do not leave animals in room
unattended.

Red Roof Inn
6890 Tower Rd.
Denver, CO 80249
303-371-5300
PET POLICY: No fee, pets under
80 lbs. Must be leashed to and
from rooms. Do not leave in
room unattended.

**Residence Inn Denver
Downtown**
2777 Zuni St.
Denver, CO 80211
303-458-5318
RATES: Single $149, double $169.
PET POLICY: Fee $15 per night,
nonrefundable. All pets and all
sizes welcome (dogs, cats, ferrets, birds, rabbits, reptiles. No
vicious animals permitted.
AMENITIES: Pet relief areas and
plenty of snacks!

The Westin Tabor Center
1672 Lawrence St.
Denver, CO 80202
303-572-9100
RATES: Single $250, double $250.
PET POLICY: No feel, all sizes
and pets welcome.

Alpine Motel
3515 N. Main Ave.
Durango, CO 81301
970-247-4042
RATES: Single $28–$74, double
$38–$84.
PET POLICY: No fee, all sizes
welcome.

AMENITIES: Convenient walking
areas.
POI: Narrow Gauge Train.
Meso Verde National Park.
Rafting. Jeep Tours.

Armhouse Bed & Breakfast
281 Silver Queen S. Bldg
Durango, CO 81301
970-382-9780
PET POLICY: Fee $20 per night.

Durango Days Inn
1700 County Rd. 203
Durango, CO 81301
970-259-1430
PET POLICY: No fee.

Drury Inn & Suites
9445 E. Dry Creek Rd.
Englewood, CO 80112
303-694-3400
PET POLICY: No fee, pets under
30 lbs.

Estes Park Days Inn
700 St. Vrain Ave.
Estes Park, CO 80517
970-586-5301
PET POLICY: Fee $7.

Four Winds Motor Lodge
1120 Big Thompson Ave.
Estes Park, CO 80517
970-586-3313
PET POLICY: Fee $15, nonre-
fundable, pets up to 50 lbs.,
walking area.

Motel 6
3015 8th Ave.
Evans, CO 80620
970-351-6481
PET POLICY: No fee. Dogs under
25 lbs. preferred (larger animals by advance approval).
Do not leave animals in room
unattended.

Sleep Inn Evans
3025 8th Ave.
Evans, CO 80620
970-356-2180
RATES: Single $59, double $65.
PET POLICY: Fee $10, nonre-
fundable. Up to 50 lbs.
AMENITIES: Large Grass area.

Days Inn
3625 E. Mulberry St.
Fort Collins, CO 80524
970-221-5490
PET POLICY: Fee $5.

Lamplighter Motel
1809 N. College Ave.
Fort Collins, CO 80524
970-484-2764
PET POLICY: No fee, all sizes, do
not leave pets alone unless in
crates, no barking, large picnic
area for guests and pets.

Motel 6
3900 E. Mulberry/State Hwy. 14
Fort Collins, CO 80524
970-482-6466
PET POLICY: No fee. Dogs under
25 lbs. preferred (larger animals by advance approval).
Do not leave animals in room
unattended.

Central Motel
201 W. Platte Ave.
Fort Morgan, CO 80701
970-867-2401
RATES: Single $46–$95, double
$52–$95.
PET POLICY: Fee $5, nonrefund-
able. All sizes welcome.
POI: Riverside Park. Fort
Morgan Museum.

Caravan Inn
1826 Grand Ave.
Glenwood Springs, CO 81601
970-945-7451
RATES: Single $59, double $106.
PET POLICY: Fee $5, nonrefund-
able. All sizes welcome.
AMENITIES: Walk area. Public
park.
POI: Hot Springs Pool. Rafting,
Skiing-Aspen, Vail. Glenwood
Canyon.

Denver Days Inn & Suites
15059 W. Colfax Ave.
Golden, CO 80401
303-277-0200
PET POLICY: Fee $8.

Grand Junction Days Inn
733 Horizon Dr.
Grand Junction, CO 81506
970-245-7200
PET POLICY: $50 deposit.

U.S. Lodgings > COLORADO

Motel 6
776 Horizon Dr.
Grand Junction, CO, 81506
970-243-2628
PET POLICY: No fee. Dogs under
25 lbs. preferred (larger animals by advance approval).
Do not leave animals in room
unattended.

West Gate Inn
2210 Hwys 6 & 50
Grand Junction, CO 81505
970-241-3020
RATES: Single $52, double $62.
PET POLICY: No fee, all sizes
welcome.
POI: Colorado National
Monument.

Mountain Lakes Lodge
10480 Highway 34
Grand Lake, CO 80447
970-627-8448
RATES: Single, double $55–$95,
3-bedroom house: $115.
PET POLICY: Fee $5, all size dogs
welcome.

Woodfield Suites Hotel
9009 E. Arapahoe Rd.
Greenwood Village, CO 80111
303-799-4555
PET POLICY: No fee.

Gunnison Days Inn
701 W. Hwy. 50
Gunnison, CO 81230
970-641-0608
PET POLICY: Fee $5.

Motel 6
480 Wadsworth Blvd.
Lakewood, CO 80226
303-232-4924
PET POLICY: No fee. Dogs under
25 lbs. preferred (larger animals by advance approval).
Do not leave animals in room
unattended.

Holiday Inn
27994 US Hwy. 50 Frontage Rd.
La Junta, CO 81050
719-384-2900
RATES: Single $59, double $69.
PET POLICY: Fee $10, nonrefund-
able. All sizes and pets welcome.
AMENITIES: Hotel can provide
litter box supplies, food/water
bowls, pet treats.

**Best Western Coach House
Resort**
5542 Highway 34E
Loveland, CO 80537
970-667-7810
RATES: Single $64.95, double
$59.95.
PET POLICY: Fee $15, Deposit
$50, refundable. All sizes and
pets accepted. Do not leave in
rooms unattended.

Denver Days Inn North
36 E. 120th Ave.
Northglenn, CO 80233
303-457-0688
PET POLICY: Fee $6.

Plain Jane Sack & Snack
3 Munn Court
Ouray, CO 81427
970-325-7313
PET POLICY: No fee, all sizes and all
pets welcome. One pet-friendly
room, one pet at time, restricted
to room and yard. Owner
responsible for damages, etc.
AMENITIES: Water dish, yard.

Motel 6
960 Hwy. 50 W
Pueblo, CO 81008
719-543-8900
PET POLICY: No fee. Dogs under
25 lbs. preferred (larger animals by advance approval).
Do not leave animals in room
unattended.

**Red Feather Ranch
Bed & Breakfast**
3613 CR 68C
Red Feather Lakes, CO 80545
970-881-3715
RATES: Single $65, double $85.
PET POLICY: Fee $15, nonre-
fundable.

**Avalanche Ranch Log
Cabins & Antiques Shop**
12863 Hwy. 133
Redstone, CO 81623
877-963-9339
RATES: Single, double $70–$145
low season, $95–$175 high
season.
PET POLICY: Fee $10 per pet per
night, nonrefundable. All sizes
welcome.

AMENITIES: Dog biscuits, pet towels, 45 acres, 1200' riverfront.
POI: Hiking, fishing, skiing,
snowshoeing, 4-wheeling, hot
springs, hunting, horseback
riding, rafting.

River's Edge
15184 Highway 133
Redstone, CO 81623
970-704-0104
RATES: Single, double $85
(+$15 per person over 2 persons
in room).
PET POLICY: No fee, all size
dongs, only.
AMENITIES: Towels, treats, and
first aid supplies available.
POI: Aspen, Marron Bells,
Glenwood Hot Springs, Vail,
fly fishing, rafting, hiking,
Aspen Music Festival, skiing.

Sabeta Tower House
502 Sabeta Dr.
Ridgeway, CO 81432
303-499-3731
RATES: Double $145.
PET POLICY: Fee $100, refund-
able. All sizes, dogs, cats, ferrets, birds. Leash laws apply.
AMENITIES: Grass backyard and
many walking paths through
open fields.

American Classic Inn
7545 W. US Hwy. 50
Salida, CO 91201
719-539-6655
PET POLICY: Fee $5, nonrefund-
able. All sizes welcome.
POI: Ghost Town. Rafting,
Skiing, Fishing, Mountain
biking. Hot Springs, Golf.

Salida Super 8 Motel
525 W. Rainbow
Salida, CO 81201
719-539-6689
RATES: Single $68, double $78.
PET POLICY: No fee, All sizes
and all pets welcome.
AMENITIES: Ground floor when
available. Pet walk behind
hotel. Town pet walk area
1/2 mile.
POI: Rafting (Arkansas River),
Monarch ski Area, Hot springs
pools, historic downtown area.

U.S. Lodgings > COLORADO

Woodland Motel
903 W. 1st St.
Salida, CO 81201
719-539-4980
RATES: Single $35, double $45.
PET POLICY: No fee, all sizes
welcome.
AMENITIES: Doggie treats,
freshly laundered doggie beds.
POI: Monarch Ski area. Hiking,
biking, trails. Royal Gorge
Bridge. Whitewater rafting.

Inn at Silver Creek
Box 4222
Silver Creek, CO 80446
970-887-2131
RATES: Single $79, Studio: $99.
PET POLICY: Fee $12. All sizes
and pets welcome. Dogs must
be on leash and under control. Do not leave in room
unattended. Advise front desk
about pets when making
reservation.
AMENITIES: Field behind facilities for best friends to run.
POI: Great hiking trails (year-
round access) in Colorado
Rockies. Ponds and lakes
nearby. Rocky Mnt. Nat'l
Park 25 minute drive.

Days Inn
580 Silverthorne Ln.
Silverthorne, CO 80498
970-468-8661
RATES: Ski season: $99–$229,
Off-season: $69–$189.
PET POLICY: Fee $10 per pet per
night. All sizes accepted.

**Mountain Vista
Bed & Breakfast**
PO Box 1398, 358 Lagoon Ln.
Silverthorne, CO 80498
970-468-7700
RATES: Double $50–$100.
PET POLICY: No fee, all size dogs
accepted. Bedrooms with
shared bath, only.
AMENITIES: 4 foot fenced
backyard.
POI: Breckenridge, Vail,
Keystone, Dillon and Frisco.

The Wyman Hotel & Inn
1371 Greene St. (Main)
Silverton, CO 81433
970-387-5372
RATES: Single $90, double
$95–$180.
PET POLICY: Fee $15, nonre-
fundable. All sizes welcome.
Do not leave unattended in
room.
AMENITIES: Dog biscuits at time
of afternoon tea.
POI: Mesa Verde National Park.
Black Canyon of the Gunnison
National Park. Silverton
Narrow Gorge Railroad.

Trinidad Days Inn
702 W. Main St.
Trinidad, CO 81082
719-846-2271
PET POLICY: $20 deposit.

Lifthouse Condominiums
555 E. Lionhead Cir.
Vail, CO 81657
970-476-2340
PET POLICY: Fee $25–$100 one-
time, no other restrictions.

Motel 6
10300 S. I-70 Frontage Rd.
Wheat Ridge, CO 80033
303-467-3172
PET POLICY: No fee. Dogs under
25 lbs. preferred (larger animals by advance approval).
Do not leave animals in room
unattended.

The Vintage Hotel
100 Winter Park Dr.
Winter Park, CO 80482
970-726-8801
RATES: Single, double
$90–$185, Studios
PET POLICY: Fee $25, all sizes
accepted.

CONNECTICUT

Branford Days Inn
375 E. Main St.
Branford, CT 06405
203-488-8314
PET POLICY: No fee.

Motel 6
320 E. Main St.
Branford, CT 06405
203-483-5828
PET POLICY: No fee. Dogs under
25 lbs. preferred (larger animals by advance approval).
Do not leave animals in room
unattended.

Holiday Inn
1070 Main St.
Bridgeport, CT 6604
203-334-1234
PET POLICY: Pets allows under
20 lbs.

Ramada Inn
Interstate Hwy. 84, Exit 8
Danbury, CT 06810
203-792-3800
PET POLICY: No fee, under 100 lbs.,
don't leave in room unat-
tended, and on leash outside.

Residence Inn Danbury
22 Segar St.
Danbury, CT 06810
203-797-1256
PET POLICY: Fee $20 nonre-
fundable.

Holiday Inn
363 Roberts St.
E. Hartford, CT 6108
860-528-9611
RATES: Avg: $109.
PET POLICY: No fee, all sizes
accepted.

Motel 6
11 Hazard Ave.
Enfield, CT 06082
860-741-3685
PET POLICY: No fee. Dogs under
25 lbs. preferred (larger animals by advance approval).
Do not leave animals in room
unattended.

U.S. Lodgings > CONNECTICUT

Red Roof Inn
5 Hazard Ave.
Enfield, CT 06082
860-741-2571
PET POLICY: No fee, pets under 80 lbs. Must be leashed to and from rooms. Do not leave in room unattended.

Griswold Inn
36 Main St.
Essex, CT 06426
860-767-1776
RATES: Avg. $90–$195.
PET POLICY: No fee, all sizes accepted.

Homewood Suites Hotel
2 Farm Glen Blvd.
Farmington, CT 6032
860-321-0001
PET POLICY: One time $150 cleaning fee and guest signature on pet policy.

Homespun Farm Bed & Breakfast
306 Preston Rd.
Griswold, CT 06351
860-376-5178
RATES: Avg. $110.
PET POLICY: Fee $50, refundable. Up to 50 lbs., all pets welcome.

Capitol Hill Ramada Inn
440 Asylum St.
Hartford, CT 06103
860-246-6591
RATES: Single $85, double $95.
PET POLICY: Fee $25, all sizes accepted.

Crowne Plaza Downtown
50 Morgan St.
Hartford, CT 06120
860-549-2400
RATES: $100 (weekend)–$210 (mid-week).
PET POLICY: Fee $25, all sizes accepted.

Hartford Downtown Days Inn
207 Brainard Rd.
Hartford, CT 06114
860-247-3297
PET POLICY: No fee.

Hartford-Windsor Super 8 Motel
57 W. Service Rd.
Hartford, CT 06120
860-246-8888
RATES: Single $58, double $66.
PET POLICY: No fee, pets in smoking rooms only.

Red Roof Inn
100 Weston St.
Hartford, CT 06120
860-7240222
PET POLICY: No fee, pets under 80 lbs. Must be leashed to and from rooms. Do not leave in room unattended.

Inn at Iron Masters
229 Main St. (Rt. 44)
Lakeville, CT 06039
860-435-9844
RATES: Single $110, double $116.
PET POLICY: No fee, dogs only. Must be leashed at all times, and not left in rooms unattended. Must be at least 1 year old and fully trained. No more than 2 per room, and must notify desk when making reservations.
AMENITIES: Dog biscuit upon check-in
POI: Berkshire mountains, Appalachian Trail, Lime Rock Speedway, Trout streams, Tanglewood, Jacob's Pillow, Shakespeare Theater, Music Mountain, Yale Summer Symphony.

The Interlaken Inn
74 Interlaken Rd.
Lakeville, CT 06039
860-435-9878
RATES: $129–$319.
PET POLICY: Fee $10, per night, all sizes accepted.

Applewood Farms Inn Bed & Breakfast
528 Colonel Ledyard
Ledyard, CT 06339
860-536-2022
RATES: Single $125, double $290.
PET POLICY: No fee, all sizes and pets welcome (dogs, cats, ferrets, birds, rabbits, etc.). May be off leash if you are with them, otherwise in outdoor run, or in crate. Not allowed on beds. Horses and dogs on premises.
AMENITIES: Outdoor run fenced and covered with dog house and cement floor. 30 acres of lanes and trails. Pastures with horses. Our 2 Basset Hounds to play with.
POI: Mystic Seaport.

Red Roof Inn
10 Rowe Ave.
Milford, CT 06460
203-877-6060
PET POLICY: No fee, pets under 80 lbs. Must be leashed to and from rooms. Do not leave in room unattended.

Hartford Days Inn
Route 322
Milldale, CT 06467
860-621-9181
PET POLICY: No fee.

Harbour Inne & Cottage
15 Edgemont St.
Mystic, CT 06355
860-572-9253
RATES: Avg. $55–$300 (seasonal).
PET POLICY: Fee $10 per day, nonrefundable. All sizes and all pets welcome (dogs, cats, ferrets, birds, rabbits, reptiles).
POI: Mystic seaport museum, Marinelife Aquarium, Foxwoods Resort-Casino, Meshantucket Pequot Indian Museum, Ocean, Beach, resort area.

Motel 6
270 Foxon Blvd.
New Haven, CT 06513
203-469-0343
PET POLICY: No fee. Dogs under 25 lbs. preferred (larger animals by advance approval). Do not leave animals in room unattended.

Residence Inn New Haven
3 Long Wharf Dr.
New Haven, CT 06511
203-777-5337
RATES: $145–$170.
PET POLICY: Fee $10 per night, all sizes accepted.
AMENITIES: All suites.

Red Roof Inn
707 Colman St.
New London, CT 06320
860-444-0001
PET POLICY: No fee, pets under
80 lbs. Must be leashed to and
from rooms. Do not leave in
room unattended.

Motel 6
269 Flanders Rd.
Niantic, CT 06357
860-739-6991
PET POLICY: No fee. Dogs under
25 lbs. preferred (larger animals by advance approval).
Do not leave animals in room
unattended.

Sandpiper Motor Inn
1750 Boston Post Rd.
Old Saybrook, CT 06475
860-399-7973
RATES: Avg. $75–$135.
PET POLICY: Fee $10, all sizes
accepted.

**Roseledge Farm
Bed & Breakfast**
418 Route 164
Preston, CT 06365
860-892-4739
RATES: Avg. $85–$125.
PET POLICY: No fee, all sizes and
pets welcome. Call first.

**Howard Johnson
Express Inn**
1760 Silas Deane Hwy.
Rocky Hill, CT 06067
860-529-3341
RATES: Single $65, double $75.
PET POLICY: Fee $10, pets
accepted for one night only.

Ramada Plaza Hotel
780 Bridgeport Ave.
Shelton, CT 06484
203-929-1500
RATES: $89–$199.
PET POLICY: No fee, pets
accepted up to 20 lbs.

Residence Inn Shelton
1001 Bridgeport Ave.
Shelton, CT 06484
203-926-9000
RATES: Single $170, double $190.
PET POLICY: Fee $20 per night,
all sizes accepted.

Motel 6
625 Queen St.
Southington, CT 06489
860-621-7351
PET POLICY: No fee. Dogs under
25 lbs. preferred (larger animals by advance approval).
Do not leave animals in room
unattended.

**House on the Hill
Bed & Breakfast**
92 Woodlawn Terrace
Waterbury, CT 06710
203-757-9900
RATES: Single $150, double $150.
PET POLICY: No fee, all sizes and
all pets welcome. Do not leave
pets unattended.

Oakdell Motel
983 Hartford Rd.
Waterford, CT 06385
860-442-9446
RATES: Single $65, double $75.
PET POLICY: Fee $10, nonre-
fundable, cannot be left in
room unattended.

**Baymont Inn & Suites—
Windsor Locks**
64 Ella Grasso Turnpike
Windsor Locks, CT 06096
860-623-3336
PET POLICY: No fee.

Motel 6
3 National Dr.
Windsor Locks, CT 06096
860-292-6200
PET POLICY: No fee. Dogs under 25
lbs. preferred (larger animals by
advance approval). Do not leave
animals in room unattended.

**Sheraton Bradley Airport
Hotel**
One Bradley International Airport
Windsor Locks, CT 06096
860-627-5311
RATES: Avg. $115–$215.
PET POLICY: No fee, pets under
25 lbs. only.

DELAWARE

Bellbuoy Motel
21 Van Dyke St.
Dewey Beach, DE 19971
302-227-6000
RATES: Single, double $39–$125.
PET POLICY: Fee $6, all sizes
accepted. (No pets in July-
August).

**Country Lane
Bed & Breakfast**
7 Country Ln.
Lewes, DE 19958
302-945-1586
RATES: Single, double $85 and $95.
PET POLICY: No fee, all size dogs,
only. Dogs not permitted in
house, guest rooms, pool deck.
AMENITIES: Three kennels available on site, protected from
elements, 10 ft. concrete run,
individual entrance doors.
POI: Delaware beaches, Cape
Helopen State Park.

Quality Inn Skyways
147 N. DuPont Hwy.
New Castle, DE 19720
302-328-6666
RATES: Single, double $84.
PET POLICY: Fee $10, all sizes
accepted.

**Howard Johnson Inn
& Suites**
1119 S. College Ave.
Newark, DE 19713
302-368-8521
RATES: Single $65, double $69.
PET POLICY: Fee $10 per pet per
night. All sizes accepted.

Red Roof Inn
415 Stanton Christiana Rd.
Newark, DE 19713
302-292-2870
PET POLICY: No fee, pets under
80 lbs. Must be leashed to and
from rooms. Do not leave in
room unattended.

Motel 6
1200 W. Ave/S Hwy. 9
New Castle, DE 19720
302-571-1200
PET POLICY: No fee. Dogs under 25
lbs. preferred (larger animals by
advance approval). Do not leave
animals in room unattended.

DISTRICT OF COLUMBIA

Carlyle Suites Hotel
1731 New Hampshire Ave., NW
Washington, DC 20009
202-234-5377
PET POLICY: No fee, all sizes and all pets welcome.

Doubletree Hotels
801 New Hampshire Ave., NW
Washington, DC 20037
202-785-2000
PET POLICY: Fee $15 per day. All sizes accepted.

Hotel Washington
515 15th St., NW
Washington, DC, 20004
202-638-5900
PET POLICY: No fee, all size pets accepted.

Howard Johnson Express Inn
600 New York Ave., NE
Washington, DC 20002
202-546-9200
RATES: Single $79+, double $89+.
PET POLICY: Fee $7 per night. All sizes accepted.

Loews L'Enfant Plaza Hotel
480 L'Enfant Plaza
Washington, DC 20024
202-484-1000
RATES: Single, double $219–$289.
PET POLICY: No fee. All sizes accepted.

Marriott's Wardman Park Hotel
2660 Woodley Road NW
Washington, DC 20008
202-328-2000
RATES: Single, double 119–$319.
PET POLICY: No fee. Small pets under 30 lbs.

Motel 6
6711 Georgia Ave.
Washington, DC 20012
202-722-1600
PET POLICY: No fee. Dogs under 25 lbs. preferred (larger animals by advance approval). Do not leave animals in room unattended.

Red Roof Inn
500 H Street Northwest
Washington, DC 20001
202-289-5959
PET POLICY: No fee, pets under 80 lbs. Must be leashed to and from rooms. Do not leave in room unattended.

Renaissance Mayflower Hotel
1127 Connecticut Avenue NW
Washington, DC 20036
202-347-3000
RATES: Single, double $289–$389.
PET POLICY: Fee $50, refundable. Pets under 20 lbs.

Swissotel Washington— the Watergate
2650 Virginia Avenue, NW
Washington, DC 20037
202-965-2300
RATES: Single $235–$450, suites $700 (suite).
PET POLICY: No fee. Small pets, only.

The Jefferson
1200 16th Street, NW
Washington, DC 70036-329
202 347-2200
RATES: Single, double $309–$539.
PET POLICY: No fee. Medium size pets (dogs).

Washington, DC Days Inn
2700 New York Ave.
Washington, DC 20002
202-832-5800
PET POLICY: No fee.

Washington Suites
2500 Pennsylvania Ave.
Washington, DC 20037
202-333-8060
RATES: Suites $109–$289.
PET POLICY: Fee $15 pet day. All sizes accepted.

Westin Fairfax
2100 Massachusetts Avenue NW
Washington, DC 20008
202-293-2100
RATES: Single $199–$320.
PET POLICY: Fee $00, nonrefundable, plus $75 refundable deposit. Small pets under 25 lbs.

Willard Inter-Continental
1401 Pennsylvania Ave.
Washington, DC 20004
202-628-9100
RATES: Single, double $425–$550.
PET POLICY: No fee. Cats and Dogs only. Pet Waiver must be signed.

FLORIDA

Hampton Inn
151 N. Douglas Ave.
Altamonte Springs, FL 32714
407-869-9000
PET POLICY: Non Refundable Deposit.

Rancho Inn
240 Hwy. 98
Apalachicola, FL 32320
850-653-9435
RATES: Single, double $50–$75.
PET POLICY: Fee $6, nonrefundable. All sizes and all pets welcome.
AMENITIES: Beautiful area for walking pets.

Canoe Outpost—Peace River
2816 NW County Rd. 661
Arcadia, FL 34266
863-494-1215
PET POLICY: No fee, all sizes and all pets welcome.

Signum Resort Las Palmas
600 E. Canfield St.
Avon Park, FL 33825
863-528-2020
RATES: Single/Double $80.
PET POLICY: Fee $10, nonrefundable. Dogs and cats only, up to 50 lbs. Over 50 lbs. stay in kennel area.
POI: 10 miles from Sebring.

Orlando Days Inn
2425 Frontage Rd.
Baseball City, FL 33837
863-424-2596
PET POLICY: Fee $10.

Dancing With Dolphins
PO Box 272
Bokeelia, FL 33922
941-282-5716
RATES: $86–$129.
PET POLICY: Fee $75, nonrefundable. All sizes and pets accepted.
AMENITIES: Fenced in yard.

U.S. Lodgings > FLORIDA

Bradenton Days Inn Near the Gulf
3506 1st St. W.
Bradenton, FL 34208
941-746-1141
PET POLICY: No fee.

Motel 6
660 67 St. Cir. E
Bradenton, FL 34208
941-747-6005
PET POLICY: No fee. Dogs under 25 lbs. preferred (larger animals by advance approval). Do not leave animals in room unattended.

Park Inn & Suites
4450 47th St. W.
Bradenton, FL 34210
941-795-4633
RATES: Single $94, double $104.
PET POLICY: Fee $10, nonrefundable, all sizes welcome.
POI: Palma Sola Bay and Beach.

Ray's Canoe Hideaway & Kayak Center
1247 Hagle Park Rd.
Bradenton, FL 34202
941-747-3909
PET POLICY: No fee, all sizes and pets welcome.
AMENITIES: Water bowl. Hitching post.
POI: Canoeing and kayaking on the lake.

Tradewinds Resort
1603 Gulf Drive N.
Bradenton Beach, FL 34217
941-779-0010
RATES: Single $109, double $139.
PET POLICY: Fee $30, nonrefundable. Credit card as deposit for damages. All sizes and all pets
AMENITIES: Food dishes, fenced dog run.
POI: DeSoto Nat'l Memorial Park, Manatee Causeway, Ocean-Beach.

'Tween Waters Inn
15951 Captiva Rd.
Captiva Island, FL 33924
941-475-5161
PET POLICY: Fee $10, nonrefundable, all sizes, miles of pet-friendly beaches.

The Moorings at Carrabelle
1000 US 98
Carrabelle, FL 32322
850-697-2800
RATES: Single $75, double $75.
PET POLICY: Fee $10, nonrefundable. All sizes and pets welcome. Deposit of $50 or open credit card.

Park Place Motel
PO Box 613, 211 Second St.
Cedar Key, FL 32625
352-543-5737
RATES: Single $60, double $60.
PET POLICY: Fee $7, nonrefundable. Over 50 lbs. Some breed restrictions.

Chipley Days Inn
1593 Main St.
Chipley, FL 32428
850-638-7335
PET POLICY: Fee $10.

Holiday Inn Express
13625 ICOT Blvd.
Clearwater, FL 33760
727-536-7275
PET POLICY: No fee, under 20 lbs. Do not leave in room unattended.

Homestead Village Studios
2311 Ulmerton Rd.
Clearwater, FL, 33762
727-572-4800
RATES: Single, double $59-69
PET POLICY: Fee $75, nonrefundable.

Homewood Suites Hotel
2233 Ulmerton Rd.
Clearwater, FL 33762
727-573-1500
PET POLICY: Pets under 40 lbs. welcome for additional fee.

Best Western SeaStone Resort & Suites
445 Hamden Dr.
Clearwater Beach, FL 33767
727-441-1722
PET POLICY: Deposit $50 nonrefundable, prefer pets under 20 lbs.

Chart House Suites
850 Bayway Blvd.
Clearwater Beach, FL 33767
727-449-8007
RATES: Single $57, double $199.
PET POLICY: Fee $25, nonrefundable. Small pets, up to 25 lbs. All pets welcome.
AMENITIES: Pet walking area, special pet treats.

Space Coast Days Inn Cocoa-Interstate Highway 95-K
5600 State Route 524
Cocoa, FL 32926-242
321-636-6500
PET POLICY: Fee $10.

Cocoa Beach Days Inn Oceanfront
5600 N. Atlantic Ave.
Cocoa Beach, FL 32931
321-783-7621
PET POLICY: No fee.

Motel 6
3701 N. Atlantic Ave.
Cocoa Beach, FL 32931
321-783-3103
PET POLICY: No fee. Dogs under 25 lbs. preferred (larger animals by advance approval). Do not leave animals in room unattended.

South Beach Inn-On-The-Sea
1701 S. Atlantic Ave.
Cocoa Beach, FL 32931
321-784-3333
RATES: Single $80, double $100.
PET POLICY: Fee $10 per day, nonrefundable. All pets welcome, up to 50 lbs.
AMENITIES: Ocean front.
POI: Kennedy Space Center, Disney World.

Surf Studio Beach Resort
1801 S. Atlantic Ave.
Cocoa Beach, FL 32931
321-783-7100
RATES: Single $75, double $150.
PET POLICY: Fee $20, nonrefundable. All sizes and pets welcome (dogs, cats, birds) pets must be licensed and vaccinated, not aggressive, kept on leash.

U.S. Lodgings > FLORIDA

Crystal River Days Inn
2380 NW Hwy. 19
Crystal River, FL 34428
352-795-2111
PET POLICY: Fee $10.

**Baymont Inn & Suites—
Cutler Ridge**
10821 Caribbean Blvd.
Cutler Ridge, FL 33189
305-278-0001
PET POLICY: No fee.

Companion Cottage
246 Chris Court
Davenport, FL 33837
863-424-0999
RATES: Single, double $150.
PET POLICY: Fee $75, refundable.
All sizes and all pets welcome.
AMENITIES: Fenced in area.
Petsitting services available.
POI: Near Walt Disney World,
Universal Studios, Busch
Gardens, cypress Gardens,
beaches 60.

Motel 6
5620 US Hwy. 27 N.
Davenport, FL 33837
941-424-2521
PET POLICY: No fee. Dogs under
25 lbs. preferred (larger animals by advance approval).
Do not leave animals in room
unattended.

Super 8 Main Gate—South
5620 US Hwy. 27
Davenport, FL 33837
863-420-8888
RATES: Single $39–$120, double
$39–$120.
PET POLICY: Fee, all sizes, all pets
welcome.
AMENITIES: Open ground to
walk pets.

**Breakers Beach Oceanfront
Motel**
27 S. Ocean Ave.
Daytona Beach, FL 32118
904-252-0863
RATES: Single $68.
PET POLICY: Fee $10 a day, non-
refundable, no puppies, pet
run or walk area.
AMENITIES: Pet run or walk
area.

**Days Inn Oceanfront
Central**
1909 S. Atlantic Ave.
Daytona Beach, FL 32118
904-255-0632
RATES: Single $45–$95, double
$55–$105.
PET POLICY: Fee $15, up to 50 lbs.
POI: Daytona Speedway 10 miles
Orlando Attractions 60 miles
Old City of St. Augustine 35
miles.

**Daytona on the Beach
Days Inn**
1220 N. Atlantic Ave.
Daytona Beach, FL 32118
904-255-2745
PET POLICY: Fee $15.

**Daytona Days Inn
Speedway**
2900 International Speedway
Blvd.
Daytona Beach, FL 32124
904-255-0541
PET POLICY: Fee $4.

Fountain Beach Resort
313 S. Atlantic Ave.
Daytona Beach, FL 32114
904-255-7491
PET POLICY: Pets must be on
leash anywhere in Daytona
Beach.

La Quinta Daytona Beach
2725 International Speedway Dr.
Daytona Beach, FL 32114
904-255-7412
PET POLICY: Under 20 lbs.

Majesty's Court Motel
999 N. Atlantic Ave.
Daytona Beach, FL 32114
904-252-5396
RATES: Single $30, double $40.
PET POLICY: Fee $10, $100
damage deposit, pets must be
on leash anywhere in Daytona
Beach, shaded, pet pen available 2 hrs a day.

Atlantic Dunes Motel & Apts.
1997 S. Atlantic Ave.
Daytona Beach Shores, FL 32118
904-255-7501
PET POLICY: Small pets.

Days Inn
472 High Adams
De Funiak Springs, FL 32433
850-892-6115
PET POLICY: Fee $10.

Motel 6
405 Hwy. 98 E, #A
Destin, FL 32541
850-837-0007
PET POLICY: No fee. Dogs under
25 lbs. preferred (larger animals by advance approval).
Do not leave animals in room
unattended.

Ocean Reef Rental Agency
10221 US Hwy. 98 W.
Destin, FL 32541
850-837-3935
RATES: Single, double $70–$500.
PET POLICY: No fee, up to 25 lbs.
POI: On the Gulf of Mexico.

Dundee Days Inn
339 US Hwy. 27
Dundee, FL 33838
863-439-1591
PET POLICY: No fee.

Monticello Motel
315 Hwy. 27N, Box 128
Dundee, FL 33838
863-439-3276
RATES: Double $38.
PET POLICY: Fee $5, nonrefund-
able, up to 25 lbs. Dogs only.

Englewood Days Inn
2540 S. McCall Rd., Hwy. 776E
Englewood, FL 34224
941-474-5544
PET POLICY: Fee $4.

**On the Banks of the
Everglades Bed & Breakfast**
201 W. Broadway
Everglades City, FL 34139
888-431-1977
PET POLICY: Preapproval
required.

Luxury on the Ocean
2815 S. Oceanshore Blvd.
Flagler Beach, FL 32136
904-439-1826
RATES: Double $150.
PET POLICY: Fee $10, all sizes
welcome.
POI: Located on pet-friendly
beach. 14 miles from Marineland.

U.S. Lodgings > FLORIDA

Whale Watch Motel
2448 S. A1A
Flagler Beach, FL 32136
904-439-2545
PET POLICY: Fee $5, nonrefund-
able, all sizes, 2 dogs per room,
max., dogs allowed on beach.

**Flamingo Lodge Marina
& Outpost**
SR 9336, Everglades Nat'l Park
Flamingo, FL 33034
800-600-3813
RATES: Single $95, double $95.
PET POLICY: No fee, small pets
up to 25 lbs. All pets welcome
(dogs, cats, ferrets, birds,
rabbits, reptiles).

Baymont Inn & Suites
3800 W. Commercial Blvd.
Fort Lauderdale, FL 33309
954-485-7900
PET POLICY: No fee.

Birch Patio Motel
617 N. Birch Rd.
Fort Lauderdale, FL 33304
954-563-9540
RATES: Single $35–$50, double
$45–$65.
PET POLICY: Fee $10 a day per
pet, nonrefundable. All sizes
welcome. Dogs and cats only.

Cortleigh Resort Motel
2100 NE 33rd Ave.
Fort Lauderdale, FL 33305
954-564-5868
RATES: Single $55, double $105.
PET POLICY: No fee, dogs and
cats only, up to 25 lbs. City
ordinance requires dogs on
leash outside.
AMENITIES: Garden areas surrounding property for walking
dogs. Lots of loving provided
to all pets.

Eighteenth Street Inn
712 SE 18th St.
Fort Lauderdale, FL 33316
954-467-7841
RATES: Single $125, double $150.
PET POLICY: Fee $25, nonre-
fundable. Dogs and Cats only,
up to 50 lbs. Must be housebroken, crate trained, flea and
tick prevention.
AMENITIES: Large fenced yard
for dogs to run.

Motel 6
1801 SR 84
Fort Lauderdale, FL 33315
954-760-7999
PET POLICY: No fee. Dogs under
25 lbs. preferred (larger animals by advance approval).
Do not leave animals in room
unattended.

Venice Beach Guest Quarters
552 N. Birch Rd.
Fort Lauderdale, FL 33304
954-564-9601
RATES: Single $85, double $120.
PET POLICY: No fee, all sizes
welcome. Security deposit
required (credit card).

Baymont Inn & Suites
2717 Colonial Blvd.
Fort Myers, FL 33907
941-275-3500
PET POLICY: Fee $25, plus $50
deposit.

Best Western Springs Resort
18051 S. Tamiami Trail
Fort Myers, FL 33908
941-267-7900
RATES: Single $54–$109, double
$59–$119.
PET POLICY: Fee $8 for 1 pet,
$12 for 2, nonrefundable,
up to 50 lbs.
POI: Near beaches and area
attractions.

Crossed Palms Beach House
5791 Estero Blvd.
Fort Myers Beach, FL 33931
941-765-0416
PET POLICY: Fee $200, refund-
able deposit. All sizes and pets
welcome.
AMENITIES: Fenced yard, 3/4 sand
and 1/4 grass, with shady spots.

**Days Inn Island
Beach Resort**
1130 Estero Blvd.
Fort Myers Beach, FL 33931
941-544-4592
RATES: Single $98, double $128.
PET POLICY: Fee $35, Dogs and
cats only. Birds also accepted.
POI: Lovers Key Preserve
(5 miles). Beach resort area.

Motel 6
3350 Marinatown Ln.
Fort Myers, FL 33903
941-656-5544
PET POLICY: No fee. Dogs under
25 lbs. preferred (larger animals by advance approval).
Do not leave animals in room
unattended.

**Radisson Inn Sanibel
Gateway**
20091 Summerlin Rd.
Fort Myers, FL 33908
941-466-1200
RATES: Single $99, double $109.
PET POLICY: Fee $50 nonrefund-
able, all sizes, all pets welcome
(dogs, cats, birds, rabbits), must
be on leash.

**Ramada Inn Beachfront
Resort**
1160 Estero Blvd.
Fort Myers Beach, FL 33931
941-463-6158
PET POLICY: Fee $35, Dogs and
cats only. Also birds.

Days Inn West Fort Pierce
6651 Darter Court
Fort Pierce, FL 34945
561-466-4066
RATES: Single $39–$79, double
$44–$84.
PET POLICY: Fee $10 per pet
per stay.
AMENITIES: Free pet treats at
check-in, free upgrades based
on availability.

Days Inn
135 Miracle Strip Pkwy.
Fort Walton Beach, FL 32548
904-244-6184
PET POLICY: Fee $10.

Fort Pierce Days Inn
6651 Darter Ct.
Ft. Pierce, FL 34945
561-466-4066
RATES: Single $55–$89, double
$55–$89.
PET POLICY: Fee $10, nonre-
fundable. All sizes welcome.
AMENITIES: Dog treats. Dog walk.
POI: Grand Prix Raceway/
Amusement park 1/2 mi, NY
Mets Stadium 8 miles Manatee
Observation Ctr. 6 miles St.
Lucie County Civic Ctr. 4 miles.

U.S. Lodgings > FLORIDA

Motel 6
2500 Peters Rd.
Ft. Pierce, FL 34945
561-461-9937
PET POLICY: No fee. Dogs under 25 lbs. preferred (larger animals by advance approval). Do not leave animals in room unattended.

Baymont Inn & Suites
3905 SW 43rd St.
Gainesville, FL 32602
352-376-0004
PET POLICY: Fee $10 first night, $5 each additional night.

Gainesville Days Inn
7516 Newberry Rd.
Gainesville, FL 32606
352-332-3033
PET POLICY: Fee $5.

Motel 6
4000 SW 40th Blvd.
Gainesville, FL 32608
352-373-1604
PET POLICY: No fee. Dogs under 25 lbs. preferred (larger animals by advance approval). Do not leave animals in room unattended.

Red Roof Inn
3500 SW 42nd St.
Gainesville, FL 32608
352-336-3311
PET POLICY: No fee, pets under 80 lbs. Must be leashed to and from rooms. Do not leave in room unattended.

Holiday Inn
51 Gulf Breeze Pkwy.
Gulf Breeze, FL 32561
850-932-2214
PET POLICY: Fee; $35, nonrefundable. Call for approval.

Miami Days Inn
1950 W. 49th St.
Hialeah, FL 33012
305-823-2121
PET POLICY: Fee $10.

Fort Lauderdale Days Inn
2601 N. 29th Ave.
Hollywood, FL 33020
954-923-7300
PET POLICY: Fee $10 per night.

Indigo Beach Resort
4053 S. Surf Rd.
Hollywood, FL 33019
954-457-9550
RATES: Single $89, double $89.
PET POLICY: No fee, all size dogs and cats, only.
POI: Adjacent to Hallandale Beachfront Park. Close to many other greenbelt areas. Centered between Miami Beach and Ft. Lauderdale attractions. Midway between those city's airports.

La Quinta Inn and Suites
2620 N. 26th Ave.
Hollywood, FL 33020
954-922-2295
RATES: Single $89, double $89.
PET POLICY: No fee, dogs up to 50 lbs. All pets welcome (dogs, cats, ferrets, birds, rabbits, reptiles). Animals other than cats and dogs must remain caged.
POI: Petsmart 1/4 miles Beach 4 miles.

Swan Motel
318 Filmore St.
Hollywood, FL, 33019
954-921-1031
RATES: Single, double $35-50 seasonal.
PET POLICY: No fee. Small pets only.

Homestead Days Inn
51 S. Homestead Blvd.
Homestead, FL 33030
305-245-1260
PET POLICY: Fee $7.

Marina Bay Inn (Waterfront)
10386 Halls River Rd.
Homosassa, FL 34448
352-628-2551
RATES: 1-Bed cottages w/full kit.: $65, 2-bed: $75.
PET POLICY: No fee. All sizes and pets welcome. On the Waterfront.
AMENITIES: Free all-natural gourmet treats at check-in.
POI: Homosassa State Wildlife Park, Crystal River.

Sandy Shores Motel
816 Gulf Blvd.
Indian Rocks Beach, FL 33785
727-595-3226
RATES: Single $59, double $98.
PET POLICY: Fee $10 per stay, All sizes, all pets welcome.
POI: 2 miles from Belleair Doggy Beach.

Islamorada Bed & Breakfast
81175 Old Hwy.
Islamorada, FL 33036
305-664-9321
RATES: Single $50–$65, double $50–$65.
PET POLICY: Fee $10, nonrefundable, Dogs only, up to 50 lbs.

Baymont Inn & Suites
3199 Hartley Rd.
Jacksonville, FL 32257
904-268-9999
PET POLICY: No fee.

Days Inn Oceanfront Resort
1031 S. 1st St.
Jacksonville, FL 32250
904-249-7231
PET POLICY: Fee $25, nonrefundable. Small pets, up to 20 lbs. Do not leave pets in room unattended.

Holiday Inn
I-95 at Airport Rd.
Jacksonville, FL 32229
904-741-4404
RATES: Single, double $84–$103.
PET POLICY: No fees. No restrictions. Pet owners will get rooms with access to outside.

La Quinta Jacksonville Orange Park
8555 Blanding Blvd.
Jacksonville, FL 32244
904-778-9539
RATES: Single $55, double $55.
PET POLICY: No fee, up to 25 lbs.

Motel 6
6107 Youngerman Cir.
Jacksonville, FL 32244
904-777-6100
RATES: Single $37.99, double $43.99.
PET POLICY: No fee. Dogs under 25 lbs. preferred (larger animals by advance approval). Do not leave animals in room unattended.

U.S. Lodgings > FLORIDA

Red Roof Inn
6969 Lenoir Avenue East
Jacksonville, FL 32216
904-296-1006
PET POLICY: No fee, pets under
80 lbs. Must be leashed to and
from rooms. Do not leave in
room unattended.

Red Roof Inn
6099 Youngerman Circle
Jacksonville, FL 32244
904-777-1000
PET POLICY: No fee, pets under
80 lbs. Must be leashed to and
from rooms. Do not leave in
room unattended.

Red Roof Inn
14701 Airport Entrance Rd.
Jacksonville, FL 32218
904-741-44-88
PET POLICY: No fee, pets under
80 lbs. Must be leashed to and
from rooms. Do not leave in
room unattended.

Jasper Days Inn
Route 3, Box 133
Jasper, FL 32052
904-792-1987
PET POLICY: Fee $5.

Atlantic Shores Resort
510 South St.
Key West, FL 33040
800-598-6988
RATES: Single $75–$160, double
$80–$180.
PET POLICY: Fee $200, refund-
able. All sizes welcome.
POI: Near dog Beach, all tourist
attractions, downtown restaurants and water activities.

**Casa Alante Guest Cottages
Bed & Breakfast**
1435 S. Roosevelt Blvd.
Key West, FL 33040
305-293-0702
RATES: Single $85–$125, double
$130–$165.
PET POLICY: Fee $5, nonrefund-
able. All sizes and all pets welcome. Prior permission
required since pet-friendly
cottages are limited.
AMENITIES: Cottages have private
gated terrace where pet may join
owners for breakfast. Pets receive
ribbon wrapped Milk Bone.

**Center Court Historic Inn
& Cottages**
916 Center St.
Key West, FL 33040
305-296-9292
RATES: Single, double $128–$428.
PET POLICY: Fee $10 per night,
per pet. Pets under 75 lbs.

**Curry Mansion Inn
Bed & Breakfast**
511 Caroline St.
Key West, FL 33040
305-294-5349
RATES: Double $150–$240.
PET POLICY: No fee, up to
25 lbs. Do not leave pets in
rooms unattended.
POI: Located in the heart of
Old Town. Can walk to
attractions.

Frances Street Bottle Inn
535 Frances St.
Key West, FL 33040
305-294-8530
RATES: Single $120, double $120.
PET POLICY: No fee, all sizes and
all pets welcome.
AMENITIES: Pets welcome at
many outdoor restaurants/
bars, and beaches.
POI: Ft. Zachary Taylor State
park, Historic Seaport, near all
tourist attractions.

Sunrise Suites Resort
3685 Seaside Dr.
Key West, FL 33040
305-296-6661
PET POLICY: Fee $30 per pet per
night. One pet per unit.
Portion of fee will be donated
to local pet shelter.

The Travelers Palm
815 Catherine St.
Key West, FL 33040
305-294-9560
RATES: Double $150.
PET POLICY: Fee $10, night,
nonrefundable. Dogs up to
25 lbs., birds in cages.

Holiday Inn
7601 Black Lake Rd.
Kissimmee, FL 34747
407-396-1100
PET POLICY: $100 Non refund-
able fee.

**Larson's Lodge-
Main Gate**
6075 W. Irlo Bronson
Memorial Hwy
Kissimmee, FL, 34747
407-396-6100
RATES: Single, double $48.95–
79.95
PET POLICY: Fee $10 per night,
Deposit $150, refundable.
Small to medium dogs.

Motel 6
7455 W. Bronson Hwy.
Kissimmee, FL 34747
407-396-6422
PET POLICY: No fee. Dogs under
25 lbs. preferred (larger animals by advance approval).
Do not leave animals in room
unattended.

Orlando Days Inn
2095 E. Irlo Bronson Hwy.
Kissimmee, FL 34744
407-846-7136
PET POLICY: Fee $10.

Red Roof Inn
4970 Kyng's Heath Rd.
Kissimmee, FL 34746
407-396-0065
PET POLICY: No fee, pets under
80 lbs. Must be leashed to and
from rooms. Do not leave in
room unattended.

Lake City Days Inn
Route 16, Box 38310
Lake City, FL 32055
904-758-4224
PET POLICY: Fee $5.

Motel 6
4587 W. Hwy. 90
Lake City, FL 32055
904-755-4664
PET POLICY: No fee. Dogs under
25 lbs. preferred (larger animals by advance approval).
Do not leave animals in room
unattended.

Baymont Inn & Suites
4315 Lakeland Park Dr.
Lakeland, FL 33809
941-815-0606
PET POLICY: No fee.

U.S. Lodgings > FLORIDA

Motel 6
3120 US Hwy. 98 N
Lakeland, FL 33805
863-682-0643
PET POLICY: No fee. Dogs under 25 lbs. preferred (larger animals by advance approval). Do not leave animals in room unattended.

Villas by the Sea Resort
4456 El Mar Dr.
Lauderdale by the Sea, FL 33308
954-772-3550
RATES: Single $75–$220, double $75–$320.
PET POLICY: Fee $10 per day, $40 per week, $100 month. All sizes welcome.
POI: Ft. Lauderdale Pet Beach, parks, great shopping, Restaurants (indoor and outdoor).

Sunset Harbor
69401 Overseas Hwy.
Long Key, FL 33001
305-664-4848
PET POLICY: Fee $100, refundable, dogs and cats only.
AMENITIES: Pet beach only 5 minutes away.

MacClenny Days Inn
1499 S. 6th St.
MacClenny, FL 32063
904-259-5100
PET POLICY: No fee.

Schooner Motel
14500 Gulf Blvd.
Madeira Beach, FL 33708
727-392-5167
PET POLICY: Fee $15–$25, nonrefundable (1-3 nights). All sizes and all pets welcome (dogs, cats, ferrets, birds, rabbits). No pets in pool area.

Madison Days Inn
SR 53 Route 1
Madison, FL 32340
904-973-3330
PET POLICY: Fee $10.

Marianna Days Inn
4132 Lafayette St.
Marianna, FL 32446
850-482-4711
PET POLICY: Fee $10.

Cottage By the Seaside
317R Ocean Ave.
Melbourne Beach, FL 32951
800-863-4987
PET POLICY: No fee. Small dogs only, up to 50 lbs.

Baymont Inn & Suites—Melbourne
7200 George T Edwards Dr.
Melbourne, FL 32940
407-242-9400
PET POLICY: No fee.

Baymont Inn & Suites
3805 N.W. 107th Ave.
Miami, FL 33165
305-640-9896
PET POLICY: No fee.

Baymont Inn & Suites
3501 N.W. Le Jeune Rd.
Miami, FL 33142
305-871-1777
PET POLICY: No fee.

Howard Johnson Plaza Hotel
10775 Caribbean Blvd,
Cutler Ridge
Miami, FL 33189
305-253-9960
RATES: Single $64, double $74.
PET POLICY: Fee $15 per night. Pets accepted under 15 lbs.

Mayfair House Hotel
3000 Florida Ave.
Miami, FL 33133
305-441-0000
RATES: Single, double $209.
PET POLICY: Fee $20 per night, nonrefundable. $200 Deposit, refundable. Pets under 25 lbs. welcome.
AMENITIES: Near Doggy park.

Red Roof Inn
3401 Northwest Le Jeune Rd.
Miami, FL 33142
305-871-4221
PET POLICY: No fee, pets under 80 lbs. Must be leashed to and from rooms. Do not leave in room unattended.

Staybridge Suites by Holiday Inn
3265 NW 57th Ave.
Miami, FL 33172
305-500-9100
PET POLICY: $75 Non refundable pet fee.

Miami Beach Days Inn
100 21st St.
Miami Beach, FL 33139
305-538-6631
PET POLICY: No fee. Pets accepted up to 20 lbs. Do not leave in room unattended.

Miami Days Inn
4299 Collins Ave.
Miami Beach, FL 33140
305-673-1513
PET POLICY: No fee.

Baymont Inn & Suites
185 Bedzel Cir.
Naples, FL 34104
941-352-8400
PET POLICY: No fee.

Red Roof Inn
1925 Davis Blvd.
Naples, FL 34104
877-508-6391
RATES: Single $40–$90, double $40–$90.
PET POLICY: No fee, pets under 80 lbs. Must be leashed to and from rooms. Do not leave in room unattended.
AMENITIES: Pet walk and exercise area.

Thompson's Retreat
111 Caribbean Rd.
Naples, FL 34108
941-513-0211
RATES: Double $200.
PET POLICY: Fee $50, refundable. All sizes and pets welcome.
AMENITIES: Invisible fence. $1\frac{1}{2}$ acres running room, grass.

U.S. Lodgings > FLORIDA

**Days Inn North Fort
Myers–Cape Coral**
13353 N. Cleveland Ave.
North Fort Myers, FL 33903
941-995-0535
PET POLICY: Fee $10.

Red Roof Inn
4800 Powerline Rd.
Oakland Park, FL 33309
954-776-6333
PET POLICY: No fee, pets under
80 lbs. Must be leashed to and
from rooms. Do not leave in
room unattended.

Ocala Days Inn
3811 NW Blichton Rd.
Ocala, FL 34482
904-629-7041
PET POLICY: Fee $10.

Ocala Days Inn
3620 W. Silver Springs Blvd.
Ocala, FL 34475
904-629-0091
PET POLICY: Fee $5.

**Baymont Inn & Suites—
Orlando**
2051 Consulate Dr.
Orlando, FL 32837
407-240-0500
PET POLICY: No fee.

Days Inn International Dr.
7200 International Dr.
Orlando, FL 32819
407-351-1200
PET POLICY: Fee $10.

Holiday Inn
6515 Int'l Dr.
Orlando, FL 32819
407-351-3500
PET POLICY: 25 lbs. or less with
deposit.

Holiday Inn Hotel & Suites
5905 Kirkman Rd.
Orlando, FL 32819
407-351-3333
PET POLICY: Fee $50, nonre-
fundable. Small dogs preferred
(up to 25 lbs).

Motel 6
5300 Adanson Rd.
Orlando, FL 32810
407-647-1444
PET POLICY: No fee. Dogs under
25 lbs. preferred (larger animals by advance approval).
Do not leave animals in room
unattended.

Motel 6
5909 American Way
Orlando, FL 32819
407-351-6500
PET POLICY: No fee. Dogs under
25 lbs. preferred (larger animals by advance approval).
Do not leave animals in room
unattended.

Orlando Days Inn Airport
2323 McCoy Rd.
Orlando, FL 32809
407-859-6100
PET POLICY: Fee $10.

Red Roof Inn
9922 Hawaiian Court
Orlando, FL 32819
407-352-1507
PET POLICY: No fee, pets under
80 lbs. Must be leashed to and
from rooms. Do not leave in
room unattended.

Red Roof Inn
5621 Major Boulevard
Orlando, FL 32819
407-313-3100
PET POLICY: No fee, pets under
80 lbs. Must be leashed to and
from rooms. Do not leave in
room unattended.

Residence Inn by Marriott
7975 Canada Ave.
Orlando, FL 32819
407-345-0117
PET POLICY: Fee $10 per day
per pet. Deposit $50–$100,
refundable. Pets under 25 lbs.

Daytona Days Inn
839 S. Atlantic Ave.
Ormond Beach, FL 32176
904-677-6600
PET POLICY: Fee $15.

Daytona Days Inn
1608 N. UUS Hwy.
Ormond Beach, FL 32174
904-672-7341
PET POLICY: Fee $5.

Brazilian Court Hotel
301 Australian Ave.
Palm Beach, FL 33480
561-655-7740
PET POLICY: Fee $75 nonre-
fundable. Up to 25 lbs.

Heart of Palm Beach Hotel
10 Royal Palm Way
Palm Beach, FL 33480
561-655-5600
PET POLICY: No fee, all pets
welcome, up to 50 lbs.

Red Roof Inn
32000 U.S. 19 North
Palm Harbor, FL 34684
727-786-2529
PET POLICY: No fee, pets under
80 lbs. Must be leashed to and
from rooms. Do not leave in
room unattended.

Bayside Inn
711 W. Beach Dr.
Panama City, FL 32401
850-763-4622
RATES: Single $80, double $94.
PET POLICY: Fee $10, nonre-
fundable, all size and pets
welcome.
AMENITIES: Walk area, swimming in Bay. Puppy treat
available at front desk daily for
our "kids."
POI: Panama City Beach, Parks.

**Panama City Days Inn
23rd St.**
301 W. 23rd St.
Panama City, FL 32405
904-785-0001
PET POLICY: Fee $5.

**Panama City Days Inn
Central**
4111 W. Hwy. 98
Panama City, FL 32401
904-784-1777
PET POLICY: Fee $2.

Crowne Plaza
200 E. Gregory
Pensacola, FL 32501
800-HOLIDAY
PET POLICY: Small fee.

Gulf Beach Inn
10655 Gulf Beach Hwy.
Pensacola, FL 32507
850-492-4501
RATES: Double $85.
PET POLICY: Fee $5 per pet, non-refundable, pets up to 50 lbs.
AMENITIES: Large dog walk area, plenty of beach to play in. Large 2-acre site with private beach.
POI: Naval Aviation Museum. Gulf Islands National Seashore.

Moonshine Cabin
3450 La Mancha Way
Pensacola, FL 32501
850-206-9009
RATES: $150 per night, $750, week.
PET POLICY: Fee $25 nonrefundable, all size dogs and cats, must have flea/tick prevention.
POI: Dollywood. Ober Gatlinburg. Great Smoky National Park.

Motel 6
7226 Plantation Rd.
Pensacola, FL 32504
850-474-1060
PET POLICY: No fee. Dogs under 25 lbs. preferred (larger animals by advance approval). Do not leave animals in room unattended.

Noble Manor
Bed & Breakfast
110 W. Strong St.
Pensacola, FL 32501
850-434-9544
RATES: Single $75–$85, double $75–$85.
PET POLICY: Fee $10 refundable, up to 50 lbs., only dogs, pets must be crated at night, and when owners are absent.
AMENITIES: Crates available. Biscuit on the pillow for dogs.

Pensacola Days Inn North
7051 Pensacola Blvd.
Pensacola, FL 32505
850-476-9090
PET POLICY: Fee $12.

Ramada Inn Bayview
7601 Scenic Hwy.
Pensacola, FL 32504
850-477-7155
AMENITIES: Good walking grounds, near Pensacola Beach.

Ramada Limited
8060 Lavelle Way
Pensacola, FL 32534
850-944-0333
RATES: Single $54, double $59.
PET POLICY: Fee $25, nonrefundable.
POI: Navel Air Museum. Gulf Coast beaches.

Red Roof Inn
6919 Pensacola Boulevard
Pensacola, FL 32505
850-478-4499
PET POLICY: No fee, pets under 80 lbs. Must be leashed to and from rooms. Do not leave in room unattended.
POI: Gulf Coast beaches.

Red Roof Inn
7340 Plantation Rd.
Pensacola, FL 32504
850-476-7960
PET POLICY: No fee, pets under 80 lbs. Must be leashed to and from rooms. Do not leave in room unattended.

Shoneys Inn Pensacola
8080 N. Davis Hwy.
Pensacola, FL 32514
850-484-8070
RATES: Single $65, double $71.
PET POLICY: Fee $17, nonrefundable. All size dogs and cats, only. Pets not allowed in lobby area. Curb your dog and pick up afterward.

Travelodge
6950 Pensacola Blvd.
Pensacola, FL 32505
850 473-0222
RATES: Single $39, double $53.
PET POLICY: No fee, all sizes welcome.
POI: Naval Air Museum. Pensacola Beach. Sam's Fun City.

Perry Days Inn
2277 S. Byron Butler Pkwy.
Perry, FL 32347
904-584-5311
PET POLICY: Fee $10.

St. Petersburg Days Inn
9359 US Hwy. 19N
Pinellas Park, FL 33782
727-577-3838
PET POLICY: Fee $6.

Days Inn Plant City
301 S. Frontage Rd.
Plant City, FL 33566
813-752-0570
PET POLICY: Fee $10.

Holiday Inn
1711 N. University Dr.
Plantation, FL 33322
954-472-5600
PET POLICY: Small fee, gourmet cat/dog treats, access to designated "pet zone." Special offers, call.

Motel 6
1201 NW 31st Ave.
Pompano Beach, FL 33069
954-977-8011
PET POLICY: No fee. Dogs under 25 lbs. preferred (larger animals by advance approval). Do not leave animals in room unattended.

The Litchfield Inn
3400 Tamiami Trail
Port Charlotte, FL 33952
941-625-4181
RATES: Single $59–$99, double $59–$99.
PET POLICY: Fee $5, all sizes welcome.
POI: Port Charlotte beach 1 mile.

Port Richey Days Inn and Lodge
11736 US Hwy. 19
Port Richey, FL 34668
813-863-1502
PET POLICY: Fee $5.

Motel 6
9300 Knights Dr.
Punta Gorda, FL 33950
941-639-9585
PET POLICY: No fee. Dogs under 25 lbs. preferred (larger animals by advance approval). Do not leave animals in room unattended.

U.S. Lodgings > FLORIDA

**Allison House
Bed & Breakfast**
215 N. Madison St.
Quincy, FL 32351
850-875-2511
RATES: Single $90, double $90.
PET POLICY: No fee, pets up to 25 lbs.

Allison House Inn
215 N. Madison St.
Quincy, FL 32351
850-904-2511
PET POLICY: No fee, dogs only, up to 25 lbs.

Safety Harbor Resort & Spa
105 N. Bayshore Dr.
Safety Harbor, FL 34695
727-726-1161
RATES: Single $89.99–$199.
PET POLICY: Fee $50, nonrefundable. Up to 25 lbs.
POI: Busch Gardens. Honeymoon Island (pet-friendly).

The Castaways at Blind Pass
6460 Sanibel-Captiva Rd.
Sanibel Island, FL 33957
941-472-1252
RATES: Single, double $109–$329 (seasonal).
PET POLICY: Fee $15 per dog. All size dogs, only.

Sanford Days Inn
4650 State Rd. 46
Sanford, FL 32771
407-323-6500
PET POLICY: Fee $5.

Sarasota Days Inn Airport
4900 N. Tamiami Tr. (US 41)
Sarasota, FL 34234
813-355-9721
PET POLICY: Fee $6.

Siesta Holiday House
1221 Holly Fern Ln.
Sarasota, FL 34239
941-953-7634
RATES: Single $695/wk, double $995/wk.
PET POLICY: No fee, small dogs up to 25 lbs. Well-behaved. Must pick up after pets.

Space Coast Days Inn
180 Hwy. A1A
Satellite Beach, FL 32937
407-777-3552
PET POLICY: No fee.

Hidden Beach Villas
3605 E. County Hwy. 30-A
Seagrove Beach, FL 32459
404-822-6453
PET POLICY: No fee. Medium dogs only up to 50 lbs.

The Beach Place
5605 Avenida Del Mare
Siesta Key, FL 34242
941-346-1745
RATES: Single $110.
PET POLICY: Fee $100, refundable. All sizes welcome, must be kept on leash.
AMENITIES: Grassy areas, pet leads.
POI: Ringling Museum, Selby Botanical Gardens, 1 hr. to Busch Gardens. 2 hrs. to Disney.

Ocala Days Inn East
5001 E. Silver Springs Blvd.
Silver Springs, FL 32688
904-236-2891
PET POLICY: Fee $7.

Days Inn Oceanfront Resort
2700 N. Ocean Dr.
Singer Island, FL 33404
561-848-8661
RATES: Single $89.
PET POLICY: Fee $10, all sizes welcome.
POI: Jupiter Beach.

Ocean Blue Motel
10 Vilano Rd.
St. Augustine, FL 32084
904-829-5939
PET POLICY: $10 nonrefundable, no restrictions, all sizes.

St. Augustine Days Inn Historic
2800 Ponce De Leon Blvd.
St. Augustine, FL 32084
904-829-6581
PET POLICY: Fee $10.

St. Augustine Days Inn West
2560 State Rd. 16
St. Augustine, FL 32092
904-824-4341
PET POLICY: Fee $10.

Best Western Ocean Inn
3955 A1A S
St. Augustine Beach, FL 32084
904-471-8010
PET POLICY: Pets allowed on beach.

Holiday Inn
860 A1A Beach Blvd.
St. Augustine Beach, FL 32084
904-4712555
PET POLICY: Pets allowed on beach.

15 Sea Place
204 E. Gorrie Dr.
St. George Island, FL 32328
850-927-2666
PET POLICY: Fee $75, nonrefundable. All sizes and pets welcome (dogs, cats, birds, ferrets, rabbits, reptiles).
AMENITIES: 2 dog beds provided. Outside shower available.

Bay Street Villas & Resort Marina
7201 Bay St.
St. Pete Beach, FL 33706
727-360-5591
PET POLICY: Fee $5, up to 25 lbs. Birds also accepted. Dogs and cats need proof of shots/flea program or dip.

Blue Dolphin Apartments
7801 Boca Ciega Dr.
St. Pete Beach, FL 33706
727-367-2068
RATES: Monthly: $650.
PET POLICY: Fee $25, nonrefundable. Dogs only, up to 25 lbs., must keep on leash.
POI: Beaches.

Ritz Motel
4237 Gulf Blvd.
St. Pete Beach, FL 33706
727-360-7642
PET POLICY: Fee $3, nonrefundable, sizes up to 50 lbs., all pets welcome.

U.S. Lodgings > FLORIDA

Starke Days Inn
1101 N. Temple
Starke, FL 32091
904-964-7600
PET POLICY: Fee $5.

Baymont Inn & Suites— Sunrise
13651 NW 2nd St.
Sunrise, FL 33325
954-846-1200
PET POLICY: No fee.

Motel 6
1027 Apalachee Pkwy.
Tallahassee, FL 32301
850-877-6171
PET POLICY: No fee. Dogs under 25 lbs. preferred (larger animals by advance approval). Do not leave animals in room unattended.

Red Roof Inn
2930 Hospitality St.
Tallahassee, FL 32303
850-385-7884
PET POLICY: No fee, pets under 80 lbs. Must be leashed to and from rooms. Do not leave in

Baymont Inn & Suites
3800 W. Commercial Blvd.
Tamarac, FL 33309
954-485-7900
PET POLICY: No fee.

Baymont Inn & Suites
9202 N. 30th St.
Tampa, FL 33612
813-930-6900
PET POLICY: No fee.

Baymont Inn & Suites
602 S. Faulkenburg Rd.
Tampa, FL 33619
813-684-4007
PET POLICY: No fee.

Best Western All Suite Hotel (Busch Gardens)
3001 University Center Dr.
Tampa, FL 33612
813-971-8930
RATES: Single, double $99–$109 (seasonal).
PET POLICY: Fee $10 per pet. Pets under 75 lbs.

Motel 6
333 E. Fowler Ave.
Tampa, FL 33612
813-932-4948
PET POLICY: No fee. Dogs under 25 lbs. preferred (larger animals by advance approval). Do not leave animals in room unattended.

Motel 6
6510 N. Hwy. 301
Tampa, FL 33610
813-628-0888
PET POLICY: No fee. Dogs under 25 lbs. preferred (larger animals by advance approval). Do not leave animals in room unattended.

Red Roof Inn
5001 North U.S. 301
Tampa, FL 33610
813-62-35245
PET POLICY: No fee, pets under 80 lbs. Must be leashed to and from rooms. Do not leave in room unattended.

Red Roof Inn
10121 Horace Ave.
Tampa, FL 33619
813-681-8484
PET POLICY: No fee, pets under 80 lbs. Must be leashed to and from rooms. Do not leave in room unattended.

Red Roof Inn
2307 E. Busch Blvd.
Tampa, FL 33612
813-932-0073
PET POLICY: No fee, pets under 80 lbs. Must be leashed to and from rooms. Do not leave in room unattended.

Tampa Days Inn Airport-Stadium
2522 N. Dale Mabry
Tampa, FL 33607
813-877-6181
PET POLICY: No fee.

Wingate Inn Busch Gardens
3751 E. Flowler Ave.
Tampa, FL 33612
813-979-2828
RATES: Single, double $75.
PET POLICY: Fee $40, nonrefundable. Dogs and cats, up to 50 lbs. Do not leave in room unattended or keep in crate.

Tarpon Springs Days Inn
40050 US Hwy. 19N
Tarpon Springs, FL 34689
727-938-8000
PET POLICY: No fee.

Holiday Inn
4951 S. Washington Ave.
Titusville, FL 32780
407-269-2121
PET POLICY: Small pets only.

Space Coast Days Inn Titusville
3755 Cheney Hwy. (Hwy. 50)
Titusville, FL 32780
321-269-4480
PET POLICY: Fee $10.

Anchor Inn
10133 Gulf Boulevard
Treasure Island, FL 33706
727-360-1871
RATES: Single, double $55–$125 (seasonal).
PET POLICY: Fee $10 per pet 1st night, $6 per night thereafter. Small pets only.

Lorelei Resort
10273 Gulf Blvd.
Treasure Island, FL 33706
727-360-4351
PET POLICY: No fee, all sizes accepted.

SeaHorse Cottages & Apartments
10356 Gulf Blvd.
Treasure Island, FL 33706
727-367-2291
RATES: Single $50, double $125.
PET POLICY: Fee $6 per day, dogs and cats up to 20 lbs. Birds also. Limit to under 20 inches tall.

Motel 6
281 US Hwy. 41 Bypass North
Venice, FL 34292
941-485-8255
PET POLICY: No fee. Dogs under
25 lbs. preferred (larger animals by advance approval).
Do not leave animals in room
unattended.

Venice Days Inn
1710 S. Tamiami Trail (US 41)
Venice, FL 34293
941-493-4558
PET POLICY: Fee $30.

**Hibiscus House
Bed & Breakfast**
501 30th St.
West Palm Beach, FL 33407
561-863-5633
RATES: Single $94–$140, double
$95–$140.
PET POLICY: No fee, all sizes
welcome.

Red Roof Inn
2421 Metrocentre Blvd. E
West Palm Beach, FL 33407
561-6977710-
PET POLICY: No fee, pets under
80 lbs. Must be leashed to and
from rooms. Do not leave in
room unattended.

**West Palm Beach Days Inn
Turnpike-Airport West**
6255 Okeechobee Blvd.
West Palm Beach, FL 33417
561-686-6000
PET POLICY: Fee $10.

**West Palm Beach—
Days Inn Airport North**
2300 45th St.
West Palm Beach, FL 33407
561-689-0450
PET POLICY: Fee $10.

Wildwood Days Inn
551 E. SR 44
Wildwood, FL 34785
352-748-7766
PET POLICY: Fee $10.

Cypress Motel
5651 Cypress Gardens Rd.
Winter Haven, FL 33884
941-324-5867
RATES: Single $45–$60, double
$50–$75.
PET POLICY: Fee $10, nonre-
fundable.
AMENITIES: 21 ground floor
rooms facing pool Efficiencies
available for longer stay.
POI: 2 acres of grounds, dog
walking area, suburban location.

Winter Haven Days Inn
200 Cypress Gardens Blvd.
Winter Haven, FL 33880
863-297-1151
PET POLICY: Fee $10.

Yulee—Days Inn
3250 US Hwy. 17
Yulee, FL 32097
904-225-2011
PET POLICY: Fee $6.

GEORGIA

Red Roof Inn
5320 Glade Rd.
Acworth, GA 30101
770-974-5400
PET POLICY: No fee, pets under
80 lbs. Must be leashed to and
from rooms. Do not leave in
room unattended.

Days Inn I-75
1200 W. 4th St.
Adel, GA 31620
912-896-4574
PET POLICY: Fee $5.

Hampton Inn
1500 W. Fourth St. (I-75, Ex. 39)
Adel, GA 31620
912-896-3099
RATES: Single $63, double $65.
PET POLICY: Fee $5, nonrefund-
able. Up to 50 lbs.

Motel 6
201 S. Thornton Dr.
Albany, GA 31705
912-439-0078
PET POLICY: No fee. Dogs under
25 lbs. preferred (larger animals by advance approval).
Do not leave animals in room
unattended.

**Residence Inn Alpharetta
Windward**
5465 Windward Pkwy. W.
Alpharetta, GA 30004
770-664-0664
PET POLICY: $125 nonrefund-
able fee.

**Staybridge Suites by
Holiday Inn**
3980 N. Point Pkwy.
Alpharetta, GA 30005
770-569-7200
PET POLICY: $75 non refundable
fee.

1906 Pathway Inn
501 S. Lee St.
Americus, GA 31709
912-928-2078
RATES: Single $100, double $110.
PET POLICY: Fee $20. All pets
under 25 lbs. welcome. Other
sizes: please call.
POI: Andersonville Nat'l
Historic Site, Plains Nat'l Site,
Providence Canyon.

Ashburn Days Inn
823 E. Washington Ave.
Ashburn, GA 31714
912-567-3346
PET POLICY: No fee.

**Baymont Inn & Suites—
Atlanta-Lenox**
2535 Chantilly Dr NE
Atlanta, GA 30324
404-321-0999
PET POLICY: No fee, up to 50 lbs.

**Beverly Hills Inn
Bed & Breakfast**
65 Sheridan Dr.
Atlanta, GA 30305
404-233-8520
PET POLICY: No fee, no restrictions.

Crowne Plaza
1325 Virginia Ave.
Atlanta, GA 30344
404-768-6660
PET POLICY: No fee.

Crowne Plaza Hotel Atlanta
6345 Powers Ferry Rd.
Atlanta, GA 30339
770-9551700
PET POLICY: Fee $25, up to 25 lbs.

**Culpepper House
Bed & Breakfast**
35 Broad. St.
Atlanta, GA 30276
770-599-8182
PET POLICY: Preapproval
required "Have not turned
anyone down yet."

**Drury Inn & Suites—
Airport**
1270 Virginia Ave.
Atlanta, GA 30344
404-761-4900
PET POLICY: No fee, no restrictions.

Four Seasons Hotel Atlanta
75 Fourteenth St.
Atlanta, GA 30309
404-881-9898
PET POLICY: No fee, no restrictions.

Granada Suite Hotels
1302 W. Peachtree St.
Atlanta, GA 30309
404-876-6100
PET POLICY: Fee $25 nonre-
fundable, no size restrictions.

**Holiday Inn Select
Perimeter—Dunwoody
Area**
4386 Chamblee Dunwoody Rd.
Atlanta, GA 30341
770-457-6363
PET POLICY: Fee $100 deposit,
$25 one-time fee, supervised,
in crates.

**Masters Economy Inn
Six Flags**
4120 Fulton Industries Blvd.
Atlanta, GA 30336
404-696-4690
PET POLICY: Fee $6 per night,
no restrictions.

Motel 6
2820 Chamblee-Tucker Rd.
Atlanta, GA 30341
770-458-6626
PET POLICY: No fee. Dogs under
25 lbs. preferred (larger animals by advance approval).
Do not leave animals in room
unattended.

**Ramada Inn and
Conference Center**
418 Armour Dr.
Atlanta, GA 30324
404-873-4661
PET POLICY: No fee, no restrictions.

Red Roof Inn
4265 Shirley Drive Southwest
Atlanta, GA 30336
404-696-4391
PET POLICY: No fee, pets under
80 lbs. Must be leashed to and
from rooms. Do not leave in
room unattended.

Red Roof Inn
1960 N. Druid Hills Rd.
Atlanta, GA 30329
404-321-1653
PET POLICY: No fee, pets under
80 lbs. Must be leashed to and
from rooms. Do not leave in
room unattended.

Red Roof Inn
1200 Virginia Ave.
Atlanta, GA 30344
404-209-1800
PET POLICY: No fee, pets under
80 lbs. Must be leashed to and
from rooms. Do not leave in
room unattended.

Red Roof Inn
2822 Chamblee-Tucker Rd.
Atlanta, GA 30341
770-458-6941
PET POLICY: No fee, pets under
80 lbs. Must be leashed to and
from rooms. Do not leave in
room unattended.

**Residence Inn Atlanta
Buckhead**
2960 Piedmont Rd. NE
Atlanta, GA 30305
404-239-0677
PET POLICY: Fee $100–$125,
no size restrictions.

**Residence Inn Atlanta
Dunwoody**
1901 Savoy Dr.
Atlanta, GA 30341
770-455-4446
PET POLICY: Fee $100–$125,
no size restrictions.

**Residence Inn Atlanta
Historic Midtown**
1041 W. Peachtree St.
Atlanta, GA 30309
404-872-8885
PET POLICY: Fee $100, no size
restrictions.

**Residence Inn Atlanta
Perimeter West**
6096 Barfield Rd.
Atlanta, GA 30328
404-252-5066
PET POLICY: Fee $75 nonre-
fundable, no size restrictions.

**The Westin Atlanta North
at Perimeter Center**
7 Concourse Pkwy.
Atlanta, GA 30328
770-395-3900
PET POLICY: Fee $75 deposit,
$50 refunded, up to 75 lbs.

Motel 6
2650 Center W. Pkwy.
Augusta, GA 30909
706-736-1934
PET POLICY: No fee. Dogs under
25 lbs. preferred (larger animals by advance approval).
Do not leave animals in room
unattended.

Red Roof Inn
4328 Frontage Rd.
Augusta, GA 30909
706-228-3031
PET POLICY: No fee, pets under
80 lbs. Must be leashed to and
from rooms. Do not leave in
room unattended.

**Misty Mountain Inn
& Cottages**
4376 Misty Mountain Ln.
Blairsville, GA 30512
706-745-4786
RATES: DOUBLE $80 midweek,
$90 Fri-Sun.
PET POLICY: Fee $10 cleaning
fee. All sizes accepted.

U.S. Lodgings > GEORGIA

7 Creeks Housekeeping Cabins
5109 Horseshoe Cove Rd.
Blairsville, GA 30512
706-745-4753
RATES: Single $65, double $65.
PET POLICY: No fee, all sizes, all pets welcome (dogs, cats, ferrets, birds, rabbits, reptiles, etc.), must be housebroken, clean and quiet, do not leave alone in cabin, must be on leash outside, keep area clean, etc.
POI: Brasstown Bald (highest mountain in Ga.), Vogel State Park, Numerous waterfalls, hiking trails (including Appalachian trail), Chatthoochee National Forest.

Blue Ridge Days Inn
PO Box 1869
Blue Ridge, GA 30513
706-632-2100
PET POLICY: Fee $4.

Blue Ridge Mountain Cabins
PO Box 1102
Blue Ridge, GA 30513
706-632-8999
PET POLICY: Fee $20 per pet per stay. Puppies up to 15 months not permitted in cabins. Pets must be friendly, housebroken, deflead. Cats must be declawed. Do not leave pets unattended. Not allowed on furniture. Call first.

The Last Resort
45 Last Resort Pass
Blue Ridge, GA 30053
800-959-5562
RATES: Single $250-weekends, double $375-weekends.
PET POLICY: No fee, all sizes welcome.

Tica Cabin Rentals
699 E. Main St.
Blue Ridge, GA 30513
706-632-4448
RATES: Single $85–$125.
PET POLICY: Fee $5, nonrefundable. All size dogs, only.

Bremen Days Inn
35 Price Creek Rd.
Bremen, GA 30110
770-537-4646
PET POLICY: Fee $5.

Baymont Inn & Suites— Brunswick
105 Tourist Dr.
Brunswick, GA 31520
912-265-7725
PET POLICY: No fee.

Brunswick Days Inn Downtown
2307 Gloucester St.
Brunswick, GA 31520
912-265-8830
PET POLICY: Fee $5.

Embassy Suites Brunswick—Golden Isles
500 Mall Blvd.
Brunswick, GA 31525
912-264-6100
RATES: Single $99, double $99.
PET POLICY: Fee $10, nonrefundable., All sizes, dogs and cats only.
POI: Jekyll Island, St. Simons Island and beaches 15 minutes, Millionaires Village 20 minutes.

Motel 6
403 Butler Dr.
Brunswick, GA 31525
912-264-8582
PET POLICY: No fee. Dogs under 25 lbs. preferred (larger animals by advance approval). Do not leave animals in room unattended.

Red Roof Inn
121 Tourist Dr.
Brunswick, GA 31520
912-264-4720
PET POLICY: No fee, pets under 80 lbs. Must be leashed to and from rooms. Do not leave in room unattended.

Cairo Days Inn
35 US Hwy. 84E
Cairo, GA 31728
912-377-4400
PET POLICY: Fee $5.

Calhoun Days Inn
742 Hwy. 53 SE
Calhoun, GA 30701
706-629-8271
PET POLICY: Fee $4.

Motel 6
5657 Hwy. 20 NE
Cartersville, GA 30121
770-386-1449
PET POLICY: No fee. Dogs under 25 lbs. preferred (larger animals by advance approval). Do not leave animals in room unattended.

Baymont Inn Atlanta Airport
2480 Old National Pkwy.
College Park, GA 30349
404-766-0000
PET POLICY: No fee.

La Quinta Atlanta Airport
4874 Old National Hwy.
College Park, GA 30337
404-768-1241
RATES: Single $49–$65, double $49–$65.
PET POLICY: No fee, up to 25 lbs.
POI: 6 Flags over Ga., Ga. Dome, Turner Field, CNN Center, World of Coke.

Red Roof Inn
2471 Old National Pkwy.
College Park, GA 30349
404-761-9701
PET POLICY: No fee, pets under 80 lbs. Must be leashed to and from rooms. Do not leave in room unattended.

Baymont Inn & Suites— Columbus
2919 Warm Springs Rd.
Columbus, GA 31909
706-323-4344
PET POLICY: No fee.

Columbus Days Inn
3452 Macon Rd.
Columbus, GA 31907
706-561-4400
PET POLICY: No fee.

U.S. Lodgings > GEORGIA

Motel 6
3050 Victory Dr.
Columbus, GA 31903
706-687-7214
PET POLICY: No fee. Dogs under 25 lbs. preferred (larger animals by advance approval). Do not leave animals in room unattended.

Commerce Red Roof Inn & Suites
157 Eisenhower Dr.
Commerce, GA 30529
706-335-3640
PET POLICY: No fee, pets under 80 lbs. Must be leashed to and from rooms. Do not leave in room unattended.

Cordele Days Inn
2115 16th Ave.
Cordele, GA 31015
912-273-1123
PET POLICY: No fee.

Ramada Inn
2016 16th Ave. E.
Cordele, GA 31015
912-273-5000
RATES: Single $45, double $45.
PET POLICY: Fee $5, nonrefundable.

Best Western White Columns Inn
10130 Alcovy Rd.
Covington, GA 30209
770-786-5800
PET POLICY: Fee $25, nonrefundable.

Holiday Inn Express
10111 Alcovy Rd.
Covington, GA 30014
770-787-4900
PET POLICY: Fee $25, nonrefundable. Small dogs only.

Bend of the River Cabins & Chalets
319 Horseshoe Ln.
Dahlonega, GA 30533
706-219-2040
RATES: Double $99–$150.
PET POLICY: Fee $20, nonrefundable, keep on leash, misc. amenities.
AMENITIES: Crates, biscuits.
POI: Dahlonega town square and gold museum, Alpine Helen, State parks and National forests.

Dalton Days Inn
1518 W. Walnut Ave.
Dalton, GA 30720
706-278-0850
PET POLICY: Fee $10.

Red Roof Inn
905 Westbridge
Dalton, GA 30722
706-259-2583
PET POLICY: No fee, pets under 80 lbs. Must be leashed to and from rooms. Do not leave in room unattended.

Dawsonville Days Inn
76 N. Georgia Ave.
Dawsonville, GA 30534
706-216-4410
PET POLICY: Fee $5.

Days Inn and Suites
4300 Snapfinger Woods Dr.
Decatur, GA 30035
770-981-5670
PET POLICY: Fee $25.

Motel 6
2565 Wesley Chapel Rd.
Decatur, GA 30035
404-288-6911
PET POLICY: No fee. Dogs under 25 lbs. preferred (larger animals by advance approval). Do not leave animals in room unattended.

Hampton Inn
1725 Pineland Rd.
Duluth, GA 30096
770-931-9800
PET POLICY: Pet with fee.

Folkston Days Inn
1201 S. 2nd St.
Folkston, GA 31537
912-496-2514
PET POLICY: Fee $5.

Motel 6
5060 Frontage Rd.
Forest Park, GA 30297
404-363-6429
PET POLICY: No fee. Dogs under 25 lbs. preferred (larger animals by advance approval). Do not leave animals in room unattended.

Hogansville Days Inn
1630 Bass Cross Rd.
Hogansville, GA 30230
706-637-5400
PET POLICY: Fee $5.

Jekyll Inn
975 N. Beachview Dr.
Jekyll Island, GA 31527
912-635-2531
RATES: Single, double $69–$129 (depending upon ocean views, etc.).
PET POLICY: Fee $10 per night. No restrictions.

Seafarer Inn
700 N. Beachview Dr.
Jekyll Island, GA 31527
912-635-2202
RATES: Single, double $59–$150 (seasonal + type of room).
PET POLICY: Fee $10 per night. All sizes accepted.

Jesup Days Inn
Hwy. 3015 & 341 US Hwy. 301
Jesup, GA 31545
912-427-3751
PET POLICY: Fee $5.

Shoneys Inn Atlanta South
6358 Old Dixie Hwy.
Jonesboro, GA 30236
770-968-5018
RATES: Single $54, double $59.
PET POLICY: No fee, all sizes welcome.

Red Roof Inn
520 Roberts Court Northwest
Kennesaw, GA 30144
770-429-0323
PET POLICY: No fee, pets under 80 lbs. Must be leashed to and from rooms. Do not leave in room unattended.

Days Inn Kingsland
1050 E. King Ave.
Kingsland, GA 31548
912-729-5454
PET POLICY: Fee $10.

Lafayette Days Inn
2209 N. Main St.
Lafayette, GA 30728
706-639-9362
PET POLICY: Fee $10.

U.S. Lodgings > GEORGIA

Amerihost Inn LaGrange
107 Hoffman Dr.
LaGrange, GA 30240
706-885-9002
RATES: Single, double $69.
PET POLICY: Fee $25, nonrefundable. All size dogs and cats, only. Do not leave in room unattended.

Lagrange Days Inn Near Callaway Gardens
2606 Whitesville Rd.
LaGrange, GA 30240
706-882-8881
PET POLICY: Fee $6.

Motel 6
2575 Whitesville
LaGrange, GA 30240
706-884-1114
PET POLICY: No fee. Dogs under 25 lbs. preferred (larger animals by advance approval). Do not leave animals in room unattended.

Days Inn
4913 Timber Dr.
Lake Park, GA 31636
912-559-0229
PET POLICY: Fee $2.

Holiday Inn Express
1198 Lakes Blvd.
Lake Park, GA 31636
912-559-5181
PET POLICY: Fee $5.

Travelodge
I-75, Exit 5
Lake Park, GA 31604
912 559-0110
RATES: Single $40, double $65.
PET POLICY: No fee, all sizes welcome.
POI: Wild Adventures Theme Park.

Shoney's Inn
14227 Jones St.
Lavonia, GA 30553
706-356-8848
RATES: Single $64.95+, double $69.95+.
PET POLICY: Fee $10 per night, per pet. Pets accepted up to 50 lbs. All pets welcome.

Lawrenceville Days Inn
731 Duluth Hwy.
Lawrenceville, GA 30045
770-995-7782
PET POLICY: No fee.

La Quinta Atlanta Panola Road
2859 Panola Rd.
Lithonia, GA 30058
770-981-6411
RATES: Single $65, double $55.
PET POLICY: No fee, up to 25 lbs.
POI: Stone Mountain Park.

Hampton Inn
3680 Riverside Dr.
Macon, GA 31210
912-471-0660
PET POLICY: Fee $15.

Motel 6
4991 Harrison Rd.
Macon, GA 31206
912-474-2870
PET POLICY: No fee. Dogs under 25 lbs. preferred (larger animals by advance approval). Do not leave animals in room unattended.

Red Roof Inn
3950 River Place Dr.
Macon, GA 31210
912-477-7477
PET POLICY: No fee, pets under 80 lbs. Must be leashed to and from rooms. Do not leave in room unattended.

Drury Inn and Suites Atlanta Northwest
1170 Powers Ferry Place
Marietta, GA 30067
770 612-0900
PET POLICY: No fee, pets under 30 lbs.

Motel 6
2360 Delk Rd.
Marietta, GA 30067
770-952-8161
PET POLICY: No fee. Dogs under 25 lbs. preferred (larger animals by advance approval). Do not leave animals in room unattended.

Mcdonough Days Inn
744 Georgia 155 S.
Mcdonough, GA 30253
770-957-5261
PET POLICY: Fee $5.

Milledgeville Days Inn
2551 N. Columbia St.
Milledgeville, GA 31061
912-453-8471
PET POLICY: Fee $10.

Red Roof Inn
1348 Southlake Plaza Dr.
Morrow, GA 30260
770-968-1483
PET POLICY: No fee, pets under 80 lbs. Must be leashed to and from rooms. Do not leave in room unattended.

Days Inn
US 29 & I-85
PO Box 548
Newnan, GA 30265
770-253-8550
PET POLICY: Fee $10.

Motel 6
40 Parkway North
Newnan, GA 30265
770-251-4580
PET POLICY: No fee. Dogs under 25 lbs. preferred (larger animals by advance approval). Do not leave animals in room unattended.

Drury Inn & Suites
5655 Jimmy Carter Blvd.
Norcross, GA 30071
770-729-0060
PET POLICY: No fee, pets under 30 lbs.

Homewood Suites Hotel
450 Technology Pkwy.
Norcross, GA 30092
770-448-4663
PET POLICY: Pets must be kept in crates. Fee charged.

La Quinta Atlanta
6187 Dawson Blvd.
Norcross, GA 30093
770-448-8686
RATES: Single $65, double $55.
PET POLICY: No fee, up to 25 lbs.
POI: Lake Lanier. Stone Mountain Park.

U.S. Lodgings > GEORGIA

La Quinta Atlanta
5375 Peachtree Industrial Blvd.
Norcross, GA 30092
770-449-5144
RATES: Single $59, double $49.
PET POLICY: No fee, up to 25 lbs.
POI: Lake Lanier. Chatahoochee
State Park.

Motel 6
6015 Oakbrook Pkwy.
Norcross, GA 30093
770-446-2311
PET POLICY: No fee. Dogs under
25 lbs. preferred (larger animals by advance approval).
Do not leave animals in room
unattended.

Red Roof Inn
5171 Brook Hollow Pkwy.
Norcross, GA 30071
770-448-8944
PET POLICY: No fee, pets under
80 lbs. Must be leashed to and
from rooms. Do not leave in
room unattended.

Shoney's Inn—Atlanta, NE
2050 Willowtrail Pkwy.
Norcross, GA 30093
770-564-0492
RATES: Single $47, double $52.
PET POLICY: Fee $25, refund-
able. All size dogs and cats.

Hampton Inn
102 Hampton Court
Perry, GA 31069
912-987-7681
PET POLICY: Pet fee.

Pine Mountain Days Inn
368 S. Main Ave.
Pine Mountain, GA 31822
706-663-2121
PET POLICY: Fee $5.

White Columns Motel
Hwy. 27S
PO Box 531
Pine Mountain, GA 31822
706-663-2312
PET POLICY: No fee.

Red Roof Inn
20 Mill Creek Circle
Pooler, GA 31322
912-748-0370
PET POLICY: No fee, pets under
80 lbs. Must be leashed to and
from rooms. Do not leave in
room unattended.

Richland Days Inn
46 Nicholson St.
Richmond, GA 31825
912-887-9000
PET POLICY: Fee $5.

Chattanooga Days Inn
5435 Alabama Hwy.
Ringgold, GA 30736
706-965-5730
PET POLICY: Fee $3.

**Baymont Inn & Suites—
Roswell**
575 Holcomb Bridge Rd.
Roswell, GA 30076
770-552-0200
PET POLICY: No fee.

Royal Windsor Cottage
4490 Hwy. 356
Sautee, GA 30571
706-878-1322
RATES: Single $105, double $145.
PET POLICY: Fee $10, nonre-
fundable. Up to 25 lbs.
AMENITIES: Over 22 acres to
exercise.
POI: Anna Ruby Falls. Alpine
Helen State Park.

**Baymont Inn & Suites—
Savannah**
8484 Abercorn St.
Savannah, GA 31406
912-927-7660
PET POLICY: No fee.

**Best Western Central
Motor Inn**
45 Eisenhower Dr.
Savannah, GA 31406
912-355-1000
RATES: Single $55–$75, double
$55–$75.
PET POLICY: Fee $15, 2+ pets, $25
nonrefundable, up to 25 lbs.
POI: Historic district 5 miles.

Econo Lodge Gateway
7 Gateway Blvd. W.
Savannah, GA 31419
912-925-2280
RATES: Single $50, double $60.
PET POLICY: Fee $5, per pet,
nonrefundable. Do not leave
pets unattended in room.
AMENITIES: Pet walk.

**Joan's on Jones
Bed & Breakfast**
17 W. Jones St.
Savannah, GA 31401
912-234-3863
RATES: Single $145, double
$145.
PET POLICY: Fee $50, nonre-
fundable, up to 50 lbs., fenced
courtyard outside the door.
AMENITIES: Fenced in patio
right outside your door.
POI: Right in the heart of historic landmark district which
is very pet-friendly.

Red Roof Inn
405 Al Henderson Boulevard
Savannah, GA 31419
912-920-3535
PET POLICY: No fee, pets under
80 lbs. Must be leashed to and
from rooms. Do not leave in
room unattended.

**Savannah Days Inn
Gateway I-95**
I-95 & Hwy. 204, Exit 94
Savannah, GA 31419
912-925-3680
PET POLICY: No fee.

**The Manor House
Bed & Breakfast**
201 W. Liberty St.
Savannah, GA 31401
912-233-9597
RATES: Double $185–$225.
PET POLICY: No fee. All sizes
and all pets welcome: dogs,
cats, and birds.

**Culpepper House
Bed & Breakfast**
35 Broad St.
Senoia, GA 30276
770-599-8182
PET POLICY: Preapproval
required "Have not turned
anyone down yet."

U.S. Lodgings > GEORGIA

AmeriHost Inn Smyrna
5130 S. Cobb Dr.
Smyrna, GA 30082
404-794-1600
RATES: Single, double $79.
PET POLICY: Fee $25, nonrefundable. All size dogs and cats, only. Do not leave in room unattended.

Red Roof Inn
2200 Corporate Plaza
Smyrna, GA 30080
770-952-6966
PET POLICY: No fee, pets under 80 lbs. Must be leashed to and from rooms. Do not leave in room unattended.

Belle Tara Inn
Bed & Breakfast
300 W. Conyers St.
St. Marys, GA 31558
912-882-4199
RATES: Single $95, double $95.
PET POLICY: No fee, all sizes welcome. Must be well-behaved, and on leash when outside. Must be crated if left alone in room.
AMENITIES: Large wooded area to walk pets.
POI: Cumberland Island National Seashore, Okefenokee, Amelia Island, Jekyll Island, St. Simons Island, Fernandia beach.

Statesboro Days Inn
461 S. Main St.
Statesboro, GA 30458
912-764-5666
PET POLICY: Fee $5.

Amerihost Inn
100 N. Park Court
Stockbridge, GA 30281
770-507-6500
RATES: Single, double $69.
PET POLICY: Fee $25, nonrefundable. All size dogs and cats. Do not leave pets in room unattended.

Motel 6
7233 Davidson Pkwy.
Stockbridge, GA 30281
770-389-1142
PET POLICY: No fee. Dogs under 25 lbs. preferred (larger animals by advance approval). Do not leave animals in room unattended.

Red Roof Inn
77 Gwinco Boulevard
Suwanee, GA 30024
770-271-5559
PET POLICY: No fee, pets under 80 lbs. Must be leashed to and from rooms. Do not leave in room unattended.

Swainsboro Days Inn
654 Main St.
Swainsboro, GA 30401
912-237-9333
PET POLICY: Fee $10.

Sylvester Days Inn
909 Franklin St.
Sylvester, GA 31791
912-776-9700
PET POLICY: Fee $5.

Thomaston Days Inn
1215 Hwy. 19 N.
Thomaston, GA 30286
706-648-9260
PET POLICY: Fee $10.

Days Inn of Thomasville
15375 US 195
Thomasville, GA 31792
912-226-6025
PET POLICY: Fee $5.

Best Western
White Columns Inn
1890 Washington Rd.
Thomson, GA 30824
706-595-8000
RATES: Single $53, double $59.
PET POLICY: Fee $10, nonrefundable, all sizes welcome, also ferrets, birds, rabbits, grassy puppy walking area.
AMENITIES: Grassy puppy walking area.

Townsend Days Inn
PO Box 156
Townsend, GA 31331
912-832-4411
PET POLICY: Fee $10.

La Quinta Atlanta
Stone Mountain
1819 Mountain Industrial Blvd.
Tucker, GA 30084
770-496-1317
RATES: Single $65, double $65.
PET POLICY: No fee, up to 25 lbs.
POI: Stone Mountain Park.

Red Roof Inn
2810 Lawrenceville Hwy.
Tucker, GA 30084
770-496-1311
PET POLICY: No fee, pets under 80 lbs. Must be leashed to and from rooms. Do not leave in room unattended.

Motel 6
3860 Flat Shoals Rd.
Union City, GA 30291
770-969-0110
PET POLICY: No fee. Dogs under 25 lbs. preferred (larger animals by advance approval). Do not leave animals in room unattended.

Red Roof Inn
6710 Shanon Pkwy.
Union City, GA 30291
770-306-7750
PET POLICY: No fee, pets under 80 lbs. Must be leashed to and from rooms. Do not leave in room unattended.

Motel 6
2003 W. Hill Ave.
Valdosta, GA 31601
912-333-0047
PET POLICY: No fee. Dogs under 25 lbs. preferred (larger animals by advance approval). Do not leave animals in room unattended.

Valdosta Days Inn
1827 W. Hill Ave.
Valdosta, GA 31601
~~912~~-249-8800
PET POLICY: Fee $5.

Waycross Days Inn
2016 Memorial Dr.
Waycross, GA 31501
912-285-4700
PET POLICY: Fee $5.

HAWAII

Kamuela Country Cottage
PO Box 1346
Kamuela, HI 96743
800-971-7244
RATES: Single $150, double $150.
PET POLICY: No fee, all size dogs and cats, only.
AMENITIES: Large fenced in yard with shade for dogs. Litter boxes and litter for cats. Bowls for food and water.
POI: Beaches within 15 minutes. Wide open hills to hike with dogs. Veterinarians nearby. Volcano National Park.

IDAHO

Holiday Inn Boise Airport
3300 Vista Ave.
Boise, ID 83705
208-344-8365
RATES: Single $79–$89, double $79–$89.
PET POLICY: No fee, all pets and sizes accepted.
POI: Historic district, beach, mountains, ski area, golf course all close by.

Motel 6
2323 Airport Way
Boise, ID 83705
208-344-3506
PET POLICY: No fee. Dogs under 25 lbs. preferred (larger animals by advance approval). Do not leave animals in room unattended.

Shilo Inn Riverside
3031 Main St.
Boise, ID 83702
208-344-3521
RATES: Single $59, double $69.
PET POLICY: Fee $10, nonrefundable. All sizes, all pets welcome (dogs, cats, birds, ferrets, rabbits, reptiles).

Shilo Inn Suites, Boise Airport
4111 Broadway Ave.
Boise, ID 83705
208-343-7662
RATES: Single $49, double $59.
PET POLICY: Fee $10, nonrefundable. All sizes, all pets welcome (dogs, cats, birds, ferrets, rabbits, reptiles).

Motel 6
416 Appleway
Coeur D'Alene, ID 83814
208-664-6600
PET POLICY: No fee. Dogs under 25 lbs. preferred (larger animals by advance approval). Do not leave animals in room unattended.

Shilo Inn
702 W. Appleway
Coeur D'Alene, ID 83814
208-664-2300
RATES: Single $59, double $69.
PET POLICY: Fee $10, nonrefundable. All sizes, all pets welcome (dogs, cats, birds, ferrets, rabbits, reptiles).

Idaho Falls Days Inn
700 Lindsay Blvd.
Idaho Falls, ID 83402
208-522-2910
PET POLICY: Fee $20.

Motel 6
1448 W. Broadway
Idaho Falls, ID 83402
208-522-0112
PET POLICY: No fee. Dogs under 25 lbs. preferred (larger animals by advance approval). Do not leave animals in room unattended.

Shilo Inn Idaho Falls
780 Lindsay Blvd.
Idaho Falls, ID 83402
208-523-0088
RATES: Single $69, double $79.
PET POLICY: Fee $10, nonrefundable. All sizes, all pets welcome.

Best Western Tyrolean Lodge
260 Cottonwood
Ketchum, ID 83340
208-726-5336
RATES: Single $80, double $120.
PET POLICY: Fee $10, nonrefundable. Up to 25 lbs. In smoking rooms only.
POI: hiking, rivers.

Mark IV Motor Inn
414 N. Main St.
Moscow, ID 83843
208-882-7557
RATES: Single, double $49–$99.
PET POLICY: Fee $5 per night. Do not leave pets in room unattended. No size restrictions.

Shilo Inn Nampa Suites
1401 Shilo Dr.
Nampa, ID 83687
208-465-3250
RATES: Single $99, double $109.
PET POLICY: Fee $10, nonrefundable. All sizes, all pets welcome.

Shilo Inn—Nampa
617 Nampa Blvd.
Nampa, ID 83687
208-466-8993
RATES: Single $79, double $89.
PET POLICY: Fee $10, nonrefundable. All sizes, all pets welcome.

Pinehurst Resort Cottages
5604 Hwy. 95
New Meadows, ID 83654
208-628-3323
RATES: Single $40, double $45.
PET POLICY: Fee $3, nonrefundable. All size dogs only. Do not leave unattended, must be leashed.
POI: Hells Canyon, Heavens Gate Overlook, the Salmon and Snake rivers, rafting, jet boating, fishing.

Motel 6
291 W. Burnside Ave.
Pocatello, ID 83202
208-237-7880
PET POLICY: No fee. Dogs under 25 lbs. preferred (larger animals by advance approval). Do not leave animals in room unattended.

Rexburg Days Inn
271 S. 2nd W.
Rexburg, ID 83440
208-356-9222
PET POLICY: No fee.

Suncrest Motel
705 Challis St.
Salmon, ID 83467
208-756-2294
RATES: Single $37, double $47.
PET POLICY: Fee $3–$7, nonrefundable, all sizes welcome.
AMENITIES: Free horse corrals.

Jerry's Country Store & Motel
HC 67, Box 300
Stanley, ID 83278
208-774-3566
RATES: Single, double $65–$75.
PET POLICY: Fee $5 per pet. No restrictions. Dogs and cats only.

U.S. Lodgings > IDAHO

Motel 6
1472 Blue Lake Blvd. N
Twin Falls, ID 83301
208-734-3993
PET POLICY: No fee. Dogs under 25 lbs. preferred (larger animals by advance approval). Do not leave animals in room unattended.

Shilo Inn
1586 Blue Lakes Blvd.
Twin Falls, ID 83301
208-733-7545
RATES: Single $69, double $79.
PET POLICY: Fee $10, nonrefundable. All sizes, all pets welcome.

Best Western Wallace Inn
100 Front St.
Wallace, ID 83873
208-752-1252
RATES: Single $74, double $84.
PET POLICY: Fee $10 day, nonrefundable, up to 50 lbs., special pet rooms.
POI: Silverwood Theme Park, Silver Mtn Ski & Recreation Area, Lookout Pass Ski & Recreation Area.

Stardust Motel
410 Pine St.
Wallace, ID 83873
208-752-1213
RATES: Single $46, double $56.
PET POLICY: Fee $10, nonrefundable.

ILLINOIS

Baymont Inn & Suites
12801 S. Cicero
Alsip, IL 60658
708-597-3900
PET POLICY: No fee.

Alton Days Inn
1900 Homer M. Adams Pkwy.
Alton, IL 62002
618-463-0800
PET POLICY: Fee $10.

Red Roof Inn
22 W. Algonquin Rd.
Arlington Heights, IL 60005
847-228-6650
PET POLICY: No fee, pets under 80 lbs. Must be leashed to and from rooms. Do not leave in room unattended.

Woodfield Suites Hotel
2000 Lakeside Dr.
Bannockburn, IL 60015
847-317-7300
PET POLICY: No fee.

Benton Days Inn
711 W. Main
Benton, IL 62812
618-439-3183
PET POLICY: No fee.

Bloomington Days Inn West
1707 W. Market St.
Bloomington, IL 61701
309-829-6292
PET POLICY: No fee.

Holiday Inn
I-55 & Rt. 108
Carlinville, IL 62626
217-324-2100
PET POLICY: Fee $10.

Baymont Inn & Suites—Champaign-Urbana
302 W. Anthony Dr.
Champaign, IL 61820
217-356-8900
PET POLICY: No fee.

La Quinta Inn Champaign
1900 Center Dr.
Champaign, IL 61820-782
217-356-4000
RATES: Single $59–$66, double $71+.
PET POLICY: No fee, pets under 30 lbs.

Microtel Inn
1615 Rion Dr.
Champaign, IL 61822
217-398-4136
RATES: Single $32, double $39.
PET POLICY: Fee $20, nonrefundable. All sizes accepted.

Red Roof Inn
212 W. Anthony Dr.
Champaign, IL 61820
217-352-0101
PET POLICY: No fee, pets under 80 lbs. Must be leashed to and from rooms. Do not leave in room unattended.

Hilton Chicago and Towers
720 S. Michigan Ave.
Chicago, IL 60605
312-922-4400
RATES: Single, double $169–$469.
PET POLICY: No fee, all sizes accepted.

Hotel Monaco Chicago
225 N. Wabash Ave.
Chicago, IL 60601
312-960-8500
RATES: Single $299, double $299.
PET POLICY: No fee, all sizes, dogs, cats, ferrets, birds, rabbits, etc. Contract of liability to be signed. Keep in cage when owner not present.
AMENITIES: Beautifully appointed boutique hotel located in heart of Chicago. All rooms feature 2-line speaker phones, in-room fax/copy/printers, Nintendo 64, Movies, 24 hour room service and fitness center. Full time Concierge, and more.

Howard Johnson Hotel
9333 Skokie Blvd.
Chicago, IL 60077
847-679-4200
RATES: Single $105, double $112.
PET POLICY: No fee, small pets only.

Motel 6
162 E. Ontario St.
Chicago, IL 60611
312-787-3580
PET POLICY: No fee. Dogs under 25 lbs. preferred (larger animals by advance approval). Do not leave animals in room unattended.

Radisson Chicago
160 E. Huron St.
Chicago, IL 60611
312-787-2900
RATES: Single, double $129–$319.
PET POLICY: No fee, deposit required: $100. Pets accepted under 50 lbs. Pets in smoking rooms, only.

U.S. Lodgings > ILLINOIS

Renaissance Chicago Hotel
1 W. Wacker Dr.
Chicago, IL 60601
312-372-7200
RATES: Single $169–$299,
double $199–$319.
PET POLICY: Fee $45, nonre-
fundable. Pets accepted under
30 lbs.

Ritz Carlton Hotel
160 E. Pearson St.
Chicago, IL 60611-012
312-266-1000
RATES: Single $375–$475,
double $395–$500.
PET POLICY: No fee. Pets
accepted under 30 lbs.

Sutton Place Hotel
21 E. Bellevue
Chicago, IL 60611
312 266 2100
PET POLICY: Deposit $500
refundable. (Not charged is
using credit card).

**The Westin Michigan Ave
Chicago**
909 N. Michigan Ave.
Chicago, IL 60611
312-943-7200
RATES: Single $184–$239,
double $239–$264.
PET POLICY: No fee, small pets
only.

Travelodge
65 E. Harrison St.
Chicago, IL 60605
312 427-8000
RATES: Single, double
$79–$109.
PET POLICY: Fee $20, refundable.
Pets accepted under 15 lbs.

Drury Inn Collinsville
602 N. Bluff
Collinsville, IL 62234
618-345-7700
PET POLICY: No fee, pets under
30 lbs.

Pear Tree Inn by Drury
552 Ramada Blvd.
Collinsville, IL 62234
618-345-9500
PET POLICY: No fee. All sizes
and pets accepted. Do not
leave in rooms unattended.

Comfort Inn Danville
383 Lynch Dr.
Danville, IL 61832-937
217-443-8004
RATES: Single, double $52–$59.
PET POLICY: No fee, all size pets
accepted.

**Danville—Champaign
Knights Inn**
411 Lynch Dr.
Danville, IL 61834
217-443-3690
RATES: Single $40, double $50.
PET POLICY: Fee $5.30. All size
pets accepted.

**Baymont Inn & Suites—
Decatur**
5100 Hickory Point Frontage Rd.
Decatur, IL 62526
217-875-5800
PET POLICY: No fee.

Decatur Days Inn
333 N. Wyckles Rd.
Decatur, IL 62522
217-422-5900
PET POLICY: No fee.

Dekalb Travelodge
1116 W. Lincoln Hwy.
Dekalb, IL 60115
815 756-3398
RATES: Single $42, double $46.
PET POLICY: Fee $5, nonrefundable.
Requires manager's approval.

Red Roof Inn
1113 Butterfield Rd.
Downers Grove, IL 60515
630-963-4205
PET POLICY: No fee, pets under
80 lbs. Must be leashed to and
from rooms. Do not leave in
room unattended.

Baymont Inn & Suites
300 E. Peoria
East Peoria, IL 61611
309-694-4959
PET POLICY: No fee.

Motel 6
104 W. Camp St.
East Peoria, IL 61611
309-699-7281
PET POLICY: No fee. Dogs under 25
lbs. preferred (larger animals by
advance approval). Do not leave
animals in room unattended.

Best Inns of America
1209 N. Keller Dr.
Effingham, IL 62401
217-347-5141
RATES: Single $42.99, double
$52.99.
PET POLICY: Fee $10 only for
pets over 25 lbs.

Comfort Inn
1304 W. Evergreen Ave.
Effingham, IL 62401
217-347-5050
RATES: Single, double $55–$60.
PET POLICY: Small pets allowed.

Days Inn
Box 626
Effingham, IL 62401
217-342-9271
PET POLICY: No fee.

Econo Lodge
1205 Keller Dr.
Effingham, IL 62401
217-347-7131
RATES: Single, double $40–$50.
PET POLICY: Small pets allowed.

Howard Johnson Express Inn
1606 W. Fayette Ave.
Effingham, IL 62401
217-342-4667
RATES: Single $45, double $70.
PET POLICY: Fee $5 per pet,
nonrefundable. Up to 50 lbs.

El Paso Days Inn
630 W. Main St.
El Paso, IL 61738
309-527-7070
PET POLICY: No fee.

Baymont Inn & Suites
500 Toll Gate Rd.
Elgin, IL 60123
847-931-4800
PET POLICY: No fee.

Crowne Plaza
495 Airport Rd.
Elgin, IL 60123
847-488-9000
PET POLICY: Contact Property
Director.

Elgin Days Inn
1585 Dundee Ave.
Elgin, IL 60120
847-695-2100
PET POLICY: Fee $10.

U.S. Lodgings > ILLINOIS

Days Inn O'Hare West
1920 E. Higgins Rd.
Elk Grove Village, IL 60007
708-894-2085
PET POLICY: Fee $10.

Drury Inn Fairview Heights
12 Ludwig Dr.
Fairview Heights, IL 62208
618 398-8530
PET POLICY: No fee, pets under
30 lbs.

Chestnut Ridge
Blackjack Rd.
Galena, IL 61036
815-777-1506
RATES: Single, double $165–$255.
PET POLICY: Pets by arrangement.

Chestnut Ridge
Blackjack Rd.
Galena, IL 61036
815-777-1506
PET POLICY: Pets allowed with
permission.

**Early American Log Cabin
Settlement**
9401 Hart John Rd.
Galena, IL 61036
815-777-4200
PET POLICY: Fee charged.

Gilman Days Inn
834 Hwy. 24 W
Gilman, IL 60938
815-265-7283
PET POLICY: Fee $3.

Holiday Inn
1250 Roosevelt Rd.
Glen Ellyn, IL 60137
630-629-6000
PET POLICY: Small pets under
25 lbs., Fee.

Baymont Inn & Suites
1625 Milwaukee Ave.
Glenview, IL 60025
847-635-8300
PET POLICY: Pets permitted with
prior permission.

St. Louis Days Inn
1100 Niedringhous Ave.
Granite City, IL 62040
618-877-7100
PET POLICY: Fee $5.

Baymont Inn & Suites
5688 N. Ridge Rd.
Gurnee, IL 60031
847-662-7600
PET POLICY: No fee.

Holiday Inn
3830 179th St.
Hammond, IL 46322
219-844-2140
PET POLICY: Small pets allowed
with deposit.

Baymont Inn & Suites
2075 Barrington Rd.
Hoffman Estates, IL 60195
847-882-8848
PET POLICY: No fee.

Motel 6
1850 McDonough Rd.
Joliet, IL 60436
815-729-2800
PET POLICY: No fee. Dogs under
25 lbs. preferred (larger animals by advance approval).
Do not leave animals in room
unattended.

Red Roof Inn
2500 Hassell Rd.
Hoffman Estates, IL 60195
847-885-7877
PET POLICY: No fee, pets under
80 lbs. Must be leashed to and
from rooms. Do not leave in
room unattended.

Red Roof Inn
1750 McDonough St.
Joliet, IL 60436
815-741-2304
PET POLICY: No fee, pets under
80 lbs. Must be leashed to and
from rooms. Do not leave in
room unattended.

Chicago Days Inn
17356 S. Torrence Ave.
Lansing, IL 60438
708-474-6300
PET POLICY: No fee.

Red Roof Inn
2450 173rd St.
Lansing, IL 60438
708-895-9570
PET POLICY: No fee, pets under
80 lbs. Must be leashed to and
from rooms. Do not leave in
room unattended.

Baymont Inn & Suites
1405 W. Hudson Dr.
Litchfield, IL 62056
217-324-4556
PET POLICY: No fee.

Best Inns of America
2700 W. De Young
Marion, IL 62959
618-997-9421
PET POLICY: No fee, no restrictions.

Marion Days Inn
1802 Bittle Pt.
Marion, IL 62959
618-997-1351
PET POLICY: Fee $5.

**Baymont Inn & Suites—
Matteson**
5210 W. Southwick Dr.
Matteson, IL 60443
708-503-0999
PET POLICY: No fee.

**Isle of View
Bed & Breakfast**
205 Metropolis St.
Metropolis, IL 62960
618-524-5838
PET POLICY: No fee, pet must
stay with owner.

Motel 6
2359 69th Ave.
Moline, IL 61265
309-764-8711
PET POLICY: No fee. Dogs under
25 lbs. preferred (larger animals by advance approval).
Do not leave animals in room
unattended.

Drury Inn Mt. Vernon
PO Box 805
Mount Vernon, IL 62864
618-244-4550
PET POLICY: No fee, pets under
30 lbs.

Red Roof Inn
1698 W. Diehl Rd.
Naperville, IL 60563
630-369-2500
PET POLICY: No fee, pets under
80 lbs. Must be leashed to and
from rooms. Do not leave in
room unattended.

U.S. Lodgings > ILLINOIS

Motel 6
1600 N. Main St.
Normal, IL 61761
309-452-0422
PET POLICY: No fee. Dogs under 25 lbs. preferred (larger animals by advance approval). Do not leave animals in room unattended.

Red Roof Inn
340 Waukegan Rd.
Northbrook, IL 60062
847-205-1755
PET POLICY: No fee, pets under 80 lbs. Must be leashed to and from rooms. Do not leave in room unattended.

Peoria Days Inn
2726 W. Lake Ave.
Peoria, IL 61615
309-688-7000
PET POLICY: Fee $10.

Red Roof Inn
4031 N. War Memorial Dr.
Peoria, IL 61614
309-685-3911
PET POLICY: No fee, pets under 80 lbs. Must be leashed to and from rooms. Do not leave in room unattended.

Princeton Days Inn
2238 N. Main St.
Princeton, IL 61356
815-875-3371
PET POLICY: Fee $6.

Diamond Motel
4703 N. 12th St.
Quincy, IL 62301
217-223-1436
RATES: Single $25, double $35.
PET POLICY: No fee. All pets and sizes accepted.
AMENITIES: All rooms street level.

Quincy Riverside Days Inn
200 Maine St.
Quincy, IL 62301
217-223-6610
PET POLICY: No fee.

Rantoul Days Inn
801 W. Champaign
Rantoul, IL 61866
217-893-0700
PET POLICY: Fee $10.

Baymont Inn & Suites
662 N. Lyford Rd.
Rockford, IL 61107
815-229-8200
PET POLICY: Fee $5, nonrefundable.

Best Suites of America
7401 Walton St.
Rockford, IL 61108
815-227-1300
RATES: Single, double $65–$125.
PET POLICY: No fee. Pets under 25 lbs.

Red Roof Inn
7434 E. State St.
Rockford, IL 61108
815-398-9750
PET POLICY: No fee, pets under 80 lbs. Must be leashed to and from rooms. Do not leave in room unattended.

Drury Inn Schaumberg
600 N. Martingale
Schaumberg, IL 60173
847 517-7737
PET POLICY: No fee, pets under 30 lbs.

Holiday Inn
1550 N. Roselle Rd.
Schaumburg, IL 60195
847-310-0500
PET POLICY: Pets up to 40 lbs.

Motel 6
9408 W. Lawrence Ave.
Schiller Park, IL 60176
847-671-4282
PET POLICY: No fee. Dogs under 25 lbs. preferred (larger animals by advance approval). Do not leave animals in room unattended.

Boondock's Floating Cottages
1 E. Dupont Rd.
Seneca, IL 61360
815-357-1100
PET POLICY: Pets allowed with permission.

Sheffield Days Inn
Hwy. 40 & I-80
Sheffield, IL 61361
815-454-2361
PET POLICY: No fee.

R 'ol House
RR 4, Box 119
Shelbyville, IL 62565
217-774-2419
RATES: Double $105, Whole house: $115.
PET POLICY: No fee, all pets and sizes welcome (dogs, cats, ferrets, birds, rabbits, reptiles).
AMENITIES: Pets stay and eat free. Fenced in pet yard, also welcome in house.
POI: Lake Shelbyville.

Chicago Days Inn
19747 Frontage Rd.
Shorewood , IL 60435
815-725-2180
PET POLICY: No fee.

Red Roof Inn
17301 S. Halsted
South Holland, IL 60473
708-331-1621
PET POLICY: No fee, pets under 80 lbs. Must be leashed to and from rooms. Do not leave in room unattended.

Baymont Inn & Suites
5851 S. 6th St.
Springfield, IL 62703
217-529-6655
PET POLICY: No fee.

Drury Inn and Suites Springfield
3180 S. Dirksen Pkwy.
Springfield, IL 62703
217 529-3900
PET POLICY: No fee, pets under 30 lbs.

Lincoln Plaza Hotel
101 E. Adams St.
Springfield, IL 62701
217-523-5661
RATES: Single $50, double $55.
PET POLICY: Fee $10, nonrefundable, up to 25 lbs.

Motel 6
6011 S. 6th St.
Springfield, IL 62707
217-529-1633
PET POLICY: No fee. Dogs under 25 lbs. preferred (larger animals by advance approval). Do not leave animals in room unattended.

Pear Tree Inn Springfield
3190 S. Dirksen Pkwy.
Springfield, IL 62703
217 529-9100
PET POLICY: No fee. All sizes
and pets accepted. Do not
leave in rooms unattended.

Red Roof Inn
3200 Singer Ave.
Springfield, IL 62703
217-753-4302
PET POLICY: No fee, pets under
80 lbs. Must be leashed to and
from rooms. Do not leave in
room unattended.

Springfield Days Inn
3000 Stevenson Dr.
Springfield, IL 62703
217-529-0171
PET POLICY: No fee.

Staunton Super 8
1527 Herman Rd.
Staunton, IL 62088
618-635-5353
RATES: Single $41.88, double
$45.88–$48.88.
PET POLICY: No fee, all sizes.

Baymont Inn & Suites
7255 W. 183rd St.
Tinley Park, IL 60477
708-633-1200
PET POLICY: No fee.

Red Roof Inn
2030 Formosa Rd.
Troy, IL 62294
618-667-2222
PET POLICY: No fee, pets under
80 lbs. Must be leashed to and
from rooms. Do not leave in
room unattended.

Motel 6
1906 N. Cunningham Ave.
Urbana, IL 61802
217-344-1082
PET POLICY: No fee. Dogs under
25 lbs. preferred (larger animals by advance approval). Do
not leave animals in room
unattended.

Days Inn
1920 Kennedy Blvd.
Vandalia, IL 62471
618-283-4400

RATES: Single $46.95, double
$57.95.
PET POLICY: Fee $10, refundable.
All sizes welcome.

Travelodge
1500 N. 6th St.
Vandalia, IL 62471
618 283-2363
RATES: Single $39.95, double
$52.95.
PET POLICY: Fee $3, nonrefund-
able. All sizes welcome.

AmeriSuites—Warrenville
4305 Weaver Pkwy.
Warrenville, IL 60555
630-393-0400
PET POLICY: Fee $50, refundable.
Only pets under 30 lbs.

Baymont Inn & Suites
855 79th St.
Willowbrook, IL 60521
630-654-0077
PET POLICY: No fee.

Red Roof Inn
7535 Robert Kingery Hwy.
Willowbrook, IL 60521
630-323-8811
PET POLICY: No fee, pets under
80 lbs. Must be leashed to and
from rooms. Do not leave in
room unattended.

Concorde Country Inn
112½ Cass St.
Woodstock, IL 60098
815-338-1100
PET POLICY: Pets allowed with
prior permission.

INDIANA

Bloomington Days Inn
200 Matlock Rd.
Bloomington, IN 47402
812-336-0905
PET POLICY: No fee.

Motel 6
1800 N. Walnut St.
Bloomington, IN 47402
812-332-0820
PET POLICY: No fee. Dogs under 25
lbs. preferred (larger animals by
advance approval). Do not leave
animals in room unattended.

Columbia Days Inn
3445 Jonathan Moore Pike
Columbia, IN 47201
812-376-9951
PET POLICY: Fee $10.

Baymont Inn & Suites
20857 N. US 231 @ I-64
Dale, IN 47523
812-937-7000
PET POLICY: No fee.

Motel 6
20840 N. US Hwy. 231
Dale, IN 47523
812-937-2294
PET POLICY: No fee. Dogs under 25
lbs. preferred (larger animals by
advance approval). Do not leave
animals in room unattended.

Days Inn
1033 N. 13th St.
Decatur, IN 46733
219-728-2196
PET POLICY: Fee $5.

Red Roof Inn
2902 Cassopolis St.
Elkhart, IN 46514
219-262-3691
PET POLICY: No fee, pets under
80 lbs. Must be leashed to and
from rooms. Do not leave in
room unattended.

Super 8 Motel
345 Windsor Ave.
Elkhart, IN 46514
219-264-4457
RATES: Single $47.99, double
$61.99.
PET POLICY: No fee, up to 50 lbs.
POI: State and County parks.

Days Inn East
4819 Tecumseh Ln.
Evansville, IN 47715
812-473-7944
PET POLICY: Fee $5.

Drury Inn & Suites
100 Cross Pointe Blvd.
Evansville, IN 47715
812-471-3400
PET POLICY: No fee, pets under
30 lbs.

U.S. Lodgings > INDIANA

Drury Inn Evansville
3901 US 41N
Evansville, IN 47711
812-423-5818
PET POLICY: No fee. All sizes
and pets accepted. Do not
leave in rooms unattended.

Motel 6
4321 Hwy. 41 N
Evansville, IN 47711
812-424-6431
PET POLICY: No fee. Dogs under 25
lbs. preferred (larger animals by
advance approval). Do not leave
animals in room unattended.

Red Roof Inn
8331 E. Walnut St.
Evansville, IN 47715
812-476-3600
PET POLICY: No fee, pets under
80 lbs. Must be leashed to and
from rooms. Do not leave in
room unattended.

Sleep Inn
9791 N. By NE Blvd.
Fishers, IN, 46038
317-558-4100
RATES: Single, double $69.96–
125.95
PET POLICY: No fee, no restrictions. Hold credit card in case
of damage.

Baymont Inn & Suites
1005 W. Washington Center Rd.
Fort Wayne, IN 46825
219-489-2220
PET POLICY: No fee.

Motel 6
3003 Coliseum Blvd. W
Fort Wayne, IN 46808
219-482-3972
PET POLICY: No fee. Dogs under 25
lbs. preferred (larger animals by
advance approval). Do not leave
animals in room unattended.

Red Roof Inn
2920 Goshen Rd.
Fort Wayne, IN 46808
219-484-8641
PET POLICY: No fee, pets under
80 lbs. Must be leashed to and
from rooms. Do not leave in
room unattended.

Days Inn
2180 E. King St.
Franklin, IN 46131
317-736-8000
PET POLICY: Fee $7.

**The Pines at Patoka Lake
Village**
7900 W. 1025 S.
French Lick, IN 47432
812-936-9854
RATES: Double $69–$89 and
$60–$75.
PET POLICY: No fee, all sizes
welcome.
POI: Patoka Lake beach in
Newton Stewart Rec. Park,
Holiday World, Nature trails
on property.

Baymont Inn & Suites
RR 1, Box 252 US 41 & I 64
Haubstat, IN 47639
812-768-5878
PET POLICY: No fee.

Huntington Days Inn
2996 W. Park Dr.
Huntington, IN 46750
219-359-8989
PET POLICY: Fee $7.

Baymont Inn & Suites
2650 Executive Dr.
Indianapolis, IN 46241
317-244-8100
PET POLICY: No fee.

Baymont Inn & Suites
2349 Post Dr.
Indianapolis, IN 46219
317-897-2300
PET POLICY: No fee.

Drury Inn
9320 N. Michigan Rd.
Indianapolis, IN 46268
317-876-9777
PET POLICY: No fee, pets under
30 lbs.

Indianapolis Days Inn
4326 Sellers St.
Indianapolis, IN 46226
317-542-1031
PET POLICY: Fee $5.

**Indianapolis Days Inn &
Suites**
8275 Craig St.
Indianapolis, IN 46250
317-841-9700
PET POLICY: Fee $25.

**Knights Inn Indianapolis
South**
4909 Knights Way
Indianapolis, IN 46217
317-788-0125
RATES: Single $45, double $55.
PET POLICY: Fee $5, refundable,
all sizes welcome.

Motel 6
5151 Elmwood Dr.
Indianapolis, IN 46203
317-783-5555
PET POLICY: No fee. Dogs under 25
lbs. preferred (larger animals by
advance approval). Do not leave
animals in room unattended.

Red Roof Inn
5221 Victory Dr.
Indianapolis, IN 46203
317-788-9551
PET POLICY: No fee, pets under
80 lbs. Must be leashed to and
from rooms. Do not leave in
room unattended.

Red Roof Inn
9520 Valparaiso Court
Indianapolis, IN 46268
317-872-3030
PET POLICY: No fee, pets under
80 lbs. Must be leashed to and
from rooms. Do not leave in
room unattended.

Motel 6
2016 Old Hwy. 31 E
Jeffersonville, IN 47129
812-283-7703
PET POLICY: No fee. Dogs under 25
lbs. preferred (larger animals by
advance approval). Do not leave
animals in room unattended.

Holiday Inn Express
201 Frontage Rd.
Lafayette, IN 47905
765-449-4808
RATES: Single $80, double $80.
PET POLICY: No fee, up to 50
lbs. All pets welcome, must be
kept on leash, noise kept to
minimum level.

U.S. Lodgings > INDIANA

Red Roof Inn
4201 State Route 26 East
Lafayette, IN 47905
765-448-4671
PET POLICY: No fee, pets under
80 lbs. Must be leashed to and
from rooms. Do not leave in
room unattended.

Red Roof Inn
8290 Georgia St.
Merrillville, IN 46410
219-738-2430
PET POLICY: No fee, pets under
80 lbs. Must be leashed to and
from rooms. Do not leave in
room unattended.

Red Roof Inn
110 W. Kieffer Rd.
Michigan City, IN 46360
219-874-5251
PET POLICY: No fee, pets under
80 lbs. Must be leashed to and
from rooms. Do not leave in
room unattended.

Mishawaka Days Inn
2754 Lincolnway E.
Mishawaka, IN 46544
219-256-2300
PET POLICY: Fee $7.

Muncie Days Inn
3509 N. Everbrook Ln.
Muncie, IN 47304
317-288-2311
PET POLICY: No fee.

New Castle Days Inn
5343 State Rd. 3
New Castle, IN 47362
765-987-8205
PET POLICY: Fee $5.

Days Inn
2229 N. Michigan St.
Plymouth, IN 46563
219-935-4276
PET POLICY: Fee $5.

Days Inn
540 W. Eaton Pike
Richmond, IN 47374
317-966-7591
PET POLICY: No fee.

Seymour Days Inn
302 S. Commerce Dr.
Seymour, IN 47274
812-522-3678
PET POLICY: No fee.

Motel 6
52624 US Hwy. 31 N
South Bend, IN 46637
219-272-7072
PET POLICY: No fee. Dogs under 25
lbs. preferred (larger animals by
advance approval). Do not leave
animals in room unattended.

Days Inn
PO Box 97
Sullivan, IN 47882
812-268-6391
PET POLICY: No fee.

Drury Inn
3020 US Highway 41S
Terre Haute, IN 47802
812-238-1206
PET POLICY: No fee, pets under
30 lbs.

Motel 6
1 W. Honey Creek Dr.
Terre Haute, IN 47802
812-238-1586
PET POLICY: No fee. Dogs under 25
lbs. preferred (larger animals by
advance approval). Do not leave
animals in room unattended.

Pear Tree by Drury
3050 S. US 41
Terre Haute, IN 47802
812-234-4268
PET POLICY: No fee. All sizes
and pets accepted. Do not
leave in rooms unattended.

Tell City Days Inn
555 S. Third St.
Terre Haute, IN 47807
812-547-3474
PET POLICY: Fee $10.

Warsaw Days Inn
3521 Lake City Hwy. US 30
Warsaw, IN 46580
219-269-3031
PET POLICY: Fee $4.

Baymont Inn & Suites
7 Cumberland Dr.
Washington, IN 47501
812-254-7000
PET POLICY: No fee, deposit $50.

IOWA

Motel 6
3225 Adventureland Dr.
Altoona, IA 50009
515-967-5252
PET POLICY: No fee. Dogs under 25
lbs. preferred (larger animals by
advance approval). Do not leave
animals in room unattended.

Holiday Inn
I-80 Exit 225
Amana, IA 52203
319-668-1175
RATES: Single $89, double $99.
PET POLICY: No fee. Do not
leave unattended in room.

Baymont Inn & Suites
2500 Elwood Dr.
Ames, IA 50010
515-296-2500
PET POLICY: No fee.

Best Western Starlite Village
2601 E. 13th St.
Ames, IA 50010
515-232-9260
RATES: Single $60, double $70.
PET POLICY: No fee, small pets
only, in smoking rooms.

Comfort Inn—Ames
1605 S. Dayton Ave.
Ames, IA 50010
515-232-0689
RATES: Avg: $59.
PET POLICY: No fee, all sizes
accepted. In smoking rooms
only.

Holiday Inn
US 30 & Elwood Dr.
Ames, IA 50014
515-292-8600
RATES: Single $95, double $105.
PET POLICY: No fee, all sizes
accepted. Pets in smoking
rooms only. Must be crated if
left alone.

University Inn
316 S. Duff
Ames, IA 50010
515-232-0280
RATES: Avg: $45–$55.
PET POLICY: Fee $20, all sizes
accepted.

U.S. Lodgings > IOWA

Des Moines Days Inn
103 NE Delaware
Ankeny, IA 50021
515-965-1995
PET POLICY: Fee $5.

Fillenwarth Beach
On W. Lake Okoboji
Arnolds Park, IA 51331
712-332-5646
RATES: Single $196, double $256.
PET POLICY: No fee, all sizes
welcome.

Motel 71-30
Junction Hwy. 71 & 30
Carroll, IA 51401
712-792-1100
RATES: Single $34, double $38.
PET POLICY: No fee, all sizes
welcome.

Cedar Falls Days Inn
4117 University Ave.
Cedar Falls, IA 50613
319-277-6931
PET POLICY: Fee $5.

University Inn
4711 University Ave.
Cedar Falls, IA 50613
319-277-1412
RATES: Single $45, double
$49–$55.
PET POLICY: Fee $30, refundable.
All sizes accepted.

**Collins Plaza Hotel &
Convention Center**
1200 Collins Rd. NE
Cedar Rapids, IA 52402
319-393-6600
RATES: Avg: $72.
PET POLICY: Fee $50, all sizes
accepted.

**Comfort Inn of Cedar
Rapids North**
5055 Rockwell Dr.
Cedar Rapids, IA 52402
319-393-8247
PET POLICY: No fee all sizes
accepted. Pets in smoking
rooms. Will use deionizer.

Comfort Inn South
390 33rd Ave. SW
Cedar Rapids, IA 52404
319-363-7934
RATES: Avg: $65–$70.
PET POLICY: Fee $10, refundable.
All sizes accepted. Pets in
smoking rooms only.

Days Inn of Cedar Rapids
3245 Southgate Pl.
Cedar Rapids, IA 52404
319-365-4339
PET POLICY: No fee.

Econo Lodge
622 33rd Ave. SW
Cedar Rapids, IA 52404
319-363-8888
RATES: Avg: $50–$69.
PET POLICY: Fee $5, all sizes.

Howard Johnson Express Inn
9100 Atlantic Dr. SW
Cedar Rapids, IA 52404
319-363-3789
RATES: Single $67.95, double
$75.95.
PET POLICY: Fee $10 day, non-
refundable, dogs and cats only,
not left unattended.
AMENITIES: Grassland area to
exercise pets.
POI: Golf course, Hawkeye
Downs race track, Polar Ice-Ice
arena, Czech museum, mall,
Kirkwood College.

Red Roof Inn
3325 Southgate Court
Cedar Rapids, IA 52404
319-366-7523
PET POLICY: No fee, pets under
80 lbs. Must be leashed to and
from rooms. Do not leave in
room unattended.

Red Roof Inn
1220 Park Place
Cedar Rapids, IA 52402
319-378-8000
PET POLICY: No fee, pets under
80 lbs. Must be leashed to and
from rooms. Do not leave in
room unattended.

Shoney's Inn & Suites
2215 Blairs Ferry Rd.
Cedar Rapids, IA 52402
319-378-3948
RATES: Single $59, double $79.
PET POLICY: Fee $50, refundable.
Dogs and Cats up to 50 lbs.

PM Park
15297 Raney Dr.
Clear Lake, IA 50428
641-357-2574

RATES: Single $25, double $30.
PET POLICY: No fee, all sizes and
pets welcome.
AMENITIES: Exercise area, pet-
friendly park.

**Sheraton Four Points
Des Moines West**
11040 Hickman Rd at I-80
Clive, IA 50325
515-278-5575
RATES: Single $59–$69, double
$59–$69.
PET POLICY: No fee. Pets under
50 lbs. Do not leave in room
unattended.
POI: Local attractions, shopping
center, golf, all nearby.

Ramada Inn
2530 Holiday Rd.
Coralville, IA 52241
319-354-7770
RATES: Single $64.95, double
$79.95.
PET POLICY: Fee $5 per pet,
nonrefundable. Up to 25 lbs.
POI: parks, University,
Museums, Mall.

Red Roof Inn
200 6th St.
Coralville, IA 52241
319-337-9797
PET POLICY: No fee, pets under
80 lbs. Must be leashed to and
from rooms. Do not leave in
room unattended.

Days Inn
3619 9th Ave.
Council Bluffs, IA 51501
712-323-2200
PET POLICY: Fee $10.

Metro Hotel
3537 W. Broadway
Council Bluffs, IA 51501
712-328-3171
RATES: Single $59–$69, double
$69–$89.
PET POLICY: No fee, all sizes
accepted. Pets in smoking
rooms only.

U.S. Lodgings > IOWA

Motel 6
3032 S. Expwy
Council Bluffs, IA 51501
712-366-2405
PET POLICY: No fee. Dogs under 25 lbs. preferred (larger animals by advance approval). Do not leave animals in room unattended.

Travelodge
2325 Ave. N
Council Bluffs, IA 51501
712 328-3881
RATES: Avg: $40–$58.
PET POLICY: Fee $5, all sizes accepted.
AMENITIES: Children under 17 free in same room.

Baymont Inn & Suites
400 Jason Way Court
Davenport, IA 52807
319-386-1600
PET POLICY: No fee.

Davenport Days Inn
3202 E. Kimberly Rd.
Davenport, IA 52807
319-355-1190
PET POLICY: Fee $5.

Hampton Inn
3330 E. Kimberly Rd.
Davenport, IA 52807
319-359-3921
RATES: Single $61, double $69, suite $110.
PET POLICY: Fee $50, refundable.

Motel 6
6111 N. Brady St.
Davenport, IA 52806
319-391-8997
PET POLICY: No fee. Dogs under 25 lbs. preferred (larger animals by advance approval). Do not leave animals in room unattended.

Denison Days Inn
315 Chamberlin Dr.
Denison, IA 51442
712-263-2500
PET POLICY: Fee $5.

Baymont Inn & Suites
1390 N.W. 118th St.
Des Moines, IA 50325
515-221-9200
PET POLICY: No fee.

Best Suites
1236 74th St.
Des Moines, IA 50266
515-223-9005
RATES: Single $79, double $89.
PET POLICY: No fee, all sizes and all pets welcome. Do not leave pets unattended. Free treats at check-in.
POI: Downtown Des Moines, near State Capital, Living History Farms, Casino, Adventureland, Three Dog Bakery, Valley Junction Area (fun stuff for your pet).

Best Western Bavarian Inn
5220 NE 14th St.
Des Moines, IA 50313
515-265-5611
RATES: Avg: $59–$69.
PET POLICY: Fee $20, small pets only.

Best Western Colonial
5020 NE 14th St.
Des Moines, IA 50313
515-265-7511
RATES: Avg: $61.
PET POLICY: No fee, all sizes accepted. Do not leave in room unattended.

Des Moines Days Inn
10841 Douglas Ave.
Des Moines, IA 50322
515-278-2811
PET POLICY: No fee.

Des Moines Marriott Hotel
700 Grand Ave.
Des Moines, IA 50309
515-245-5500
RATES: Single $169, double $179.
PET POLICY: No fee, all sizes accepted.

Hickman Motor Lodge
6500 Hickman Rd.
Des Moines, IA 50322
515-276-8591
RATES: Single $38, double $46.
PET POLICY: No fee, all sizes welcome.
POI: Living history farm.

Kirkwood Civic Center Hotel
400 Walnut St.
Des Moines, IA 50309
515-244-9191
RATES: Single $65, double $79.
PET POLICY: No fee, call first for availability.

Motel 6
4940 NE 14th St (50313)
Des Moines, IA 50316
515-266-5456
PET POLICY: No fee. Dogs under 25 lbs. preferred (larger animals by advance approval). Do not leave animals in room unattended.

Red Roof Inn
4950 NE 14th St.
Des Moines, IA 50313
515-266-6800
PET POLICY: No fee, pets under 80 lbs. Must be leashed to and from rooms. Do not leave in room unattended.

Savery Hotel and Spa
401 Locust St.
Des Moines, IA 50309
515-244-2151
RATES: Single $74, double $139.
PET POLICY: Fee $35, refundable. All sizes accepted.

Super 8 Lodge Des Moines
4755 Merle Hay Rd.
Des Moines, IA 50322
515-278-8858
RATES: Single $59, double $69.
PET POLICY: Fee $25, no size restrictions.
POI: Dog Show at Iowa State Fairgrounds. Vet less than 1 mile away, Petco pet store, Saylorville Lake.

Valley West Inn
11001 University Ave.
Des Moines, IA 50325
515-225-2222
RATES: Single $72, double $70.
PET POLICY: Fee $20, refundable. Small dogs only, in smoking rooms.

U.S. Lodgings > KANSAS

Best Western Midway Hotel
3100 Dodge St.
Dubuque, IA 52003
319-557-8000
RATES: Avg: $85–$99.
PET POLICY: No fee, all sizes accepted. Do not leave in room unattended.

Days Inn—Dubuque
1111 Dodge St.
Dubuque, IA 52003
319-583-3297
RATES: Single $69, double $69.
PET POLICY: No fee, all sizes, dogs and cats only.

Motel 6
2670 Dodge St.
Dubuque, IA 52003
319-556-0880
PET POLICY: No fee. Dogs under 25 lbs. preferred (larger animals by advance approval). Do not leave animals in room unattended.

Grinnell Days Inn
Hwy. 146
Grinnell, IA 50112
515-236-6710
PET POLICY: Fee $5.

Days Inn Mason City
2301 4th St. SW
Mason City, IA 50401
515-423-4444
PET POLICY: No fee.

Missouri Valley Days Inn
1967 Hwy. 30
Missouri Valley, IA 51555
712-642-4003
PET POLICY: Fee $5.

Ramada Limited
1200 E. Baker
Mount Pleasant, IA 52641
319038509571
RATES: Single $64.95, double $69.95.
PET POLICY: Fee $10 day, non-refundable, only dogs and cats, not to be left unattended in room.
AMENITIES: Large grassy area for exercise.
POI: Iowa Wesleyan College, Old Thresher's Museum, Harlan House, Theater Museum, historic community.

Days Inn of Ottumwa
206 Church St.
Ottumwa, IA 52501
515-682-8131
PET POLICY: No fee.

Baymont Inn & Suites
3101 Singing Hills Blvd.
Sioux City, IA 51106
712-233-2302
PET POLICY: No fee.

Motel 6
6166 Harbor Dr.
Sioux City, IA 51111
712-277-3131
PET POLICY: No fee. Dogs under 25 lbs. preferred (larger animals by advance approval). Do not leave animals in room unattended.

Davenport Days Inn
2889 N. Plainview Dr.
Walcott, IA 52773
319-284-6600
PET POLICY: Fee $5.

Comfort Inn of Waterloo
1945 La Porte Rd.
Waterloo, IA 50702
319-234-7411
RATES: Single $55, double $60.
PET POLICY: No fee, all sizes welcome. Pets in smoking rooms only.
AMENITIES: Lots of grass.

Motel 6
2343 Logan Ave.
Waterloo, IA 50703
319-236-3238
PET POLICY: No fee. Dogs under 25 lbs. preferred (larger animals by advance approval). Do not leave animals in room unattended.

Best Suites
1236 74th St.
West Des Moines, IA 50266
515-223-9005
RATES: Single $79, double $89.
PET POLICY: No fee, all sizes and all pets welcome. Do not leave pets unattended.
AMENITIES: Free treats at check-in.
POI: Downtown Des Moines, near State Capital, Living History Farms, Casino, Adventureland, Three Dog Bakery, Valley Junction Area (fun stuff for your pet).

Motel 6
7655 Office Plaza Drive North
West Des Moines, IA 50266
515-267-8885
PET POLICY: No fee. Dogs under 25 lbs. preferred (larger animals by advance approval). Do not leave animals in room unattended.

Williamsburg Days Inn
2214 U Ave.
Williamsburg, IA 52361
319-668-2097
PET POLICY: No fee.

KANSAS

Best Western Crown Motel
2320 S. Range
Colby, KS 67701
913-462-3943
RATES: Single $50–$80, double $60–$80.
PET POLICY: No fee, all sizes welcome.
AMENITIES: 35 acres of trees and grass.
POI: Museum 1/2 mile. Junior College 1 mile.

Colby Days Inn
I-70 & Hwy. 25
Colby, KS 67701
785-462-8691
PET POLICY: No fee.

Emporia Days Inn
3032 W. Hwy. 50
Emporia, KS 66801
316-342-1787
PET POLICY: No fee.

Motel 6
2630 W. 18th Ave.
Emporia, KS 66801
316-343-1240
PET POLICY: No fee. Dogs under 25 lbs. preferred (larger animals by advance approval). Do not leave animals in room unattended.

Best Western Red Baron Hotel
Bypass US 50 & US 83
Garden City, KS 67846
316-275-4164
PET POLICY: No fee, all sizes and pets welcome (ferrets, birds, etc.).
AMENITIES: Several large grassy areas for dogs.
POI: Single $46, double $55.

U.S. Lodgings > KANSAS

Best Western Wheat Lands Motor Inn
1311 E. Fulton St.
Garden City, KS 67846
316-276-2387
RATES: Single $51, double $63.
PET POLICY: No fee, all sizes and all pets welcome (ferrets, birds, etc.).
AMENITIES: Several large grassy areas for dogs.

Great Bend Days Inn
4701 10th
Great Bend, KS 67530
316-792-8235
PET POLICY: No fee.

Hays Days Inn
3205 N.Vine
Hays, KS 67601
785-628-8261
RATES: Single $45–$50, double $50–$65.
PET POLICY: Fee $5, all sizes welcome. Specific rooms for pets, not allowed unattended in rooms.
AMENITIES: Park in back of the hotel.
POI: Tours sponsored by Visitors Bureau-by appt., Old Fort Hays.

Motel 6
3404 Vine St.
Hays, KS 67601
785-625-4282
PET POLICY: No fee. Dogs under 25 lbs. preferred (larger animals by advance approval). Do not leave animals in room unattended.

Red Roof Inn
115 S. Highway 75
Holton, KS 66436
785-364-3172
PET POLICY: No fee, pets under 80 lbs. Must be leashed to and from rooms. Do not leave in room unattended.

Hampton Inn
1401½ E. 11th Ave.
Hutchinson, KS 67501
800-HAMPTON
PET POLICY: Small pets only.

Days Inn
1024 S. Washington St.
Junction City, KS 66441
785-762-2727
RATES: Single $45, double $55.
PET POLICY: No fee, all sizes and all pets welcome.
AMENITIES: Dog walking area provided.

Motel 6
1931 Lacy Dr.
Junction City, KS 66441
785-762-2215
PET POLICY: No fee. Dogs under 25 lbs. preferred (larger animals by advance approval). Do not leave animals in room unattended.

Lawrence Days Inn
2309 Iowa St.
Lawrence, KS 66047
785-843-9100
RATES: Single, double $62.
PET POLICY: No fee. All size dogs and cats in 2-story building only.
POI: University of Kansas, Kansas City.

Viking Motel
446 Harrison
Lindsborg, KS 67456
785-227-3336
RATES: Single $45, double $49.
PET POLICY: No fee, small dogs and cats only (under 25 lbs). Do not leave pets in room unattended. May refuse pets, so call first.

Motel 6
510 Tuttle Creek Blvd.
Manhattan, KS 66502
785-537-1022
PET POLICY: No fee. Dogs under 25 lbs. preferred (larger animals by advance approval). Do not leave animals in room unattended.

Oak Tree Inn
1127 Pony Express Blvd.
Marysville, KS 66508
785-562-1234
RATES: Single $49, double $52.
PET POLICY: Fee $10, non-refundable. All size dogs and cats welcome.
POI: Ferry Landing Park, Historic Courthouse, Pony Express Museum, Union Pacific Steam.

Comfort Inn
6401 E. Frontage Rd.
Merriam, KS 66202
913-262-2622
RATES: Single $64.95, double $69.95.
PET POLICY: Fee $5, nonrefundable. All size dogs and cats. Do not leave in room unattended.
POI: Outskirts of Kansas City, 25 miles from airport.

Drury Inn Shawnee Mission—Merriam
9009 Shawnee Mission Pkwy.
Merriam, KS 66202
913 236-9200
PET POLICY: No fee, pets under 30 lbs.

Newton Days Inn
105 Manchester
Newton, KS 67114
316-283-3330
PET POLICY: Fee $10.

Kansas Kountry Inn
3538 US Hwy. 20
Oakley, KS 67748
785-672-3131
RATES: Single $40, double $50.
PET POLICY: Fee, all sizes and all pets welcome.

Ottawa Days Inn
1641 S. Main
Ottawa, KS 66067
785-242-4842
PET POLICY: No fee.

Chase Suites Hotel by Woodfin
6300 W. 110th St.
Overland Park, KS 66211
913-491-3333
RATES: Single $99, double $129.
PET POLICY: Fee $10 per pet per day, nonrefundable. $150 deposit (refundable). All sizes welcome.
AMENITIES: Gift bag upon arrival.
POI: Shawnee Mission Dog Park, 3 Dog Bakery.

Drury Inn Overland Park
10951 Metcalf Ave.
Overland Park, KS 66210
913 345-1500
PET POLICY: No fee, pets under 30 lbs.

U.S. Lodgings > KENTUCKY

Red Roof Inn
6800 W. 108th St.
Overland Park, KS 66211
913-341-0100
PET POLICY: No fee, pets under 80 lbs. Must be leashed to and from rooms. Do not leave in room unattended.

Russell Days Inn
1225 S. Fossall St.
Russell, KS 67665
785-483-6660
PET POLICY: No fee.

Best Western Mid-America Inn
1846 N. 9th St.
Salina, KS 67401
785-827-0356
RATES: Single $56.95, double $59.95.
PET POLICY: No fee, all sizes and pets welcome (dogs, cats, birds, rabbits, ferrets, reptiles).

Motel 6
635 W. Diamond Dr.
Salina, KS 67401
785-827-8397
PET POLICY: No fee. Dogs under 25 lbs. preferred (larger animals by advance approval). Do not leave animals in room unattended.

Oak Tree Inn
US 40, HCl, Box 558
Sharon Springs, KS 67758
785-852-4665
RATES: Single $59, double $59.
PET POLICY: Fee $10, nonrefundable. All sizes, all pets welcome.
POI: Wallace County Museum.

Motel 6
709 Fairlawn Rd.
Topeka, KS 66606
785-272-8283
PET POLICY: No fee. Dogs under 25 lbs. preferred (larger animals by advance approval). Do not leave animals in room unattended.

Topeka Days Inn
1510 S. W. Wanamaker Rd.
Topeka, KS 66604
913-272-8538
PET POLICY: No fee.

Oak Tree Inn
1177 E. 16th
Wellington, KS 67152
316-326-8191
RATES: Single $55.95, double $65.95.
PET POLICY: Fee $5, nonrefundable. Up to 25 lbs., only dogs and cats.

Holiday Inn
5500 W. Kellogg
Wichita, KS 67209
316-943-2181
PET POLICY: Fee $25. All sizes accepted.

Motel 6
5736 W. Kellogg
Wichita, KS 67209
316-945-8440
PET POLICY: No fee. Dogs under 25 lbs. preferred (larger animals by advance approval). Do not leave animals in room unattended.

Quality Inn Airport
600 S. Holland
Wichita, KS 67209
316-722-8730
PET POLICY: Fee $20 refundable deposit.

Ramada Inn Wichita
7335 E. Kellogg
Wichita, KS 67207
316-685-1281
PET POLICY: Fee $10.

Wichita Days Inn
9100 E. Kellogg
Wichita, KS 67207
316-685-0371
PET POLICY: Fee $6.

KENTUCKY

Days Inn
12700 State Rd. 180
Ashland, KY 41101
606-928-3600
PET POLICY: No fee.

Knights Inn
7216 US Route 60
Ashland, KY 41102
606-928-9501
RATES: Single $38, double $43.
PET POLICY: Fee $5 per dog. No large pets, please.

Ramada Inn
523 N. Third St.
Bardstown, KY 40004
502-349-0363
RATES: Single $60, double $65.
PET POLICY: Fee $10 per pet, nonrefundable. Under 40 lbs.

Beaver Dam Days Inn
1750 US Hwy. 231
Beaver Dam, KY 42320
270-274-0851
PET POLICY: Fee $10.

Days Inn
Rte. 595 & I95
Berea, KY 40403
606-986-7373
PET POLICY: Fee $5.

Baymont Inn & Suites
165 Three Springs Rd.
Bowling Green, KY 42104
270-843-3200
PET POLICY: Deposit $10.

Bowling Green Days Inn
4617 Scottsville Rd.
Bowling Green, KY 42104
270-781-6470
PET POLICY: Fee $10.

Drury Inn
3250 Scottsville Rd.
Bowling Green, KY 42104
270-842-7100
PET POLICY: No fee, pets under 30 lbs.

Motel 6
3139 Scottsville Rd.
Bowling Green, KY 42104
270-843-0140
PET POLICY: No fee. Dogs under 25 lbs. preferred (larger animals by advance approval). Do not leave animals in room unattended.

Days Inn Carrollton
61 Inn Rd.
Carrollton, KY 41008
502-732-9301
PET POLICY: No fee.

Baymont Inn & Suites
174 Adams Rd.
Corbin, KY 40701
606-523-9040
PET POLICY: No fee.

U.S. Lodgings > KENTUCKY

Corbin Days Inn
I-75 & US 25W
Corbin, KY 40701
606-528-8150
PET POLICY: Fee $10.

Days Inn
2010 N. Mulberry
Elizabethtown, KY 42701
502-769-5522
PET POLICY: Fee $5.

Red Roof Inn
2009 N. Mulberry St.
Elizabethtown, KY 42701
270-765-4166
PET POLICY: No fee, pets under 80 lbs. Must be leashed to and from rooms. Do not leave in room unattended.

Baymont Inn & Suites
1805 Airport Exchange Blvd.
Erlanger, KY 41018
606-746-0300
PET POLICY: No fee.

Red Roof Inn
7454 Turfway Rd.
Florence, KY 41042
606-647-2700
PET POLICY: No fee, pets under 80 lbs. Must be leashed to and from rooms. Do not leave in room unattended.

Baymont Inn & Suites
12759 Fort Campbell Blvd.
Ft. Campbell, KY 42262
270-439-0022
PET POLICY: No fee.

Lexington Days Inn
US 127
Frankfort, KY 40601
502-875-2200
PET POLICY: No fee.

Days Inn of Georgetown
385 Delaplain Rd.
Georgetown, KY 40324
502-863-5000
PET POLICY: Fee $5.

Oak Tree Inn
1075 Richmond Rd.
Irvine, KY 40336
606-723-2600
RATES: Single $44.95, double $49.95.

PET POLICY: Fee $5, nonrefundable. All sizes and all pets welcome (dogs, cats, ferrets, birds, rabbits, reptiles).
POI: Bybee Pottery 10 minutes away, Natural Bridge State Park 30 minutes away, Fort Boonesboro State Park 30 minutes away, Cedar Village Restaurant.

Louisville Days Inn
I-71 & SR 53
LaGrange, KY 40031
502-222-7192
PET POLICY: No fee.

B&B at Silver Springs Farm
3710 Leestown Rd.
Lexington, KY 40511
859-255-1784
PET POLICY: Fee $40, nonrefundable, pets in crate is left alone, on leash other times, not allowed near horse paddock.

Days Inn Lexington
1987 N. Broadway
Lexington, KY 40505
859-299-1202
PET POLICY: Fee 10.

Holiday Inn
1950 Newtown Pike
Lexington, KY 40511
859-233-0512
RATES: Single $109.99, double $119.95.
PET POLICY: Fee $25, nonrefundable. Up to 50 lbs.
POI: Kentucky Horse Park.

Motel 6
2260 Elkhorn Rd.
Lexington, KY 40505
606-293-1431
PET POLICY: No fee. Dogs under 25 lbs. preferred (larger animals by advance approval). Do not leave animals in room unattended.

Red Roof Inn
100 Canebrake Dr.
Lexington, KY 40509
859-543-1877
PET POLICY: No fee, pets under 80 lbs. Must be leashed to and from rooms. Do not leave in room unattended.

Red Roof Inn
2651 Wilhite Dr.
Lexington, KY 40503
859-277-9400
PET POLICY: No fee, pets under 80 lbs. Must be leashed to and from rooms. Do not leave in room unattended.

Red Roof Inn
1980 Haggard Court
Lexington, KY 40505
859-293-2626
PET POLICY: No fee, pets under 80 lbs. Must be leashed to and from rooms. Do not leave in room unattended.

Shoney's Inn
2753 Richmond Rd.
Lexington, KY 40509
859-269-4999
RATES: Single $58, double $63.
PET POLICY: Fee $5, nonrefundable. All pets welcome, up to 25 lbs.
AMENITIES: One mile from park w/lake.

Holiday Inn Express
400 GOP St.
London, KY 40741
606-878-7654
RATES: Single $62–$75, double $62–$75.
PET POLICY: No fee, dogs only, up to 50 lbs.

London Days Inn
2035 W. 192 Bypass
London, KY 40741
606-864-7331
PET POLICY: Fee $5.

Red Roof Inn
110 Melcon Ln.
London, KY 40741
606-862-8844
PET POLICY: No fee, pets under 80 lbs. Must be leashed to and from rooms. Do not leave in room unattended.

Breckinridge Inn
2800 Breckinridge Ln.
Louisville, KY 40220
502-456-5050
PET POLICY: Fee $25 for small dogs, $50 for big dogs.

U.S. Lodgings > KENTUCKY

Executive West Hotel
830 Phillips Ln.
Louisville, KY 40209
502-367-2251
RATES: Single $84, double $94.
PET POLICY: Fee $100, nonre-
fundable. All sizes and all pets
welcome (dogs, casts, ferrets,
birds, rabbits, reptiles).
AMENITIES: Large grass area.

Holiday Inn
3317 Fern Valley Rd.
Louisville, KY 40213
502-964-3311
PET POLICY: Fee $25.

Inn at Woodhaven
401 S. Hubbards Ln.
Louisville, KY 40207
502-895-1011
PET POLICY: No fee, must notify
owner.

Louisville Days Inn
1850 Embassy Sq. Blvd.
Louisville, KY 40299
502-491-1040
PET POLICY: Fee $6.

Motel 6
3200 Kemmons Dr.
Louisville, KY 40218
502-473-0000
PET POLICY: No fee. Dogs under 25
lbs. preferred (larger animals by
advance approval). Do not leave
animals in room unattended.

Red Roof Inn
9330 Blairwood Rd.
Louisville, KY 40222
502-426-7621
PET POLICY: No fee, pets under
80 lbs. Must be leashed to and
from rooms. Do not leave in
room unattended.

Red Roof Inn
4704 Preston Hwy.
Louisville, KY 40213
502-968-0151
PET POLICY: No fee, pets under
80 lbs. Must be leashed to and
from rooms. Do not leave in
room unattended.

Residence Inn by Marriott
120 N. Hurstbourne Pkwy.
Louisville, KY 40222
502-425-1821
PET POLICY: Fee $75 for length
of stay.

**The Seelbach Louisville's
Grand Hotel**
500 Fourth Ave.
Louisville, KY 40202
502-585-3200
RATES: Single $109–$279, double
$109–$279.
PET POLICY: Fee $50, refundable.
All sizes welcome.

Days Inn Madisonville
1900 Lantaff Blvd.
Madisonville, KY 42431
502-821-8620
PET POLICY: Fee $5.

Motel 6
1460 S. Main St.
Morgantown, KY 42261
270-526-9481
PET POLICY: No fee. Dogs under 25
lbs. preferred (larger animals by
advance approval). Do not leave
animals in room unattended.

Mt. Sterling Days Inn
705 Maysville Rd.
Mt. Sterling, KY 40353
859-498-4680
RATES: Single $38, double $43.
PET POLICY: Fee $5, nonrefund-
able. All sizes welcome.
AMENITIES: Dog walk area.

Motel 6
4585 Frederica St.
Owensboro, KY 42301
270-686-8606
PET POLICY: No fee. Dogs under 25
lbs. preferred (larger animals by
advance approval). Do not leave
animals in room unattended.

Owensboro Days Inn
3720 New Hartford Rd.
Owensboro, KY 42301
502-684-9621
PET POLICY: No fee.

Baymont Inn & Suites
5300 Old Cairo Rd.
Paducah, KY 42001
270-442-6666
PET POLICY: No fee.

Days Inn
3901 Hinkleville Rd.
Paducah, KY 42001
502-442-7501
PET POLICY: Fee $10.

Drury Inn
3975 Hinkleville Rd.
Paducah, KY 42001
502-443-3313
PET POLICY: No fee, pets under
30 lbs.

Drury Suites—Paducah
120 McBride Ln.
Paducah, KY 42001
502-441-0024
PET POLICY: No fee. All sizes
and pets accepted. Do not
leave in rooms unattended.

Motel 6
5120 Hinkleville Rd.
Paducah, KY 42001
270-443-3672
PET POLICY: No fee. Dogs under 25
lbs. preferred (larger animals by
advance approval). Do not leave
animals in room unattended.

Pear Tree Inn by Drury
4910 Hinkleville Rd.
Paducah, KY 42001
270-444-7200
PET POLICY: No fee. All sizes
and pets accepted. Do not
leave in rooms unattended.

Days Inn Paintsville
512 S. Mayo Trail
Paintsville, KY 41240
606-789-3551
PET POLICY: Fee $5.

Days Inn
2109 Belmont Dr.
Richmond, KY 40475
606-624-5769
PET POLICY: Fee $5.

Red Roof Inn
111 Bahama Court
Richmond, KY 40475
859-625-0084
PET POLICY: No fee, pets under
80 lbs. Must be leashed to and
from rooms. Do not leave in
room unattended.

U.S. Lodgings > KENTUCKY

Louisville Days Inn
I-65 & KY 44
Shepherdsville, KY 40165
502-543-3011
PET POLICY: No fee.

Springfield Days Inn
324 Lincoln Dr.
Springfield, KY 40069
270-926-1013
PET POLICY: Fee $10.

Winchester Days Inn
1100 Interstate Dr.
Winchester, KY 40391
606-744-9111
PET POLICY: No fee.

LOUISIANA

Alexandria Days Inn
1146 MacArthur Dr.
Alexandria, LA 71303
316-443-1841
PET POLICY: Fee $10.

Motel 6
546 MacArthur Dr.
Alexandria, LA 71301
318-445-2336
PET POLICY: No fee. Dogs under 25 lbs. preferred (larger animals by advance approval). Do not leave animals in room unattended.

Arcadia Days Inn
1061 Hwy. 151
Arcadia, LA 71001
318-263-3555
PET POLICY: No fee.

Baton Rouge Days Inn
10245 Airline Hwy.
Baton Rouge, LA 70816
225-291-8152
PET POLICY: Fee $5.

Baymont Inn & Suites—Baton Rouge
10555 Rieger Rd.
Baton Rouge, LA 70809
225-291-6600
PET POLICY: No fee.

Homewood Suites Hotel
5860 Corporate Blvd.
Baton Rouge, LA 07080
225-927-1700
PET POLICY: fee.

Motel 6
9901 Gwen Adele Ave.
Baton Rouge, LA 70816
215-924-2130
PET POLICY: No fee. Dogs under 25 lbs. preferred (larger animals by advance approval). Do not leave animals in room unattended.

Red Roof Inn
11314 Boardwalk Dr.
Baton Rouge, LA 70816
225-275-6600
PET POLICY: No fee, pets under 80 lbs. Must be leashed to and from rooms. Do not leave in room unattended.

Baymont Inn & Suites
2717 Village Ln.
Bossier City, LA 71112
318-742-7890
PET POLICY: No fee.

Motel 6
210 John Wesley Blvd.
Bossier City, LA 71112
318-742-3472
PET POLICY: No fee. Dogs under 25 lbs. preferred (larger animals by advance approval). Do not leave animals in room unattended.

Le Jardin Sur Le Bayou
256 Lower Country Dr.
Bourg, LA 70343
504-594-2722
RATES: Single $90, double $90.
PET POLICY: No fee, all sizes welcome.

Quality Inn Marina
5353 Paris Rd.
Chalmette, LA 70043
504-277-5353
RATES: Single $59, double $65.
PET POLICY: Fee $25, nonrefundable.
POI: French Quarter. Jazzland Theme Park. Aquarium of America. Chalmette National Battlefield.

Days Inn—Delhi
113 Snider Rd.
Delhi, LA 71232
318-878-9000
RATES: Single $40, double $48.
PET POLICY: Fee $10, nonrefundable. Pets up to 50 lbs. In smoking rooms only.

Colonial Inn of Louisiana
I-12, US 51
Hammond, LA 70403
504-345-2953
PET POLICY: Fee $8, nonrefundable, no restrictions.

Jennings Days Inn
2502 Port Dr.
Jennings, LA 70546
318-824-6550
PET POLICY: Fee $5.

New Orleans Days Inn Airport-Kenner
1300 Veterans Memorial Blvd.
Kenner, LA 70062
504-469-2531
PET POLICY: No fee.

Lafayette Days Inn
1620 N. University at I-10
Lafayette, LA 70506
318-237-8880
PET POLICY: No fee.

Red Roof Inn
1718 N. University Ave.
Lafayette, LA 70507
337-233-3339
PET POLICY: No fee, pets under 80 lbs. Must be leashed to and from rooms. Do not leave in room unattended.

Lake Charles Days Inn
1010 N. Martin Luther King Hwy.
Lake Charles, LA 70601
318-433-1711
PET POLICY: No fee.

Motel 6
335 Hwy. 171
Lake Charles, LA 70601
337-433-1773
PET POLICY: No fee. Dogs under 25 lbs. preferred (larger animals by advance approval). Do not leave animals in room unattended.

Oak Tree Inn
7875 Airline Hwy.
Livonia, LA 70755
225-637-2590
RATES: Single $49, double $55.
PET POLICY: Fee $5, nonrefundable. All sizes and all pets welcome.

U.S. Lodgings > LOUISIANA

POI: 20 miles to Baton Rouge, 15 miles to Satterfields River Walk, 15 miles to New Roads historic area, also camping, fishing, hunting area.

Motel 6
1501 US Hwy. 165 Bypass
Monroe, LA 71202
318-322-5430
PET POLICY: No fee. Dogs under 25 lbs. preferred (larger animals by advance approval). Do not leave animals in room unattended.

Natchitoches Days Inn
1000 College Ave.
Natchitoches, LA 71457
318-352-4428
PET POLICY: Fee $10.

Red Roof Inn
1718 N. University Ave.
Lafayette, LA 70507
337-233-3339
PET POLICY: No fee, pets under 80 lbs. Must be leashed to and from rooms. Do not leave in room unattended.

Ambassador Hotel
535 Tchoupitoulas St.
New Orleans, LA 70130
504-527-5271
PET POLICY: Fee $25 per pet. All sizes accepted. Do not leave unattended in room.

Drury Inn & Suites
820 Poydras St.
New Orleans, LA 70112
504-529-7800
PET POLICY: No fee, pets under 30 lbs.

Essam's House Bed & Breakfast
3660 Gentilly Boulevard
New Orleans, LA 70122
504-947-3401
RATES: cottage $85.
PET POLICY: No fee. Pets allowed only in cottage.

La Quinta New Orleans Crowder
8400 I-10 Service Rd.
New Orleans, LA 70127
504-246-5800
RATES: Single, double $65.99+.
PET POLICY: No fee. Must have credit card on file in case of damage.

Motel 6
12330 I-10 Service Rd.
New Orleans, LA 70128
504-240-2862
PET POLICY: No fee. Dogs under 25 lbs. preferred (larger animals by advance approval). Do not leave animals in room unattended.

Windsor Court Hotel
300 Gravier St.
New Orleans, LA 70130
504-523-6000
RATES: Single, double $195–$500.
PET POLICY: Deposit $250, $100 refundable. Pets under 20 lbs.

Opolousas Days Inn
1649 I-49 Service Rd S.
Opolousas, LA 70570
800-DAYSINN
PET POLICY: Fee $20.

Motel 6
2800 I-10 Frontage Rd.
Port Allen, LA 70767
225-343-5945
PET POLICY: No fee. Dogs under 25 lbs. preferred (larger animals by advance approval). Do not leave animals in room unattended.

Super 8 Motel, Baton Rouge West
I-10 & Hwy. 415
Port Allen, LA 70767
225-381-9134
RATES: Single $40, double $45.
PET POLICY: Fee $5, nonrefundable. All sizes welcome.
AMENITIES: Enclosed grass courtyard to walk pets.

Holiday Inn
401 N. Service Rd., I-20
Ruston, LA 71270
318-255-5901
PET POLICY: Kennels.

Lake Rosemound Inn
10473 Lindsey Ln.
St. Francisville, LA 70775
225-635-3176
RATES: Single $75, double $125.
PET POLICY: No fee, all sizes welcome.
AMENITIES: 190-acre lake.

Red Roof Inn
7296 Greenwood Rd.
Shreveport, LA 71119
318-938-5342
PET POLICY: No fee, pets under 80 lbs. Must be leashed to and from rooms. Do not leave in room unattended.

Shreveport Days Inn
4935 W. Monkhouse Rd.
Shreveport, LA 71109
318-636-0080
PET POLICY: Fee $5.

Guest Lodge
58512 Tyler Dr.
Slidell, LA 70459
504-641-2153
RATES: Single $42,00, double $45.
PET POLICY: Fee $10, refundable. Up to 40 lbs.
POI: French Quarter, 2 casinos, Jazz Land Theme park, NASA Stennis Center, Gulf Coast casinos.

Motel 6
136 Taos St.
Slidell, LA 70458
504-649-7925
PET POLICY: No fee. Dogs under 25 lbs. preferred (larger animals by advance approval). Do not leave animals in room unattended.

Baymont Inn & Suites
503 Constitution Dr.
West Monroe, LA 71292
318-387-2711
PET POLICY: No fee.

Red Roof Inn
102 Constitution Dr.
West Monroe, LA 71292
318-388-2420
PET POLICY: No fee, pets under 80 lbs. Must be leashed to and from rooms. Do not leave in room unattended.

MAINE

Bangor Days Inn Airport
250 Odlin Rd.
Bangor, ME 04401
207-942-8272
RATES: Single $49, double $89.
PET POLICY: Fee $6, nonrefundable. All sizes and all pets accepted. Exotic animals (rabbits, ferrets, reptiles, birds) should be cages.
AMENITIES: Grassy walking area next to parking lot.
POI: Coles Land Transportation Museum, Blackbeard's Amusement Park.

Motel 6
1100 Hammond St.
Bangor, ME 04401
207-947-6921
PET POLICY: No fee. Dogs under 25 lbs. preferred (larger animals by advance approval). Do not leave animals in room unattended.

Bar Harbor Days Inn
120 Eden St.
Bar Harbor, ME 04609
207-288-3321
PET POLICY: No fee.

Hutchins Mountain View Cottages
RR 2, Box 1190
Bar Harbor, ME 04609
800-775-4833
RATES: Single $68, double $84.
PET POLICY: No fee, all sizes welcome.
AMENITIES: Large field and walking trails.
POI: Acadia National Park.

Primrose Inn
73 Mt. Desert St.
Bar Harbor, ME 04609
207-288-4031
PET POLICY: One pet-friendly room.

The Country Inn on Penobscot Bay
90 Northport Ave. (Rt. 1)
Belfast, ME 04915
207-338-5715
RATES: Single, double $65–$165 (seasonal).
PET POLICY: Fee $15 per night. All sizes accepted.

The Briar Lea Bed & Breakfast
150 Maryville Rd.
Bethel, ME 04217
207-824-4717
RATES: Single $69, double $79.
PET POLICY: Fee $10, nonrefundable. All sizes, dogs and cats.

The Lawnmeer Inn
Route 27 S.
Boothbay Harbor, ME 04575
800-633-7645
PET POLICY: Fee $10 per night, nonrefundable. Pets must be under personal control.

Pleasant Mountain Inn
Box 246
Bridgton, ME 04009
207-932-4505
RATES: Single $50, double $60.
PET POLICY: Fee $10. Deposit $50, refundable. All sizes and pets welcome. Do not leave pets in room for long periods of time unless in crates.
AMENITIES: Large field and lake suitable for pets to swim.

Breezemere Farm Inn
71 Breezemere Rd.
Brooksville, ME 04617
207-326-8628
RATES: Cabin: $790 per week.
PET POLICY: Fee $25, nonrefundable. All size dogs and cats only. Pets must be under owner's control at all times. Must behave well around other pets and farm animals. Up-to-date w/vaccinations.
POI: Mountains, National Park, East Penobscot Bay.

Bucksport Motor Inn
151 Main St.
Bucksport, ME 04416
207-469-3111
RATES: Single $40.65–$65, double $45–$75.
PET POLICY: No fee, must be leashed and not left unattended in room.

Camden Harbour Inn
83 Bayview St.
Camden, ME 03843
207-236-4200
PET POLICY: Fee $20 per night, nonrefundable.

Inn By the Sea
40 Bowery Beach Rd.
Cape Elizabeth, ME, 04107
207-799-3134
RATES: Single $139-289, double $169-568
PET POLICY: No fee. All size dogs accepted. Specific pet rooms assigned.
AMENITIES: Pet Room Service menu, doggie dishes, treats and towels. Dogs registered in computer and pictures taken for "Family Photo" album, and website.

Sheepscot River Inn
306 Eddy Rd.
Edgecomb, ME 04556
207-882-6343
RATES: Single $70–$100, double $80–$120.
PET POLICY: No fee, all sizes and all pets welcome (dogs, cats, ferrets, birds, rabbits, reptiles). Pets allowed in suits and cottages. Keep on leash, do not leave alone for extended periods of time.
AMENITIES: Biscuits at front desk.

Twilite Motel
147 Bucksport Rd.
Ellsworth, ME 04605
207-667-8165
RATES: Single $74, double $89.
PET POLICY: Fee $10, nonrefundable. All sizes. Do not leave pets in room unattended, and scoop!
AMENITIES: Large lawn and country setting.
POI: Acadia National Park, Bar Harbor, Maine.

Mount Blue Motel
Wilton Rd.
Farmington, ME 04938
207-778-6004
PET POLICY: Fee $7, nonrefundable. All sizes welcome, do not leave pet unattended.

U.S. Lodgings > MAINE

Mount Blue Motel
454 Wilton Rd.
Farmington, ME 04938
207-778-6004
RATES: Single $40, double $55.
PET POLICY: Fee $7, nonrefundable. All sizes welcome, do not leave pet unattended.
POI: Close to 3 ski areas, shopping, restaurants, hiking, swimming and golf.

Freeport Inn
335 US 1S
Freeport, ME, 04032
207-865-3106
RATES: Single, double $59-95-99.95+ (seasonal)
PET POLICY: No fees. All sizes and pets accepted.
POI: L.L. Bean, 25 acres on Cousins River.

Cabot Cove Cottages
7 S. Main St., Box 1153
Kennebunkport, ME 04046
800-962-5424
RATES: Single $90–$125, double $115–$160.
PET POLICY: Fee $7 per night per pet, nonrefundable. No Pit bulls, Rotweilers, or Dobermans.
AMENITIES: Towels, water bowls, can stay alone in cottage if quiet.
POI: Row boats on cove, 7 minutes to drive to beach, 12 minutes to walk to downtown, whale watching tours, golf courses, walk to restaurants.

Lodge at Turbat's Creek
PO Box 2722
Kennebunkport, ME 04046
207-967-8700
RATES: Single $75–$139, double $75–$139.
PET POLICY: No fee.

Herbert Hotel
Main St.
Kingfield, ME 04947
207-265-2000
RATES: Single $45, double $59.
PET POLICY: No fee, no restrictions, all pets welcome (dogs, cats, ferrets, birds, rabbits, reptiles).
POI: Sugarloaf USA, golf course.

Motel 6
516 Pleasant St.
Lewiston, ME 04240
207-782-6558
PET POLICY: No fee. Dogs under 25 lbs. preferred (larger animals by advance approval). Do not leave animals in room unattended.

Old Colonial Motel
61 W. Grand Ave.
Old Orchard Beach, ME 04064
207-934-9862
RATES: Single $60–$115, double $65–$175.
PET POLICY: No fee, all pets welcome (dogs, cats, birds, ferrets, rabbits). July 1 to Labor Day, pets must be 40 lbs. or less.
AMENITIES: Pets allowed on beach before Memorial Day and after Labor day. During season, before 10 a.m., after 5 p.m. Free dog treats.

Andrews Lodging Bed & Breakfast
417 Auburn St.
Portland, ME 04103
207-797-9157
RATES: Single $89, double $175.
PET POLICY: Fee $10 per day. Designated rooms, prior approval required.

Motel 6
One Riverside St.
Portland, ME 04103
207-775-0111
PET POLICY: No fee. Dogs under 25 lbs. preferred (larger animals by advance approval). Do not leave animals in room unattended.

Northern Lights Motel
72 Houlton Rd.
Presque Isle, ME 04769
207-764-4441
RATES: Single $32.95, double $39.95.
PET POLICY: Fee $10, all size dogs and cats. Call about other pets.
AMENITIES: Large walking area out back.
POI: 5 miles to State Park.

Crescent Lake Cottages
7 Cottage Ln.
Raymond, ME 04071
207-655-3393
RATES: Single $545 wk, double $595 wk.
PET POLICY: Fee $20 week, nonrefundable, all size dogs and cats, ferrets, birds, rabbits.
AMENITIES: Fenced-in beach area. Dog runs.
POI: Sebago Lake Region.

The Birches
PO Box 81, Birches Rd.
Rockwood, ME 04478
800-825-9453
PET POLICY: Fee $8 per night or $40 per week, lots of walking room for pets.

Best Western Merry Manor Inn
700 Main St.
South Portland, ME 04106
207-774-6151
RATES: Single $99–$119, double $109–$129.95.
PET POLICY: No fee, all sizes and all pets welcome.

Sunrise Motel
Bar Harbor Rd., Rt. 3
Trenton, ME 04605
207-667-8452
PET POLICY: Fee $5 per night, large lawn for exercise, all sizes.

Trenton Days Inn
Route 1
Trenton, ME 04605
207-667-9506
PET POLICY: Fee $10.

Ne'R Beach Motel
US 1, Box 389
Wells, ME 04054
207-646-2636
RATES: Single $64–$89, double $79–$104.
PET POLICY: Fee $8 per pet per day, nonrefundable. All sizes welcome.
POI: Moody and Wells beach.

U.S. Lodgings > MAINE

Whispering Pines Motel
Rt. 2, 183 Lake Rd.
Wilton, ME 04294
207-645-3721
RATES: Single $41.40, double $88.
PET POLICY: Fee $3 day, all sizes
welcome. Dogs must be on
leash, cannot be left alone in
room.
AMENITIES: Treats.
POI: Mt. Blue State Park,
Sugar Loaf USA.

MARYLAND

Days Inn
783 W. Bel Air Ave.
Aberdeen, MD 21001
410-272-5782
PET POLICY: Dogs only.

Red Roof Inn
988 Hospitality Way
Aberdeen, MD 21001
410-273-7800
PET POLICY: No fee, pets under
80 lbs. Must be leashed to and
from rooms. Do not leave in
room unattended.

Annapolis Days Inn
1542 Whitehall Rd./Rt. 50
Annapolis, MD 21401
410-974-4440
PET POLICY: No fee.

Radisson Hotel
210 Holiday Court
Annapolis, MD, 21401
410-224-3150
RATES: Single, double $89-169
PET POLICY: No fee, all sizes and
pets accepted.

Holiday Inn West
1800 Belmont Ave.
Baltimore, MD 21244
410-265-1400
PET POLICY: Fee $10 a night,
nonrefundable.

Motel 6
1654 Whitehead Court
Baltimore, MD 21207
410-265-7660
PET POLICY: No fee. Dogs under 25
lbs. preferred (larger animals by
advance approval). Do not leave
animals in room unattended.

Holiday Inn
4095 Powder Mill Rd.
Beltsville, MD 20705
301-937-4422
PET POLICY: Small pets under
20 lbs.

Days Inn—Camp Springs-Andrews AFB
5001 Mercedes Blvd.
Camp Springs, MD 20746
301-423-2323
PET POLICY: Fee $10.

Motel 6
5701 Allentown Rd.
Camp Springs, MD 20746
301-702-1061
PET POLICY: No fee. Dogs under 25
lbs. preferred (larger animals by
advance approval). Do not leave
animals in room unattended.

The River Inn at Rolph's Wharf
1008 Rolph's Wharf Rd.
Chestertown, MD 21620
410-778-6347
RATES: Double $105.
PET POLICY: Fee $10, nonrefund-
able. All size dogs and cats. Do
not leave in room unattended.
AMENITIES: 5 acres to run on.
Beach to go swimming by
Chester River.
POI: Historic Chestertown 2
miles away. Outdoor beach bar
by pool so you can eat and
not have to leave your dog in
the room.

Easton Days Inn
Mile Marker 67
Easton, MD 21601
410-822-4600
PET POLICY: Fee $8.

Motel 6
223 Belle Hill Rd.
Elkton, MD 21921
410-392-5020
PET POLICY: No fee. Dogs under 25
lbs. preferred (larger animals by
advance approval). Do not leave
animals in room unattended.

Holiday Inn
2 Montgomery Village Ave.
Gaithersburg, MD 20879
301-948-8900
PET POLICY: Pets 15 lbs. and under.

Red Roof Inn
497 Quince Orchard Rd.
Gaithersburg, MD 20878
301-977-3311
PET POLICY: No fee, pets under
80 lbs. Must be leashed to and
from rooms. Do not leave in
room unattended.

Baltimore Days Inn
6600 Ritchie Hwy.
Glen Burnie, MD 21061
410-761-8300
PET POLICY: No fee.

Savage River Lodge
PO Box 655
Grantsville, MD 21536
301-689-3200
RATES: Single $160, double $180.
PET POLICY: Fee $20, nonrefund-
able. All sizes and pets welcome. Deposit required, $100,
refundable. Pets not allowed in
lodge, only in cabins.
AMENITIES: Homemade dog
biscuits each morning with
people muffin baskets.

Motel 6
11321 Massey Blvd.
Hagerstown, MD 21740
301-582-4445
PET POLICY: No fee. Dogs under 25
lbs. preferred (larger animals by
advance approval). Do not leave
animals in room unattended.

Ramada Hagerstown
901 Dual Hwy.
Hagerstown, MD 21740
301-733-5100
PET POLICY: Small fee, gourmet
cat/dog treats, access to
designated "pet zone." Special
offers, call.

Red Roof Inn
7306 Parkway Drive South
Hanover, MD 21076
410-712-4070
PET POLICY: No fee, pets under
80 lbs. Must be leashed to and
from rooms. Do not leave in
room unattended.

U.S. Lodgings > MARYLAND

Red Roof Inn
8000 Washington Blvd.
Jessup, MD 20794
410-796-0380
PET POLICY: No fee, pets under 80 lbs. Must be leashed to and from rooms. Do not leave in room unattended.

Motel 6
3510 Old Annapolis Rd.
Laurel, MD 20724
301-497-1544
PET POLICY: No fee. Dogs under 25 lbs. preferred (larger animals by advance approval). Do not leave animals in room unattended.

Red Roof Inn
9050 Lanham Severn Rd.
Lanham, MD 20706
301-731-8830
PET POLICY: No fee, pets under 80 lbs. Must be leashed to and from rooms. Do not leave in room unattended.

Oak Tree Inn
12310 Winchester Rd., SW
LaVale, MD 21502
301-729-6700
RATES: Single $69.95, double $69.95.
PET POLICY: Fee $5, nonrefundable. All sizes and all pets (dogs, cats, birds).

Days Inn
21847 Three Notch Rd.-Rt. 235
Lexington Park, MD 20653
301-863-6666
PET POLICY: Fee $4.

Motel 6
5179 Raynor Ave.
Linthicum Heights, MD 21090
410-636-9070
PET POLICY: No fee. Dogs under 25 lbs. preferred (larger animals by advance approval). Do not leave animals in room unattended.

Red Roof Inn
827 Elkridge Landing Rd.
Linthicum Heights, MD 21090
410-850-7600
PET POLICY: No fee, pets under 80 lbs. Must be leashed to and from rooms. Do not leave in room unattended.

Georgia Belle Motel Suites & Lodge
12000 Coastal Hwy.
Ocean City, MD 21842
410-250-4000
RATES: Vary monthly, call for latest rates.
PET POLICY: Fee $25 for stay. No pets in July and August. No size restrictions.

Sheraton Fontainebleau Hotel
10100 Ocean Hwy.
Ocean City, MD, 21842
410-524-3535
RATES: Single, double $79-289
PET POLICY: Fee $25. Up to 50 lbs. accepted, but are flexible. Sign agreement, leave number if pet's alone in room. Restricted number of pet rooms.
AMENITIES: Pet area out back near beach.

Red Roof Inn
6170 Oxon Hill Rd.
Oxon Hill, MD 20745
301-567-8030
PET POLICY: No fee, pets under 80 lbs. Must be leashed to and from rooms. Do not leave in room unattended.

Days Inn
1540 Ocean Hwy.
Pocomoke City, MD 21851
410-957-3000
PET POLICY: No fee.

Red Roof Inn
16001 Shady Grove Rd.
Rockville, MD 20850
301-987-0965
PET POLICY: No fee, pets under 80 lbs. Must be leashed to and from rooms. Do not leave in room unattended.

The Inn at Perry Cabin
308 Watkins Ln.
St. Michaels, MD 21663
410-745-2200
RATES: Single, double $435.
PET POLICY: Fee $50, nonrefundable. All size dogs and cats. Please advise us when making reservations of number and names of pets.

AMENITIES: Welcome gifts on check-in. Canine Room Service Menu prepared to order. Also available is "Man's Best Friend" picnic basket.

Rambler Motel
US 15 at Jct State Rd. 550
Thurmont, MD 21788
301-271-2424
RATES: Single $52, double $62.
PET POLICY: No fee, up to 50 lbs. Dogs and Cats only. Do not leave unattended in room.

Red Roof Inn
111 W. Timonium Rd.
Timonium, MD 21093
410-666-0380
PET POLICY: No fee, pets under 80 lbs. Must be leashed to and from rooms. Do not leave in room unattended.

Baltimore Days Inn
8801 Loch Raven Blvd.
Towson, MD 21286
410-882-0900
PET POLICY: Fee $15.

Days Inn of Waldorf
11370 Days Court
Waldorf, MD 11370
301-932-9200
PET POLICY: Fee $10.

Howard Johnson Express Inn
3125 Crain Hwy.
Waldorf, MD 20602
301-932-5090
RATES: Single $45.95, double $54.40.
PET POLICY: Fee $10, nonrefundable, no cats. Dogs up to 50 lbs.
AMENITIES: All rooms are ground floor with outside entrances. All have grassy areas close by.
POI: Washington, DC, Southern Maryland, historic sites, Andrews AFB, Pax River Naval Base.

Days Inn—Westminster
25 S. Cranberry Rd.
Westminster, MD 21157
410-857-0500
PET POLICY: Fee $5.

U.S. Lodgings > MARYLAND

The Boston Inn
533 Baltimore Blvd.
Westminster, MD 21157
410-848-9095
RATES: Single $52, double $58.
PET POLICY: Fee $50, refundable,
no cats.

Red Roof Inn
310 E. Potomac St.
Williamsport, MD 21795
301-582-3500
PET POLICY: No fee, pets under
80 lbs. Must be leashed to and
from rooms. Do not leave in
room unattended.

MASSACHUSETTS

Wyndham Andover
123 Old River Rd.
Andover, MA 01810
978-975-3600
PET POLICY: No fee. Pets under
25 lbs.

Baymont Inn & Suites
446 Southbridge St.
Auburn, MA 01501
508-832-7000
PET POLICY: No fee.

Cape Cod's Lamb & Lion Inn
2504 Main St., Box 511
Barnstable, MA 02630
508-362-6823
RATES: Single $85, double $160.
PET POLICY: Fee $15, nonrefund-
able. All sizes and all pets welcome (dogs, cats, ferrets, birds,
rabbits, reptiles). Do not leave
pets in room unattended.
Must be leashed. Groomed
prior to visit.
AMENITIES: Cookies on arrival.
Bowels and dishes when
needed.

Jenkins Inn & Restaurant
7 W. St., Route 122
Barre, MA 01005
978-355-6444
RATES: Single $130, double $130.
PET POLICY: Fee $5, refundable.
All sizes, dogs and cats only,
do not leave unattended in
room. Keep on leash going in
and out.

Boston Days Inn Braintree
190 Wood Rd.
Braintree, MA 02184
781-848-1260
PET POLICY: No fee.

Motel 6
125 Union St.
Braintree, MA 02184
781-848-7890
PET POLICY: No fee. Dogs under 25
lbs. preferred (larger animals by
advance approval). Do not leave
animals in room unattended.

Best Western at Historic Concord
740 Elm St.
Concord, MA 01742
508-369-6100
RATES: Single $104, double
$119.
PET POLICY: Fee $10, nonre-
fundable. All sizes and all pets
welcome.

Motel 6
1668 Worcester Rd.
Framingham, MA 01702
508-620-0500
PET POLICY: No fee. Dogs under 25
lbs. preferred (larger animals by
advance approval). Do not leave
animals in room unattended.

Red Roof Inn
650 Cochituate Rd.
Framingham, MA 01701
508-872-4499
PET POLICY: No fee, pets under
80 lbs. Must be leashed to and
from rooms. Do not leave in
room unattended.

Augusta House Bed & Breakfast
49 South St.
Great Barrington, MA 01230
413-528-3064
RATES: Avg: $65–$125 seasonal.
PET POLICY: Fee $10 per night,
nonrefundable. Deposit $50,
refundable. All size dogs welcome. Limit 1 pet per room.
Deposit required, must be
leashed outside. Do not leave
unattended in room, and dogs
not allowed in common
rooms during breakfast.

POI: Tanglewood, Berkshire
Theatre Festival, Jacobs Pillow,
Butternut and Catamount Ski
areas.

Candlelight Motor Inn
208 Mohawk Tr.
Greenfield, MA 01301
413-772-0101
RATES: Single $56, double $72.
PET POLICY: Fee $10, non-
refundable.
AMENITIES: Grass area.

Cascade Motor Lodge
201 Main St.
Hyannis, MA 02601
508-775-9717
RATES: Single $44–$68.
PET POLICY: No fee, all size dogs
and cats only. Do not leave
pets in room unattended.
AMENITIES: Large walking area.
POI: One block from Martha's
Vinyard and Nantucket ferries.

Mt. View Motel
499 S. Main St.
Lanesborough, MA 01237
413-442-1009
RATES: Single $55–$125, double
$65–$135.
PET POLICY: Fee $10, nonrefund-
able. Dogs, cats, and birds only.
POI: Near resort area.

Motel 6
48 Commercial St.
Leominster, MA 01453
078-537-8161
PET POLICY: No fee. Dogs under 25
lbs. preferred (larger animals by
advance approval). Do not leave
animals in room unattended.

Red Roof Inn
60 Forbes Blvd.
Mansfield, MA 02048
508-339-2323
PET POLICY: No fee, pets under
80 lbs. up to 80 lbs. 2 pets per
room, grassy areas for walking
dogs, sign a damage release.

Hidden Hill Cottages
41 Hidden Hill Ln.
Martha's Vineyard, MA 02568
508-693-2809
RATES: Double $125–$160.

U.S. Lodgings > MASSACHUSETTS

PET POLICY: Fee $75 (week), nonrefundable. All sizes, dogs and cats and birds accepted. Do not leave unattended in rooms for more than 2 hours. Please clean up.
AMENITIES: Treats for pets.

McComb Days Inn
2298 Delaware Ave.
McComb, MA 39648
601-684-5566
PET POLICY: Fee $8.

Days Inn—Plymouth-Middleboro
Rte. 105 N.
Middleboro, MA 02346
508-946-4400
PET POLICY: No fee.

Skaket Beach Motel
203 Cranberry Hwy.
Orleans, MA 02653
508-255-1020
RATES: Single $75, double $85.
PET POLICY: Fee $9, nonrefundable. All sizes, but dogs and cats only. No pets in July and August. Must not be left alone in rooms.

BayShore & Chandler House
493 Commercial St.
Provincetown, MA 02657
508-487-9133
RATES: Single $75–$135, double $98–$185.
PET POLICY: Fee $15, nonrefundable. All sizes and all pets welcome (dogs, cats, ferrets, birds, rabbits).
AMENITIES: Dog bowls.

Gabriel's Apartments & Guest Rooms
104 Bradford St.
Provincetown, MA 02657
508-487-3232
RATES: Single $100, double $150.
PET POLICY: Fee $10 per night. All sizes and pets welcome (dogs, cats, ferrets, birds, rabbits, reptiles). Deposit $50, refundable.
AMENITIES: Dog biscuits in rooms, water bowls outside, fenced in yard.
POI: Provincetown downtown.

Pilgrim House Inn
306 Commercial St.
Provincetown, MA 02657
508-487-6424
RATES: Double $135.
PET POLICY: No fee, all sizes and all pets welcome. Pets allowed in apartments only.
POI: National seashore across from Provincetown Bay.

Taunton Days Inn
Route 44
Raynham, MA 02767
508-824-8647
PET POLICY: No fee.

Holiday Inn Express
909 Hingham St.
Rockland, MA 2370
781-871-5660
PET POLICY: Pet Paw Program.

Salem Inn
7 Summer St.
Salem, MA 01970
978-741-0680
RATES: Single, double $119–$169.
PET POLICY: Fee $15, all sizes and pets welcome.

Colonial Traveler Motor Court
1753 Broadway
Saugus, MA 01906
781-233-6700
RATES: Single $89, double $99.
PET POLICY: Refundable fee, all sizes welcome.

Motel 6
821 Fall River Ave.
Seekonk, MA 02771
508-336-7800
PET POLICY: No fee. Dogs under 25 lbs. preferred (larger animals by advance approval). Do not leave animals in room unattended.

Race Brook Lodge
864 S. Undermountain Rd.
Sheffield, MA 01257
888-725-6343
PET POLICY: Larger room for families w/pets.

Red Roof Inn
367 Turnpike Rd.
Southborough, MA 01772
508-481-3904
PET POLICY: No fee, pets under 80 lbs. Must be leashed to and from rooms. Do not leave in room unattended.

Motel 6
1314 Route 28
South Yarmouth, MA 02664
508-394-4000
PET POLICY: No fee. Dogs under 25 lbs. preferred (larger animals by advance approval). Do not leave animals in room unattended.

Windjammer Motel
192 S. Shore Dr.
South Yarmouth, MA 02664
508-398-2370
PET POLICY: Fee $30, up to 50 lbs., limit 1 pet.

Publick House Historic Inn
State Rd. 131, On the Common
Sturbridge, MA 01566
508-347-3313
RATES: Double $100.
PET POLICY: Fee $5, nonrefundable. All sizes and all pets welcome. Pets allowed only in Country Motor Lodge bldg.

Sturbridge Days Inn
66-68 Haynes St. Old Route 15
Sturbridge, MA 01566
508-347-3391
PET POLICY: Fee $5.

Motel 6
95 Main St.
Tewksbury, MA 01876
078-851-8677
PET POLICY: No fee. Dogs under 25 lbs. preferred (larger animals by advance approval). Do not leave animals in room unattended.

U.S. Lodgings > MASSACHUSETTS

Cape Cod Claddagh Inn
77 W. Main St., Rt. 28
West Harwich, MA 02671
508-432-9628
RATES: Single $95, double $150.
PET POLICY: No fee, all sizes
welcome. Do not leave pets in
room unattended.
AMENITIES: Wooded area.
Biking and Hiking trails.
Beach.
POI: Conservation area.
Beaches. Trips to Martha's
Vinyard and Nantucket.

Red Roof Inn
1254 Riverdale St.
West Springfield, MA 01089
413-731-1010
PET POLICY: No fee, pets under
80 lbs. Must be leashed to and
from rooms. Do not leave in
room unattended.

Jericho Valley Inn
2541 Hancock Rd.
Williamstown, MA 01267
413-458-9511
PET POLICY: No fee, all sizes
welcome.

Red Roof Inn
19 Commerce Way
Woburn, MA 01801
781-935-7110
PET POLICY: No fee, pets under
80 lbs. Must be leashed to and
from rooms. Do not leave in
room unattended.

Crowne Plaza
10 Lincoln Square
Worcester, MA 1608
508-791-1600
PET POLICY: No fee.

MICHIGAN

Linda's Lighthouse Inn
5965 Pte. Tremble Rd.
Algonac, MI 48001
810-794-2992
RATES: Single $85, double $95.
PET POLICY: Fee $15, nonrefund-
able. All sizes welcome.
AMENITIES: Outside balcony.
POI: Algonac State Park,
Algonac Waterfront Park, St.
Johns Marsh, lighthouses.

Motel 6
3764 S. State St.
Ann Arbor, MI 48108
734-665-9900
PET POLICY: No fee. Dogs under 25
lbs. preferred (larger animals by
advance approval). Do not leave
animals in room unattended.

Red Roof Inn
3621 Plymouth Rd.
Ann Arbor, MI 48105
734-996-5800
PET POLICY: No fee, pets under
80 lbs. Must be leashed to and
from rooms. Do not leave in
room unattended.

Battle Creek Days Inn
4786 Beckley Rd.
Battle Creek, MI 49017
616-979-3561
PET POLICY: No fee.

Baymont Inn & Suites
4725 Beckley Rd.
Battle Creek, MI 49017
616-979-5400
PET POLICY: Dogs Only.

Motel 6
4775 Beckley Rd.
Battle Creek, MI 49015
616-979-1141
PET POLICY: No fee. Dogs under 25
lbs. preferred (larger animals by
advance approval). Do not leave
animals in room unattended.

Red Roof Inn
45501 N. Expressway
Service Dr.
Belleville, MI 48111
734-697-2244
PET POLICY: No fee, pets under
80 lbs. Must be leashed to and
from rooms. Do not leave in
room unattended.

Red Roof Inn
1630 Mall Dr.
Benton Harbor, MI 49022
616-927-2484
PET POLICY: No fee, pets under
80 lbs. Must be leashed to and
from rooms. Do not leave in
room unattended.

Baymont Inn & Suites
41211 Ford Rd.
Canton Twp., MI 48187
734-981-1808
PET POLICY: No fee.

Pine River Motel
102 Lafayette
Cheboygan, MI 49721
231-627-5119
RATES: Single $30–$40, double
$40–$50.
PET POLICY: Fee $10, nonrefund-
able. All sizes, dogs only. Do
not leave in room unattended.
AMENITIES: A big runway.

**Quality Inn Convention
Center & Suites**
1000 Orleans Blvd.
Coldwater, MI 49036
517-278-2017
RATES: Seasonal room rates.
PET POLICY: Fee varies, refundable. Up to 50 lbs., all pets
welcome (dogs, cats, ferrets,
birds, rabbits). No snakes.
AMENITIES: Outdoor walking trail.

Red Roof Inn
348 S. Willowbrook Rd.
Coldwater, MI 49036
517-279-1199
PET POLICY: No fee, pets under
80 lbs. Must be leashed to and
from rooms. Do not leave in
room unattended.

**Best Western—
Greenfield Inn**
3000 Enterprise Dr.
Dearborn, MI 48101
313-271-1600
PET POLICY: $100 deposit,
refundable.

The Ritz-Carlton
300 Town Center Dr.
Dearborn, MI 48101
313-441-2000
PET POLICY: Fee $200 non-
refundable.

Red Roof Inn
24130 Michigan Ave.
Dearborn, MI 48124
313-278-9732
PET POLICY: No fee, pets under
60 lbs. Must be leashed to and
from rooms. Do not leave in
room unattended.

U.S. Lodgings > MICHIGAN

Holiday Inn
300 E. Bay St.
East Tawas, MI 48730
517-362-8601
PET POLICY: Pets allowed with signed pet waiver.

Escanaba Days Inn
2603 N. Lincoln Rd.
Escanaba, MI 49829
906-789-1200
PET POLICY: Fee $30.

Motel 6
38300 Grand River Ave.
Farmington Hills, MI 48335
238-471-0590
PET POLICY: No fee. Dogs under 25 lbs. preferred (larger animals by advance approval). Do not leave animals in room unattended.

Red Roof Inn
24300 Sinacola Court
Northeast
Farmington Hills, MI 48335
248-478-8640
PET POLICY: No fee, pets under 80 lbs. Must be leashed to and from rooms. Do not leave in room unattended.

Howard Johnson Express Inn
G-3277 Miller Rd.
Flint, MI 48507
810-733-5910
RATES: Single $45, double $60.
PET POLICY: Fee $10, nonrefundable, all sizes welcome.

Motel 6
2324 Austin Pkwy.
Flint, MI 48507
810-767-7100
PET POLICY: No fee. Dogs under 25 lbs. preferred (larger animals by advance approval). Do not leave animals in room unattended.

Red Roof Inn
G-3219 Miller Rd.
Flint, MI 48507
810-733-1660
PET POLICY: No fee, pets under 80 lbs. Must be leashed to and from rooms. Do not leave in room unattended.

Drury Inn & Suites
260 S. Main
Frankenmuth, MI 48734
517-652-2800
PET POLICY: No fee, pets under 30 lbs.

Downtown Motel
208 S. Otsego Ave.
Gaylord, MI 49735
517-732-5010
RATES: Single $40, double $50.
PET POLICY: No fee. All sizes and all pets welcome. Do not leave in room unattended.

Red Roof Inn
510 S. Wisconsin
Gaylord, MI 49735
517-731-6331
PET POLICY: No fee, pets under 80 lbs. Must be leashed to and from rooms. Do not leave in room unattended.

Baymont Inn & Suites
2873 Kraft Ave S.E.
Grand Rapids, MI 49512
616-956-3300
PET POLICY: No fee.

Days Inn—Downtown
310 Pearl St. NW
Grand Rapids, MI 49504
616-235-7611
PET POLICY: Fee $10.

Motel 6
3524 28th St SE
Grand Rapids, MI 49512
616-957-3511
PET POLICY: No fee. Dogs under 25 lbs. preferred (larger animals by advance approval). Do not leave animals in room unattended.

Peaches Bed & Breakfast
29 Gay Ave. SE
Grand Rapids, MI 49503
616-454-8000
RATES: Double $88.
PET POLICY: Fee $10, nonrefundable. All sizes welcome. Dogs preferred.
POI: Van Andel Arena. Meijer Gardens.

Red Roof Inn
5131 E. 28th St.
Grand Rapids, MI 49512
616-942-0800
PET POLICY: No fee, pets under 80 lbs. Must be leashed to and from rooms. Do not leave in room unattended.

Days Inn
W8176 S. US 2
Iron Mountain, MI 49801
906-774-2181
PET POLICY: Fee $7.

Holiday Inn
2000 Holiday Inn Dr.
Jackson, MI 49202
517-783-2681
PET POLICY: $15 cleaning fee.

Baymont Inn & Suites
2203 S. 11th St.
Kalamazoo, MI 49009
616-372-7999
PET POLICY: No fee.

Motel 6
3704 Van Rick Rd.
Kalamazoo, MI 49002
616-344-9255
PET POLICY: No fee. Dogs under 25 lbs. preferred (larger animals by advance approval). Do not leave animals in room unattended.

Red Roof Inn
5425 W. Michigan Ave.
Kalamazoo, MI 49009
616-375-7400
PET POLICY: No fee, pets under 80 lbs. Must be leashed to and from rooms. Do not leave in room unattended.

Hampton Inn
525 N. Canal Rd.
Lansing, MI 48917
517-627-8381
PET POLICY: Pets under 50 lbs. Deposit required.

Hawthorn Suites
901 Delta Commerce Dr.
Lansing, MI 48917
517-886-0600
PET POLICY: Fee $125 non-refundable for length of stay.

Lansing Days Inn
6501 S. Pennsylvania
Lansing, MI 48911
517-393-1650
PET POLICY: Fee $10.

Motel 6
7326 W. Saginaw Hwy.
Lansing, MI 48917
517-321-1444
PET POLICY: No fee. Dogs under 25
lbs. preferred (larger animals by
advance approval). Do not leave
animals in room unattended.

Red Roof Inn
7412 W. Saginaw Hwy.
Lansing, MI 48917
517-321-7246
PET POLICY: No fee, pets under
80 lbs. Must be leashed to and
from rooms. Do not leave in
room unattended.

Ludington House
501 E. Ludington Ave.
Ludington, MI 49431
231-845-7769
PET POLICY: Dogs accepted by
reservation.

**Naders Lakeshore Motor
Lodge**
612 N. Lakeshore Dr.
Ludington, MI 49431
231-843-8757
RATES: Must call for rates.
PET POLICY: No fee, all sizes and
all pets welcome. Must be
leashed, and do not leave in
room unattended.
POI: Lake Michigan Public
Beach. Ludington State Park.

**Bed & Breakfast at
Ludington**
2458 S. Beaune Rd.
Ludington, MI 49431
231-843-0768
RATES: Single $50, double $60.
PET POLICY: Fee $12 per night,
nonrefundable. Only dogs and
cats. Kittens on premises.
AMENITIES: Acres without roads.
Two fine trails.

Baymont Inn & Suites
109 S. Nicolet St.
Mackinaw City, MI 49701
231-436-7737
PET POLICY: No fee.

Motel 6
206 N. Nicolet St.
Mackinaw City, MI 49701
231-436-8961
PET POLICY: No fee. Dogs under 25
lbs. preferred (larger animals by
advance approval). Do not leave
animals in room unattended.

Super 8 Motel
601 N. Huron Ave.
Mackinaw City, MI 49701
616-436-5252
PET POLICY: Less than 10 lbs.,
must be confined.

Val-Ru Motel
14394 N. Mackinaw Hwy.
Mackinaw City, MI 49701
231-436-7691
PET POLICY: Fee $5 per day per
pet. All sizes welcome. Credit
card deposit. Must pick up
after pets.
AMENITIES: Large run area for
pets.
POI: Pet-friendly boats to
Mackinac Island.

Red Roof Inn
32511 Concord Dr.
Madison Heights, MI 48071
248-583-4700
PET POLICY: No fee, pets under
80 lbs. Must be leashed to and
from rooms. Do not leave in
room unattended.

Hillside Motel
1675 US 31 S.
Manistee, MI 49660
231-723-2584
PET POLICY: Fee $5, up to 50
lbs., prior notice, 1 per room,
dogs only.

Ramada Inn
412 W. Washington
Marquette, MI 49855
906-228-6000
RATES: Single $94, double $99.
PET POLICY: No fee, all sizes
welcome.
POI: 2 large parks within a
couple of blocks.

Travelodge
1010 M-28 E.
Marquette, MI 49855
906-249-1712
RATES: Single $42.95, double
$49.95.
PET POLICY: Fee $5, nonrefund-
able.
AMENITIES: Lots of room for pet
exercise.
POI: Close to Lake Superior.
Close to casino.

Westwood Suites
2782 US Hwy. 41 W
Marquette, MI 49855
906-226-2314
RATES: Single $50, double $55.
PET POLICY: Fee $6, nonrefund-
able. All sizes welcome.

Monroe Days Inn
1440 N. Dixie Hwy.
Monroe, MI 48162
734-289-4000
PET POLICY: Fee $25.

Comfort Inn Munising
M-28 E, Box 276
Munising, MI 49862
906-387-2493
RATES: Single $98, double $98.
PET POLICY: No fee, all sizes
welcome. Pet in smoking
rooms only.

Terrace Motel
420 Prospect
Munising, MI 49862
906-387-2735
RATES: Single $48, double $52.
PET POLICY: Fee $3, nonrefund-
able. Up to 50 lbs.
POI: Waterfalls, Pictured Rocks
National Lakeshore, Hiawatha
National Forest.

Bel Aire Motel
4240 Airline Rd.
Muskegon, MI 49444
616-733-2196
PET POLICY: Under 10 lbs.

Seaway Motel
631 W. Norton Ave.
Muskegon, MI 49441
616-733-1220
PET POLICY: Pets accepted under
10 lbs.

U.S. Lodgings > MICHIGAN

Scott's Superior Inn & Cabins
277 Lakeshore Rd.
Ontonagon, MI 49953
906-884-4866
PET POLICY: No fee.

The Pines Motel
8228 US 31 N.
Pentwater, MI 49449
231-869-5128
RATES: Single $40–$70, double $50–$80.
PET POLICY: Fee $5, nonrefundable. All sizes welcome. Do not leave pets unattended.
POI: Lake Michigan, Fishing/charters, Golf.

Comfort Inn
1314 US 31 N
Petoskey, MI 49770
231-347-3220
RATES: Double $48.75.
PET POLICY: No fee, all sizes welcome.

Port Huron Days Inn
2908 Pine Grove
Port Huron, MI 48060
810-984-1522
PET POLICY: Fee $10.

Red Roof Inn
39700 Ann Arbor Rd.
Plymouth, MI 48170
734-459-3300
PET POLICY: No fee, pets under 80 lbs. Must be leashed to and from rooms. Do not leave in room unattended.

Red Roof Inn
2580 Crooks Rd.
Rochester Hills, MI 48309
248-853-6400
PET POLICY: No fee, pets under 80 lbs. Must be leashed to and from rooms. Do not leave in room unattended.

Baymont Inn & Suites
9000 Wickham Rd.
Romulus, MI 48174
734-722-6000
PET POLICY: No fee.

Crowne Plaza
8000 Merriman Rd.
Romulus, MI 48174
734-729-2600
PET POLICY: No fee.

Detroit Days Inn
9501 Middlebelt Rd.
Romulus, MI 48174
734-946-4300
PET POLICY: Fee $25.

Motel 6
9095 Wickham
Romulus, MI 48174
734-595-7400
PET POLICY: No fee. Dogs under 25 lbs. preferred (larger animals by advance approval). Do not leave animals in room unattended.

Red Roof Inn
7680 Merriman Rd.
Romulus, MI 48174
734-641-9006
PET POLICY: No fee, pets under 80 lbs. Must be leashed to and from rooms. Do not leave in room unattended.

Baymont Inn & Suites
20675 13 Mile Rd.
Roseville, MI 48066
810-296-6910
PET POLICY: No fee.

Red Roof Inn
31800 Little Mack Rd.
Roseville, MI 48066
810-296-0310
PET POLICY: No fee, pets under 80 lbs. Must be leashed to and from rooms. Do not leave in room unattended.

Best Western Saginaw
1408 S. Outer Dr.
Saginaw, MI 48601
517-755-7010
RATES: Single, double $69.
PET POLICY: No fee, all sizes and pets welcome.

Crowne Plaza
400 Johnson St.
Saginaw, MI 48607
517-753-6608
PET POLICY: No fee.

Red Roof Inn
966 S. Outer Dr.
Saginaw, MI 48601
517-75-48414
PET POLICY: No fee, pets under 80 lbs. Must be leashed to and from rooms. Do not leave in room unattended.

Grand Motel
1100 E. Portage Ave.
Sault Ste. Marie, MI 49783
906-632-2141
RATES: Single $40–$60, double $44–$64.
PET POLICY: No fee, must be housebroken and quiet.

Royal Motel
1707 Ashmun St.
Sault Ste. Marie, MI 49783
906-632-6323
PET POLICY: No fee, up to 25 lbs.

Red Roof Inn
27660 Northwestern Hwy.
Southfield, MI 48034
248-353-7200
PET POLICY: No fee, pets under 80 lbs. Must be leashed to and from rooms. Do not leave in room unattended.

Baymont Inn & Suites
12888 Reeck Rd.
Southgate, MI 48195
734-374-3000
PET POLICY: No fee.

Baymont Inn & Suites
2601 W. Marquette Woods Rd.
Stevensville, MI 49127
616-428-9111
PET POLICY: No fee.

Hampton Inn
5050 Red Arrow Hwy.
Stevensville, MI 49127
616-429-2700
PET POLICY: Pets with deposit.

Red Roof Inn
21230 Eureka Rd.
Taylor, MI 48180
734-374-1150
PET POLICY: No fee, pets under 80 lbs. Must be leashed to and from rooms. Do not leave in room unattended.

U.S. Lodgings > MICHIGAN

Tecumseh Inn
1445 W. Chicago Blvd.
Tecumseh, MI 49286
517-423-7401
RATES: Single $51, double $60.
PET POLICY: No fee, $25 refundable deposit. All sizes welcome.
POI: Dundee, Irish Hills, Hidden Lake Gardens.

Drury Inn
575 W. Big Beaver Rd.
Troy, MI 48084
810-528-3330
PET POLICY: No fee, pets under 30 lbs.

Red Roof Inn
2350 Rochester Court
Troy, MI 48083
248-689-4391
PET POLICY: No fee, pets under 80 lbs. Must be leashed to and from rooms. Do not leave in room unattended.

Firefly Resort
15657 Lake Shore Rd.
Union Pier, MI 49129
616-469-0245
RATES: Single $85, double $125.
PET POLICY: Fee $20, nonrefundable. All sizes, all pets welcome. Must clean up after.
AMENITIES: Private beach access.

Sweethaven Resort
9517 Union Pier Rd.
Union Pier, MI 49129
616-469-0332
RATES: Single $135, double $175.
PET POLICY: No fee, all sizes welcome. Must be responsible for any damages by pets.
AMENITIES: 9 acres of woods.

Baymont Inn & Suites
45311 Park Ave.
Utica, MI 48315
810-731-4700
PET POLICY: No fee.

Baymont Inn & Suites
30900 Van Dyke Ave.
Warren, MI 48093
810-574-0550
PET POLICY: No fee.

Motel 6
8300 Chicago Rd.
Warren, MI 48093
810-26-9300
PET POLICY: No fee. Dogs under 25 lbs. preferred (larger animals by advance approval). Do not leave animals in room unattended.

Red Roof Inn
7001 Convention Blvd.
Warren, MI 48092
810-268-9020
PET POLICY: No fee, pets under 80 lbs. Must be leashed to and from rooms. Do not leave in room unattended.

La Hacienda Motel
969 W. Houghton Ave.
West Branch, MI 48661
517-345-2345
RATES: Single $40, double $50.
PET POLICY: No fee. All sizes and all pets welcome. Do not leave in room unattended.

Lake Land Motel
1002 E. Colby St.
Whitehall, MI 49461
231-894-5644
RATES: Single $30–$60, double $35–$65.
PET POLICY: Fee $5, nonrefundable.
AMENITIES: Large field to walk pets.
POI: Parks and beaches.

MINNESOTA

Skyline Motel
605 30th Ave. W.
Alexandria, MN 56308
320-763-3175
RATES: Single $45, double $55.
PET POLICY: No fee, all sizes and all pets welcome. Do not leave pets unattended in room.

Thayer's Historic Bed & Breakfast
60 W. Elm St, Hwy. 55
Annandale, MN 55302
320-274-8222
RATES: Single $125, double 245.
PET POLICY: Fee $20, nonrefundable. Dogs and cats only. Must have note from vet stating pet is free of fleas and parasites.

Austin Days Inn
700 16th Ave. NW
Austin, MN 55912
507-433-8600
PET POLICY: No fee.

Holiday Inn
1701 4th St. NW
Austin, MN 55912
507-433-1000
PET POLICY: Pets in smoking room.

Best Western Bemidji
2420 Paul Bunyan Dr.
Bemidji, MN 56601
218-759-7709
RATES: Single $49, double $65.
PET POLICY: No fee, all sizes welcome. Pets in smoking rooms only. Credit card must be on file.

Holiday Inn Express
2422 Ridgeway Ave. NW
Bemidji, MN 56601
218-751-2487
PET POLICY: Small pets allowed if attended.

Baymont Inn & Suites
7815 Nicollet Ave. S.
Bloomington, MN 55420
612-881-7311
PET POLICY: No fee.

Brainerd Days Inn
Hwy. 210 & 371 N.
Brainerd, MN 56401
218-829-0391
PET POLICY: Fee $5.

Red Roof Inn
12920 Aldrich Avenue South
Burnsville, MN 55337
952-890-1420
PET POLICY: No fee, pets under 80 lbs. Must be leashed to and from rooms. Do not leave in room unattended.

Baymont Inn & Suites— Minneapolis
6415 James Cir. N.
Brooklyn Center, MN 55430
612-561-8400
PET POLICY: No fee.

U.S. Lodgings > MINNESOTA

**Holiday Inn Express Hotel
& Suites**
9333 Springbrook Dr.
Coon Rapids, MN 55433
612-792-9292
PET POLICY: With restrictions.

Holiday Inn
1155 Hwy. 10 E
Detroit Lakes, MN 56501
218-847-2121
RATES: Single $129, double
$129.
PET POLICY: No fee, all sizes and
pets welcome (dogs, cats,
birds, ferrets, rabbits, reptiles).

**Best Western Downtown
Motel**
131 W. 2nd St.
Duluth, MN 55802
218-727-6851
RATES: Single $40, double $55.
PET POLICY: No fee, all sizes and
all pets welcome.

Duluth Days Inn
909 Cottonwood Ave.
Duluth, MN 55811
218-727-3110
PET POLICY: No fee.

Motel 6
200 S. 27th Ave. West
Duluth, MN 55806
218-723-1123
PET POLICY: No fee. Dogs under 25
lbs. preferred (larger animals by
advance approval). Do not leave
animals in room unattended.

**Holiday Inn Express Hotel
& Suites**
1950 Rahncliff Court
Eagan, MN 55122
651-681-9266
PET POLICY: Small pets allowed
if attended.

Fergus Falls Days Inn
610 Western Ave. N
Fergus Falls, MN 56537
218-739-3311
PET POLICY: No fee.

Grand Rapids Days Inn
311 E. Hwy. 3
Grand Rapids, MN 55744
219-326-3457
PET POLICY: Deposit required.

Hibbing Days Inn
1520 Hwy. 37
Hibbing, MN 55746
218-263-8306
PET POLICY: No fee.

Hinckley Days Inn
104 Grindstone Court
Hinckley, MN 55037
320-384-7751
PET POLICY: Fee $5, small pets
only. Smoking rooms only!
Do not leave in room
unattended.

International Falls Days Inn
2331 Hwy. 53 S.
International Falls, MN 56649
218-283-9441
PET POLICY: No fee.

Mankato Days Inn
1285 Range St.
Mankato, MN 56002
507-387-3332
PET POLICY: No fee.

Crowne Plaza
618 2nd Ave. S.
Minneapolis, MN 55402
612-338-2288
PET POLICY: No fee.

**Hilton Minneapolis—
St. Paul Airport**
3800 E. 80th St.
Minneapolis, MN 55425
612-854-2100
RATES: Vary with Season.
PET POLICY: No fee, all sizes and
pets welcome.

Monticello Days Inn
200 E. Oakwood Dr.
Monticello, MN 55362
612-295-1111
PET POLICY: Fee $5.

Moorhead Days Inn
1010 Holiday Dr.
Moorhead, MN 56560
218-233-7531
PET POLICY: Fee $10.

Motel Mora
301 State Hwy. 65
Mora, MN 55051
320-679-3262
RATES: Single $33, double $62.
PET POLICY: Fee $5, nonrefund-
able. Pets up to 50 lbs.

Archer House
212 Division St.
Northfield, MN 55057
507-645-5661
RATES: Regular rooms
$45–$55, suites $40–$75,
weekends $115–$140.
PET POLICY: No fee, all sizes and
pets accepted.

Oakdale Motel
1418 S. Oak Ave.
Owatonna, MN 55060
507-451-5480
RATES: Single $36–$45, double
$46–$65.
PET POLICY: Fee $7, nonrefund-
able. All sizes accepted.
POI: Kaplan Woods. Kohlmier
Lake.

Cross Point Resort
29870 Crosspoint Ln.
Pelican Rapids, MN 56572
218-863-8593
RATES: Cabin: $55.
PET POLICY: No fee for single
nights. Weekly fee, $25.
All sizes and all pets welcome.

Leisure Lane Resort
20473 Leisure Dr.
Pelican Rapids, MN 56572
218-863-4490
PET POLICY: Fee $35, No restric-
tions, all sizes.

Red Roof Inn
2600 Annapolis Lane North
Plymouth, MN 55441
612-553-1751
PET POLICY: No fee, pets under
80 lbs. Must be leashed to and
from rooms. Do not leave in
room unattended.

Red Wing Days Inn
955 7th St.
Red Wing, MN 55066
651-388-3568
PET POLICY: Fee $7.50.

Motel 6
7640 Cedar Ave S
Richfield, MN 55423
612-861-4491
PET POLICY: No fee. Dogs under 25
lbs. preferred (larger animals by
advance approval). Do not leave
animals in room unattended.

U.S. Lodgings > MINNESOTA

Kahler Inn and Suites
9 N.W. Third Ave. & W.
Center St.
Rochester, MN 55901-289
507-289-8646
RATES: Single $99, double $99.
PET POLICY: No fee, up to 50
lbs., must be in smoking rooms.

Motel 6
2107 W. Frontage Rd.
Rochester, MN 55901
507-282-6625
PET POLICY: No fee. Dogs under 25
lbs. preferred (larger animals by
advance approval). Do not leave
animals in room unattended.

Rochester Days Inn South
111 28th St. SE
Rochester, MN 55904
507-286-1001
PET POLICY: No fee.

Holiday Inn Hotel & Suites
75 S. 37th Ave.
St. Cloud, MN 56301
320-253-9000
RATES: Single $74.95, double
$74.95.
PET POLICY: No fee, owner must
be with pet at all times. Pets
not allowed in public areas.
POI: Quarry Park Reserve.

Motel 6
815 1st St S
St. Cloud, MN 56387
320-253-7070
PET POLICY: No fee. Dogs under 25
lbs. preferred (larger animals by
advance approval). Do not leave
animals in room unattended.

St. Cloud Days Inn
420 SE Hwy. 10
St. Cloud, MN 56304
320-253-0500
PET POLICY: No fee.

**Lakeshore Motor Inn
Downtown**
404 N. 6th Ave.
Virginia, MN 55792
218-741-3360
RATES: Single $39, double $52.
PET POLICY: No fee.
POI: Adjoining walking path
around lake.

Willmar Days Inn
225 28th St. SE
Willmar, MN 56201
320-231-1275
PET POLICY: No fee.

Hampton Inn
1450 Weir Dr.
Woodbury, MN 55125
651-578-2822
PET POLICY: Pets less than 25 lbs.

**Holiday Inn Express Hotel
& Suites**
9840 Norma Ln.
Woodbury, MN 55125
651-702-0200
PET POLICY: Pets allowed in
smoking rooms.

Red Roof Inn
1806 Wooddale Dr.
Woodbury, MN 55125
651-738-7160
PET POLICY: No fee, pets under
80 lbs. Must be leashed to and
from rooms. Do not leave in
room unattended.

Days Inn—Worthington
207 Oxford St.
Worthington, MN 56187
507-376-6155
PET POLICY: Fee $6.

MISSISSIPPI

Lofty Oaks Inn
17288, Hwy. 67
Biloxi, MS 39552
228-392-6722
RATES: Single $99, double $125.
PET POLICY: Fee $10, nonre-
fundable. All sizes welcome.
POI: 15 minutes to beaches.

Motel 6
2476 Beach Blvd.
Biloxi, MS 39531
228-388-5130
PET POLICY: No fee. Dogs under
25 lbs. preferred (larger animals by advance approval).
Do not leave animals in room
unattended.

Days Inn—Clarksdale
1910 State St.
Clarksdale, MS 38614
601-624-4391
PET POLICY: Fee $8.

Holiday Inn
506 Hwy. 45 N.
Columbus, MS 39701
662-328-5202
PET POLICY: Small pets accepted.

Motel 6
1203 Hwy. 45 North
Columbus, MS 39705
652-327-4450
PET POLICY: No fee. Dogs under 25
lbs. preferred (larger animals by
advance approval). Do not leave
animals in room unattended.

Greenville Days Inn
PO Box 1139
Greenville, MS 38701
662-335-1999
PET POLICY: Fee $5.

Motel 6
9355 US Hwy. 49
Gulfport, MS 39503
228-863-1890
PET POLICY: No fee. Dogs under 25
lbs. preferred (larger animals by
advance approval). Do not leave
animals in room unattended.

Shoney's Inn of Gulfport
9375 Hwy. 49
Gulfport, MS 39503
228-868-8500
RATES: Single $45–$65, double
$49–$69.
PET POLICY: Fee $25, refundable.
All size dogs and cats.

Baymont Inn & Suites
123 Plaza Dr.
Hattiesburg, MS 39402
601-264-8380
PET POLICY: No fee.

Hattiesburg Days Inn
6518 Hwy. 49 N.
Hattiesburg, MS 39401
601-544-6300
PET POLICY: Fee $6.

Motel 6
6508 US Hwy. 49
Hattiesburg, MS 39401
601-544-6096
PET POLICY: No fee. Dogs under 25
lbs. preferred (larger animals by
advance approval). Do not leave
animals in room unattended.

U.S. Lodgings > MISSOURI

Holiday Inn Express
601 Hwy. 82 W.
Indianola, MS 38751
602-887-7477
PET POLICY: $25 Deposit.

Crowne Plaza
200 E. Amite St.
Jackson, MS 39201
601-969-5100
PET POLICY: No fee, Deposit
$125–$150, refundable. No
size restrictions.

Motel 6
6145 I-55 N
Jackson, MS 39213
601-956-8848
PET POLICY: No fee. Dogs under 25
lbs. preferred (larger animals by
advance approval). Do not leave
animals in room unattended.

Red Roof Inn
700 Larson St.
Jackson, MS 39202
601-969-5006
PET POLICY: No fee, pets under
80 lbs. Must be leashed to and
from rooms. Do not leave in
room unattended.

Baymont Inn & Suites
1400 Roebuck Dr.
Meridian, MS 39301
601-693-2300
PET POLICY: No fee.

Meridian Days Inn
145 Hwy. 11 & 80E
Meridian, MS 39301
601-483-3812
RATES: Single $45, double $55.
PET POLICY: Fee $5 per pet,
nonrefundable. All sizes
welcome.

Cedar Grove Plantation
617 Kingston Rd.
Natchez, MS 39120
601-445-0585
RATES: Single $120–$225,
double $120–$225.
PET POLICY: No fee, all sizes
welcome, dogs and cats, only.
Pets not allowed in guest
rooms, dogs must be leashed
or kept in kennels, provided.
Not allowed in rooms.
AMENITIES: Kennels on premises.
Kennels have dog houses.

Days Inn
I-20 & Hwy. 15
Newton, MS 39345
601-683-3361
PET POLICY: Fee $8.

Biloxi Days Inn
7305 Washington Ave.
Ocean Springs, MS 39564
228-872-8255
PET POLICY: Fee $5.

Oxford Days Inn
1101 Frontage Rd.
Oxford, MS 38655
662-234-9500
PET POLICY: Fee $5.

Philadelphia Days Inn
1009 Holland Ave.
Philadelphia, MS 39350
601-650-2590
PET POLICY: Fee $5.

Jackson Days Inn
1035 Hwy. 49S
Richland, MS 39218
601-932-5553
PET POLICY: Fee $5.

Homewood Suites Hotel
853 Centre St.
Ridgeland, MS 39157
601-899-8611
PET POLICY: Non refundable
deposit required.

Red Roof Inn
810 Adcock St.
Ridgeland, MS 39157
601-956-7707
PET POLICY: No fee, pets under
80 lbs. Must be leashed to and
from rooms. Do not leave in
room unattended.

Tunica Days Inn
2440 Casino Strip Resort Blvd.
Robinsonville, MS 38664
601-363-9996
PET POLICY: No fee.

Red Roof Inn
1500 McCullough Blvd.
Tupelo, MS 38804
662-844-1904
PET POLICY: No fee, pets under
80 lbs. Must be leashed to and
from rooms. Do not leave in
room unattended.

Tupelo Days Inn
1015 N. Gloster
Tupelo, MS 38804
662-842-0088
PET POLICY: No fee.

Battlefield Inn
4137 I-20, N. Frontage Rd.
Vicksburg, MS 39183
601-638-5811
RATES: Single $55, double $68.
PET POLICY: Fee $5, nonrefund-
able, all sizes, not unattended,
portable kennel on site.
AMENITIES: Dog walking area.
POI: Next to National Military
park, near city park.

MISSOURI

Drury Inn
1201 Drury Ln.
Arnold, MO 63010
314-296-9600
PET POLICY: No fee, pets under
30 lbs.

Baymont Inn and Suites
2375 Green Mountain Dr.
Branson, MO 65616
417-336-6161
PET POLICY: No fee.

Days Inn of Branson
3524 Keeter St.
Branson, MO 65616
417-334-5544
RATES: Single $80, double $105.
PET POLICY: Fee $10.

Motel 6
2825 Green Mountain Dr.
Branson, MO 65616
417-335-8990
PET POLICY: No fee. Dogs under 25
lbs. preferred (larger animals by
advance approval). Do not leave
animals in room unattended.

Peachtree Inn
2450 Green Mountain Dr.
Branson, MO 65616
417-335-5900
PET POLICY: Deposit $25,
refundable. Pets under 20 lbs.
Pets must be kept in carriers
when leaving in room.

U.S. Lodgings > MISSOURI

Red Roof Inn
220 S. Wildwood Dr.
Branson, MO 65616
417-335-4500
PET POLICY: No fee, pets under
80 lbs. Must be leashed to and
from rooms. Do not leave in
room unattended.

Settle Inn of Branson
3050 Green Mountain Dr.
Branson, MO 65616
417-335-4700
RATES: Single $49–$149.
PET POLICY: Fee $8. All sizes and
pets accepted.

Red Roof Inn
3470 Hollenberg Dr.
Bridgeton, MO 63044
314-291-3350
PET POLICY: No fee, pets under
80 lbs. Must be leashed to and
from rooms. Do not leave in
room unattended.

Butler Days Inn
100 S. Fran Ave.
Butler, MO 64730
660-679-4544
PET POLICY: Fee $5.

Drury Lodge
104 S. Vantage Dr.
Cape Girardeau, MO 63701
573-334-7151
PET POLICY: No fee. All sizes
and pets accepted. Do not
leave in rooms unattended.

Pear Tree Inn by Drury
3248 Williams St.
Cape Girardeau, MO 63701
314-334-3000
PET POLICY: No fee. All sizes
and pets accepted. Do not
leave in rooms unattended.

Baymont Inn & Suites
2500 I-70 Drive S.W.
Columbia, MO 65203
573-445-1899
PET POLICY: No fee.

**Days Inn Hotel &
Conference Center**
1900 I-70 Drive SW
Columbia, MO 65203
573-445-8511
RATES: Single $49.95, double
$69.95.
PET POLICY: Fee $5 per pet,
nonrefundable. Up to 25 lbs.
POI: Parks, golf courses, hiking,
biking trails, University,
museums.

Drury Inn
1000 Knipp St.
Columbia, MO 65203
573-445-1800
PET POLICY: No fee, pets under
30 lbs.

Motel 6
1800 I-70 Dr SW
Columbia, MO 65203
573-445-8433
PET POLICY: No fee. Dogs under 25
lbs. preferred (larger animals by
advance approval). Do not leave
animals in room unattended.

Red Roof Inn
201 E. Texas Ave.
Columbia, MO 65202
573-442-0145
PET POLICY: No fee, pets under
80 lbs. Must be leashed to and
from rooms. Do not leave in
room unattended.

Travelodge
900 Vandiver Dr.
Columbia, MO 65202
573 449-1065
RATES: Single $49.95, double
$69.95.
PET POLICY: Fee $5 per pet,
nonrefundable. Up to 25 lbs.
POI: Parks, golf courses, hiking,
biking trails, University,
museums.

Drury Inn & Suites
11980 Olive Street Rd.
Creve Coeur, MO 63141
314-989-1100
PET POLICY: No fee, pets under
30 lbs.

Oak Tree Inn
1608 Hwy. Business 60 W.
Dexter, MO 63841
573-624-5800
RATES: Single $46.95, double
$49.95.
PET POLICY: Fee $5, nonrefund-
able. Up to 25 lbs., all pets
welcome.

Rock Eddy Bluff Farm
10245 Maries Rd., #511
Dixon, MO 65459
573-759-6081
RATES: Single $110, double $110.
PET POLICY: No fee, all sizes welcome. Do not leave unattended
in room except in crate. Pets
must stay off furniture.
AMENITIES: Room to roam and
explore.
POI: On-site canoeing fishing,
hiking, swimming, Ozark River,
scenic views.

Scenic Rivers Motel
231 N. 2nd St.
Ellington, MO 63638
573-663-7722
RATES: Single $38, double $43.
PET POLICY: No fee, pets wel-
come up to 50 lbs.
POI: Clearwater Lake, Current
River, Blue Springs.

Drury Inn Southwest
1088 S. Highway Dr.
Fenton, MO 63026
314-343-7822
PET POLICY: No fee, pets under
30 lbs.

Pear Tree Inn by Drury
1100 S. Highway Dr.
Fenton, MO 63026
314-343-8820
PET POLICY: No fee. All sizes
and pets accepted. Do not
leave in rooms unattended.

Baymont Inn & Suites
1303 Veterans Blvd.
Festus, MO 63028
636-937-2888
PET POLICY: No fee.

Drury Inn
1001 Veterans Blvd.
Festus, MO 63028
314-933-2400
PET POLICY: No fee, pets under
30 lbs.

U.S. Lodgings > MISSOURI

Red Roof Inn
307 Dunn Rd.
Florissant, MO 63031
314-831-7900
PET POLICY: No fee, pets under 80 lbs. Must be leashed to and from rooms. Do not leave in room unattended.

Loganberry Inn Bed & Breakfast
310 W. Seventh St.
Fulton, MO 65251
573-642-9229
PET POLICY: Fee $15 incl. biscuits/food, dogs and cats only, no other restrictions.

Travelodge
105 Sunny Ln. Dr.
Grain Valley, MO 23185
816 224-3420
RATES: Single $49.95, double $69.95.
PET POLICY: Fee $7 per pet, nonrefundable. Up to 50 lbs.

Days Inn
4070 Market St.
Hannibal, MO 63401
314-248-1700
PET POLICY: No fee.

Pear Tree Inn by Drury
1317 Hwy. 84
Hayti, MO 63851
314-359-2702
PET POLICY: No fee. All sizes and pets accepted. Do not leave in rooms unattended.

Baymont Inn & Suites
318 Taylor Rd.
Hazelwood, MO 63042
314-731-4200
PET POLICY: No fee.

Red Roof Inn
13712 E. 42nd Terrace
Independence, MO 64055
816-373-2800
PET POLICY: No fee, pets under 80 lbs. Must be leashed to and from rooms. Do not leave in room unattended.

Drury Inn & Suites
225 Drury Ln.
Jackson, MO 63755
573-243-9200
PET POLICY: No fee, pets under 30 lbs.

Jackson Days Inn
517 Jackson Blvd.
Jackson, MO 63755
573-243-3577
PET POLICY: No fee.

Motel 6
1624 Jefferson St.
Jefferson City, MO 65109
573-634-4220
PET POLICY: No fee. Dogs under 25 lbs. preferred (larger animals by advance approval). Do not leave animals in room unattended.

Drury Inn
3601 Range Line Rd.
Joplin, MO 64804
417-781-8000
PET POLICY: No fee, pets under 30 lbs.

Motel 6
3031 S. Range Line Rd.
Joplin, MO 64804
417-781-6400
PET POLICY: No fee. Dogs under 25 lbs. preferred (larger animals by advance approval). Do not leave animals in room unattended.

Westwood Motel
1700 W. 30th St.
Joplin, MO 64804
417-782-7212
RATES: Single $36, double $39.
PET POLICY: Fee $5, nonrefundable, pets up to 50 lbs. accepted (dogs and cats only). Do not leave unattended in room.

Baymont Inn & Suites
8601 Hillcrest
Kansas City, MO 64138
816-822-7000
PET POLICY: No fee.

Chase Suite Hotel by Woodfin
9900 NW Prairie View Rd.
Kansas City, MO 64153
816-891-9009
RATES: Single $79, double $89.
PET POLICY: Fee $50, nonrefundable. Up to 50 lbs.
AMENITIES: Convenient area to walk pets.

Drury Inn & Suites-Airport
7900 NW Tiffany Springs Pkwy.
Kansas City, MO 64163
816-880-9700
PET POLICY: No fee, pets under 30 lbs.

Drury Inn—Stadium
3830 Blue Ridge Cutoff
Kansas City, MO 64133
816-923-3000
PET POLICY: No fee. All sizes and pets accepted. Do not leave in rooms unattended.

Hampton Inn
1051 N. Cambridge
Kansas City, MO 64120
816-483-7900
RATES: Single $79, double $89.
PET POLICY: Fee $5, nonrefundable. All sizes and all pets welcome.

Homewood Suites Hotel
7312 N. Polo Dr.
Kansas City, MO 64153
816-880-9880
PET POLICY: Deposit required.

Kansas City Days Inn
11120 NW Ambassador Dr.
Kansas City, MO 64190
816-746-1666
PET POLICY: Fee $6.

Motel 6
8230 NW Prairie View Rd.
Kansas City, MO 64151
816-741-6400
PET POLICY: No fee. Dogs under 25 lbs. preferred (larger animals by advance approval). Do not leave animals in room unattended.

Red Roof Inn
3636 NE Randolph Rd.
Kansas City, MO 64161
816-452-8585
PET POLICY: No fee, pets under 80 lbs. Must be leashed to and from rooms. Do not leave in room unattended.

Su Casa B&B
9004 E. 92nd St.
Kansas City, MO 64138
816-965-5647
PET POLICY: Fee $10 per dog, $25 per horse. Accommodates dogs and horses. Call first. Pets must be housebroken.

U.S. Lodgings > MISSOURI

Kearny Days Inn
400 Platte-Clay Way
Kearney, MO 64060
816-628-2288
PET POLICY: Fee $5.

Kennett Days Inn
110 Independence Ave.
Kennett, MO 63857
573-888-9860
PET POLICY: Fee $10.

Budget Host Village Inn
1304 S. Baltimore
Kirksville, MO 63501
660-665-3722
RATES: Single $40, double $50.
PET POLICY: Fee $5, nonrefundable.
POI: Truman University, restaurants.

Holiday Inn
Business Hwy. 54
Lake Ozark, MO 65049
573-365-2334
PET POLICY: Fee $5.

Days Inn at the Lake
2560 S. Outer Rd.
Lake St. Louis, MO 63367
314-625-1711
PET POLICY: Fee $5.

Drury Inn—Westport
12220 Dorsett Rd.
Maryland Heights, MO 63043
314-576-9966
PET POLICY: No fee. All sizes
and pets accepted. Do not
leave in rooms unattended.

Days Inn of Mountain Grove
300 E. 19th St.
Mountain Grove, MO 65711
417-926-5555
PET POLICY: Fee $6.

Baymont Inn & Suites
2214 Taney
North Kansas City, MO 64116
816-221-1200
PET POLICY: No fee.

Rambler Inn Motel
1401 E. Austin St.
Nevada, MO 64772
417-667-3351
RATES: Single $38, double $44.
PET POLICY: Fee $5, nonrefundable. All sizes, dogs, cats, birds,
and rabbits. Pet-owner
responsible for damages.
POI: 1 miles from Champion
Diamonds. 1 miles from golf
course. 2 hrs. from Osage Beach.
1 hr. from Stockton Lake.

Oak Grove Days Inn
101 N. Locust
Oak Grove, MO 64075
816-690-8700
RATES: Single $49.95, double
$59.95.
PET POLICY: Fee $10, nonrefundable. All sizes welcome.
POI: Kansas City.

Comfort Inn—KCI
1200 Hwy. 92
Platte City, MO 64079
816-858-5430
RATES: Single $50, double $60.
PET POLICY: Fee $3 per night
per pet, nonrefundable. Up to
50 lbs.
POI: Weston, MO historic town.
Shiloh Springs.

Drury Inn
2220 N. Westwood Blvd.
Poplar Bluff, MO 63901
314-686-2451
PET POLICY: No fee, pets under
30 lbs.

Pear Tree Inn by Drury
2218 N. Westwood Blvd.
Poplar Bluff, MO 63901
573-785-7100
PET POLICY: No fee. All sizes
and pets accepted. Do not
leave in rooms unattended.

Days Inn
1207 Kings Hwy.
Rolla, MO 65401
314-341-3700
PET POLICY: No fee.

Drury Inn
2006 N. Bishop
Rolla, MO 65401
314-364-4000
PET POLICY: No fee, pets under
30 lbs.

Baymont Inn & Suites
1425 S. Fifth St.
St. Charles, MO 63301
636-946-6936
PET POLICY: No fee.

Red Roof Inn
2010 Zumbehl Rd.
St. Charles, MO 63303
636-947-7770
PET POLICY: No fee, pets under
80 lbs. Must be leashed to and
from rooms. Do not leave in
room unattended.

Drury Inn
4213 Frederick Blvd.
St. Joseph, MO 64506
816-364-4700
PET POLICY: No fee, pets under
30 lbs.

Motel 6
4021 Frederick Blvd.
St. Joseph, MO 64506
816-232-2311
PET POLICY: No fee. Dogs under 25
lbs. preferred (larger animals by
advance approval). Do not leave
animals in room unattended.

Baymont Inn & Suites
12330 Dorsett Rd.
St. Louis, MO 63043
314-878-1212
PET POLICY: No fee.

Drury Inn—Gateway Arch
4th & Market St.
St. Louis, MO 63102
314-231-3003
PET POLICY: No fee, pets under
30 lbs.

Drury Inn & Suites
711 N. Broadway
St. Louis, MO 63102
314-231-8100
PET POLICY: No fee, pets under
30 lbs.

U.S. Lodgings > MISSOURI

Drury Inn—St. Louis Airport
10490 Natural Bridge
St. Louis, MO 63134
314-423-7700
PET POLICY: No fee. All sizes and pets accepted. Do not leave in rooms unattended.

Holiday Inn South
4234 Butler Hill Rd.
St. Louis, MO 63129
314-894-0700
RATES: Single $89, double $99.
PET POLICY: Fee $50, refundable. All sizes welcome.

Motel 6
4021 Frederick Blvd.
St. Joseph, MO 64506
816-232-2311
PET POLICY: No fee. Dogs under 25 lbs. preferred (larger animals by advance approval). Do not leave animals in room unattended.

Red Roof Inn
5823 Wilson Ave.
St. Louis, MO 63110
314-645-0101
PET POLICY: No fee, pets under 80 lbs. Must be leashed to and from rooms. Do not leave in room unattended.

Red Roof Inn
11837 Lackland Rd.
St. Louis, MO 63146
314-991-4900
PET POLICY: No fee, pets under 80 lbs. Must be leashed to and from rooms. Do not leave in room unattended.

Drury Inn— St. Louis-St. Peters
80 Mid Rivers Mall Dr.
St. Peters, MO 63376
314-397-9700
PET POLICY: No fee. All sizes and pets accepted. Do not leave in rooms unattended.

Best Western Montis Inn
14086 Highway 2
St. Robert, MO, 65583
573-336-4299
RATES: Single, double $55
PET POLICY: No fee. All sizes and pets accepted. Do not leave pets in room unattended.

Days Inn
Hwy. Z, 14125
St. Robert, MO 65583
314-336-5556
PET POLICY: No fee.

Econo Lodge
305 Hwy. 8
St. Robert, MO 65583
314-336-7272
RATES: Single $49.95, double $59.95.
PET POLICY: No fee, pets up to 25 lbs. Only one pet per room.
POI: Ft. Leonardwood Military Training Base.

Red Roof Inn
129 St. Robert's Boulevard
St. Robert, MO 65583
573-336-2510
PET POLICY: No fee, pets under 80 lbs. Must be leashed to and from rooms. Do not leave in room unattended.

Pear Tree Inn by Drury
2602 Read E. Malone
Sikeston, MO 63801
573-471-8660
PET POLICY: No fee. All sizes and pets accepted. Do not leave in rooms unattended.

Sikeston Days Inn
1330 S. Main St.
Sikeston, MO 63801
573-471-3930
PET POLICY: No fee.

Baymont Inn & Suites
3776 S. Glenstone
Springfield, MO 65804
417-889-8188
PET POLICY: No fee.

Drury Inn & Suites
2715 N. Glenstone Ave.
Springfield, MO 65803
417-863-8400
RATES: Single 49.99+, suites $99–$129.
PET POLICY: No fee. All sizes and pets accepted. Do not leave in room unattended.

Motel 6
3114 N. Kentwood
Springfield, MO 65803
417-833-0880
PET POLICY: No fee. Dogs under 25 lbs. preferred (larger animals by advance approval). Do not leave animals in room unattended.

Pear Tree Inn by Drury
2745 N. Glenstone
Springfield, MO 65803
416-869-0001
PET POLICY: No fee. All sizes and pets accepted. Do not leave in rooms unattended.

Red Roof Inn
2655 N. Glenstone
Springfield, MO 65803
417-518-31210
PET POLICY: No fee, pets under 80 lbs. Must be leashed to and from rooms. Do not leave in room unattended.

Springfield Days Inn
621 W. Sunshine
Springfield, MO 65807
417-862-0153d
PET POLICY: Fee $10.

Baymont Inn & Suites
275 N. Service Rd.
Sullivan, MO 63080
513-860-3333
PET POLICY: No fee.

Econo Lodge Sullivan
307 N. Service Rd.
Sullivan, MO 63080
573-468-3136
RATES: Single $39, double $49.
PET POLICY: No fee, all sizes and all pets welcome.
POI: Meremac Caverns, Meramec Park, Fischer Cave, Onondaga Cave State Park, Sullivan Airport, Sullivan County Club golf course.

Dogwood Acres Resort
HCR 69, Box 373
Sunrise Beach, MO 65079
573-374-5956
RATES: Single $55, double $75.
PET POLICY: Fee $75, refundable.
All sizes and pets welcome.
Pets must be on leash, and
must be cleaned up before
entering. Shedding and loud
dogs not welcome.
AMENITIES: 10 wooded acres, on
Lake of the Ozarks.

Days Inn West Plains
US 63N
PO Box 278
West Plains, MO 65775
417-256-4135
PET POLICY: Fee $5.

Ramada Inn
1301 Preacher Roe Blvd.
West Plains, MO 65775
417-256-8191
RATES: Single $43, double $50.
PET POLICY: Fee $10, nonrefund-
able. All sizes and pets welcome (dogs, cats, birds, ferrets,
rabbits, reptiles).

MONTANA

Best Western Buck's T-4 Lodge
46625 Gallatin Rd.
Big Sky, MT 59716
406-995-4111
RATES: Single $89, double $109.
PET POLICY: Fee $5, nonrefund-
able, all pets welcome, up to
50 lbs.
POI: Yellowstone National Park,
Big Sky Ski and Summer
Resort.

Cherry Tree Inn
823 N. Broadway
Billings, MT 59101
406-252-5603
RATES: Single $35, double $45.
PET POLICY: No fee, all sizes
welcome. Do not leave in
room unattended.

Days Inn
843 Pkwy. Ln.
Billings, MT 59101
406-252-4007
PET POLICY: No fee.

Motel 6
5400 Midland Rd.
Billings, MT 59101
406-252-0093
PET POLICY: No fee. Dogs under 25
lbs. preferred (larger animals by
advance approval). Do not leave
animals in room unattended.

Red Roof Inn
5353 Midland Rd.
Billings, MT 59102
406-248-7551
PET POLICY: No fee, pets under
80 lbs. Must be leashed to and
from rooms. Do not leave in
room unattended.

Days Inn
1321 N. 7th St.
Bozeman, MT 59715
406-587-5251
PET POLICY: No fee.

Ramada Limited
2020 Wheat Dr.
Bozeman, MT 59715
406-585-2626
RATES: Single $49–$89, double
$59–$99.
PET POLICY: No fee, all sizes
welcome.
AMENITIES: Exit directly from
room or outside.
POI: Yellowstone National park.
National Forest 10 miles.

Royal 7 Motel
310 N. 7th Ave.
Bozeman, MT 59715
406-587-3103
RATES: Single, double
$32.75–$51.75.
PET POLICY: No fee. All sizes
accepted. Smoking rooms only.

Western Motel
121 Central Ave.
Browning, MT 59417
406-338-7572
PET POLICY: No deposit required.

War Bonnet Inn
2100 Cornell Ave.
Butte, MT 59701
406-494-7800
RATES: Single $69, double $79.
PET POLICY: Fee $8 per pet per
night, nonrefundable. All sizes
and all pets welcome.
POI: Walking path along creek
and park nearby.

Big Sky Motel
209 S. Main
Choteau, MT 59422
406-466-5318
RATES: Single $38, double $44.
PET POLICY: Fee $5, nonrefund-
able. Do not leave unattended
in room, walk on leash. Keep
off beds and furniture.
AMENITIES: Large park nearby
and fields behind motel.
POI: Near Glacier National
Park, Bob Marshall
Wilderness, Freezeout Bird
Sanctuary.

Glacier Gateway Inn
1121 E. Railroad. St.
Cut Bank, MT 59427
406-873-5544
RATES: Single $46, double $56.
PET POLICY: No fee, up to 25 lbs.

Hotel Albert Bed & Breakfast
#7 Yellowstone Trail, Box 144
DeBorgia, MT 59830
406-678-4303
RATES: Single $56, double $64.
PET POLICY: Fee $5 per pet,
nonrefundable. Up to 50 lbs.
No cats due to allergies.

Torrey Mountain Log Cabin Rentals
4849 Argenta Rd.
Dillon, MT 59725
406-683-4706
RATES: Cabins: $100.
PET POLICY: No fee, all sizes and
pets welcome.
AMENITIES: Lots of room for
pet-walking.
POI: Foothills of Beaverhead
Nat'l Forest, Bannack State
Park, Crystal Park, Virginia
City, Nevada City, Yellowstone
Nat'l Park (3 hours).

Jacobson's Scenic View Cottages
PO Box 216
East Glacier Park, MT 59434
406-226-4422
PET POLICY: No fee, under 25 lbs.

U.S. Lodgings > NEBRASKA

Best Western Sundowner Inn
1018 Front St.
Forsyth, MT 59327
406-356-2115
RATES: Single $55–$65, double $70–$85.
PET POLICY: Fee $3, nonrefundable. All pets and all sizes welcome. Do not leave pets unattended in room. Cats must be kenneled if left alone. Owners responsible for any damages.
AMENITIES: Dog walking area adjacent to motel.

Glendive Days Inn
2000 N. Merrill Ave.
Glendive, MT 59330
406-365-6011
PET POLICY: No fee.

Great Falls Days Inn
101 14th Ave. NW
Great Falls, MT 59404
408-727-6565
PET POLICY: Fee $5.

Appleton Inn Bed & Breakfast
1999 Euclid Ave.
Helena, MT 59601
406-443-7330
RATES: Single $85, double $125.
PET POLICY: No fee, up to 50 lbs.
POI: Spring Meadow Lake. Mount Helena park.

Helena Days Inn
2001 Prospect Ave.
Helena, MT 59601
406-442-3280
PET POLICY: No fee.

Motel 6
800 N. Oregon St.
Helena, MT 59601
406-442-9990
PET POLICY: No fee. Dogs under 25 lbs. preferred (larger animals by advance approval). Do not leave animals in room unattended.

Shilo Inn
2020 Prospect Ave.
Helena, MT 59601
406-442-0320
RATES: Single $69, double $79.
PET POLICY: Fee $10, nonrefundable. All sizes, all pets welcome.

Kalispell Grand Hotel
100 Main St.
Kalispell, MT 59901
406-755-8100
RATES: Single $63, double $78.
PET POLICY: No fee, all sizes welcome.
POI: City park.

Days Inn—Westgate
8600 Truck Stop Rd.
Missoula, MT 59802
406-721-9776
PET POLICY: Fee $5.

Motel 6
3035 Expo Pkwy Commerce Center
Missoula, MT 59808
406-549-6665
PET POLICY: No fee. Dogs under 25 lbs. preferred (larger animals by advance approval). Do not leave animals in room unattended.

Elkhorn Mountain Inn
1 Jackson Creek
Montana City, MT 59634
406-442-6625
RATES: Single $53.99, double $60.25.
PET POLICY: Fee $5, nonrefundable.
POI: Rural location with plenty of room for pets to roam and explore.

O'Haire Manor Motel
204 2nd St. S.
Shelby, MT 59474
406-434-5555
RATES: Single $35, double $45.
PET POLICY: Fee $5, nonrefundable. Do not leave unattended in room.

NEBRASKA

Flying Bee Beefmaster Ranch
6755 County Rd. 42
Bayard, NE 69334
308-783-2885
RATES: Single $55, double $65.
PET POLICY: No fee, all sizes and pets welcome. Must be on leash and under control at all times.
AMENITIES: Corrals and water hydrants provided for horses/mules or other livestock.

Westerner Motel
300 Oak St.
Chadron, NE 69337
308-432-5577
RATES: Single $39.88, double $49.88.
PET POLICY: No fee, all pets welcome. Cats must be in smoking room.

Columbus Days Inn
371 33rd Ave.
Columbus, NE 68601
402-564-2527
PET POLICY: Fee $7.

Grand Island Days Inn
Hwys 281 & 2
Grand Island, NE 68803
308-384-8624
PET POLICY: Fee $7.50.

Lazy V Motel
2703 E. Hwy. 30
Grand Island, NE 68801
308-384-0700
RATES: Single $30, double $38.
PET POLICY: Fee $3. Up to 50 lbs.

Motel 6
101 Talmadge
Kearney, NE 68847
308-338-0705
PET POLICY: No fee. Dogs under 25 lbs. preferred (larger animals by advance approval). Do not leave animals in room unattended.

Budget Host Minute Man Motel
801 Plum Creek Pkwy.
Lexington, NE 68850
308-324-5544
RATES: Single $34–$38, double $40–$44.
PET POLICY: Fee $5 per pet, nonrefundable. All size dogs welcome, keep leashed, and walk in pet areas only. Do not leave unattended in rooms.
POI: Dawson County Museum, Heartland Military Museum, Antiques Capital of central Nebraska, Johnson Lake Rec. Area, Family Aquatic Center.

Lexington Days Inn
Hwy. 283 & Commerce Rd.
Lexington, NE 68850
308-324-6440
PET POLICY: Fee $6.

U.S. Lodgings > NEBRASKA

Baymont Inn & Suites
3939 26th St. - N.
Lincoln, NE 68521
402-477-1100
PET POLICY: No fee.

Lincoln Days Inn
1140 Calvert St.
Lincoln, NE 68502
402-423-7111
PET POLICY: No fee.

Motel 6
3001 NW 12th St.
Lincoln, NE 68521
402-475-3211
PET POLICY: No fee. Dogs under 25 lbs. preferred (larger animals by advance approval). Do not leave animals in room unattended.

Red Roof Inn
6501 N. 28th St.
Lincoln, NE 68504
402-438-4700
PET POLICY: No fee, pets under 80 lbs. Must be leashed to and from rooms. Do not leave in room unattended.

Staybridge Suites by Holiday Inn
2701 Fletcher Ave.
Lincoln, NE 68504
402-438-7829
PET POLICY: $75 Non refundable fee.

McCook Days Suites
901 N. Hwy. 83
McCook, NE 69001
308-345-7115
PET POLICY: Fee $20.

Oak Tree Inn
80700 Hwy. 26
Morrill, NE 69358
308-247-2111
RATES: Single $45, double $50.
PET POLICY: Fee $5, nonrefundable, all size pets welcome.
POI: Scottsbluff monument.

Norfolk Country Inn
1201 S. 13th St.
Norfolk, NE 68701
402-371-4430

RATES: Single $50, double $56.
PET POLICY: No fee, all size dogs and cats, only. Must be housebroken and quiet. Do not leave in room unattended.
AMENITIES: 2 large grassy exercise areas.
POI: Ta-Ha-Zooka Park 1miles Cowboy Trail. Museum. Ashfall Fossil Bed within 50 miles.

Sands Motor Inn
501 Halligan Dr.
North Platte, NE 69101
308-532-0151
RATES: Single $49.95, double $55.95.
PET POLICY: Fee $5, nonrefundable, all sizes and all pets welcome.
POI: Summer months: Buffalo Bill State Park, State wide celebration in June-rodeo, evening entertainment by well known singers. Worlds largest railroad terminal.

Ogallala Days Inn
601 Stagecoach Trail
Ogallala, NE 69153
308-284-6365
RATES: Single $45–$60, double $54–$70.
PET POLICY: Fee $6, all sizes welcome. No male, unneutered cats.
POI: Adjacent Lake and walk path. Lake McConaught (9 mi).

Baymont Inn & Suites
10760 M St.
Omaha, NE 68127
402-592-5200
PET POLICY: No fee.

Crowne Plaza Suites
655 N. 108th Ave.
Omaha, NE 68154
402-496-0850
PET POLICY: No fee.

Homewood Suites Hotel
7010 Hascall St.
Omaha, NE 68106
402-397-7500
PET POLICY: Pets allowed with $150 deposit ($50 nonrefundable).

Motel 6
10708 M St.
Omaha, NE 68127
402-331-3161
PET POLICY: No fee. Dogs under 25 lbs. preferred (larger animals by advance approval). Do not leave animals in room unattended.

Paxton Days Inn
I-80 Ex 145
Paxton, NE 69155
308-239-4510
PET POLICY: Fee $10.

Holiday Inn
664 Chase Blvd.
Sidney, NE 69162
308-254-2000
RATES: Single $89.99, double $89.99.
PET POLICY: Fee $10, nonrefundable, all sizes.

Sidney Motor Lodge
2031 Illinois St.
Sidney, NE 69162
308-254-4581
RATES: Single $42, double $48.
PET POLICY: No fee, all sizes and all pets welcome.

Holiday Inn
803 E. Hwy. 20
Valentine, NE 69201
402-376-3000
PET POLICY: Small pets only.

NEVADA

Best Inn & Suites
650 W. Front St.
Battle Mountain, NV 89820
702-635-5200
RATES: Single $45, double $47.
PET POLICY: No fee, all sizes welcome.
AMENITIES: Pet area with benches.

Lake Mead Resort & Marina
322 Lakeshore Rd.
Boulder City, NV 89005
702-293-2074
PET POLICY: Fee $5 per night. Deposit $25, refundable.

U.S. Lodgings > NEVADA

Days Inn
3103 N. Carson St.
Carson City, NV 89701
702-883-3343
PET POLICY: Fee $10.

Motel 6
2749 S. Carson St.
Carson City, NV 89701
775-885-7710
PET POLICY: No fee. Dogs under 25
lbs. preferred (larger animals by
advance approval). Do not leave
animals in room unattended.

Motel 6
3021 Idaho St.
Elko, NV 89801
775-738-4337
PET POLICY: No fee. Dogs under 25
lbs. preferred (larger animals by
advance approval). Do not leave
animals in room unattended.

Oak Tree Inn
95 Spruce Rd.
Elko, NV 89802
775-777-2222
RATES: Single $49, double $69.
PET POLICY: Fee $5, nonrefund-
able. All sizes, all pets welcome.

**Once Upon A Time
Bed & Breakfast**
537 14th St.
Elko, NV 89801
775-738-1200
RATES: Double $65–$95.
PET POLICY: No fee, all sizes and
all pets welcome. Must get
along with lodging's Giant
Schnauzer.
AMENITIES: Fenced back yard.
Doggy door to outside. Water.

Shilo Inn
2401 Mountain City Hwy.
Elko, NV 89801
775-738-5522
RATES: Single $59, double $69.
PET POLICY: Fee $10, nonrefund-
able. All sizes, all pets welcome.

Best Western Parkview Inn
921 Las Vegas Blvd. N.
Las Vegas, NV 89101
702-385-1213

RATES: Single $45, double $45.
PET POLICY: Fee $8, nonrefund-
able. All sizes welcome. Please
call ahead for additional
restrictions.
POI: Fremont St. Experience
strip. Las Vegas motor speedway.
Lake Mead recreation area.

Crowne Plaza
4255 S. Paradise Rd.
Las Vegas, NV 89109
702-369-4400
PET POLICY: No fee, pets in
smoking rooms only.

La Quinta Inn
3782 Las Vegas Blvd. S.
Las Vegas, NV 89109
800-531-5900
PET POLICY: No fee, 1 pet per
room, under 20 lbs.

La Quinta Inn
7101 Cascade Valley Rd.
Las Vegas, NV 89128
702-360-1200
PET POLICY: No fee, under 25 lbs.

Motel 6
195 E. Tropicana Ave.
Las Vegas, NV 89109
702-798-0728
PET POLICY: No fee. Dogs under 25
lbs. preferred (larger animals by
advance approval). Do not leave
animals in room unattended.

Residence Inn by Marriott
3225 Paradise Rd.
Las Vegas, NV, 89109
702-796-9300
RATES: Studios: $109-149.
Penthouses: $149-219
PET POLICY: Fee one-time $50,
nonrefundable. Plus $10 nonre-
fundable fee per night. All sizes

Vagabond Inn—Las Vegas
3265 Las Vegas Blvd. S.
Las Vegas, NV 89109
702-735-5102
RATES: Single $54, double $59.
PET POLICY: Fee $10, all sizes
and pets welcome (dogs, cats,
ferrets, birds, rabbits, reptiles).
Do not leave unattended in
room.

**Riverside Resort
Hotel & Casino**
1650 S. Casino Dr.
Laughlin, NV 89039
702-298-2535
PET POLICY: Fee $8, $100
deposit, under 10 lbs.

Days Inn
701 E. Seventh St.
Reno, NV 89512
775-786-4070
PET POLICY: Fee $10.

Motel 6
1400 Stardust St.
Reno, NV 89503
775-747-7390
PET POLICY: No fee. Dogs under 25
lbs. preferred (larger animals by
advance approval). Do not leave
animals in room unattended.

**Old Pioneer Garden
Bed & Breakfast**
2805 Unionville Rd.
Unionville, NV 89418
775-538-7585
RATES: Single $85.
PET POLICY: No fee, all sizes
welcome. Must be under
owners control at all times.
AMENITIES: Wide open spaces
for hiking.
POI: Hundreds of miles of free
access BLM land.

Motel 6
1600 Winnemucca Blvd.
Winnemucca, NV 89445
775-623-1180
PET POLICY: No fee. Dogs under 25
lbs. preferred (larger animals by
advance approval). Do not leave
animals in room unattended.

Lake Tahoe Vacation Condo
PO Box 12519
Zephyr Cove, NV 89448
775-586-8662
RATES: $150–$350.
PET POLICY: Fee $25, nonre-
fundable. All sizes and pets
welcome. Max. of 2 per rental.
POI: Lake Resort Area, National
Park, near Casinos, 3 miles
from Heavenly Ski Resort,
beaches, forest, walking trails.

U.S. Lodgings > NEVADA

Lake Village Resort
301 Hwy. 50
Zephyr Cove, NV 89448
775-589-6065
RATES: Single $145, double $195.
PET POLICY: Fee $100, refundable, all sizes, dogs only, must be kenneled in room if unattended.
AMENITIES: For $20 per dog, per night, your pet can accompany you in your enjoyment of the lovely wooded grounds surrounding the Lake Village Resort Townhomes.
POI: Heavenly Ski Resort. Pet-friendly outdoor cafes for you and your pooch to enjoy.

NEW HAMPSHIRE

King Birch Motor Lodge
RT 11-D
Alton Bay, NH 03810
603-875-2222
RATES: Cabins: $125.
PET POLICY: Fee $25, nonrefundable. All pets welcome. Must be on leash, pick up after pets, do not leave pets in rooms unattended.
AMENITIES: 10 acres for pet-walking, kennels by appointment for day trips, local 24-hour vet, swimming for pets and owners.

Horse Haven Bed & Breakfast
462 Raccoon Hill Rd.
Concord-Salisbury, NH 03268
603-648-2101
RATES: Single $50, double $75.
PET POLICY: Fee $5 per stay, all sizes and pets welcome (dogs, cats, ferrets, birds, rabbits, reptiles).
POI: Flyball training course, 35 acres to romp, walking trails, nearby river for swimming. Dog sitting, fenced in area, and very pet-friendly owners.

Tanglewood Motel & Cottages
Rt. 16, White Mountain Hwy.
Conway, NH 03818
603-447-5932

PET POLICY: No fee, all sizes and all pets welcome (dogs, cats, ferrets, birds, rabbits, reptiles). Pets in cottages only, do lot leave unattended unless in cages. Must scoop.
AMENITIES: Lots of exercising trails. river swimming.

Dover/Durham Days Inn
481 Central Ave.
Dover, NH 03820
603-742-0400
PET POLICY: No fee.

Black Dog Manor Bed & Breakfast
25 Auburn St.
Franklin, NH 03235
603-934-0322
RATES: Double $75.
PET POLICY: Fee $5. All sizes. Dogs only. Do not leave pets in room unattended. Proof of Rabies and Bordatella vaccines requiredd. No dog bathing in bathrooms.
AMENITIES: Large fenced-in backyard. Kennel run provided for outdoor enclosure. Indoor kennel available in basement. 50% fee donated to humane society if rooms left in adequate condition.

Colonial Comfort Inn
370 Main St.
Gorham, NH 03581
603-466-2732
RATES: Please call.
PET POLICY: No fee, all sizes and all pets welcome.
POI: White Mt. National Forest, hiking areas.

Top Notch Motor Inn
265 Main St.
Gorham, NH 03581
603-466-5496
RATES: Single $44–$139, double $54–$139.
PET POLICY: No fee, up to 25 lbs., well-groomed dogs, only.
POI: Mt. Washington. Story Land. Santa's Village.

Swiss Chalets Village Inn
Rt. 16A
Intervale, NH 03845
603-356-2232

RATES: Single, double $39–$159.
PET POLICY: Fee $15, nonrefundable. All sizes welcome.
AMENITIES: 1-acre pet walk field.
POI: White Mountain National Forest.

Dana Place Inn
Rt. 16, Pinkham Notch
Jackson, NH 03846
800-537-9276
PET POLICY: No fee, designated rooms, not allowed in common areas of Inn. Seasonal.

The Village House
PO Box 359, Rt. 16A
Jackson, NH 03846
603-383-6666
RATES: Single $60, double $120.
PET POLICY: No fee, all sizes and well-behaved pets welcome.

Whitneys' Inn—Jackson
Five Mile Cir. Rd.
Jackson, NH 03846
603-383-8916
RATES: Single $95 Double 105.
PET POLICY: Fee $25 one time fee, nonrefundable. All sizes welcome.
AMENITIES: Pet blankets.
POI: Storyland. Mtn. Trails and streams.

Days Inn
175 Key Rd.
Keene, NH 03431
603-352-7616
PET POLICY: Fee $10.

Parker's Motel
Rt. 3, Box 100
Lincoln, NH 03251
603-745-8341
RATES: Single $79, double $89.
PET POLICY: Fee $5, nonrefundable. All sizes, dogs and cats only.

Red Roof Inn
519 State Route 106
Loudon, NH 03307
603-225-8399
PET POLICY: No fee, pets under 80 lbs. Must be leashed to and from rooms. Do not leave in room unattended.

U.S. Lodgings > NEW JERSEY

Days Hotel Manchester
55 John E. Devine Dr.
Manchester, NH 03101
603-668-6110
PET POLICY: No fee.

Merrimack Days Inn
242 Daniel Webster Hwy.
Merrimack, NH 03054
603-429-4600
PET POLICY: No fee.

Residence Inn by Marriott
246 Daniel Webster
Merrimack, NH 03054
603-424-8100
RATES: Single: $110+.
PET POLICY: Fee $50, plus $5 per day per pet. Pets prohibited from certain areas. Must notify housekeeping. Do not leave in room unattended.

Motel 6
2 Progress Ave.
Nashua, NH 03062
603-889-4151
PET POLICY: No fee. Dogs under 25 lbs. preferred (larger animals by advance approval). Do not leave animals in room unattended.

Red Roof Inn
77 Spitbrook Rd.
Nashua, NH 03060
603-888-1893
PET POLICY: No fee, pets under 80 lbs. Must be leashed to and from rooms. Do not leave in room unattended.

Good Harvest Inn
Rt. 16 - 302
North Conway, NH 03860
603-356-2073
PET POLICY: No fee, all sizes accepted.

Isaac E. Merrill House Inn
720 Kearsarge Rd.
North Conway, NH 03847
603-356-9041
PET POLICY: Dogs only, cannot be left in room unattended.

Sunnybrook Cottages
Rt. 16
PO Box 1429
North Conway, NH 03818
603-447-3922

RATES: Single, double $79–$104 (seasonal).
PET POLICY: Fee $10 per stay. All sizes accepted.

Motel 6
3 Gosling Rd.
Portsmouth, NH 03801
603-334-6606
PET POLICY: No fee. Dogs under 25 lbs. preferred (larger animals by advance approval). Do not leave animals in room unattended.

Red Roof Inn
15 Red Roof Ln.
Salem, NH 03079
603-898-6422
PET POLICY: No fee, pets under 80 lbs. Must be leashed to and from rooms. Do not leave in room unattended.

Fieldstone Country Inn
125 Fieldstone Ln., Box 456
Twin Mountain, NH 03595
603-846-5646
RATES: Double $65–$95.
PET POLICY: No fee, all sizes welcome. Do not leave unattended in room, not allowed in common rooms.
AMENITIES: Pet sitting if arranged ahead.
POI: Hiking, cross country skiing.

Dunroamin' Inn
759 Lancaster Rd.
Whitefield, NH 03598
603-837-3010
PET POLICY: Fee $10, nonrefundable. Dogs and cats, only. Up to 50 lbs. Must be supervised and not left in room unattended.
AMENITIES: Large outside area to exercise pet. Large rooms so pets won't feel confined.

NEW JERSEY

Days Inn—Absecon-Atlantic City
224 E. White Horse Pike
Absecon, NJ 08201
609-652-2200
PET POLICY: Fee $20.

Marquis De Lafayette Hotel
501 Beach Ave.
Cape May, NJ 08204
609-884-3500
PET POLICY: Fee $20 per day, nonrefundable.

High Point Country Inn
1328 Rt. 23
Colesville, NJ 07461
973-702-1860
RATES: Single $40+, double $74–$84.
PET POLICY: Fee $5. No restrictions.

Red Roof Inn
860 New Durham Rd.
Edison, NJ 08817
732-248-9300
PET POLICY: No fee, pets under 80 lbs. Must be leashed to and from rooms. Do not leave in room unattended.

Motel 6
244 Rt 18
East Brunswick, NJ 08816
732-390-4545
PET POLICY: No fee. Dogs under 25 lbs. preferred (larger animals by advance approval). Do not leave animals in room unattended.

Ramada Inn and Conference Center
130 Route 10 W.
East Hanover, NJ 07936
973-386-5622
RATES: Single $119, double $129.
PET POLICY: Small, up to 25 lbs., on 1st floor only.
AMENITIES: First floor only.

Crystal Motor Lodge
170 Main St.
Eatontown, NJ 07724
908-542-4900
RATES: Single $70, double $85.
PET POLICY: Fee $10, nonrefundable, up to 50 lbs.

Newark Airport Hilton
1170 Spring St.
Elizabeth, NJ 07201
908-351-3900
PET POLICY: No fee, Small pets preferred.

U.S. Lodgings > NEW JERSEY

Town House Motel
351 Franklin St.
Hightstown, NJ 08520
609-448-2400
RATES: Single $69, double $74.
PET POLICY: Fee $10, nonre-
fundable, all sizes, all pets welcome (ferrets, birds, rabbits,
reptiles, etc.).

Red Roof Inn
3203 Brunswick Pike
Lawrenceville, NJ 08648
609-896-3388
PET POLICY: No fee, pets under
80 lbs. Must be leashed to and
from rooms. Do not leave in
room unattended.

Fountain's Motel
160 Ocean Ave.
Long Branch, NJ 07740
732-222-7200
RATES: Single $70, double $85.
PET POLICY: Fee $10, nonre-
fundable, up to 50 lbs.

Red Roof Inn
208 New Rd.
Monmouth Junction, NJ
08852
732-821-8800
PET POLICY: No fee, pets under
80 lbs. Must be leashed to and
from rooms. Do not leave in
room unattended.

Red Roof Inn
603 Fellowship Rd.
Mount Laurel, NJ 08054
856-234-5589
PET POLICY: No fee, pets under
80 lbs. Must be leashed to and
from rooms. Do not leave in
room unattended.

Crystal Inn
706 Hwy. 35
Neptune, NJ 07753
732-776-9000
RATES: Single $70, double $85.
PET POLICY: Fee $10, nonre-
fundable, up to 50 lbs.

New York City Days Inn
2750 Tonnelle Ave.
North Bergen, NJ 07047
201-348-3600
PET POLICY: No fee.

Surf 16 Motel
1600 Surf Ave.
North Wildwood, NJ 08260
609-522-1010
PET POLICY: Fee $10 per pet per
nigh, nonrefundable. All sizes
welcome.

Crossings Motor Inn
3420 Haven Ave.
Ocean City, NJ 08226
609-398-4433
RATES: Avg: $69–$145.
PET POLICY: Fee $15, nonrefund-
able. All sizes and pets welcome.
Pets allowed from 1st weekend in May until end of June.
Then, after Labor Day until
closing.

Red Roof Inn
855 U.S. 46
Parsippany, NJ 07054
973-334-3737
PET POLICY: No fee, pets under
80 lbs. Must be leashed to and
from rooms. Do not leave in
room unattended.

Motel 6
1012 Stelton Rd.
Piscataway, NJ 08854
732-981-9200
PET POLICY: No fee. Dogs under 25
lbs. preferred (larger animals by
advance approval). Do not leave
animals in room unattended.

Crowne Plaza
2 Harmon Plaza
Secaucus, NJ 7084
201-348-6900
PET POLICY: No fee.

Red Roof Inn
15 Meadowlands Pkwy.
Secaucus, NJ 07094
201-319-1000
PET POLICY: No fee, pets under
80 lbs. Must be leashed to and
from rooms. Do not leave in
room unattended.

Holiday Inn
4701 Station Rd.
South Plainfield, NJ 7080
908-753-5500
RATES: Single $134, double $134.
PET POLICY: No fee, up to 50 lbs.

Red Roof Inn
11 Centre Plaza
Tinton Falls, NJ 07724
732-389-4646
PET POLICY: No fee, pets under
80 lbs. Must be leashed to and
from rooms. Do not leave in
room unattended.

High Point Country Inn
1328 Rt. 23
Wantage, NJ 07461
973-702-1860
RATES: Single $70, double $80.
PET POLICY: Fee $5, nonrefund-
able. Must clean up after pet.
POI: Near High Point State
Park.

Wrightstown Days Inn
507 E. Main St.
Wrightstown, NJ 08562
609-723-6900
PET POLICY: Fee $20.

NEW MEXICO

Holiday Inn Express
1401 S. White Sands Blvd.
Alamogordo, NM 88310
800-HOLIDAY
PET POLICY: With deposit.

Motel 6
251 Panorama Blvd.
Alamogordo, NM 88310
505-434-5970
PET POLICY: No fee. Dogs under 25
lbs. preferred (larger animals by
advance approval). Do not leave
animals in room unattended.

**Albuquerque Days Inn
Northeast**
10321 Hotel Ave NE
Albuquerque, NM 87123
505-275-0599
PET POLICY: Fee $5.

Albuquerque Days Inn West
6031 Iliff Rd. NW
Albuquerque, NM 87105
505-836-3297
PET POLICY: Fee $5.

Albuquerque Days Inn East
13317 Central Ave. NE
Albuquerque, NM 87123
505-294-3297
PET POLICY: Fee $5.

U.S. Lodgings > NEW MEXICO

Baymont Inn & Suites—Albuquerque
7439 Pan America Freeway NE
Albuquerque, NM 87109
505-345-7500
PET POLICY: No fee.

Casa del Granjero Bed & Breakfast
414 C. de Baca Ln., NW
Albuquerque, NM 87114
505-897-4144
PET POLICY: Pet accepted, but must be outdoors in stable, only.

Howard Johnson Express Inn
7630 Pan American Freeway
Albuquerque, NM 87109
505-828-1600
RATES: Single $49, double $55.
PET POLICY: Fee $5 per day, all sizes welcome. Must be housebroken.
AMENITIES: Plenty of vacant land nearby.

Motel 6
13141 Central Ave NE
Albuquerque, NM 87123
505-294-4600
PET POLICY: No fee. Dogs under 25 lbs. preferred (larger animals by advance approval). Do not leave animals in room unattended.

Plaza Inn—Albuquerque
900 Medical Arts Ave. NE
Albuquerque, NM 87102
505-243-5693
PET POLICY: No fee. Pets welcome up to 50 lbs.

Red Roof Inn
6015 Iliff Road Southwest
Albuquerque, NM 87121
505-831-3400
PET POLICY: No fee, pets under 80 lbs. Must be leashed to and from rooms. Do not leave in room unattended.

Best Western
2111 Sosimo Padilla Blvd.
Belen, NM 87002
505-861-3181

RATES: Single $59.95, double $64.95.
PET POLICY: Fee $5, nonrefundable. All sizes and all pets welcome (dogs, cats, ferrets, birds, rabbits, reptiles).
POI: Quiet location 30 miles from Albuquerque.

Carlsbad Inn
2019 S. Canal St.
Carlsbad, NM 88220
505-887-1171
RATES: Single $35, double $45.
PET POLICY: Fee $5, all pets must be attended at all times.
POI: Carlsbad Caverns.

Carlsbad Days Inn
3910 National Parks Hwy.
Carlsbad, NM 88220
505-887-7800
PET POLICY: Deposit required.

Motel 6
3824 National Parks Hwy.
Carlsbad, NM 88220
505-885-0011
PET POLICY: No fee. Dogs under 25 lbs. preferred (larger animals by advance approval). Do not leave animals in room unattended.

Best Western Kokopelli Lodge
702 S. 1st St.
Clayton, NM 88415
505-374-2589
RATES: Single $59–$169, double $69–$149.
PET POLICY: Fee $5, nonrefundable, up to 50 lbs., dogs and cats only. Limited rooms, call first, grassy area for exercise.
AMENITIES: Big grassy area for exercise.

Clovis Days Inn
1720 Mabry Dr.
Clovis, NM 88101
505-762-2971
PET POLICY: Fee $3.

Motel 6
2620 Mabry Dr.
Clovis, NM 88101
505-762-2995
PET POLICY: No fee. Dogs under 25 lbs. preferred (larger animals by advance approval). Do not leave animals in room unattended.

Deming Motel
500 W. Pine St.
Deming, NM 88030
505-546-2737
RATES: Double, Queen, King: $25–$60.
PET POLICY: Fee $3 (plus tax), nonrefundable. Up to 50 lbs. Special designated rooms for pets.
POI: Rockhound State Park, Pancho Villa State Park, Springs Canyon Park. Several parks in the city.

Deming Days Inn
1601 E. Pine St.
Deming, NM 88030
505-546-8813
PET POLICY: Fee $5.

Motel 6
I-10 & Motel Dr.
Deming, NM 88031
505-546-2623
PET POLICY: No fee. Dogs under 25 lbs. preferred (larger animals by advance approval). Do not leave animals in room unattended.

Wagon Wheel Motel
1109 W. Pine St.
Deming, NM 88031
505-546-2681
RATES: Single $28, double $31.
PET POLICY: No fee, up to 50 lbs.
POI: City of Rocks. Pancho Villa State Park. Faywood Hot Springs.

El Capitan Motel
1300 E. Hwy. 66
Gallup, NM 87301
505-863-6828
RATES: Single $25, double $30.
PET POLICY: No fee, all sizes, dogs and cats only.

Gallup Days Inn East
1603 W. Hwy. 66
Gallup, NM 87301
505-863-3891
PET POLICY: Fee $5.

Gallup Days Inn West
3201 W. Hwy. 66
Gallup, NM 87301
505-863-6889
PET POLICY: Fee $5.

U.S. Lodgings > NEW MEXICO

Motel 6
3306 W. 66
Gallup, NM 87301
505-863-4492
PET POLICY: No fee. Dogs under
25 lbs. preferred (larger animals by advance approval). Do
not leave animals in room
unattended.

Red Roof Inn
3304 W. Highway 66
Gallup, NM 87301
505-722-7765
PET POLICY: No fee, pets under
80 lbs. Must be leashed to and
from rooms. Do not leave in
room unattended.

Motel 6
1505 E. Santa Fe Ave.
Grants, NM 87020
505-285-4607
PET POLICY: No fee. Dogs under 25
lbs. preferred (larger animals by
advance approval). Do not leave
animals in room unattended.

Sands Motel
112 McArthur St.
Grants, NM 87020
505-287-2996
RATES: Single $31, double $36.
PET POLICY: Fee $5–$10, nonre-
fundable, all sizes welcome.
AMENITIES: Walking area behind
motel.
POI: Several national Parks.
State park with lake.

Baymont Inn & Suites
1500 Hickory Dr.
Las Cruces, NM 88005
505-523-0100
PET POLICY: No fee.

Hampton Inn
755 Avenida de Mesilla
Las Cruces, NM, 88005
505-526-8311
RATES: Single, double $55-57
PET POLICY: No fee, no restrictions. All sizes pets welcome.

Holiday Inn De Las Cruces
201 E. University Ave.
Las Cruces, NM 88001
505-526-4411

RATES: Single $79, double $84.
PET POLICY: Fee $25, refund-
able. All sizes welcome.
POI: New Mexico State
University, Downtown, Old
Historic Mesilla.

Las Cruces Days Inn
2600 S. Valley Dr.
Las Cruces, NM 88005
505-526-4441
PET POLICY: Fee $5.

Motel 6
235 La Posada Ln.
Las Cruces, NM 88001
505-525-1010
PET POLICY: No fee. Dogs under 25
lbs. preferred (larger animals by
advance approval). Do not leave
animals in room unattended.

**TRH Smith Mansion
Bed & Breakfast**
909 N. Alameda Blvd.
Las Cruces, NM 88005
505-525-2525
RATES: Single $75, double $75.
PET POLICY: Fee $15 nonrefund-
able, medium to 50 lbs., dogs,
cats, rabbits, crate when left in
room.
AMENITIES: Large yard available
for exercise.

**Lordsburg Days Inn &
Suites**
1100 W. Motel Dr.
Lordsburg, NM 88045
505-542-3600
RATES: Single $63, double $65.
PET POLICY: Fee $7, refundable.
POI: Gila National Forest,
Coronado National Forest.

Los Lunas Days Inn
1919 Main St.
Los Lunas, NM 87031
505-865-5995
PET POLICY: No fee.

Motel 6
3307 N. Main St.
Roswell, NM 88201
505-625-6666
PET POLICY: No fee. Dogs under
25 lbs. preferred (larger animals by advance approval). Do
not leave animals in room
unattended.

Roswell Days Inn
1310 N. Main St.
Roswell, NM 88201
505-623-4021
PET POLICY: No fee.

**Alexander's Inn Bed &
Breakfast**
529 E. Palace Ave.
Santa Fe, NM 87501
505-986-1431
PET POLICY: Fee $20, nonre-
fundable. All sizes welcome.

**El Paradero Bed &
Breakfast**
220 W. Manhattan Ave.
Santa Fe, NM 85701
505-988-1177
RATES: Single $80–$100, double
$90–$140.
PET POLICY: Fee $10, nonrefund-
able, all sizes welcome. Do not
leave in room unattended.
POI: Hiking, National Forests.

Eldorado Hotel
309 W. San Francisco St.
Santa Fe, NM 87501
505-988-4455
PET POLICY: No fee. Please
advise about pet upon making
reservation. All sizes accepted.

**Hacienda Nicholas
Bed & Breakfast Inn**
320 E. Marcy St.
Santa Fe, NM 87501
505-992-8385
RATES: Single $95–$160, double
$95–$160.
PET POLICY: Fee $20, nonrefund-
able. All sizes welcome.
POI: Plaza. Bandalier National
Park. Santa Fe National Forest.

Hotel Santa Fe
1501 Paseo De Peralta
Santa Fe, NM 87501
505-982-1200
RATES: Single $109, double $256.
PET POLICY: Fee $20, nonrefund-
able. All sizes welcome.
AMENITIES: Special pet check-in.

**Inn of the Turquoise Bear
Bed & Breakfast**
342 E. Buena Vista St.
Santa Fe, NM 87501
505-983-0798

U.S. Lodgings > NEW YORK

PET POLICY: Fee $20, nonrefundable. Up to 50 lbs. All pets welcome (dogs, cats, ferrets, birds, rabbit).

Inn On the Alameda
303 E. Alameda
Santa Fe, NM 87501
505-984-2121
PET POLICY: Fee $20 a night, under 30 lbs.

Motel 6
3007 Cerrillos Rd.
Santa Fe, NM 87505
505-473-1380
PET POLICY: No fee. Dogs under 25 lbs. preferred (larger animals by advance approval). Do not leave animals in room unattended.

Residence Inn Santa Fe
1698 Galisteo St.
Santa Fe, NM 87505
505-988-7300
PET POLICY: Fee $10 per day, $150 deposit, refundable.

Santa Fe Days Inn
2900 Cerrillos Rd.
Santa Fe, NM 87505
505-424-3297
PET POLICY: Fee $10.

**The Madeleine
Bed & Breakfast Inn**
106 Faithway
Santa Fe, NM 97501
525-982-3456
RATES: Single $80–$165, double $80–$165.
PET POLICY: Fee $20, nonrefundable. All sizes welcome.
POI: Plaza. Bandalier National Park. Santa Fe National Forest.

Days Inn of Santa Rosa
1830 Will Rogers Dr.
Santa Rosa, NM 88435
505-472-5985
PET POLICY: No fee.

Motel 6
3400 Will Rogers Dr.
Santa Rosa, NM 88435
505-472-3045
PET POLICY: No fee. Dogs under 25 lbs. preferred (larger animals by advance approval). Do not leave animals in room unattended.

Days Inn
1333 Paseo Del Pueblo Sur
Taos, NM, 87571
505-758-2230
RATES: Single $44.50, double $60.15 ($5 extra for each additional adult)
PET POLICY: No fee, no restrictions. Call in advance. Do not leave pets unattended in room. Pets not permitted in lobby.

Quality Inn Taos
1043 Camino Del Pueblo Sur
Taos, NM, 87571
505-758-2200
RATES: Single, double $59-94
PET POLICY: Fee $7 per night. No restrictions.

Motel 6
2900 E. Tucumcari Blvd.
Tucumcari, NM 88401
505-461-4791
PET POLICY: No fee. Dogs under 25 lbs. preferred (larger animals by advance approval). Do not leave animals in room unattended.

Safari Motel
722 E. Tucumcari Blvd.
Tucumcari, NM 88401
505-461-3642
RATES: Single $36, double $42.
PET POLICY: Fee $3, nonrefundable. All sizes welcome.
AMENITIES: Large exercise area.

Tucumcari Days Inn
2623 S. First St.
Tucumcari, NM 88401
505-461-3158
PET POLICY: Fee $5.

Oak Tree Inn
Hwy. 285, 60 & 54
Vaughn, NM 88353
505-584-8733
RATES: Single $59, double $64.
PET POLICY: Fee $5, nonrefundable. Up to 50 lbs., only dogs and cats.
POI: Billy the Kid Museum 57 miles, Santa Rosa Lake 37 miles.

NEW YORK

Ambassador Motor Inn
1600 Central Ave.
Albany, NY 12205
518-456-8982
RATES: Single $60, double $75.
PET POLICY: Fee $50 refundable, must sign pet contract, large grassy area available.
AMENITIES: Large grassy area.
POI: State Capital.

Crowne Plaza
10 Eyck Plaza
Albany, NY 12207
518-462-6611
PET POLICY: No fee.

Howard Johnson Hotel
416 Southern Blvd.
Albany, NY 12209
518-462-6555
RATES: Single $65, double $75.
PET POLICY: No fee, all sizes welcome.
POI: Pepsi Arena, RPI, State Capital, State Offices.

Mansion Hill Inn
115 Philip St.
Albany, NY 12202
518-465-2038
RATES: Single $145, double $175.
PET POLICY: No fee, all sizes welcome.

Motel 6
100 Watervliet Ave.
Albany, NY 12206
518-438-7447
PET POLICY: No fee. Dogs under 25 lbs. preferred (larger animals by advance approval). Do not leave animals in room unattended.

Red Roof Inn
188 Wolf Rd.
Albany, NY 12205
518-459-1971
PET POLICY: No fee, pets under 80 lbs. Must be leashed to and from rooms. Do not leave in room unattended.

U.S. Lodgings > NEW YORK

Red Roof Inn
42 Flint Rd.
Amherst, NY 14226
716-689-7474
RATES: Single $29–$99, double
$34–$99.
PET POLICY: No fee, pets under
80 lbs. Must be leashed to and
from rooms. Do not leave in
room unattended.
POI: University of N.Y. at Buffalo.
Albright Knox Art Gallery.

Red Roof Inn
42 Flint Rd.
Amherst, NY, 14226
716-689-7474
RATES: Single $29.00-$99.00,
double $34.00-$99.00
PET POLICY: No fee, pets under
80 lbs. accepted. Must be leashed
to and from rooms. Do not
leave in room unattended.
POI: University of N.Y. at Buffalo.
Albright Knox Art Gallery.

Auburn Days Inn
37 William St.
Auburn, NY 13021
315-252-7567
PET POLICY: No fee.

Holiday Inn
75 North St.
Auburn, NY 13021
315-253-4531
PET POLICY: Pets under 40 lbs.

Caboose Motel
8620 State Rt. 415
Avoca, NY 14809
607-566-2216
RATES: Single $37, double
$46–$51.
PET POLICY: No fee, up to 50 lbs.
Do not leave pets unattended
in rooms.
POI: Wineries, Corning Glass
Museum.

Batavia Days Inn
200 Oak St.
Batavia, NY 14020
716-343-1440
PET POLICY: Fee $10.

Bath Days Inn
330 W. Morris St.
Bath, NY 14810
607-776-7644
PET POLICY: No fee.

Motel 6
1012 Front St.
Binghamton, NY 13905
607-771-0400
PET POLICY: No fee. Dogs under 25
lbs. preferred (larger animals by
advance approval). Do not leave
animals in room unattended.

Binghamton Super 8 Motel
Route 11, Upper Court St.
Binghamton, NY 13904
607-775-3443
RATES: Single $39.95, double
$44.95.
PET POLICY: Fee $10, refundable.
All sizes and all pets welcome.
Do not leave pets in room
unattended.

Red Roof Inn
146 Maple Dr.
Bowmansville, NY 14026
716-633-1100
PET POLICY: No fee, pets under
80 lbs. Must be leashed to and
from rooms. Do not leave in
room unattended.

Days Inn
NYS Rt. 13
Canastota, NY 13032
315-697-3309
PET POLICY: No fee.

Best Western University Inn
90 E. Main St.
Canton, NY 13617
315-386-8522
PET POLICY: Fee $50, non-
refundable.

Catskill Days Inn
I-87
Catskill, NY 12414
518-943-5800
PET POLICY: Fee $5.

Inn at Lake Joseph
400 St. Joseph Rd.
Catskill Mountains, NY 12777
845-791-9506
RATES: Single $200, double $220.
PET POLICY: Fee $20, nonre-
fundable. Pets welcome in carriage house and cottage
rooms.
AMENITIES: Room to roam.

The Hedges
180 Sanford Ave.
Clinton, NY 13323
315-853-3031
PET POLICY: No fee, all sizes and
all pets welcome.
AMENITIES: Convenient walking
area for pets.

**Best Western Inn of
Cobleskill**
12 Campus Dr. Extension
Cobleskill, NY 12043
518-234-4321
RATES: Single $91–$101.
PET POLICY: No fee, all sizes
welcome.

Travelers Motor Inn
1630 Central Ave.
Colonie, NY 12205
518-456-0222
PET POLICY: Pets must be in
carrier and not left in room
unattended.

Forget Me Not Farm
420 Sibley Gulf Rd.
Cooperstown, NY 13326
607-547-8871
RATES: Single, double $100.
PET POLICY: No fee, all sizes and
all pets welcome. Must have
current Rabies certificate, and
prior approval of management.
POI: National Baseball Hall of
Fame, Farmers Museum, Howe
Caverns, Fennimore House.

Hotel Pratt
50 Pioneer St.
Cooperstown, NY 13326
607-431-1022
RATES: Week: $600, Weekend:
$400.
PET POLICY: Fee $50, refundable.
All sizes and all pets welcome.
Must control behavior and
noise.
POI: National Baseball Hall of
Fame, Farmers Museum, Howe
Caverns, Fennimore House.

Dansville Daystop
Commerce Dr.
Dansville, NY 14437
716-335-6023
PET POLICY: No fee.

U.S. Lodgings > NEW YORK

Days Inn
10455 Bennett Rd.
Dunkirk, NY 14063
716-673-1351
PET POLICY: No fee.

Bend in the Road Guest House
58 Spring Close Hwy.
East Hampton, NY 11937
631-324-4592
RATES: Single $100, double $175.
PET POLICY: No fee, all size dogs (also ferrets, birds, rabbits).
AMENITIES: Dog friendly swimming pool with steps built in, 20-acre farm for running, free of traffic.
POI: Beaches.

Dutch Motel
488 Montauk Hwy.
East Hampton, NY 11937
631-324-4550
RATES: Single $150, double $200.
PET POLICY: Fee $10 per night, one pet per room., up to 25 lbs.
POI: 1 miles from town, 2 miles pet-friendly beach, close to train station and bus stop.

Residence Inn Syracuse
6420 Yorktown Cir.
East Syracuse, NY 13057
315-432-4488
PET POLICY: Fee $100 nonrefundable, plus $5 per day.

The Jefferson Inn Bed & Breakfast
3 Jefferson St.
Ellicottville, NY 14731
716-699-5869
PET POLICY: Fee $10, nonrefundable. Dogs only, well-behaved or cages. Pets in efficiency units only, not B&B.

Holiday Inn
1 Holiday Plaza 760 E. Water
Elmira, NY 14901
607-734-4211
PET POLICY: Smoking rooms only.

Motel 6
485 Hamilton St.
Geneva, NY 14456
315-789-4050

PET POLICY: No fee. Dogs under 25 lbs. preferred (larger animals by advance approval). Do not leave animals in room unattended.

Red Roof Inn
5370 Camp Rd.
Hamburg, NY 14075
716-648-7222
PET POLICY: No fee, pets under 80 lbs. Must be leashed to and from rooms. Do not leave in room unattended.

Sandy Creek Manor House
1960 Redman Rd.
Hamlin, NY 14464
716-964-7528
RATES: Single $60, double $85.
PET POLICY: Fee $5 per pet per day, nonrefundable. All sizes welcome.
POI: Hamlin Beach State Park, Creek in back.

Wyndham Wind Watch Hotel
1717 Motor Pkwy.
Hauppauge, NY 11749
631-232-9800
PET POLICY: Fee $100, refundable. Pets under 30 lbs.

Rochester Days Inn
4853 W. Henrietta Rd.
Henrietta, NY 14467
716-334-9300
PET POLICY: No fee.

Red Roof Inn
4820 W. Henrietta Rd.
Henrietta, NY 14467
716-359-1100
PET POLICY: No fee, pets under 80 lbs. Must be leashed to and from rooms. Do not leave in room unattended.

Motel 6
4133 Rt 17
Horseheads, NY 14845
607-739-2525
PET POLICY: No fee. Dogs under 25 lbs. preferred (larger animals by advance approval). Do not leave animals in room unattended.

St. Charles Hotel
16-18 Park Pl.
Hudson, NY 12534
518-822-9900
RATES: Single $79, double $99.
PET POLICY: Fee $75 refundable, all pets available.

Columbia Bed & Breakfast
228 Columbia St.
Ithaca, NY 14850
607-272-0204
RATES: Single $125, double $195(Suite).
PET POLICY: Fee $25, nonrefundable. All size dogs. Pets must be on vet prescribed flea treatment, provide own bed, not permitted on furniture.
AMENITIES: Welcome dish of biscuits on arrival. Comparable treats for other pets.
POI: Walking trails, pet-friendly restaurants, Ithaca's downtown center, Ithaca College and Cornell.

La Tourelle Country Inn
1150 Danby Rd (96B)
Ithaca, NY 14850
607-273-2734
RATES: Single $99, double $150.
PET POLICY: No fee, all sizes welcome. Specific pet rooms.
AMENITIES: 70 acres. Access to outside through room door.
POI: State park. Cornell Vet School.

Meadow Court Inn
529 S. Meadow St.
Ithaca, NY 14850
607-273-3885
RATES: Single $50, double $75.
PET POLICY: Fee $10, nonrefundable, all sizes welcome.

Red Roof Inn
1980 E. Main St. Box 455
Jamestown, NY 14733
716-665-3670
PET POLICY: No fee, pets under 80 lbs. Must be leashed to and from rooms. Do not leave in room unattended.

U.S. Lodgings > NEW YORK

Red Roof Inn
590 Fairview St.
Johnson City, NY 13790
607-729-8940
PET POLICY: No fee, pets under 80 lbs. Must be leashed to and from rooms. Do not leave in room unattended.

Holiday Inn
503 Washington Ave.
Kingston, NY 12401
845-338-0400
RATES: Single, double $119 (seasonal).
PET POLICY: No fees, no restrictions.

Best Western–Golden Arrow Hotel
150 Main St.
Lake Placid, NY 12946
518-523-3353
RATES: Single, double $89–$169.
PET POLICY: Fee $25, nonrefundable. No size restrictions. Pets must be leashed when walking through hotel. Clean-up bags provided.

Green Haven Resort Motel
Lake Shore Dr.
Lake George, NY 12845
518-668-2489
PET POLICY: No pets July and August.

Lake House on Lake George
PO Box 195
Lake George, NY 12824
518-668-5545
RATES: 3-day midweek: $500 up to 4 persons, $3,000 full week up to 10 persons.
PET POLICY: Fee $40. All size dogs accepted.
AMENITIES: Private house on lake for swimming w/pet

Lake Placid Resort-Holiday Inn
1 Olympic Dr.
Lake Placid, NY, 12946
518-523-2556
RATES: Single, double $69-199
PET POLICY: No fee. Do not leave pets unattended at any time. Need to sign damage waiver.

Microtel Inn
7 Rensselaer Ave.
Latham, NY 12110
518-782-9161
RATES: Single $52.95, double $89.95.
PET POLICY: No fee, all sizes welcome.

Knights Inn—Liverpool-Syracuse
430 Electronics Pkwy.
Liverpool, NY 13088
315-453-6330
PET POLICY: Fee $5, nonrefundable, all sizes welcome.

Middletown Motel
501 Rt. 211 E.
Middletown, NY 10940
845-342-2535
RATES: Single $59.95, double $79.95.
PET POLICY: Fee $50, $35 of which is refundable, per dog. Pets in nonsmoking rooms.

Days Inn—Middletown
Rt. 17M
PO Box 279
New Hampton, NY 10958
914-374-2411
PET POLICY: No fee.

Dorinda's Bed & Breakfast
50 Marakill Ln.
New Paltz, NY 12561
914-255-6793
RATES: Garden Apartment: $125.
PET POLICY: No fee, all sizes and pets welcome. Do not leave in Apt. unattended. Must be accompanied by owner at all times.
AMENITIES: Lots of open spaces available.

Crowne Plaza
304 E. 42nd St.
New York, NY 10017
212-986-8800
PET POLICY: Fee $500 deposit, refundable, small dogs, don't leave unattended.

Crowne Plaza Hotel Manhattan
1605 Broadway
New York, NY 10019
212-977-4000
PET POLICY: $50 refundable fee; 30 lbs. or less; sign waiver for damages; not allowed in room along.

Dumont Plaza Suites
150 E. 34th St.
New York, NY 10016
212-481-7600
PET POLICY: $300 refundable fee; small dogs; case-by-case basis.

Four Seasons Hotel New York
57 E. 57th St.
New York, NY 10022
212-758-5700
PET POLICY: No fee; under 15 lbs.; can't leave alone in room.

Hilton New York and Towers
1335 Avenue Of the Americas
New York, NY 10019
212-586-7000
PET POLICY: No fee; under 15 lbs.

Hotel Plaza Athenée, New York
37 E. 64th St.
New York, NY 10021
212 734-9100
PET POLICY: No fee; any size, well-behaved.

Le Parker Meridien
118 W. 57th St.
New York, NY 10019
212-245-5000
PET POLICY: $50 nonrefundable fee; 50 lbs. limit.

Mayflower Hotel On the Park
15 Central Park West
New York, NY 10023
212-265-0060
PET POLICY: No fee; any size, sign a disclaimer form.

Millennium Broadway
145 W. 44th St.
New York, NY 10036
212-768-4400
PET POLICY: No fee; small and medium size dogs.

U.S. Lodgings > NEW YORK

Morgans
237 Madison Ave.
New York, NY 10016
212-686-0300
PET POLICY: $50 refundable fee;
very small cats, dogs; sign a
waiver.

New York Marriott Marquis
1535 Broadway
New York, NY 10036
212-398-1900
PET POLICY: No fee, small pets;
responsible for any damages.

New York Palace Hotel
455 Madison Ave.
New York, NY 10022
212-888-7000
PET POLICY: No fee; up to 10 lbs.,
no snakes.

Novotel New York
226 W. 52nd St.
New York, NY 10019
212-315-0100
PET POLICY: No fee; any size.

Peninsula New York Hotel
700 Fifth Ave.
New York, NY 10019
212-956-2888
RATES: Single $550–$690,
double $550–$690.
PET POLICY: No fee; under 25
lbs., must be kept in cage or
kennel. Must sign waiver form
for damages.
AMENITIES: Doggy treats.
POI: Central Park. Rockefeller
Center. Tiffany's, Saks, St.
Patrick's Cathedral.

Red Roof Inn
6 W. 32nd St.
New York, NY 10001
212-643-7100
PET POLICY: No fee, pets under
80 lbs. Must be leashed to and
from rooms. Do not leave in
room unattended.

Regent Hotel
55 Wall St.
New York, NY 10005
212-845-8600
PET POLICY: No fee; under 25
lbs.; owner must be present,
responsible for damages.

**Renaissance New York
Hotel**
714 Seventh Ave.
New York, NY 10036
212-765-7676
PET POLICY: $65 nonrefundable
fee, any size.

Sheraton Manhattan Hotel
790 Seventh Ave.
New York, NY 10019
212-581-3300
PET POLICY: No fee; any size.

Soho Grand Hotel
310 W. Broadway
New York, NY 10013
212-965-3000
PET POLICY: No fee; any size;
2 floors just for pets, pet-beds,
menu, etc.

The Carlyle
35 E. 76th St.
New York, NY 10023
212-744-1600
PET POLICY: No fee; small pets.

The Drake Swissotel
440 Park Ave.
New York, NY 10022
212-421-0900
PET POLICY: No fee; small pets;
sign a waiver.

The Envoy Club
377 E. 33rd St.
New York, NY 10016
212-481-4600
PET POLICY: No fee; any size.

The Lowell
28 E. 63rd St.
New York, NY 10021
212-838-1400
PET POLICY: No fee; under 20 lbs.

The Marmara—Manhattan
301 E. 94th St.
New York, NY 10128
212-427-3100
RATES: Single $4,500 month,
double $8,600 month.
PET POLICY: No fee, all sizes and
pets welcome (dogs, cats,
birds, ferrets, rabbits, reptiles).
Minimum 30 day stay.
AMENITIES: Extended Stay Hotel.

The Pierre
2 E. 61st St.
New York, NY 10021
212-838-8000
PET POLICY: No fee; under 15
lbs. Can't leave along in room,
full trained, sign affidavit, on
leash at all.

The Plaza
Fifth Ave. &
Central Park South
New York, NY 10019
212-759-3000
PET POLICY: No fee, under 15
lbs., sign a waiver.

TriBeCa Grand
2 Avenue of the Americas
New York, NY 10013
212-519-6600
PET POLICY: No fee, any size.

Lake Ontario Motel
3330 Lockport-Olcott Rd.
Newfane, NY 14108
716-778-9821
RATES: Single $39, double $59.
PET POLICY: Fee $5–$10, all
sizes, all pets welcome (dogs,
cats, ferrets, birds, rabbits,
reptiles, etc.).

Niagara Rainbow Motel
7900 Niagara Falls Blvd.
Niagara Falls, NY 14304
716-283-1760
RATES: Single $29.99, double
$34.99–$89.99.
PET POLICY: No fee, all sizes
welcome.
AMENITIES: Cabins.
POI: Niagara Falls.

**Niagara Falls Riverview at
the Falls Days Inn**
401 Buffalo Ave.
Niagara Falls, NY 14303
716-285-2541
PET POLICY: Fee $10.

Days Inn Ogdensburg
1200 Paterson St.
Ogdensburg, NY 13669
315-343-3200
PET POLICY: Fee $7.

Oswego Days Inn
101 State Route 104
Oswego, NY 13126
315-343-3136
PET POLICY: No fee.

**Best Western Lodge
on the Green**
3171 Canada Rd.
Painted Post, NY 14870
607-962-2456
PET POLICY: No fee, all sizes and
pets welcome (dogs, cats, ferrets,
birds, rabbits, reptiles).

Residence Inn
9 Gerhard Rd.
Plainview, NY 11803
516-433-6200
PET POLICY: Fee $100, non-
refundable.

**Baymont Inn & Suites—
Plattsburgh**
16 Plaza Blvd.
Plattsburgh, NY 12901
518-562-4000
PET POLICY: No fee.

Crowne Plaza
70 State St.
Rochester, NY 14614
716-546-3450
PET POLICY: No fee.

**Econo Lodge—
Rochester South**
940 Jefferson Rd.
Rochester, NY 14623
716-427-2700
RATES: Single $59, double $69.
PET POLICY: No fee, all sizes and
pets welcome (dogs, cats, ferrets,
birds, rabbits, reptiles).

Hampton Inn
500 Center Pl. Dr.
Rochester, NY 14615
716-663-6070
PET POLICY: No fee.

Holiday Inn
173 Sunrise Hwy. Rt 27
Rockville Centre, NY 11570
516-678-1300
RATES: Single $149.
PET POLICY: Fee $15, nonrefund-
able. All sizes welcome.

Adirondack Motel
23 Lake Flower Ave.
Saranac Lake, NY 12983
518-891-2116
RATES: Single $55–$130, double
$55–$130.
PET POLICY: Fee $7 for 2nd pet,
all sizes welcome, keep pets
on leash, must clean up, etc.
POI: Lake Placid.

The Point
HCR 1, Box 65
Saranac Lake, NY 12983
800-255-3530
RATES: Single, double $1,300
per night.
PET POLICY: No fee. All size
dogs and cats only.
AMENITIES: Dog beds provided

Albany Days Inn
167 Nott Terrace
Schenectady, NY 12308
518-370-3297
PET POLICY: No fee.

Skaneateles Suites
W. Genesee St.
Skaneateles, NY 13152
315-685-7568
RATES: Suites $95–$150.
PET POLICY: Fee $25, nonrefund-
able. All sizes and pets welcome.
Pets must be controlled at all
times.

Oak Tree Inn
606 Major's Path
Southampton, NY 11968
631-287-2057
RATES: Double $100–$250.
PET POLICY: No fee, all size
dogs, only. Do not leave in
room unattended.

Southampton Inn
91 Hill St.
Southampton, NY 11968
631-283-6500
PET POLICY: All sizes welcome.

Red Roof Inn
6614 N. Thompson Rd.
Syracuse, NY 13206
315-437-3309
PET POLICY: No fee, pets under
80 lbs. Must be leashed to and
from rooms. Do not leave in
room unattended.

**Sheraton University Hotel
& Conference Center**
801 University Ave.
Syracuse, NY 13210
315-475-3000
PET POLICY: Fee $50, nonre-
fundable.

**Syracuse Days Inn
University**
6609 Thompson Rd.
Syracuse, NY 13206
315-437-5998
RATES: Single $49.99–$69.99,
double $59.99–$79.99.
PET POLICY: Fee $10, nonrefund-
able. Pets in smoking rooms
only.

Westwood Guest Cottage
286 Fred Braun Rd.
Unadilla, NY 13849
607-369-7306
RATES: Single, double $150.
PET POLICY: No fee, all size dogs
and cats only.
AMENITIES: Pets can be left in
room while guests sightsee. All
pets free to exercise, walk on
our 11 acres of meadows and
woods.
POI: Nature hiking.

Motel 6
150 N. Genesee St.
Utica, NY 13502
315-797-8743
PET POLICY: No fee. Dogs under 25
lbs. preferred (larger animals by
advance approval). Do not leave
animals in room unattended.

Red Roof Inn
20 Weaver St.
Utica, NY 13502
315-724-7128
PET POLICY: No fee, pets under
80 lbs. Must be leashed to and
from rooms. Do not leave in
room unattended.

Algonquin Motel
PO Box 528, Rt. 30
Wells, NY 12190
518-924-2751
RATES: Single $45, double $53.
PET POLICY: No fee, all size dogs
and cats only.
POI: The great outdoors of the
Adirondacks.

U.S. Lodgings > NORTH CAROLINA

Woodland Bed & Breakfast
12 Woodland Ave.
Westhampton Beach, NY
11978
631-288-1681
RATES: Single $80, double $135.
PET POLICY: Fee $5, nonrefundable. All size dogs welcome.
AMENITIES: Fenced in backyard.

Adirondack Meadows Bed & Breakfast
277 Lake Shore Rd.
Willsboro, NY 12996
877-963-4075
RATES: Single $65, double $65.
PET POLICY: Fee $10, nonrefundable. All sizes welcome, crates preferred. Do not leave unattended. No pets on beds/furniture.
AMENITIES: Friendly Golden Retriever in residence.
POI: Adirondack Park, Lake Champlain, hiking, swimming, historical sites.

NORTH CAROLINA

Asheville Days Inn
201 Tunnel Rd.
Asheville, NC 28805
828-252-4000
PET POLICY: Fee $15.

Best Inns—Asheville
1435 Tunnel Rd.
Asheville, NC 28805
828-298-4000
RATES: Single $41–$59, double $48–$69.
PET POLICY: No fee, up to 25 lbs. Do not leave in room unattended. Leash policy.
POI: Biltmore Estate. Chimney Rock Park (23 miles), Downtown Asheville (5 miles).

Dunromin
501 Biltmore Ave.
Asheville, NC 28801
828-658-3345
RATES: Single $150, double $175.
PET POLICY: Fee $100, refundable. Dogs only, up to 50 lbs.
AMENITIES: Yard, shade, country atmosphere.
POI: Ashville N.C. Biltmore Estate, Great Smoky Mountain National Park. Hiking trails.

Motel 6
1415 Tunnel Rd.
Asheville, NC 28805
828-299-3040
PET POLICY: No fee. Dogs under 25 lbs. preferred (larger animals by advance approval). Do not leave animals in room unattended.

Red Roof Inn
16 Crowell Rd.
Asheville, NC 28806
828-667-9803
PET POLICY: No fee, pets under 80 lbs. Must be leashed to and from rooms. Do not leave in room unattended.

The Banner Elk Inn Bed & Breakfast
Route 3, Box 1134
Banner Elk, NC 28604
704-898-6223
RATES: Single $100, double $110.
PET POLICY: No fee for Inn, $100 for cottages. All sizes welcome.
AMENITIES: Park across the street.

Linville Cottage Inn
PO Box 508
Banner Elk, NC 28646
704-733-6557
RATES: Single, double $125–$150.
PET POLICY: No fee. All sizes and pets accepted.

Biscoe Days Inn
531 E. Main St.
Biscoe, NC 27209
910-428-2525
PET POLICY: Fee $5.

Linville Cottage Inn
PO Box 508
Boone, NC 28646
704-733-6557
RATES: Single, double $125–$150.
PET POLICY: No fee. All sizes and pets accepted.

Trout Cove Cabins
1629 Trout Cove Rd.
Brasstown, NC 28902
888-389-3584
RATES: Single $425 (weekly).
PET POLICY: No fee, all size dogs only. Must call first.
AMENITIES: 184 acres with numerous well tended trails over mountains and near water.

POI: Natahala National Park, Fires Creek Bear Sanctuary, Lake Chatuge, Appalachian Trail, John C. Campbell Folk School, golf courses, craft and antiques stores.

Hidden Creek Cabins
126 Hidden Creek Ln., Box 973
Bryson City, NC 28713
828-507-5627
RATES: $85–$100 per night.
PET POLICY: Fee $15, nonrefundable, all sizes accepted.
AMENITIES: 4 cabins nestled along banks of large Trout Creek in heart of the Great Smoky Mountains. Feature fireplace, hot tub, satellite TV/VCR, full kitchen/bath, campfire pits, hiking trails. Private and secluded.
POI: Near Cherokee Great Smoky Mountain Railroad, white water rafting, antiques, National Park,

Comfort Inn
978 Plantation Dr.
Burlington, NC 27215
910-227-3681
RATES: Single $55.95, double $64.31.
PET POLICY: Fee $15, nonrefundable, all size dogs and cats, only.

Red Roof Inn
2133 W. Hanford Rd.
Burlington, NC 27215
336-227-1270
PET POLICY: No fee, pets under 80 lbs. Must be leashed to and from rooms. Do not leave in room unattended.

Ridgetop Cabin Rentals
Route 5, Box 643
Burnsville, NC 28714
828-675-5511
RATES: Double $85.
PET POLICY: No fee, all size dogs and cats, only.

U.S. Lodgings > NORTH CAROLINA

Red Roof Inn Cary
1800 Walnut St.
Cary, NC 27511
919-469-3400
PET POLICY: No fee. Dogs under 25 lbs. preferred. Larger animals accepted with prior approval. Do not leave pets in room unattended.

Charlotte Days Inn
118 E. Woodlawn Rd.
Charlotte, NC 28217
704-525-5500
PET POLICY: Fee $10.

Drury Inn & Suites
415 W. W.T. Harris Blvd.
Charlotte, NC 28262
704-593-0700
RATES: Single, double $78–$112.
PET POLICY: No fee, up to 25 lbs. Keep in crate.

Homewood Suites Hotel
2770 Yorkmont Rd.
Charlotte, NC 28208
704-357-0500
PET POLICY: Prior approval and fees may apply.

Motel 6
3420 I-85 Service Rd South
Charlotte, NC 28208
704-394-4993
PET POLICY: No fee. Dogs under 25 lbs. preferred (larger animals by advance approval). Do not leave animals in room unattended.

Red Roof Inn
3300 I-85 South
Charlotte, NC 28208
704-392-2316
PET POLICY: No fee, pets under 80 lbs. Must be leashed to and from rooms. Do not leave in room unattended.

Red Roof Inn
5116 N. I-85
Charlotte, NC 28206
704-596-8222
PET POLICY: No fee, pets under 80 lbs. Must be leashed to and from rooms. Do not leave in room unattended.

Red Roof Inn
131 Red Roof Dr.
Charlotte, NC 28217
704-529-1020
PET POLICY: No fee, pets under 80 lbs. Must be leashed to and from rooms. Do not leave in room unattended.

Staybridge Suites by Holiday Inn
7924 Forest Pine Rd.
Charlotte, NC 28273
704-527-6767
PET POLICY: $75 non refundable fee.

Baymont Inn & Suites
PO Box 1865 Acquoni Rd.
Cherokee, NC 28719
828-497-2102
PET POLICY: No fee.

Hampton Inn
19501 Statesville Rd.
Cornelius, NC 28031
704-892-9900
RATES: Single $69, double $69.
PET POLICY: Fee $25, nonrefundable. All sizes welcome.
POI: Many parks around lakes, Davidson College.

Holiday Inn— Lake Norman
19901 Holiday Ln.
Cornelius, NC 28031
704-892-9120
RATES: Single $79.95, double $79.95.
PET POLICY: Fee $25, all size and all pets welcome. Pets have designated rooms (NC law). Designated walking area available.
AMENITIES: Designated walking area available.
POI: 10 miles north of Charlotte, Jetton Park on the lake is a wonderful exercise and play area for pets.

Best Western Skyland Inn
5400 Hillsborough Rd.
Durham, NC 27705
919-383-2508
RATES: Single, double $48–$64.
PET POLICY: Fee $5, all sizes and pets accepted.

Carolina Duke Motor Inn
2517 Guess Rd.
Durham, NC 27705
919-286-0771
RATES: Single $39.98, double $47.98.
PET POLICY: Fee $3, nonrefundable, dogs only.
AMENITIES: Area for walking.

Durham Days Inn
I-85 & Redwood Rd.
Durham, NC 27704
919-688-4338
PET POLICY: Fee $10.

La Quinta Inn & Suites
1919 W. Park Dr.
Durham, NC 27713
919-484-1422
PET POLICY: No fee. Pets accepted under 20 lbs. only.

Red Roof Inn
5623 Chapel Hill Boulevard
Durham, NC 27707
919-489-9421
PET POLICY: No fee, pets under 80 lbs. Must be leashed to and from rooms. Do not leave in room unattended.

Red Roof Inn
1915 North Pointe Dr.
Durham, NC 27705
919-471-9882
PET POLICY: No fee, pets under 80 lbs. Must be leashed to and from rooms. Do not leave in room unattended.

Red Roof Inn
4405 Highway 55
Durham, NC 27713
919-361-1950
PET POLICY: No fee, pets under 80 lbs. Must be leashed to and from rooms. Do not leave in room unattended.

Wyndham Garden Hotel
4620 S. Miami Blvd.
Durham, NC 27703
919-941-6066
PET POLICY: No fee, all size dogs and cats.
AMENITIES: Welcome treat for dogs and cats.

U.S. Lodgings > NORTH CAROLINA

Elizabeth City Days Inn
308 S. Hughes Blvd.
Elizabeth, NC 27909
252-335-4316
PET POLICY: No fee.

Motel 6
2076 Cedar Creek Rd.
Fayetteville, NC 28301
910-485-8122
PET POLICY: No fee. Dogs under 25 lbs. preferred (larger animals by advance approval). Do not leave animals in room unattended.

Red Roof Inn
1569 Jim Johnson Rd.
Fayetteville, NC 28303
910-321-1460
PET POLICY: No fee, pets under 80 lbs. Must be leashed to and from rooms. Do not leave in room unattended.

Mill House Lodge
1150 W. Blue Ridge Rd.
Flat Rock, NC 28731
828-693-6077
RATES: Single $45–$75, double $65–$175.
PET POLICY: Fee $15–$35, based on size of unit and length of stay, nonrefundable. Dogs and cats up to 50 lbs. Dogs must be on leash.

Franklin Days Inn
1320 E. Main St.
Franklin, NC 28734
828-524-6491
PET POLICY: No fee.

Days Inn Gastonia— Charlotte
1700 N. Chester St.
Gastonia, NC 28052
704-864-9981
PET POLICY: Fee $15.

Mountain View Lodge and Cabins
PO Box 90
Glendale Springs, NC 28629
800-903-6811
RATES: Single $65, double $110.
PET POLICY: Fee $7, nonrefundable. All sizes and pets welcome (dogs, cats, ferrets, birds, rabbits, reptile.) Must be on leash or respond to voice commands.

AMENITIES: Grassy lawn for walking, running and sniffing. Wooded areas. Cookies every day. Pickup bags provided.
POI: Trails everywhere. New River for fishing, canoeing, swimming. Grandfather Mountain. Numerous State Parks.

Linville Cottage Inn
PO Box 508
Grandfather Mountain, NC 28646
704-733-6557
RATES: Single, double $125–$150.
PET POLICY: No fee. All sizes and pets accepted.

River House Inn & Restaurant
1896 Old Field Creek Rd.
Grassy Creek, NC 28631
336-982-2109
RATES: Avg: $115–$150.
PET POLICY: No fee, all sizes and all pets welcome. Pets must be clean and well-trained. No barking permitted.
AMENITIES: 180 acres on North Fork of New River in Ashe Cnty mountains. Hiking and swimming with POI: Near state parks.

Drury Inn & Suites
3220 High Point Rd.
Greensboro, NC 27404
336-856-9696
PET POLICY: No fee, pets under 30 lbs.

Motel 6
605 S. Regional Rd.
Greensboro, NC 27409
336-668-2085
PET POLICY: No fee. Dogs under 25 lbs. preferred (larger animals by advance approval). Do not leave animals in room unattended.

Red Roof Inn
301 SE Greenville Blvd.
Greenville, NC 27858
252-756-2792
PET POLICY: No fee, pets under 80 lbs. Must be leashed to and from rooms. Do not leave in room unattended.

The AmeriSuites Hotel
1619 Stanley Rd.
Greensboro, NC 27407
336-852-1443
PET POLICY: Under 10 lbs.

Havelock Days Inn
1220 E. Main St.
Havelock, NC 28532
252-447-1122
PET POLICY: Fee $5.

Beechtree Inn Bed & Breakfast
Route 1, Box 517
Hertford, NC 27944
252-426-7815
PET POLICY: No fee, pets allowed with owners in selected rooms.

Holiday Inn Express
2250 Hwy. 70 SE
Hickory, NC 28602
828-328-2081
RATES: Single $79, double $79.
PET POLICY: Fee $25, nonrefundable. All sizes and all pets welcome.

Red Roof Inn
1184 Lenoir Rhyne Blvd.
Hickory, NC 28602
828-323-1500
PET POLICY: No fee, pets under 80 lbs. Must be leashed to and from rooms. Do not leave in room unattended.

Fire Mountain Inn and Cabins
PO Box 2772
Highlands, NC 28741
828-526-4446
RATES: Cabins: $175.
PET POLICY: Fee $150, refundable. Dogs only, up to 50 lbs. Must confirm by name in reservation letter.
AMENITIES: Over 75 acres of open pasture for dogs to run, backing up on 336 acres of springs, streams, ponds, etc.
POI: Nantahala Nat'l Forest, Great Smokey Mnts Nat'l Park, Appalachian Trail, Blue Ridge Pkwy.

U.S. Lodgings > NORTH CAROLINA

Kelsey & Hutchinson Lodge
450 Spring St.
Highlands, NC 28714
828-526-4746
PET POLICY: Fee $15, nonrefundable. All size dogs and cats and birds.

Red Roof Inn
13830 Statesville Rd.
Huntersville, NC 28070
704-875-7880
PET POLICY: No fee, pets under 80 lbs. Must be leashed to and from rooms. Do not leave in room unattended.

Ramada Inn Resort & Conference Center
1701 S. Virginia Dare Trail
Kill Devil Hills, NC 27948
252-441-2151
PET POLICY: Fee $5, nonrefundable, all sizes welcome.

Linville Cottage Inn
PO Box 508
Linville Falls, NC 28646
828-733-6557
RATES: Single, double $125–$150.
PET POLICY: No fee. All sizes and pets accepted.

Parkview Lodge & Cabins
Hwy. 221 & Blue Ridge Pkwy.
Linville Falls, NC 28647
828-765-4787
RATES: Single $49, double $64.
PET POLICY: Fee $10, nonrefundable. All sizes and pets welcome.

Days Inn
3030 N. Roberts Ave.
Lumberton, NC 28358
910-738-6401
PET POLICY: Keep in kennel.

Alamo Motel & Cottages
1485 Soco Rd.
Maggie Valley, NC 28751
800-467-7485
RATES: Single $40, double $65.
PET POLICY: Fee $5, nonrefundable. All sizes welcome.

POI: Great Smokey Mountains National Park, Blue Ridge Parkway, Biltmore Estate, Ghost Town Amusement Park.

Country Cabins
171 Bradley St.
Maggie Valley, NC 28751
828-926-0612
RATES: Single $100, double $115–$130.
PET POLICY: Fee $50–$20, nonrefundable. All sizes welcome. Pets must be leashed outside.
AMENITIES: Room to roam. Trees to sniff.

Maggie Mountain Villas and Chalet
60 Twin Hickory Ln.
Maggie Valley, NC 28751
828-926-4258
800-308-1808
PET POLICY: Fee $8 night for 1st pet, $4 for each additional.

Moore Realty
119 E. Altoona St.
Nags Head, NC 27959
252-480-1480
RATES: $775–$2,150 per week, depends on time of year.
PET POLICY: Fee $50 nonrefundable (week).
AMENITIES: Pet towels (after swim).

The Beach House
PO Box 1671
Nags Head, NC 27959
252-480-1480
RATES: $675–$1750 for 8 pers./week.
PET POLICY: Fee $50, nonrefundable. All sizes and pets welcome (dogs, cats, ferrets, birds, rabbits, reptiles).
AMENITIES: Pet towels, scoops for pickup.

Corinne's Studio Apartments
33 Silver Lake Rd.
Ocracoke Island, NC 27960
252-928-5851
RATES: Double $50–$110.
PET POLICY: Fee $10, refundable. All sizes and all pets welcome. Do not leave pets in room unattended, or keep in cage.

Baymont Inn & Suites
1001 Aerial Center Pkwy.
Raleigh, NC 27560
919-481-3600
PET POLICY: No fee.

Holiday Inn
4100 Glenwood Ave.
Raleigh, NC 27612
919-782-8600
PET POLICY: With deposit.

Motel 6
3921 Arrow Dr.
Raleigh, NC 27612
919-782-7071
PET POLICY: No fee. Dogs under 25 lbs. preferred (larger animals by advance approval). Do not leave animals in room unattended.

Red Roof Inn
3520 Maitland Dr.
Raleigh, NC 27610
919-231-0200
PET POLICY: No fee, pets under 80 lbs. Must be leashed to and from rooms. Do not leave in room unattended.

Red Roof Inn
1370 N. Wesleyan Blvd.
Rocky Mount, NC 27803
252-984-0907
PET POLICY: No fee, pets under 80 lbs. Must be leashed to and from rooms. Do not leave in room unattended.

Days Inn
1810 Lutheran Synod Dr.
Salisbury, NC 28144
704-633-4211
PET POLICY: Fee $6.

William & Garland Motel
Box 204, Hwy. 58
Salter Path, NC 28575
252-247-3733
RATES: Single, double $49–$69.
PET POLICY: Fee $5 per pet. All pets welcome up to 50 lbs. Must be quiet and well-behaved.

Woodlands Inn of Sapphire
1305 US 64 W.
Sapphire, NC 28774
828-966-4709

U.S. Lodgings > NORTH DAKOTA

RATES: Single $70.
PET POLICY: Fee $5 per night, nonrefundable. Up to 25 lbs.
POI: Waterfalls, hiking, national forest, golf, fishing, antiquing.

Shelby Days Inn
US 74 W. at Neisler St.
Shelby, NC 28152
704-482-6721
PET POLICY: No fee.

Red Roof Inn
1508 E. Broad St.
Statesville, NC 28625
704-878-2051
PET POLICY: No fee, pets under 80 lbs. Must be leashed to and from rooms. Do not leave in room unattended.
AMENITIES: Large grassy areas for dogs/walkers

Sea Star Motel
2108 N. New River Dr.
Surf City, NC 28445
800-343-0087
PET POLICY: Fee $10, nonrefundable, pets allowed on beach, on leash. No puppies.

Thomasville Days Inn
895 Lake Rd.
Thomasville, NC 27360
336-472-6600
PET POLICY: Fee $25.

Days Inn Fayetteville—North
Route 1, Box 216BB
Wade, NC 28395
910-323-1255
PET POLICY: Fee $6, All sizes accepted.

Wadesboro Days Inn
209 E. Caswell St.
Wadesboro, NC 28170
704-694-7070
PET POLICY: Fee $6.

Days Inn
1611 Roanoke Rapids Rd.
Weldon, NC 27890
919-536-4867
PET POLICY: Fee $6.

Anderson Guest House
520 Orange St.
Wilmington, NC, 28401
910-343-8128
RATES: Rates vary. Studios, $115
PET POLICY: Fee $10 per night. No restrictions.

Motel 6
2828 Market on US 17/74 Bus
Wilmington, NC 28403
910-762-0120
PET POLICY: No fee. Dogs under 25 lbs. preferred (larger animals by advance approval). Do not leave animals in room unattended.

Landfall Park Hampton Inn & Suites
1989 Eastwood Rd.
Wilmington, NC 28403
910-256-9600
RATES: Single $99, double $99.
PET POLICY: Fee $45+, non-refundable. All sizes and all pets welcome (dogs, cats, birds, ferrets, rabbits, reptiles). Call for details.
AMENITIES: Near Ocean/Beach, Resort area, airport, Shell Island (pet-friendly).

Augustus T Zevely Inn
803 S. Main
Winston-Salem, NC 27101
336-748-9299
RATES: Single $100, double $110.
PET POLICY: No fee, only one pet per room, up to 50 lbs.
POI: Old Salem historical district.

Holiday Inn Select
5790 University Pkwy.
Winston-Salem, NC 27104
336-767-9595
RATES: Single, double $89.
PET POLICY: Fee $25, nonrefundable. Only dogs and cats under 25 lbs.

Motel 6
3810 Patterson Ave.
Winston-Salem, NC 27105
336-661-1588
PET POLICY: No fee. Dogs under 25 lbs. preferred (larger animals by advance approval). Do not leave animals in room unattended.

Yanceville Days Inn
1858 NC Hwy. 86
Yanceyville, NC 27379
336-694-9494
PET POLICY: Fee $8.

NORTH DAKOTA

Buckboard Inn
1191 1st Ave. NW
Beach, ND 58621
701-872-4794
RATES: Single $32.81, double $45.53.
PET POLICY: No fee, all size and all pets welcome (dogs, cats, birds).

Bismarck Days Inn
1300 E. Capitol Ave.
Bismark, ND 58501
701-223-9151
PET POLICY: No fee.

Motel 6
2433 State St.
Bismarck, ND 58501
701-255-6878
PET POLICY: No fee. Dogs under 25 lbs. preferred (larger animals by advance approval). Do not leave animals in room unattended.

Budget Host 4U Motel
704 Hwy. 12W
Bowman, ND 58623
701-523-3243
RATES: Single $28–$34, double $36–$44.
PET POLICY: No fee, all sizes welcome.
POI: Theodore Roosevelt National Park.

Comfort Inn
215 Hwy. 2 E
Devils Lake, ND 58301
701-662-6760
RATES: Single $50, double $60.
PET POLICY: Fee $10, refundable.
AMENITIES: Walk way.

Days Inn Devils Lake
Route 5, Box 8
Devils Lake, ND 58301
701-662-5381
PET POLICY: Fee $3.

U.S. Lodgings > NORTH DAKOTA

Nodak Motel
600 E. Villard St.
Dickinson, ND 58601
701-225-5119
RATES: Single $31.50, double $45.
PET POLICY: No fee, all size and all pets welcome (dogs, cats, birds, ferrets, rabbits, reptiles). In smoking rooms only.
POI: Theodore Roosevelt National Park, ND Cowboy Hall of Fame, 30 minutes from Little Missouri.

Fargo Airport/ Dome Days Inn
1507 19th Ave. N
Fargo, ND 58102
701-232-0000
PET POLICY: Fee $15.

Holiday Inn Express
1040 40th St.
Fargo, ND 58103
701-282-2000
PET POLICY: Small pets allowed if attended.

Motel 6
1202 36th St S
Fargo, ND 58103
701-232-9251
PET POLICY: No fee. Dogs under 25 lbs. preferred (larger animals by advance approval). Do not leave animals in room unattended.

Red Roof Inn
901 38th St.
Fargo, ND 58103
701-282-9100
PET POLICY: No fee, pets under 80 lbs. Must be leashed to and from rooms. Do not leave in room unattended.

Days Inn
3101 34th St. S.
Grand Forks, ND 58201
701-775-0060
PET POLICY: Call for permission.

Jamestown Days Inn
824 SW 20th St.
Jamestown, ND 58401
701-251-9085
PET POLICY: No fee, All sizes accepted.

Days Inn
2100 4th St. SW
Minot, ND 58701
701-852-3646
RATES: Single $40, double $53.
PET POLICY: No fee, dogs only, up to 50 lbs.

West Fargo Days Inn
525 E. Main Ave.
West Fargo, ND 58078
701-281-0000
PET POLICY: Fee $15.

OHIO

Akron Days Inn South-Airport
3237 S. Arlington Rd.
Akron, OH 44312
330-644-1204
PET POLICY: No fee.

Red Roof Inn
2939 S. Arlington Rd.
Akron, OH 44312
330-644-7748
PET POLICY: No fee, pets under 80 lbs. Must be leashed to and from rooms. Do not leave in room unattended.

Red Roof Inn
99 Rothrock Rd.
Akron, OH 44321
330-666-0566
PET POLICY: No fee, pets under 80 lbs. Must be leashed to and from rooms. Do not leave in room unattended.

Residence Inn by Marriott
120 Montrose W. Ave.
Akron, OH 44321
330-666-4811
RATES: Studio Suites $75, Penthouse: $150.
PET POLICY: Fee $75–$150 (depends upon accommodation), nonrefundable. All sizes welcome.
AMENITIES: Pet walk area. Scoops.
POI: State Parks.

Days Inn—Ashland
1423 CR 1575
Ashland, OH 44805
419-289-0101
PET POLICY: No fee.

Holiday Inn Express Hotel & Suites
1392 TR 743
Ashland, OH 44805
419-281-2900
RATES: Single $79, double $79.
PET POLICY: Fee $35, refundable. All pets welcome, up to 50 lbs. Do not leave unattended in rooms, walk in designated area.

Ho Hum Motel
3801 N. Ridge W.
Ashtabula, OH 44004
440-969-1136
RATES: Single $40–$50, double $55–$65.
PET POLICY: Fee $5, non-refundable.
POI: Lake Erie.

Red Roof Inn
24801 Rockside Rd.
Bedford Heights, OH 44146
440-439-2500
PET POLICY: No fee, pets under 80 lbs. Must be leashed to and from rooms. Do not leave in

Bellville Days Inn
880 Rte 97
Bellville, OH 44813
419-886-3800
PET POLICY: Fee $5.

Youngstown Days Inn
8392 Market St.
Boardman, OH 44512
330-758-2371
PET POLICY: Fee $4.

Dayton Days Inn Brookville
100 Parkview Dr.
Brookville, OH 45309
513-833-4003
PET POLICY: Fee $10.

Bucyrus Days Inn
1515 N. Sandusky St.
Bucyrus , OH 44820
419-562-3737
PET POLICY: Fee $10.

Days Inn
3970 Convenience Cir.
Canton, OH 44718
216-493-8883
PET POLICY: No fee.

Chillicothe Days Inn
1250 N. Bridge St.
Chillicothe, OH 45601
614-775-7000
PET POLICY: Fee $5.

Cincinnati Days Inn
I-275 & US 42
Cincinnati, OH 45241
513-554-1400
PET POLICY: No fee.

Motel 6
3960 Nine Mile Rd.
Cincinnati, OH 45255
513-752-2262
PET POLICY: No fee. Dogs under 25
lbs. preferred (larger animals by
advance approval). Do not leave
animals in room unattended.

Red Roof Inn
11345 Chester Rd.
Cincinnati, OH 45246
513-771-5141
PET POLICY: No fee, pets under
80 lbs. Must be leashed to and
from rooms. Do not leave in
room unattended.

Red Roof Inn
5300 Kennedy Ave.
Cincinnati, OH 45213
513-531-6589
PET POLICY: No fee, pets under
80 lbs. Must be leashed to and
from rooms. Do not leave in
room unattended.

Woodfield Suites Hotel
11029 Dowlin Dr.
Cincinnati, OH 45241
513-771-0300
PET POLICY: No fee.

Baymont Inn & Suites
4222 W. 150 St.
Cleveland, OH 44135
216-251-8500
PET POLICY: No fee.

Marriott Cleveland Airport
4277 W. 150th St.
Cleveland, OH 44135
216-252-5333
PET POLICY: Fee $50 nonrefund-
able deposit.

Red Roof Inn
1363 W. McPherson Hwy.
Clyde, OH 43410
419-547-6660
PET POLICY: No fee, pets under
80 lbs. Must be leashed to and
from rooms. Do not leave in
room unattended.

**Columbus Days Inn
University**
3160 Olentangy River Rd.
Columbus, OH 43202
614-261-0523
PET POLICY: No fee.

Motel 6
1289 E. Dublin-Granville Rd.
Columbus, OH 43229
614-846-9860
PET POLICY: No fee. Dogs under 25
lbs. preferred (larger animals by
advance approval). Do not leave
animals in room unattended.

Motel 6
7480 N. High St.
Columbus, OH 43235
614-431-2525
PET POLICY: No fee. Dogs under 25
lbs. preferred (larger animals by
advance approval). Do not leave
animals in room unattended.

Red Roof Inn
7474 N. High St.
Columbus, OH 43235
614-846-3001
PET POLICY: No fee, pets under
80 lbs. Must be leashed to and
from rooms. Do not leave in
room unattended.

Red Roof Inn
900 E. Dublin-Granville
Columbus, OH 43229
614-888-7440
PET POLICY: No fee, pets under
80 lbs. Must be leashed to and
from rooms. Do not leave in
room unattended.

Days Inn
3636 N. Dixie Dr.
Dayton, OH 44514
937-275-5603
PET POLICY: Fee $25.

Motel 6
7130 Miller Ln.
Dayton, OH 45414
937-898-3606
PET POLICY: No fee. Dogs under 25
lbs. preferred (larger animals by
advance approval). Do not leave
animals in room unattended.

Red Roof Inn
7370 Miller Ln.
Dayton, OH 45414
937-898-1054
PET POLICY: No fee, pets under
80 lbs. Must be leashed to and
from rooms. Do not leave in
room unattended.

**Baymont Inn & Suites—
Dublin**
6145 Park Center Cir.
Dublin, OH 43017
614-792-8300
PET POLICY: No fee.

**Red Roof Inn (Columbus)
Dublin**
5125 Post Rd.
Dublin, OH 43017
614-764-3993
PET POLICY: No fee. Dogs under
25 lbs. preferred. Larger animals accepted with prior
approval. Do not leave pets in
room unattended.

Red Roof Inn
2580 Colonel Glenn Hwy.
Fairborn, OH 45324
937-426-6116
PET POLICY: No fee, pets under
80 lbs. Must be leashed to and
from rooms. Do not leave in
room unattended.

Fostoria Days Inn
601 Findlay St.
Fostoria, OH 44830
419-435-6511
PET POLICY: No fee.

Red Roof Inn
1900 Stringtown Rd.
Grove City, OH 43123
614-87-58543
PET POLICY: No fee, pets under
80 lbs. Must be leashed to and
from rooms. Do not leave in
room unattended.

U.S. Lodgings > OHIO

Red Roof Inn
1214 Corporate Dr.
Holland, OH 43528
419-866-5512
PET POLICY: No fee, pets under 80 lbs. Must be leashed to and from rooms. Do not leave in room unattended.

Baymont Inn & Suites
6161 Quarry Ln.
Independence, OH 44131
216-447-1133
PET POLICY: No fee.

Red Roof Inn
6020 Quarry Ln.
Independence, OH 44131
216-447-0030
PET POLICY: No fee, pets under 80 lbs. Must be leashed to and from rooms. Do not leave in room unattended.

Lima Days Inn
1250 Neubrecht Rd.
Lima, OH 45801
419-227-6515
PET POLICY: Fee $10.

Motel 6
1800 Harding Hwy.
Lima, OH 45804
419-228-0456
PET POLICY: No fee. Dogs under 25 lbs. preferred (larger animals by advance approval). Do not leave animals in room unattended.

Baymont Inn & Suites
268 E. Highland Rd.
Macedonia, OH 44056
330-468-5400
PET POLICY: No fee.

Baymont Inn & Suites
120 Standor Ave.
Mansfield, OH 44903
419-774-0005
PET POLICY: No fee.

Hampton Inn
1051 N. Lexington Springmill Rd.
Mansfield, OH 44906
419-747-5353
PET POLICY: Pets allowed in smoking rooms only.

Marietta Knights Inn
506 Pike St.
Marietta, OH 45750
740-373-7373
RATES: Single $40, double $50.
PET POLICY: Fee $5, non-refundable.
AMENITIES: Walking area, park nearby.
POI: Fenton Glass, Historic downtown Marietta.

Marion Days Inn
1838 Marion-Mt. Gilead Rd.
Marion, OH 43302
740-389-4651
PET POLICY: Fee $5.

Marysville Days Inn
16510 Square Dr.
Marysville, OH 43040
937-644-8821
PET POLICY: No fee.

Baymont Inn & Suites
9918 Escort Dr.
Mason, OH 45040
513-459-1111
PET POLICY: No fee.

Cincinnati Days Inn
19 Mason-Montgomery Rd.
Mason, OH 45040
513-398-3297
PET POLICY: No fee.

Red Roof Inn
9847 Bardes Rd.
Mason, OH 45040
513-398-3633
PET POLICY: No fee, pets under 80 lbs. Must be leashed to and from rooms. Do not leave in room unattended.

Homewood Suites Hotel
1410 Arrowhead Rd.
Maumee, OH 43537
419-897-0980
PET POLICY: Deposit required.

Red Roof Inn
1570 Reynolds Rd.
Maumee, OH 43537
419-893-0292
PET POLICY: No fee, pets under 80 lbs. Must be leashed to and from rooms. Do not leave in room unattended.

Toledo-Maumee Days Inn
150 Dussel Dr.
Maumee, OH 43537
419-893-9960
PET POLICY: No fee.

Baymont Inn & Suites—Mayfield Heights
1421 Golden Gate Blvd.
Mayfield Heights, OH 44124
440-442-8400
PET POLICY: No fee.

Homewood Suites Hotel
3100 Contemporary Ln.
Miamisburg, OH 45342
937-432-0000
PET POLICY: fee.

Motel 6
8101 Springboro Pike
Miamisburg, OH 45342
937-434-8750
PET POLICY: No fee. Dogs under 25 lbs. preferred (larger animals by advance approval). Do not leave animals in room unattended.

Red Roof Inn
222 Byers Rd.
Miamisburg, OH 45342
937-866-0705
PET POLICY: No fee, pets under 80 lbs. Must be leashed to and from rooms. Do not leave in room unattended.

Red Roof Inn
17555 Bagley Rd.
Middleburg Heights, OH 44130
440-243-2441
PET POLICY: No fee, pets under 80 lbs. Must be leashed to and from rooms. Do not leave in room unattended.

Motel 6
6880 Sunset Strip Ave NW
North Canton, OH 44720
330-494-7611
PET POLICY: No fee. Dogs under 25 lbs. preferred (larger animals by advance approval). Do not leave animals in room unattended.

Red Roof Inn
5353 Inn Circle Ct NW
North Canton, OH 44720
330-499-1970

U.S. Lodgings > OHIO

PET POLICY: No fee, pets under 80 lbs. Must be leashed to and from rooms. Do not leave in room unattended.

Baymont Inn & Suites
1154 Professional Dr.
Perrysburg, OH 43551
419-872-0000
PET POLICY: No fee.

Toledo-Perrysburg Days Inn
10667 Fremont Pike
Perrysburg, OH 43551
419-874-8771
PET POLICY: No fee.

Red Roof Inn
1051 Tiffany South
Poland, OH 44514
330-758-1999
PET POLICY: No fee, pets under 80 lbs. Must be leashed to and from rooms. Do not leave in room unattended.

Red Roof Inn
2449 Brice Rd.
Reynoldsburg, OH 43068
614-864-3683
PET POLICY: No fee, pets under 80 lbs. Must be leashed to and from rooms. Do not leave in room unattended.

College Hill Motel
10987 State Rd.
Rio Grande, OH 45674
740-245-5326
RATES: Single $34, double $43.
PET POLICY: No fee, up to 25 lbs.

Red Roof Inn
6100 U.S. Route 250
Sandusky, OH 44870
419-609-9000
PET POLICY: No fee, pets under 80 lbs. Must be leashed to and from rooms. Do not leave in room unattended.

Homewood Suites Hotel
2670 E. Kemper Rd.
Sharonville, OH 45241
513-772-8888
PET POLICY: Pets under 40 lbs. Welcome for additional fee.

Motel 6
3850 Hauck Rd.
Sharonville, OH 45241
513-]563-1123
PET POLICY: No fee. Dogs under 25 lbs. preferred (larger animals by advance approval). Do not leave animals in room unattended.

Red Roof Inn
2301 Sharon Rd.
Sharonville, OH 45241
513-771-5552
PET POLICY: No fee, pets under 80 lbs. Must be leashed to and from rooms. Do not leave in room unattended.

Baymont Inn & Suites
12150 Springfield Pike
Springdale, OH 45246
513-671-2300
PET POLICY: No fee.

Red Roof Inn
68301 Red Roof Ln.
St. Clairsville, OH 43950
740-695-4057
PET POLICY: No fee, pets under 80 lbs. Must be leashed to and from rooms. Do not leave in room unattended.

Cleveland Days Inn Airport-South
9029 Pearl Rd.
Strongsville, OH 44136
216-234-3575
PET POLICY: Fee $5.

Red Roof Inn
15385 Royalton Rd.
Strongsville, OH 44136
440-238-0170
PET POLICY: No fee, pets under 80 lbs. Must be leashed to and from rooms. Do not leave in room unattended.

Motel 6
5335 Heatherdowns Blvd.
Toledo, OH 43614
419-865-2308
PET POLICY: No fee. Dogs under 25 lbs. preferred (larger animals by advance approval). Do not leave animals in room unattended.

Red Roof Inn
3530 Executive Pkwy.
Toledo, OH 43606
419-536-0118
PET POLICY: No fee, pets under 80 lbs. Must be leashed to and from rooms. Do not leave in room unattended.

Toledo Days Inn
1800 Miami St.
Toledo, OH 43605
419-666-5120
PET POLICY: Fee $10.

Van Wert Days Inn
820 N. Washington St.
Van Wert, OH 45891
419-238-5222
PET POLICY: No fee.

Holiday Inn Express
2417 State Rt. 60
Vermilion, OH 44089
440-967-8770
RATES: Single $79, double $79.
PET POLICY: Fee $35, refundable. All pets welcome, up to 50 lbs. Do not leave unattended in room, not allowed in public areas, lobby, etc. Walk in designated areas.

Wapakoneta Days Inn
1659 Bellefontaine St.
Wapakoneta, OH 45895
419-738-2184
PET POLICY: Fee $10.

Red Roof Inn
29595 Clemens Rd.
Westlake, OH 44145
440-892-7920
PET POLICY: No fee, pets under 80 lbs. Must be leashed to and from rooms. Do not leave in room unattended.

Red Roof Inn
4166 State Route 306
Willoughby, OH 44094
440-946-9872
PET POLICY: No fee, pets under 80 lbs. Must be leashed to and from rooms. Do not leave in room unattended.

U.S. Lodgings > OHIO

Days Inn—North
1610 Motor Inn Dr.
Youngstown, OH 44420
216-759-3410
PET POLICY: Fee $10.

Red Roof Inn
1051 N. Canfield-Niles Rd.
Youngstown, OH 44515
330-793-9851
PET POLICY: No fee, pets under 80 lbs. Must be leashed to and from rooms. Do not leave in room unattended.

Red Roof Inn
4929 E. Pike Rd.
Zanesville, OH, 43701
740-453-6300
PET POLICY: No fee, pets under 80 lbs. accepted. Must be leashed to and from rooms. Do not leave in room unattended.

OKLAHOMA

Best Western Altus
2804 N. Main St.
Altus, OK 73521
405-482-9300
RATES: Single $55, double $65.
PET POLICY: No fee, all sizes dogs and cats accepted. Also birds and rabbits.

Days Inn
3202 N. Main St.
Altus, OK 73521
405-477-2300
PET POLICY: No fee.

Motel 6
120 Holiday Dr.
Ardmore, OK 73401
580-226-7666
PET POLICY: No fee. Dogs under 25 lbs. preferred (larger animals by advance approval). Do not leave animals in room unattended.

Days Inn
4302 W. Doolin
Blackwell, OK 74631
580-363-2911
RATES: Single $45, double $50.
PET POLICY: Fee $5, all sizes welcome.

Motel 6
2500 E. Hwy. 66
Elk City, OK 73644
580-225-6661
PET POLICY: No fee. Dogs under 25 lbs. preferred (larger animals by advance approval). Do not leave animals in room unattended.

Elk City Days Inn
1100 Hwy. 34
Elk City, OK 73644
580-225-9210
PET POLICY: No fee.

Enid Days Inn
200 N. Van Buren
Enid, OK 73703
580-234-0080
PET POLICY: No fee.

Econo Lodge
923 Hwy. 54 E
Guymon, OK 73942
580-338-5431
RATES: Single $39–$50, double $60–$80.
PET POLICY: Fee $5, nonrefundable. Up to 25 lbs. Do not leave in room unattended, or must be kept in crate.
POI: Golf, Lake, tennis, parks, fishing, paddle boats, Rodeo Arena.

Green Country Inn
Hwy. 59 N.
Heavener, OK 74937
918-653-7801
RATES: Single $49.95, double $53.95.
PET POLICY: Fee $10, nonrefundable. All sizes, all pets welcome.

Summerside Inn
PO box 242
Ketchum, OK 74349
918-782-3301
PET POLICY: Small, well-behaved.

Lawton Days Inn
3110 Cache Rd.
Lawton, OK 73505
580-353-3104
PET POLICY: No fee.

Motel 6
202 SE Lee Blvd.
Lawton, OK 73501
580-355-9765
PET POLICY: No fee. Dogs under 25 lbs. preferred (larger animals by advance approval). Do not leave animals in room unattended.

Days Inn
1217 S. George Nigh Expressway
McAlester, OK 74501
918-426-5050
PET POLICY: Fee $15.

Motel 6
6166 Tinker Diagonal
Midwest City, OK 73110
405-737-6676
PET POLICY: No fee. Dogs under 25 lbs. preferred (larger animals by advance approval). Do not leave animals in room unattended.

Motel 6
1417 N. Moore Ave.
Moore, OK 73160
405-799-6616
PET POLICY: No fee. Dogs under 25 lbs. preferred (larger animals by advance approval). Do not leave animals in room unattended.

Days Inn
900 S. 32nd St.
Muskogee, OK 74401
918-683-3911
PET POLICY: Fee $5.

Motel 6
903 S. 32nd St.
Muskogee, OK 74401
918-683-8369
PET POLICY: No fee. Dogs under 25 lbs. preferred (larger animals by advance approval). Do not leave animals in room unattended.

Motel 6
12121 N. I-35 Service Rd.
Oklahoma City, OK 73131
405-478-4030
RATES: Single $39.95, double $44.99.
PET POLICY: No fee. Dogs under 25 lbs. preferred (larger animals by advance approval). Do not leave animals in room unattended.

Oklahoma City Days Inn
2616 So I-35
Oklahoma City, OK 73129
405-677-0521
PET POLICY: Fee $15.

Red Roof Inn
309 S. Meridian Ave.
Oklahoma City, OK 73108
405-947-8777
PET POLICY: No fee, pets under
80 lbs. Must be leashed to and
from rooms. Do not leave in
room unattended.

The AmeriSuites Hotel
3201 W. Memorial Rd.
Oklahoma City, OK 73134
405-749-1595
RATES: Single, double $79–$89.
PET POLICY: No fee. Pets under
20 lbs.

Ponca City Days Inn
1415 E. Bradley
Ponca City, OK 74604
405-767-1406
PET POLICY: Fee $10.

Pryor Days Inn
US Hwy. 69 S. & 69A
Pryor, OK 74362
918-825-7600
PET POLICY: Fee $10.

Roland Days Inn
207 Cherokee Blvd.
Roland, OK 74954
918-427-1000
PET POLICY: Fee $10.

Motel 6
4981 N. Harrison St.
Shawnee, OK 74804
405-275-5310
PET POLICY: No fee. Dogs under 25
lbs. preferred (larger animals by
advance approval). Do not leave
animals in room unattended.

Best Western Stillwater
600 E. McElroy
Stillwater, OK 74075
405-377-7010
RATES: Single, double $65.
PET POLICY: No fee, dogs and
cats under 25 lbs.

Days Inn
5010 W. 6th St.
Stillwater, OK 74074
405-743-2570
PET POLICY: No fee.

Motel 6
5122 W. 6th Ave.
Stillwater, OK 74074
405-624-0433
PET POLICY: No fee. Dogs under 25
lbs. preferred (larger animals by
advance approval). Do not leave
animals in room unattended.

Baymont Inn & Suites
4530 E. Skelly Dr.
Tulsa, OK 74135
918-488-8777
PET POLICY: No fee.

Days Inn—West
5525 W. Skelly Dr.
Tulsa, OK 74107
918-446-1561
PET POLICY: Fee $8.

Holiday Inn Express
9010 E. 71st St.
Tulsa, OK 74133
918-459-5321
PET POLICY: No fee.

Tulsa Days Inn
8201 E. Skelly Dr.
Tulsa , OK 74129
918-665-6800
PET POLICY: Deposit.

Motel 6
5828 W. Skelly Dr.
Tulsa, OK 74107
918-445-0223
PET POLICY: No fee. Dogs under 25
lbs. preferred (larger animals by
advance approval). Do not leave
animals in room unattended.

Weatherford Days Inn
1019 E. Main St.
Weatherford, OK 73096
580-772-5592
PET POLICY: Fee $15.

Hampton Inn
1351 Canadian Court
Yukon, OK 73099
405-350-6400
PET POLICY: Special restrictions
apply for pets.

OREGON

**Best Western Pony Soldier
Motor Inn**
315 Airport Rd.
Albany, OR 97321
541-928-6322
RATES: Single $69, double $92.
PET POLICY: No fee, all sizes and
pets welcome (dogs, cats, ferrets,
birds, rabbits, reptiles).
AMENITIES: 1/3-acre lawn area
with trees and picnic tables.

Motel 6
2735 E. Pacific Blvd.
Albany, OR 97321
541-926-4233
PET POLICY: No fee. Dogs under 25
lbs. preferred (larger animals by
advance approval). Do not leave
animals in room unattended.

**Clementine's
Bed & Breakfast**
847 Exchange St.
Astoria, OR 97103
503-325-2005
RATES: Single, double $125.
PET POLICY: Fee $5, all size dogs
and cats.

Shilo Inn Beaverton
990 SW Canyon Rd.
Beaverton, OR 97225
503-297-2551
RATES: Single $69, double $79.
PET POLICY: Fee $10, nonrefund-
able. All sizes, all pets welcome.

US Suites of Portland
10220 SW 152nd Ave.
Beaverton, OR 976007
503-443-2033
RATES: Single $119, double $149.
PET POLICY: Fee $300, refund-
able. All sizes and pets
welcome, including dogs, cats,
birds, and reptiles.
AMENITIES: Pet sitting services
available. Parks nearby.
POI: Near Willamette River
with access for pets to run
and swim.

Shilo Inn Suites Hotel
3105 O B Riley Rd.
Bend, OR 97701
541-389-9600
PET POLICY: Fee $10, nonrefund-
able. All sizes, all pets welcome.

U.S. Lodgings > OREGON

Burns Days Inn
577 W. Monroe
Burns, OR 97720
541-573-2047
PET POLICY: No fee.

Surfsand Resort
Oceanfront and Gower
Cannon Beach, OR 97110
503-436-2274
RATES: Single $179, double $249.
PET POLICY: Fee $10, nonrefundable. All sizes and all pets welcome.
AMENITIES: Walking Papers and Treats at check-in.

Agency Lake Resort
37000 Modoc Pt. Rd.
Chiloquin, OR 97624
541-783-2489
PET POLICY: Fee $2, all sizes okay, 1-acre exercise area, must be on leash, dogs and cats only.

Motel 6
1445 Bayshore Dr.
Coos Bay, OR 97420
541-267-7171
PET POLICY: No fee. Dogs under 25 lbs. preferred (larger animals by advance approval). Do not leave animals in room unattended.

Trollers Lodge
355 SW Hwy. 101, Box 800
Depoe Bay, OR 97341
541-765-2287
RATES: $59 + tax, double $93 + tax.
PET POLICY: Fee $7, nonrefundable. All sizes and all pets welcome (dogs, cats, birds, ferrets, rabbits). Do not leave pets unattended in room unless caged.
AMENITIES: Samantha, Dir. Of Pet Services (part Lab), provides welcome note and treats on arrival. Loves to play with four-legged guests.

Motel 6
3690 Glenwood Dr.
Eugene, OR 97403
541-687-2395
PET POLICY: No fee. Dogs under 25 lbs. preferred (larger animals by advance approval). Do not leave animals in room unattended.

Park Motel
85034 Hwy. 101
Florence, OR 97439
541-997-2634
PET POLICY: Fee $6, nonrefundable, all sizes welcome, cannot be left unattended in room, 6 acres of lawns for exercise, etc.

Motel 6
1800 Northeast 7th St.
Grants Pass, OR 97526
541-474-1331
PET POLICY: No fee. Dogs under 25 lbs. preferred (larger animals by advance approval). Do not leave animals in room unattended.

Motel 6
5136 S. 6th St.
Klamath Falls, OR 97603
541-884-2110
PET POLICY: No fee. Dogs under 25 lbs. preferred (larger animals by advance approval). Do not leave animals in room unattended.

Shilo Inns
1880 NW 6th St.
Grants Pass, OR 97526
541-479-8391
RATES: Single $69, double $79.
PET POLICY: Fee $10, nonrefundable. All sizes, all pets welcome.

Vagabond Lodge
4070 Westcliff Dr.
Hood River, OR 97031
541-386-2992
RATES: Double $45–$54, suites $86–$98 (seasonal).
PET POLICY: No fees. All sizes accepted. Pets cannot sleep on beds.

Shilo Inn Klamath Falls
2500 Almond St.
Klamath Falls, OR 97601
541-885-7980
RATES: Single $89, double $99.
PET POLICY: Fee $10, nonrefundable. All sizes, all pets welcome.
POI: Mountains.

Crowne Plaza
14811 Kruse Oaks Blvd.
Lake Oswego, OR 97035
503-624-8400
PET POLICY: No fee.

Sailor Jack's Inn
1035 N.W. Harbor Ave.
Lincoln City, OR 97367
541-994-3696
RATES: Single, double $39.95–$65.95 (seasonal).
PET POLICY: Fee $10 per pet. All sizes accepted.

Shilo Inn Lincoln City
1501 NW 40th Pl.
Lincoln City, OR 97367
541-994-2199
RATES: Single $109, double $119.
PET POLICY: Fee $10, nonrefundable. All sizes, all pets welcome.

Motel 6
2400 Biddle Rd.
Medford, OR 97504
541-779-0550
PET POLICY: No fee. Dogs under 25 lbs. preferred (larger animals by advance approval). Do not leave animals in room unattended.

Pear Tree Motel
3730 Fern Valley Rd.
Medford, OR 97504
541-535-4445
PET POLICY: No fee. All sizes and pets accepted. Do not leave in rooms unattended.

Shilo Inn Medford
2111 Biddle Rd.
Medford, OR 97504
541-770-5151
RATES: Single $69, double $79.
PET POLICY: Fee $10, nonrefundable. All sizes, all pets welcome.

Shilo Inn
501 Sitka Ave.
Newberg, OR 97132
503-537-0303
RATES: Single $59, double $69.
PET POLICY: Fee $10, nonrefundable. All sizes, all pets welcome.

Holiday Inn Newport at Agate Beach
3019 N. Coast Hwy.
Newport, OR 97365
541-265-9411
RATES: Single $109–$124.
PET POLICY: Fee $10 per pet per stay. All sizes welcome. Do not leave unattended in room.

U.S. Lodgings > OREGON

AMENITIES: Doggie bags with treats. Great beach access.
POI: Agate Beach access, Oyaquira Bay Lighthouse, Newport's Historic Bayfront.

Shilo Inn—Newport Oceanfront
536 SW Elizabeth St.
Newport, OR 97365
541-265-7701
RATES: Single $99, double $109.
PET POLICY: Fee $10, nonrefundable. All sizes, all pets welcome.

Holiday Inn
1249 Tapadera Ave.
Ontario, OR 97914
541-889-8621
PET POLICY: Fee $10.

Motel 6
275 NE 12th St.
Ontario, OR 97914
541-889-6617
PET POLICY: No fee. Dogs under 25 lbs. preferred (larger animals by advance approval). Do not leave animals in room unattended.

Motel 6
325 SE Nye Ave.
Pendleton, OR 97801
541-276-3160
PET POLICY: No fee. Dogs under 25 lbs. preferred (larger animals by advance approval). Do not leave animals in room unattended.

Red Lion Inn—Indian Hills
304 SE Nye Ave.
Pendleton, OR 97801
541-276-6111
RATES: Single, double $59–$69.
PET POLICY: Deposit $20, refundable. All sizes and pets accepted.

Travelodge
411 SW Dorion Ave.
Pendleton, OR 97801
541 276-7531
RATES: Single $55, double $65.
PET POLICY: Fee, $10, nonrefundable, all sizes welcome.
POI: Pendleton Underground Tours, World Famous Round-Up Grounds, Umatilla Historical Museum, antique stores.

Days Inn—Portland North
9930 N. Whitaker Rd.
Portland, OR 97217
503-289-1800
RATES: Single $65, double $75, Kitchenette: $80.
PET POLICY: Fee $15, all sizes welcome.
AMENITIES: Dog treat at check-in, pet pick-up station. Delta Park in back for walking pets.
POI: Exposition Center ½ mi, Portland Speedway, Portland Meadows, Jantzen Beach Super center. Downtown, 4 miles.

Four Points Sheraton
50 SW Morrison at Front Ave.
Portland, OR 97204
503-221-0711
PET POLICY: No fee, all sizes and pets welcome (dogs, cats, birds, ferrets, rabbits, reptiles).

Hotel Vintage Plaza
422 SW Broadway
Portland, OR 97205
503-228-1212
RATES: Single $150, double $150.
PET POLICY: No fee, all sizes and pets welcome. Do not leave pets unattended in rooms. On leash in public areas of hotel. Must not be aggressive toward pets or people.
AMENITIES: Bottled water, Dispoz-A-Scoop, VIP treatment.
POI: 7 blocks from Tom McCall Waterfront park, Closest pet restroom is 1 block.

Motel 6
3104 SE Powell Blvd.
Portland, OR 97202
503-238-0600
PET POLICY: No fee. Dogs under 25 lbs. preferred (larger animals by advance approval). Do not leave animals in room unattended.

Red Roof Inn
11207 NE Holman St.
Portland, OR 97220
503-382-3820
PET POLICY: No fee, pets under 80 lbs. Must be leashed to and from rooms. Do not leave in room unattended.

Residence Inn by Marriott Portland Downtown
1710 NE Multnomah
Portland, OR 97232
503-288-1400
RATES: Single $139–$144, double $165–$189.
PET POLICY: Fee $50, nonrefundable. All sizes and all pets welcome (dogs, cats, birds, ferrets, rabbits, reptiles). Must keep restrained for housekeeping to service room.
AMENITIES: Walking area.

River Place Hotel
1510 SW Harbor Way
Portland, OR 97201
503-228-3233
RATES: Single $219, double $239.
PET POLICY: Fee $100 nonrefundable. All sizes welcome.
AMENITIES: Walking, bowls, blankets, special food mats, biscuits.
POI: Waterfront park, Walk along the Esplanade.

U.S. Suites
10220 SW Nimbus
Portland, OR 97223
503-443-2033
RATES: Single $99–$129, double $119–$149.
PET POLICY: Fee $150–$300, nonrefundable.

Motel 6
2247 S. Hwy. 97
Redmond, OR 97756
541-923-2100
PET POLICY: No fee. Dogs under 25 lbs. preferred (larger animals by advance approval). Do not leave animals in room unattended.

Anchor Bay Inn
1821 Hwy. 101 Ave.
Reedsport, OR 97467
541-271-2149
RATES: Single $49, double $59.
PET POLICY: Fee $5, nonrefundable. All pets up to 50 lbs. Birds also. Must take pet with you when you leave the room.
AMENITIES: Pick up bags.

U.S. Lodgings > OREGON

Motel 6
1401 Hawthorne Ave NE
Salem, OR 97301
503-371-8024
PET POLICY: No fee. Dogs under 25 lbs. preferred (larger animals by advance approval). Do not leave animals in room unattended.

Aloha Inn
441 2nd Ave.
Seaside, OR 97138
503-738-9581
PET POLICY: Fee $7, nonrefundable. All sizes welcome.

Comfort Inn Boardwalk
545 Broadway
Seaside, OR 97138
503-738-3011
RATES: Single $78, double $88.
PET POLICY: Fee $7 nonrefundable.
POI: 3 blocks to the beach.

Shilo Inn Seaside East
900 S. Holladay
Seaside, OR 97138
503-738-0549
RATES: Single $89, double $99.
PET POLICY: Fee $10, nonrefundable. All sizes, all pets welcome.

Shilo Inn Eugene/Springfield
3350 Gateway
Springfield, OR 97477
541-747-0332
RATES: Single $69, double $79.
PET POLICY: Fee $10, nonrefundable. All sizes, all pets welcome.

Summer Lake Inn
31501 Hwy. 31
Summer Lake, OR 97640
541-943-3983
RATES: All cabins: $100–$125.
PET POLICY: Fee $10 per stay (up to 10 days), nonrefundable. All size dogs welcome, no cats.
AMENITIES: Places to swim, large area for running.
POI: Wide open spaces, no people, mountains and high desert.

The Dalles Days Inn
2500 W. Sixth
The Dalles, OR 97058
541-296-1191
PET POLICY: Fee $10.

Shilo Inn
3223 Bret Clodfelter Way
The Dalles, OR 97058
541-298-5502
RATES: Single $69, double $79.
PET POLICY: Fee $10, nonrefundable. All sizes, all pets welcome.

Motel 6
17959 SW McEwan Rd.
Tigard, OR 97224
503-684-0760
PET POLICY: No fee. Dogs under 25 lbs. preferred (larger animals by advance approval). Do not leave animals in room unattended.

Shilo Inn Portland I-5
7300 SW Hazel Fern Rd.
Tigard, OR 97224
503-639-2226
RATES: Single $59, double $69.
PET POLICY: Fee $10, nonrefundable. All sizes, all pets welcome.

Shilo Inn—Washington Square
10830 SW Greenburg Rd.
Tigard, OR 97223
503-620-4320
RATES: Single $59, double $69.
PET POLICY: Fee $10, nonrefundable. All sizes, all pets welcome.

Shilo Inn—Tillamook
2515 N. Main St.
Tillamook, OR 97141
503-842-7971
RATES: Single $89, double $99.
PET POLICY: Fee $10, nonrefundable. All sizes, all pets welcome.

1900 Sears & Roebuck Home
484 N. 10th St.
Vale, OR 97918
541-473-9636
RATES: Double $65.
PET POLICY: No fee, all sizes and pets welcome. Pets not allowed in B&B home, but kept in kennels or in heated building. Horses, $10, includes hay. All pets must be vaccinated.
AMENITIES: Horses and hunting dogs welcome.

Shilo Inn
1609 E. Harbor Dr.
Warrenton, OR 97146
503-861-2181
RATES: Single $89, double $99.
PET POLICY: Fee $10, nonrefundable. All sizes, all pets welcome.

Fireside Resorts Motel
1881 Hwy. 101 North
Yachats, OR 97498
541-547-3636
RATES: Single, double $69–$130.
PET POLICY: Fee $7 per day (maximum 2 pets in room).

PENNSYLVANIA

Days Inn Conference Center
1151 Bulldog Dr.
Allentown, PA 18104
610-395-3731
PET POLICY: Fee $15.

Red Roof Inn
1846 Catasauqua Rd.
Allentown, PA 18103
610-264-5404
PET POLICY: No fee, pets under 80 lbs. Must be leashed to and from rooms. Do not leave in room unattended.

Motel 6
1500 Sterling St.
Altoona, PA 16602
814-946-7601
PET POLICY: No fee. Dogs under 25 lbs. preferred (larger animals by advance approval). Do not leave animals in room unattended.

Days Inn
State Rd. 8, I-80 & Route 8
Barkeyville, PA 16038
814-786-7901
PET POLICY: No fee.

Janey Lynn Motel
3567 Business Route 220
Bedford, PA 15522
814-634-9515
RATES: Single $23–$45, double $28–$60.
PET POLICY: Fee $5, up to 25 lbs., only dogs and cats, must be clean.

U.S. Lodgings > PENNSYLVANIA

Howard Johnson Hotel
100 Davis St.
Bradford, PA 16701
814-362-4501
RATES: Single $64, double $71.
PET POLICY: Fee $50, refundable.
All sizes welcome.
POI: Zippo Lighter/Case Knife
Museum, Penn-Brad Oil
Museum, Kinzua Railroad
Bridge, Eldred.

Days Inn
139 Pittsburgh Rd.
Butler, PA 16001
412-287-6761
PET POLICY: No fee.

Days Inn Carlisle
101 Alexander Spring Rd.
Carlisle, PA 17013
717-258-4147
PET POLICY: Fee $6.

Motel 6
1153 Harrisburg Pike
Carlisle, PA 17013
717-249-7622
PET POLICY: No fee. Dogs under 25
lbs. preferred (larger animals by
advance approval). Do not leave
animals in room unattended.

Quality Inn Carlisle
1255 Harrisburg Pike
Carlisle, PA 17013
717-243-6000
RATES: Single $65.99, double
$65.99.
PET POLICY: No fee, one pet per
room.
POI: Carlisle fairgrounds, U.S.
Army War College.

Days Inn
30 Falling Spring Rd.
Chambersburg, PA 17201
717-263-1288
PET POLICY: No fee.

Clarion Days Inn
Rt 69 & I-80
Clarion, PA 16214
814-226-8682
PET POLICY: Fee $5.

Red Roof Inn
1454 Beers School Rd.
Coraopolis, PA 15108
412-264-5678

PET POLICY: No fee, pets under
80 lbs. Must be leashed to and
from rooms. Do not leave in
room unattended.

Red Roof Inn
20009 U.S.19 & Marguerite Rd.
Cranberry Township, PA
16066
724-776-5670
PET POLICY: No fee, pets under
80 lbs. Must be leashed to and
from rooms. Do not leave in
room unattended.

Red Roof Inn
300 Red Roof Inn Rd.
Danville, PA 17821
570-275-7600
PET POLICY: No fee, pets under
80 lbs. Must be leashed to and
from rooms. Do not leave in
room unattended.

Econo Lodge
387 Ben Franklin Hwy.
Douglassville, PA 19518
610-385-3016
RATES: Single $42, double $89.
PET POLICY: Fee $10, nonrefund-
able, all sizes welcome, must
be caged when owner not in
room.
POI: Hopewell State Park,
Daniel Boone homestead.

Days Inn
2415 Nazareth Rd.
Easton, PA 18042
610-253-0546
PET POLICY: Fee $5.

Days Inn
7415 Schultz Rd.
Erie, PA 16509
814-868-8521
PET POLICY: Fee $5.

Holiday Inn
18W 18th St.
Erie, PA 16501
814-456-2961
RATES: Single, double
$79–$95–$139.95.
PET POLICY: No fee. Pets under
25 lbs.

Motel 6
7875 Peach St.
Erie, PA 16509
814-864-4811
PET POLICY: No fee. Dogs under 25
lbs. preferred (larger animals by
advance approval). Do not leave
animals in room unattended.

Red Roof Inn
7865 Perry Hwy.
Erie, PA 16509
814-868-5246
PET POLICY: No fee, pets under
80 lbs. Must be leashed to and
from rooms. Do not leave in
room unattended.

Red Roof Inn
49 Industrial Hwy.
Essington, PA 19029
610-521-5090
PET POLICY: No fee, pets under
80 lbs. Must be leashed to and
from rooms. Do not leave in
room unattended.

**Best Western Valley
Forge/Exton**
815 N. Pottstown Pke
Exton, PA 19341
610-363-1100
RATES: Single, double
$79–$109.
PET POLICY: No fee, all sizes and
pets welcome. Pets not permitted in lobby, restaurant, or
bar. Many access doors for
pets in and out.
AMENITIES: Big wooded area in
back. Access doors to outside.

Best Inn
301 Steinwehr Ave.
Gettysburg, PA 17325
717-334-1188
PET POLICY: No fee. All sizes
accepted. Do not leave in
room unattended for long
periods of time.

Travelodge
613 Baltimore St.
Gettysburg, PA 17325
800 578-7878
PET POLICY: No fee. All sizes
accepted.

U.S. Lodgings > PENNSYLVANIA

Sweetwater Farm B&B
50 Sweetwater Rd.
Glen Mills, PA 19342
610-459-4711
RATES: Single, double $200.
PET POLICY: Fee $25, nonre-
fundable. All size dogs and cats
only. Pets welcome in cottages
only.
AMENITIES: Horses and goats on
property.
POI: Brandywine Valley, State
Parks, Chadds Ford.

Baymont Inn
200 N. Mountain Rd.
Harrisburg, PA 17112
717-540-99339
RATES: Single $65, double $75.
PET POLICY: No fee, all sizes
welcome. Do not leave pets
unattended in room.
POI: Hershey Park 9 miles.
Gettysburg 20 miles.

Baymont Inn & Suites
990 Eisenhower Blvd.
Harrisburg, PA 17112
717-939-8000
PET POLICY: No fee.

Comfort Inn
525 S. Front St.
Harrisburg, PA 17104
717-233-1611
PET POLICY: Fee $15 per night
per pet, no size restrictions.

Days Inn—Harrisburg
800 Eisenhower Blvd.
Harrisburg, PA 17057
717-939-4147
PET POLICY: No fee.

Red Roof Inn
400 Corporate Circle
Harrisburg, PA 17110
717-657-1445
PET POLICY: No fee, pets under
80 lbs. Must be leashed to and
from rooms. Do not leave in
room unattended.

Red Roof Inn
950 Eisenhower Boulevard
Harrisburg, PA 17111
717-939-1331
PET POLICY: No fee, pets under
80 lbs. Must be leashed to and
from rooms. Do not leave in
room unattended.

Warrior Ridge Hideaway
PO Box 36
Hesston, PA 16647
814-231-0683
RATES: Single $109–$179, double
$269–$289.
PET POLICY: Fee $10, (1 night
or 1 week) nonrefundable. All
size dogs and cats.
POI: Near Raystown Lake.

Philadelphia Days Inn
245 Easton Rd.
Horsham, PA 19044
215-674-2500
PET POLICY: Fee $10.

Motel 6
430 Napoleon Place
Johnstown, PA 15901
814-536-1114
PET POLICY: No fee. Dogs under 25
lbs. preferred (larger animals by
advance approval). Do not leave
animals in room unattended.

Kane View Motel
RD 1 Box 91A
Kane, PA 16735
814-837-8600
RATES: Single $46, double $48.
PET POLICY: Fee $5, nonrefund-
able.
AMENITIES: Backyard with 3 acres.

Motel 6
815 W. Dekalb Pike
King of Prussia, PA 19406
610-265-7200
PET POLICY: No fee. Dogs under 25
lbs. preferred (larger animals by
advance approval). Do not leave
animals in room unattended.

Red Roof Inn
3100 Cabot Boulevard West
Langhorne, PA 19047
215-750-6200
PET POLICY: No fee, pets under
80 lbs. Must be leashed to and
from rooms. Do not leave in
room unattended.

Daum's Country Living
2220 Maple Dr.
Leeper, PA 16233
814-744-8381

RATES: Avg: $135 per night.
PET POLICY: No fee, all sizes and
pets welcome. Do not leave in
room unattended unless
crated. Must be housebroken.
POI: Cook Forest State Park,
Allegheny National Forest.

General Sutter Inn
14 E. Main St.
Lititz, PA 17543
717-626-2115
PET POLICY: No fee, free dog
biscuits, all sizes welcome.

Comfort Inn
300 Gateway Dr.
Mansfield, PA 16933
570-662-3000
RATES: Single $65, double $75.
PET POLICY: Fee $10, all size
pets accepted.

Pittsburgh Days Inn
924 Sheraton Dr.
Mars, PA 18046
724-772-2700
PET POLICY: No fee.

**Best Western Inn at
Hunt's Landing**
900 Route 6 & 209
Matamoras, PA 18336
570-491-2400
RATES: Single, double $84–$129.
PET POLICY: No fee. No restric-
tions.

Days Inn of Meadville
240 Conneaut Lake Rd.
Meadville, PA 16335
814-337-4264
PET POLICY: Fee $5.

Harrisburg Days Inn
1012 Wesley Dr.
Mechanicsburg, PA 17055
717-766-3700
PET POLICY: Fee $25.

Holiday Inn
I-80 & US 150 N.
Milesburg, PA 16853
814-355-7521
RATES: Single $85, double $85.
PET POLICY: No fee, all sizes and
all pets welcome (dogs, cats,
ferrets, birds, rabbits, reptiles).

U.S. Lodgings > PENNSYLVANIA

Days Inn—Monroeville
2727 Mosside Blvd.
Monroeville, PA 15146
412-856-1610
PET POLICY: Fee $5.

Red Roof Inn
2729 Mosside Boulevard
Monroeville, PA 15146
412-856-4738
PET POLICY: No fee, pets under 80 lbs. Must be leashed to and from rooms. Do not leave in room unattended.

Days Inn
353 Lewisberry Rd.
New Cumberland, PA 17070
717-774-4156
PET POLICY: Fee $15.

Ramada Inn
110 Main St.
New Stanton, PA 15672
724-925-6755
PET POLICY: Fee $10 nonrefundable, prefer small pets.

Crowne Plaza
1800 Market St.
Philadelphia, PA 19103
215-561-7500
RATES: Single $159, double $169.
PET POLICY: Fee $25, plus $100 refundable deposit. Rooms cleaned only if pet is in crate.

Motel 6
211 Beecham Dr.
Pittsburgh, PA 15205
412-922-9400
PET POLICY: No fee. Dogs under 25 lbs. preferred (larger animals by advance approval). Do not leave animals in room unattended.

Philadelphia Marriott
1201 Market St.
Philadelphia, PA 19107
215-625-2900
PET POLICY: Fee $100 nonrefundable.

Pittsburgh Days Inn
100 Kisow Dr.
Pittsburgh, PA 15205
412-922-0120
PET POLICY: Fee $10.

Red Roof Inn
6404 Steubenville Pike
Pittsburgh, PA 15205
412-787-7870
PET POLICY: No fee, pets under 80 lbs. Must be leashed to and from rooms. Do not leave in room unattended.

Westin Convention Center
1000 Penn Ave.
Pittsburgh, PA, 15222
412-281-3700
RATES: Single, double $79+.
PET POLICY: No fee, all pets and sizes welcome. Must sign damage waiver.

Pittston Days Inn
307 Rt 315
Pittston, PA 18640
570-654-3301
PET POLICY: Fee $10.

Days Inn
29 High St.
Pottstown, PA 19464
610-970-1101
PET POLICY: Fee $10.

Econo Lodge
387 Ben Franklin Hwy.
Pottstown, PA 19518
610-385-3016
PET POLICY: Fee $10, nonrefundable, all sizes welcome, must be caged when owner not in room.

Cottage at Ross Mill Farm
PO Box 498
Ruchland, PA 18956
215-322-1539
RATES: Single, double $100.
PET POLICY: No fee. All sizes and pets welcome.
AMENITIES: Cottages for 6 people and pets with large, enclosed area with shelter for pets when owner is away. Lots of woods and streams. Pets are part of the experience of staying at the cottage.

Hampton Inn
US 11 and 15
Selinsgrove, PA 17870
570-743-2223
PET POLICY: Deposit required.

Pegasus Bed & Breakfast
Woodtown Rd.
Shohola, PA 18458
570-296-4017
RATES: Room w/bath: $75, shared bath: $65.
PET POLICY: No fee. All sizes accepted.
AMENITIES: cottage.

Days Inn—Somerset
220 Waterworks Rd.
Somerset, PA 15501
814-445-9200
PET POLICY: No fee.

Holiday Inn
202 Harmon St.
Somerset, PA 15501
814-445-9611
RATES: Single $69–$89, double $79–$99.
PET POLICY: No fee, up to 50 lbs.
POI: Idlewild Amusement Park, Georgian Place factory shops, Frank Lloyd Wright "Fallingwater", Jennerstown speedway.

Spring Valley Bed & Breakfast
RR 1, Box 117
Spring Creek, PA 16436
814-489-3695
RATES: Single $99, double $159.
PET POLICY: No fee, all size dogs, only.
AMENITIES: 35 acres of country to hike. Horseback riding on premises.

Days Inn Penn State
240 Pugh St.
State College, PA 16801
814-238-8454
PET POLICY: Fee $10.

Motel 6
1274 N. Atherton St.
State College, PA 16803
814-234-1600
PET POLICY: No fee. Dogs under 25 lbs. preferred (larger animals by advance approval). Do not leave animals in room unattended.

U.S. Lodgings > PENNSYLVANIA

Rimrock Country Cottages
425 Rimrock Dr.
Stroudsburg, PA 18360
570-629-2360
RATES: Single, double $125.
PET POLICY: No fee, all sizes and pets welcome (dogs, cats, birds, ferrets, rabbits, reptiles). Animals must be on leash outside. Must clean up after pets.
POI: Resort area.

Red Roof Inn
3100 Lincoln Hwy.
Trevose, PA 19053
215-244-9422
PET POLICY: No fee, pets under 80 lbs. Must be leashed to and from rooms. Do not leave in room unattended.

Holiday Inn
210 Ludlow St.
Warren, PA 16365
814-726-300
PET POLICY: Fee with signed waiver.

Motel 6
1283 Motel 6 Dr.
Washington, PA 15301
724-223-8040
PET POLICY: No fee. Dogs under 25 lbs. preferred (larger animals by advance approval). Do not leave animals in room unattended.

Red Roof Inn
1399 W. Chestnut St.
Washington, PA 15301
724-228-5750
PET POLICY: No fee, pets under 80 lbs. Must be leashed to and from rooms. Do not leave in room unattended.

Radisson Hotel Sharon
Route 18 & I-80
West Middlesex, PA 16159
724-528-2501
RATES: Single $90, double $95.
PET POLICY: No fee, up to 25 lbs.

Pocono Days Inn
State Rd. 940
White Haven, PA 18661
717-443-0391
PET POLICY: Fee $5.

**Holiday Inn/
TGI Friday's Complex**
880 Kidder St.
Wilkes-Barre, PA 18702
570-824-8901
RATES: Single $84.
PET POLICY: No fee, All pets welcome.

Red Roof Inn
1035 Highway 315
Wilkes-Barre, PA 18702
717-829-6422
PET POLICY: No fee, pets under 80 lbs. Must be leashed to and from rooms. Do not leave in room unattended.

Wilkes-Barre Days Inn
760 Kidder St.
Wilkes-Barre, PA 18702
570-826-0111
PET POLICY: No fee.

City View Inn
US 15
Williamsport, PA 17701
717-326-2601
PET POLICY: No fee, all sizes and pets welcome.

Motel 6
125 Arsenal Rd.
York, PA 17404
717-846-6260
PET POLICY: No fee. Dogs under 25 lbs. preferred (larger animals by advance approval). Do not leave animals in room unattended.

Red Roof Inn
323 Arsenal Rd.
York, PA 17402
717-843-8181
PET POLICY: No fee, pets under 80 lbs. Must be leashed to and from rooms. Do not leave in room unattended.

RHODE ISLAND

Babcock House
7 Florence Ave.
Newport, RI 02840
401-851-2016
PET POLICY: Fee $50, refundable. All size dogs and cats.
AMENITIES: Fenced-in yard.

Bannister's Wharf
1 Bannisters Wharf
Newport, RI 02840
401-846-4500
RATES: Single $75–$275, double $75–$275.
PET POLICY: No fee, all sizes and all pets welcome. Owner responsible for any damages.

Bidlack's Bed & Breakfast
80 Bliss Mine Rd.
Newport, RI 02840
401-849-3691
RATES: Double $150.
PET POLICY: No fee, all pets welcome. Up to 50 lbs.
AMENITIES: 1 block from city park, walking distance to beach, big yard, accommodations are a 3-room
POI: Newport Mansions, Cliff Walk, Beaches, Sailing, Historical sites.

Inn on Bellevue
30 Bellevue Ave.
Newport, RI 02840
401-848-6242
RATES: Single/Double $90–$175.
PET POLICY: No fee, all sizes and pets welcome. Please call if pets are over 50 lbs., or exotic.

Motel 6
Rt 114 at Coddington Hwy.
249 JT Connell Hwy.
Newport, RI 02840
401-848-0600
PET POLICY: No fee. Dogs under 25 lbs. preferred (larger animals by advance approval). Do not leave animals in room unattended.

SeaView Inn
240 Aquidneck Ave.
Newport, RI 02842
401-846-5000
RATES: Double $79–$179.
PET POLICY: Fee $10 per night. All sizes welcome. $25 damage deposit.
POI: Ocean view rooms. 1.5 miles to downtown.

U.S. Lodgings > SOUTH CAROLINA

The Kings' Rose
Bed & Breakfast Inn
1747 Moorsfield Rd.
South Kingstown, RI 02879
401-783-5222
RATES: Single $110, double $150.
PET POLICY: No fee. Do not
leave pet unattended in room.
POI: University of RI campus
beach, many state beaches, US
Wildlife Refuge, Newport
mansions nearby.

Larchwood Inn
521 Main St.
Wakefield, RI 02879
401-783-5454
RATES: Single $90, double $130.
PET POLICY: Fee $5, nonrefund-
able, pets not allowed in
public areas.
POI: Newport, Mystic Seaport,
Foxwoods Casino, Block Island.

Crowne Plaza
801 Greenwich Ave.
Warwick, RI 2886
401-732-6000
PET POLICY: No fee.

Motel 6
20 Jefferson Boulevard
Warwick, RI 02888
401-467-9800
PET POLICY: No fee. Dogs under 25
lbs. preferred (larger animals by
advance approval). Do not leave
animals in room unattended.

SOUTH CAROLINA

Days Inn—Downtown
1204 Richland Ave. W.
Aiken, SC 29801
803-649-5524
PET POLICY: Fee $10.

Anderson Days Inn
1007 Smith Mill Rd.
Anderson, SC 29625
864-375-0375
PET POLICY: No fee.

Days Inn—Port Royal
1660 S. Ribaut
Beaufort, SC 29935
803-524-1551
PET POLICY: Deposit required.

Camden SC Bed &
Breakfast
127 Union St.
Camden, SC 29020
803-432-2366
RATES: Single, double $85.
PET POLICY: No fee, all sizes and
all pets welcome. Pets not
allowed in dining room.

Days Inn—Airport Coliseum
2998 W. Montague Ave.
Charleston, SC 29418
843-747-4101
PET POLICY: Fee $6.

Motel 6
2551 Ashley Phosphate Rd.
Charleston, SC 29418
843-572-6590
PET POLICY: No fee. Dogs under 25
lbs. preferred (larger animals by
advance approval). Do not leave
animals in room unattended.

Cheraw Days Inn
820 Market St.
Cheraw, SC 29520
843-537-5554
PET POLICY: Fee $5.

Baymont Inn & Suites
911 Bush River Rd.
Columbia, SC 29210
803-798-3222
PET POLICY: No fee.

Baymont Inn & Suites
1538 Horseshoe Dr.
Columbia, SC 29223
803-736-6400
PET POLICY: No fee.

Columbia Days Inn
133 Plumbers Rd.
Columbia, SC 29203
803-754-4408
PET POLICY: Fee $7.

Motel 6
1776 Burning Tree Rd.
Columbia, SC 29210
803-798-9210
PET POLICY: No fee. Dogs under 25
lbs. preferred (larger animals by
advance approval). Do not leave
animals in room unattended.

Red Roof Inn
7580 Two Notch Rd.
Columbia, SC 29223
803-736-0850
PET POLICY: No fee, pets under
80 lbs. Must be leashed to and
from rooms. Do not leave in
room unattended.

Red Roof Inn
10 Berryhill Rd.
Columbia, SC 29210
803-798-9220
PET POLICY: No fee, pets under
80 lbs. Must be leashed to and
from rooms. Do not leave in
room unattended.

Florence Days Inn
2111 W. Lucas St.
Florence, SC 29501
843-665-4444
PET POLICY: No fee.

Motel 6
1834 W. Lucas Rd.
Florence, SC 29501
843-667-6100
PET POLICY: No fee. Dogs under 25
lbs. preferred (larger animals by
advance approval). Do not leave
animals in room unattended.

Red Roof Inn
2690 David McLeod Blvd.
Florence, SC 29501
843-678-9000
PET POLICY: No fee, pets under
80 lbs. Must be leashed to and
from rooms. Do not leave in
room unattended.

Days Inn Charlotte
South—Carowinds
3482 Carowinds Blvd.
Fort Mill, SC 29715
803-548-8000
PET POLICY: Fee $5.

Motel 6
255 Carowinds Blvd.
Fort Mill, SC 29708
803-548-9656
PET POLICY: No fee. Dogs under 25
lbs. preferred (larger animals by
advance approval). Do not leave
animals in room unattended.

U.S. Lodgings > SOUTH CAROLINA

Hampton Inn
I-85 Exit 90, Hwy. 105 &
Nancy Creek Rd.
Gaffney, SC 29341
864-206-0011
PET POLICY: Fee $10.

Red Roof Inn
132 New Painter Rd.
Gaffney, SC 29341
864-206-0200
PET POLICY: No fee, pets under
80 lbs. Must be leashed to and
from rooms. Do not leave in
room unattended.

Spartanburg Days Inn
I-85 & Hwy. 11
Gaffney, SC 29341
864-489-7172
PET POLICY: No fee.

Charleston Days Inn
1430 Redbank Rd.
Goose Creek, SC 29445
843-797-6000
PET POLICY: Fee $10.

Crowne Plaza
851 Congaree Rd.
Greenville, SC 29607
864-297-6300
PET POLICY: Fee $50, non-
refundable.

Days Inn
831 Congaree Rd.
Greenville, SC 29607
864-288-6221
PET POLICY: Fee $10.

Guesthouse Suites Plus
48 McPrice Court
Greenville, SC 29615
864-297-0099
RATES: Single $90, double $110.
PET POLICY: Fee $100, nonre-
fundable. Up to 25 lbs.
POI: Bilo Center. Palmetto
Expo. Center. Downtown
Greenville.

Motel 6
224 Bruce Rd.
Greenville, SC 29605
864-277-8630
PET POLICY: No fee. Dogs under 25
lbs. preferred (larger animals by
advance approval). Do not leave
animals in room unattended.

Red Roof Inn
2801 Laurens Rd.
Greenville, SC 29607
864-297-4458
PET POLICY: No fee, pets under
80 lbs. Must be leashed to and
from rooms. Do not leave in
room unattended.

Days Inn Stateline
I-95 & US 17
PO Box 1150
Hardeeville, SC 29927
803-784-2281
PET POLICY: Fee $5.

Motel 6
224 Bruce Rd.
Greenville, SC 29605
864-277-8630
PET POLICY: No fee. Dogs under 25
lbs. preferred (larger animals by
advance approval). Do not leave
animals in room unattended.

Ocean Breeze
50 Ocean Breeze
Hilton Head, SC 29928
717-657-0177
RATES: Weekly Rates: $550–
$3250.
PET POLICY: Fee $500.
Refundable All pets welcome,
dogs must be on leash outside.
POI: Ocean beaches.

Red Roof Inn
5 Regency Pkwy.
Hilton Head Island, SC 29928
843-686-6808
PET POLICY: No fee, pets under
80 lbs. Must be leashed to and
from rooms. Do not leave in
room unattended.

Sunset Rentals
PO Box 7258
Hilton Head, SC 29938
843-785-6767
RATES: Single $100.
PET POLICY: Fee $500, refund-
able. Up to 50 lbs., cats and
dogs only. Current (30 days)
health certificate and shot
record.

Lake City Days Inn
170 S. Ron McNair Blvd.
Lake City, SC 29560
843-394-3269
PET POLICY: No fee.

The Red Horse Inn
310 N. Campbell Rd.
Landrum, SC 29356
864-895-4968
PET POLICY: Fee $50, refund-
able. Prefer small, pets. Larger
sizes require cleaning fee
and/or crate.

Myrtle Beach Days Inn
1564 Hwy. 17 N
Little River, SC 29566
843-249-3535
PET POLICY: Fee $10.

Camden Days Inn
529 Hwy. 601
Lugoff, SC 29078
803-438-6990
PET POLICY: Fee $6.

Days Inn of Manning
I-95 & US 301
Manning, SC 29102
803-473-2596
PET POLICY: Fee $5.

**Fannie Kate's Inn &
Restaurant**
127 S. Main St.
McCormick, SC 29835
864-465-0051
RATES: Single, double $85.
PET POLICY: Fee $25, refundable.
All size dogs and cats, only.
AMENITIES: Will walk dogs if
desired by owner.

Red Roof Inn
301 Johnnie Dodds Blvd.
Mt Pleasant, SC 29464
843-884-1411
PET POLICY: No fee, pets under
80 lbs. Must be leashed to and
from rooms. Do not leave in
room unattended.

El Dorado Motel
2800 S. Ocean Blvd.
Myrtle Beach, SC 29577
843-626-3559
PET POLICY: Fee $50 deposit,
$10 daily fee, up to 25 lbs.

La Quinta Inn & Suites
1561 21st Ave.
Myrtle Beach, SC 29577
843-916-8801
PET POLICY: Fee none, up to 25
lbs.

U.S. Lodgings > SOUTH CAROLINA

Mariner Hotel
7003 N. Ocean Blvd.
Myrtle Beach, SC, 29572
843-449-5281
RATES: Single, double $49-139
PET POLICY: Fee $9 per night,
Deposit, $100, refundable. No
restrictions.

Myrtle Beach Days Inn
3209 Hwy. 17 S.
Myrtle Beach, SC 29582
843-272-6196
PET POLICY: Fee $10.

Palm Crest Motel
701 S. Ocean Blvd.
Myrtle Beach, SC 29577
843-448-7141
RATES: Single, double $51–$85
(seasonal changes) Rooms
w/kitchenettes.
PET POLICY: No fee, all sizes
accepted ("no elephants,
please").

Red Roof Inn
2801 S. Kings Hwy.
Myrtle Beach, SC 29577
843-626-4444
PET POLICY: No fee, pets under
80 lbs. Must be leashed to and
from rooms. Do not leave in
room unattended.

Sportsman Motor Inn
1405 S. Ocean Blvd.
Myrtle Beach, SC 29577
843-334-4311
PET POLICY: Fee $12, plus $50
refundable deposit. Dogs and
Cats up to 25 lbs., also, birds.
Pet septic tank and walking
area.

St. John's Inn
6803 N. Ocean Blvd.
Myrtle Beach, SC 29572
843-449-5251
PET POLICY: Fee $50 deposit,
$10 daily fee, up to 50 lbs.

Super 8 Motel
3450 Hwy. 17S Bypass
Myrtle Beach, SC 29577
843-293-6100
PET POLICY: No pets over 30 lbs.

The Sportsman Motor Inn
1405 S. Ocean Blvd.
Myrtle Beach, SC 29577
843-448-4311
RATES: Double $70.
PET POLICY: Fee $12 per night,
$50 refundable security, full-
grown pets, only, under 20 lbs.
AMENITIES: Pet septic tank.
Walking area.
POI: Pavilion. Broadway at the
Beach.

Newberry Days Inn
Rt 1 Winnsboro Rd.
Newberry, SC 29108
803-276-2294
PET POLICY: No fee.

Back to the Beach
1416 S. Ocean Blvd.
North Myrtle Beach, SC
29582
888-BEACH-40
RATES: From $79 per night up
to $1495 per week.
PET POLICY: Fee $100 week,
nonrefundable, all sizes and all
pets welcome. Dogs and cats
must have proof of current
vaccination.
AMENITIES: Pet fee waived to
max. $100 per visit.
POI: Near Ocean/Beach, 225
outlet stores.

Red Roof Inn
7480 Northwoods Blvd.
North Charleston, SC 29406
843-572-9100
RATES: Single $49.99, double
$54.99.
PET POLICY: No fee, pets under
80 lbs. Must be leashed to and
from rooms. Do not leave in
room unattended.
POI: 12 miles to downtown
Charleston. 3 miles east of
Charleston Southern University.

Retreat Myrtle Beach
500 Main St.
North Myrtle Beach, SC
29582
800-645-3618
PET POLICY: Fee $100 over 30 lbs.
$50 under 30 lbs., for length
of stay. All size pets welcome.
POI: Oceanfront/1st block.

Orangeburg Days Inn
Rt. 2 Box 215
Orangeburg, SC 29115
803-534-0500
PET POLICY: Fee $7.

Richburg Days Inn
Hwy. 9 & I-77, Ex. 65
Richburg, SC 29729
803-789-5555
PET POLICY: Fee $5.

Holiday Inn
I-95 & US 78
St. George, SC 29477
843-563-4581
RATES: Single, double $79.
PET POLICY: No fee, all animals
(with fur) accepted, all sizes,
no reptiles, pet menu, treats,
walking area.
AMENITIES: Large pet walk and
play field.

St. George Days Inn
128 Interstate Dr.
St. George, SC 29477
843-563-4027
PET POLICY: Fee $5.

St. George Economy Motel
125 Motel Dr.
St. George, SC 29477
843-563-2360
RATES: Single $31.95, double
$39.95.
PET POLICY: No fee, all sizes and
all pets welcome (dogs, cats,
ferrets, birds, rabbits, reptiles).

Comfort Inn
249 Britain St.
Santee, SC 29142
803-854-3221
RATES: Single $59.95, double
$59.95.
PET POLICY: Fee $10, nonrefund-
able, all sizes welcome.

Days Inn
9078 Old Hwy. #6
Santee, SC 29142
803-854-2175
PET POLICY: Fee $6.

U.S. Lodgings > SOUTH CAROLINA

Main Street Motel
700 W. Main St.
Spartanburg, SC 29301
864-583-8471
RATES: Single $30, double $45.
PET POLICY: Fee $5 per day,
small animals (no reptiles or
farm animals).
AMENITIES: Large lawn for
walking dogs.

Motel 6
105 Jones Rd.
Spartanburg, SC 29303
864-573-6383
PET POLICY: No fee. Dogs under 25
lbs. preferred (larger animals by
advance approval). Do not leave
animals in room unattended.

Residence Inn by Marriott
9011 Fairforest Rd.
Spartanburg, SC 29301
864-576-3333
RATES: Single $99, double $109.
PET POLICY: Fee $150, non-
refundable. Dogs and cats only.

Spartanburg Days Inn
100 Hearon Cir.
Spartanburg, SC 29303
864-503-9048
PET POLICY: No fee.

**Magnolia House
Bed & Breakfast**
230 Church St.
Sumter, SC 29150
803-775-6694
RATES: Single $85, double $95.
PET POLICY: No fee, all sizes and
all pets welcome. Must be
friendly and kept on leash. Do
not leave in room unattended.

Turbeville Days Inn
I-95 and Hwy. 378
Turbeville, SC 29162
843-659-8060
PET POLICY: Fee $5.

Winnsboro Days Inn
Hwy. 34 & 321
Winnsboro, SC 29180
803-635-1447
PET POLICY: Fee $5.

Point South Days Inn
Jct I-95 Ex 33 & US 17
Yemassee, SC 29945
843-726-8156
PET POLICY: Fee $5.

SOUTH DAKOTA

Motel 6
1815 5th Ave.
Belle Fourche, SD 57717
605-892-6663
PET POLICY: No fee. Dogs under 25
lbs. preferred (larger animals by
advance approval). Do not leave
animals in room unattended.

Chamberlain Days Inn
I-90, Ex. 260
Chamberlain, SD 57325
605-734-4111
PET POLICY: No fee.

The Guest House
201 E. Mott Ave.
Chamberlain, SD 57325
605-734-5815
RATES: Single, double $65.
PET POLICY: No fee, all pets
welcome. No restrictions.
AMENITIES: Fenced yard.
POI: Furnished guest house,
near marine, hiking trails,
beach on Missouri River.

Custer Days Inn
532 Crook St.
Custer, SD 57730
605-673-4500
PET POLICY: Fee $5.

Deadwood Days Inn
Hwy. 85 S.
Deadwood, SD 57732
605-578-1294
PET POLICY: Fee $10.

Prairie Vista Inn
Hwy. 212 E.
Faith, SD 57626
605-967-2343
RATES: Single $49, double $55.
PET POLICY: Fee $50, refundable.
All sizes welcome. Do not
leave pets in room unattended.
POI: Hometown of the T-Rex-
Sue. 2 hrs. to Mt. Rushmore
and Black Hills. 1½ hrs. from
Sturgis,

Fort Pierre Motel
211 S. First St.
Fort Pierre, SD 57532
605-223-3111
RATES: Single $38, double $46.

PET POLICY: No fee, all sizes
welcome.
AMENITIES: Exercise area. Dog
treats.
POI: Lily Park. City Park.

Coachlight Motel
1000 W. Havens St.
Mitchell, SD 57301
605-996-5686
RATES: Single $36, double $44.
PET POLICY: No fee, all sizes
welcome.

Motel 6
1309 S. Ohlman St.
Mitchell, SD 57301
605-996-0530
PET POLICY: No fee. Dogs under 25
lbs. preferred (larger animals by
advance approval). Do not leave
animals in room unattended.

Days Inn
520 W. Sioux Ave.
Pierre, SD 57501
605-224-0411
PET POLICY: No fee.

Apollo Motel
2400 Mt. Rushmore Rd.
Rapid City, SD 57701
605-343-9331
PET POLICY: Fee $25 refundable
deposit, up to 30 lbs.

Knights Inn
2401 Mt. Rushmore Rd.
Rapid City, SD 57701
605-348-1453
PET POLICY: No fee, dogs only,
all sizes accepted.

Motel 6
620 E. Latrobe St.
Rapid City, SD 57701
605-343-3687
PET POLICY: No fee. Dogs under 25
lbs. preferred (larger animals by
advance approval). Do not leave
animals in room unattended.

Baymont Inn
3200 Meadow Ave.
Sioux Falls, SD 57106
605-362-0835
RATES: Single $54–$79, double
$59–$89.
PET POLICY: No fee, all sizes and
pets welcome (dogs, cats,
ferrets, birds, rabbits, reptiles).

U.S. Lodgings > TENNESSEE

Motel 6
3009 W. Russell St.
Sioux Falls, SD 57107
605-336-7800
PET POLICY: No fee. Dogs under 25 lbs. preferred (larger animals by advance approval). Do not leave animals in room unattended.

Sioux Falls Days Inn
5001 N. Cliff Ave.
Sioux Falls, SD 57104
605-331-5959
PET POLICY: Fee Call for information.

Royal Rest Motel
444 Main St.
Spearfish, SD 57783
605-642-3842
RATES: Single $40, double $50.
PET POLICY: No fee, up to 50 lbs. ended.

Sturges Days Inn
HC 55 Box 348
Sturges, SD 57785
605-347-3027
PET POLICY: No fee.

Hitching Post Motel
211 10th Ave.
Wall, SD 57790
605-279-2133
RATES: Single $40–$44, double $44–$50.
PET POLICY: No fee, all sizes welcome.
AMENITIES: Walk area.
POI: National Park.

TENNESSEE

Nashville Days Inn
501 Collins Park Dr.
Antioch, TN 37013
615-731-7800
PET POLICY: Fee $8.

Athens Days Inn
2541 Decatur Pike
Athens, TN 37303
423-745-5800
PET POLICY: No fee.

Motel 6
2002 Whitaker Rd.
Athens, TN 37303
419-745-4441
PET POLICY: No fee. Dogs under 25 lbs. preferred (larger animals by advance approval). Do not leave animals in room unattended.

Ramada Limited
115 County Rd. 247
Athens, TN 37303
423-745-1212
RATES: Single, double $49.95–$59.95.
PET POLICY: Fee $6. All sizes accepted.

Baymont Inn & Suites
108 W. Park Dr.
Brentwood, TN 37027
615-376-4666
PET POLICY: No fee.

Red Roof Inn
8097 Moores Ln.
Brentwood, TN 37027
615-309-8860
PET POLICY: No fee, pets under 80 lbs. Must be leashed to and from rooms. Do not leave in room unattended.

Residence Inn Nashville Brentwood
206 Ward Cir.
Brentwood, TN 37027
615-371-0100
RATES: Single $99, double $129.
PET POLICY: Fee $100–$150 nonrefundable, up to 25 lbs., one pet per room.

Chattanooga Days Inn
101 E. 20th St.
Chattanooga, TN 37408
423-267-9761
PET POLICY: Fee $5.

Holiday Inn
2345 Shallowford Village Dr.
Chattanooga, TN 37421
423-855-2898
PET POLICY: Pets up to 30 lbs.

Holiday Inn Express
7024 McCucheon Rd.
Chattanooga, TN 37421
423-490-8560
PET POLICY: Pets up to 30 lbs.

Red Roof Inn
6521 Ringgold Rd.
Chattanooga, TN 37412
423-894-6720
PET POLICY: No fee, pets under 80 lbs. Must be leashed to and from rooms. Do not leave in room unattended.

Motel 6
2440 Williams St.
Chattanooga, TN 37408
423-265-7300
PET POLICY: No fee. Dogs under 25 lbs. preferred (larger animals by advance approval). Do not leave animals in room unattended.

Red Roof Inn
7014 Shallowford Rd.
Chattanooga, TN 37421
423-899-0143
PET POLICY: No fee, pets under 80 lbs. Must be leashed to and from rooms. Do not leave in room unattended.

Days Inn of Clarksville
76 Connector Rd.
Clarksville, TN 37043
615-358-3194
PET POLICY: No fee.

Red Roof Inn
197 Holiday Dr.
Clarksville, TN 37040
931-905-1555
PET POLICY: No fee, pets under 80 lbs. Must be leashed to and from rooms. Do not leave in room unattended.

Baymont Inn & Suites
107 Interstate Drive NW
Cleveland, TN 37312
423-339-1000
PET POLICY: No fee.

Cleveland Days Inn
2550 Georgetown Rd.
Cleveland, TN 37311
615-476-2112
PET POLICY: No fee.

Columbia Days Inn
1504 Nashville Hwy.
Columbia, TN 38401
931-381-3297
PET POLICY: Fee $5.

U.S. Lodgings > TENNESSEE

Baymont Inn & Suites
1161 S. Jefferson
Cookeville, TN 38506
931-525-6668
PET POLICY: No fee.

Days Inn
1296 Bunker Hill Rd.
Cookeville, TN 38501
615-528-1511
PET POLICY: Call for details.

Crossville Days Inn
305 Executive Dr.
Crossville, TN 38555
931-484-9691
PET POLICY: Fee $5, nonrefundable.

Best Western Dayton
7835 Rhea County Hwy.
Dayton, TN 37321
423-775-6560
RATES: Single $55, double $59.
PET POLICY: Fee $3, per night, nonrefundable. Pets welcome in our single story bldg, only. Under 25 lbs.

North Chattanooga Days Inn Dayton
3914 Rhea County Hwy.
Dayton, TN 37321
615-775-9718
PET POLICY: No fee.

Baymont Inn & Suites
1085 E. Christie Dr.
Dickson, TN 37055
615-740-1000
PET POLICY: No fee.

Dickson Days Inn
Hwy. 46 & I-40
Dickson, TN 37055
615-446-7561
PET POLICY: No fee.

Motel 6
I-65 & Bryson Rd.
Elkton, TN 38455
931-468-2594
PET POLICY: No fee. Dogs under 25 lbs. preferred (larger animals by advance approval). Do not leave animals in room unattended.

Elizabethton Days Inn
505 W. Elk Ave.
Elizabethton, TN 37643
423-543-3344
PET POLICY: No fee.

Fayetteville Days Inn
1651 Huntsville Hwy.
Fayetteville, TN 37334
931-433-6121
PET POLICY: No fee.

Baymont Inn & Suites— Nashville South
4207 Franklin Commons Court
Franklin, TN 37064
615-791-7700
PET POLICY: No fee.

Nashville Days Inn Franklin
4217 S. Carothers Rd.
Franklin, TN 37064
615-790-1140
PET POLICY: No fee.

Baymont Inn & Suites— Goodlettsville
120 Cartwright Ct.
Goodlettsville, TN 37072
615-851-1891
PET POLICY: No fee.

Motel 6
323 Cartwright St.
Goodlettsville, TN 37072
615-859-9674
PET POLICY: No fee. Dogs under 25 lbs. preferred (larger animals by advance approval). Do not leave animals in room unattended.

Red Roof Inn
110 Northgate Dr.
Goodlettsville, TN 37072
615-859-2537
PET POLICY: No fee, pets under 80 lbs. Must be leashed to and from rooms. Do not leave in room unattended.

Shoney's Inn
100 Northcreek Blvd.
Goodlettsville, TN 37072
615-851-1067
RATES: Single $49–$69, double $55–$65.
PET POLICY: Fee $25, refundable. Dogs and Cats only, all sizes accepted.
AMENITIES: Bag of treats at check-in.

Greeneville Days Inn
935 E. Andrew Johnson Hwy.
Greeneville, TN 37743
423-639-2156
PET POLICY: Fee $10.

Nolichuckey Bluffs
297 Kinser Park Ln.
Greeneville, TN 37743
800-842-4690
RATES: Single $90, double $90.
PET POLICY: Fee $25, refundable. All sizes and all pets welcome (dogs, cats, birds, rabbits). Pets in log cabin, only.
POI: Dollywood. Biltmore House. Appalachian Trail.

Holladay Days Inn
13845 Hwy. 641
Holladay, TN 38341
901-847-2278
PET POLICY: Fee $20.

Hurricane Mills Days Inn
15415 Hwy. 13 S.
Hurricane, TN 37078
931-296-7647
PET POLICY: Deposit.

Baymont Inn & Suites
2370 N. Highland Ave.
Jackson, TN 38305
901-664-1800
PET POLICY: No fee.

Jackson Days Inn
1919 Hwy. 45 Bypass
Jackson, TN 38305
901-668-3444
PET POLICY: No fee.

Jackson Days Inn North Hollywood
2239 N. Hollywood Dr.
Jackson, TN 38305
901-668-4840
PET POLICY: No fee.

Kimball Days Inn
72 Dixie Lee Junction
Jasper, TN 37347
423-837-7933
PET POLICY: Fee $6.

Apple Valley Resort
1850 Paul Dr.
Jefferson City, TN 37760
800-545-8106

U.S. Lodgings > TENNESSEE

RATES: Single $100, double $135.
PET POLICY: No fee, all sizes welcome.
POI: Pigeon Forge. Gatlinburg.

Days Inn
PO Box 299
Jellico, TN 37762
423-784-7281
PET POLICY: Fee $5.

Nashville Days Inn
201 Gifford Pt.
Joelton, TN 37080
615-876-3261
PET POLICY: No fee.

Days Inn
2312 Brown Mill Rd.
Johnson City, TN 37604
423-282-2211
PET POLICY: No fee.

Red Roof Inn
210 Broyles Dr.
Johnson City, TN 37601
423-282-3040
PET POLICY: No fee, pets under 80 lbs. Must be leashed to and from rooms. Do not leave in room unattended.

Knoxville Days Inn
495 Gallaher Rd.
Kingston, TN 37763
865-376-2127
PET POLICY: Fee $5.

Knoxville Days Inn Kingston
495 Gallaher Rd.
Kingston, TN 37763
865-376-2069
PET POLICY: Fee $20.

Baymont Inn & Suites
11341 Campbell Lakes Dr.
Knoxville, TN 37922
865-671-1010
PET POLICY: No fee.

Holiday Inn Knoxville
1315 Kirby Rd.
Knoxville, TN 37909
865-584-3911
RATES: Single $80–$90, double $80–$90.
PET POLICY: Fee $10, nonrefundable. 50% of fee is donated to Humane Society.

AMENITIES: Special rooms with crate. Sample dog and cat food. Covered patio.
POI: Univ. Tenn. Vet School.

Knoxville Days Inn West
326 Lovell Rd.
Knoxville, TN 37922
865-966-5801
PET POLICY: No fee.

Motel 6
402 Lovell Rd.
Knoxville, TN 37922
865-675-7200
PET POLICY: No fee. Dogs under 25 lbs. preferred (larger animals by advance approval). Do not leave animals in room unattended.

Quality Inn North
6712 Central Ave. Pike
Knoxville, TN 37912
865-689-6600
RATES: Single $49.95, double $54.95.
PET POLICY: Fee $10, nonrefundable. All sizes welcome.

Red Roof Inn
5640 Merchants Center Blvd.
Knoxville, TN 37912
865-689-7100
PET POLICY: No fee, pets under 80 lbs. Must be leashed to and from rooms. Do not leave in room unattended.

Red Roof Inn
209 Advantage Place
Knoxville, TN 37922
865-691-1664
PET POLICY: No fee, pets under 80 lbs. Must be leashed to and from rooms. Do not leave in room unattended.

The Lamb's Inn
620 N. Main St.
Lake City, TN 37769
865-426-2171
RATES: Single $29–$39, double $39–$53.
PET POLICY: No fee, all sizes welcome.

Days Inn
914 Murfreesboro Rd.
Lebanon, TN 37087
615-444-5635
PET POLICY: Fee $5.

Days Inn & Suites
2259 Hillsboro Rd.
Manchester, TN 37355
931-728-9530
RATES: Single $49.95, double $55.
PET POLICY: Fee $6, non-refundable.

Red Roof Inn
95 Expressway Dr.
Manchester, TN 37355
931-728-5177
PET POLICY: No fee, pets under 80 lbs. Must be leashed to and from rooms. Do not leave in room unattended.

Baymont Inn & Suites—Memphis/Airport
3005 Millbranch Rd.
Memphis, TN 38116
901-396-5411
PET POLICY: No fee.

Baymont Inn & Suites—Memphis/East
6020 Shelby Oaks Dr.
Memphis, TN 37134
901-377-2233
PET POLICY: No fee.

Drury Inn Memphis
1556 Sycamore View
Memphis, TN 38134
901 373-8200
PET POLICY: No fee, pets under 30 lbs.

Memphis Days Inn
3839 Elvis Presley Blvd.
Memphis, TN 38116
901-346-5500
RATES: Single $77, double $87.
PET POLICY: Fee $10, nonrefundable. All sizes welcome.
POI: Graceland.

Motel 6
1321 Sycamore View Rd.
Memphis, TN 38134
901-382-8572
PET POLICY: No fee. Dogs under 25 lbs. preferred (larger animals by advance approval). Do not leave animals in room unattended.

U.S. Lodgings > TENNESSEE

Motel 6
1117 E. Brooks Rd.
Memphis, TN 38116
901-346-0992
PET POLICY: No fee. Dogs under 25 lbs. preferred (larger animals by advance approval). Do not leave animals in room unattended.

Ramada Inn Midtown
1837 Union Ave.
Memphis, TN 38104
901-278-4100
RATES: Single, double $59–$69, suites $89–$129.
PET POLICY: Fee $15 per pet. Must use "Do Not Disturb" sign on door if you leave pet in room.

Red Roof Inn
3875 American Way
Memphis, TN 38118
901-363-2335
PET POLICY: No fee, pets under 80 lbs. Must be leashed to and from rooms. Do not leave in room unattended.

Red Roof Inn
210 S. Pauline St.
Memphis, TN 38104
901-528-0650
PET POLICY: No fee, pets under 80 lbs. Must be leashed to and from rooms. Do not leave in room unattended.

Monteagle Days Inn
742 Dixie Lee Ave.
Monteagle, TN 37356
931-924-2900
PET POLICY: No fee.

Holiday Inn
2227 Old Fort Pkwy.
Murfreesboro, TN 37129
615-896-2420
PET POLICY: Small pets allowed.

Motel 6
114 Chaffin Pl
Murfreesboro, TN 37130
615-890-8524
PET POLICY: No fee. Dogs under 25 lbs. preferred (larger animals by advance approval). Do not leave animals in room unattended.

Murfreesboro Days Inn
2036 S. Church St.
Murfreesboro, TN 37130
615-893-1090
PET POLICY: No fee.

Red Roof Inn
2282 Armory Dr.
Murfreesboro, TN 37129
615-893-0104
PET POLICY: No fee, pets under 80 lbs. Must be leashed to and from rooms. Do not leave in room unattended.

Baymont Inn & Suites—Nashville/Airport
531 Donelson Pike
Nashville, TN 37214
615-885-3100
PET POLICY: No fee.

Drury Inn Nashville South
341 Harding Place
Nashville, TN 37211
615 834-7170
PET POLICY: No fee, pets under 30 lbs.

Drury Inn—Airport
555 Donelson Pike
Nashville, TN 37211
800-378-7946
PET POLICY: No fee, pets under 30 lbs.

Homewood Suites Hotel
2640 Elm Hill Pike
Nashville, TN 37210
615-884-8111
PET POLICY: $200 deposit, $100 refundable.

Nashville Days Inn
1400 Brick Church Pk
Nashville, TN 37207
615-228-5977
PET POLICY: Fee $7.

Motel 6
420 Metroplex Dr.
Nashville, TN 37211
615-833-8887
PET POLICY: No fee. Dogs under 25 lbs. preferred (larger animals by advance approval). Do not leave animals in room unattended.

Pear Tree Inn Nashville South
343 Harding Place
Nashville, TN 37211
615 834-4242
PET POLICY: No fee. All sizes and pets accepted. Do not leave in rooms unattended.

Red Roof Inn
510 Claridge Dr.
Nashville, TN 37214
615-872-0735
PET POLICY: No fee, pets under 80 lbs. Must be leashed to and from rooms. Do not leave in room unattended.

Red Roof Inn
4271 Sidco Dr.
Nashville, TN 37204
615-832-0093
PET POLICY: No fee, pets under 80 lbs. Must be leashed to and from rooms. Do not leave in room unattended.

Red Roof Inn
2460 Music Valley Dr.
Nashville, TN 37214
615-889-0090
PET POLICY: No fee, pets under 80 lbs. Must be leashed to and from rooms. Do not leave in room unattended.

Super 8 Motel
350 Harding Pl.
Nashville, TN 37211
615-834-0620
RATES: Single $49, double $54.
PET POLICY: Fee $5 per pet per day, nonrefundable. Up to 50 lbs., dogs and cats only.

Holiday Inn
1010 Cosby Rd.
Newport, TN 37822
423-623-8622
RATES: Single $65.95, double $65.95.
PET POLICY: No fee, pets up to 25 lbs.
POI: Dollywood. Whitewater rafting. Biltmore House. Pigeon Forge. Gatlinburg.

U.S. Lodgings > TEXAS

Motel 6
255 Heritage Blvd.
Newport, TN 37821
423-623-1850
PET POLICY: No fee. Dogs under 25 lbs. preferred (larger animals by advance approval). Do not leave animals in room unattended.

Knoxville Days Inn
Oak Ridge
206 S. Illinois
Oak Ridge, TN 37830
865-483-5615
PET POLICY: Fee $4.

Oakland Days Inn
6805 Hwy. 64
Oakland, TN 38060
800-DAYSINN
PET POLICY: Fee $5.

Motel 6
336 Henderson Chapel Rd.
Pigeon Forge, TN 37863
865-908-1244
PET POLICY: No fee. Dogs under 25 lbs. preferred (larger animals by advance approval). Do not leave animals in room unattended.
POI: Dollywood.

Mountain Mist
Rentals & Realty
2225 Pkwy., Ste. 1, Box 1324
Pigeon Forge, TN 37868
800-634-5814
RATES: Cabins: $135–$150.
PET POLICY: Fee $50–$100 non-refundable, all sizes and all pets welcome. Must clean up after pets.

Baymont Inn & Suites
7534 Conner Rd.
Powell, TN 37849
865-947-7500
PET POLICY: No fee.

The Wild Heart Ranch
1070 Old Sewanee Rd.
Sewanee, TN 37375
423-837-0849
RATES: Single $75, double $100.
PET POLICY: No fee, all sizes and pets welcome, including horses. Proper animal supervision is only requirement.

AMENITIES: Stables, barn, pastures.
POI: Franklin State Forest (6,941 acres), horseback riding trails, fully stocked lake, bathhouse, campsites, spelunking caves.

Nashville Days Inn Smyrna
1300 Plaza Dr.
Smyrna, TN 37167
615-355-6161
PET POLICY: Fee $10.

Sweetwater Days Inn
229 Hwy. 68
Sweetwater, TN 37874
423-337-4200
PET POLICY: Fee $5.

Boyette's Resort
Rt. 1, Box 1230
Tiptonville, TN 38079
901-253-6523
RATES: Single $45.50, double $60.29.
PET POLICY: No fee, pets up to 25 lbs., pets not to be left unattended in cottages.

Twin Valley Ranch Bed & Breakfast Horse Ranch
2484 Old Chihowee Rd.
Walland, TN 37886
865-984-0980
RATES: Single $85.
PET POLICY: No fee, all sizes welcome. Must get permission.
AMENITIES: Trails for hiking. Paddocks for horses.
POI: Horseback riding, fishing, swimming. Dollywood. Great Smokey National Park.

White Pine Days Inn
3670 Roy Messer Hwy.
White Pine, TN 37890
865-674-2573
PET POLICY: Fee $5.

Baymont Inn & Suites
5612 Lenox Ave.
Whitebridge, TN 37209
615-353-0700
PET POLICY: No fee.

TEXAS

Abilene Days Inn
1702 I-20 E
Abilene, TX 79601
915-672-6433
PET POLICY: No fee.

Holiday Inn Express
1625 State Hwy. 351
Abilene, TX 79601
915-673-5271
PET POLICY: Small pets allowed.

Motel 6
4951 W. Stamford St.
Abilene, TX 79603
915-672-8462
PET POLICY: No fee. Dogs under 25 lbs. preferred (larger animals by advance approval). Do not leave animals in room unattended.

Alvin Days Inn
110 E. Hwy. 6
Alvin, TX 77511
281-331-5227
PET POLICY: Fee $10.

Hampton Inn
1700 I-40 East
Amarillo, TX, 79103
806-372-1425
PET POLICY: No fee. All sizes accepted. Do not leave pets unattended in rooms.
POI: King: $64, double $69

Motel 6
3930 I-40 E
Amarillo, TX 79103
806-374-6444
PET POLICY: No fee. Dogs under 25 lbs. preferred (larger animals by advance approval). Do not leave animals in room unattended.

Motel 6
2032 Paramount Blvd.
Amarillo, TX 79109
3806-55-6554
PET POLICY: No fee. Dogs under 25 lbs. preferred (larger animals by advance approval). Do not leave animals in room unattended.

U.S. Lodgings > TEXAS

Red Roof Inn
1620 Interstate 40 East
Amarillo, TX 79103
806-374-2020
PET POLICY: No fee, pets under
80 lbs. Must be leashed to and
from rooms. Do not leave in
room unattended.

**Baymont Inn & Suites—
Arlington**
2401 Diplomacy Dr.
Arlington, TX 76011
817-633-2400
PET POLICY: No fee.

Dallas Days Inn
1195 N. Watson Rd.
Arlington, TX 76011
817-649-8881
PET POLICY: Fee $5.

**La Quinta Inn Dallas
Arlington Conference
Center**
825 N. Watson Rd.
Arlington, TX 76011
817-640-4142
PET POLICY: Dogs under 20 lbs.

Motel 6
2626 E. Randol Mill Rd.
Arlington, TX 76011
817-649-0147
PET POLICY: No fee. Dogs under 25
lbs. preferred (larger animals by
advance approval). Do not leave
animals in room unattended.

Austin Days Inn
3105 N. IH-35
Austin, TX 78722
512-478-1631
PET POLICY: No fee.

Baymont Inn & Suites
150 Parker Dr.
Austin, TX 78728
512-246-2800
PET POLICY: No fee.

**Clarion Inn &
Suites Conf. Ctr.**
2200 S. I-35
Austin, TX 78704
512-444-0561
PET POLICY: Pets in smoking
rooms only.

**Drury Inn and Suites
Austin North**
6711 Interstate 35 North
Austin, TX 78752
512 467-9500
PET POLICY: No fee, pets under
30 lbs.

**Drury Inn Austin
Highland Mall**
919 E. Koenig Ln.
Austin, TX 78751
512 454-1144
PET POLICY: No fee, pets under
30 lbs.

Holiday Inn
3401 S. I-35
Austin, TX 78741
512-448-2444
PET POLICY: Pets allowed with
deposit.

Homewood Suites Hotel
10925 Stonelake Blvd.
Austin, TX 78759
512-349-9966
PET POLICY: $75 Non refundable
fee, trained pets accepted up
to 15 lbs.

Motel 6
5330 N. Interregional Hwy.
Austin, TX 78751
512-467-9111
PET POLICY: No fee. Dogs under 25
lbs. preferred (larger animals by
advance approval). Do not leave
animals in room unattended.

Red Roof Inn
4701 S. I-35
Austin, TX 78744
502-448-0091
PET POLICY: No fee, pets under
80 lbs. Must be leashed to and
from rooms. Do not leave in
room unattended.

Red Roof Inn
8210 N. Interregional Hwy.
Austin, TX 78753
512-835-2200
PET POLICY: No fee, pets under
80 lbs. Must be leashed to and
from rooms. Do not leave in
room unattended.

Residence Inn Austin South
4537 S. Interstate 35
Austin, TX 78744
512-912-1100
PET POLICY: Fee $100, non-
refundable.

**Baymont Inn & Suites—
Baytown**
5215 I-10 E.
Baytown, TX 77521
281-421-7300
PET POLICY: No fee.

Holiday Inn Express
5222 I-10 E.
Baytown, TX 77524
281-421-7200
PET POLICY: No fee.

Beaumont Days Inn
30 N. IH 10
Beaumont, TX 77702
409-838-0581
PET POLICY: Fee $5.

Motel 6
1155 I-10 South
Beaumont, TX 77701
409-835-5913
PET POLICY: No fee. Dogs under 25
lbs. preferred (larger animals by
advance approval). Do not leave
animals in room unattended.

Big Spring Days Inn
2701 S. Gregg St.
Big Spring, TX 79720
915-267-5237
PET POLICY: Deposit required.

Brady Days Inn
2108 S. Bridge St.
Brady, TX 76825
915-597-0789
PET POLICY: No fee.

Brenham Days Inn
201 Hwy. 290 Loop E.
Brenham, TX 77833
409-830-1110
PET POLICY: No fee.

Motel 6
2255 N. Expwy
Brownsville, TX 78520
956-546-4699
PET POLICY: No fee. Dogs under 25
lbs. preferred (larger animals by
advance approval). Do not leave
animals in room unattended.

Red Roof Inn
2377 N. Expressway 83
Brownsville, TX 78520
956-504-2300
PET POLICY: No fee, pets under
80 lbs. Must be leashed to and
from rooms. Do not leave in

Brownwood Days Inn
515 E. Commerce
Brownwood, TX 76801
915-646-2551
PET POLICY: Fee $5.

Days Inn
1204 C C Woodson Rd.
Brownwood, TX 76801
915-643-5611
PET POLICY: No fee.

**Fort Worth Days Inn
Burleson**
329 S. Burleson Blvd.
Burleson, TX 76028
817-447-1111
PET POLICY: Fee $5.

Canton Days Inn
109 S
Canton, TX 75103
903-567-6588
PET POLICY: Fee $5.

Red Roof Inn
1720 S. Broadway
Carrollton, TX 75006
972-245-1700
PET POLICY: No fee, pets under
80 lbs. Must be leashed to and
from rooms. Do not leave in
room unattended.

Centerville Days Inn
PO Box 729
Centerville, TX 75833
903-536-7175
PET POLICY: Fee $7.

Days Inn
T15545 I-10 E
Channelview, TX 77530
713-457-3000
PET POLICY: No fee.

Cleburne Days Inn
101 N. Ridgeway Dr.
Cleburne, TX 76031
817-645-8836
PET POLICY: No fee.

Holiday Inn
1503 S. Texas Ave.
College Station, TX 77840
409-693-1736
PET POLICY: Small pets allowed.

Motel 6
2327 Texas Ave South
College Station, TX 77840
979-696-3379
PET POLICY: No fee. Dogs under 25
lbs. preferred (larger animals by
advance approval). Do not leave
animals in room unattended.

Baymont Inn & Suites
1506 I-45 S.
Conroe, TX 77301
409-539-5100
PET POLICY: No fee.

Days Inn Corpus Christi
901 Navigation Blvd.
Corpus Christi, TX 78404
361-888-8599
RATES: Single $45, double $50.
PET POLICY: Fee $10 per night,
up to 25 lbs. nonsmoking
rooms.
POI: CC Beach, Padre Island,
USS Lexington, Texas State,
Aquarium, Greyhound Racing.

Drury Inn Corpus Christi
2021 N. Padre Island
Corpus Christi, TX 78408
361 289-8200
PET POLICY: No fee, pets under
30 lbs.

Motel 6
8202 S. Padre Island Dr.
Corpus Christi, TX 78412
361-991-8858
PET POLICY: No fee. Dogs under 25
lbs. preferred (larger animals by
advance approval). Do not leave
animals in room unattended.

Ramada Ltd.
5501 IH-37 at McBride
Corpus Christi, TX 78408
361-289-5861
RATES: Single $69, double $79.
PET POLICY: Fee $15, nonre-
fundable. Up to 50 lbs.
POI: Greyhound Race Track.

Red Roof Inn
6805 S. Padre Island Dr.
Corpus Christi, TX 78412
361-992-9222
PET POLICY: No fee, pets under
80 lbs. Must be leashed to and
from rooms. Do not leave in
room unattended.

Red Roof Inn
6301 Interstate Highway 37
Corpus Christi, TX 78409
361-289-6925
PET POLICY: No fee, pets under
80 lbs. Must be leashed to and
from rooms. Do not leave in

**Surfside Condominium
Apartments**
15005 Windward Dr.
Corpus Christi, TX 78418
800-548-4585
RATES: Avg. $115.
PET POLICY: Fee $15 per day
per pet, nonrefundable. All
pets welcome, up to 50 lbs.
AMENITIES: Pet walking area.
POI: Close to beach.

Corsicana Days Inn
2018 Hwy. 287
Corsicana, TX 75110
903-872-0659
PET POLICY: Fee $6.

Crowne Plaza
14315 Midway Rd.
Dallas, TX 75244
972-980-8877
PET POLICY: No fee.

Crowne Plaza
7050 Stemmons Frwy.
Dallas, TX 75247
214-630-8500
PET POLICY: No fee.

Crowne Plaza Suites
7800 Alpha Rd.
Dallas, TX 75240
972-233-7600
PET POLICY: No fee.

Drury Inn Dallas North
2421 Walnut Hill Ln.
Dallas, TX 75229
972 484-3330
PET POLICY: No fee, pets under
30 lbs.

U.S. Lodgings > TEXAS

Harvey Hotel—Dallas
7815 LBJ Freeway
Dallas, TX 75251
972-960-7000
RATES: Single, double
$69–$109.
PET POLICY: Fee $50, refundable.
All sizes accepted.

Homewood Suites Hotel
9169 Markville Dr.
Dallas, TX 75243
972-437-6966
PET POLICY: Pets under 50 lbs.
With $50 non refundable fee.

Le Meridien Dallas
650 N. Pearl St.
Dallas, TX 75201
214 979 9000
RATES: Single, double
$189–$220.
PET POLICY: No fee, small pets
only.

Motel 6
2753 Forest Ln.
Dallas, TX 75234
972-620-2828
PET POLICY: No fee. Dogs under 25
lbs. preferred (larger animals by
advance approval). Do not leave
animals in room unattended.

Motel 6
2660 Forest Ln.
Dallas, TX 75234
972-484-9111
PET POLICY: No fee. Dogs under 25
lbs. preferred (larger animals by
advance approval). Do not leave
animals in room unattended.

Red Roof Inn
1550 Empire Central Dr.
Dallas, TX 75235
214-638-5151
PET POLICY: No fee, pets under
80 lbs. Must be leashed to and
from rooms. Do not leave in
room unattended.

Red Roof Inn
8108 E.R.L Thornton Blvd.
Dallas, TX 75228
214-388-8741
PET POLICY: No fee, pets under
80 lbs. Must be leashed to and
from rooms. Do not leave in
room unattended.

Red Roof Inn
10335 Gardner Rd.
Dallas, TX 75220
972-506-8100
PET POLICY: No fee, pets under
80 lbs. Must be leashed to and
from rooms. Do not leave in

**Residence Inn Dallas by
Marriott—Northpark**
10333 N. Central Expressway
Dallas, TX 75231
214-750-8220
RATES: Single $129, double $159.
PET POLICY: Fee $100, nonre-
fundable. Small, up to 25 lbs.

**The Mansion
On Turtle Creek**
2821 Turtle Creek Blvd.
Dallas, TX 75219
AMENITIES: 214–$559–$2100.
PET POLICY: Fee $100, nonre-
fundable. Dogs accepted up to
75 lbs.

Del Rio Days Inn
3808 Hwy. 90 W.
Del Rio, TX 78840
830-775-0585
RATES: Single $43, double $53.
PET POLICY: Fee $5, all sizes,
dogs and cats, birds, rabbits,
pets must be on leash,
Monthly Fee $50 per month.

Motel 6
2115 Ave _F_
Del Rio, TX 78840
830-774-2115
PET POLICY: No fee. Dogs under 25
lbs. preferred (larger animals by
advance approval). Do not leave
animals in room unattended.

Ramada Inn
2101 Ave. F
Del Rio, TX 78840
830-775-1511
RATES: Single $60, double $70.
PET POLICY: No fee, up to 50 lbs.

Motel 6
615 N. Hwy. 75
Denison, TX 75020
903-465-4446
PET POLICY: No fee. Dogs under 25
lbs. preferred (larger animals by
advance approval). Do not leave
animals in room unattended.

Motel 6
4125 Interstate 35 North
Denton, TX 76207
940-566-4798
PET POLICY: No fee. Dogs under 25
lbs. preferred (larger animals by
advance approval). Do not leave
animals in room unattended.

Red Roof Inn
1401 N. Beckley Rd.
De Soto, TX 75115
972-224-7100
PET POLICY: No fee, pets under
80 lbs. Must be leashed to and
from rooms. Do not leave in
room unattended.

Travelodge
3205 I-40 East
East Amarillo, TX 79104
806 372-8171
RATES: Truckers: $35, Single,
double $38–$42.
PET POLICY: Fee $10, nonrefund-
able per stay. Pets accepted up
to 25 lbs.

Bastrop Days Inn
4102 Hwy. 71
East Bastrop, TX 78602
512-321-1157
PET POLICY: Fee $20.

**Baymont Inn & Suites—
El Paso-East**
7944 Gateway Blvd. E.
El Paso, TX 79915
915-591-3300
PET POLICY: No fee.

**Baymont Inn & Suites—
El Paso-West**
7620 N. Mesa St.
El Paso, TX 79912
915-525-2999
PET POLICY: No fee.

El Paso Days Inn
10635 Gateway W.
El Paso, TX 79935
915-595-1913
PET POLICY: Fee $25.

Howard Johnson Inn
8887 Gateway W.
El Paso, TX 79925
915-591-9471

U.S. Lodgings > TEXAS

RATES: Single $53, double $58.
PET POLICY: No fee, all pets welcome, other than dogs and cats must be cages, pet walk area available.
AMENITIES: Pet walk area.
POI: Petsmart, Mexico.

Motel 6
11049 Gateway Blvd. W
El Paso, TX 79935
915-594-8533
PET POLICY: No fee. Dogs under 25 lbs. preferred (larger animals by advance approval). Do not leave animals in room unattended.

Motel 6
1330 Lomaland Dr.
El Paso, TX 79935
915-592-6386
PET POLICY: No fee. Dogs under 25 lbs. preferred (larger animals by advance approval). Do not leave animals in room unattended.

Red Roof Inn
11400 Chito Samaniego Dr.
El Paso, TX 79936
915-599-8877
PET POLICY: No fee, pets under 80 lbs. Must be leashed to and from rooms. Do not leave in room unattended.

Red Roof Inn
7530 Remcon Circle
El Paso, TX 79912
915-587-9977
PET POLICY: No fee, pets under 80 lbs. Must be leashed to and from rooms. Do not leave in room unattended.

Travelodge
6400 Montana Ave.
El Paso, TX 79925
915 726-1368
RATES: Single $53, double $62.
PET POLICY: Fee $10, nonrefundable. All sizes welcome.
AMENITIES: Gardens.

Super 8 Motel
800 E. Dickinson Blvd.
Fort Stockton, TX 79735
915-336-9711
RATES: Single $42.95, double $56.50.

PET POLICY: Fee $8 per pet, nonrefundable. All sizes welcome.
POI: Historic sites 2-4 blocks away. Beautiful park 2 blocks away.

American Inn
7301 W. Freeway
Fort Worth, TX 76116
817-244-7444
PET POLICY: No fee, all sizes accepted.

Fort Worth Days Inn
42131-35W. S. Fwy
Fort Worth, TX 76115
817-923-1987
PET POLICY: No fee.

Fort Forth Days Inn
8500 I-30 & Las Vegas Tri.
Fort Worth, TX 76108
817-246-4961
PET POLICY: Fee $5.

Green Oaks Park Hotel
6901 W. Freeway
Fort Worth, TX 76116
817 738-7311
RATES: Single $79, double $84, suites $99–$149.
PET POLICY: Fee $30 per night per pet. Pets up to 50 lbs.

Hampton Inn West
2700 Cherry Ln.
Fort Worth, TX 76116
817-560-4180
RATES: Single, double $69–$84.
PET POLICY: No fee. Pets up to 25 lbs.

Holiday Inn
100 Altamesa E. Blvd.
Fort Worth, TX 76134
817-293-3088
RATES: Single, double $69–$79.
PET POLICY: No fee. Pets up to 50 lbs.

Holiday Inn Express Hotel & Suites
4609 City Lake Blvd. West
Fort Worth, TX 76109
817-292-4900
RATES: Single, double $79–$89, suites $99–$159.
PET POLICY: Fee $25. Quiet dogs, well-behaved.

La Quinta Inn— Fort Worth West
7888 I-30W
Fort Worth, TX 76108
817-246-5511
RATES: Double $66.67–$125, King Size: $74.58–$130.
PET POLICY: No fee, all sizes accepted.

Motel 6
1236 Oakland Blvd.
Fort Worth, TX 76103
817-834-7361
PET POLICY: No fee. Dogs under 25 lbs. preferred (larger animals by advance approval). Do not leave animals in room unattended.

Motel 6
6600 S. Frwy
Fort Worth, TX 76134
817-293-8595
PET POLICY: No fee. Dogs under 25 lbs. preferred (larger animals by advance approval). Do not leave animals in room unattended.

Ramada Inn Midtown
1401 S. University Dr.
Fort Worth, TX 76107
817-336-9311
RATES: Single $68+, double $72+.
PET POLICY: Fee $25, nonrefundable. All sizes accepted.

Renaissance Worthington Hotel
200 Main St.
Fort Worth, TX 76102
817-870-1000
RATES: Single, double $159–$189.
PET POLICY: No fee: all sizes accepted. Must sign pet waiver.

Residence Inn Fort Worth River Plaza
1701 S. University Dr.
Fort Worth, TX 76107
817-870-1011
RATES: All Suites $115–$159.
PET POLICY: Fee $5 per day. All sizes accepted.

Gainesville Days Inn
Rt 2, Box 13A
Gainesville, TX 76240
940-665-5555
PET POLICY: Fee $7.

U.S. Lodgings > TEXAS

Cottage-By-The-Beach Rentals
810 Ave. L
Galveston, TX 77550
409-770-9332
RATES: Cottages: $95–$250 night.
PET POLICY: No fee, all pets welcome.
AMENITIES: Private, fenced in yard. Paved driveway to eliminate burrs, etc. Hose to wash pets. Nearby Vet.
POI: Moody Gardens, Houston Six Flags, Galveston Historical district, Carnival Cruise Lines, fishing, surfing, sailing, beaches, Dickens Christmas Festival.

Motel 6
7404 Ave J Broadway
Galveston, TX 77554
409-740-3794
PET POLICY: No fee. Dogs under 25 lbs. preferred (larger animals by advance approval). Do not leave animals in room unattended.

Motel 6
436 W. I-30 and Beltline Rd.
Garland, TX 75043
972-226-7140
PET POLICY: No fee. Dogs under 25 lbs. preferred (larger animals by advance approval). Do not leave animals in room unattended.

Red Roof Inn
13700 LBJ Freeway
Garland, TX 75041
972-686-0202
PET POLICY: No fee, pets under 80 lbs. Must be leashed to and from rooms. Do not leave in room unattended.

Georgetown Days Inn
209 N. IH 35
Georgetown, TX 78628
512-863-5572
PET POLICY: No fee.

La Quinta Inn Georgetown
333 N. I-35
Georgetown, TX 78628
512-869-2541
RATES: Double $69.
PET POLICY: No fee, all sizes welcome.

Baymont Inn & Suites
301 Capitol St.
Grapevine, TX 76051
817-329-9300
PET POLICY: No fee.

Embassy Suites Outdoor World
2401 Bass Pro Dr.
Grapevine, TX 76051
972-724-2600
RATES: Single, double: $119 weekends, $199 weekdays.
PET POLICY: No fee, small dogs and cats only, up to 25 lbs.
AMENITIES: Outdoor bathroom area for pets on site.
POI: In the heart of Dallas/Ft. Worth.

La Quinta Inn Harlingen
1002 S. Expressway 83
Harlingen, TX, 78552
956-428-6888
RATES: Single, double $79.99+.
PET POLICY: No fee. Prefer small dogs, but will take any size (clean) dogs.

Oak Tree Inn
1051 N. Market St.
Hearne, TX 77859
979-279-5599
RATES: Single $54, double $64.
PET POLICY: Fee $5, nonrefundable. All sizes and all pets welcome.
POI: Bryan College Station.

Baymont Inn & Suites
6790 Southwest Freeway
Houston, TX 77074
713-784-3838
PET POLICY: No fee.

Baymont Inn & Suites
12701 North Freeway
Houston, TX 77060
281-875-2000
PET POLICY: No fee.

Comfort Suites— Near the Galleria
6221 Richmond Ave.
Houston, TX 77057
713-787-0004
RATES: Single $98, double $98.
PET POLICY: Fee $25, nonrefundable, all sizes and all pets welcome.

Drury Inn and Suites Houston Hobby
7902 Mosley
Houston, TX 77061
713 941-4300
PET POLICY: No fee, pets under 30 lbs.

Drury Inn and Suites Houston Near the Galleria
1615 W. Loop South
Houston, TX 77027
713 963-0700
PET POLICY: No fee, pets under 30 lbs.

Drury Inn and Suites Houston West
1000 N. Highway 6
Houston, TX 77079
281 558-7007
PET POLICY: No fee, pets under 30 lbs.

Hawthorn Suites— Houston Southwest
6910 S.W. Freeway
Houston, TX 77074
713-785-3415
RATES: Single $79+$5 p, day for pet, double $99+$5 p, day for pet.
PET POLICY: Fee $15, nonrefundable. Up to 50 lbs.
AMENITIES: Lots of room to exercise pets.
POI: Grooming, vet services, pet stores nearby.

Holiday Inn
15222 JFK Blvd.
Houston, TX 77032
281-449-2311
PET POLICY: Pets allowed with deposit.

Homewood Suites Hotel
7655 W. FM 1960
Houston, TX 77070
281-955-5200
PET POLICY: Small pet fee.

Houston Days Inn
4640 S. Main St.
Houston, TX 77002
713-523-3777
PET POLICY: Fee $20.

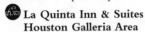

U.S. Lodgings > TEXAS

Houston Days Inn North
9025 North Freeway
Houston, TX 77037
281-820-1500
PET POLICY: Deposit required.

**La Quinta Inn & Suites
Houston Galleria Area**
1625 W. Loop South
Houston, TX 77027
713-355-3440
PET POLICY: No fee. Pets under
20 lbs.

**La Quinta Inn Houston
Astrodome**
9911 Buffalo Speedway
Houston, TX 77054
713-668-8082
PET POLICY: No fee. Pets under
20 lbs.

**La Quinta Inn Houston
Brookhollow**
11002 Northwest Freeway
Houston, TX 77092
713-688-2581
PET POLICY: No fee. Pets under
20 lbs.

**La Quinta Inn Houston
Cyfair**
13290 Fm 1960 West
Houston, TX 77065
281-469-4018
PET POLICY: No fee. Pets under
20 lbs.

**La Quinta Inn Houston
Greenspoint**
6 North Belt East
Houston, TX 77060
281-447-6888
PET POLICY: No fee. Pets under
20 lbs.

Motel 6
2900 W. Sam Houston Pkwy
South
Houston, TX 77042
713-334-9188
PET POLICY: No fee. Dogs under 25
lbs. preferred (larger animals by
advance approval). Do not leave
animals in room unattended.

Motel 6
5555 W. 34th St.
Houston, TX 77092
713-682-8588

PET POLICY: No fee. Dogs under 25
lbs. preferred (larger animals by
advance approval). Do not leave
animals in room unattended.

Quality Inn & Suites
9041 Westheimer
Houston, TX 77063
713-783-1400
RATES: Single $49, double $59.
PET POLICY: Fee $25, nonrefund-
able, all sizes and all pets welcome (dogs, cats, birds, rabbits,
ferrets, reptiles, etc.).

Red Roof Inn
12929 Northwest Freeway
Houston, TX 77040
713-939-0800
PET POLICY: No fee, pets under
80 lbs. Must be leashed to and
from rooms. Do not leave in
room unattended.

Red Roof Inn
2960 W. Sam Houston
Parkway South
Houston, TX 77042
713-785-9909
PET POLICY: No fee, pets under
80 lbs. Must be leashed to and
from rooms. Do not leave in
room unattended.

Red Roof Inn
9005 Airport Blvd.
Houston, TX 77061
713-943-3300
RATES: Single $49.99, double
$54.99.
PET POLICY: No fee, pets under
80 lbs. Must be leashed to and
from rooms. Do not leave in
room unattended.

Red Roof Inn
15701 Park Ten Place
Houston, TX 77084
281-579-7200
PET POLICY: No fee, pets under
80 lbs. Must be leashed to and
from rooms. Do not leave in
room unattended.

**Red Roof Inn Houston
Hobby Airport**
9005 Airport Boulevard
Houston, TX 77061
713-943-3300

PET POLICY: No fee, small pets
up to 25 lbs., must be on a
leash and within voice com-
mand always.

Red Lion Hotel
2525 W. Loop South
Houston, TX 77027
713-961-3000
RATES: Single $134–$154, dou-
ble $144–$164.
PET POLICY: Fee $25 for stay,
Deposit $100, $75 refundable.

**Residence Inn—
Houston Clear Lake**
525 Bay Area Blvd.
Houston, TX 77058
281-486-2424
RATES: Single $119, double $145.
PET POLICY: Fee $50, nonrefund-
able. All sizes and pets welcome (dogs, cats, ferrets, birds,
rabbits, reptiles).
AMENITIES: Large walking/
play area.

Residence Inn by Marriott
9965 Westheimer
Houston, TX 77042
713-974-5454
RATES: Single $109.
PET POLICY: Fee $50, nonrefund-
able. All sizes and pets welcome (dogs, cats, birds, ferrets,
rabbits, reptiles).

**Robin's Nest
Bed & Breakfast Inn**
4104 Greeley
Houston, TX 77006
713-528-5821
RATES: Single $89–$120, double
$99–$120.
PET POLICY: Fee $20, nonrefund-
able, all cats accepted, call about
dogs, usually older preferred,
must be well-behaved. Treats
available.
POI: Parks, running tracks,
groomers, huge pet stores
where the animals are welcome.

U.S. Lodgings > TEXAS

Shoneys Inn & Suites
12323 Katy Freeway
Houston, TX 77079
281-493-5626
RATES: Single $57, double $62.
PET POLICY: Fee $25, nonre-
fundable. Pets up to 50 lbs. All
pets accepted.
POI: Kay mills Mall, Bear Creek
Park, Houston Arboretum.

**Shoney's Inn & Suites,
Houston, SW**
6687 SW Freeway
Houston, TX 77074
713-776-2633
RATES: Single $55–$75, double
$59–$79.
PET POLICY: Fee $25, nonre-
fundable. All size dogs and
cats. Rooms cleaned only
with guests present. Do not
leave pets in room unat-
tended.

**Towne Place Suites by
Marriott**
1050 Bay Area Blvd.
Houston, TX 77058
281-286-2132
RATES: Single $86, double $109.
PET POLICY: Fee $60, nonre-
fundable. All sizes and pets
welcome (dogs, cats, ferrets,
birds, rabbits, reptiles).

Holiday Inn Express
201 W. Hill Park Cir.
Huntsville, TX 77340
409-293-8800
PET POLICY: Fee $10.

Motel 6
122 I-45
Huntsville, TX 77340
936-291-6927
PET POLICY: No fee. Dogs under 25
lbs. preferred (larger animals by
advance approval). Do not leave
animals in room unattended.

Drury Inn
4210 W. Airport Freeway
Irving, TX 75062
972-986-1200
PET POLICY: No fee, pets under
30 lbs.

Motel 6
7800 Heathrow Dr.
Irving, TX 75063
972-915-3993
PET POLICY: No fee. Dogs under 25
lbs. preferred (larger animals by
advance approval). Do not leave
animals in room unattended.

Red Roof Inn
8150 Esters Boulevard
Irving, TX 75063
972-929-0020
PET POLICY: No fee, pets under
80 lbs. Must be leashed to and
from rooms. Do not leave in
room unattended.

Red Roof Inn
2611 W. Airport Freeway
Irving, TX 75062
972-570-7500
PET POLICY: No fee, pets under
80 lbs. Must be leashed to and
from rooms. Do not leave in
room unattended.

**Residence Inn—
Dallas Las Colinas**
950 Walnut Hill Ln.
Irving, TX 75038
972-580-7773
RATES: Single $139, double $149.
PET POLICY: Fee $50, nonrefund-
able. Pets up to 50 lbs. All pets
welcome (dogs, cats, ferrets,
birds, rabbits, reptiles).
POI: Close to downtown Dallas
and Fort Worth.

**Staybridge Suites by
Holiday Inn**
1201 Executive Cir.
Irving, TX 75038
972-465-9400
PET POLICY: $75 non refundable
fee.

Ozona Daystop
820 Loop 466
Iziba, TX 76943
915-392-2631
PET POLICY: No fee.

Jasper Days Inn
1730 S. Wheeler
Jasper, TX 75951
409-384-6816
PET POLICY: Fee $5.

Junction Days Inn
111 S. Martinez St.
Junction, TX 76849
915-446-3730
PET POLICY: Fee $4.

Kenedy Days Inn
453 N. Sunset Strip
Kenedy, TX 78119
510-583-2521
PET POLICY: Fee $5.

Holiday Inn
3430 Hwy. 77 S.
Kingsville, TX 78363
361-595-5753
PET POLICY: Small pets allowed.

Holiday Inn
800 Garden St.
Laredo, TX 78040
956-727-5800
PET POLICY: Small pets.

Motel 6
5310 San Bernardo Ave.
Laredo, TX 78041
956-725-8187
PET POLICY: No fee. Dogs under 25
lbs. preferred (larger animals by
advance approval). Do not leave
animals in room unattended.

Red Roof Inn
1006 W. Calton Rd.
Laredo, TX 78041
956-712-0733
PET POLICY: No fee, pets under
80 lbs. Must be leashed to and
from rooms. Do not leave in
room unattended.

Lindale Days Inn
13307 CR 472
Lindale, TX 75771
903-882-7800
PET POLICY: Fee $10.

Crescent Park Motel
Hwy. 385 & 84
Littlefield, TX 79339
806-385-4464
RATES: Single $32, double $40.
PET POLICY: Fee $5, nonrefund-
able. Up to 50 lbs.

Hampton Inn
112 S. Access Rd.
Longview, TX 75603
903-758-0959
PET POLICY: Special restrictions
apply for pets.

U.S. Lodgings > TEXAS

Lubbock Days Inn
2401 4th St.
Lubbock, TX 79415
806-747-7111
PET POLICY: No fee.

Motel 6
909 66th St.
Lubbock, TX 79412
806-45-5541
PET POLICY: No fee. Dogs under 25 lbs. preferred (larger animals by advance approval). Do not leave animals in room unattended.

Holiday Inn
4306 S. 1st St.
Lufkin, TX 75901
409-639-3333
PET POLICY: Fee $5.

Motel 6
1110 S. Timberland Dr.
Lufkin, TX 75091
936-637-7850
PET POLICY: No fee. Dogs under 25 lbs. preferred (larger animals by advance approval). Do not leave animals in room unattended.

Lytle Days Inn
19525 McDonald St.
Lytle, TX 78052
830-772-4777
PET POLICY: Fee $5.

Marshall Days Inn
PO Box 1836
Marshall, TX 75672
903-927-1718
PET POLICY: No fee.

Drury Inn Mcallen
612 W. Expressway 83
Mcallen, TX 78501
956 687-5100
PET POLICY: No fee, pets under 30 lbs.

Motel 6
700 W. Expwy 83
Mcallen, TX 78501
956-687-3700
PET POLICY: No fee. Dogs under 25 lbs. preferred (larger animals by advance approval). Do not leave animals in room unattended.

McKinney Days Inn
2104 N. Central Expressway
McKinney, TX 75070
972-548-8888
PET POLICY: No fee.

Dallas Days Inn
3601 Hwy. 80
Mesquite, TX 75150
972-279-6561
PET POLICY: Fee $5.

Midland Days Inn
1003 S. Midkiff Ave.
Midland, TX 79701
915-697-3155
PET POLICY: No fee.

Motel 6
1000 S. Midkiff Rd.
Midland, TX 79701
915-697-3197
PET POLICY: No fee. Dogs under 25 lbs. preferred (larger animals by advance approval). Do not leave animals in room unattended.

Mineral Wells Days Inn
3701 E. Hubbard St.
Mineral Wells, TX 76067
940-325-6961
PET POLICY: Fee $6.

Mount Pleasant Days Inn
2501 W. Ferguson
Mount Pleasant, TX 75455
903-577-0152
PET POLICY: Fee $10.

Nacogdoches Days Suites
2724 North St.
Nacogdoches, TX 75961
409-564-3726
PET POLICY: Fee $5.

Holiday Inn
1051 I-35 E.
New Braunfels, TX 78130
830-625-8017
PET POLICY: $50 non refundable fee.

Motel 6
1275 IH-35
New Braunfels, TX 78130
830-626-0600
PET POLICY: No fee. Dogs under 25 lbs. preferred (larger animals by advance approval). Do not leave animals in room unattended.

Odem Days Inn
Hwy. 77 S.
Odem, TX 78370
512-368-2166
PET POLICY: No fee.

Best Western Garden Oasis
110 W. I-20
Odessa, TX 79761
915-337-3006
RATES: Single $55, double $68.
PET POLICY: No fee, all sizes welcome. Do not leave in rooms unattended. Responsible for damages.
POI: Car Museum-14 miles Meteor crater 14 miles UTPB-6 miles.

Holiday Inn Hotel & Suites
6201 E. Bus. I-20
Odessa, TX 79760
915-362-2311
PET POLICY: No fee.

Motel 6
200 E. I-20 Service Rd.
Odessa, TX 79766
915-333-4025
PET POLICY: No fee. Dogs under 25 lbs. preferred (larger animals by advance approval). Do not leave animals in room unattended.

Odessa Days Inn
3075 E. Business Loop 20
Odessa, TX 79761
915-335-8000
PET POLICY: Deposit required.

Motel 6
4407 27th St.
Orange, TX 77632
409-883-4891
PET POLICY: No fee. Dogs under 25 lbs. preferred (larger animals by advance approval). Do not leave animals in room unattended.

Ozona Daystop
820 Loop 466
Ozona, TX 76943
915-392-2631
PET POLICY: No fee.

Palestine Days Inn
1100 Palestine Ave.
Palestine, TX 75801
903-729-3151
PET POLICY: No fee.

U.S. Lodgings > TEXAS

Plainview Days Inn
3600 Olton Rd.
Plainview, TX 79072
806-293-2561
PET POLICY: No fee.

Best Western Park Suites Hotel
640 Park Blvd. E.
Plano, TX 75074
972-578-2243
RATES: Suite $95–$145 (kitchenette).
PET POLICY: Fee $20 for pets over 15 lbs.

Motel 6
2550 N. Central Expwy
Plano, TX 75074
972-578-1626
PET POLICY: No fee. Dogs under 25 lbs. preferred (larger animals by advance approval). Do not leave animals in room unattended.

Red Roof Inn
301 Ruisseau Dr.
Plano, TX 75023
972-881-8191
PET POLICY: No fee, pets under 80 lbs. Must be leashed to and from rooms. Do not leave in room unattended.

Residence Inn by Marriott
5001 Whitestone Ln.
Plano, TX 75024
972-473-6761
RATES: Single, double $69.
PET POLICY: Fee $150, nonrefundable. All sizes and pets welcome.
AMENITIES: Running areas. open pasture, pooper scoopers, dog dishes.

The Days Inn Port Lavaca
2100 N. Hwy. 35
Port Lavaca, TX 77979
512-552-4511
PET POLICY: Fee $8.

Ranger Days Inn
I-20 Ex 349, Box 16-C
Ranger, TX 76470
254-647-1176
PET POLICY: Fee $5.

Robstown Days Inn
320 Hwy. 77 S.
Robstown, TX 78380
361-387-9416
PET POLICY: Fee $5.

San Angelo Days Inn
4613 S. Jackson
San Angelo, TX 76903
915-658-6594
PET POLICY: No fee.

Aloha Inn
1435 Austin Hwy.
San Antonio, TX 78209
210-828-0933
RATES: Single $45, double $55.
PET POLICY: Fee 10% of room rate, nonrefundable. Up to 25 lbs. Sign pet agreement.
AMENITIES: Small fenced run.

Drury Inn & Suites
201 N. St. Mary's St.
San Antonio, TX 78205
210-212-5200
PET POLICY: No fee, pets under 30 lbs.

Drury Inn and Suites San Antonio Airport
95 NE Loop 410
San Antonio, TX 78216
210 366-9300
PET POLICY: No fee, pets under 30 lbs.

Motel 6
16500 IH-10 W
San Antonio, TX 78257
210-697-0731
PET POLICY: No fee. Dogs under 25 lbs. preferred (larger animals by advance approval). Do not leave animals in room unattended.

Motel 6
9400 Wurzbach Rd.
San Antonio, TX 78240
210-593-0013
PET POLICY: No fee. Dogs under 25 lbs. preferred (larger animals by advance approval). Do not leave animals in room unattended.

Pear Tree Inn by Drury— San Antonio Airport
143 NE Loop 410
San Antonio, TX 78216
210 366-9300

PET POLICY: No fee. All sizes and pets accepted. Do not leave in rooms unattended.

Red Roof Inn
6880 N.W. Loop 410
San Antonio, TX 78238
210-509-3434
PET POLICY: No fee, pets under 80 lbs. Must be leashed to and from rooms. Do not leave in room unattended.

Red Roof Inn
6861 Highway 90 West
San Antonio, TX 78227
210-675-4120
PET POLICY: No fee, pets under 80 lbs. Must be leashed to and from rooms. Do not leave in room unattended.

Red Roof Inn
333 Wolf Rd.
San Antonio, TX 78216
210-340-4055
PET POLICY: No fee, pets under 80 lbs. Must be leashed to and from rooms. Do not leave in room unattended.

San Antonio Days Inn
4039 E. Houston St.
San Antonio, TX 78220
210-333-9100
PET POLICY: No fee.

San Antonio Days Inn Northeast
3443 Interstate Hwy. 35 N.
San Antonio, TX 78219
210-225-4040
PET POLICY: No fee.

Staybridge Suites by Holiday Inn
4320 Spectrum One
San Antonio, TX 78230
210-558-9009
PET POLICY: $75 non refundable fee.

Woodfield Suites Hotel
100 W. Durango Blvd.
San Antonio, TX 78204
210-212-5400
PET POLICY: No fee.

U.S. Lodgings > TEXAS

San Benito Days Inn
1451 W. Expressway 83 & 77
San Benito, TX 78586
956-399-3891
PET POLICY: Fee $10.

San Marcos Days Inn
1005 Interstate Hwy. 35 N.
San Marcos, TX 78666
512-353-5050
PET POLICY: No fee.

Holiday Inn
2950 N. Hwy. 123 Bypass
Seguin, TX 78155
830-372-0860
PET POLICY: $25 pet deposit
refundable with room check.

Purple Sage Motel
1501 E. Coliseum Dr.
Snyder, TX 79550
915-573-5491
RATES: Single $43–$53, double
$51–$61.
PET POLICY: No fee, all sizes and
pets welcome (dogs, cats, ferrets,
birds, rabbits, reptiles). Room
must be paid by credit card.
AMENITIES: Area to walk dogs.

Snyder Days Inn
800 E. Coliseum Dr.
Snyder, TX 79549
915-573-1166
PET POLICY: Fee $5.

Days Inn
1312 Service Rd.
Sonora, TX 76950
915-387-3516
PET POLICY: Fee $2.

South Padre Island Days Inn
3913 Padre Blvd.
South Padre Island, TX 78597
210-761-7831
PET POLICY: Fee $20.

Motel 6
4013 Padre Blvd.
South Padre Island, TX 78597
956-761-7911
PET POLICY: No fee. Dogs under 25
lbs. preferred (larger animals by
advance approval). Do not leave
animals in room unattended.

Red Roof Inn
24903 N. I-45
Spring, TX 77380
281-367-5040
PET POLICY: No fee, pets under
80 lbs. Must be leashed to and
from rooms. Do not leave in
room unattended.

Holiday Inn
2865 W. Washington
Stephenville, TX 76401
254-968-5256
PET POLICY: Fee $100, refund-
able. Large dogs welcome, all
pets welcome.

Drury Inn and Suites
13770 Southwest Freeway
Sugar Land, TX 77478
281 277-9700
PET POLICY: No fee, pets under
30 lbs.

Shoney's Inn & Suites
14444 SW Freeway
Sugar Land, TX 77478
281-565-6655
RATES: Single $55–$75, double
$59–$79.
PET POLICY: Fee $25, nonrefund-
able. All size dogs and cats.

Holiday Inn
1495 E. Industrial Dr.
Sulphur Springs, TX 75482
903-885-0562
PET POLICY: Small pets allowed.

Motel 6
510 Northwest Georgia
Sweetwater, TX 79556
915-235-4387
PET POLICY: No fee. Dogs under 25
lbs. preferred (larger animals by
advance approval). Do not leave
animals in room unattended.

Motel 6
1100 N. General Bruce Dr.
Temple, TX 76504
254-778-0272
PET POLICY: No fee. Dogs under 25
lbs. preferred (larger animals by
advance approval). Do not leave
animals in room unattended.

Holiday Inn Express
5401 N. State Line Ave.
Texarkana, TX 75503
903-792-3366
PET POLICY: Fee and deposit.

Motel 6
1924 Hampton Rd.
Texarkana, TX 75503
903-793-1413
PET POLICY: No fee. Dogs under 25
lbs. preferred (larger animals by
advance approval). Do not leave
animals in room unattended.

**Drury Inn and Suites
Houston Woodlands**
28099 Interstate 45 North
The Woodlands, TX 77380
281 362-7222
PET POLICY: No fee, pets under
30 lbs.

Motel 6
3236 Gentry Pkwy.
Tyler, TX 75702
903-595-6691
PET POLICY: No fee. Dogs under 25
lbs. preferred (larger animals by
advance approval). Do not leave
animals in room unattended.

Tyler Days Inn North
3300 Mineola Hwy.
Tyler, TX 75702
903-595-2451
PET POLICY: Fee $6.

**Best Western Inn of
Van Horn**
1705 W. Broadway
Van Horn, TX 79855
915-283-2410
RATES: Single $42, double $46.
PET POLICY: No fee, all sizes
welcome.

Van Horn Days Inn
600 E. Broadway
Van Horn, TX 79855
915-283-1007
PET POLICY: Fee $4–$8.

Best Western Village Inn
1615 Expressway
Vernon, TX 76384
940-552-5417
RATES: Single $49, double $53.
PET POLICY: No fee, up to 25 lbs.
$5 for medium and large dogs.

Vernon Days Inn
3110 Expressway
Vernon, TX 76384
940-552-9982
PET POLICY: No fee.

U.S. Lodgings > TEXAS

Motel 6
3120 Jack Kultgen Fwy
Waco, TX 76706
254-662-4622
PET POLICY: No fee. Dogs under 25 lbs. preferred (larger animals by advance approval). Do not leave animals in room unattended.

Waco Days Inn
1504 Interstate Hwy. 35 N.
Waco, TX 76705
254-799-8585
PET POLICY: No fee.

Holiday Inn Express
1702 E. Expressway 83
Westaco, TX 78596
956-969-9920
PET POLICY: No fee.

Comfort Inn of Wichita Falls
1750 Maurine St.
Wichita Falls, TX 76304
940-322-2477
RATES: Single $52, double $55.
PET POLICY: Fee $10, nonrefundable, all sizes, no restrictions.

Motel 6
1812 Maurine St.
Wichita Falls, TX 76306
940-322-8817
PET POLICY: No fee. Dogs under 25 lbs. preferred (larger animals by advance approval). Do not leave animals in room unattended.

Red Roof Inn
1032 Central Freeway
Wichita Falls, TX 76305
940-766-6881
PET POLICY: No fee, pets under 80 lbs. Must be leashed to and from rooms. Do not leave in room unattended.

Travelodge
1740 Maurine St.
Wichita Falls, TX 76304
940-767-5653
RATES: Single $52, double $55.
PET POLICY: Fee $10, nonrefundable, all sizes, no restrictions.

Toenail Moon Retreat
3200 FM 3237
Wimberley, TX 78676
512-328-6887
RATES: Single $75, double $85–$105.
PET POLICY: Fee $15, nonrefundable, all sizes and all pets welcome (dogs, cats, ferrets, birds, rabbits, reptiles). Must be flea-free, and have current vaccines. Must be leashed on property.
AMENITIES: Deep water swimming. Enclosed decks.

UTAH

Kokopelli Inn
Hwy. 191, Box 27
Bluff, UT 84512
435-672-2322
RATES: Single $45, double $45.
PET POLICY: Fee $10 per pet per night, nonrefundable. Up to 50 lbs.
POI: River rafting, horseback riding, Jeep tours,. Near Monument Valley, Canyon Lands, Hovenweep National Park.

Cedar City Days Inn
1204 S. Main
Cedar City, UT 84720
435-867-8877
PET POLICY: Fee $10.

Motel 6
1620 W. 200 North
Cedar City, UT 84720
435-586-9200
PET POLICY: No fee. Dogs under 25 lbs. preferred (larger animals by advance approval). Do not leave animals in room unattended.

**Rainbow Country
Bed & Breakfast Inn**
586 E. 300 S.
Escalante, UT 84726
801-826-4567
RATES: Single $40–$60, double $45–$65.
PET POLICY: No fee, all sizes welcome.
AMENITIES: Pet-friendly hiking trails.
POI: National monument.

Motel 6
946 E. Main, Box 358
Green River, UT 84525
435-564-3436
PET POLICY: No fee. Dogs under 25 lbs. preferred (larger animals by advance approval). Do not leave animals in room unattended.

Danish Viking Lodge
989 S. Main
Heber City, UT 84032
435-654-2202
RATES: Single $45, double $55.
PET POLICY: Fee $10, nonrefundable. Up to 50 lbs.
POI: Olympic Venue. 7 ski resorts. 3 lakes. 2 golf courses.

Motel 6
650 W. State - Villa Park
Hurricane, UT 84737
435-635-4010
PET POLICY: No fee. Dogs under 25 lbs. preferred (larger animals by advance approval). Do not leave animals in room unattended.

Shilo Inn
296 W. 100 North
Kanab, UT 84741
435-644-2562
RATES: Single $79, double $89.
PET POLICY: Fee $10, nonrefundable. All sizes, all pets welcome.

Logan Days Inn
364 S. Main
Logan, UT 84321
435-753-5623
PET POLICY: No fee.

Homewood Suites Hotel
844 E. Fort Union
Midvale, UT 84047
801-561-5999
PET POLICY: Pets under 30 lbs. $75 non refundable cleaning fee.

Motel 6
7263 S. Catalpa
Midvale, UT 84047
801-561-0058
PET POLICY: No fee. Dogs under 25 lbs. preferred (larger animals by advance approval). Do not leave animals in room unattended.

U.S. Lodgings > VERMONT

Motel 6
1089 N. Main St.
Moab, UT 84532
435-259-6686
PET POLICY: No fee. Dogs under 25 lbs. preferred (larger animals by advance approval). Do not leave animals in room unattended.

Best Western High Country Inn
1335 W. 12th St.
Ogden, UT 84404
801-394-9474
RATES: Single $59, double $69.
PET POLICY: No fee, all sizes welcome.

Motel 6
1455 Washington Blvd.
Ogden, UT 84404
801-627-4560
PET POLICY: No fee. Dogs under 25 lbs. preferred (larger animals by advance approval). Do not leave animals in room unattended.

Park City's Best Ski Lodge
Park City, UT 84098
877-428-0847
RATES: Single $135, double $190.
PET POLICY: No fee, all sizes, all pets welcome. Fenced yard.
AMENITIES: Fenced yard.
POI: Near the Canyon's ski area.

Days Inn
1675 N. 200W
Provo, UT 84604
801-375-8600
PET POLICY: No fee.

Motel 6
1600 S. University Ave.
Provo, UT 84601
801-375-5064
PET POLICY: No fee. Dogs under 25 lbs. preferred (larger animals by advance approval). Do not leave animals in room unattended.

Days Inn
333 Main St.
Richfield, UT 84701
801-896-6476
PET POLICY: No fee.

Days Inn Thunderbird Lodge & Art Gallery
150 N. 1000 E
St. George, UT 84770
801-673-6123
PET POLICY: Fee $20.

Days Inn— Salt Lake City Airport
1900W N. Temple
Salt Lake City, UT 84116
801-539-8538
PET POLICY: Deposit required.

Motel 6
1990 W. N. Temple St.
Salt Lake City, UT 84116
801-364-1053
PET POLICY: No fee. Dogs under 25 lbs. preferred (larger animals by advance approval). Do not leave animals in room unattended.

Quality Inn—City Center
154 W. 600 S
Salt Lake City, UT 84101
801-521-2930
RATES: Single $59, double $69.
PET POLICY: No fee.
POI: 3 major parks: Liberty, Pioneer, Galivan.

Best Western Cottontree Inn
1455 N. 1750 West
Springville, UT 84663
801-489-3641
RATES: Single $54, double $59.
PET POLICY: Fee $10 per pet. All sizes accepted.

Springville Days Inn
520 S. 2000 W.
Springville, UT 84683
801-491-0300
PET POLICY: Fee $25.

Motel 6
1092 W. Highway 40
Vernal, UT 84078
435-789-0666
PET POLICY: No fee. Dogs under 25 lbs. preferred (larger animals by advance approval). Do not leave animals in room unattended.

Motel 6
561 E. Wendover Blvd.
Wendover, UT 84083
435-665-2267
PET POLICY: No fee. Dogs under 25 lbs. preferred (larger animals by advance approval). Do not leave animals in room unattended.

Baymont Inn & Suites
2229 W. City Center Court
West Valley City, UT 84119
801-886-1300
PET POLICY: No fee.

VERMONT

Arcady at the Sunderland Lodge
6249 Route 7A
Arlington, VT 05250
802-362-1176
RATES: Single, double $85 (Holiday: $120).
PET POLICY: Fee $10. All sizes and pets welcome. Basic pet-handling rules apply.
AMENITIES: Huge backyard to run pets.

Inn at Maplemont Farm
PO Box 11
Barnet, VT 05821
802-633-4880
PET POLICY: No fee, all sizes and pets welcome (dogs, cats, ferrets, birds, rabbits). Do not leave pets in room unattended. Pets on premises.

Alexandra Bed & Breakfast
916 Orchard Rd.
Bennington, VT 05201
802-442-5619
PET POLICY: Call innkeeper first.

Molly Stark Motel
829 Marlboro Rd.
Brattleboro, VT 05301
802-254-2440
RATES: Single $45, double $75.
PET POLICY: Fee $5, nonrefundable. Up to 50 lbs.

Motel 6
1254 Putney Rd, Rt 5N
Brattleboro, VT 05301
802-254-6007
PET POLICY: No fee. Dogs under 25 lbs. preferred (larger animals by advance approval). Do not leave animals in room unattended.

U.S. Lodgings > VERMONT

Super 8—Burlington
1016 Shelburne Rd.
Burlington, VT 05403
802-862-6421
RATES: Single $49–$79, double $59–$89.
PET POLICY: No fee, all sizes and all pets welcome.
AMENITIES: Walking area behind hotel.

Town & Country Motel
490 Shelburne Rd.
Burlington, VT 05401
802-862-5786
RATES: Single $59, double $69.
PET POLICY: Fee $5 per night per dog, nonrefundable, all sizes welcome, dogs only, treats available.
AMENITIES: Treats, field nearby for walking pets.
POI: One mile from 14-mile bike path along Lake Champlain. National Park, Beach.

Old Town Farm Inn
665 Vt. Rte. 10
Chester, VT 05143
802-875-2346
RATES: Single $110, double $120.
PET POLICY: Fee $10, nonrefundable. Dogs and Cats, only. Must be quiet. Deer on property.
POI: Okemo Mountain, Fletcher Farm (Calvin Coolidge birthplace).

Days Inn
23 College Pkwy.
Colchester, VT 05446
802-655-0900
PET POLICY: Fee $5.

Motel 6
74 S. Park Dr.
Colchester, VT 05446
802-654-6860
PET POLICY: No fee. Dogs under 25 lbs. preferred (larger animals by advance approval). Do not leave animals in room unattended.

The Inn on the Common
1162 N. Craftsbury Rd. Box 75
Craftsbury Common, VT 05827
802-586-9619

RATES: Single $170, double $300.
PET POLICY: Fee $15, nonrefundable. All sizes welcome.
AMENITIES: Play time with the Inn's dog Tyler.

Barrows House
PO Box 98
Dorset, VT 05251
802-639-4455
RATES: Single $185 MAP, double $225 MAP.
PET POLICY: Fee $20 per day, all size dogs, only. Do not leave in room unattended, or they must be crated.

Silver Maple Lodge & Cottages
RR 1, Box 8
Fairlee, VT 05045
802-333-4326
RATES: Single $65, double $69.
PET POLICY: No fee, all sizes and pets welcome.

Deer Run Motor Inn
RR 1, Box 260
Jeffersonville, VT 05464
802-644-8866
RATES: Single, double $50–$65.
PET POLICY: Fee $8, nonrefundable.

Cortina Inn & Resort
103 US Route 4
Killington, VT 05751
802-773-3333
RATES: Single $99–$169, double $124–$189.
PET POLICY: Fee $5, nonrefundable, all pets welcome (dogs, cats, ferrets, rabbits, birds, reptiles, etc.). Pets must be in carrier/crate with water and food. Not in lobbies or public areas, feed outside or in bathroom, walking trails, etc.). Treats available.
AMENITIES: Fresh baked treats on arrival. Pet sitters, list of kennels, pet grooming facilities available on request.

Frog's Leap Inn
RR 1, Box 107, Route 100
Londonderry, VT 05148
802-824-3019

RATES: Double $125.
PET POLICY: Fee $10 per pet per day, nonrefundable, must be restrained outside, outdoor kennels and trails available.
AMENITIES: Outdoor kennel. Trails.
POI: Green Mountain National Park. Lowell Lake. Echo Lake. Jamaica State Park.

Cavenish Pointe Inn
Rt. 103, Box 525
Ludlow, VT, 05149
802-226-7688
RATES: Summer: $59-99, Winter: $79-219
PET POLICY: Fee $20 per night. 9 pet rooms available. No size restrictions.

Forest Echo Farm
967 Tinney Rd.
Mt. Holly, VT 05758
802-258-4544
RATES: Cabins: $400 week + tax.
PET POLICY: No fee, all size dogs only. Must be friendly with other digs and people. Must be under owners control at all times.
POI: Hiking, cross-country skiing on property, nearest town: Ludlow, restaurants, antique stores, bakeries, farmstands, near Okemo and Killington for skiing, etc.

Putney Inn
Depot Rd.
Putney, VT 05346
802-387-5517
PET POLICY: Fee $10 per night, all sizes welcome.

Aime's Motel
RR1, Box 332
St. Johnsbury, VT 05819
802-748-3194
RATES: Single $40, double $55.
PET POLICY: No fee, all sizes welcome. Do not leave pets in rooms unattended.
AMENITIES: We provide bedding for pets.

U.S. Lodgings > VIRGINIA

Three Stallion Inn
Stock Farm Rd.
Randolph, VT 05060
802-728-5575
RATES: Single $100–$135,
double $127–$162.
PET POLICY: Fee $25 per night,
nonrefundable. All size dogs
and cats. $200 damage deposit
required, refundable. Only two
rooms are available for pets.
AMENITIES: 35 km trails on
1300 acres for hiking, snowshoeing, x-c skiing. Pets are
welcome on trails.

**Best Western Windjammer
Inn & Conference Center**
1076 Williston Rd.
South Burlington, VT 05403
802-863-1125
RATES: Single $59–$89, double
$69–$95.
PET POLICY: Fee $5 per day, all
sizes welcome.

**Honeywood Country
Lodge**
4527 Mountain Rd.
Stowe, VT 05672
802-253-4124
PET POLICY: Fee $6 per pet, non-
refundable. All sizes welcome.

Mountaineer Inn
3343 Mountain Rd.
Stowe, VT 0572
802-253-7525
RATES: Single $90, double $90.
PET POLICY: Fee $5, nonrefund-
able. All sizes and pets welcome.
POI: Smugglers Notch all seasons. 5.5 mile paved recreation
path, hiking, climbing, swimming, biking, snowmobiling,
drawn sleigh rides. Pet-
friendly summer concerts,
Waterberry State Park.

Northern Lights Lodge
4441 Mountain Rd.
Stowe, VT 05672
802-253-8541
PET POLICY: Fee $10, nonre-
fundable. All size dogs, only.
Please do not leave your dogs
in the room unattended for
more than a few hours.

**Topnotch at Stowe
Resort & Spa**
4000 Mountain Rd.
Stowe, VT 05672
802-253-8585
PET POLICY: No fee, all sizes
accepted. Not allowed in
Condominiums or Townhouses.

**Arcady at the
Sunderland Lodge**
6249 Route 7A
Sunderland, VT 05250
802-362-1176
RATES: Single, double $85
(Holiday: $120).
PET POLICY: Fee $10. All sizes
and pets welcome. Basic pet-
handling rules apply.
AMENITIES: Huge backyard to
run pets.

Basin Harbor Club
Basin Harbor Rd.
Vergennes, VT 05491
802-475-2311
RATES: Single $109–$350,
double $119–$400.
PET POLICY: Fee $7.50, refundable,
all sizes and all pets welcome.

Powderhound Resort
Rt. 100, Box 369
Warren, VT 05674
800-548-4022
RATES: Single, double $70–$125.
PET POLICY: No fee, no restric-
tions.

Snow Goose Inn
Box 366, Route 100
West Dover, VT 05356
802-464-3984
RATES: Double $150.
PET POLICY: Fee $25, nonrefund-
able, all sizes and all pets wel-
come. Must have own beds.
AMENITIES: 3 acres of woodlands.

Inn at Quail Run
106 Smith Rd.
Wilmington, VT 05363
802-464-3362
PET POLICY: Fee $15 per night,
all sizes welcome.

The Winslow House
492 Woodstock Rd.
Woodstock, VT 05091
802-457-1820

RATES: Single $95, double $150.
PET POLICY: No fee, all size dogs
and cats. Do not leave pets in
room unattended.
AMENITIES: Area for walking dog.

VIRGINIA

Red Roof Inn
5975 Richmond Hwy.
Alexandria, VA 22303
703-960-5200
PET POLICY: No fee, pets under
80 lbs. Must be leashed to and
from rooms. Do not leave in
room unattended.

Washington DC Days Inn
6100 Richmond Hwy.
Alexandria, VA 22303
703-329-0500
PET POLICY: Fee $10.

Best Western Key Bridge
1850 N. Fort Myer Dr.
Arlington, VA 22209
703-522-0400
PET POLICY: Fee $25, designated
rooms, must be in crate.

Crowne Plaza
1489 Jefferson Davis Hwy.
Arlington, VA 22202
703-416-1600
PET POLICY: No fee.

**Executive Club Suites—
Arlington**
108 S. Courthouse Rd.
Arlington, VA 22209
703-522-2582
RATES: Single $120, double $215.
PET POLICY: Fee $50, plus $250
refundable deposit. All sizes
and pets welcome.

**Quality Hotel Courthouse
Plaza**
1200 N. Courthouse Rd.
Arlington, VA 22201
703-524-4000
PET POLICY: Fee $10 daily, $25
one-time, must be in crate.

Quality Inn—Iwo Jima
1501 Arlington Blvd.
Arlington, VA 22209
703-524-5000
PET POLICY: Fee $10 daily,
designated rooms.

U.S. Lodgings > VIRGINIA

Sky Chalet Mountain Lodges
Rt. 263, 280 Sky Chalet Ln.
Basye, VA 22810
540-856-2147
RATES: Single $49, double $79.
PET POLICY: No fee, all sizes
welcome. Must be on leach
outside, quiet, well-behaved.
AMENITIES: Treats for pets in
delivered continental break-
fast. Woods, hiking places, etc.
POI: Lake Laura, George
Washington Nat'l Forest,
Skyline Drive, Luray Caverns,
Shenandoah Caverns,
Shenandoah Vineyards, Bryce
Resort.

Elmo's Rest
2122 Sheep Creek Rd.
Bedford, VA 24523
540-586-3707
PET POLICY: Fee $50, nonrefund-
able, all sizes accepted, under
control.

Cape Charles Days Inn
29108 Lankford Hwy.
Cape Charles, VA 23310
757-331-1000
PET POLICY: Fee $8.

Carmel Church Days Inn
PO Box 70
Carmel Church, VA 22546
804-448-2011
PET POLICY: Fee $6.

Days Inn University Area
1600 Emmet St.
Charlottesville, VA 22901
804-293-9111
PET POLICY: Fee $5.

Red Roof Inn
1309 W. Main St.
Charlottesville, VA 22903
804-295-4333
PET POLICY: No fee, pets under
80 lbs. Must be leashed to and
from rooms. Do not leave in
room unattended.

Super 8 Motel
390 Greenbrier Dr.
Charlottesville, VA 22901
802-973-0888
RATES: Single $40–$75, double
$40–$75.
PET POLICY: Fee $6, nonrefund-
able, all sizes welcome.

Holiday Inn
1200 5th St.
Charlottesville, VA, 22902
804-977-5100
RATES: Single, double $64.95–
109.95
PET POLICY: Fee $7.50 per night.
All sizes and pets accepted.

Motel 6
701 Woodlake Dr.
Chesapeake, VA 23320
757-420-2976
PET POLICY: No fee. Dogs under 25
lbs. preferred (larger animals by
advance approval). Do not leave
animals in room unattended.

Red Roof Inn
724 Woodlake Dr.
Chesapeake, VA 23320
757-523-0123
PET POLICY: No fee, pets under
80 lbs. Must be leashed to and
from rooms. Do not leave in
room unattended.

Chester Days Inn
2410 W. Hundred Rd.
Chester, VA 23831
804-748-5871
PET POLICY: Fee $6.

The Garden & Sea Inn
PO Box 275
Chincoteague Area, VA 23415
800-824-0672
RATES: Single, double $75–$185.
PET POLICY: No fee, all sizes and
pets welcome. Must be quiet
in room and on-leash outside.
AMENITIES: Fenced runs.

Christiansburg Days Inn
PO Box 768
Christiansburg, VA 24068
540-382-0261
PET POLICY: Fee $5.

Days Inn
30 Colonial Ave.
Colonial Beach, VA 22443
804-224-0404
PET POLICY: Fee $10.

Danville Days Inn
1309 Piney Forest Rd.
Danville, VA 24540
804-836-6745
PET POLICY: No fee.

Comfort Inn Emporia
1411 Skippers Rd.
Emporia, VA 23847
804-348-3282
RATES: Single, double
$49.95–$69.95.
PET POLICY: No fee, no size
restrictions. Do not leave pets
unattended in rooms.

Emporia Days Inn
921 W. Atlantic St.
Emporia, VA 23847
804-634-9481
PET POLICY: Fee $6.

**Holiday Inn Fairfax-
FairOaks Mall**
11787 Lee Jackson Memorial
Hwy.
Fairfax, VA 22033
703-352-2525
PET POLICY: No fee for pets
under 20 lbs. Fees may go as
high as $100 depending on
size of pets. Call first.

**Cascade Mountain Inn &
Restaurant**
96 Cascade Trail
Fancy Gap, VA 24328
540-728-2300
RATES: Single, double $45–$55.
PET POLICY: No fee, up to 50
lbs., all pets welcome, including birds.

**Doe Run Lodge at
Groundhog Mountain**
Milepost 189, Blue Ridge
Pkwy.
Fancy Gap, VA 24343
540-398-2212
RATES: Double $139. Special:
up to $234.
PET POLICY: Fee $25, nonrefund-
able, all pets welcome.
AMENITIES: Chalets w/2-bed-
room, 2-bath w/kitchenette,
living room, private balcony,
apprx. 900 sq. ft living space.
Units have refrigerators,
TV/VCRs, hair dryers, coffee
makers, wood-burning fire-
places/woodstoves. Firewood
provided. Hike, fish, tennis.
Pool.
POI: Area to walk pets.

U.S. Lodgings > VIRGINIA

Dunning Mills Inn
2305C Jefferson Davis Hwy.
Fredericksburg, VA 22401
540-373-1256
RATES: Single $69, double $73.
PET POLICY: Fee $5, all sizes,
all pets welcome (dogs, cats,
ferrets, birds, rabbits, etc.).

**Fredericksburg Days Inn
North**
14 Simpson Rd.
Fredericksburg, VA 22406
540-373-5340
PET POLICY: Fee $5.

**Fredericksburg Days Inn
South**
5316 Jefferson Davis Hwy.
Fredericksburg, VA 22408
540-898-6800
PET POLICY: Fee $5.

Motel 6
401 Warrenton Rd.
Fredericksburg, VA 22405
540-371-5443
PET POLICY: No fee. Dogs under 25
lbs. preferred (larger animals by
advance approval). Do not leave
animals in room unattended.

Quality Inn Fredericksburg
543 Warrenton Rd.
Fredericksburg, VA 22406
540-373-0000
PET POLICY: Fee $8, nonrefund-
able.

Homewood Suites Hotel
4100 Innslake Dr.
Glen Allen, VA 23060
804-217-8000
PET POLICY: Pets under 35 lbs.
$150 non refundable cleaning
fee.

The Hummingbird Inn
PO Box 147
Goshen, VA 24439
540-997-9065
RATES: Avg: $120.
PET POLICY: Fee $20 (one-time
charge), nonrefundable. Dogs
only, up to 50 lbs. Must be
neutered, over 1 year old.
Specific pet-friendly rooms.

Hampton Days Inn
1918 Coliseum Dr.
Hampton, VA 23666
804-826-4810
PET POLICY: Fee $6.

Red Roof Inn
1925 Coliseum Dr.
Hampton, VA 23666
757-838-1870
PET POLICY: No fee, pets under
80 lbs. Must be leashed to and
from rooms. Do not leave in
room unattended.

**Harrisonburg Days Inn
James Madison Univ.**
1131 Forest Hill Rd.
Harrisonburg, VA 22801
540-433-9353
PET POLICY: Fee $5.

Motel 6
10 Linda Ln.
Harrisonburg, VA 22801
540-433-6939
PET POLICY: No fee. Dogs under 25
lbs. preferred (larger animals by
advance approval). Do not leave
animals in room unattended.

Village Inn
4979 S. Valley Pike (Route 11)
Harrisonburg, VA 22801
800-736-7355
RATES: Single $50, double $60.
PET POLICY: Fee $5, all sizes,
only dogs and cats. Extensive
yards and fields for pets.
AMENITIES: Quiet, Scenic rural
setting. Extensive yards and
fields for pets to play.

The Tides Resorts
480 King Carter Dr.
Irvington, VA 22480
800-843-3746
RATES: Singles: $319, double
$384.
PET POLICY: No fee, all sizes
welcome. Dogs must be on
leash when on grounds.

**Leesburg Days Inn
Downtown**
721 E. Market St. On Us 7 &
Us 15 Bypass
Leesburg, VA 20175
703-777-6622
PET POLICY: No fee.

Days Inn Keydet General
325 W. Midland Trail
Lexington, VA 24450
540-463-2143
PET POLICY: No fee.

The Hummingbird Inn
30 Wood Ln.
PO Box 147
Lexington, VA 24439
540-997-9065
RATES: Avg: $120.
PET POLICY: Fee $20 (one-time
charge), nonrefundable. Dogs
only, up to 50 lbs. Must be
neutered, over 1 year old.
Specific pet-friendly rooms.

**The Inn at Meander
Plantation**
HCR 5, Box 460A
Locust Dale, VA 22948
540-672-4912
RATES: Single, double $150.
PET POLICY: Fee $20 per stay,
nonrefundable. All sizes wel-
come. Limit 2 pets at one time.
AMENITIES: Rural area great for
walking with pets.

Luray Days Inn
138 Whispering Hill Rd.
Luray, VA 22835
540-743-4521
PET POLICY: Fee $10.

Shenandoah River Cabins
6502 S. Page Valley Rd.
Luray, VA 22835
540-743-4159
RATES: Single $90, double $140.
PET POLICY: Fee $10, all sizes
and all pets welcome.

Red Roof Inn
10610 Automotive Dr.
Manassas, VA 20109
703-335-9333
PET POLICY: No fee, pets under
80 lbs. Must be leashed to and
from rooms. Do not leave in
room unattended.

Days Inn—Oyster Point
1829 Fishing Point Dr.
Newport News, VA 23606
757-873-6700
PET POLICY: Fee $10.

U.S. Lodgings > VIRGINIA

Motel 6
797 J Clyde-Morris Blvd.
Newport News, VA 23601
757-595-6336
PET POLICY: No fee. Dogs under 25 lbs. preferred (larger animals by advance approval). Do not leave animals in room unattended.

Newport News Days Inn
14747 Warwick Blvd.
Newport News, VA 23602
804-874-0201
PET POLICY: No fee.

Motel 6
853 N. Military Hwy.
Norfolk, VA 23502
757-461-2380
PET POLICY: No fee. Dogs under 25 lbs. preferred (larger animals by advance approval). Do not leave animals in room unattended.

Norfolk Days Inn
1631 Bayville St.
Norfolk, VA 23503
757-583-4521
PET POLICY: No fee.

Quality Inn
6280 Northampton Blvd.
Norfolk, VA 23502
757-461-6251
PET POLICY: Fee $25.

Raphine Days Inn
584 Oakland Cir.
Raphine, VA 24472
540-377-2604
PET POLICY: Fee $5.

Red Roof Inn
5701 B Chamberlayne Rd.
Richmond, VA 23227
804-266-3739
PET POLICY: No fee, pets under 80 lbs. Must be leashed to and from rooms. Do not leave in room unattended.

Red Roof Inn
4350 Commerce Rd.
Richmond, VA 23234
804-271-7240
PET POLICY: No fee, pets under 80 lbs. Must be leashed to and from rooms. Do not leave in room unattended.

Red Roof Inn
100 Greshamwood Place
Richmond, VA 23225
804-745-0600
PET POLICY: No fee, pets under 80 lbs. Must be leashed to and from rooms. Do not leave in room unattended.

Residence Inn Richmond West
2121 Dickens Rd.
Richmond, VA 23230
804-285-8200
RATES: Tiered rates from $124 to 84, based on length of stay.-
PET POLICY: Fee $125, non-refundable.

Richmond Days Inn
1600 Robin Hood Rd.
Richmond, VA 23220
804-353-1287
PET POLICY: Fee $2.

Richmond Days Inn
2100 Dickens Rd.
Richmond, VA 23230
804-282-3300
PET POLICY: Fee $6.

Wyndham Garden Hotel— Richmond Airport
4700 S. Laburnum Ave.
Richmond, VA 23231
804-226-4300
PET POLICY: Fee $25, nonre-fundable. Up to 50 lbs., dogs and cats only. Do not leave pets in room unattended.

Patrick Henry Hotel
617 S. Jefferson St.
Roanoke, VA 24011
540-345-8811
PET POLICY: Small pets only.

Roanoke Days Inn Civic Center—Downtown
535 Orange Ave.
Roanoke, VA 24016
540-342-4551
PET POLICY: No fee.

Baymont Inn & Suites
140 Sheraton Dr.
Salem, VA 24153
540-562-2717
PET POLICY: No fee.

Richmond Days Inn Airport
5500 Williamsburg Rd.
Sandston, VA 23150
804-222-2041
PET POLICY: No fee.

High Meadows Vineyard Inn
55 High Meadows Ln.
Scottsville, VA 24590
804-286-2218
RATES: e-mail for rates.
PET POLICY: Fee $20, non-refundable.
AMENITIES: Lots of room to run.

Ashton Country House
1205 Middlebrook Ave.
Staunton, VA 24401
800-296-7819
PET POLICY: Fee $10, non-refundable.

Days Inn
Rt. 2, Box 414
Staunton, VA 24401
540-337-3031
PET POLICY: No fee.

Staunton Days Inn
273 D Bells Ln.
Staunton, VA 24402
540-248-0888
PET POLICY: Fee $6.

Suffolk Days Inn
1526 Holland Rd.
Suffolk, VA 23434
757-539-5111
PET POLICY: No fee.

Daystop Roanoke
US 220
Troutville, VA 24175
540-992-3100
PET POLICY: No fee.

Roanoke Daystop Troutville
PO Box 305
Troutville, VA 24175
540-992-6041
PET POLICY: No fee.

Days Inn Oceanfront
Oceanfront & 32nd St.
Virginia Beach, VA 23451
757-428-7233
PET POLICY: No fee.

U.S. Lodgings > WASHINGTON

Days Inn Virginia Beach Expressway
4600 Bonney Rd.
Virginia Beach, VA 23462
757-473-9745
PET POLICY: No fee.

Red Roof Inn
5745 Northampton Blvd.
Virginia Beach, VA 23455
757-460-3414
PET POLICY: No fee, pets under 80 lbs. Must be leashed to and from rooms. Do not leave in room unattended.

Red Roof Inn
196 Ballard Court
Virginia Beach, VA 23462
757-490-0225
PET POLICY: No fee, pets under 80 lbs. Must be leashed to and from rooms. Do not leave in room unattended.

Waynesboro Days Inn
2060 Rosser Ave.
Waynesboro, VA 22980
540-943-1101
PET POLICY: Fee $10.

Heritage Inn
1324 Richmond Rd.
Williamsburg, VA 23185
800-782-3800
PET POLICY: No fee, no restrictions, grassy area, prefer in kennel if left alone.

Holiday Inn
3032 Richmond Rd.
Williamsburg, VA 23185
757-565-2600
PET POLICY: Deposit required.

Motel 6
3030 Richmond Rd.
Williamsburg, VA 23185
757-565-3433
PET POLICY: No fee. Dogs under 25 lbs. preferred (larger animals by advance approval). Do not leave animals in room unattended.

Red Roof Inn
824 Capitol Landing Rd.
Williamsburg, VA 23185
757-259-1948
PET POLICY: No fee, pets under 80 lbs. Must be leashed to and from rooms. Do not leave in room unattended.

Days Inn Winchester
2951 Valley Ave.
Winchester, VA 22601
540-667-1200
PET POLICY: Fee $6.

Woodbridge Days Inn Potomac Mills—Dale City
14619 Potomac Mills Rd.
Woodbridge, VA 22192
703-494-4433
PET POLICY: No fee.

Motel 6
220 Lithia Rd.
Wytheville, VA 24382
540-228-7988
PET POLICY: No fee. Dogs under 25 lbs. preferred (larger animals by advance approval). Do not leave animals in room unattended.

WASHINGTON

Bellingham Days Inn
125 E. Kellog Rd.
Bellingham, WA 98226
360-671-6200
PET POLICY: Fee $7.

Motel 6
3701 Byron
Bellingham, WA 98225
360-671-4494
PET POLICY: No fee. Dogs under 25 lbs. preferred (larger animals by advance approval). Do not leave animals in room unattended.

Quality Inn Baron Suites
100 E. Kellogg Rd.
Bellingham, WA 98226
360-647-8000
PET POLICY: Fee $25 nonrefundable.

Val-U-Inn
805 Lakeway Dr.
Bellingham, WA 98226
360-671-9600
RATES: Single $54.
PET POLICY: Fee $5 per night, nonrefundable, up to 50 lbs. Dogs only.

Inn at Semi-Ah-Moo—A Wyndham Resort
9565 Semiahmoo Pkwy.
Blaine, WA 98230
360-371-2000
PET POLICY: Fee $50. No restrictions.

Howard Johnson Plaza Hotel & Conference Center
5640 Kitsap Way
Bremerton, WA 98312
360-373-9900
RATES: Single $75, double $85.
PET POLICY: Fee $50 refundable, up to 25 lbs.
POI: Seabeck beach/park.

Centralia Travelodge
1325 Lake Shore Dr.
Centralia, WA 98531
360 736-9344
RATES: Single $55, double $60.
PET POLICY: Fee $5, nonrefundable. All sizes welcome.

Motel 6
1310 Belmont Ave.
Centralia, WA 98531
360-330-2057
PET POLICY: No fee. Dogs under 25 lbs. preferred (larger animals by advance approval). Do not leave animals in room unattended.

Nordlig Motel
101 W. Grant St.
Chewelah, WA 99109
509-935-6704
RATES: Single, double $45.95–$51.65.
PET POLICY: Fee $3. All sizes accepted. Do not leave unattended in rooms.

Motel 6
222 Bridge St.
Clarkston, WA 99403
509-758-1631
PET POLICY: No fee. Dogs under 25 lbs. preferred (larger animals by advance approval). Do not leave animals in room unattended.

U.S. Lodgings > WASHINGTON

Stewart Lodge
805 W. First St.
Cleelum, WA 98922
509-674-4548
RATES: Single $52, double $70.
PET POLICY: Fee $5, nonrefundable.
POI: Lake Cleelum. Yakima Lake.

Colville Comfort Inn
166 NE Canning Dr.
Colville, WA 99114
509-684-2010
RATES: Single $66, double $85.
PET POLICY: No fee, all size dogs and cats, only.

Edmonds Harbor Inn
130 W. Dayton
Edmonds, WA 98020
425-771-5021
RATES: Single $89, double $99.
PET POLICY: Fee $10, nonrefundable.
POI: Kingston Ferry, 1½ blocks from beach.

Motel 6
224 128th St SW
Everett, WA 98204
425-353-8120
PET POLICY: No fee. Dogs under 25 lbs. preferred (larger animals by advance approval). Do not leave animals in room unattended.

Travelodge City Center
3030 Broadway
Everett, WA 98201
425 259-6141
RATES: Single $59.95, double $69.95.
PET POLICY: Fee $5, nonrefundable, dogs only, all sizes. Do not leave in room unattended.

Kalaloch Lodge
157151 Hwy. 101
Forks, WA 98331
360-962-2271
RATES: Single $93, double $93.
PET POLICY: Fee $10 per night, nonrefundable. All sizes welcome.

Mt. Baker Lodging
7425 Mt. Baker Rd.
Glacier, WA 98266
360-599-2453
PET POLICY: No fee, all size domesticated pets welcome.

Motel 6
1885 15th Pl NW
Issaquah, WA 98027
425-392-8405
PET POLICY: No fee. Dogs under 25 lbs. preferred (larger animals by advance approval). Do not leave animals in room unattended.

Summerwalk at Klahanie
3850 Klahanie Dr. SE
Issaquah, WA 98029
425-557-2200
PET POLICY: Fee $200, refundable. All size dogs and cats. Limit of two 80 lb. dogs, combined limit.
AMENITIES: Hundreds of acres of walking trails, near parks and lakes. Apartment community
POI: Near Cascade mountain range. 15 min. to Lake Washington.

Seattle Days Inn South Seattle/Kent
1711 W. Meeker St.
Kent, WA 98032
253-854-1950
PET POLICY: No fee.

Island Tyme Bed & Breakfast
4940 S. Bayview Rd.
Langley, WA 98260
360-221-5078
RATES: Single $95, double $95.
PET POLICY: No fee, all sizes and all pets welcome.

Anchorage Cottages
2209 Blvd. N.
Long Beach, WA 98631
360-642-2351
RATES: Single $78.50, double $92.50.
PET POLICY: Fee $6, nonrefundable. Dogs and cats only, up to 50 lbs. Keep on leashes. Two dogs per cottage.
AMENITIES: Dog washing area after beach-play. Dog towels provided.

Ocean Lodge Motel-1
208 Balstad Ave. W.
Long Beach, WA 98631
360-642-5400
RATES: 1st Fl.: $55, 2nd Fl.: $60, 3rd Fl: $70 (ocean view).

PET POLICY: Fee $5, sometimes. No size restrictions for 1st floor. Under 20 lbs. for 2nd and 3rd floors.

Ocean Lodge Motel-2
208 Balstad Ave. W.
Long Beach, WA 98631
360-642-5400
RATES: 1st Fl.: $55, 2nd Fl.: $60, 3rd Fl: $70 (ocean view).
PET POLICY: Fee $5, sometimes. No size restrictions for 1st floor. Under 20 lbs. for 2nd and 3rd floors.

FedWold Cottage & Gardens
80 Port Stanley Rd.
Lopez Island, WA 98261
360-468-3062
RATES: Single $98–$86, double $98–$86.
PET POLICY: No fee, all sizes and all pets welcome.

Holiday Inn Express Hotel & Suites
19103 Hwy. 2
Monroe, WA 98272
360-863-1900
PET POLICY: Fee $25.

Motel 6
2822 Wapato Dr.
Moses Lake, WA 98837
509-766-0250
PET POLICY: No fee. Dogs under 25 lbs. preferred (larger animals by advance approval). Do not leave animals in room unattended.

Shilo Inn
1819 E. Kittleson
Moses Lake, WA 98837
509-765-9317
RATES: Single $69, double $79.
PET POLICY: Fee $10, nonrefundable. All sizes, all pets welcome.

Travelodge
316 S. Pioneer Way
Moses Lake, WA 98837
509 765-8631
RATES: Single $59.95, double $69.95.
PET POLICY: Fee $5, nonrefundable, dogs only, all sizes. Do not leave in room unattended.

U.S. Lodgings > WASHINGTON

Mt. Baker Lodging
7425 Mt. Baker Rd.
Mount Baker, WA 98266
360-599-2453
RATES: Single $110, double $245.
PET POLICY: No fee, all size
domesticated pets welcome.
POI: Mt. Baker ski area. Mt.
Baker National Forest. Silver
Lake State Park.

Best Western College Way Inn
300 W. College Way
Mount Vernon, WA 98273
360-424-4287
RATES: Single $58–$71, double
$68–$81.
PET POLICY: Fee $10 per night,
nonrefundable. All sizes welcome.

Days Inn, Mt. Vernon
2009 Riverside Dr.
Mount Vernon, WA 98273
360-424-4141
PET POLICY: No fee.

**Harbor View Motel
and RV Park**
3204 281st St.
Ocean Park, WA 98640
360-665-4959
RATES: Single $45, double $50.
PET POLICY: Fee $3. All sizes and
pets welcome (dogs, cats,
ferrets, birds, rabbits, reptiles).
Do not leave pets in rooms
or vehicles unattended.
POI: Numerous state parks,
world's longest beach (28 miles),
clamming, crabbing, fishing,

Discovery Inn
1031 Discovery Ave. SE
Ocean Shores, WA 98569
360-289-3371
RATES: Single $60, double $60.
PET POLICY: Fee $10, pets on
first floor only.
AMENITIES: Pet run.
POI: Beaches, parks, boating.

Nautilus Condos
PO Box 128
Ocean Shores, WA 98569
360-289-2722
RATES: Double $70–$135.

PET POLICY: Two dogs maxi-
mum, no cats. Do not leave
animals alone in room or car.
Must be leashed on property.
Read pet policy on their site.
AMENITIES: Towels, dog duty
area, dog treats, wash facilities.
POI: Casino, Olympic National
Forest, ferry to Westport.

Puget View Guest House
7924 61st Ave. NE
Olympia, WA 98516
360-413-9474
RATES: Single $89–$119, double
$99–$129.
PET POLICY: Fee $10 per night
per pet, nonrefundable. Prior
approval required.

Camaray Motel
1320 Main St.
Oroville, WA 98844
509-476-3684
PET POLICY: No fee.

Sandpiper Beach Resort
4159 State Road 109
Pacific Beach, WA 98571
360-276-4580
RATES: Single, double $55–$165
(seasonal).
PET POLICY: Fee $10 per pet. All
sizes accepted.

Poulsbo's Inn
18680 Hwy. 305
Poulsbo, WA 98370
360-779-3921
RATES: Single $77, double $77.
PET POLICY: Fee $10 per pet per
night. Up to 50 lbs.

Sandy Hook Beach Cabin
14532 Sandy Hook Rd, NE
Poulsbo, WA 98370
206-842-4260
RATES: Cabin: Single and
Double $50.
PET POLICY: No fee, all sizes and
pets welcome (dogs, cats, ferrets, birds, rabbits, reptiles).
Limit of 2 dogs, must be
housebroken. No allowed in
pool or beds. Cats on property so dogs must be con-
tained.
AMENITIES: Pet-friendly beach,
dog dishes provided.

POI: Suquamish Indian
Museum, Keyport Undersea
museum, Winery tours, golf,
tennis, kayaking and canoe
rentals, bi-plane rides, hiking,
casino gaming, antiquing.

**Quality Inn Paradise Creek
Motor Inn**
SE 1400 Bishop Blvd.
Pullman, WA 99163
509-332-0500
RATES: Single $64.99, double
$74.99.
PET POLICY: No fee, all sizes and
pets welcome.
AMENITIES: Beautiful 8 mile
walking trail that starts from
our parking lot.
POI: One of the best vet colleges
in the country with special
rates for owners of pet patients.

Motel 6
1751 Fowler St.
Richland, WA 99352
509-783-1250
PET POLICY: No fee. Dogs under 25
lbs. preferred (larger animals by
advance approval). Do not leave
animals in room unattended.

Shilo Inn Richland
50 Comstock
Richland, WA 99352
509-946-4661
RATES: Single $69, double $79.
PET POLICY: Fee $10, nonrefund-
able. All sizes, all pets welcome.

Crowne Plaza
1113 6th Ave.
Seattle, WA 98101
206-464-1980
PET POLICY: No fee.

Homewood Suites by Hilton
206 Western Ave. W.
Seattle, WA 98119
206-281-9393
RATES: Single $149, double
$169.
PET POLICY: Fee $20 per day
(max. $140), nonrefundable.
All sizes welcome.
POI: Seattle Center, Space
Needle, Seattle waterfront.

U.S. Lodgings > WASHINGTON

Motel 6
16500 Pacific Hwy. South
Seattle, WA 98188
206-246-4101
PET POLICY: No fee. Dogs under 25
lbs. preferred (larger animals by
advance approval). Do not leave
animals in room unattended.

Motel 6
18900 47th Ave S
Seattle, WA 98188
206-241-1648
PET POLICY: No fee. Dogs under 25
lbs. preferred (larger animals by
advance approval). Do not leave
animals in room unattended.

Pensione Nichols
1923 First Ave.
Seattle, WA 98101
206-441-7125
RATES: Single $75, double $95.
PET POLICY: No fee, all sizes
welcome. (No children!).
POI: In Seattle's Pike Place.
Walking distance to Space
Needle and Waterfront.

Red Roof Inn
16838 International Blvd.
Seattle, WA 98188
206-248-0901
PET POLICY: No fee, pets under
80 lbs. Must be leashed to and
from rooms. Do not leave in
room unattended.

**Travelodge by
the Space Needle**
200 6th Ave N.
Seattle, WA 98109
206 441-7878
RATES: Single $119, double
169.
PET POLICY: Fee $5., nonrefund-
able, only dog, all sizes, do not
leave unattended in room.

**Vagabond Inn—
Space Needle**
325 Aurora Ave North
Seattle, WA 98109
206-441-0400
RATES: Single $79, double $89.
PET POLICY: Fee $10, dogs and
cats only, up to 50 lbs.

Seaview Motel & RV Park
3728 Pacific Hwy.
Seaview, WA 98644
360-642-2450
RATES: Single $48, double $54.
PET POLICY: No fee, all size dogs
only. Cats, ferrets, and other
animals on approval. First pet
free, additional animals $5 per
day.
AMENITIES: Dogs allowed on
28-mile peninsula if on-leash.
POI: National and State Historic
area, North Head and Cape
Disappointment Lighthouses,
Ft. Canby, Ledbetter, Loomis
Lake, and Pacific Pines State
Parks, hiking, leash-free beach.

Best Inn & Suites
6309 E. Broadway
Spokane, WA 99212
509-535-7185
RATES: Single $49, double $49.
PET POLICY: No fee, all sizes and
all pets welcome (dogs, cats,
ferrets, birds, rabbits, etc.).

Budget Inn
110 E. 4th Ave.
Spokane, WA 99202
509-838-6101
RATES: Single $39, double $49.
PET POLICY: No fee, all sizes and
all pets welcome.

Motel 6
1508 S. Rustle St.
Spokane, WA 99224
509-459-6120
PET POLICY: No fee. Dogs under 25
lbs. preferred (larger animals by
advance approval). Do not leave
animals in room unattended.

Park Lane Motel
4412 E. Sprague Ave.
Spokane, WA 99212
509-535-1626
RATES: Single $47.50, double
$57.50.
PET POLICY: No fees, no restrictions, up to 50 lbs.
AMENITIES: With reservations
pet gets welcome bone.
POI: Our 2-acre fenced grass
walking area.

Shangri-La Motel
2922 W. Government Way
Spokane, WA 99204
509-747-2066
RATES: Single $42.95, double
$46.95.
PET POLICY: No fee, pets up to
50 lbs.
POI: Riverside State Park.

Shilo Inn
923 E. 3rd Ave.
Spokane, WA 99202
509-535-9000
RATES: Single $79, double $89.
PET POLICY: Fee $10, nonrefund-
able. All sizes, all pets welcome.

Spokane Days Inn Airport
4212 W. Sunset Blvd.
Spokane, WA 99224
509-747-2021
PET POLICY: Fee $10.

Travelodge
W-33 Spokane Falls Blvd.
Spokane, WA 99201
509 623-9727
RATES: Single, double $59.95.
PET POLICY: Fee $10, nonrefund-
able, up to 50 lbs.
AMENITIES: Dog bones at check
in, grassy area for pet walking.
POI: Opera House, Riverfront
park.

Motel 6
1811 S. 76th St.
Tacoma, WA 98408
253-473-7100
PET POLICY: No fee. Dogs under 25
lbs. preferred (larger animals by
advance approval). Do not leave
animals in room unattended.

Shilo Inn
7414 S. Hosmer
Tacoma, WA 98408
253-475-4020
RATES: Single $69, double $79.
PET POLICY: Fee $10, nonrefund-
able. All sizes, all pets welcome.

Tacoma Days Inn
3021 Pacific Hwy.
Tacoma, WA 98424
253-922-3500
PET POLICY: No fee.

U.S. Lodgings > WEST VIRGINIA

Tacoma Days Inn
Tacoma Mall
6802 Tacoma Mall Blvd.
Tacoma, WA 98409
253-475-5900
PET POLICY: Fee $20.

Summertide Resort,
RV Park, Marina
1578 NE Northshore Rd.
Tahuya Hood Canal, WA 98588
360-275-9313
RATES: Single $80, double $100.
PET POLICY: Fee $5, refundable.
All sizes and all pets welcome.
Must be on leash at all times,
must clean up, and never leave
unattended. No barking or
disturbing others.
AMENITIES: Waterfront for dogs
to swim, trails to exercise,
fresh water stream, walking
and jogging areas for pets.

Holiday Inn Express Hotel
& Suites
13101 NE 27th Ave.
Vancouver, WA 98686
360-576-1040
RATES: Single $79, double $79.
PET POLICY: Fee $35, + 10 per
day, nonrefundable. All sizes
welcome.

Homewood Suites Hotel
701 SE Columbia Shores Blvd.
Vancouver, WA 98661
360-750-1100
RATES: Single $109, double $109.
PET POLICY: Fee $35 + $10 per
day, nonrefundable. All sizes
welcome.

Shilo Inn Downtown
Vancouver
401 E. 13th St.
Vancouver, WA 98660
360-696-0411
RATES: Single $59, double $69.
PET POLICY: Fee $10, nonrefund-
able. All sizes, all pets welcome.

Shilo Inn Hazel Dell
13206 Hwy. 99
Vancouver, WA 98686
360-573-0511
RATES: Single $59, double $69.
PET POLICY: Fee $10, nonrefund-
able. All sizes, all pets welcome.

Economy Inn
700 N. Wenatchee Ave.
Wenatchee, WA 98801
509-663-8133
RATES: Single $45, double $55.
PET POLICY: Fee $10, non-
refundable, all sizes and all
pets welcome.

Welcome Inn
232 N. Wenatchee Ave.
Wenatchee, WA 98801
509-663-7121
RATES: Single $39.95, double
$69.95.
PET POLICY: Fee $5, nonrefund-
able, dogs only, all sizes. Do
not leave pets in room alone.

Alaskan Motel
708 N. First St.
Westport, WA 98595
360-268-9133
RATES: Single $30–$40, double
$40–$60.
PET POLICY: Fee $10, nonre-
fundable. All size dogs, only.
Do not leave pets in room
unattended. Leash-law in
affect.
AMENITIES: Dog walking area.
Towels for dogs for after-
beach cleaning or for beds.
POI: Room to roam, 1¼ miles
from ocean beach and harbor.

Motel 6
1104 N. 1st St.
Yakima, WA 98901
509-454-0080
PET POLICY: No fee. Dogs under 25
lbs. preferred (larger animals by
advance approval). Do not leave
animals in room unattended.

WEST VIRGINIA

Comfort Inn
1909 Harper Rd.
Beckley, WV 25801
304-255-2161
RATES: Single $49, double $88.
PET POLICY: No fee, all sizes and
all pets welcome (dogs, cats,
ferrets, birds, rabbits, reptiles).
AMENITIES: Large grassy exercise
area, welcome treats at check-
in, pets welcome in all rooms
with no restrictions or deposit.

POI: New River Gorge Nat'l
Park, Little Beaver State Park,
Hiking tails, Whitewater rafting, skiing, horseback riding,
exhibition coal mine, golf.

Charleston Days Inn
6400 MacCorkle Ave.
Charleston, WV 25304
304-925-1010
PET POLICY: No fee.

Embassy Suites
300 Court St.
Charleston, WV 25301
304-347-8700
RATES: Single, double
$119–$159.
PET POLICY: No fee for small
pets. Fee for large dogs $50,
refundable.

Motel 6
6311 MacCorkle Ave SE
Charleston, WV 25304
304-925-0471
PET POLICY: No fee. Dogs under 25
lbs. preferred (larger animals by
advance approval). Do not leave
animals in room unattended.

Cheat River Lodge
Rt. 1, Box 115
Elkins, WV, 26241
304-636-2301
RATES: Single, double $58-146
PET POLICY: Fee $5-10, all sizes
and pets welcome.

Fairmont Days Inn
228 Middletown Rd.
Fairmont, WV 26554
304-366-5995
PET POLICY: Fee $10.

Red Roof Inn
50 Middletown Rd.
Fairmont, WV 26554
304-366-6800
PET POLICY: No fee, pets under
80 lbs. Must be leashed to and
from rooms. Do not leave in
room unattended.

Super 8 Motel
2208 Pleasant Valley Rd.
Fairmont, WV 26504
304-363-1488
PET POLICY: No fee, no restrictions.

U.S. Lodgings > WEST VIRGINIA

Days Inn
5196 US Rt. 60
Huntington, WV 25705
304-733-4477
PET POLICY: Up to 10 lbs.

Radisson Hotel Huntington
1001 3rd Ave.
Huntington, WV 25701
304-525-1001
PET POLICY: Pets under 30 lbs.

Red Roof Inn
5190 US Route 60 E
Huntington, WV 25705
304-733-3737
PET POLICY: No fee, pets under
80 lbs. Must be leashed to and
from rooms. Do not leave in
room unattended.

Stone Lodge
5600 US Rt. 60 E.
Huntington, WV 25705
304-736-3451
PET POLICY: No fee, all sizes, in
older section only, boarding
facilities nearby.

Red Roof Inn
PO Box 468/Putnam Village
Shopping Center
Hurricane, WV 25526
304-757-6392
PET POLICY: No fee, pets under
80 lbs. Must be leashed to and
from rooms. Do not leave in
room unattended.

Red Roof Inn
6305 MacCorkle Avenue SE
Kanawha City, WV 25304
304-925-6953
PET POLICY: No fee, pets under
80 lbs. Must be leashed to and
from rooms. Do not leave in
room unattended.

Days Inn
635 N. Jefferson St.
Lewisburg, WV 24901
304-645-2345
PET POLICY: Fee $10.

Days Inn
209 Viking Way
Martinsburg, WV 25401
304-263-1800
PET POLICY: No fee.

Holiday Inn
1400 Saratoga Ave.
Morgantown, WV 26505
304-599-1680
PET POLICY: Fee $10.

Mt. Nebo Days Inn
Rt 18 S, HC 76, Box 700
Mt. Nebo, WV 26679
304-872-5151
PET POLICY: No fee.

Motel 6
3604½ E. 7th St.
Parkersburg, WV 26101
304-424-5100
PET POLICY: No fee. Dogs under 25
lbs. preferred (larger animals by
advance approval). Do not leave
animals in room unattended.

Red Roof Inn
3714 E. 7th St.
Parkersburg, WV, 26101
304-485-1741
PET POLICY: No fee, pets under
80 lbs. accepted. Must be
leashed to and from rooms.
Do not leave in room unattended.

Park Motel
34 N. Main St.
Petersburg, WV 26847
304-257-4656
PET POLICY: Fee $5, all sizes.

Days Inn
347 Meadowfield Ln.
Princeton, WV 24740
304-425-8100
PET POLICY: No fee.

Sleep Inn
1015 Oakvale Rd.
Princeton, WV 24740
304-431-2800
PET POLICY: No fee. Medium
dogs only.

Red Roof Inn
4006 MacCorkle Avenue SW
South Charleston, WV 25309
304-744-1500
PET POLICY: No fee, pets under
80 lbs. Must be leashed to and
from rooms. Do not leave in
room unattended.

Wheeling Days Inn
I-70 & Dallas Pike
Traidelphia, WV 26059
304-547-0610
PET POLICY: No fee.

WISCONSIN

Woodfield Suites Hotel
3730 W. College Ave.
Appleton, WI 54914
920-734-7777
PET POLICY: No fee.

**Best Western—
Arrowhead Lodge**
600 Oasis Rd.
Black River Falls, WI 54615
715-284-9471
RATES: Single $79.95, double
$99.95.
PET POLICY: No fee, all sizes and
pets welcome (dogs, cats,
birds, ferrets, reptiles, rabbits).
Do not leave in room unat-
tended, cages or crates required.
AMENITIES: Adjacent to large
wooded area.
POI: On a lake.

Black River Falls Days Inn
919 Hwy. 54
Black River Falls, WI 54015
715-284-4333
PET POLICY: No fee.

Baymont Inn & Suites
20391 W. Bluemound Rd.
Brookfield, WI 53045
262-782-9100
PET POLICY: No fee.

Motel 6
20300 W. Bluemound Rd.
Brookfield, WI 53045
262-786-7337
PET POLICY: No fee. Dogs under 25
lbs. preferred (larger animals by
advance approval). Do not leave
animals in room unattended.

East Shore Inn
N3049 US Hwy. 151
Chilton, WI 53014
920-849-4230
RATES: Double $75.
PET POLICY: Fee $5, nonrefund-
able. Use crates, must be non-
aggressive, housebroken.

U.S. Lodgings > WISCONSIN

AMENITIES: Walking path, large lawn.
POI: County park (Calumet), lake access nearby.

Lake Aire Motel
5732 183rd St.
Chippewa Falls, WI 54729
715-723-2231
RATES: Single $34, double $39.
PET POLICY: No fee, up to 50 lbs., cannot be left in room unattended.
AMENITIES: 2-acre walking area.
POI: Wissota State Park, Heritage House, Ervin Park, Leinenkugals Brewery.

Holiday Inn Express
7184 Morrisonville Rd.
DeForest, WI 53532
608-846-8686
PET POLICY: Small pets allowed if attended at all times.

Baymont Inn & Suites
2801 Hillside Dr.
Delafield, WI 53018
262-646-8500
PET POLICY: No fee.

Holiday Inn Express Hotel & Suites
3030 Golf Rd.
Delafield, WI 53018
414-646-7077
PET POLICY: Small pets allowed if attended.

Eagle River Days Inn
844 N. Railroad. St.
Eagle River, WI 54521
715-479-5151
PET POLICY: No fee.

The Edgewater Inn
5054 Hwy. 70W
Eagle River, WI 54521
715-479-4011
RATES: Single $59.95, double $69.95 (Off-season rates available).
PET POLICY: Fee $10, nonrefundable, all sizes welcome.
AMENITIES: Inn and resort on the Eagle River chain of 28 lakes. 6 cottages and 13 motel rooms on 2.5 acres. All size pets welcome.
POI: We are on the water and pets are welcomed to swim.

Days Inn—West
6319 Truax Ln.
Eau Claire, WI 54701
715-874-5550
PET POLICY: Fee $25.

The Feathered Star
6202 Highway 42
Egg Harbor, WI 54209
920-743-4066
PET POLICY: Fee $8, all sizes and all pets welcome.
AMENITIES: Large outdoor area for pets to exercise.

Fenmore Hills Motel
5814 Hwy. 18W
Fennimore, WI 53809
608-822-3281
RATES: Single $56, double $65.
PET POLICY: No fee, all sizes welcome. Dogs and cats only. Do not leave in room unattended.
AMENITIES: Open country setting.
POI: Historical sites, tourist attractions, The House on the Rock, Riverboat casino.

Baymont Inn & Suites
77 Holiday Ln.
Fond du Lac, WI 54935
920-921-4000
PET POLICY: No fee.

Fond du Lac Days Inn
107 N. Pioneer Rd.
Fond du Lac, WI 54935
920-923-6790
PET POLICY: Fee $6.

Holiday Inn
625 W. Rolling Meadows Dr.
Fond du Lac, WI 54937
920-923-1440
PET POLICY: Deposit $100.

Baymont Inn & Suites
5110 N. Port Washington Rd.
Glendale, WI 53217
414-964-8484
PET POLICY: No fee.

Woodfield Suites Hotel
5423 N. Port Washington Rd.
Glendale, WI 53217
414-962-6767
PET POLICY: No fee.

Baymont Inn & Suites
2840 S. Oneida St.
Green Bay, WI 54304
920-494-7887
PET POLICY: No fee.

Days Inn—City Center
406 N. Washington St.
Green Bay, WI 54301
920-435-4484
PET POLICY: No fee.

Motel 6
1614 Shawano Ave.
Green Bay, WI 54303
920-494-6730
PET POLICY: No fee. Dogs under 25 lbs. preferred (larger animals by advance approval). Do not leave animals in room unattended.

Northwoods Motel
9854 N. State Hwy. 27
Hayward, WI 54843
715-634-8088
RATES: Single $50.
PET POLICY: Fee $5, nonrefundable. Dogs only with kennel and leash.

Ross' Teal Lake Lodge & Golf Club
12425 N. Ross Rd.
Hayward, WI 54843
715-462-3631
RATES: Single 95, double $300.
PET POLICY: Fee $5 per pet per day. All sizes and pets welcome. Two pets per guest home.

Hazelhurst Inn Bed & Breakfast
6941 Hwy. 51
Hazelhurst, WI, 54531
715-356-6571
RATES: Single, double $59.95-69.95 (includes full-breakfast)
PET POLICY: Fee $10, one-time fee. All sizes accepted. Do not leave dogs unattended at any time.
AMENITIES: Kennels and runs available. Hiking trails for people and pets in back.

Hurley Days Inn
850 N. 10th Ave.
Hurley, WI 54534
715-561-3500
PET POLICY: No fee.

U.S. Lodgings > WISCONSIN

Baymont Inn & Suites
616 Midland Rd.
Janesville, WI 53546
608-758-4545
PET POLICY: No fee.

Motel 6
3907 Milton Ave.
Janesville, WI 53546
608-756-1742
PET POLICY: No fee. Dogs under 25
lbs. preferred (larger animals by
advance approval). Do not leave
animals in room unattended.

Days Inn—Johnson Creek
4545 W. Linmar Ln.
Johnson Creek, WI 53038
414-699-8000
PET POLICY: Fee $50.

Baymont Inn & Suites
7540 118th Ave.
Kenosha, WI 53158
262-857-7911
PET POLICY: No fee.

**Days Inn Hotel &
Conference Center**
101 Sky Harbour Dr.
La Crosse, WI 54603
608-783-1000
RATES: Single $79.99, double
$89.99.
PET POLICY: Fee $10, nonre-
fundable. Up to 50 lbs., dogs
and cats only. In smoking
rooms only.
POI: Mississippi River,
Grandad's Bluff, M&M Llama
Ranch, St. Rose Convent,
Chael, Norskedalen, Amish
Country.

Motel 6
E 10892 Fern Dell Rd.
Lake Delton, WI 53940
608-254-5000
PET POLICY: No fee. Dogs under 25
lbs. preferred (larger animals by
advance approval). Do not leave
animals in room unattended.

**Americinn—
Madison South-Monona**
101 W. Broadway
Madison, WI 53716
608-222-8601
RATES: Single $64.90, double
$69.90.

PET POLICY: No fee, all sizes
welcome.
AMENITIES: Small exercise area
with trees. Pet Park 3 miles.
POI: State Capitol, University of
Wisconsin, Alliant Expo
Center.

Baymont Inn & Suites
8102 Excelsior Dr.
Madison, WI 53717
608-831-7711
PET POLICY: No fee.

Crowne Plaza
4402 E. Washington Ave.
Madison, WI 53704
608-244-4703
PET POLICY: No fee.

Days Inn—Madison
4402 E. Broadway Service Rd.
Madison, WI 53716
608-223-1800
PET POLICY: Fee $50.

Holiday Inn Express
722 John Nolan Dr.
Madison, WI 53713
608-255-7400
PET POLICY: Small pets allowed.

Motel 6
1754 Thierer Rd.
Madison, WI 53704
608-241-8101
PET POLICY: No fee. Dogs under 25
lbs. preferred (larger animals by
advance approval). Do not leave
animals in room unattended.

Red Roof Inn
4830 Hayes Rd.
Madison, WI 53704
608-241-1787
PET POLICY: No fee, pets under
80 lbs. Must be leashed to and
from rooms. Do not leave in
room unattended.

Woodfield Suites Hotel
5217 Terrace Dr.
Madison, WI 53704
608-245-0123
PET POLICY: No fee.

Manitowoc Days Inn
908 Washington St.
Manitowoc, WI 54220
920-682-8271
PET POLICY: No fee.

**Best Western Holiday
Manor Motor Lodge**
1815 N. Broadway
Menomonie, WI 54751
715-235-9651
RATES: Single, double $59–$86.
PET POLICY: Fee $10 per pet.
Pet owners assigned rooms
with outside doors.

Motel 6
2100 Stout St.
Menomonie, WI 54751
715-235-6901
PET POLICY: No fee. Dogs under 25
lbs. preferred (larger animals by
advance approval). Do not leave
animals in room unattended.

Baymont Inn & Suites
5442 N. Lovers Ln. Rd.
Milwaukee, WI 53225
414-535-1300
PET POLICY: No fee.

Motel 6
5037 S. Howell Ave.
Milwaukee, WI 53207
414-482-4414
PET POLICY: No fee. Dogs under 25
lbs. preferred (larger animals by
advance approval). Do not leave
animals in room unattended.

Baymont Inn & Suites
7141 S. 13th St.
Oak Creek, WI 53154
414-762-2266
PET POLICY: No fee.

Red Roof Inn
6360 S. 13th St.
Oak Creek, WI 53154
414-764-3500
PET POLICY: No fee, pets under
80 lbs. Must be leashed to and
from rooms. Do not leave in
room unattended.

Baymont Inn & Suites
5377 N. Kinney Coley Rd.
Onalaska, WI 54650
608-783-7191
PET POLICY: No fee.

Baymont Inn & Suites
1950 Omro Rd.
Oshkosh, WI 54902
920-233-4190
PET POLICY: No fee.

U.S. Lodgings > WISCONSIN

Park Plaza International Hotel & Convention Ctr.
1 N. Main St.
Oshkosh, WI 54901
920-231-5000
RATES: Single $75, double $85.
PET POLICY: No fee. Small to 25 pounds.

Super 8 Motel
1581 W. S. Park Ave.
Oshkosh, WI 54903
920-426-2885
PET POLICY: No fee, up to 25 lbs., all pets welcome.

Plover Days Inn
5253 Harding Ave.
Plover, WI 54467
715-341-7300
PET POLICY: No fee.

Best Western Quiet House
Hwy. 18-35S-60S
Prairie Du Chien, WI 53821
608-326-4777
PET POLICY: Fee $15.

Brisbois Motor Inn
533 N. Marquette Rd.
Prairie Du Chien, WI 53821
608-326-8404
PET POLICY: Fee $5, pets in smoking rooms only.

Currier's Lakeview Resort Motel
2010 E. Sawyer St.
Rice Lake, WI 54868
715-234-7474
RATES: Single $35, double $85.
PET POLICY: No fee. All sizes and all pets welcome.
AMENITIES: Large grounds for walking and playing.

Kinni Creek Lodge & Outfitters
545 N. Main
River Falls, WI 54022
715-425-7378
PET POLICY: Boarding available nearby.

Baymont Inn & Suites
2932 Kohler Memorial Dr.
Sheboygan, WI 53081
920-457-2321
PET POLICY: No fee.

Best Value Inn—Parkway
3900 Motel Rd.
Sheboygan, WI 53081
920-458-8338
RATES: Single $37.90, double $46.90.
PET POLICY: Fee $5 per dog per visit, nonrefundable. No puppies unless caged.
AMENITIES: 9 acres to run.
POI: Terry Andre State park close by with 2 miles of beach. Black River Trail.

Best Nights Inn
303 W. Wisconsin Ave.
Sparta, WI 54656
800-201-0234
PET POLICY: No fee, all sizes welcome. Credit card must be on file in case of damages.

Justin Trails Bed & Breakfast
7452 Kathryn Ave.
Sparta, WI 54656
608-269-4522
PET POLICY: Fee $12, per pet per day, nonrefundable. All sizes welcome. No smoking on premises.
AMENITIES: 8 miles hiking trails.

Baymont Inn & Suites
4917 Main St.
Stevens Point, WI 54481
715-344-1900
PET POLICY: No fee.

Cottage Retreat
133 N. 8th Place
Sturgeon Bay, WI 54235
920-743-0967
RATES: Double $50–$150.
PET POLICY: No fee, all sizes and all pets welcome.
AMENITIES: Acres of woods, plenty of wildlife.
POI: 6 state parks and dozens of county parks. Located in middle of Door County, WI (Midwest's vacation capital).

Holiday Inn Express
13339 Hospitality Ct.
Sturtevant, WI 53177
414-884-0200
PET POLICY: Small pets allowed if attended.

Best Western Bridgeview Motor Inn
415 Hammond Ave.
Superior, WI 54880
715-392-8174
RATES: Single $50, double $65.
PET POLICY: No fee, all sizes and all pets welcome. Do not leave pets in room unattended.

Holiday Inn Express
101 Aviation Way
Watertown, WI 53094
92-262-1910
PET POLICY: With deposit.

Baymont Inn & Suites
110 Grand Seasons Dr.
Waupaca, WI 54981
715-258-9212
PET POLICY: No fee.

Baymont Inn & Suites
1910 Stewart Ave.
Wausau, WI 54401
715-842-0421
PET POLICY: No fee.

Wausau Days Inn
4700 Rib Mountain Drive.
Wausau, WI 54401
715-355-5501
PET POLICY: Fee $10.

Madison Days Inn
6311 Rostad Dr.
Windsor/Deforest, WI 53598
608-846-7473
PET POLICY: Fee $50 Deposit.

Delton Oaks Resort
730 E. Hiawatha Dr.
Wisconsin Dells, WI, 53965
888-374-6257
PET POLICY: Fee $10 per night (3 night minimum).
POI: Single, double $110-185

Rodeway Inn
350 W. Munroe St.
Wisconsin Dells, WI, 53965
888-888-6050
PET POLICY: Fee $10, no size limits.

U.S. Lodgings > WISCONSIN

Super 8 Motel
800 Co Highway H
PO Box 467
Wisconsin Dells, WI, 53965
608-254-6464
PET POLICY: No fee. All sizes
and pets welcome. Do not
leave in room unattended.
POI: Single, double $51-58 (seasonal)

WYOMING

Motel 6
100 Flat Iron Dr.
Buffalo, WY 82834
307-684-7000
PET POLICY: No fee. Dogs under 25
lbs. preferred (larger animals by
advance approval). Do not leave
animals in room unattended.

Casper Days Inn
301 E. E. St.
Casper, WY 82601
307-234-1159
RATES: Single $55, double $65.
PET POLICY: No fee, all sizes
welcome.
AMENITIES: Dog walk.

Motel 6
1150 Wilkins Cir.
Casper, WY 82601
307-234-3903
PET POLICY: No fee. Dogs under 25
lbs. preferred (larger animals by
advance approval). Do not leave
animals in room unattended.

Shilo Inn
I-15 & Curtis Rd.
Casper, WY 82636
307-577-7429
RATES: Single $59.99, double $69.
PET POLICY: Fee $10, nonrefundable. All sizes, all pets welcome
(dogs, cats, birds, ferrets, rabbits,
reptiles).

Westridge Motel
955 Cy Ave.
Casper, WY 82601
307-234-8911
RATES: Single $35, double $39.
PET POLICY: Fee $5, nonrefundable, all sizes welcome. Must
be housetrained.
AMENITIES: Pet walking area.
POI: Restaurant is next door.

Days Inn Cheyenne
2360 W. Lincoln Way
Cheyenne, WY 82001
307-778-8877
PET POLICY: No fee.

Motel 6
1735 Westland Rd.
Cheyenne, WY 82001
307-635-6806
PET POLICY: No fee. Dogs under 25
lbs. preferred (larger animals by
advance approval). Do not leave
animals in room unattended.

Oak Tree Inn
1625 Stillwater Ave.
Cheyenne, WY 82001
307-778-6620
RATES: Single $59, double $62.
PET POLICY: Fee $5, nonrefundable. All sizes, all pets welcome
(dogs, cats, ferrets, birds).
POI: Frontier Days.

Best Western Sunset Motor Inn
1601 8th St.
Cody, WY 82414
307-587-4265
RATES: Single $49–$59, double
$59–$69.
PET POLICY: No fee, up to 50
lbs. Must inform the desk.
POI: Resort area.

Heart2Heart Ranch Bed, Barn, Breakfast
483 Rd. 2AB
Cody, WY 82414
307-287-2906
RATES: Double $80 (seasonal).
PET POLICY: No fee, all sizes and all
pets welcome. Pen for dogs, but
they are also allowed in guest
rooms. Horses also accepted.
AMENITIES: No fee for animals,
except horses, since they will
be fed ($10 night).

Black Bear Country Inn
505 N. Ramshom
Dubois, WY 82513
307-455-2344
RATES: Single Under $50.
PET POLICY: No fee, all sizes
welcome. Dogs only.
POI: Teton - Yellowstone
National Park, Teddy Bear
Shop on premises.

Motel 6
261 Bear River Dr.
Evanston, WY 82930
307-789-0791
PET POLICY: No fee. Dogs under 25
lbs. preferred (larger animals by
advance approval). Do not leave
animals in room unattended.

Gillette Days Inn
910 E. Boxelder Rd.
Gillette, WY 82718
307-682-3999
PET POLICY: Fee $10.

Motel 6
2105 Rodgers Dr.
Gillette, WY 82716
307-686-8600
PET POLICY: No fee. Dogs under 25
lbs. preferred (larger animals by
advance approval). Do not leave
animals in room unattended.

Oak Tree Inn
1170 W. Flaming Gorge Way
Green River, WY 82935
307-875-4889
RATES: Single $59, double $69.
PET POLICY: Fee $5, nonrefundable, all size pets welcome.

Holiday Inn
115 E. Park
PO Box 1323
Hot Springs, WY 82443
307-864-3131
PET POLICY: Please advise of pets.

Motel 6
600 S. Hwy. 89
Jackson, WY 83001
307-733-1620
PET POLICY: No fee. Dogs under 25
lbs. preferred (larger animals by
advance approval). Do not leave
animals in room unattended.

Red Lion Wyoming Inn
930 W. Broadway
Jackson, WY 83002
307-734-0035
RATES: Single, double
$129–$199.
PET POLICY: No fee. All sizes
accepted.

U.S. Lodgings > WYOMING

Holiday Inn
2313 Soldier Springs Rd.
Laramie, WY 82070
307-742-6611
RATES: Single $74.
PET POLICY: No fee, up to 50
lbs. Pets in designated rooms.

Motel 6
621 Plaza Ln.
Laramie, WY 82070
307-742-2307
PET POLICY: No fee. Dogs under 25
lbs. preferred (larger animals by
advance approval). Do not leave
animals in room unattended.

Pines Motel
248 E. Wentworth
Newcastle, WY 82701
307-746-4334
RATES: Single $38, double $45.
PET POLICY: No fee, pets up to
50 lbs. Owner responsible for
cleanup.
POI: Black Hills, Mount
Rushmore, Crazy Horse.

Days Inn of Rawlins
2222 E. Cedar
Rawlins, WY 82301
307-324-6615
PET POLICY: No fee.

Days Inn
909 W. Main St.
Riverton, WY 82501
307-856-9677
PET POLICY: Fee $5.

Holiday Inn
1675 Sunset Dr.
Rock Springs, WY 82901
307-382-9200
PET POLICY: Fee $10.

Motel 6
2615 Commercial Way
Rock Springs, WY 82901
307-362-1850
PET POLICY: No fee. Dogs under 25
lbs. preferred (larger animals by
advance approval). Do not leave
animals in room unattended.

**Best Western Inn at
Sundance**
2719 E. Cleveland St.
Sundance, WY 82729
307-283-2800
RATES: Single $65, double $65.
PET POLICY: Fee $25, refund-
able. Pets up to 50 lbs.
POI: Near Devil's Tower Nat'l
Monument, Mt. Rushmore.

Motel 6
95 16th St.
Wheatland, WY 82201
307-322-1800
PET POLICY: No fee. Dogs under 25
lbs. preferred (larger animals by
advance approval). Do not leave
animals in room unattended.

Canada

Up the street from our petswelcome.com offices, there's a Canadian family that owns Rory, a Nova Scotia Duck Tolling. Rory is an intelligent, shining-eyed beauty who, in human company, is well behaved and maintains a Canadian reserve that stands in stark contrast to the undisciplined and riotous behavior of the Gordon Setters and Vizslas in our office. However, get Rory outside into the woods and fields, and he's the first one to swan dive into a mud puddle and roll around with joyful abandon, while our suddenly mild-mannered dogs look on with a sense of awe and reverence. For many of us in the office, Rory is a blast of fresh Canadian air who, at least in a romantic fashion, seems to capture and personify the spirit of our neighbors to the north. Because of Rory, more than one of us has packed our bags and headed up there with our pets to discover for ourselves the wide open spaces and cosmopolitan cities that are a haven of people- and pet-friendliness.

If you decide to head up to Canada, make sure you meet all the requirements to get your pet through customs. Upon arrival, all animals are subject to veterinary inspection. If evidence or suspicion of disease is found, the animals may be refused entry into Canada. Dogs and domestic cats entering the country from the United States will need certification, signed by a licensed veterinarian, that they have been vaccinated against rabies during the preceding 36-month period. Visitors wishing to bring a dog or domestic cat into Canada from a country other than the United States should contact Agriculture Canada: 905-676-2545.

ALBERTA

Banff Rocky Mountain Resort
1029 Banff Ave.
Banff, AB T0L 0C0
403-762-5531

Best Western Siding 29 Lodge
453 Marten St.
Banff, AB T0L 0C0
403-762-5575
RATES: Single $85–$195, double $85–$195.
PET POLICY: No fee, all sizes welcome.

Castle Mountain Village
PO Box 1655
Banff, AB T0L 0C0
403-762-3868

Driftwood Inn
Banff Ave.
Banff, AB T0L 0C0
403-762-4496
RATES: Single $95, double $105.
PET POLICY: Fee $10, nonrefundable. All sizes and pets welcome.

Red Carpet Motor Inn
524 Banff Ave.
Banff, AB T0L 0C0
403-762-4184

Spruce Grove Motel
Box 471
Banff, AB T0L 0C0
403-762-2112
RATES: Double $50–$80.
PET POLICY: No fee, all sizes welcome. No male cats.
POI: Unlimited hiking and walking trails (on leash only).

Heritage Inn
1303 2nd St., W.
Brooks, AB T1R 1B8
403-362-6666

Super 8 Motel-Brooks
1240 Cassils Rd., E.
Brooks, AB T1R 1B6
403-362-8000

The Douglas Country Inn
PO Box 463
Brooks, AB T1R 1B5
403-362-2873

Canadian Lodgings > ALBERTA

Best Western Hospitality Inn
135 Southland Dr. SE
Calgary, AB T2J 5X5
403-278-5050

Best Western Village Park Inn
1804 Crowchild TR, NW
Calgary, AB T2M 3Y7
403-289-0241

Blackfoot Inn
5940 Blackfoot Trail S.
Calgary, AB T2H 2B5
403-252-2253

Budget Host Motor Inn
4420 16th Ave., NW
Calgary, AB T3B 0M4
403-288-7115

Calgary West Days Inn
1818 16th Ave. NW
Calgary, AB T2M 0L8
403-289-1961

**Calgary Westways
Guesthouse**
216 25 Ave. SW
Calgary, AB T2S OL1
403-229-1758

Calgary-days Inn
2369 Banff Trail NW
Calgary, AB T2M 4L2
403-289-5571

Carriage House
9030 Macleod Trail S.
Calgary, AB T2H 0M4
403-253-1101

Coast Plaza At Calgary
1316 33 St. NE
Calgary, AB T2A6B6
403-248-8888

Delta Bow Valley
209 4th Ave. SE
Calgary, AB T2G OC6
403-266-1980

Econo Lodge Banff Trail
2231 Banff Trail
Calgary, AB T2M 4L2
403-289-1921

Elbow River Inn
1919 Macleod Trail SE
Calgary, AB T2G4S1
403-269-6771

Flamingo Motor Hotel
7505 Macleod Rd., S
Calgary, AB T2H 0L8
403-252-4401

Glenmore Inn
2720 Glenmore Tr., SE
Calgary, AB T2C 2E6
403-279-8611

Holiday Inn
1250 McKinnon Dr. NE
Calgary, AB T2E 7T7
403-230-1999
PET POLICY: No fee.

Holiday Inn
119 12 Ave. SW
Calgary, AB T2R 2G8
403-266-4611
PET POLICY: Pets allowed with
restrictions.

Holiday Inn Express
2227 Banff Trail NW
Calgary, AB T2M 4L2
403-289-6600
PET POLICY: No fee.

Holiday Inn Macleod Trail
4206 Macleod Trail S.
Calgary, AB T2G 2R7
403-287-2700
RATES: Single $104, double $104.
PET POLICY: Fee $20, nonrefund-
able, dogs and cats only, all
sizes, first floor only.
AMENITIES: Side door entrance
to avoid lobby if desired.

**Quality Hotel &
Conference Centre**
3828 Macleod Trail
Calgary, AB T2G 2R2
403-243-5531

Quality Inn Motel Village
2359 Banff Trail NW
Calgary, AB T2M 4L2
403-289-1973

**Radisson Hotel Calgary
Airport**
2120 16 Ave. NE
Calgary, AB T2E 1L4
403-291-4666
PET POLICY: Fee, $10, all sizes
welcome. Smoking rooms
only.

**Radisson Hotel Calgary
Airport**
2120 16th Ave. NE
Calgary, AB T2E 1L4
403-291-4666
RATES: Single $100, double $100.
PET POLICY: No fee. All pets
welcome.

Ramada Crowchild Inn
5353 Crowchild Trail, NW
Calgary, AB T3A 1W9
403-288-5353

Ramada Hotel Downtown
708 8th Ave. SW
Calgary, AB T2P 1H2
403-263-7600

**Super 8 Motel Calgary
Airport**
3030 Barlow Trl., NE
Calgary, AB T1Y 1A2
403-291-9888

Super 8 Motel Northwest
1904 Crowchild Tr., NW
Calgary, AB T2M 3Y7
403-289-9211

The Palliser Hotel
133 9th Ave. SW
Calgary, AB T2P 2M3
403-262-1234

The Westin Calgary
320 4th Ave. SW
Calgary, AB T2P 2S6
403-266-1611

Travelodge
9206 MacLeod Trail S.
Calgary, AB T7S 1N3
403-253-7070

Travelodge
2750 Sunridge Blvd, NE
Calgary, AB T2J 0P5
403-291-1260
RATES: Single $79–$119, double
$89–$129.
PET POLICY: No fee, all sizes and
all pets welcome (dogs, cats,
birds, ferrets, rabbits, reptiles).
Do not leave unattended
unless in cage.
AMENITIES: Full grass area and
large parking lot available for
walking pets.

Canadian Lodgings > ALBERTA

Travelodge
6216 48th Ave.
Camrose, AB T4V 0K6
780-672-3377

Quality Resort Chateau Canmore
1720 Bow Valley Trail
Canmore, AB T1W 2X3
403-678-6699

Rocky Mountain Ski Lodge
Box 8070
Canmore, AB T1W 2T8
403-678-5445

Rundle Ridge Chalets
1100 Harvie Heights Rd.
Canmore, AB T1W 2W2
403-678-5387

The Drake Inn
909 Railway Ave.
Canmore, AB T1W 1P3
403-678-5131

The Stockade Log Cabins
1050 Harvie Heights Rd.
Canmore, AB T1W 2W2
403-678-5212

Wild Rose Bed & Breakfast
305 Lady MacDonald Crescent
Canmore, AB T1W 1H5
403-609-2860
RATES: Single Can $50, double Can $85.
PET POLICY: Fee $5 nonrefundable, which includes dog food (up to 50 lbs.); dogs only.
AMENITIES: Fenced kennel in the backyard; walking and hiking trails start from house.

Flamingo Motel
848 Main St., S
Cardston, AB T0K 0K0
403-653-3952

Howard Johnson Express Inn
37-8 Ave. W., Box 308
Cardston, AB T0K 0K0
403-653-4481

Bluebird Motel
5505 1st St., W
Claresholm, AB T0L 0T0
403-625-3395

Bow River Inn
3 Westside Dr.
Cochrane, AB T0L 0W0
403-932-7900

New Frontier Motel
1002 8th Ave.
Cold Lake, AB T0A 0V0
403-639-3030

Green Acres Motel
200 2nd Ave.
Dead Man's Flats, AB T1W 2W4
403-678-5344

Pigeon Mountain Motel
PO Box 8038
Dead Man's Flats, AB T1W 2T8
403-678-5756

Big Sky Country Bed & Breakfast
Box 5, Site 3, RR 1
DeWinton, AB T0L 0X0
403-256-1545

Alberta Place
10049 103rd St.
Edmonton, AB T5J 2W7
780-423-1565
RATES: Single, double $155–$350.
PET POLICY: Fee $10 per day, nonrefundable.

Argyll Plaza Hotel
9933 63rd Ave.
Edmonton, AB T6E 6C9
403-438-5876

Best Western Cedar Park Inn
5116 Calgary Tr., Northbound
Edmonton, AB T6H 2H4
403-434-7411

Campus Tower Hotel
11145 87th Ave.
Edmonton, AB T6G 0Y1
780-439-6060

Campus Tower Hotel
11145 87th Ave.
Edmonton, AB T6G 0Y1
403-439-6060

Chateau Louis Hotel & Conference Center
11727 Kingsway Ave.
Edmonton, AB T5G3A1
780-452-7770

Comfort Inn Edmonton
17610 100th Ave.
Edmonton, AB T5S 1S9
780-484-4415

Continental Inn
16625 Stony Plain Rd.
Edmonton, AB T5P 4A8
403-484-7751

Convention Inn
4404 Calgary Trail
Edmonton, AB T6J 5H2
403-434-6415

Crowne Plaza
10111 Bellamy Hill
Edmonton, AB T5J 1N7
780-428-6611
PET POLICY: No fee.

Delta Edmonton Centre Suite Hotel
10222 102nd St.
Edmonton, AB T5A 4C5
403-429-3900

Edmonton House Suite Hotel
10205 100 Ave.
Edmonton, AB T5J 4B5
780-420-4000

Edmonton Inn
11830 Kingsway Ave.
Edmonton, AB T5G0X5
780-454-9521

Edmonton-days Inn
10041 106th St.
Edmonton, AB T5J 1G3
403-423-1925

Holiday Inn
4520 76th Ave.
Edmonton, AB T6B 0A5
780-468-5400
RATES: Single $79, double $79.
PET POLICY: No fee, small pets accepted up to 25 lbs.
AMENITIES: Surprise check-in bag of toys.

Holiday Inn
4235 Calgary Trail N.
Edmonton, AB T6J 5H2
780-438-1222
PET POLICY: No fee.

Canadian Lodgings > ALBERTA

Holiday Inn Express Hotel & Suites
10017-179 A. St.
Edmonton, AB T5S 2L7
403-483-4000
PET POLICY: No fee.

Hotel Macdonald
10065 100th St.
Edmonton, AB T5J 0N6
780-424-5181
RATES: Single Can.$199, double
Can. $219.
PET POLICY: Fee $20, up to 50 lbs.
Do not leave pets unattended
in room.
AMENITIES: Half of fee goes to
local SPCA shelter.
POI: Walking trails below hotel.

Howard Johnson Plaza Hotel
10010 104th St.
Edmonton, AB T5J 0Z1
780-423-2450

Mayfield Inn And Suites
16615 109th Ave.
Edmonton, AB T5P4K8
780-484-0821

The Westin Edmonton
10135 100th St.
Edmonton, AB T5J ON7
780-426-3636

Travelodge
10320 45th Ave. S.
Edmonton, AB T5W 0Z4
780-436-9770

Travelodge
3414 118th Ave.
Edmonton, AB T5S 1A7
780-474-0456

Travelodge
18320 Stony Plain Rd.
Edmonton, AB T6H 5K3
780-483-6031

The Guest House
4411 4th Ave.
Edson, AB T7E 1B8
403-723-4486

D.J. Motel
416 Main St.
Fort Macleod, AB T0L 0Z0
403-553-4011

RATES: Single Can. $44+, double
Can. $54+.
PET POLICY: No fee, all sizes
welcome. Pets in smoking
rooms only.
POI: RCMP Museum,
Wilderness Park on river.

Kozy Motel
433 24th St.
Fort Macleod, AB T0L 0Z0
403-553-3115

Red Coat Inn Motel
359 Main St.
Fort Macleod, AB T0L 0Z0
403-553-4434
RATES: Single Can. $54+,
double Can.$60+.
PET POLICY: No fee, all sizes
welcome.
AMENITIES: Baby sitting.
POI: RCMP Museum,
Wilderness Park on river.

Sunset Motel
104 Hwy. 3W
Fort Macleod, AB T0L 0Z0
403-553-4448

Travelodge
9713 Hardin St.
Fort McMurray, AB T9H 1L2
780-743-3301

Stanford Inn
11401 100 Ave.
Grande Prairie, AB T8V 5M6
780-539-5670

The Lodge Motor Inn
10909 100th Ave.
Grande Prairie, AB T8V 3J9
403-539-4700

Crestwood Hotel
678 Carmichael Ln.
Hinton, AB T7V 1S9
403-865-4001

Holiday Inn
393 Gregg Ave.
Hinton, AB T7V 1N1
780-865-3321
PET POLICY: No fee.

Canadia Pacific Jasper Park Lodge
Hwy. 16, Box 40
Jasper, AB T0E 1E0
403-852-3301

RATES: Single $149–$709,
double $149–$709.
PET POLICY: Fee $30 per night,
nonrefundable; primarily dogs
and cats, but other types will
be considered.

Canadia Pacific Jasper Park Lodge
Hwy. 16
Jasper, AB T0E 1E0
403-852-3301
PET POLICY: Fee $30 per night,
nonrefundable; primarily dogs
and cats, but other types will
be considered.

Lobstick Lodge
94 Geikie St.
Jasper, AB T0E 1E0
403-852-4471

Sunwapta Falls Resort
Hwy. 93
Jasper, AB T0E 1E0
403-852-4852

Best Western Denham Inn
5207 50th Ave.
Leduc, AB T9E 6V3
403-986-2241

Lethbridge Lodge Hotel
320 Scenic Dr.
Lethbridge, AB T1J 4B4
403-328-1123

Lethbridge Super 8 Lodge
2210 7th Ave. S.
Lethbridge, AB T1J 1M7
403-329-0100

Pepper Tree Inn
1142 Mayor Magrath Dr.
Lethbridge, AB T1K 2P7
403-438-4436

Quality Inn Lethbridge
1030 Mayor Magrath Dr. S.
Lethbridge, AB T1K 2P8
403-328-6636

The Parkside Inn
1009 Mayor Magrath Dr., S.
Lethbridge, AB T1K 2P7
403-438-3466

Travelodge
526 Mayor Magrath Dr.
Lethbridge, AB T1J 3M2
403-327-5701

Canadian Lodgings > ALBERTA

Everlasting Bed & Breakfast
PO Box 500
Lloydminster, AB S9V 0Y6
403-875-0004

Tropical Inn
5621 44th St.
Lloydminster, AB T9V 0B2
403-875-7000

Wayside Inn
5411 44th St.
Lloydminster, AB T9V 0A9
780-875-4404

West Harvest Inn
5620 44 St.
Lloydminster, AB T9V 0B6
403-875-6113

Best Western Inn
722 Redcliff Dr.
Medicine Hat, AB T1A 5E3
403-527-3700

Imperial Inn
3282 13th Ave., SE
Medicine Hat, AB T1B 1H8
403-527-8811

**Medicine Hat Lodge Hotel
& Convention Centre**
1051 Ross Glen Dr., SE
Medicine Hat, AB T1B 3T8
403-529-2222

Ranchmen Motel
1617 Bomford Crescent, SW
Medicine Hat, AB T1A 5E7
402-527-2263

Super 8 Motel
1280 Trans-Canada Way, SE
Medicine Hat, AB T1B 1J5
403-528-8888

Nakoda Lodge
PO Box 149
Morley, AB T0L 1N0
403-881-3949

Nisku Inn
Box 9801, Edmonton Int.
Airport
Nisku, AB T5J 2T2
403-955-7744

Okotoks Country Inn
59 River Side Gate
Okotoks, AB T0L 1T0
403-938-1999

RATES: Single $75, double $85.
PET POLICY: Fee $5, nonrefund-
able. All sizes, dogs and cats
only. $100 refundable deposit.
Pets in smoking rooms only.
Do not leave unattended in
rooms.
AMENITIES: Dog biscuits.
POI: Beside the river.

Traveller's Motor Hotel
9510 100th St.
Peace River, AB T8S 1S9
403-624-3621

Heritage Inn
919 Waterton
Pincher Creek, AB T0K 1W0
403-627-5000

Pincher Creek Super 8 Motel
1307 Freebairn Ave.
Pincher Creek, AB T0K 1W0
403-627-5671

Whiskey Point Resort
Box 309
Quathiaski Cove, AB V0P 1N0
800-622-5311

Holiday Inn
6500 67th St.
Red Deer, AB T4P 1A2
403-342-6567
PET POLICY: No fee.

Travelodge
2807 50th Ave.
Red Deer, AB T4R 1H6
403-346-2011

Holiday Inn Express
4715 45th St., P.O. Box 1447
Rocky Mountain, AB T0M 1T0
800-HOLIDAY
PET POLICY: No fee.

Chinook Inn
Hwy. 11, 59th Ave.
Rocky Mountain House, AB
T0M 1T0
403-845-2833

Franklin's Inn
2016 Sherwood Dr.
Sherwood Park, AB T8A 3X3
780-467-1234
RATES: Single $75, double $81.
PET POLICY: Fee $5, nonrefund-
able; only dogs and cats up to
50 lbs. $100 refundable
deposit.

POI: West Edmonton Mall, Elk
Island National Park,
Strathcona Wilderness Centre,
Millennium Place, Ukrainian
Cultural Village.

**Ramada Limited
Edmonton East**
30 Broadway Blvd.
Sherwood Park, AB T8H 2A2
780-467-6727

St. Albert Inn
156 St. Albert Rd.
St. Albert, AB T9N 0P5
403-459-5551

Ramada Inn Stony Plain
3301 43rd Ave.
Stony Plain, AB T7Z 1L1
780-963-0222

Stony Plain
4620 48th St.
Stony Plain, AB T7Z 1L4
780-963-3444

Travelodge
74 Boulder Blvd.
Stony Plain, AB T1J 3M2
780-963-1161
PET POLICY: Fee $100, refund-
able. Up to 50 lbs. Do not
leave in room unattended.
Cats must be kept in kennel.

Heritage Inn
4830 46th Ave.
Taber, AB T1G 2A4
403-223-4424

Rose's Rest Bed & Breakfast
Box 772
Turner Valley, AB T0L 2A0
403-933-4174

Raven Motor Inn
4710 50th St.
Valleyview, AB T0H 3N0
403-524-3383

Bayshore Inn
111 Waterton Ave.
Waterton Park, AB T0K 2M0
403-859-2211

East Glen Motel
East Service Rd., Hwy. 44
Westlock, AB T0G 2L0
403-349-3138

Canadian Lodgings > BRITISH COLUMBIA

Wayside Inn
4103 56th St.
Wetaskiwin, AB T9A 1V2
403-352-6681

Travelodge
5003 50 St.
Whitecourt, AB T7S 1N3
780-778-2216

BRITISH COLUMBIA

Best Western Villager West Motor Inn
61 10th St. SW
Salmon Arm, BC V1E 1E4
250-832-9793
RATES: Single $60–$80, double $65–$95.
PET POLICY: Fee $5, nonrefundable. All sizes and pets welcome. Do not leave in room unattended.
POI: Shuswap Lake.

100 Mile House Super 8
989 Alder Ave.
100 Mile House, BC V0K 2E0
250-395-8888

Red Coach Inn
170 Cariboo Hwy. N.
100 Mile House, BC V0K 2E0
250-395-2266

Econo Lodge
32111 Marshall Rd.
Abbotsford, BC V2T 1A3
604-859-3171

Holiday Inn Express
2073 Clearbrook Rd.
Abbotsford, BC V2T 2X1
604-859-6211
PET POLICY: No fee.

Howard Johnson Resort Hotel
P.O. Box 39, 1681 Cowichan Bay Rd.
Abbotsford, BC V0R 1N0
250-748-6222

Quality Inn Abbotsford
1881 Sumas Way
Abbotsford, BC V2S 4L5
604-853-1141

Mountain Springs Motel
253 Yellowhead Hwy.
Barriere, BC V0E 1E0
250-672-0090

Glacier Mountain Lodge
Box 27, 869 Shell Rd.
Blue River, BC V0E1J0
250-673-2393
RATES: Call toll free or e-mail for rates.
PET POLICY: Fee $5 per pet, nonrefundable. All pets welcome up to 50 lbs. Must be well behaved, clean and quiet and cannot be left alone in room.

Mike Wiegele Heli Ski Village
Harwood Dr.
Blue River, BC V0E 1J0
250-673-8381

Mountain Shores Resort & Marina
RR 1, Box 6, Site 9
Boswell, BC V0B 1A0
250-223-8258

401 Motor Inn
2950 Boundary Rd.
Burnaby, BC V5M 3Z9
604-438-3451

Accent Inn Vancouver Burnaby
3777 Henning Dr.
Burnaby, BC V5C 6N5
604-473-5000
RATES: Single $99–$129, double $109–$139.
PET POLICY: No fee, small pets only.

Burns Lake Motor Inn
Hwy. 16E
Burns Lake, BC V0J 1E0
250-692-7545

Bonaparte Motel
1395 Hwy. 97N
Cache Creek, BC V0K 1H0
250-457-9693

Tumbleweed Motel
PO Box 287
Cache Creek, BC V0K 1H0
250-457-6522

Whiskey Point Resort
Box 309
Cambell River, BC V0P 1N0
800-622-5311

Best Western Austrian Chalet
462 S. Island Hwy.
Campbell River, BC V9W 1A5
250-923-4231

Campbell River Lodge & Fishing Resort
1760 Island Hwy.
Campbell River, BC V9W 2E7
250-287-7446
RATES: Single $55–$79, double $60–$94.
PET POLICY: Fee $6, nonrefundable. Pets up to 25 lbs.

Campbell River Super 8 Motel
340 S. Island Hwy.
Campbell River, BC V9W 1A5
250-286-6622

Chase Country Inn Motel
576 Coburn St.
Chase, BC V0E 1M0
250-679-3333

Fuller Lake Motel
9300 Trans Canada Hwy.
Chemainus, BC V0R 1K0
250-246-3282

Stagecoach Inn
5413 S. Access Rd.
Chetwynd, BC V0C 1J0
250-788-9666

Best Western Rainbow Country Inn
43971 Industrial Way
Chilliwack, BC V2R 3A4
604-795-3828

Comfort Inn Chilliwack
45405 Luckakuck Way
Chilliwack, BC V2R 3C7
604-858-0636

Holiday Inn
45920 1st Ave.
Chilliwack, BC V2P 7K1
604-795-4788
PET POLICY: Small pets

Rainbow Motor Inn
45620 Yale Rd. W.
Chilliwack, BC V2P 2N2
604-792-6412

Canadian Lodgings > BRITISH COLUMBIA

Travelodge
45466 Yale Rd. W.
Chilliwack, BC V2R 3Z8
604-792-4240

New Horizon Motel
2037 Hwy. 3
Christina Lake, BC V0H 1E0
250-447-9312

Royal Inn Bed & Breakfast
1 Chase Rd.
Christina Lake, BC V0H 1E0
250-447-9090

Dunn Lake Resort
Box 9020
Clearwater, BC V0E 1N0
250-674-2344

Jasper Way Inn
57 E. Old North Thompson
Hwy.
Clearwater, BC V0E 1N0
250-674-3345

**Blue Heron Landing Bed &
Breakfast**
126 Croteau Rd.
Comox, BC V9M 2P8
250-339-4973

Holiday Inn
631 Lougheed Hwy.
Coquitlam, BC V3K 3S5
604-931-4433
PET POLICY: No fee.

**Best Western Collingwood
Inn**
1675 Cliffe Ave.
Courtenay, BC V9N 2K6
250-338-1464
RATES: Single Can. $82, double
Can. $92.
PET POLICY: Fee $8 per pet per
day. Up to 50 lbs. 2 pets maxi-
mum.
POI: Crown Isle golfing. Mount
Washington skiing.

**Quality Inn & Suites
Kingfisher**
4330 S. Island Hwy.
Courtenay, BC V9N 8H9
250-338-1323
PET POLICY: Fee $8 per day per
pet, nonrefundable. 2 pets
maximum.

Travelodge
2605 S Island Hwy.
Courtenay, BC V9N 2L8
250-334-4491

Inn of the South
803 Cranbrook St.
Cranbrook, BC V1C 3S2
250-489-4301

Model A Inn
1908 Cranbrook St., N.
Cranbrook, BC V1C 3T1
250-489-4600

Ponderosa Motel & RV Park
500 Van Horne St., S.
Cranbrook, BC V1C 4H3
250-426-6114
PET POLICY: No fee, up to 50 lbs.;
all pets welcome, including birds.

Ponderosa Motel & RV Park
500 Van Horne St. S
Cranbrook, BC V1C 4W7
250-426-6114
RATES: Single $40, double $55.
PET POLICY: No fee. All pets
welcome up to 50 lbs.

City Centre Motel
220 15th Ave., N.
Creston, BC V0B 1G0
250-428-2257

Downtowner Motor Inn
1218 Canyon St.
Creston, BC V0B 1G0
250-428-2238
RATES: Single $48, double $54.
PET POLICY: Fee $4, nonrefund-
able. Pets up to 50 lbs. No
more than 2 pets per room.
POI: 30 minutes to lake. Wildlife
center.

Sunset Motel
2705 Canyon St.
Creston, BC V0B 1G0
250-428-2229

Ramada Limited
1748 Alaska Ave.
Dawson Creek, BC V1G 1P4
250-782-8595
RATES: Single $72, double $79.
PET POLICY: Fee $10, nonre-
fundable. Only dogs and cats.
Up to 50 lbs.
AMENITIES: 4 acres of grass land.
POI: Overlooking rolling hills, 7
blocks to museum.

The George Dawson Inn
11705 8th St.
Dawson Creek, BC V1G 4N9
250-782-9151

Best Western Tsawwassen Inn
1665 56th St.
Delta, BC V4L 2B2
604-943-8221

Peggy's Bed & Breakfast
5813 Grove Ave.
Delta, BC V4K 2B3
604-940-3322
RATES: Single $30, double $50.
PET POLICY: Fee $10, refund-
able. Up to 50 lbs. Dogs and
cats only. One dog at a time.
AMENITIES: Large enclosed yard.
Dog sitting available.
POI: Deas Island park, which
has dog friendly trails; nearby
dyke that stretches for a few
kilometres; hidden trails near
the village of Ladner; Vancouver
(30 minutes away) with shopping and cultural events; lots
of pet-friendly parks.

River Run Cottages
24551 River Rd., W
Delta, BC V4K 1R9
604-946-7778

**Best Western Cowichan
Valley Inn**
6474 Trans-Canada Hwy. 1
Duncan, BC V9L 3W8
250-748-2722

Flacon Nest Motel
5867 Trans-Canada Hwy. 1
Duncan, BC V9L 3R9
250-748-8188

**Silver Bridge Inn &
Conference Centre**
140 Trans-Canada Hwy. 1
Duncan, BC V9L 3P7
250-748-4311

Howard Johnson Inn
1902 George St.
Enderby, BC V0E 1V0
250-838-6825

**The Cat's Pyjamas Bed &
Breakfast**
159 Brickyard Rd.
Enderby, BC V0E 1V0
250-838-9509

Canadian Lodgings > BRITISH COLUMBIA

Fernie Westways Guest House
Box 658
Fernie, BC V0B 1M0
250-423-3058

Super 8 Motel-Fernie
2021 Hwy. 3
Fernie, BC V0B 1M1
250-423-6788

Kicking Horse Lodge
100 Centre St.
Field, BC V0A 1G0
250-343-6303

Travelodge
4711 50th Ave. S
Fort Nelson, BC V0C 1R0
250-774-3911

Driftwood Village Resort
205 Bluff Rd. E.
Galiano Island, BC V0N 1P0
250-539-5457
RATES: Single $80, double $125.
PET POLICY: Fee $5–$10. All
sizes and pets welcome. Must
be on leash. Clean up after
dogs.
AMENITIES: 2 acres of grounds
for walking.

Cedars Inn
895 Sunshine Coast Hwy.
Gibsons, BC V0N 1V0
604-886-3008

Best Western Mountain View Inn
1024 11th St., N.
Golden, BC V0A 1H0
250-344-2333

Golden Rim Motor Inn
1416 Golden View Rd.
Golden, BC V0A 1H0
250-344-7281

Imperial Motel
7389 Riverside Dr.
Grand Forks, BC V0H 1H0
250-442-5566

Western Traveller
1591 Central Ave.
Grand Forks, BC V0H 1H0
250-443-5566

Harrison Hot Springs Resort
100 Esplanade
Harrison Hot Springs, BC
V0M 1K0
604-796-2244

Alpine Motel
505 Old Hope-Princeton Way
Hope, BC V0X 1L0
604-869-9931

Inn-Towne Motel
510 Trans-Canada Hwy.
Hope, BC V0X 1L0
604-869-7276

Maple Leaf Motor Inn
377 Old Hope Princeton Way
Hope, BC V0X 1L0
604-869-7107

Quality Inn Hope
350 Old Hope Princeton Way
Hope, BC V0X 1L0
604-869-9951

Swiss Chalets
456 Trans-Canada Hwy.
Hope, BC V0X 1L0
604-869-9020

Windsor Motel
778 3rd Ave.
Hope, BC V0X 1L0
604-869-9944

Olde Osprey Inn Bed & Breakfast
RR 1
Kaleden, BC V0H 1K0
250-497-7134

Accent Inn - Kamloops
1325 Columbia St W
Kamloops, BC V2C 6P4
250-374-8877
RATES: Single $79–$119, double
$89–$129.
PET POLICY: No fee, small pets
up to 25 lbs.

Casa Marquis Motor Inn
530 Columbia St.
Kamloops, BC V2C 2V1
250-372-7761
RATES: Single $49, double $69.
PET POLICY: Fee $5 nonrefund-
able, small dogs only.
POI: Located near area suitable
for walking your pet.

Courtesy Motel
1773 Trans-Canada Hwy. E.
Kamloops, BC V2C 3Z6
250-372-8533

Days Inn
1285 Trans-Canada Hwy. W.
Kamloops, BC V2E 2J7
250-374-5911

Fountain Motel
506 Columbia St.
Kamloops, BC V2C 2V1
250-374-4451

Grandview Motel
463 Grandview Terrace
Kamloops, BC V2C 3Z3
250-372-1312

Hospitality Inn-Kamloops
500 W. Columbia St.
Kamloops, BC V2C1K6
250-374-4164

Howard Johnson Inn
610 W. Columbia St.
Kamloops, BC V2C 1L1
250-374-1515

Kings Motor Inn
1775 Trans-Canada Hwy. E.
Kamloops, BC V2C 3Z6
250-372-2800

Lamplighter Motel
1901 Trans-Canada Hwy. E.
Kamloops, BC V2C 3Z9
250-372-3386

Roche Lake Resort
PO Box 669
Kamloops, BC V2C 5L7
250-828-2007

Thompson Hotel & Conference Center
650 Victoria St.
Kamloops, BC V2C 2B4
250-374-1999

Thrift Inn
2459 Trans-Canada Hwy. E.
Kamloops, BC V2C 4A9
250-374-2488

Travelodge
430 Columbia St.
Kamloops, BC V2C 2T5
250-372-8202

Canadian Lodgings > BRITISH COLUMBIA

Accent Inn Kelowna
1140 Harvey Ave.
Kelowna, BC V1Y 6E7
250-862-8888
RATES: Single $79–$119, double
$89–$129.
PET POLICY: No fee, small pets
up to 25 lbs.

Big White Motor Lodge
1891 Parkinson Wayu
Kelowna, BC V1Y 7V6
250-860-3982

**Grand Resort And
Conference Ctr**
1310 Water St.
Kelowna, BC V1Y 9P3
250-763-4500

Howard Johnson Inn
1652 Gordon Dr.
Kelowna, BC V1Y 3H1
250-762-5444

Oasis Motor Inn
1884 Gordon Dr.
Kelowna, BC V1Y 3H7
250-0763-5396

Pandosy Inn
3327 Lakeshore Rd.
Kelowna, BC V1W 3S9
250-762-5858

Ramada Lodge Hotel
2170 Harvey Ave.
Kelowna, BC V1Y 6G8
250-860-9711
RATES: Single $99, double $109.
PET POLICY: Fee $10, nonrefund-
able, all pets welcome, up to
50 lbs. Do not leave unattended
in room.
AMENITIES: Provincial park
nearby that allows dogs.

Safari Inn
1651 Powick Rd.
Kelowna, BC V1X 4L1
250-765-9889

Town And Country Motel
2629 Hwy. 97 N.
Kelowna, BC V1X 4J6
250-860-7121

**Holiday Inn Express Hotel
& Suites**
8750 204th St.
Langley, BC V1M 2Y5
604-882-2000

RATES: Single $99, double $109.
PET POLICY: Fee $10, nonre-
fundable, pets up to 50 lbs.
POI: Pet-friendly parks and
walking trails nearby.

Travelodge
21653 Fraser Hwy.
Langley, BC V3A 4H1
604-533-4431

Travelodge
20470 88th Ave.
Langley, BC V1M 2Y6
604-888-4891

Westward Inn
19650 Fraser Hwy.
Langley, BC V3A 4C7
604-534-9238

Malahat Bungalows Motel
PO Box 48
Malahat, BC V0R 2L0
250-478-3011

Manning Park Resort
Hwy. 3
Manning Park, BC V0X 1R0
250-840-8822

Best Western Maple Ridge
21735 Lougheed Hwy.
Maple Ridge, BC V2X 2S2
604-463-5111

Bob's Bed & Breakfast
21089 Dewdney Trunk Rd.
Maple Ridge, BC V2X 3G1
604-463-5052

Travelodge
21650 Lougheed Hwy.
Maple Ridge, BC V2X 2S1
604-467-1511

North Country Lodge
PO Box 567
McBride, BC V0J 2E0
250-569-0001

Coquihalla Motor Inn
3571 Vought St.
Merritt, BC V1K 1C5
250-378-3567

Douglas Motel
2702 Nicola Ave.
Merritt, BC V1K 1B8
250-378-9244
RATES: Single $40–$80, double
$50–$100.

PET POLICY: No fee, all sizes,
dogs and cats only. Do not
leave unattended in rooms
and keep off beds and sofas.
Leash rules apply.
AMENITIES: Large side yard and
nearby fields for exercise.
POI: In May there is a long
weekend dog show.

Merritt Motor Inn
3561 Vought St.
Merritt, BC V1K 1C5
250-378-8830

The Selkirk Inn
210 W. 6th Ave.
Nakusp, BC V0G 1R0
250-265-3666

**Nanaimo-Days Inn
Harbourview**
809 Island Hwy. S.
Nanaimo, BC V9R 5K1
250-754-8171

Port O'Call Motel
505 N. Terminal Ave.
Nanaimo, BC V9S 4K1
250-753-3421

Travelodge
96 Terminal Ave. N.
Nanaimo, BC V9S 4J2
250-754-6355

Alpine Motel
1120 Halls Mines Rd.
Nelson, BC V1L 1G6
250-352-5501
RATES: Single $40, double $80.
PET POLICY: Fee $20, nonrefund-
able. All pets welcome.
POI: Kokanee Glacier Provincial
Park, hiking, biking, fishing.

Elkin Creek Guest Ranch
Box 22
Nemaiah Valley, BC V0L 1X0
604-700-0945

Canyon Court Motel
1748 Capilano Rd.
North Vancouver, BC V7P 3B4
604-988-3181

Cedar Hill
1095 W. Keith Rd
North Vancouver, BC V7P 1Y6
604-988-9629

Canadian Lodgings > BRITISH COLUMBIA

Southwind Inn
PO Box 1500
Oliver, BC V0H 1T0
250-498-3442

Vaseux Lake Lodge
9710 Sundial Rd.
Oliver, BC V0H 1H0
250-498-0516
RATES: Single, double $150–$195.
PET POLICY: Fee $50, nonrefundable; call ahead for permission. Do not leave unattended in townhouses. Quiet dogs only.
AMENITIES: Fido welcome package: bed, beach towel, dishes, toys and treats. Pets welcome on beach and in lake.

Mount Kobau Motor Inn
PO Box 431
Osoyoos, BC V0H 1V0
250-495-7322

Best Western Bayside Inn
240 Dogwood St.
Parksville, BC V9P 2H5
250-248-8333

Gray Crest Seaside Resort
1115 E. Island Hwy.
Parksville, BC V9P 2E2
250-248-6513

Tigh Na Mara Resort Hotel
1095 E. Island Hwy.
Parksville, BC V9P 2E5
250-248-2072

V.I.P. Motel
414 West Island Hwy.
Parksville, BC V9P 1K8
250-248-3244
RATES: Single $59, double $94.
PET POLICY: No fee, all sizes and all pets welcome. Do not leave pets unattended in rooms, and walk off property.
AMENITIES: Dog run available if needed.

Timber Inn
3483 Hwy. 95
Parson, BC V0A 1L0
250-348-2228

Pemberton Creekside Bed & Breakfast
1344 Elmswood Dr.
Pemberton, BC V0N 1L0
604-894-6520

RATES: Single, double $89.
PET POLICY: Fee $20, nonrefundable. Dogs only, all sizes. Must have shots up to date and be spayed or neutered.
AMENITIES: Kennels and blankets available.

Bel-Air Motel
2670 Skaha Lake Rd.
Penticton, BC V2A 6G1
250-492-6111

Golden Sands Resort
1028 Lakeshore Dr.
Penticton, BC V2A 1C1
250-492-4210

Penticton Lakeside Resort & Conference Centre
21 Lakeshore Dr., W.
Penticton, BC V2A 7M5
250-493-8221

Ramada Courtyard Inn
1050 Eckhardt Ave. W.
Penticton, BC V2A 2C3
250-492-8926

Spanish Villa Resort
890 Lakeshore Dr., W.
Penticton, BC V2A 1C1
250-492-2922

Waterfront Inn
3688 Parkview St.
Penticton, BC V2A 6H1
250-492-8228

Alberni Inn
3805 Redford St.
Port Alberni, BC V9Y 3S2
250-723-9405

Tyee Village Motel
4151 Redford St.
Port Alberni, BC V9Y 3R6
250-723-8133

Best Western Poco Inn
1545 Lougheed Hwy.
Port Coquitlam, BC V3B 1A5
604-941-6216

C-View Bed & Breakfast
6170 Hardy Bay
Port Hardy, BC V0N 2P0
250-949-7560

Connaught Motor Inn
1550 Victoria St.
Prince George, BC V2L 2L2
250-562-4441

Ramada Hotel Downtown Prince George
444 George St.
Prince George, BC V2L 1R6
604-563-0055

Aleeda Motel
900 3rd Ave., W.
Prince Rupert, BC V8J 1M8
250-627-1367

Alpine Meadows Bed & Breakfast
RR 1
Pritchard, BC V0E 2P0
250-577-3726

Taku Resort
616 Taku Rd.
Quadra Island, BC V0P 1H0
250-285-3031

Whiskey Point Resort
Box 309
Quadra Island, BC V0P 1N0
800-622-5311
RATES: Single $64, double $69.
PET POLICY: Fee $5, nonrefundable. Maximum 2 pets per room.
AMENITIES: Walking trails and protected yard to play in.
POI: Near beaches and hiking trails. Relaxed island environment that welcomes pets.

Old Duch Inn
2690 Island Hwy., W.
Qualicum Beach, BC V9K 1G8
250-752-6914

The Shorewater Condominium Resort
3295 Island Hwy. W.
Qualicum Beach, BC V9K 2C6
250-752-6901

Whiskey Point Resort
Box 309
Quathiaski Cover, BC V0P 1N0
250-285-2201

Talisman Inn
753 Front St.
Quesnel, BC V2J 2L2
250-992-7247
PET POLICY: No fee, all sizes and pets welcome (dogs, cats, ferrets, birds, rabbits). Only ground-floor rooms available.

Canadian Lodgings > BRITISH COLUMBIA

Travelodge
524 Front St.
Quesnel, BC V2J 2K6
250-992-7071

Valhalla Motel & Family Restaurant
2010 Valhalla Rd.
Quesnel, BC V2J 4C1
250-747-1111

Cedar Motel
7593 Main St. W.
Radium Hot Springs,
BC V0A 1M0
250-347-9463

Chalet Eurpe
5063 Madsen Rd.
Radium Hot Springs,
BC V0A 1M0
250-347-9305
PET POLICY: Fee $10, nonrefundable. Dogs only, any size on approval.
AMENITIES: Great walking trails right from back door.

Howard Johnson Resort Hotel
5425 Hwy. 93
Radium Hot Springs,
BC V0A 1M0
250-347-9341

Lido Motel
4876 McKay St.
Radium Hot Springs,
BC V0A 1M0
250-347-9533

Sunset Motel
4883 McKay St.
Radium Hot Springs,
BC V0A 1M0
250-347-9863

Best Western Wayside Inn
1901 LaForme Blvd.
Revelstoke, BC V0E 2S0
250-837-6161

Boulder Mountain Inn
Box 1125
Revelstoke, BC V0E 2S0
250-837-9573

Swiss Chalet Motel
1101 Victoria Rd.
Revelstoke, BC V0E 2S0
250-837-4650

The Regent Inn
112 1st St. E.
Revelstoke, BC V0E 2S0
250-837-2107

Accent Inn Vancouver Airport
10551 St. Edwards Dr.
Richmond, BC V6X 3L8
604-273-3311
RATES: Single $84–$124, double $94–$134.
PET POLICY: No fee, small pets up to 25 lbs.

Delta Pacific Resort & Conference Centre
10251 St. Edwards Dr.
Richmond, BC V6X 2M9
604-278-9611

Delta Vancouver Airport Hotel & Marina
3500 Cessna Dr.
Richmond, BC V7B 1C7
604-278-1241

Marriott Vancouver Airport
7571 Westminster Hwy.
Richmond, BC V6X 1A3
604-276-2112

Radisson President Hotel & Suites
8181 Cambie Rd.
Richmond, BC V6X 2X9
604-276-8181

Swiss Alps Inn
1199 Nancy Green Hwy.
Rossland, BC V0G 1Y0
250-362-7364

Quality Inn Waddling Dog
2476 Mount Newton Cross Rd.
Saanichton, BC V8M 2B8
250-652-1146

Victoria/Saanichton Super 8 Motel
2477 Mount Newton Cross Rd.
Saanichton, BC V8M 2B7
250-652-6888

Best Western Villager West Motor Inn
61 10th St. SW
Salmon Arm, BC V1E 1E4
250-832-9793

RATES: Single $60–$80, double $65–$95.
PET POLICY: Fee $5, nonrefundable. All sizes and pets welcome. Do not leave in room unattended.
POI: Shuswap Lake.

Cinnamon Stick Bed & Breakfast
1801 28th Ave. NE
Salmon Arm, BC V1E 3X2
250-832-4808

Salmon Arm Super 8 Motel
2901 10th Ave. Ne
Salmon Arm, BC V1E 4N1
250-832-8812

The Coast Shuswap Lodge
200 Trans-Canada Hwy.
Salmon Arm, BC V1E 4P6
250-832-7081

Travelodge
2401 Trans Canada Hwy. W.
Salmon Arm, BC V1E 4P7
250-832-9721

Eagles Nest Bed & Breakfast
115 Sollitt Rd.
Salt Spring Island, BC V8K 2J5
250-537-2129

Lakeside Country Inn
1001 Savona Access Rd.
Savona, BC V0K 2J0
250-373-2528

Best Western Emerald Isle Motor Inn
2306 Beacon Ave.
Sidney, BC V8L 1X2
250-656-4441

Cedarwood Motel
9522 Lochside Dr.
Sidney, BC V8L 1N8
250-656-5551

Victoria Airport Travelodge
2280 Beacon Ave.
Sidney, BC V8L 1X1
250-656-1176
RATES: Single $99, double $115.
PET POLICY: Fee $100, refundable.
POI: Butchart Gardens; 15 minutes to airport and 5 minutes to ferries.

Canadian Lodgings > BRITISH COLUMBIA

Aspen Motor Inn
4628 Yellowhead Hwy.
Smithers, BC V0J 2N0
250-847-4551

**Manzer Lodge
Bed & Breakfast**
3007 Manzer Rd.
Sooke, BC V0S 1N0
250-642-6632

**Ocean Wilderness
Country Inn**
109 W. Coast Rd.
Sooke, BC V0S 1N0
250-646-2116

Sooke Harbour House
1528 Whiffen Spit Rd.
Sooke, BC V0S 1N0
250-642-3421
RATES: Single, double
$125–$300.
PET POLICY: Fee $20, refundable.
All size dogs and cats. Must be
well behaved.
AMENITIES: Sleeping baskets or
beds, water and food dishes, toys
and a copy of our pet "rules."
POI: Overlooking harbour and
Juan Defuca Strait.

Summerland Motel
2107 Tait St.
Summerland, BC V0H 1Z0
250-494-4444

**Days Hotel—
Surrey City Center**
9850 King George Hwy.
Surrey, BC V3T 4Y3
604-588-9511

Ramada Limited
19225 Hwy. 10
Surrey, BC V3S 8V9
604-576-8388
RATES: Single $80.
PET POLICY: Fee $10, per pet
per night., nonrefundable. All
size pets welcome (dogs, cats,
ferrets, birds, rabbits).
POI: Horseback riding, winery,
annual rodeo.

Sheraton Guildford Hotel
15269 104th Ave.
Surrey, BC V3R 1N5
604-582-9288
RATES: Single $149–$199, double $149–$249.

Sheraton Guildford Hotel
15269 104th Ave.
Surrey, BC V3R 1N5
604-582-9288

Alpine House Motel
4326 Lakelse Ave.
Terrace, BC V8G 1N8
250-635-7216

Coast Inn of the West
4620 Lakelse Ave.
Terrace, BC V8G 1R1
250-638-8141
RATES: Single $85, double $95.
PET POLICY: No fee, up to 50 lbs.

Crab Dock Guest House
310 Olsen Rd.
Tofino, BC V0R 2Z0
250-725-2911

Crystal Cove Beach Resort
1165 Cedarwood Pl.
Tofino, BC V0R 2Z0
250-725-4213

Gull Cottage Bed & Breakfast
1254 Lynn Rd.
Tofino, BC V0R 2Z0
250-725-3177

The Wickaninnish Inn
Osprey Ln. & Chesterman
Beach
Tofino, BC V0R 2Z0
800-333-4604

Tauca Lea by the Sea
1971 Harbour Crescent
Ucluelet-Long Beach,
BC V0R 3A0
250-726-4625
RATES: Single $170, double
$210.
PET POLICY: Fee $30, nonrefund-
able. All size dogs, only. Do
not leave unattended in rooms.
Must be on leash at resort.

Chalet Continental
1450 5th Ave.
Valemount, BC V0E 2Z0
250-566-9787

The Mountaineer Inn
PO Box 217
Valemount, BC V0E 2Z0
250-566-4477

2400 Motel
2400 Kingsway
Vancouver, BC V5R 5G9
604-434-2464

Bosmans Hotel
1060 Howe St.
Vancouver, BC V6Z 1P5
604-682-3171

**Coast Vancouver Airport
Hotel**
1041 Sw Marine Dr.
Vancouver, BC V6P 6L6
604-263-1555

**Four Seasons Hotel
Vancouver**
791 W. Georgia St.
Vancouver, BC V6C 2T4
604-689-9333

**Golden Tulip Georgian
Court Hotel**
773 Beatty St.
Vancouver, BC V6B 2M4
604-682-5555

Holiday Inn
711 W. Broadway
Vancouver, BC V5K 3Y2
604-879-0511
PET POLICY: No fee.

Holiday Inn Hotel & Suites
1110 Howe St.
Vancouver, BC V6Z 1R2
604-684-2151
PET POLICY: No fee.

Hotel Vancouver
900 W. Georgia St.
Vancouver, BC V6C 2W6
604-684-3131

**Metropolitan Hotel
Vancouver**
645 Howe St.
Vancouver, BC V6C 2Y9
604-687-1122

Pacific Palisades Hotel
1277 Robson St.
Vancouver, BC V6E 1C4
604-688-0461

Quality Hotel Downtown
1335 Howe St.
Vancouver, BC V6Z 1R7
604-682-0229

Canadian Lodgings > BRITISH COLUMBIA

Renaissance Vancouver Harbourside
1133 W. Hastings St.
Vancouver, BC V6E 3T3
604-689-9211

Sutton Place Hotel
845 Burrard St.
Vancouver, BC V6Z 2K6
604-682-5511
RATES: Single $220, double $220.
PET POLICY: Fee $150, non-refundable, only dogs and cats up to 25 lbs.
AMENITIES: Welcome cookies on arrival, Sit and Stay program, pet registry and Polaroid, $5 gift certificate at Three Dog Bakery.

Sylvia Hotel
1154 Gilford St.
Vancouver, BC V6G 2P6
604-681-9321

The London Guard Motel
2227 Kingsway St.
Vancouver, BC V5N 2T6
604-430-4646

The Pan Pacific Hotel Vancouver
999 Canada Pl.
Vancouver, BC V6C 3B5
604-662-8111

The Waterfront
900 Canada Pl. Way
Vancouver, BC V6C 3L5
604-691-1991

The Westin Bayshore Resort & Marina
1601 Bayshore Dr.
Vancouver, BC V6G2V4
604-682-3377
RATES: Call for current rates.
PET POLICY: No fee, only dogs and cats.
POI: Overlooks 1,000-acre Stanley Park; minutes from historic Gastown.

Best Western Lodge & Conference Centre
3914 32nd St.
Vernon, BC V1T 5P1
250-545-3385

Comfort Inn Vernon
4204 32nd St.
Vernon, BC V1T 5P4
250-542-4434

Falcon-Nest
5620 Neil Rd.
Vernon, BC V1B 3J5
250-545-1759

Schell Motel
2810 35th St.
Vernon, BC V1T 6B5
250-545-1351

The Maria Rose Bed & Breakfast
8083 Aspen Rd.
Vernon, BC V1B 3M9
250-549-4773
RATES: Single $60, double $75.
PET POLICY: Fee $5, nonrefundable. Up to 25 lbs.
AMENITIES: Acres of trees.
POI: Beaches, provincial parks, mountain resort.

Travelodge
3000 28th Ave.
Vernon, BC V1T 1W1
250-545-2161

Accent Inn - Victoria
3233 Maple St.
Victoria, BC V8X 4Y9
250-475-7500
RATES: Single $79–$119, double $89–$129.
PET POLICY: No fee, small pets up to 25 lbs.

Admiral Motel
257 Belleville St.
Victoria, BC V8V 1X1
250-388-6267
PET POLICY: No fee. Pets must be in special rooms (usually smoking rooms). All sizes accepted.

Blue Ridge Inn
3110 Douglas St.
Victoria, BC V8Z 3K4
250-388-4345

Dashwood Seaside Manor
1 Cook St.
Victoria, BC V8V 3W6
250-385-5517

Doric Motel
3025 Douglas St.
Victoria, BC V8T 4N2
250-386-2481

Executive House Hotel
777 Douglas St.
Victoria, BC V8W 2B5
250-388-5111

Forgett-Me-Nott Bed & Breakfast
4388 Northridge Crescent
Victoria, BC V8Z 4Z3
250-744-2047
RATES: Double $65 - $75.
PET POLICY: No fee. All size dogs and cats.
AMENITIES: Pet-sitting service available. Walking trails along Colquitz Creek across the street.
POI: Close to Elk and Beaver Lake Parks and beaches.

Harbour Towers Hotel
345 Quebec St.
Victoria, BC V8V 1W4
250-385-2405

Malahat Bungalows Motel
300 Trans Canada Hwy.
Victoria, BC V0R 2L0
250-478-3011
PET POLICY: No fee, all size pets welcome. Pets must be under control at all times.

Ocean Pointe Resort Hotel & Spa
45 Songhees Rd.
Victoria, BC V9A 6T3
250-360-2999

Oxford Castle Inn
133 Gorge Rd. E.
Victoria, BC V9A 1L1
250-388-6431

Quality Inn-Waddling Dog
2476 Mt. Newton Cross Rd.
Victoria, BC V8M 2B8
250-652-1146
RATES: Single $80, double $90.
PET POLICY: Fee $5, nonrefundable, all sizes, only dogs and cats.
AMENITIES: Resident Basset Hound "John."
POI: Surrounded by great fishing, golf courses, nature parks and beaches.

Canadian Lodgings > MANITOBA

Robin Hood Motel
136 Gorge Rd. E.
Victoria, BC V9A 1L4
250-388-4302
RATES: Single $46–$69, double
$51–$84.
PET POLICY: Fee $5, nonrefund-
able. Dogs only, up to 50 lbs.
POI: 2 kilometres from
Victoria's beautiful Inner
Harbour.

Ryan's Bed & Breakfast
224 Superior St.
Victoria, BC V8V 1T3
250-389-0012

Shamrock Motel
675 Superior St.
Victoria, BC V8V 1V1
250-385-8768

The Empress
721 Government St.
Victoria, BC V8W 1W5
250-384-8111

Holiday Inn
213 - 2569 Dobbin Rd.
Westbank, BC V4T 2J6
250-768-8879
PET POLICY: No fee.

Delta Whistler Resort
4050 Whistler Way
Whistler, BC V0N 1BO
604-932-1982

Edgewater Lodge
8841 Hwy. 00
Whistler, BC V0N 1B0
604-932-0688

Listel Whistler Hotel
4121 Village Green
Whistler, BC V0N 1B4
604-932-1133
PET POLICY: Fee $15, nonre-
fundable. All sizes welcome.

**Residence Inn
Whistler/Blackcomb**
4899 Painted Cliff Rd.
Whistler, BC V0N 2B4
604-905-3400

Tantalus Lodge
4200 Whistler Way
Whistler, BC V0N 1B4
604-932-4146

The AnneRose Inn
3016 St. Anton Way
Whistler, BC V0N 1B3
604-938-9868
PET POLICY: $250 damage
deposit (refundable), no
restrictions on size or type,
keep crated if alone, males
must be neutered.

The Chateau Whistler Resort
4599 Chateau Blvd.
Whistler, BC V0N 1B4
604-938-8000

Drummond Lodge Motel
1405 Cariboo Hwy.
Williams Lake, BC V2G 2W3
250-392-5334

Overlander Hotel
1118 Lakeview Crescent
Williams Lake, BC V2G 1A3
250-392-3321

**Williams Lake Super 8
Motel**
1712 Broadway Ave. S.
Williams Lake, BC V2G 2W4
250-398-8884

Fort Yale Motel
31265 Trans-Canada Hwy.
Yale, BC V0K 2S0
604-863-2216

MANITOBA

Comfort Inn Brandon
925 Middleton Ave.
Brandon, MB R7C 1A8
204-727-6232

Super 8 Motel Brandon
1570 Highland Ave.
Brandon, MB R7C 1A7
204-729-8024

Polar Inn
15 Franklin St.
Churchill, MB R0B 0E0
204-675-8878

Rodeway Inn Motel
10 Hwy. S.
Dauphin, MB R7N 2V4
204-638-5102

Country Resort by Carlson
10 Centre St.
Gimli, MB R0C 1B0
204-642-8565

Manitobah Inn
Box 867
Portage La Prairie,
MB R1N 3C3
204-857-9792

**The Russell Inn hotel &
Conference Center**
PO Box 578
Portage La Prairie,
MB R0J 1W0
204-773-2186

Westgate Inn Motel
1010 Saskatchewan Ave. E.
Portage La Prairie,
MB R1N 0K1
204-239-5200

Solmundon Gesta Hus
Box 76
Riverton, MB R0C 2R0
204-279-2088

Daerwood Motor Inn
162 Main St.
Selkirk, MB R1A 1R3
204-482-7722

Wescana Inn
439 Fischer Ave.
The Pas, MB R9A 1M3
204-623-5446

**Country Inns & Suites
By Carlson**
70 Thompson Dr. N.
Thompson, MB R8N1Y8
204-778-8879
RATES: Call for rates.
PET POLICY: Fee $10 nonrefund-
able. Up to 50 lbs.
POI: Paint Lake, Pisew Falls.

Best Western Carlton Inn
220 Carlton St.
Winnipeg, MB R3C 1P5
204-942-0881

Charter House Hotel
330 York At Hargrove
Winnipeg, MB R3C 0N9
204-942-0101

Comfort Inn Airport
1770 Sargent Ave.
Winnipeg, MB R3H 0C8
204-783-5627

Canadian Lodgings > MANITOBA

Comfort Inn South
3109 Pembina Hwy.
Winnipeg, MB R3T 4R6
204-269-7390
PET POLICY: No fee, no size
restrictions, can't be left unattended in room, must walk off
property.

**Country Inn & Suites
by Carlson**
730 King Edward St.
Winnipeg, MB R3H 1B4
204-783-6900

Crowne Plaza
350 St. Mary Ave.
Winnipeg, MB R3C 3J2
204-942-0551
PET POLICY: No fee.

Delta Winnipeg
288 Portage Ave.
Winnipeg, MB R3C 0B8
204-956-0410
PET POLICY: No fee, no size limit,
must be in room with your pet.

**Gordon Downtowner
Motor Hotel**
330 Kennedy St.
Winnipeg, MB R3B 2M6
204-943-5581

Holiday Inn Winnipeg South
1330 Pembina Hwy.
Winnipeg, MB R3T 2B4
204-452-4747
RATES: Single $159, double $169.
PET POLICY: No fee. All pets
welcome. Owner responsible
for pet's behavior.
POI: Adjacent to community park.

**International Inn-
Best Western**
1808 Wellington Ave.
Winnipeg, MB R3H 0G3
204-786-4801

Norlander Inn
1792 Pembina Hwy.
Winnipeg, MB R3T 2G2
204-269-6955

Place Louis Riel Suites
190 Smith St.
Winnipeg, MB R3C 1J8
204-947-6961

Quality Inn Winnipeg
635 Pembina Hwy.
Winnipeg, MB R3M 2L4
204-453-8247

Ramada Marlborough Hotel
331 Smith St.
Winnipeg, MB R3B 2G9
204-942-6411

The Lombard
2 Lombard Pl.
Winnipeg, MB R3B 0Y3
204-957-1350

Viscount Gort Hotel
1670 Portage Ave.
Winnipeg, MB R3J 0C9
204-775-0451

Windsor Park Inn
1034 Elizabeth Rd.
Winnipeg, MB R2J 1B3
204-253-2641

NEW BRUNSWICK

Atlantic Host Inn
PO Box 910
Bathurst, NB E2A 4H7
506-548-3335

**Best Western Danny's Inn
& Conference Centre**
PO Box 180
Bathurst, NB E2A 3Z2
506-546-6621

Comfort Inn Bathurst
1170 St. Peter Ave.
Bathurst, NB E2A 2Z9
506-547-8000

Country Inn And Suites
777 St Peter Ave.
Bathurst, NB E2A 2Y9
506-548-4949

**Keddys Bathurst
Htl Conv Ctr**
80 Main St.
Bathurst, NB E2A 1A3
506-546-6691

Comfort Inn Campbellton
111 Val D'amour Rd
Campbellton, NB E3N 3G9
506-753-4121

Howard Johnson Hotel
157 Water St.
Campbellton, NB E3N 3H2
506-753-4133

Cocagne Motel
PO Box 119
Cocagne, NB E0A 1K0
506-576-6657

**Best Western Manoir
Adelaide**
385 Adelaide St.
Dalhousie, NB E0K 1B0
506-684-5681

Carriage House Inn
230 University Ave.
Fredericton, NB E3B 4H7
506-452-9924

Comfort Inn
255 Prospect St. W.
Fredericton, NB E3B 5Y4
506-453-0800

**Country Inn And Suites
Frederic**
445 Prospect St. W.
Fredericton, NB E3B 6B8
506-459-0035

Howard Johnson Hotel
Lower St. Mary's Trans Canada
Hwy. #2
Fredericton, NB E3B 5E3
506-460-5500

Keddy's Inn
368 Forest Hill Rd.
Fredericton, NB E3B 5G2
506-454-4461

Lord Beaverbrook Hotel
659 Queen St.
Fredericton, NB E3B 5A6
506-455-3371

Wandlyn Inn Federation
958 Prospect St.
Fredericton, NB E3B2T8
506-452-7658
RATES: Call for rates.
PET POLICY: No fee. All dogs
and cats welcome.

Wandlyn Inn Fredericton
958 Prospect St.
Fredericton, NB E3B 2T8
506-462-4444
PET POLICY: No fee, only dogs
and cats, up to 50 lbs.

Canadian Lodgings > NEW BRUNSWICK

Holiday Inn
35 Mactaquac Rd.
French Village, NB E3E 1L2
506-363-5111
PET POLICY: No fee.

Auberge Pres-du-Lac Inn
TCH Box 6
Grand Falls, NB E0J 1M0
506-473-1300

Comfort Inn Miramichi
201 Edward St.
Miramichi, NB E1A 2Y7
506-622-1215
PET POLICY: No fee, all sizes and pets welcome. Must have kennel in room and pets cannot be left alone in room.
POI: French Fort Cove, Richie Wharf.

Country Inn & Suites by Carlson
333 King George Hwy.
Miramichi, NB E1V 2Y7
506-627-1999

Comfort Inn
201 Edward St.
Mirimichi, NB E1V2Y7
506-622-1215
RATES: Single, double Can.$68.40–$75.60.
PET POLICY: No fee. All pets welcome. Require kennels. Pets cannot be left alone in room.
POI: French Fort Cove, Ritchie Wharf.

Beacon Light Motel
1062 Mountain Rd.
Moncton, NB E1C 2T1
506-384-1734

Best Western Crystal Palace Hotel
499 Paul St.
Moncton, NB E1A 6S5
506-858-8584

Colonial inns
42 Highfield St.
Moncton, NB E1C 8T6
506-382-3395

Comfort Inn East
20 Maplewood Dr.
Moncton, NB E1A 6P9
506-859-6868

Comfort Inn Magnetic Hill
2495 Mountain Rd.
Moncton, NB E1G 2W4
506-384-3175

Country Inn & Suites by Carlson
2475 Mountain Rd.
Moncton, NB E1C 8M7
506-852-7000

Delta Beausejour
750 Main St.
Moncton, NB E1C 1E6
506-854-4344

Holiday Inn Express
2515 Mouuntain Rd.
Moncton, NB E1C BR7
506-384-1050
PET POLICY: No fee.

Keddys Brunswick Hotel
1005 Main St.
Moncton, NB E1A 7A7
506-854-2210
RATES: Single $75, double $85.
PET POLICY: No fee.

Pine Cone Motel
RR #1
Penobsquis, NB E0E 1L0
506-433-3958

Marshlands Inn
55 Bridge St.
Sackville, NB E0A 3C0
506-536-0170

Colonial Inns
175 City Rd.
Saint John, NB E2L 3T5
506-652-3000

Comfort Inn Saint John
1155 Fairville Blvd.
Saint John, NB E2M 5T9
506-674-1873

Country Inn & Suites by Carlson
1011 Fairville Blvd.
Saint John, NB E2M 5T9
506-635-0400

Delta Brunswick
39 King St.
Saint John, NB E2L 4W3
506-648-1981

Garden House Bed & Breakfast
28 Garden St.
Saint John, NB E2L 3K3
506-646-9093

Howard John Hotel
400 Main St. at Chesley Dr.
Saint John, NB E2K 4N5
506-642-2622

Keddys Fort Howe Hotel
10 Portland At Main St.
Saint John, NB E2K 4H8
506-657-7320

Park Plaza Motel
607 Rothesay Ave.
Saint John, NB E2H 2G9
506-633-4100

Regent Motel
2121 Ocean West Way
Saint John, NB E2M 5H6
506-672-8273

Saint John Hilton
1 Market Square
Saint John, NB E2L 4Z6
506-693-8484

Shadow Lawn Inn
3180 Rothesay Rd.
Saint John, NB E2E 5V7
506-847-7539

Terrace Motel
2131 Ocean West Way
Saint John, NB E2M 5H6
506-672-9670

Kingsbrae Arms Relais & Chateaux
219 King St.
St. Andrews, NB E5B 1Y1
506-529-1897
RATES: Single $620, double $700 (week).
PET POLICY: No fee, all sizes, dogs only, must be well behaved.
AMENITIES: Dog bones on arrival with masters' chocolate truffles.
POI: Near Algonquin Links Golf Course.

The Algonquin
184 Adolphus St.
St. Andrews, NB E0G 2X0
506-529-8823

Canadian Lodgings > NEW BRUNSWICK

**Granite Town Hotel
& Country Inn**
79 Main St.
St. George, NB E0G 2Y0
506-755-6415

**Lake Digdeguash Four
Seasons Chalets**
PO Box 296
St. George, NB E3L 2X2
506-755-2737

Loon Bay Lodge
PO Box 101
St. Stephen, NB E3L 2W9
506-466-1240

St. Stephen Inn
99 King St.
St. Stephen, NB E3L 2C6
506-466-1814

Daigle's Motel
68 Bridge St.
St-Leonard, NB E0L 1M0
506-423-6351

Econo Lodge Sussex
1015 Main St.
Sussex, NB E4E 2M6
506-433-2220

Quality Inn Fairway
PO Box 1757
Sussex, NB E0E 1P0
506-433-3470

Stiles Motel Hill View
827 Main St.
Woodstock, NB E7M 2E9
506-328-6671

McCready's Motel
Young's Cover Rd.
Youngs Cover Rd.,
NB E0E 1S0
506-362-2916

NEWFOUNDLAND

Comfort Inn Corner Brook
41 Maple Valley Rd.
Corner Brook, NF A2H 6T2
709-639-1980

Holiday Inn
48 West St.
Corner Brook, NF A2H 2Z2
709-634-5381
PET POLICY: No fee.

Albatross Hotel
PO Box 450
Gander, NF A1V 1W8
709-256-3956

Comfort Inn Gander
112 Trans Canada Hwy.
Gander, NF AIV 1P8
709-256-3535

Sinbads Motel
Bennett Dr.
Gander, NF A1V 1W8
709-651-2678

Mount Peyton Motor Hotel
213 Lincoln Rd.
Grand Falls, NF A2A 1P8
709-489-2251

**Terra Nova Hospitality
Home & Cottages**
General Delivery
Port Blandford, NF A0C 2G0
709-543-2260

Ventureland Cottages
General Delivery
Portland Creek, NF A0K 4G0
709-898-2490

Best Western Travellers Inn
199 Kenmount Rd.
St. John's, NF A1B 3P9
709-722-5540

**Delta St. John's Hotel &
Conference Centre**
120 New Gower St.
St. John's, NF A1C 6K4
709-739-6404

Holiday Inn
180 Portugal Cove Rd.
St. John's , NF A1B 2N2
709-722-0506
PET POLICY: No fee.

Quality Hotel Downtown
2 Hill O'Chips
St. John's, NF A1C 6B1
709-754-7788

**The Battery
Hotel & Suites**
100 Signal Hill Rd.
St. John's, NF A1A 1B3
709-576-0040
RATES: Single, double $99.
PET POLICY: No fee. All sizes
and pets accepted.

The Battery Hotel & Suites
100 Signal Hill Rd.
St. John's, NF A1A 1B3
800-563-8181

Holiday Inn
44 Queen St.
Stephenville, NF A2N 2M5
709-643-6666
PET POLICY: No fee.

NOVA SCOTIA

Auberge Wandlyn Inn
PO Box 275
Amherst, NS B2H 3Z2
902-667-3331

Comfort Inn Amherst
143 S. Albion St.
Amherst, NS B4H 2X2
902-667-0404

Maritime Inn Antigonish
158 Main St.
Antigonish, NS B2G 2B7
902-863-4001

Silver Dart Lodge
PO Box 399
Baddeck, NS B0E 1B0
902-295-2340

Coastal Inn Esquire
771 Bedford Hwy.
Bedford, NS B4A 1EG
902-465-7777

The Travelers Motel
773 Bedford Hwy.
Bedford, NS B4A 1A4
902-835-3394
RATES: Single $69, double $69.
PET POLICY: No fee, up to 50 lbs.

Grand View Motel
Hwy. 3
Black Point, NS B0J 1B0
902-857-9776

Bridgetown Motor Inn
396 Granville St.
Bridgetown, NS B0S 1C0
902-665-4403

Auberge Wandlyn Inn
50 North St.
Bridgewater, NS B0S 1C0
902-543-7131

Canadian Lodgings > NOVA SCOTIA

Comfort Inn Bridgewater
49 North St.
Bridgewater, NS B4V 2V7
902-543-1498

Windjammer Motel
4070 Route 3
Chester, NS B0J 1J0
902-275-3567
RATES: Single $60, double $65.
PET POLICY: No fee, all sizes
welcome.
AMENITIES: Large yard.
POI: Peggy Cove.

Laurie's Motor Inn
Main St.
Cheticamp, NS B0E 1H0
902-224-2400

Park View Motel Limited
PO Box 117
Cheticamp, NS B0E 1H0
902-224-3232

Le Manoir Samson Inn
1768 Route 1
Church Point, NS B0W 1M0
902-769-2526

Best Western Mic Mac Hotel
313 Prince Albert Rd.
Dartmouth, NS B2Y 1N3
902-469-5850

Comfort Inn Dartmouth
456 Windmill Rd.
Dartmouth, NS B3A 1J7
902-463-9900

**Country Inn & Suites by
Carlson**
1 Yorkshire Ave.
Dartmouth, NS B3A 1J7
902-465-4000

Future Inns
20 Highfield Park Dr.
Dartmouth, NS B3A 3S8
902-465-6555

Holiday Inn
99 Wyse Rd.
Dartmouth, NS B3A 1L9
902-463-1100
PET POLICY: No fee.

Keddy's Dartmouth Inn
9 Braemar Dr.
Dartmouth, NS B2Y 3H6
902-469-0331

Ramada Plaza Hotel
240 Brownlow Ave.
Dartmouth, NS B3B 1X6
902-468-8888

Admiral Digby Inn
441 Shore Rd.
Digby, NS B0V 1A0
902-245-2531

Markland Coastal Resort
802 Dingwall Rd.
Dingwall, NS B0C 1G0
902-383-2246

MacLellans Cottages
RR I
Economy, NS B0M 1J0
902-647-2209

**Inn at the Vinyard
Bed & Breakfast**
264 Old Post Rd.
Grand Pre, NS B0P 1M0
902-542-9554

Chebucto Inn
6151 Lady Hammond Rd.
Halifax, NS B3K 2R9
902-453-4330

Citadel Halifax Hotel
1960 Brunswick St.
Halifax, NS B3J 2G7
902-422-1391

Days Inn Halifax
636 Bedford Hwy.
Halifax, NS B3M 2L8
902-443-3171

Delta Barrington
1875 Barrington St.
Halifax, NS B3J 3L6
902-429-7410

Delta Halifax
1990 Barrington St.
Halifax, NS B3J 1P2
902-425-6700

Econo Lodge Halifax
560 Bedford Hwy.
Halifax, NS B3M 2L8
902-443-0303

Holiday Inn Express
133 Kearney Lake Rd.
Halifax, NS B3M 4P3
902-445-1100

RATES: Single $99, double $119.
PET POLICY: No fee, up to 50
lbs. Pets must be attended to
at all times.
AMENITIES: Dog treats.
POI: Peggy's Cove, 45 kilometres
away.

Holiday Inn Select
1980 Robie St.
Halifax, NS B3H 3G5
902-423-1161
PET POLICY: No fee.

Prince George Hotel
1725 Market St.
Halifax, NS B3J 3N9
902-425-1986

Sheraton Halifax Hotel
1919 Upper Water St.
Halifax, NS B3J 3J5
902-421-1700

Wandlyn Inn Halifax
50 Bedford Hwy.
Halifax, NS B3M 2J2
902-443-0416

Seascape Cottages
Ferry Rd.
Heatherton, NS B0H 1R0
902-386-2825

Keltic Lodge
Middle Head Peninsula
Ingonish Beach, NS B0C 1L0
902-285-2880

Allen's Motel
384 Park St.
Kentville, NS B3N 1M9
902-678-2683

Auberge Wandlyn Inn
3230 Hwy. 1
Kentville, NS B3R 1B9
902-678-8311

Sun Valley Motel
905 Park St.
Kentville, NS B3N 3V7
902-678-7368

Liscombe Lodge
Guysborough County
Liscomb, NS B0J 2A0
902-779-2307

Boscawen Inn
150 Cumberland St.
Lunenburg, NS B0J 2C0
902-634-3325

Canadian Lodgings > NOVA SCOTIA

Homeport Motel & Inn
167 Victoria Rd.
Lunenburg, NS B0J 2C0
902-634-8234

Bayview Pines Country Inn
678 Oakland Rd.
Mahone Bay, NS B0J 2E0
902-624-9970
RATES: Single Can. $80, double
Can. $85.
PET POLICY: No fee. All pets
welcome, up to 50 lbs.

Ocean Trail Retreat
RR1
Mahone Bay, NS B0J 2E0
902-624-8824

The Normaway Inn
691 Egypt Rd.
Margaree Valley, NS B0E 2C0
902-248-2987

Cape View Motel & Cottages
PO Box 9, Almon River
Mavillette, NS B0W 2Y0
902-645-2258

Comfort Inn New Glasgow
740 Westville Rd.
New Glasgow, NS B2H 2J8
902-755-6450

**Country Inn & Suites by
Carlson**
700 Westville Rd.
New Glasgow, NS B2H 2J8
902-928-1333

Clansman Motel
PO Box 216
North Sydney, NS B2A 3M3
902-794-7226
RATES: Single $80, double $90.
PET POLICY: No fee, pets
accepted up to 50 lbs.
POI: Lots of room to walk.
Wooded area.

**Marquis of Dufferin
Seaside Inn**
RR 1
Port Dufferin, NS B0J 2R0
902-654-2696

**Cove Motel & Mariner
Dining Room**
PO Box 119
Port Hastings, NS B0E 2T0
902-747-2700

Keddy's Inn
PO Box 50
Port Hastings, NS B0E 2T0
902-625-0460

**MacPuffin Motel
Wandlyn Inn**
PO Box 558
Port Hastings, NS B0E 2V0
902-625-0621

**Maritime Inn Port
Hawkesbury**
717 Reeves St.
Port Hawkesbury, NS B0E
2V0
902-625-0320

Stonehame Chalets
RR 3
Scotsburn, NS B0K 1R0
902-485-3468

**MacKenzie's Motel &
Cottages**
260 Water St.
Shelburne, NS B0T 1W0
902-875-2842

Mountain Gap Resort
PO Box 504
Smiths Cover, NS B0V 1A0
902-245-5841

Comfort Inn Sydney
368 Kings Rd.
Sydney, NS B1S 1A8
902-562-0200

Delta Sydney
300 Esplanade
Sydney, NS B1P 1A7
902-562-7500

Sydney Days Inn
480 Kings Rd.
Sydney, NS B1S 1A8
902-539-6750

Gowrie House Country Inn
139 Shore Rd.
Sydney Mines, NS B1V 1A6
902-544-1050

**Best Western Glengarry
Trade & Convention Centre**
150 Willow St.
Truro, NS B2N 4Z6
902-893-4311

Comfort Inn Truro
12 Meadow Dr.
Truro, NS B2N 5V4
902-893-0330

Keddy's Inn
437 Prince St.
Truro, NS B2N 1E6
902-895-1651

Palliser Resort
Tidal Bore Rd.
Truro, NS B2N 5G6
902-893-8951

Tidal Bore Inn
29 Truro Heights Rd.
Truro, NS B2N 5A9
902-895-9241

Best Western Mermaid Motel
545 Main St.
Yarmouth, NS B5A 1J6
902-742-7821

Capri Motel
8-12 Herbert St.
Yarmouth, NS B5A 1J6
902-742-7168

Comfort Inn Yarmouth
96 Starrs Rd.
Yarmouth, NS B5A 2T5
902-742-1119

Lakelawn Motel
641 Main St.
Yarmouth, NS B5A1K2
902-742-3588
RATES: Single $59, double $79.
PET POLICY: No fee. Small pets
only.

Rodd Colony Harbour Inn
Hawthorne St.
Yarmouth, NS B5A 3K7
902-742-9194

**Rodd Grand Hotel Conv
Ctr**
417 Main St.
Yarmouth, NS B5A 4B2
902-742-2446

NORTHWEST TERRITORIES

Iglu Hotel
Box 179
Baker Lake, NT X0C 0A0
819-793-2801

Canadian Lodgings > ONTARIO

Snowshoe Inn
PO Box 1000
Fort Providence, NT X0E 0L0
867-699-3511
RATES: Single $95, double $115.
PET POLICY: Fee $50 refundable.
All sizes and all pets welcome.

Arctic Char Inn
General Delivery
Holman, NT X0E 0S0
403-396-3531

Navigator Inn
PO Box 158
Iqaluit, NT X0A 0H0
819-979-6201

Rayuka Inn
Box 308
Norman Wells, NT X0E 0V0
403-587-2354

Yellowknife Inn
PO Box 490
Yellowknife, NT X1A 2N4
403-873-2601

ONTARIO

Trapper Jack's Motel
Box 105
Algoma Mills, ON P0R 1A0
705-849-2341

Red Pine Motor Inn
497 Victoria St. E.
Alliston, ON L0M 1A0
705-435-4381

Angus Village Motel
174 Mill St.
Angus, ON L0M 1B0
705-424-6362

Jack's Lake Lodge
Box 690
Apsley, ON K0L 1A0
705-656-4291

Gull Lake Cottages
RR 1
Arden, ON K0H 1B0
613-336-2341

Rock Glen Motel
Box 217, RR 1, Hwy. 7
Arkona, ON N0M 1B0
519-828-3838

Cedar Cover Park
Box 158
Arnprior, ON K7S 3H4
613-623-3133

Twin Maples Motel
175 Daniel St. S.
Arnprior, ON K1S 2L9
613-623-4271

Vacation Inn
70 Madawaska Blvd.
Arnprior, ON K7S 1S5
613-623-7991

The Pines Motel
RR 11
Atikoikan, ON P0T 1C0
807-597-6767

Indiaonta Resort
Box 1289
Atikokan, ON P0T 1C0
807-947-2581

Radisson Motel
310 Mackenzie Ave. E.
Atikokan, ON P0T 1C0
807-597-2766

White Otter Inn
710 Mackenzie Ave. E.
Atikokan, ON P0T 1C0
807-597-2747

Elm Motel
530 Talbot St. E.
Aylmer, ON N5H 2W2
519-773-8136

Mayes Family Cottages
Box 10, RR 1
Baileboro, ON K0L 1B0
705-939-6490

**Best Western Sword
Motor Inn**
146 Hastings St.
Bancroft, ON K0L 1C0
613-332-2474
RATES: Single $100, double $100.
PET POLICY: No fee, up to 25
lbs., do not leave pets in room
unattended.
AMENITIES: Large exercise area.

Somerset Inn
RR 3
Bancroft, ON K0L 1C0
613-339-3100

Barrie Huronia Motel
240 Bradford St.
Barrie, ON L4N 3B6
705-728-3340

Best Western Royal Oak Inn
35 Hart Dr.
Barrie, ON L4N 5M3
605-721-4848

Comfort Inn Barrie
75 Hart Dr.
Barrie, ON L4N 5M3
705-722-3600

Lake Simcoe Motel
114 Blake St.
Barrie, ON L4M 1K3
705-728-3704

Travelodge
55 Hart Dr.
Barrie, ON L4M 3B9
705-734-9500

Travelodge
300 Bayfield St.
Barrie, ON L4N 5M3
705-722-4466

Mountain View Motel
RR 1, Box 101
Barry's Bay, ON K0J 1B0
613-756-2757

The Little Inn of Bayfield
Main St.
Bayfield, ON N0M 1G0
519-565-2611

Crestwind Hotel
Box 149
Beardmore, ON P0T 1G0
807-875-2132

Green Acres Motel
Box 426
Belle River, ON N0R 1A0
519-727-6102

Best Western Bellevile
387 N. Front St.
Belleville, ON K8P 3C8
613-969-1112

Casa Marina
RR 1
Belleville, ON K8N 4Z1
613-962-5790

Canadian Lodgings > ONTARIO

Comfort Inn Belleville
200 N. Park St.
Belleville, ON K8P 2Y9
613-966-7703

Quality Inn Belleville
407 N. Front St.
Belleville, ON K8P 3C8
613-962-9211

Ramada Inn on the Bay & Conference Resort
11 Bay Bridge Rd.
Belleville, ON K8P 3P6
613-968-3411

Voyager Motor Inn
RR 5
Belleville, ON K8N 4Z5
613-962-8641

Queen's Motel
RR 1
Blenheim, ON N0P 1A0
519-676-5477

Auberge Eldo Inn
Box 156
Blind River, ON P0R 1B0
705-356-2255

Friendship Inn
181 Causley St., Hwy. 1
Blind River, ON P0R 1B0
705-356-2249

MacIver's Missisaugua Motel
Box 502
Blind River, ON P0R 1B0
705-356-7441

Old Mill Motel
Hwy. 17 & Woodward
Blind River, ON P0R 1B0
705-356-2274

Bloomfield Inn
29 Stanley St. W.
Bloomfield, ON K0K 1G0
613-393-3301

Keewanee Lodge Motel
RR 1
Bobcaygeon, ON K0M 1A0
705-738-2878

Riverside Lodge
84 Front St. E.
Bobcaygeon, ON K0M 1A0
705-738-2193

Sunnyside Camp
Box 53
Bonfield, ON P0H 1E0
705-776-2401

Bellwood Motel
133 Manitoba St.
Bracebridge, ON P1L 1S3
705-645-4424

Islander Inn
320 Taylor Rd.
Bracebridge, ON P1L 1K1
705-645-2235

Comfort Inn Brampton
5 Rutherford Rd. S.
Brampton, ON L6W 3J3
905-452-0600

Holiday Inn Select
30 Peel Centre Dr.
Brampton, ON L6T 4G3
905-792-9900
PET POLICY: No fee.

Welcominn
30 Clark Blvd.
Brampton, ON L6W 1X3
416-454-1300

Bell City Motel
901 Colborne St. E.
Brantford, ON N3S 3T3
519-756-5236

Best Western Brant Park Inn & Conference Centre
19 Holiday Dr.
Brantford, ON N3T 5W5
519-753-8651

Brantford-Days Inn
460 Fairview Dr.
Brantford, ON N3R 7A9
519-759-2700

Comfort Inn Brantford
58 King George Rd.
Brantford, ON N3R 5K4
519-753-3100

Harbourview Motel & marina
Box 1719
Brighton, ON K0K 1H0
613-475-1515

Presqu'ile Beach Motel
243 Main St. W.
Brighton, ON K0K 1H0
613-475-1010
RATES: Single $51, double $59.
PET POLICY: No fee, all sizes welcome.

Britt Motor Inn
RR 1
Britt, ON P0G 1A0
705-383-2343

M & R Motel
Box 144
Britt, ON P0G 1A0
705-383-2491

Comfort Inn Brockville
7777 Kent Blvd.
Brockville, ON K6V 6N7
613-345-0042

Seaway Motel
Box 11, RR 1
Brockville, ON K6V 5T1
613-342-1357

Bavarian Inn
49 Taylor St.
Bruce Mines, ON P0R 1C0
705-785-3447

Russ Haven Resort
Pickerel Lake Rd.
Burks Falls, ON P0A 1C0
705-382-2027

Comfort Inn Burlington
3290 S. Service Rd.
Burlington, ON L7N 3M6
905-639-1700

Crestwood Motel
527 Plains Rd. E.
Burlington, ON L7T 2E2
416-634-6119

Holiday Inn
3063 S. Service Rd.
Burlington, ON L7N 3E9
905-639-4443
PET POLICY: No fee.

Town & Country Motel
517 Plains Rd. E.
Burlington, ON L7T 2E2
905-634-2383

Canadian Lodgings > ONTARIO

Travelodge
2020 Lakeshore Rd.
Burlington, ON L7R 3B9
905-681-0762

Barryvale Lodge
RR 2
Calabogie, ON K0J 1H0
613-752-2392

Jocko's Beach Motel
RR 3
Calabogie, ON K0J 1H0
613-752-2107

Cambridge-Days Inn
650 Hespeler Rd.
Cambridge, ON N1R 6J8
519-622-1070

Comfort Inn Cambridge
220 Holiday Inn Dr.
Cambridge, ON N3C 1Z4
519-658-1100

Holiday Inn
200 Holiday Inn Dr.
Cambridge, ON N3C 1Z4
519-658-4601
PET POLICY: No fee.

**Langdon Hall Country
House Hotel & Spa**
RR 33
Cambridge, ON N3H 4R8
519-740-2100

Motel Riviera
352 Front St. N.
Campbellford, ON K0L 1L0
705-653-1771

Trent House Motel
149 Queen St. N.
Campbellford, ON K0L 1 L0
705-653-2190

McKee's Camp
Box 1113
Capreol, ON P0M 1H0
705-858-3529

Cedars Motel
RR 2
Carleton Pl., ON K7C 3P2
613-257-2047

Alford's Bed & Breakfast
Box 17
Chaffey's Locks, ON K0G 1E0
613-359-1173

Riverside Motel
116 Cherry St.
Chapeau, ON P0M 1K0
705-864-0440

Motel Chapeau
72 Cedar St.
Chapeau, ON P0M 1K-0
705-864-0290

Chatham Motel
659 Grand Ave. E.
Chatham, ON N7L 1X6
519-352-4670

Comfort Inn Chatham
1100 Richmond St.
Chatham, ON N7M 5J5
519-352-5500

Flamingo Motel
421 Grand Ave. E.
Chatham, ON N7L 1X4
519-354-5130

Kent Motel
420 Grand Ave. E.
Chatham, ON N7L 1X2
519-352-9222

Luxury Inn
25 Michener Rd.
Chatham, ON N7L 4B8
519-354-3366

Rainbow Motel
RR 1
Chatham, ON N7M 5J1
519-351-6610

Travellers Motel
RR 5
Chatham, ON N7M 5J5
519-351-3874

Key Motel
RR 3
Chatsworth, ON N0H 1G0
519-794-2350

Tudor Lodge Motel
1665 London Rd.
Clearwater, ON N7T 7H2
519-542-7716

Cloyne Motor Inn
Box 130
Cloyne, ON K0H 1K0
613-336-8779

Marle Lake Lodge
RR 2
Cloyne, ON K0H 1K0
613-336-2213

Best Western Cobourg Inn
930 Burnham St.
Cobourg, ON K9A 2X9
905-372-2105
RATES: Call for rates.
PET POLICY: No fee, pets up to
50 lbs. Do not leave pets in
room unattended.
POI: Next to large conservation
area (Rotary Park) and on
Cobourg Trail.

Comfort Inn Cobourg
121 Densmore Rd.
Cobourg, ON K9A 4J9
905-372-7007

Hillside Motel
Box 351
Cobourg, ON K9A 4K8
905-372-2158

**Northumberland Heights
Country Inn**
RR 5
Cobourg, ON K9A 4J8
905-372-7500

Tom's Motel
428 King St. E.
Cobourg, ON K9A 1M6
905-372-9421

Chimo Motel
Box 2336
Cochrane, ON P0L 1C0
705-272-6555

Golden Gate Motel
Box 1930
Cochrane, ON P0L 1C0
705-272-5498

**Northern Lites Motel
& Restaurant**
PO Box 1720
Cochrane, ON P0L 1C0
705-272-4281

Island View Cottages
Box 170
Coe Hill, ON K0L 1P0
613-337-5533

Severn Falls Motel
Box 315, RR 1
Coldwater, ON L0K 1E0
705-686-7955

Canadian Lodgings > ONTARIO

Best Western Collingwood
1 Basalm St.
Collingwood, ON L94 3J4
705-444-2144
PET POLICY: No fee, all sizes
welcome. Do not leave pets in
room unattended.

Blue Mountain Auberge
138 Happy Valley Rd.
Collingwood, ON L9Y 3Z2
705-445-1497
RATES: Single $79.95, double
$99.95.
AMENITIES: No traffic, pets can
run.

Blue Mountain Motel
Box 2152, RR 2
Collingwood, ON L9Y 3Z1
705-445-1146

Mariner Motor Hotel
305 Hume St.
Collingwood, ON L9Y 1W2
705-445-3330

Moore's Motel
RR 3
Collingwood, ON L9Y 3Z2
705-445-2478

Sea & Ski motel
530 First St.
Collingwood, ON L9Y 1C1
705-445-9422

Thriftlodge Collingwood
RR #3 Hwy. 26 W
Collingwood, ON L9Y 3Z2
705-445-1674
RATES: Single $80, double $100.
PET POLICY: Fee $5 per night,
nonrefundable. Smoking
rooms only. Do not leave pets
unattended in rooms.
AMENITIES: Large grassy, treed
walking area.
POI: Blue Mountain skiing,
Wasaga beach, Georgian trails,
walking, hiking, biking.

Sand Bay Camp
RR 2
Combermere, ON K0J 1L0
613-756-5060

Black Forest Inn
26 King St.
Conestogo, ON N0B 1N0
519-664-2223

Birch Hill Camp
Box 118
Corbeil, ON P0H 1K0
705-752-1273
PET POLICY: No fee. All pets
accepted.

**Best Western Parkway Inn
& Conference Centre**
1515 Vincent Massey Dr.
Cornwall, ON K6H 5R6
613-932-0451

Holiday Inn Express
1625 Vincent Massey Dr.
Cornwall, ON K6H 5R6
613-937-0111
PET POLICY: No fee.

**Radisson Hotel Toronto
East-Don Valley**
1250 Eglinton
Don Mills, ON M3C 1J3
416-449-4111

White Towers Motel
120 Donald St., ON L4N 5G7
705-726-0208

**Montecassino Place Suites
Hotel**
3710 Chesswood Dr.
Downsview, ON M3J2W4
416-630-8100

Best Western Motor Inn
349 Government Rd.
Dryden, ON P8N 2Z5
807-223-3201
RATES: Single $70, double $80.
PET POLICY: No fee, all sizes
welcome. Pets must be quiet.
AMENITIES: Large running field
behind hotel.

Comfort Inn Dryden
522 Government Rd.
Dryden, ON P8N 2P5
807-223-3893

Clear Lake Inn
955 Hwy. 6 S.
Espanola, ON P5E 1N9
705-869-1748

Lake Aspey Resort
300 Lake Aspey Rd.
Espanola, ON P5E 1T1
800-559-6583

Holiday Inn Select
970 Dixon Rd.
Etobicoke, ON M9W 1J9
416-675-7611
PET POLICY: No fee.

Travelodge
445 Rexdale Blvd.
Etobicoke, ON M9W 6K5
416-740-9500

Hipwell's Motel
299 Hwy. 20W
Fonthill, ON L0S 1E0
905-892-3588

Comfort Inn Fort Erie
1 Hospitality Dr.
Fort Erie, ON L2A 6G1
905-871-8500

**YesterDays Resort &
Conference Centre**
Hwy. 607A, Box 100
French River, ON P0M 1A0
705-857-3383

The 1000 Islands Motel
550 King St. E.
Gananoque, ON K7G 1H2
613-382-3911

The Colonial Resort
780 King St. W.
Gananoque, ON K7G 2H5
613-382-8390

Sunny Point Cottages
Rosseau Rd.
Georgian Bay, ON P0C 1K0
705-378-2505

Chimo Hotel
1199 Joseph Cyr St.
Gloucester, ON K1J 7T4
613-744-1060

Comfort Inn
1252 Michael St.
Gloucester, ON K1J 7T1
613-744-2900

Travelodge
1486 Innes Rd.
Gloucester, ON K1B 3V5
613-745-1133

The Victoria Inn
5316 Harwood Rd.
Gores Landing, ON K0K 2E0
905-342-3261

Canadian Lodgings > ONTARIO

Howard Johnson Inn
1165 Muskoka Rd. S.
Gravenhurst, ON P1P 1K6
705-687-7707

Howard Johnson Inn & Suites
4 Windward Dr.
Grimsby, ON L3M 1Y6
905-309-7171

Best Western Emerald Inn - Guelph
106 Carden St.
Guelph, ON N1H 3A3
519-836-1331

Comfort Inn Guelph
480 Silvercreek Pkwy.
Guelph, ON N1H 7R5
519-763-1900

Guelph Super 8 Motel
281 Woodlawn Rd. W.
Guelph, ON N1H 7K7
519-836-5850

Guelph-Days Inn
785 Gordon St.
Guelph, ON N1G 1Y8
519-822-9112

Holiday Inn
601 Scottsdale Dr.
Guelph, ON N1G 3E7
519-836-0231
PET POLICY: No fee.

Howard Johnson Plaza Hotel
112 King St. E.
Hamilton, ON L8N 1A8
905-546-8111

Ramada Plaza Hotel
150 King St. E.
Hamilton, ON L8N 1B2
905-528-3451

Sheraton Hamilton
116 King St. W.
Hamilton, ON L8P 4V3
905-529-5515

Highland Court
208 W. Main St.
Huntsville, ON P1H 1Y1
705-789-4424

Tulip Inn
211 Arrowhead Park Rd.
Huntsville, ON P1H 2J4
705-789-4001
RATES: Single $74.95, double $84.95.
PET POLICY: No fee, all sizes welcome.
AMENITIES: 11 acres of woodland.
POI: River/beach on site. Arrowhead park next door.

Travelodge
20 Samnah Crescent
Ingersoll, ON N5C 3J7
519-425-1100

Estok Motor Inn
Hwy. 17
Iron Bridge, ON P0R 1H0
705-843-2100

Travelodge
Hwy. 17 E.
Iron Bridge, ON P0R 1H0
705-843-0262

McAuley Motel
RR 3
Johnstown, ON K0E 1T0
613-925-3076

Comfort Inn Kapuskasing
172 Government Rd. E.
Kapuskasing, ON P5N 2W9
705-335-8583

Comfort Inn Kenora
1230 Hwy. 17 E.
Kenora, ON P9N 1L9
807-468-8845

Travelodge
800 Sunset Strip (Hwy. 17 E.)
Kenora, ON P9N 1L9
807-468-3155

Whispering Pines Motel
Longbow Lake Post Office
Kenora, ON P0X 1H0
807-548-4025

Comfort Inn Hwy. 401
55 Warne Crescent
Kingston, ON K7L 4V4
613-546-9500

Comfort Inn Midtown
1454 Princess St. (Hwy. 2)
Kingston, ON K7M 3E5
613-549-5550

Holiday Inn
1 Princess St.
Kingston, ON K7L 1A1
613-549-8400
PET POLICY: No fee.

Howard Johnson Confederation Place Hotel
237 Ontario St.
Kingston, ON K7L 2Z4
613-549-6300
RATES: Single $99, double $139.
PET POLICY: No fee, all sizes and all pets welcome.
AMENITIES: Grassy area for walking pets.

Strathview Bed & Breakfast
3651 Moreland-Dixon Rd.
Kingston, ON K0H 1X0
613-353-6355

The Executive Motel
794 Hwy. 2 E.
Kingston, ON K7L 4V1
613-549-1620

Comfort Inn Kirkland Lake
455 Government Rd. W.
Kirkland Lake, ON P0K 1A0
705-567-4909

Comfort Inn Kitchener
2899 King St. E.
Kitchener, ON N2A 1A6
519-894-3500

Four Points Hotel Kitchener
105 King St. E.
Kitchener, ON N2G 2K8
519-744-4141

Holiday Inn
30 Fairway Rd.
Kitchener, ON N2A 2N2
519-893-1211
PET POLICY: No fee.

Howard Johnson Hotel
133 Weber St.
Kitchener, ON N2A 1C2
519-893-1234

Rodeway Suites Conestoga
55 New Dundee Rd.
Kitchener, ON N2G 3W5
519-895-2272

Canadian Lodgings > ONTARIO

**Lake Edge Cottages
Bed & Breakfast**
45 Lake Edge Rd, RR #4
Lakefield, ON K0L 2H0
705-652-9080
RATES: Single $95, double $110.
PET POLICY: No fee, all sizes,
dogs, cats and birds welcome.
AMENITIES: Dog/cat-sitting
available with advance notice.
Student will meet your pet
and sit with it in your cottage
while you are absent. Hourly
charge for this service.

Comfort Inn Leamington
279 Erie St. S.
Leamington, ON N8H 3C4
519-326-9071

Sun Parlor Motel
135 Talbot St. W.
Leamington, ON N8H 1N2
519-326-6131

Wigle's Colonial Motel
133 Talbot St. E.
Leamington, ON N8H 1L6
519-326-3265

**Best Western Lamplighter
Inn**
591 Wellington Rd. S.
London, ON N6C 4R3
519-681-7151

Comfort Hotel Downtown
374 Dundas St.
London, ON N6B 1V7
519-661-0233

Comfort Inn London
1156 Wellington Rd.
London, ON N6E 1M3
519-685-9300

**Delta London Armouries
Hotel**
325 Dundas St.
London, ON N6B 1T9
519-679-6111

Four Points Hotel London
1150 Wellington Rd. S.
London, ON N6E 1M3
519-681-0600

Hilton London Ontario
300 King St.
London, ON N6B1S2
519-439-1661

Howard Johnson Inn
1170 Wellington Rd. S.
London, ON N6E 1M3
519-681-1550

Quality Suites Suites
1120 Dearness Dr.
London, ON N6E 1N9
519-680-1024

Station Park Inn
242 Pall Mall St.
London, ON N6A5P6
519-642-4444

Colonial Inn Motel
Hwy. 7
Madoc, ON K0K 2K0
613-473-2221

Peninsula Inn
PO Box 597
Marathon, ON P0T 2E0
807-229-0651

Comfort Inn Northeast
8330 Woodbine Ave.
Markham, ON L3R 2N8
905-477-6077

Mohawk Motel
335 Sauble St.
Massey, ON P0P 1P0
705-865-2722

Comfort Inn Airport West
1500 Matheson Blvd. At Dixie
Mississauga, ON L4W 3Z4
905-624-6900

**Delta Meadowvale Resort
& Conference Centre**
6750 Mississauga Rd.
Mississauga, ON L5N 2L3
905-821-1981

Dodge Suites Hotel
5050 Orbitor Dr.
Mississauga, ON L4W 4X2
905-238-9600

**Four Points Hotel Toronto
Airport**
5444 Dixie Rd.
Mississauga, ON L4W 2L2
905-624-1144

Holiday Inn
100 Britannia Rd. E.
Mississauga, ON L4Z 2G1
905-890-5700
PET POLICY: No fee.

Novotel Hotel Mississauga
3670 Hurontario St.
Mississauga, ON L5B 1P3
905-896-1000

**Radisson Hotel Toronto-
Mississauga**
2501 Argentia Rd.
Mississauga, ON L5N 4G8
905-858-2424

**Sheraton Gateway in
Toronto International
Airport**
Box 3000
Mississauga, ON L5P 1C4
905-672-7000

Toronto Airport Hilton
5875 Airport Rd.
Mississauga, ON L4V 1N1
905-677-9900

**Toronto-Days Inn
Mississauga**
4635 Tomken Rd.
Mississauga, ON L4W 1J9
905-238-5480

Memquisit Lodge Inc.
RR 1
Monetville, ON P0M 2K0
705-898-2355

**Mount Hope
Super 8 Motel**
2975 Homestead Dr.
Mount Hope, ON L0R 1W0
905-679-3355

Monterey Inn
2259 Hwy. 16
Nepean, ON K2E 6Z8
613-226-5813

Rideau Heights Motor Inn
72 Rideau Heights Dr.
Nepean, ON K2E 7A6
613-226-4152

The Luxor Hotel
350 Moodie Dr.
Nepean, ON K2H 8G3
613-726-1717

Comfort Inn Newmarket
1230 Journey's End Cir.
Newmarket, ON L3Y 7V1
905-895-3355

Canadian Lodgings > ONTARIO

Ashbury Motel
7800 Lundy's Ln.
Niagara Falls, ON L2H 1H1
416-356-8280

Aston Villa Motel
7939 Lundy's Ln.
Niagara Falls, ON L2H 1H3
416-357-3535

**Best Western Fallsview
Motor Hotel**
5551 Murray St.
Niagara Falls, ON L2G 2J4
905-356-0551
PET POLICY: No fee, all sizes
welcome.

Caravan Motel
8511 Lundy's Ln.
Niagara Falls, ON L2H 1H5
416-357-1104

Clarion Old Stone Inn
5425 Robinson St.
Niagara Falls, ON L2G 7L6
416-357-1234

Comfort Inn
5640 Stanley Ave.
Niagara Falls, ON L2G 3X5
800-221-2222

**Comfort Inn
North of the Falls**
4009 River Rd.
Niagara Falls, ON L2E 3E9
905-356-0131

Continental Inn
5756 Ferry St.
Niagara Falls, ON L2G 1S7
416-356-2449

Days Inn Fallsview District
6408 Stanley Ave.
Niagara Falls, ON L2G 3Y5
905-356-5877

Diplomat Inn
5983 Stanley Ave.
Niagara Falls, ON L2G 3Y2
416-357-9564

Edgecliff Motel
4615 Cataract Ave.
Niagara Falls, ON L2E 3M3
416-354-1688

Empire Motel
5046 Centre St.
Niagara Falls, ON L2G 3N9
416-357-2550

Falls Manor Motel
7104 Lundy's Ln.
Niagara Falls, ON L2G 1W2
416-358-3211

Flamingo Motor Inn
7701 Lundyu's Ln.
Niagara Falls, ON L2H 1H3
905-356-4646

Glengate Motel
5534 Stanley Ave.
Niagara Falls, ON L2G 3X2
905-357-1333

Inn on the Hill
5785 Ferry St.
Niagara Falls, ON L2G 1S8
416-358-3559

La Riviera Motel
5427 Ferry St.
Niagara Falls, ON L2G 1S2
416-356-0211

Mayside Motel
5450 Kitchener St.
Niagara Falls, ON L2G 1B8
416-358-7844

Melody Motel
13065 Lundy's Ln.
Niagara Falls, ON L2E 6S4
416-227-1023

**Niagara Parkway Court
Motel**
3708 Main St.
Niagara Falls, ON L2G 6B1
905-295-3331

Rodeway Inn & Suites
7720 Lundy's Ln.
Niagara Falls, ON L2H 1H1
905-358-9833

Sunset Inn
5803 Stanley Ave.
Niagara Falls, ON L2G 3X8
905-354-7513

Universal Inn
6000 Stanley Ave.
Niagara Falls, ON L2G 3Y1
905-358-6243
PET POLICY: Fee $10, refund-
able, up to 50 lbs.

Best Western North Bay
700 Lakeshore Dr.
North Bay, ON P1A 2G4
705-474-5800

Comfort Inn Hwy. 17
1200 O'Brien St.
North Bay, ON P1B 9B3
705-476-5400

Comfort Inn South
676 Lakeshore Dr.
North Bay, ON P1A 2G4
705-494-9444

Travelodge
718 Lakeshore Dr.
North Bay, ON P1B 8G4
705-472-7171

Travelodge
1525 Seymour St.
North Bay, ON P1A 2G4
705-495-1133

**Quality Hotel & Executive
Suites**
754 Bronte Rd.
Oakville, ON L6J 4Z3
905-847-6667

Comfort Inn Orillia
75 Progress Dr.
Orillia, ON L3V 6H1
705-327-7744

Travelodge
600 Sundial Dr.
Orillia, ON L3V 6N3
705-325-2233

Comfort Inn Oshawa
605 Bloor St. W.
Oshawa, ON L1J 5Y6
905-434-5000

Holiday Inn
1011 Bloor St. E.
Oshawa, ON L1H 7K6
905-576-5101
PET POLICY: No fee.

Days Inn - Downtown
319 Rideau St.
Ottawa, ON K1N5Y4
613-789-5555
RATES: Single $105, double $115.
PET POLICY: No fee, all sizes
welcome.
POI: Nearby parks.

Canadian Lodgings > ONTARIO

Delta Ottawa Hotel & Suites
361 Queen St.
Ottawa, ON K1R 7S9
613-238-6000

Howard Johnson Hotel
140 Slater St.
Ottawa, ON K1P 5H6
613-238-2888

Le Chateau Laurier
1 Rideau St.
Ottawa, ON K1N 8S7
613-241-1414

Les Suites Hotel
130 Besserer St.
Ottawa, ON K1N 9M9
613-232-2000

Lord Elgin Hotel
100 Elgin St.
Ottawa, ON K1P 5K8
613-235-3333
RATES: Single $115, double $125.
PET POLICY: No fee, pets up to
50 lbs.

Marriott Ottawa
100 Kent St.
Ottawa, ON K1P 5R7
613-238-1122

**Natural Choice Vegetarian
B&B & Spa**
263 Mcleod St.
Ottawa, ON K2P 1A1
613-563-4399
RATES: Single $85+
PET POLICY: No fee, all sizes
welcome, please call first.
AMENITIES: Dog park across street.
POI: Museum of Nature, Rideau
Canal, restaurants, shops.

Novotel Ottawa
33 Nicholas St.
Ottawa, ON K1N 9M7
613-230-3033

Quality Hotel Downtown
290 Rideau St.
Ottawa, ON K1N 5Y3
613-789-7511

Ramada Hotel & Suites
111 Cooper St.
Ottawa, ON K2P 2E3
613-238-1331

Sheraton Ottawa Hotel
150 Albert St.
Ottawa, ON K1P 5G2
613-238-1500

Southway Inn
2431 Bank St.
Ottawa, ON K1V 8R9
613-737-0811

The Westin Ottawa
11 Colonel By Dr.
Ottawa, ON K1N 9H4
613-560-7000

Travelodge
2098 Montreal Rd.
Ottawa, ON K1R 5A7
613-745-1531

Travelodge
402 Queen St.
Ottawa, ON K1R 5A7
613-236-1133

Webb's Motel
1705 Carling Ave.
Ottawa, ON K2A 1C8
613-728-1881

Best Western Inn on the Bay
1800 2nd Ave. E.
Owen Sound, ON N4K 5RI
519-371-9200

Comfort Inn Owen Sound
955 9th Ave. E.
Owen Sound, ON N4K 6N4
519-371-5500

Crystal Motel
672 10th St. W.
Owen Sound, ON N4K 3R9
519-372-2929

**Owen Sound Motor Inn
Econo Lodge**
485 9th Ave. E.
Owen Sound, ON N4K 3E2
519-371-3011

Best Western Georgian Inn
48 Joseph St.
Parry Sound, ON P2A 2G5
705-746-5837

Comfort Inn Parry Sound
120 Bowes St.
Parry Sound, ON P2A 2L7
705-746-6221

Jolly Roger Inn
Hwy. 400
Parry Sound, ON P2A 2W8
705-746-2461

**Maple Leaf Resort &
Cottages**
58 Otter Lake Rd. (RR #2)
Parry Sound, ON P2A 2W8
705-267-2584
RATES: Call for rates.
PET POLICY: No fee, all size dogs
and cats welcome. Pet counts
as person according to maxi-
mum-occupancy rules.
AMENITIES: Pets allowed in lake
and country hiking trails.

Sunny Point Cottages & Inn
Rosseau Rd.
Parry Sound, ON P0C 1K0
705-378-2505
RATES: Cottage single $147,
cottage double $147.
PET POLICY: No fee, all sizes
welcome. Must be kept on
leash.
AMENITIES: Privacy. 100-acre
resort.
POI: Boats, miniputt, kayaks,
canoes, paddle boats, fire-
places, tennis, hot tubs/sauna.

**Best Western Pembroke Inn
& Conference Center**
One International Dr.
Pembroke, ON K8A 6W5
613-735-0131

Comfort Inn Pembroke
959 Pembroke St. E.
Pembroke, ON K8A 3M3
613-735-1057

Comfort Inn Peterborough
1209 Lansdowne St.
Peterborough, ON K9J 7M2
705-740-7000

Holiday Inn
150 George St. N.
Peterborough, ON K9J 3G5
705-743-1144
PET POLICY: No fee.

King Bethune House
270 King St.
Peterborough, ON K9J 2S2
705-743-4101

Canadian Lodgings > ONTARIO

RATES: Single $84, double $104.
PET POLICY: Fee $10 per day, nonrefundable, all sizes welcome.
POI: Trent Severn Waterway, River Park, Peterborough Zoo, Reptile Zoo, Caves, Theatres, dining.

Quality Inn Peterborough
1074 Lansdowne St.
Peterborough, ON K9J 1Z9
705-748-6801

Robyn's Motel
RR 7
Peterborough, ON K6J 6X8
705-745-3225

Comfort Inn Pickering
533 Kingston Rd.
Pickering, ON L1V 3N7
905-831-6200

Ducks Dive Charters & Cottages
RR #3, 5535 Long Pt. Rd.
Picton, ON K0K 2T0
613-476-3764

Merrill Inn
343 Main St. E.
Picton, ON K0K 2T0
613-476-7451

Motel De Champlain
200 Hwy. 17
Plantagenet, ON K0B 1L0
613-673-5220

Colonial Fireside Inn
1350 Pembroke St.
Poembroke, ON K8A 7A3
613-732-2623

Comfort Inn Port Hope
Hwy. 401 & Hwy. 28
Port Hope, ON L1A 3V9
905-885-7000

The Carlyle Inn
86 John St.
Port Hope, ON L1A 2Z2
905-885-8686

Huron Sands Motel
20 Sunova Beach Rd.
Providence Bay, ON P0P 1T0
705-377-4616

The Renfrew Inn
760 Gibbons Rd.
Renfrew, ON K7V 4A2
613-432-8109

Carlingview Airport Inn
221 Carlingview Dr.
Rexdale, ON M9W5E8
416-675-3303

Wyndham Briston Place
950 Dixon Rd.
Rexdale, ON M9W 5N4
416-675-9444

The Clansmen Motel
RR 2
Richards Landing, ON P0R 1J0
705-246-2581

Sheraton Parkway Toronto North Hotel
600 Hwy. 7 E.
Richmond Hill, ON L4B 1B2
905-881-2121

Best Western Guildwood Inn
1400 Venetian Blvd.
Sarnia, ON N7T 7W6
519-337-7577

Drawbridge Inn
283 N. Christina St.
Sarnia, ON N7T5V4
519-337-7571
RATES: Single, double $79–$100.
PET POLICY: No fee, all sizes welcome.
POI: Centenial Park close by. Canatara Park 5–10 minute drive.

Holiday Inn
1498 Venetian Blvd.
Sarnia, ON N7T 7W6
519-336-4130
PET POLICY: No fee.

Travelodge
332 Bay St.
Sault Ste Marie, ON P6A 1X1
705-759-1400

Ambassador Motel
1275 Great Northern Rd.
Sault Ste. Marie, ON P6A 5K7
705-759-6199

Bel-Air Motel
398 Pim St.
Sault Ste. Marie, ON P6B 2V1
705-945-7950

Comfort Inn Sault Ste. Marie
333 Great Northern Rd.
Sault Ste. Marie, ON P6B 4Z8
705-759-8000

Crown Motel
184 Great Northern Rd.
Sault Ste. Marie, ON P6B 4Z3
705-254-6441

Glenview Vacation Cottages
2611 Great Northern Rd.
Sault Ste. Marie, ON P6A 5K7
705-759-3436

Holiday Inn
208 St. Mary's River Dr.
Sault Ste. Marie, ON P6A 5V4
705-949-0611
PET POLICY: No fee.

Holiday Motel
435 Trunk Rd.
Sault Ste. Marie, ON P6A 3T1
705-759-8608

Northlander Motel
243 Great Northern Rd.
Sault Ste. Marie, ON P6B 4Z2
705-254-6452

Ramada Inn & Convention Center
229 Great Northern Rd.
Sault Ste. Marie, ON P6B 4Z2
705-942-2500

Villa Inn Motel
724 Great Northern Motel
Sault Ste. Marie, ON P6B 5A3
705-942-2424

Comfort Inn Simcoe
85 The Queensway E.
Simcoe, ON N3Y 4M5
519-426-2611

Comfort Inn St. Catharines
2 Dunlop Dr.
St. Catharines, ON L2R 1A2
905-687-8890

Holiday Inn
2 N. Service Rd.
St. Catharines, ON L2N 4G9
905-934-8000
PET POLICY: No fee.

Canadian Lodgings > ONTARIO

Howard Johnson Hotel & Conference Center
89 Meadowvale Dr.
St. Catharines, ON L2N 3Z8
905-934-5400

Comfort Inn St. Thomas
100 Centennial Ave.
St. Thomas, ON N5R 5B2
519-633-4082

Comfort Inn Hwy. 17
440 2nd Ave. N.
Sudbury, ON P3B 4A4
705-560-4502

Comfort Inn Hwy. 69
2171 Regent St. S.
Sudbury, ON P3E 5V3
705-522-1101

Days Inn Sudbury
117 Elm St.
Sudbury, ON P3C 1T3
705-674-7517

Howard Johnson Hotel
390 Elgin St. S.
Sudbury, ON P3B 1B4
705-675-1273

Travelodge
1401 Paris St.
Sudbury, ON P3E 3B6
705-522-1100
RATES: Single $100, double $130.
PET POLICY: No fee, all sizes and all pets welcome (dogs, cats, ferrets, birds, rabbits, reptiles). Pets in smoking rooms only on first and second floors.
POI: Bell Park, Nepahwin Beach.

Carolyn Beach Motel
One Lakeside Dr.
Thessalon, ON P0R 1L0
705-842-3330

Best Western Crossroads Motor Inn
655 W. Arthur St.
Thunder Bay, ON P7E 5R6
807-577-4241

Best Western Nor'Wester Hotel & Suites
2080 Hwy. 61
Thunder Bay, ON P7C 4Z2
807-473-9123

Comfort Inn Thunder Bay
660 W. Arthur St.
Thunder Bay, ON P7E 5R8
807-475-3155

Ritz Motel
2600 Arthur St. E.
Thunder Bay, ON P7E 5P4
807-623-8189

Rose Valley Lodge & Restaurant
RR#1, S. Gillies
Thunder Bay, ON P0T 2V0
807-473-5448

Super 8 Motel
439 Memorial Ave.
Thunder Bay, ON P7B 3Y6
807-344-2612

Travelodge
698 Arthur St. W.
Thunder Bay, ON P7B 3Y7
807-473-1600

Travelodge
450 Memorial Ave.
Thunder Bay, ON P7E 5R8
807-345-2343

Victoria Inn
555 W. Arthur St.
Thunder Bay, ON P7E 5RS
807-577-8481

Super 8 Motel-Tillsonburg
92 Simcoe St.
Tillsonburg, ON N4G 2J1
519-842-7366

Comfort Inn Timmins
939 Algonquin Blvd. E.
Timmins, ON P4N 7J5
705-264-9474

Ramada Inn
1800 Riverside Dr.
Timmins, ON P4N 7J5
705-267-6241
RATES: Single $73, double $83.
PET POLICY: No fee. All sizes accepted ("no horses").

Travelodge
1136 Riverside Dr.
Timmins, ON P4R 1A2
705-360-1122

Allenby Guiest House
223 Strathmore Blvd.
Toronto, ON M4J 1P4
416-461-7095

Best Western Toronto Airport-Carlton Place
33 Carlson Ct.
Toronto, ON M9W 6H5
416-675-1234

Cambridge Suite Hotel
15 Richmond St E.
Toronto, ON M5C 1N2
416-368-1990

Comfort Inn
3306 Kingston Rd.
Toronto, ON M1M 1P8
416-269-7400

Comfort Inn
66 Norfinch Dr.
Toronto, ON M3N 1X1
416-736-4700

Crowne Plaza Toronto Don Valley
1250 Eglinton Ave. E
Toronto, ON M3C 1J3
416-449-4111
RATES: Single Can.$129, double Can.$159.
PET POLICY: Fee $25, nonrefundable, dogs and cats only, up to 50 lbs.
AMENITIES: Looking at special menu. Walking trail, located in parklands.
POI: Onterio Science Centre, Metro Zoo, paramount Canada's Wonderland, Toronto beaches.

Delta Chelsea Inn
33 Gerrard Street West
Toronto, ON M5G 1Z4
416-595-1975
PET POLICY: No fee. Small cats and dogs only.

Delta Toronto Airport Hotel
801 Dixon Rd.
Toronto, ON M9W 1J5
416-675-6100
PET POLICY: Fee $50 for 5-day and longer stay. Under 5 days, $50 refundable damage deposit.

Canadian Lodgings > ONTARIO

Delta Toronto East
2035 Kennedy Rd.
Toronto, ON M1T 3G2
416-299-1500
PET POLICY: Deposit $30.

Heritage Inn/toronto
385 Rexdale Blvd.
Toronto, ON M9W1R9
416-742-5510

Holiday Inn
370 King St. W.
Toronto, ON M5V 1J9
416-599-4000
PET POLICY: No fee.

**Hotel Inter-Continental
Toronto**
220 Bloor St. W.
Toronto, ON M5S 1T8
416-960-5200

**Howard Johnson
Clarington Hotel**
143 Duke St., Brownsville
Toronto, ON L1C 2W4
905-623-3373

Howard Johnson Express Inn
2420 Surveyor Rd.
Toronto, ON L5N 4E6
905-858-8600

Howard Johnson Inn
89 Ave. Rd.
Toronto, ON M5R 2G3
416-964-1220

**Le Royal Meridien
The King Edward Hotel**
37 King Street East
Toronto, ON M5C 1E9
416-863-9700
RATES: Single $205+, double
$285–$625.
PET POLICY: No fee. Small pets
under 35 lbs.

Metropolitan Hotel Toronto
108 Chestnut St.
Toronto, ON M5G1R3
416-977-5000

Novotel North York Hotel
3 Park Home Ave.
Toronto, ON M2N 6L3
416-733-2929

Novotel Toronto Center
45 The Esplanade
Toronto, ON M5E 1W2
416-367-8900
RATES: Single, double $115–$260.
PET POLICY: Fee $20. Maximum
of 2 pets per room.

Novotel-Toronto Airport
135 Carlingview Dr.
Toronto, ON M9W 5E7
416-798-9800

**Quality Hotel & Suites
Toronto Airport East**
2180 Islington Ave.
Toronto, ON M9P 3P1
416-240-9090

Quality Hotel Midtown
280 Bloor St. W.
Toronto, ON M5S 1V8
416-968-0010
RATES: Single $140–$150,
double $165.
PET POLICY: No fee, all size pets
accepted.

Quality Inn-Toronto East
22 Metropolitan Rd.
Toronto, ON M1R 2T6
416-293-8171

Quality Suites
262 Carlinview Dr.
Toronto, ON M9W 5G1
416-674-8442

**Radisson Suite Hotel
Toronto Airport**
640 Dixon Rd.
Toronto, ON M9W 1J1
416-242-7400
RATES: Single $129–$209,
double $189–$209.
PET POLICY: No fee. Small pets
preferred. Must be crated in
room.

Regal Constellation
900 Dixon Rd.
Toronto, ON M9W 1J7
416-675-1500

Royal York
100 Front St. W.
Toronto, ON M5J 1E3
416-368-2511

Toronto Colony Downtown
89 Chestnut St.
Toronto, ON M5G 1R1
416-977-0707

**Toronto-Days Inn
Downtown**
30 Carlton St.
Toronto, ON M5B 2E9
416-977-6655

**Triumph Howard Johnson
Plaza Hotel**
2737 Keele St. N. York
Toronto, ON M3M 2E9
416-636-4656

**Venture Inn-
Toronto Airport**
925 Dixon Rd.
Toronto, ON M9W 1J8
416-674-2222

Comfort Inn Trenton
68 Monogram Pl.
Trenton, ON K8V 6S3
613-965-6660

Holiday Inn
Hwy. 401 & Glen Miller Rd.
Trenton, ON K8V 5R1
613-394-4855
PET POLICY: No fee.

Park Place Motel
43 Victoria St.
Tweed, ON K0K 3J0
613-478-3134

Bon Air Motel
268 Main St.
Wasaga Beach, ON L0L 2P0
705-429-6364

Comfort Inn Waterloo
190 Weber St. N.
Waterloo, ON N2J 3H4
519-747-9400

Waterloo Inn
475 King St. N.
Waterloo, ON N2J 2Z5
519-884-0220

Canadian Lodgings > ONTARIO

**Kinniwabi Pines
Motel/Cottages**
132 Hwy. 17S, PO Box 1429
Wawa, ON P0S 1K0
705-856-7302
RATES: Single $50, double $60,
cottage $70.
PET POLICY: Fee $6, nonrefund-
able, must stay off beds and
furniture. Smoking rooms only.
POI: High Falls, Sandy Beach,
Silver Falls.

Parkway Motel
PO Box 784
Wawa, ON P0S 1K0
705-856-7020

Sportsman's Motel
45 Mission Rd.
Wawa, ON P0S 1K0
705-856-2272

The Mystic Isle Motel
PO Box 557
Wawa, ON P0S 1K0
705-856-1737

**Wawa Northern Lights
Motel**
Hwy. 17
Wawa, ON P0S 1K0
705-856-1900

**Best Western Rose City
Suites**
300 Prince Charles Dr.
Welland, ON L3C 7B3
905-732-0922

Comfort Inn Welland
870 Niagara St.
Welland, ON L3C 1M3
905-732-4811

Canadiana Motel
732 Dundas St. E.
Whitby, ON L1N 2J7
905-668-3686

Quality Suites East Suites
1700 Champlain Ave.
Whitby, ON L1N 6A7
905-432-8800

**Comfort Inn Ambassador
Bridge**
2765 Huron Church Rd.
Windsor, ON N9E 3Y7
519-972-1331

Comfort Inn Windsor
2955 Dougall Ave.
Windsor, ON N9E 1S1
519-966-7800

**Days Inn Downtown
Windsor**
675 Goyeau St.
Windsor, ON N9A 1H3
519-258-8411

Hilton Windsor
277 Riverside Dr. W.
Windsor, ON N9A 5K4
519-973-5555

Holiday Inn Select
1855 Huron Church Rd.
Windsor, ON N9C 2L6
519-966-1200
PET POLICY: No fee.

Howard Johnson Express Inn
2130 Division Rd.
Windsor, ON N8W 1Z7
800-446-4656

**Quality Suites
Downtown Suites**
250 Dougall Ave.
Windsor, ON N9A 7C6
519-977-9707

**Radisson Riverfront
Windsor**
333 Riverside Dr W.
Windsor, ON N9A 5K4
519-977-9777
RATES: Single $149, double $159.
PET POLICY: No fee, pets up to
25 lbs. Must sign pet responsi-
bility agreement form.
POI: Casino, Commerica Park,
Raceway.

**Quality Inn & Convention
Centre**
580 Bruin Blvd.
Woodstock, ON N4V 1E5
519-537-5586

**Country View Motel & RV-
Park Camping Resort**
Hwy. 22
Wyoming, ON N0N 1T0
519-845-3394

PRINCE EDWARD ISLAND

Bay Vista Motor Inn
RR 1
Cavendish, PE C0A 1E0
902-963-2225

**Cavendish Bosom Buddies
Cottages**
19 Keppoch Rd.
Cavendish, PE G1A 7T8
902-963-3449

Cavendish Maples Cottages
29 Westhaven Crescent
Cavendish, PE C1E 1L6
902-963-2818

Sundance Cottages
RR 2
Cavendish, PE C0A 1N0
902-963-2149
RATES: Single $100, double $100.
PET POLICY: Fee $7, nonrefund-
able. All sizes welcome.
POI: Prince Edward National
Park, Green Gables House,
Rainbow Valley, golfing, fish-
ing, deep-sea fishing, great
dining.

**Best Western
MacLaughlan Hotel**
238 Grafton St.
Charlottetown, PE C1A 1L5
902-892-2461

**Charlottetown Hotel –
A Rodd Classic Hotel**
PO Box159
Charlottetown, PE C1A 7K4
902-894-7371

Comfort Inn Charlottetown
112 Trans Canada Hwy.
Charlottetown, PE C1E 1E7
902-566-4424

Delta Prince Edward
18 Queen St.
Charlottetown, PE C1A 8B9
902-566-2222

**Holiday Inn Express
Hotel & Suites**
Trans Canada Hwy. #1
Charlottetown, PE C1A 8L4
902-892-1201
PET POLICY: No fee.

Canadian Lodgings > QUEBEC

Thriftlodge by Rodd
PO Box 651
Charlottetown, PE C1A 7L3
902-892-2481

Sunny King Motel
PO Box 159
Cornwall, PE C0A 1H0
902-566-2209

St. Lawrence Motel
RR 2
North Rustico, PE C0A 1N0
902-963-2053

Rodd Brudenell River Resort
PO Box 67
Roseneath, PE C0A 1G0
902-652-2332

Anne's Ocean View Haven Bed & Breakfast
Kinloch Rd.
Stratford, PE C1A 7N7
902-569-4644

Quality Inn Garden of the Gulf
618 Water St., E.
Summerside, PE C1N 2V5
902-436-2295

Rodd Mill River Resort & Conference Centre
PO Box 399
Woodstock, PE C0B 1V0
902-859-3555

QUEBEC

Chateau Cartier Resort Hotel
1170 Aylmer Rd
Aylmer, PQ J9H SE1
819-778-0000

Gite Aux Trois Pains
3 rue des Pins c.p. 127
Baie-Des-Sables, PQ G0J 1C0
877-210-2910
RATES: Single $40, double $50.
PET POLICY: No fee, all sizes welcome.
POI: Jardins De Metis.

Gite de l'Anse Beaumont
19 rue de l'Anse
Beaumont, PQ G0R 1C0
418-833-1199

Comfort Inn East
240 Boul. Sainte-anne
Beauport, PQ G1E 3L7
418-666-1226

Hotel Ramada Quebec City East
321 Sainte Anne Blvd.
Beauport, PQ G1E 3L4
418-666-2828

Berthierville-Days Inn
760 Rue Gadoury
Berthierville, PQ J0K 1A0
450-836-1621

Comfort Inn South Shore
96 Boul. De Mortagne
Boucherville, PQ J4B 5M7
450-641-2880

Best Western Hotel National
7746 boul Taschereau
Brossard, PQ J4X 1C2
514-466-6756

Comfort Inn South
7863 Boul. Taschereau
Brossard, PQ J4Y 1A4
450-678-9350

Comfort Inn Chicoutimi
1595 Boul. Talbot
Chicoutimi, PQ G7H 4C3
418-693-8686

Le Nouvel Hotel La Sagueneenne
250 des Sagueneens
Chicoutimi, PQ G7H 3A4
418-545-8326

Best Western Hotel International
13000 Cote de Liesse
Dorval, PQ H9P 1B8
514-631-4811

Comfort Inn Aeroport
340 Av Michel Jasmin
Dorval, PQ H9P 1C1
514-636-3391

Travelodge
1010 Herron Rd
Dorval, PQ H9S 1B3
514-631-4537

Comfort Inn Drummondville
1055 Rue Hains
Drummondville, PQ J2C 6G6
819-477-4000

Hotel le Dauphin
600 boul St-Joseph
Drummondville, PQ J2C 2C1
819-478-4141

Motel Adams
2 rue Adams
Gaspe, PQ G0C 1R0
418-368-2244

Comfort Inn Gatineau
630 Boul. La Gappe
Gatineau, PQ J8T 9Z6
819-243-6010

Hotel Le Castel
901 rue Principale
Granby, PQ J2G 2Z5
514-378-9071

Holiday Inn
2 Montcalm St.
Hull, PQ J8X 4B4
819-778-3880
PET POLICY: No fee.

Days Inn La Pocatiere
235 Rt. 132
La Pocatiere, PQ G0R 1Z0
418-856-1688

Le Manoir du Lac Delage
40 Ave. du Lac
Lac-Delage, PQ G0A 4P0
418-848-2551

Comfort Inn
1255 boul Duplessis
L'Ancienne-Lorette,
PQ G2G 2B4
418-872-5900

Comfort Inn Laval
2055 Auto. Des Laurentides
Laval, PQ H7S 1Z6
450-686-0600

Hilton Montréal/Laval
2225, Autoroute Des Laurentides
Laval, PQ H7S 1Z6
450-682-2225

Canadian Lodgings > QUEBEC

Hotel/Motel Ideal Ste-Rose
379 boul Labelle
Laval, PQ H7L 3A3
514-625-0773

Quality Suites Suites
2035 Auto. Des Laurentides
Laval, PQ H7S 1Z6
450-686-6777

La Paysanne Motel
32 rue Queen
Lennoxville, PQ J1M 1H9
819-569-5585

Comfort Inn Levis
10 Du Vallon E.
Levis, PQ G6V 9J3
418-835-5605

Hotel Motel Ideal La Barre
2019 boul Taschereau
Longeuil, PQ J4K 2Y1
514-677-9101

Gite du Carrefour
11 ave St-Laurent Ouest
Louiseville, PQ J5V 1J3
819-228-4932

Motel La Marina
1032 ave du Phare Ouest
Matane, PQ G4W 3M9
418-562-3234

Crowne Plaza
505 Sherbrooke St. E.
Montreal, PQ H2L 1K2
514-842-8581
PET POLICY: No fee.

Delta Montreal
450 Sherbrooke St W.
Montreal, PQ H3A 2T4
514-286-1986

Holiday Inn
420 Sherbrooke St. W.
Montreal, PQ H3A 1B4
514-842-6111
PET POLICY: No fee.

Holiday Inn
6500 Cote de Liesse
Montreal, PQ H4T 1E3
514-739-3391
PET POLICY: No fee.

Hotel Auberge Universal Montreal
5000 rue Sherbrooke Est
Montreal, PQ H1V 1A1
514-253-3365

Hotel Du Parc
3625 Ave. Du Parc
Montreal, PQ H2X 3P8
514-288-6666

Hotel Inter-Continental Montreal
360 rue St-Antoine Ouest
Montreal, PQ H2Y 3X4
514-987-9900

Hotel Omni Mont-royal
1050 Sherbrooke St. W.
Montreal, PQ H3A 2R6
514-284-1110

Le Centre Sheraton Hotel
1201 Rene-Levesque Blvd. W.
Montreal, PQ H3B 2L7
514-878-2000

Loews Hotel Vogue
1425 rue De La Montangne
Montreal, PQ H3G 1Z3
514-285-5555

Lord Berri Hotel
1199 Berri St.
Montreal, PQ H2L 4C6
514-845-9236

Novotel Montreal Centre
1180 de la Montagne
Montreal, PQ H3G 1Z1
514-861-6000
RATES: Single $159, double $159.
PET POLICY: No fee. Up to 50
lbs. Owner responsible for
damages or noise. Pets not
allowed in restaurant.
POI: Across the street from
Molson center, 2-minute walk
from Crescent Street with its
nightlife and St. Catherine
Street for its shopping.

Quality Hotel Downtown
3440 Av Du Parc
Montreal, PQ H2X 2H5
514-849-1413

Residence Inn Montreal Downtown
2045 Peel St.
Montreal, PQ H3A 1T6
514-982-6064

Wandlyn Inn Montreal
7200 Sherbrooke St E.
Montreal, PQ H1N 1E7
514-256-1613

Travelodge
50, Boul, René-Lévesque W
Montréal, PQ H2Z 1A2
514-874-9090

Au Pic de L'Aurore
1 Rt. 132
Percé, PQ G0C 2L0
418-782-2166

Bonaventure Pavillon Cote Surprise
367 Rt. 132
Percé, PQ G0C 2L0
418-782-2166

Hotel Motel Manoir de Percé
212 boul Perron
Percé, PQ G0C 2L0
418-782-2022

Motel Le Mirage
288 Rt. 132
Percé, PQ G0C 2L0
418-782-5151

Hotel du Lac Carling
2255 Route 327 Nord
Pine Hill, PQ J0V 1A0
514-533-9211

Comfort Inn
700 boul St-Jean
Pointe-Claire, PQ J9R 3K2
514-697-6210

Holiday Inn
6700 Trans-Canada Hwy.
Pointe-Claire, PQ H9R 1C2
514-697-7110
PET POLICY: No fee.

Quality Suites
6300 Trans-Canada Hwy.
Pointe-Claire, PQ H9R 1B9
514-426-5060

Canadian Lodgings > QUEBEC

Chateau Grande-Allee
601 Grande-Allee
Quebec, PQ G1R 2K4
418-647-4433

Hotel Chateau Bellevue
16 rue de la Porte
Quebec, PQ G1R 4M9
418-692-2573

Hotel Chateau Laurier
695 Grande-Allee Est
Quebec, PQ G1R 2K4
418-522-8108

Hotel Le Manoir LaFayette
661 rue Grande Allee Est
Quebec, PQ G1R 2K4
418-522-2652

L'Hotel du Vieux Quebec
1190 rue St-Jean
Quebec, PQ G1R 1S6
418-692-1850
PET POLICY: No fee, all size dogs
and cats, only.

Loews Le Concorde
1225 Pl. Montcalm
Quebec, PQ G1R 4W6
418-647-2222

Quality Suites Quebec
1600 Rue Bouvier
Quebec, PQ G2K 1N8
418-622-4244

Quebec Hilton
1100 boul Rene Levesque E
Quebec, PQ G1R 5P5
418-647-2411

Comfort Inn Rimouski
455 Boul. St-germain Ouest
Rimouski, PQ G5L 3P2
418-724-2500

Riviere-du-loup-Days Inn
182 Fraser
Riviere Du Loup, PQ G5R 1C8
418-862-6354

Comfort Inn Riviere-du-loup
85 Boul. Cartier
Riviere-du-loup, PQ G5R 4X4
418-867-4162

Comfort Inn Rock Forest
4295 Boul. Bourque
Rock Forest, PQ J1N 1S4
819-564-4400

Comfort Inn Rouyn-noranda
1295 Av Lariviere
Rouyn-noranda, PQ J9X 6M6
819-797-1313

Hotel Valleyfield
40 ave du Centenaire
Salaberry-de-Velleyfield, PQ
J6S 3L6
514-373-1990

Comfort Inn Sept-iles
854 Boul. Laure
Sept-iles, PQ G4R 1Y7
418-968-6005

Auberge Motel l'Escapade
3383 rue Garnier
Shawinigan, PQ G9N 6R4
819-539-6911

Motel Safari
4500 12e Ave.
Shawinigan-Sud, PQ G9N 6T5
819-536-2664

Delta Sherbrooke
2685 King St. W.
Sherbrooke, PQ J1L 1C1
819-822-1989

Motel La Reserve
4235 rue King Ouest
Sherbrooke, PQ J1L 1N7
819-566-6464

Auberge Manoir de Tilly
3854 Chemin de Tilly
St-Antoine-de-Tilly,
PQ G0S 2C0
418-886-2407

Motel Beaurivage
245 1 ere Ave. Ouest
Ste-Anne-des-Monts,
PQ G0E 2G0
418-763-2291

Comfort Inn
7320 boul Wilfrid-Hamel
Ste-Foy, PQ G2G 1C1
418-872-5038

Holiday Inn
3125 Hochelaga Blvd.
Ste-Foy, QC G1V 4A8
418-653-4901
PET POLICY: No fee.

Motel L'Abitation
2828 boul Laurier
Ste-Foy, PQ G1V 2M1
418-653-7267

Motel Oncle Sam
7025 boul Wilfrid-Hamel
Ste-Foy, PQ G2G 1B6
418-872-1488

Auberge des Gallant
1171 chemin St-Henri
Ste-Marthe, PQ J0P 1W0
514-459-4241

Hotel sur la Colline
357 Rt. 117
St-Faustin, PQ J0T 2G0
819-688-2102

Auberge du Faubourg
280 ave de Gaspe Ouest
St-Jean-Port-Joli, PQ G0R 3G0
418-598-6455

Comfort Inn
700 rue Gadbois
St-Jean-Sur-Richelieu,
PQ J3A 1V1
514-359-4466

Hotel Gouverneur St-Jean-Sur-Richelieu
725 boul du Seminaire Nord
St-Jean-Sur-Richelieu,
PQ J3B 8H1
514-348-7376

Days Inn Montreal Airport
4545 Cote Vertu Ouest
St-Laurent, PQ H4S 1C8
514-332-2720

Quality Hotel Dorval
7700 Cote de Liesse
St-Laurent, PQ H4T 1E7
514-731-7821

Manoir Sant-Sauveur
246 chemin du Lac Millette
St-Sauveur-des-Monts,
PQ J0R 1R3
514-227-1811

Comfort Inn Thetford Mines
123 Boul. Smith S.
Thetford Mines, PQ G6G 7S7
418-338-0171

Canadian Lodgings > QUEBEC

Delta Trois-Rivieres
1620 rue Notre-Dame
Trois-Rivieres, PQ G9A 6E5
819-376-1991

Le Gite du Huard
42 rue St-Louis
Trois-Rivieres, PQ G9A 1T5
819-375-8771

Comfort Inn
6255 rue Corbeil
Trois-Rivieres-Ouest,
PQ G8Z 4P9
819-371-3566

Comfort Inn Val D'or
1665 3ieme Av
Val D'or, PQ J9P 1V9
819-825-9360

SASKATCHEWAN

Eastview Wilderness Guest Ranch
Box 66
Arborfield, SK S0E 0A0
306-769-4138

Lakeview Lodge Motel
447 Saskatchewan St.
Elbow, SK S0H 1J0
306-854-4444

Best Western Westridge Motor Inn
100 12 Ave. NW
Kindersley, SK S0L 1S0
306-463-4687

Imperial 400 Motel
4320 44 St.
Lloydminster, SK S9V 1R5
306-825-4400

Heritage Inn
1590 Main St. N.
Moose Jaw, SK S6H 7N7
306-693-7550
RATES: Single $75, double $85.
PET POLICY: No fee, all size dogs and cats only. Must be under owner's control at all times.

Prarie Oasis Motel
1400 9th Ave. N.E.
Moose Jaw, SK S6H 4N9
306-693-8888

Super 8 Motel-Moose Jaw
1706 Main St. N.
Moose Jaw, SK S6A 4P1
306-692-8888

Happy Inn
992 101 St.
North Battleford, SK S9A 0Z3
306-445-9425

Tropical Inn
1001 Battleford Rd.
North Battleford, SK S9A 2W3
306-446-4700

Comfort Inn Prince Albert
3863 2nd Ave. W.
Prince Albert, SK S6W 1A1
306-763-4466

Imperial 400 Motel
3580 2nd Ave. W.
Prince Albert, SK S6V 5G2
306-764-6881

Travelodge
3551 2nd Ave. W.
Prince Albert, SK S6V 5G1
306-764-6441
RATES: Single $72, double $82.
PET POLICY: Fee $50, refundable. All sizes welcome.
POI: Shopping, theatre, museums, casino, parks.

Centennial Motel
PO Box 190
Quill Lake, SK S0A 3E0
306-383-2322

Spring Valley Guest Ranch
Box 10
Ravenscrag, SK S0N 0T0
306-295-4124

Comfort Inn Regina
3221 E. Eastgate Dr.
Regina, SK S4Z 1A4
306-789-5522

Imperial 400 Inn – Regina
4255 Albert St S.
Regina, SK S4S3R6
306-584-8800

Inn And Suites Regina
3321 East Gate Bay
Regina, SK S4Z 1A4
306-789-9117

Ramada Hotel & Convention Center
1818 Victoria Ave.
Regina, SK S4P 0R1
306-569-1666
RATES: Single $72 weekend, $87 corp.; double $72 weekend, $97 corp.
PET POLICY: No fee, all sizes and all pets welcome (dogs, cats, birds, ferrets, rabbits, reptiles).
POI: Wascana Park, largest city centre urban park in North America, RCMP Museum, Casino Regina, Royal Saskatchewan Museum, Imax – Science Centre.

Sherwood House Motel
3915 Albert St.
Regina, SK S4S 3R4
306-586-3131

Super 8 Motel
2730 Victoria Ave. E.
Regina, SK S4N 6M5
306-789-8833

Travelodge regina East
1110 Victoria Ave. E.
Regina, SK S4N 7A9
306-565-0455
PET POLICY: No fee, all sizes welcome. Pets must be in smoking rooms.

Inn And Suites Saskatoon
617 Cynthia St.
Saskatoon, SK S7L 6B7
306-934-3900

Best Western Inn & Suites
1715 Idlwyld Dr. N.
Saskatoon, SK S7L 1B4
306-244-5552

Comfort Inn Saskatoon
2155 Northridge Dr.
Saskatoon, SK S7L 6X6
306-934-1122

Delta Bessborough
601 Spadina Crescent E.
Saskatoon, SK S7K 3G8
306-244-5521

Imperial 400 Inn – Saskatoon
610 Idylwyld Dr N.
Saskatoon, SK S7L0Z2
306-244-2901

Canadian Lodgings > YUKON

Quality Hotel Downtown
90 22nd St.
Saskatoon, SK S7K 3T6
306-244-2311

Caravel Motel
705 N. Service Rd., NE
Swift Current, SK S9H 3X6
306-773-8385

Comfort Inn Swift Current
1510 S. Service Rd. E.
Swift Current, SK S9H 3X6
306-778-3994

**Imperial 400 Inn –
Swift Current**
1150 Begg St. E.
Swift Current, SK S9H 3Z4
306-773-2033

Rodeway Inn Motel
1200 S. Service Rd. E.
Swift Current, SK S9H 3X6
306-773-4664

Safari Inn Motel
810 S. Service Rd. E.
Swift Current, SK S9H 3T9
306-773-4608

Westwind Motel
155 Begg St. W.
Swift Current, SK S9H 3S8
306-773-1441

**Country Pioneer Style
Bed & Breakfast**
RR 1
Tisdale, SK S0E 1T0
306-873-4100

Perfect Inns
238 Sims Ave.
Weyburn, SK S4H 2J8
306-842-2691

Imperial 400 Inn – Yorkton
207 Broadway E.
Yorkton, SK S3N3K7
306-783-6581

Travelodge
345 Broadway St. W.
Yorkton, SK S3N 0N8
306-783-6571

YUKON

**Westmark Inn/Beaver
Creek**
Alaska Hwy.
Beaver Creek, YT Y0B 1A0
867-862-7501

Westmark Inn
PO Box 420
Dawson City, YT Y0B 1G0
867-993-5542

**White Ram Manor
Bed & Breakfast**
7th Ave. & Harper St.
Dawson City, YT Y0B 1G0
867-993-5772

Gateway Motel
Box 5460
Haines Junction, YT Y0B 1L0
867-634-2371

High Country Inn
4051 4th Ave.
Whitehorse, YT Y1A 1H1
867-667-4471
RATES: Double
$Can.99–$Can.209.
PET POLICY: Fee $15, up to 50
lbs. Pets restricted to ground-
floor rooms.
POI: Park next door, river-front
walks two blocks away.

**The Town and Mountain
Hotel**
401 Main St.
Whitehorse, YT Y1A 2B6
867-668-7644

Westmark Klondike Inn
2288 2nd Ave.
Whitehorse, YT Y1A1C8
867-668-4747

Westmark Whitehorse
201 Wood St.
Whitehorse, YT Y1A 3T3
867-668-4700

CAMPGROUNDS

Taking your dog into the wilderness (it's not a good idea to take cats or other pets) can be extremely rewarding. If you own a dog who really loves to go for walks and be outside, taking him on a trail for a hike into the woods will make him one extremely happy puppy. With all the sensory stimulation that the outdoors provides, you'll see a side of your pet that you might not have witnessed before, especially if you live in an urban, or even suburban, area. Watching your dog fully engaged, tail wagging, nose to the ground and in the air, and prancing back and forth with his tongue lolling is an experience that we recommend to every dog owner. Just make sure that you and your pet are in shape for the hike. And, no matter how tempted you are, *never* take your dog off the leash. Even dogs that are well trained and obedient might fly off at the sight of another animal or other distraction and most likely will get disoriented and/or lost in the unfamiliar surroundings.

When camping with your pet, here are some basic rules you should follow:

- *Always* call before going. Requirements change all the time.

- Almost all campgrounds—private or public—that accept pets require them to be on a 6-foot leash. Many will not permit the animal to sleep outdoors and either require the pet to be kept in a crate or kept in the tent.

- Always clean up after your animal. Even though you're outside, somebody's going to be walking where you did, so treat your campsite like you would your own property.

- Even if leashed, your pet should never be left unattended. There's always the possibility of an unpleasant encounter with other animals or travelers.

- Find out about the hazardous plant life in the area, especially poisonous plants and other plants, like cactus and poison ivy, that can physically hurt your pet.

- During your stay, be vigilant in checking your pet for ticks, foot injuries and dehydration. Give your pet fresh drinking water, and don't let her drink from questionable sources found in the wilderness.

- Take your pet to the veterinarian when you get home to make sure she's as healthy as when you left.

ALABAMA

Wind Creek State Park
4325 AL Hwy. 128
Alexander City, AL 35010
256-329-0845

Claude D. Kelley State Park
580 H. Kyle
Atmore, AL 36502
334-862-2511

Chewacla State Park
124 Shell Toomer Pkwy.
Auburn, AL 36830
334-887-5621

Roland Cooper State Park
285 Deer Run Dr.
Camden, AL 36726
334-682-4050

Lake Lurleen State Park
13226 Lake Lurleen
Coker, AL 35452
205-339-1558

Big Bridge Campground
21899 County Rd. 222
Crane Hill, AL 35053
256-287-0440

KOA
2350 Dead Lake Rd.
Creola, AL 36525
334-675-0320

Cheaha State Park
Route 1, Box 77-H
Delta, AL 36258
256-488-5111

Chickasaw State Park
26955 US Hwy. 43
Gallion, AL 36742
334-295-8230

Bucks Pocket State Park
393 County Rd. 174
Grove Oak, AL 35975
256-659-2000

Gulf State Park
20115 State Hwy. 135
Gulf Shores, AL 36542
334-948-6353

U.S. Campgrounds > ARIZONA

Lake Guntersville State Park
7966 Alabama Hwy. 227
Guntersville, AL 35976
256-571-5455

KOA
250 Fisher Rd.
Hope Hull, AL 36043
334-288-0728

Monte Sano State Park
5105 Nolen Ave.
Huntsville, AL 35801
256-534-3757

Mountain Lakes Resort
1345 Murphy Hill Rd.
Langston, AL 35755
800-330-3550

KOA
22191 Hwy. 216
McCalla, AL 35111
205-477-2778

Ozark Trav-L-Park
4000 U.S. 231 N.
Ozark, AL 36360
334-774-3219

KOA
222 Hwy. 33
Pelham, AL 35124
205-664-8832

Oak Mountain State Park
PO Box 278
Pelham, AL 35124
205-620-2527

Styx River Resort
25301 Water World Rd.
Robertsdale, AL 36567
800-330-3550

Joe Wheeler State Park
Rt. 4, Box 369-A
Rogersville, AL 35652
256-247-1184

Paul M. Grist State Park
1546 Grist Rd.
Selma, AL 36701
334-872-5846

Meaher State Park
5200 Battleship Pkwy. East
Spanish Fort, AL 36577
334-626-5529

**Rickwood Caverns
State Park**
370 Rickwood Park Rd.
Warrior, AL 35180
205-647-9692

ALASKA

Anchorage RV Park
7300 Oilwell Rd.
Anchorage, AK 99504
907-338-7275

**Oceanview RV Park &
Campground**
PO Box 18035
Coffman Cove, AK 99918
907-329-2015

Kenai Princess RV Park
Cooper Landing, AK 99572
907-595-1425

Denali Riverside RV Park
Milepost 240, Parks Hwy.
Denali National Park, AK
99755
888-778-7700

Denali RV Park & Motel
Box 155V
Denali National Park, AK
99755
800-478-1501

River's Edge RV Park
4140 Boat St.
Fairbanks, AK 99709
800-770-3343

Port Chilkoot Camper Park
PO Box 1589
Haines, AK 99827
907-766-2000

**McKinley RV &
Campground**
PO Box 340
Healy, AK 99743
907-683-2379

**The Driftwood Inn RV
Park**
135 W. Bunnell Ave.
Homer, AK 99603
907-235-8019

Santaland RV Park
PO Box 55317
North Pole, AK 99705
888-488-9123

Back Track Camper Park
PO Box 375
Skagway, AK 99840
888-778-7700

TOK RV Village
PO Box 739
Tok, AK 99780
907-883-5877

Eagle's Rest RV Park
PO Box 610
Valdez, AK 99686
907-835-2373

ARIZONA

KOA
1540 S. Tomahawk Rd.
Apache Junction, AZ 85219
602-982-4015

KOA
PO Box 357
Ash Fork, AZ 86320
520-637-2521

KOA
Box 1060
Benson, AZ 85602
520-586-3977

KOA
Box 569
Black Canyon City, AZ 85324
602-374-5318

Ehrenberg KOA
Ehrenberg-Parker Hwy.
Ehrenberg, AZ 85334
520-923-7863

Flagstaff KOA
5803 N. Hwy. 89
Flagstaff, AZ 86004
520-526-9926

Holbrook KOA
102 Hermosa Dr.
Holbrook, AZ 86025
520-524-6689

U.S. Campgrounds > ARIZONA

KOA
3820 N. Roosevelt
Kingman, AZ 86401
520-757-4397

Picacho KOA
PO Box 368
Picacho, AZ 85241
520-466-7401

Seligman KOA
801 E. Hwy. 66, Box 156
Seligman, AZ 86337
520-422-3358

KOA
1000 Circle Pines Rd.
Williams, AZ 86046
520-635-2626

Williams KOA
5333 Hwy. 64
Williams, AZ 86046
520-635-2307

ARKANSAS

KOA
3539 N. Hwy. 71
Alma, AR 72921
501-632-2704

KOA
221 Frost Rd.
Arkadelphia, AR 71923
870-246-4922

Millwood State Park
1564 Hwy. 32 E.
Ashdown, AR 71822
870-898-2800

DeGray Lake Resort
Route 3, Box 490
Bismark, AR 71929
501-865-2801

White Oak Lake
Route 2, Box 28
Bluff City, AR 71722
870-685-2748

Bull Shoals State Park
PO Box 205
Bull Shoals, AR 72619
870-431-5521

Mount Nebo State Park
Route 3, Box 374
Dardanelle, AR 72834
501-229-3655

KOA
15020 Hwy. 187 S.
Eureka Springs, AR 72632
501-253-8036

Woolly Hollow State Park
82 Woolly Hollow Rd.
Greenbrier, AR 72058
501-679-2098

Lake Poinsett State Park
5752 State Park Ln.
Harrisburg, AR 72432
870-578-2064

**West Memphis/Shell Lake
KOA**
P.O. Box 151
Heth, AR 72346
800-562-2140

Boxhound Resort RV Park
1313 Tri-Lake Dr.
Horseshoe Bend, AR 72512
501-670-4496

KOA
838 McClendon Rd.
Hot Springs, AR 71901
501-624-5912

Lake Catherine State Park
1200 Catherine Park Rd.
Hot Springs, AR 71913
501-844-4176

Withrow Springs State Park
Route 3, Box 29
Huntsville, AR 72740
501-559-2593

Jacksonport State Park
PO Box 8
Jacksonport, AR 72075
870-523-2143

Moro Bay State Park
6071 Hwy. 15 S.
Jersey, AR 71651
870-463-8555

Lake Frierson State Park
7904 Hwy. 141
Jonesboro, AR 72401
870-932-2615

Daisy State Park
HC-71, Box 66
Kirby, AR 71950
870-398-4487

Lake Chicot State Park
2542 Hwy. 257
Lake Village, AR 71653
870-265-5480

Best Holiday Trav-L-Park
7037 I-55 #1
Marion, AR 72364
501-739-4801

Logoly State Park
PO Box 245
McNeil, AR 71752
870-695-3561

KOA
30 Kamper Ln.
Morrilton, AR 72110
501-354-8262

Petit Jean State Park
1285 Petit Jean Mountain Rd.
Morrilton, AR 72110
501-727-5441

Lake Ouachita State Park
5451 Mountain Pine Rd.
Mountain Pine, AR 71956
501-767-9366

Lake Fort Smith State Park
PO Box 4
Mountainburg, AR 72946
501-369-2469

**Crater of Diamonds
State Park**
Route 1
Murfreesboro, AR 71958
870-285-3113

KOA
7820 Crystal Hill Rd.
North Little Rock, AR 72118
501-758-4598

**Battlefield Inn,
Motel & RV Park**
14753 Hwy. 62 E.
Pea Ridge, AR 72751
501-451-1188

U.S. Campgrounds > CALIFORNIA

Old Davidsonville State Park
7953 Hwy. 166 S.
Pocahontas, AR 72455
870-892-4708

Lake Charles State Park
3705 Hwy. 25
Powhatan, AR 72458
870-878-6595

KOA
PO Box 456
Rogers, AR 72757
501-451-8566

Lake Dardanelle State Park
2428 Marina Rd.
Russellville, AR 72801
501-967-5516

Cane Creek State Park
PO Box 96
Star City, AR 71667
870-628-4714

KOA
8225 Camper Ln.
Texarcana, AR 71858
870-772-0751

Crowley's Ridge State Park
Box 97
Walcott, AR 72474
870-573-6751

Devil's Den State Park
11333 W. Arkansas Highway 74
West Fork, AR 72774
501-761-3325

Village Creek State Park
201 CR 754
Wynne, AR 72396
870-238-9406

CALIFORNIA

Auburn KOA
3550 KOA Way
Auburn, CA 95602
530-885-0990

Chila Vista KOA
111 N. 2nd Ave.
Chila Vista, CA 91910
619-427-3601

Cloverdale KOA
PO Box 600
Cloverdale, CA 95425
707-894-3337

Crescent City KOA
4241 Hwy. 101 N.
Crescent City, CA 95531
707-464-5744

Eureka KOA
4050 N. Hwy. 101
Eureka, CA 95503
707-725-3359

Fortuna KOA
2189 Riverwalk Dr.
Fortuna, CA 95540
707-725-3359

**Lake Tulloch RV
Campground & Marina**
14448 Tulloch Rd.
Jamestown, CA 95327
209-881-0107

KOA
2851 E. 8 Mile Rd.
Lodi, CA 95420
209-334-0309

Loomis KOA
3945 Taylor Rd.
Loomis, CA 95650
916-652-6737

KOA
PO Box 276
Lost Hills, CA 93249
805-797-2719

Manchester KOA
Box 266
Manchester, CA 95459
707-882-2375

KOA
Box 545, Hwy. 140
Midpines, CA 05345
209-966-2201

KOA
900 N. Mt. Shasta Blvd.
Mt. Shasta City, CA 96067
916092604029

Needles KOA
5400 National Old Trails Hwy.
Needles, CA 92363
760-326-4207

Petaluma KOA
20 Rainsville Rd.
Petaluma, CA 94952
707-763-1492

KOA
2200 N. White Ave.
Pomona, CA 91768
909-593-8915

KOA
280 N. Boulder Dr.
Redding, CA 96003
530-246-0101

KOA
1707 Cable Canyon Rd.
San Bernardino, CA 92407
909-887-4098

KOA
900 Anzar Rd.
San Juan Bautista, CA 95045
408-623-4263

Santa Cruz KOA
1186 San Andreas Rd.
Santa Cruz, CA 95076
831-722-2377

KOA
4765 Santa Margarita Lake
Rd.
Santa Margarita, CA 93453
805-438-5618

KOA
5101 E. Lerdo Hwy.
Shafter, CA 93263
805-399-3107

KOA
4655 Rock Barn Rd.
Shingle Springs, CA 95682
530-676-2267

KOA
7749 KOA Rd.
Shingletown, CA 96088
530-474-3133

KOA
Box 11552
South Lake Tahoe, CA 96155
530-577-3693

KOA
16530 Stoddard Wells Rd.
Victorville, CA 92392
760-245-6867

U.S. Campgrounds > CALIFORNIA

KOA
7480 Ave. 308
Visalia, CA 94391
559-651-0544

KOA
15627 Hwy. 178
Weldon, CA 93283
760-378-2001

KOA
3951 Lake Rd.
West Sacreamento, CA 95691
916-371-6771

KOA
Box 946
Willits, CA 95490
707-459-6179

KOA
Box 967, 35250 Outer Hwy. 15
Yermo, CA 92398
760-254-2311

COLORADO

KOA
6900 Juniper Ln.
Alamosa, CO 81101
719-589-9757

Mancos State Park
PO Box 1697
Arboles, CO 81121
970-883-2208

Cherry Creek State Park
4201 S. Parker Rd.
Aurora, CO 80014
303-699-3860

KOA
27700 CR 303
Buena Vista, CO 81211
719-395-8318

KOA
PO Box 528
Canon City, CO 81215
719-275-6116

Crawford State Park
PO Box 147
Carwford, CO 81415
970-921-5721

KOA
6527 S I-25
Castle Rock, CO 80104
303-681-2568

Pearl Lake State Park
PO Box 750
Clark, CO 80428
970-879-3922

Steamboat Lake State Park
PO Box 750
Clark, CO 80428
970-879-3922

Colorado River State Park-Island Acres
PO Box 700
Clifton, CO 81520
970-434-3388

KOA
3238 E I-70 Business
Clifton, CO 81520
970-434-6644

Vega State Park
PO Box 186
Collbran, CO 81624
970-487-3407

KOA
27432 E. Hwy. 160
Cortez, CO 81321
970-565-9301

KOA
21435 US Hwy. 50
Cotopaxi, CO 81223
719-275-9308

KOA
2800 E. US 40
Craig, CO 81625
970-824-5105

KOA
PO Box 699
Cripple Creek, CO 80813
719-689-3376

KOA
1675 Hwy. 92
Delta, CO 81416
970-874-3918

**The Flying A
RV Park & Motel**
676 Hwy. 50
Delta, CO 81416
970-874-9659

Mueller State Park
PO Box 49
Divide, CO 80814
719-687-2366

KOA
13391 CR 250
Durango, CO 81301
970-247-4499

KOA
30090 US Hwy. 160
Durango, CO 81301
970-247-0783

KOA
2051 Big Thompson Ave.
Estes, CO 80517
970-586-2888

KOA
8100 Bandley Dr.
Fountain, CO 80817
719-382-7575

**Golden Gate Canyon
State Park**
3873 Hwy. 46
Golden, CO 80403
303-582-3707

KOA
661 Hwy. 46
Golden, CO 80403
303-582-9979

KOA
105 Country Rd. 50
Gunnison, CO 81230
970-641-1358

KOA
Box 445
Hudson, CO 80642
303-536-4763

Bonny State Park
30010 Rd. 3
Idalia, CO 80735
970-354-7306

U.S. Campgrounds > CONNECTICUT

KOA
26680 Hwy. 50
La Junta, CO 81050
719-384-9580

Eleven Mile State Park
4229 County Rd. 92
Lake George, CO 80827
719-748-3401

KOA
5385 Hwy. 50
Lamar, CO 81052
719-336-7625

KOA
Box 600, 6670 N. Hwy. 287
LaPorte, CO 80535
970-493-9758

KOA
575 Colorado Ave.
Limon, CO 80828
719-775-2151

Chatfield State Park
11500 N. Roxborough Park Rd.
Littleton, CO 80125
303-791-7275

Highline State Park
1800 11.8 Rd.
Loma, CO 81524
970-858-7208

Barbour Ponds State Park
4995 Weld County Rd. 24
Longmont, CO 80501
303-678-9402

Boyd Lake State Park
3720 N. County Rd. 11-C
Loveland, CO 80538
970-669-1739

KOA
200 N. Cedar
Montrose, CO 81401
970-249-9177

San Luis State Park
PO Box 175
Mosca, CO 81146
719-378-2020

KOA
0581 Country Rd. 241
New Castle, CO 81647
970-984-2240

Stagecoach State Park
PO Box 98
Oak Creek, CO 80467
970-736-2436

Jackson Lake State Park
26363 County Rd. 3
Orchard, CO 80649
970-645-2551

KOA
PO Box J
Ouray, CO 81427
970-325-4736

KOA
9040 I-25 S.
Pueblo, CO 81004
719-676-3376

KOA
4131 I-25 N.
Pueblo, CO 81008
719-542-2273

Pueblo State Park
640 Pueblo Reservoir Rd.
Pueblo, CO 81005
719-561-9320

Ridgway State Park
28555 Hwy. 550
Ridgway, CO 81432
970-626-5822

Rifle Falls State Park
0050 Rd. 219
Rifle, CO 81650
970-625-1607

Rifle Gap State Park
0050 Rd. 219
Rifle, CO 81650
970-625-1607

Sylvan State Park
0050 Rd. 219
Rifle, CO 81650
970-625-1607

Arkansas Headwaters State Park
PO Box 126
Salida, CO 81201
719-539-7289

KOA
3603 Lincoln Ave.
Steamboat Springs, CO 80487
970-879-0273

North Sterling State Park
24005 County Rd. 330
Sterling, CO 80751
970-522-3657

KOA
Box 597
Strasburg, CO 80136
303-622-9274

Trinidad State Park
32610 Hwy. 12
Trinidad, CO 81082
719-846-6951

KOA
53337 Hwy. 14
Walden, CO 80480
970-723-4310

State Forest State Park
2746 Jackson County Rd. 14
Walden, CO 80480
970-723-8366

Lathrop State Park
70 County Rd. 502
Walsenburg, CO 81089
719-738-2376

KOA
Box 130
Wellington, CO 80549
970-568-7486

CONNECTICUT

Brialee RV & Tent Park
174 Laurel Ln., Box 125
Ashford, CT 06278
860-429-8359

Salt Rock Campground
120 Scotland Rd.
Baltic, CT 06330
860-822-8728

Acorn Acres
135 Lake Rd.
Bozrah, CT 06334
860-859-1020

Nickerson Park
Rt. 198
Chaplin, CT 06235
860-455-0007

U.S. Campgrounds > CONNECTICUT

River Road Campground
13 River Rd.
Clinton, CT 06413
860-669-2238

Riverdale Farm Campsite
111 River Rd.
Clinton, CT 06413
860-669-5388

Lone Oak Campground
360 Norfolk Rd.
East Canaan, CT 06024
860-824-7051

Wolf's Den Campground
256 Town St.
East Haddam, CT 06423
860-873-9681

Markham Meadows
7 Markham Rd.
East Hampton, CT 06424
860-267-8012

Nelson's Family Campground
71 Mott Hill Rd.
East Hampton, CT 06424
860-267-5300

Hide-Away-Cove Family Campground
1060 North Rd.
East Killingly, CT 06243
860-774-1128

Stateline Campresort
Route 101
East Killingly, CT 06243
860-774-3016

Aces High RV Park
301 Chesterfield Rd.
East Lyme, CT 06333
860-739-5585

Charlie Brown Campground
100 Chaplin Rd.
Eastford, CT 06242
860-974-0142

Peppertree Camping
Rt. 198
Eastford, CT 06242
860-974-1439

Mohawk Campground
Route 4
Goshen, CT 06756
860-491-2231

Valley in the Pines
Lucas Rd.
Goshen, CT 06756
860-491-2032

Little City Campground
741 Little City Rd.
Higganum, CT 06441
860-345-4886

Campers World
Edmond Rd.
Jewett City, CT 06351
860-376-2340

Lake Williams Campground
1742 Exeter Rd.
Lebanon, CT 06249
860-642-7761

Water's Edge Family Campground
271 Leonard Bridge Rd.
Lebanon, CT 06249
860-642-7470

Deer Haven Campground
15 Kenyon Rd.
Lisbon, CT 06351
860-376-1081

Ross Hill park
170 Ross Hill Rd.
Lisbon, CT 06351
860-376-9606

Hemlock Hill Camp Resorts
Hemlock Hill Rd.
Litchfield, CT 06759
860-567-2267

Looking Glass Hill Campground
Route 202
Litchfield, CT 06759
860-567-2050

White Memorial Family Campground
Bantam Lake
Litchfield, CT 06759
860-567-0089

Camp Niantic-By-The-Atlantic
271 W. Main St.
Niantic, CT 06357
860-739-9308

West Thompson Lake Campground
Reardon Rd.
North Grosvenordale, CT 06255
860-923-2982

Highland Orchards Resort Park
118 Pendleton Hill Rd.
North Stonington, CT 06359
860-599-5101

M.H.G. RV Park
Route 184
North Stonington, CT 06359
860-535-0501

Pequot ledge Campground & Cabins
157 Doyle Rd.
Oakdale, CT 06370
860-859-0682

Seaport Campground
Route 184
Old Mystic, CT 06372
860-536-4044

River Bend Campground
41 Pond St.
Oneco, CT 06373
860-564-3440

Gentile's Campground
Mt. Tobe Rd.
Plymouth, CT 06782
860-283-8437

Hidden Acres Family Campground
47 River Rd.
Preston, CT 06365
860-887-9633

Strawberry Park Resort Campground
Pierce Rd.
Preston, CT 06365
860-886-1944

U.S. Campgrounds > FLORIDA

Salem Farms Campground
39 Alexander Rd.
Salem, CT 06420
860-859-2320

Witch Meadow Lake Campground
139 Witch Meadow Rd.
Salem, CT 06420
860-859-1542

Highland Campground
42 Toleration Rd., Box 305
Scotland, CT 06264
860-423-5684

Mineral Springs Campground
135 Leonard Rd.
Stafford Springs, CT 06076
860-684-2993

Roaring Brook Campground
8 South Rd.
Stafford Springs, CT 06076
860-684-7086

Sterling Park Campground
177 Gibson Hill Rd.
Sterling, CT 06377
860-564-8777

Branch Brook Campground
435 Watertown Rd.
Thomaston, CT 06787
860-283-8144

Del-Aire Campground
704 Shenipsit Lake Rd.
Tolland, CT 06084
860-875-8325

Countryside Campground
75 Cook Hill Rd.
Voluntown, CT 06384
860-376-0029

Nature's Campsites
Route 49N
Voluntown, CT 06384
860-376-4203

Circle "C" Campground
21 Bailey Rd.
Volyntown, CT 06384
860-564-4534

Moosemeadow Camping Resort
Moosemeadow Rd.
Willington, CT 06279
860-429-7451

Rainbow Acres Family Campground
150 Village Hill Rd.
Willington, CT 06279
860-684-5704

White Pines Campsites
232 Old North Rd.
Winsted, CT 06098
860-379-0124

Black Pond Campsites
Route 197
Woodstock, CT 06281
860-974-2065

Chamberlain Lake Campground
1397 Route 197
Woodstock, CT 06281
860-974-0567

MANNA Campground
1728 Route 198
Woodstock, CT 06281
860-974-3910

DELAWARE

Lums Pond State Park
1068 Howell School Rd.
Bear, DE 19701
302-368-6989

Jim's Hide A Way
Dagsboro, DE 19939
302-539-6095

Tuckahoe Acres Camping Resort
Dagsboro, DE 19939
302-539-1841

Killens Pond State Park
525 Killens Pond Rd.
Felton, DE 19943
302-284-3412

The Houston G&R Campground
4075 Gun & Rod Club Rd.
Houston, DE 19954
302-398-8108

Trap Pond State Park
RD 2, Box 331
Laurel, DE 19956
302-875-2392

Cape Henlopen State Park
42 Cape Henlopen Dr.
Lewes, DE 19958
320-645-2103

Tall Pines
221 Tall Pines
Lewes, DE 19958
302-684-0300

Holly Lake Campsites
RD Box 141
Millsboro, DE 19966
302-945-3410

Pine Tree Campsites
Ocean View, DE 19970
302-539-7006

Sandy Cove Campsite
RD 1, Box 256
Ocean View, DE 19970
302-539-6245

3 Seasons Camping Resort
727 Country Club Rd.
Rehoboth Beach, DE 19971
302-227-2564

Big Oaks Family Campgrounds
Box 53
Rehoboth Beach, DE 19971
302-645-6838

Delaware Seashore State Park
Inlet 850
Rehoboth Beach, DE 19971
302-539-7202

FLORIDA

Traveler's Campground
17701 April Blvd.
Alachua, FL 32615
904-462-2505

Alligator Point Campground
Route 1, P.O. Box 3392
Alligator Po, FL 32346
850-349-2525

U.S. Campgrounds > FLORIDA

KOA
1320 Alligator Dr.
Alligator Point, FL 32346
850-349-2525

Orlando Green Acres RV Resort
9701 Forest City Rd.
Altomonte Springs, FL 32714
800-894-8563

Arcadia Peace River Campground
2998 NW Hwy. 70
Arcadia, FL 34266
800-559-4011

Yogi Bear's Jellystone Park
9770 SW County Rd. 769
Arcadia, FL 34266
800-795-9733

Parramore's Campground
1675 S. Moon Rd.
Astor, FL 32102
800-516-2386

Fish Haven Lodge
Box 1, Fish Haven Rd.
Auburndale, FL 33823
941-984-1183

Lake Bonnet Village Campground
2900 E. Lake Bonnet Rd.
Avon Park, FL 33825
941-385-7010

Sunny Acres RV Resort
P.O. Box 238
Bagdad, FL 32530
850-623-0576

Breezy Pines RV Estates
P.O. Box 430191 Big Pin
Big Pine Key, FL 33043
305-872-9041

Bonita Beach Trailer Park
27800 Meadow Ln.
Bonita Springs, FL 33923
800-654-9907

Winter Quarters RV Resort
800 Kay Rd.
Bradenton, FL 34202
800-678-2131

Sumter Oaks RV Park
4602 County Route 673
Bushnell, FL 33513
352-793-1333

Mango-Oak Manor
190 Oak Manor Dr.
Cape Canaver, FL 32920
407-799-0741

Cedar Key RV Park
P.O. Box 268
Cedar Key, FL 32625
352-543-5150

Rainbow Country RV Campground
11951 SW Shiloh Rd.
Cedar Key, FL 32625
352-543-6268

KOA
Rt. 1, Box 1248
Chattahoochee, FL 32324
850-442-6657

NW Florda Campground & Music
677 Griffin Rd.
Chipley, FL 32428
850-638-0362

Chokoloskee Island Park
75 Hamilton Ln.
Chokoloskee, FL 33925
941-695-2414

Clearwater Travel Resort
2946 Gulf to Bay Blvd.
Clearwater, FL 34619
800-831-1204

Travel Towne Travel Trailer Resort
29850 US Hwy. 19 N
Clearwater, FL 34621
813-784-2500

Thousand Trails
2110 Hwy. 27 S
Clermont, FL 34711
800-723-1217

Okeechobee Landings, Inc. RV
420 Holiday Blvd.
Clewiston, FL 33440
800-322-5933

Oceanus Mobile Village & RV Park
152 Crescent Beach Dr.,
Cocoa Beach, FL 32931
407-783-3871

Crescent City Campground
Route 2, Box 25
Crescent Cit, FL 32112
800-634-3968

Crystal Isles RV Resort
11419 W. Ft. Island Tra
Crystal Rive, FL 34429
888-RVFORME

Travelers Rest Resort, Inc.
29129 Johnston Rd.
Dade City, FL 33523
800-565-8114

Deer Creek RV Golf Resort
4200 US Hwy. 27 N
Davenport, FL 33837
800-424-2931

Mouse Mountain RV Resort
7500 Osceola Polk Line Rd.
Davenport, FL 33837
941-424-2791

Daytona Beach Campground
4601 Clyde Morris Blvd.
Daytona Beach, FL 32119
904-761-2663

Nova Family Campground
1190 Herbert St.
Daytona Beach, FL 32119
904-767-0095

Camping on the Gulf Holiday
10005 W. Emerald Coast
Destin, FL 32541
850-837-6334

Destin RV Park
150 Regions Way
Destin, FL 32541
850-837-6215

RV Park
362 Miramar Beach Dr.
Destin, FL 32550
850-837-3529

U.S. Campgrounds > FLORIDA

Citrus Hills RV Park
5311 E. State Route 60
Dover, FL 33527
813-737-4770

Tampa East Green Acres Travel
4630 McIntosh Rd.
Dover, FL 33527
800-45-GREEN

Dunedin Beach Campground
2920 Alt 19 N
Dunedin, FL 34698
800-345-7504

Horseshoe Cove RV Resort
5100 60th St.
E. Bradenton, FL 34203
800-291-3446

Pleasant Lake RV Resort
6633 53rd Ave.
E. Bradenton, FL 34203
800-283-5076

Ho-Hum RV Resort Park
2132 Hwy. 98
E. Carrabell, FL 32322
888-88HOHUM

Morgan's RV Park
4411 State Route 542
E. Lakeland, FL 33801
941-665-9631

Arrowhead Campsites
4820 Hwy. 90
E. Marianna, FL 32446
850-482-5583

Royal Coachmen Resort
1070 Laurel Rd.
E. Nokomis, FL 34275
800-548-8678

Bulow RV Resort
P.O. Box 1328
Flagler Beach, FL 32136
800-RV-BULOW

Flagler By The Sea
2981 N. Oceanshore Blvd
Flagler Beach, FL 32136
800-434-2124

Picnickers Campground-Shelltown
2455 N. Oceanshore Blvd
Flagler Beach, FL 32136
800-553-2381

Southern Comfort RV Resort
345 E. Palm Dr.
Florida City, FL 33034
305-248-6909

Pine Lake RV Park
21036 US Hwy. 231
Fountain, FL 32438
850-722-1401

The Outpost
4576 Hwy. 3280
Freeport, FL 32439
850-835-2779

Lily Lake Golf Resort
500 US Hwy. 27
Frostproof, FL 33843
941-635-3685

Buglewood RV Resort
2121 NW 29th Ct.
Ft. Lauderdale, FL 33311
800-487-7395

Candlelight Park
5731 S. State Route 7
Ft. Lauderdale, FL 33314
954-791-5023

Kozy Kampers RV Park
3631 W. Commerical Blvd
Ft. Lauderdale, FL 33309
954-731-8570

Twin Lakes Travel Park
3055 Burris Rd.
Ft. Lauderdale, FL 33314
800-327-8182

Yacht Haven Park & Marina
2323 State Route 84
Ft. Lauderdale, FL 33312
800-581-2322

Ocklawaha Canoe Outpost RV Park
15260 NE 152nd Pl.
Ft. McCoy, FL 32134
352-236-4606

Cypress Woods RV Resort
5551 Luckett Rd.
Ft. Myers, FL 33905
800-414-9879

Cypress Woods RV Resort
Ft. Myers, FL 33905
941-694-2191

Fort Myers Beach RV Resort
16299 San Carlos Blvd.
Ft. Myers, FL 33908
800-553-7484

Fort Myers Beach RV Resort
Ft. Myers, FL 33905
941-466-7171

Garden RV Park
2830 Garden St.
Ft. Myers, FL 33917
941-995-7417

Gulf Air Travel Park
17279 San Carlos Blvd.
Ft. Myers, FL 33931
941-466-8100

Mar-Good RV Park, Cottages, Marina
Ft. Myers, FL 33905
941-392-6383

Seminole Campground
8991 Triplett Rd.
Ft. Myers, FL 33917
941-543-2919

Seminole Campground
Ft. Myers, FL 33905
941-543-2919

Shady Acres Travel Park
Ft. Myers, FL 33905
941-267-8448

Shady Acres Travel Park
19370 S. Tamiami Tr.
Ft. Myers, FL 33908
941-267-8448

Swan Lake Village & RV Resort
2400 N. Tamiami Tr.
Ft. Myers, FL 33903
941-995-3397

U.S. Campgrounds > FLORIDA

The Groves RV Campground
16175 John Morris Rd.
Ft. Myers, FL 33908
941-466-5909

The Groves RV Resort
Ft. Myers, FL 33905
941-466-4300

The Plantation RV Resort
Ft. Myers, FL 33905
941-275-1575

The Plantation, an RV Condo Resort
P.O. Box 60686
Ft. Myers, FL 33906
800-710-8819

Upriver Campground Resort
17021 Upriver Dr.
Ft. Myers, FL 33917
800-848-1652

Upriver Campground Resort
Ft. Myers, FL 33905
941-543-3330

Woodsmoke Camping Resort
19551 US Hwy. 41
Ft. Myers, FL 33908
800-231-5053

Ebb Tide RV Park
1725 Main St.
Ft. Myers Beach, FL 33931
941-463-5444

Ebb Tide RV Park
Ft. Myers Beach, FL 33931
941-463-5444

Gulf Air Travel Park
Ft. Myers Beach, FL 33931
941-466-8100

San Carlos RV Park
18701 San Carlos Blvd.
Ft. Myers Beach, FL 33931
800-525-7275

San Carlos RV Park
Ft. Myers Beach, FL 33931
941-466-3133

Road Runner Travel Resort
5500 St. Lucie Blvd
Ft. Pierce, FL 34946
800-833-7108

Playground RV Park
777 Beal Pkwy.
Ft. Walton Beach, FL 32547
850-862-3513

Port Cove RV Park & Marina
110 Georgetown Landing
Georgetown, FL 32139
800-980-5263

Mar-Good RV Park Cottages & Marina
321 Pear Tree Ave.
Goodland, FL 34140
941-394-6383

Paradise Island RV Resort
2900 S. US Hwy. 27
Haines City, FL 33844
800-831-2207

High Springs Campground
24004 NW Old Bellamy Rd
High Springs, FL 32643
904-454-1688

River's Edge RV Campground
P.O. Box 189
Holt, FL 32564
800-339-CAMP

Miami-Homestead KOA
20675 SW 162nd Ave.
Homestead, FL 33187
800-562-7732

The Boardwalk
100 NE 6th Ave.
Homestead, FL 33030
305-248-2487

Camp N Water
11465 W. Priest Ln.
Homosassa, FL 34448
352-628-2000

Citrus Cnty Chassahowitzka River
8600 W. Miss Maggie Dr.
Homosassa, FL 34446
352-382-2200

Gulf Coast Nudist Resort
13220 Houston Ave.
Hudson, FL 34667
813-868-1061

Indian Rocks Beach RV Resort
601 Gulf Blvd.
Indian Rocks, FL 34635
800-354-7559

Shawnee Trail Campground
2000-C Bishop's Point
Inverness, FL 34450
800-834-7595

Fiesta Key KOA
P.O. Box 618 - Mile Mar
Islamorada, FL 33001
800-562-7730

Flamingo Lake RV Resort
3640 Newcomb Rd.
Jacksonville, FL 32218
800-782-4323

Kathryn Abbey Hanna Park
500 Wonderwood Dr.
Jacksonville, FL 32233
904-249-4700

KOA
PO Box 18244
Jacksonville, FL 32229
912-729-3232

Jennings Outdoor Resort Campground
Route 1, Box 221
Jennings, FL 32053
904-938-3321

West Jupiter Camping Resort
17801 N. 130th Ave.
Jupiter, FL 33478
888-746-6073

America Outdoors
97450 Overseas Hwy.
Key Largo, FL 33037
305-852-8054

Calusa Camp Resort
325 Calusa Rd.
Key Largo, FL 33037
305-451-0232

U.S. Campgrounds > FLORIDA

Florida Keys RV Resort
100003 Overseas Hwy.
Key Largo, FL 33037
305-451-6090

Rock Harbor Marina
36 E. 2nd St
Key Largo, FL 33037
305-852-2025

Jabour's Trailer Court
223 Elizabeth St.
Key West, FL 33040
305-294-5723

Sugarloaf Key KOA
Box 469
Key West, FL 33042
305-745-3549

Kissimmee Campground
2643 Alligator Ln.
Kissimmee, FL 34746
407-396-6851

KOA
4771 W. Bronson Hwy.
Kissimmee, FL 34746
407-396-2400

**Orange Grove
Campground**
2425 Old Fineland Rd.
Kissimmee, FL 34746
800-3CAMPING

Orlando-Kissimmee KOA
4771 W. Irlo Bronson Hw
Kissimmee, FL 34746
800-562-7791

**Ponderosa Park
Campground**
1983 Boggy Creek Rd.
Kissimmee, FL 34744
407-847-6002

Sherwood Forest RV Park
5300 W. Irlo Bronson Hw
Kissimmee, FL 34746
800-548-9981

**Tropical Palms Fun
Resort & Campground**
2650 Holiday Trl
Kissimmee, FL 34746
800-64-PALMS

Yogi Bear's Jellystone Park
8555 W. Irlo Bronson, U
Kissimmee, FL 34747
800-776-YOGI

**Disney's For Wilderness
Camping**
P.O. Box 10000
Lake Buena Vista, FL 32830
407/WDISNEY

**Fort Summit Camping
Resort**
P.O. Box 22182
Lake Buena Vista, FL 32830
800-424-1880

KOA
Rt. 16, Box 243
Lake City, FL 32055
904-752-9131

Wagon Wheel RV Resort
Route 3, Box 176
Lake City, FL 32024
904-752-2279

Wayne's RV Resort
Route 17, Box 501
Lake City, FL 32024
904-752-5721

Idlewild Lodge & RV Park
4110 County Rd. 400
Lake Panasoffkee, FL 33538
352-793-7057

Camp Florida Resort
1525 US Hwy. 27 S
Lake Pl., FL 33852
941-699-1991

**Cypress Isle RV
Park & Marina**
2 Cypress Isle Ln.
Lake Placid, FL 33852
863-465-5241

**Camping Resort of the
Palm Beaches**
5332 Lake Worth Rd.
Lake Worth, FL 33463
800-247-9650

Valencia Estates & RV Park
3325 Barstow Hwy., SR 98 S
Lakeland, FL 33803
800-645-9033

A Camper's World
Route 1, Box 164B
Lamont, FL 32336
850-997-3300

Lee's Travel Park
1610 Belcher Rd.
Largo, FL 33771
888-510-8900

Holiday Travel Resort
28229 County Rd. 33
Leesburg, FL 34748
800-428-5334

KOA
33951 Spinnaker
Lillian, FL 36549
334-961-1717

**The Spirit of Suwannee
Music Park**
3076 95th Dr.
Live Oak, FL 32060
904-364-1683

Fiesta Key KOA
Box 618
Long Key, FL 33001
305-664-4922

Lion Country Safari KOA
2000 Lion Country Safari Rd.
Loxahatchee, FL 33470
561-793-9797

**Sunsport Gardens Nudist
Retreat**
14125 North Rd.
Loxahatchee, FL 33470
800-551-7117

Camp Nebraska RV Park
10314 N. Nebraska Ave.
Lutz, FL 33612
813-971-3460

Hidden River Ranch
P.O. Box 345
MacClenny, FL 32063
912-843-2603

Jolly Roger Travel Park
59275 Overseas Hwy.
Marathon, FL 33050
800-995-1525

U.S. Campgrounds > FLORIDA

Pelican Motel & Trailer Park
59151 Overseas Hwy.
Marathon, FL 33050
305-289-0011

Marineland Camping Resort
9741 Ocean Shore Blvd.
Marineland, FL 32086
904-471-4700

Jim Hollis' River Rendezvous
Route 2, Box 635
May, FL 32066
800-53305276

Sportsman Cove
P.O. Box 107
McIntosh, FL 32664
352-591-1435

Rustic Sands Resort Campground
HC03 800 N. 15th St.
Mexico Beach, FL 32456
850-648-5229

Gator Park
24050 SW 8th St.
Miami, FL 33187
800-559-2205

KOA
20675 SW 162 Ave.
Miami, FL 33187
305-233-5300

Kobe Trailer Park
11900 NE 16th Ave.
Miami, FL 33161
305-893-5121

Cedar Pines Campground
6436 Robie Rd.
Milton, FL 32570
850-623-8869

KOA
4513 W. Main St.
Mims, FL 32754
407-269-7361

Northgate Travel Park
3277 First Ave.
Mims, FL 32754
407-267-0144

Lakeside at Barth
855 Barth Rd.
Molino, FL 32577
850-587-2322

KOA
Rt 2, Box 5160
Monticello, FL 32344
850-997-3890

Woodlands Camp
15749 County Rd. 455
Montverde, FL 34756
407-469-2792

Meadowlark Campground
12525 Williams Rd. SW
Moore Haven, FL 33471
941-675-2243

Club Naples
3180 Beck Blvd.
Naples, FL 34114
888-795-2780

Crystal Lake RV Resort
160 County Rd. 951 N
Naples, FL 34119
800-322-4525

Endless Summer RV Estates
2 Tina Ln., Radio Rd.
Naples, FL 33942
941-643-1511

Kountree Kampinn RV Resort
5200 County Rd. 951
Naples, FL 34114
941-775-4340

Naples KOA
1700 Barefoot Williams Rd.
Naples, FL 33962
941-774-5455

Port of the Islands RV Resort
12425 Union Rd
Naples, FL 34114
800-319-4447

Silver Lakes RV Resort
1001 Silver Lakes Blvd.
Naples, FL 33961
800-843-2836

Emeral Beach RV Park
8899 Navarre Pkwy.
Navarre, FL 32566
850-939-3431

Navarre Beach Campground
9201 Navarre Pkwy.
Navarre, FL 32566
850-939-2188

KOA
1300 Old Mission Rd.
New Smyrna Beach, FL 32168
904-427-3581

Lake Awesome
899 Knights Tr.
Nokomis, FL 34275
800-437-9397

Sunseekers RV Park
North Ft. Myers, FL 33918
941-731-1303

Swan Lake Village & RV Resort
North Ft. Myers, FL 33918
941-995-3397

Ocala KOA
3200 SW 38th Ave.
Ocala, FL 34474
352-237-2138

Bob's Big Bass RV Park
12766 Hwy. 441 SE
Okeechobe, FL 34974
941-763-2638

Zachary Taylor Camping Resort
2995 US Hwy. 441 SE
Okeechobe, FL 34974
888-282-6523

Fijian RV Park
6500 SE Hwy. 441
Okeechobee, FL 34974
888-646-2267

Okeechobee KOA
4276 Hwy. 441 S.
Okeechobee, FL 34974
941-763-0231

Joa Navatto Old Town Campground
Hwy. 349, Box 522
Old Town, FL 32680
352-542-9500

U.S. Campgrounds > FLORIDA

Suwannee River KOA
P.O. Box 460
Old Town, FL 32680
800-562-7635

KOA
1440 E. Minnesota Ave.
Orange City, FL 32763
904-775-3996

Village Park Luxury RV Park
2300 E. Graves Ave.
Orange City, FL 32763
904-775-2545

Whiteys Fish Camp
2032 County Rd. 220
Orange Park, FL 32073
904-269-4198

KOA
12345 Narcoossee Rd.
Orlando, FL 32827
407-277-5075

Ocean Village Camper Resort
2162 Ocean Shore Blvd.
Ormond Beach, FL 32176
904-441-1808

On Ocean Seaside RV & Trailer
1047 Ocean Shore Blvd.
Ormond Beach, FL 32176
904-441-0900

Sunshine Holiday Camper Resort
1701 N. US Hwy. 1
Ormond Beach, FL 32174
904-672-3045

St. John's Campground
US Hwy. 17, Route 3
Palatka, FL 32131
904-328-4470

Bay Aire RV Park
2242 US Hwy. Alt 19 N
Palm Harbor, FL 34683
813-784-4082

Caladesi Travle Trailer Park
205 Dempsey Rd.
Palm Harbor, FL 34683
813-784-362

KOA
37061 US 19 N.
Palm Harbor, FL 34684
727-937-8412

Palm Harbor Resort
2119 Alt 19 N
Palm Harbor, FL 34683
813-785-3401

Sherwood Forest RV Resort
251 US Hwy. Alt 19
Palm Harbor, FL 34683
800-413-9762

Fiesta Grove RV Resort
8615 Bayshore Rd.
Palmetto, FL 34221
941-722-7661

Fisherman's Cove RV Resort
100 Palmview Rd.
Palmetto, FL 34221
941-729-3685

Frog Creek Campground
8515 Bayshore Rd.
Palmetto, FL 34221
800-771-3764

Winterset Travel Trailer RV Park
8515 US Hwy. 41 N
Palmetto, FL 34221
800-263-3984

Holiday Park & Campground
14 Coastal Hwy.
Panacea, FL 32346
850-98405757

Ocean Park RV Resort
23026 Panama City Beach
Panama City, FL 32413
850-235-0306

Panama City Beach KOA
8800 Thomas Dr.
Panama City, FL 32408
800-562-2483

Pine Glen Motor Coach & RV Park
11930 Panama City Beach
Panama City, FL 32407
850-230-8353

KOA
8800 Thomas Dr.
Panama City Beach, FL 32408
850-234-5731

All Star RV Campground
13621 Perdino Key Dr.
Pensacola, FL 32507
800-245-3602

Southern Oaks
3641 Hwy. 19 S
Perry, FL 32347
800-339-5421

Cape San Blas Camping Resort
P.O. Box 645
Port St. Joe, FL 32457
850-229-6800

Gulf View RV Resort
10205 Burnt Store Rd.
Punta Gorda, FL 33950
941-639-3978

KOA
6800 Golf Course Blvd.
Punta Gorda, FL 33982
941-637-1188

Punta Gorda RV Resort
3701 Baynard Dr.
Punta Gorda, FL 33950
941-639-2010

Sun-N-Shade Campground
14880 Tamiami Tr.
Punta Gorda, FL 33955
941-639-5388

Whippoorwill Sportsmans Lodge
3129 Cooks Landing Rd.
Quincy, FL 32351
850-875-2605

Alafia River RV Resort
9812 Gilbsonton Dr.
Riverview, FL 33569
813-677-1997

Space Coast RV Resort
820 Barnes Blvd.
Rockledge, FL 32955
407-636-2873

U.S. Campgrounds > FLORIDA

Hide-A-Way RV Resort
2206 Chaney Dr.
Ruskin, FL 33570
800-607-2532

Lone Pine RV Park
201 11th Ave NW
Ruskin, FL 33570
813-645-6532

River Oaks RV Resort
201 Stephens Rd.
Ruskin, FL 33561
800-645-6311

Twelve Oaks RV Resort
6300 State Route 46 W
Sanford, FL 32771
800-633-9529

Emerald Coast RV Resort
7525 W. Scenic Hwy. 30
Santa Rosa, FL 32459
800-BEACH-RV

Crystal Lake RV Park
P.O. Box 362
Scottsmoor, FL 32775
407-268-8555

Buttonwood Bay RV Resort
10001 US Hwy. 27 S
Sebring, FL 33870
800-289-2522

Sebring Grove RV Resort
4105 US Hwy. 27
Sebring, FL 33870
941-382-1660

Tanglewood RV Resort
4545 US Hwy. 27 N
Sebring, FL 33870
800-386-4545

Lazy Days Campground Resort
6130 Lazy Days Blvd.
Seffner, FL 33584
800-626-7800

Holiday Campground
10000 Park Blvd.
Seminole, FL 34647
800-354-7559

Silver Springs Campers Garden
3151 NE 56th Ave.
Silver Springs, FL 34488
800-640-3733

South Bay RV Campground
100 Levee Rd.
South Bay, FL 33493
561-992-9045

Deer Haven RV Park
2812 Hwy. 2321
Southport, FL 32409
850-265-6205

Bryn Mawr Ocean Resort
4850 Hwy. A1A
St. Augustine, FL 32084
904-471-3353

Cooksey's Camping Resort
2795 State Rd. 3
St. Augustine, FL 32084
904-471-3171

Indian Forest Campground
1555 State Route 207
St. Augustine, FL 32086
800-233-4324

KOA
9950 KOA Rd.
St. Augustine, FL 32095
904-824-8309

North Beach Camp Resort
4125 Coastal Hwy.
St. Augustine, FL 32095
800-542-8316

Ocean Grove RV Resort
4225 Hwy. A1
St. Augustine, FL 32084
800-342-4007

Peppertree Beach Club
4825 Hwy. A1A
St. Augustine, FL 32084
800-325-2267

St. Augustine Beach KOA
525 W. Pope Rd.
St. Augustine, FL 32084
800-562-4022

Stagecoach RV Park, Inc.
2711 County Rd. 208
St. Augustine, FL 32092
904-824-2319

State Park Campground of America
1425 State Rd. 16
St. Augustine, FL 32095
904-824-4016

Gator RV Resort
5755 E. Irlo Bronson Hw
St. Cloud, FL 34771
888-252-0020

Ft. Myers–Pine Island KOA
5120 Stringfellow Rd.
St. James City, FL 33956
800-562-8505

St. Petersburg KOA
5400 95th St. N.
St. Petersburg, FL 33708
727-392-2233

KOA
1475 S. Walnut St.
Starke, FL 32091
904-964-8484

Boyd's Key West Campground
6401 Maloney Ave.
Stock Island, FL 33040
305-294-1465

Bluewater Key RV Resort
P.O. Box 409
Sugarloaf Key, FL 33044
800-237-2266

Lazy Lakes Campground
P.O. Box 440179
Sugarloaf Key, FL 33044
800-354-5524

Tallahassee RV Park
6504 Mahan Dr.
Tallahassee, FL 32308
850-878-7641

Bay Bayou Traveler
12622 Memorial Hwy.
Tampa, FL 33635
813-855-1000

U.S. Campgrounds > IDAHO

**Great Outdoors RV-
Golf Resort**
135 Plantation Dr.
Titusville, FL 32780
800-621-2267

Oak Acres Campground
326 Goff Rd
Venus, FL 33960
941-465-2795

KOA
8850 N. US 1, Box 337
Wabasso, FL 32970
561-589-5682

Crystal Lake Village
237 Maxwell Rd.
Wauchula, FL 33873
800-661-3582

**Little Charlie Creek
RV Park**
1850 Heard Bridge Rd.
Wauchula, FL 33873
941-773-0088

Trailer Gardens
1444 Old Okeechobee Rd.
West Palm Beach, FL 33401
561-659-2817

Kelly's RV-MH Park
RR1, Box 370
White Spring, FL 32096
904-397-2616

KOA
882 E. SR 44
Wildwood, FL 34785
352-748-2774

Wayside RV Park
1201 S. Main St.
Wildwood, FL 34785
800-241-4133

**Orlando Winter Garden
Campgro**
13905 W. Colonia Dr.
Winter Garden, FL 34787
407-656-1415

State Stop Campground
700 W. Hwy. 50 (AKA 144)
Winter Garden, FL 34787
407-656-8000

Hunters Run RV Estates
37041 Chancey Rd.
Zephyrhills, FL 33541
813-783-1133

Jim's RV Park
35120 Hwy. 54 W
Zephyrhills, FL 33541
813-782-5610

Leisure Days RV Resort
34533 Leisure Days Dr.
Zephyrhills, FL 33541
813-788-2631

**Smitty's Country Style
RV Campground**
30846 State Route 54 W
Zephyrhills, FL 33543
813-973-4301

GEORGIA

KOA
2523 Redbud Rd. NE
Calhoun, GA 30701
706-629-7511

KOA
800 Cass-White Rd. NW
Cartersville, GA 30121
770-382-7330

KOA
5473 Mt. Olive
Commerce, GA 30529
706-335-5535

KOA
373 Rockhouse Rd.
Cordele, GA 31015
912-273-5454

KOA
PO Box 967
Forsyth, GA 31029
912-994-2019

KOA
2000 Old US 41 Hwy.
Kennesaw, GA 30152
770-427-2046

KOA
291 Mt. Olive Rd.
McDonough, GA 30253
770-957-2610

KOA
Box 309
Richmond Hill, GA 31324
912-756-3396

**Chattanooga South/
Lookout Mtn. KOA**
199 KOA Blvd.
Ringgold, GA 30736
800-562-4167

**Lookout Mtn./Chattanooga
West KOA**
Box 490
Trenton, GA 30752
800-562-1239

IDAHO

Indian Springs
3249 Indian Springs Rd.
American Falls, ID 83211
202-226-2174

Pipeline
American Falls, ID 83211
202-236-6860

Carroll's Travel Plaza
Rt.1, Box 20A
Arco, ID 83213
208-527-3504

**Aspen Acres Golf Club
& RV Park**
4179 E., 1100 N
Ashton, ID 83420
208-652-3524

Cave Falls
Ashton, ID 83420
208-652-7442

**Jessen's RV and
Bed & Breakfast**
Box 11, 1146 S
Ashton, ID 83420
208-652-3356

Pole Bridge Campground
Forest Rd.
Ashton, ID 83420
208-652-7742

Riverside Campground
Forest Rd.
Ashton, ID 83420
208-652-7442

U.S. Campgrounds > IDAHO

Warm River Campground
Ashton, ID 83420
208-652-7442

Silverwood RV Park
N. 26225 Hwy. 95
Athol, ID 83801
208-583-3400

Big Eddy Campground
Banks, ID 83602
208-365-7000

Canyon Campground
Banks, ID 83602
208-365-7000

Cold Springs Campground
Banks, ID 83602
208-365-7000

**Swinging Bridge
Campground**
Banks, ID 83602
208-365-7000

**Bayview Scenic Motel &
RV Park**
P.O. Box 70
Bayview, ID 83803
208-683-2215

**MacDonald's Hudson Bay
Resort**
P.O. Box 38
Bayview, ID 83803
208-683-2211

Scenic Bay Marina
P.O. Box 36
Bayview, ID 83803
208-683-2243

**Riverside RV &
Campground**
Box 432
Bellevue, ID 83313
208-788-2020

Boise KOA
7300 Federal Way
Boise, ID 83706
208-345-7673

Hi Valley RV Park
10555 Hwy. 55
Boise, ID 83703
208-939-8080

Mountain View RV Park
2040 Airport Way
Boise, ID 83705
208-345-4141

On the River RV Park
6000 Glenwood
Boise, ID 83714
208-375-7432

Shafer Butte
Boise, ID 83714
208-364-4242

Willow Creek
Boise, ID 83714
208-364-4242

Bonners Ferry Resort
Rt. 4. Box 4700, 6438 S. Main
Bonners Ferry, ID 83805
208-267-2422

Deep Creek Resort
Rt. 4, Box 628
Bonners Ferry, ID 83805
208-267-2729

Idyl Acres RV Park
HCR 61, Box 170
Bonners Ferry, ID 83805
208-267-3629

Meadow Creek
Bonners Ferry, ID 83805
208-267-5561

**Town and Country Motel
& RV Park**
Route 4, Box 4664
Bonners Ferry, ID 83805
208-267-7915

Banbury Hot Springs
Route 3, Box 408
Buhl, ID 83316
208-543-2098

Miracle Hot Springs
P.O. Box 171
Buhl, ID 83316
208-543-6002

Brownlee Campground
Cambridge, ID 83610
208-549-2420

Frontier Motel & RV Park
P.O. Box 178, 240 S. Superior St.
Cambridge, ID 83610
208-257-3851

Woodhead Park
Cambridge, ID 83610
800-422-3143

High-Five Campground
Carey, ID 83320
208-436-4187

Littlewood Reservoir
Carey, ID 83320
208-436-4187

**Arrowhead RV Park on
the River**
P.O. Box 337
Cascade, ID 83611
208-382-4534

**Aurora Motel – RV Park
& Storage**
P.O. Box 799
Cascade, ID 83611
208-382-4948

Big Sage Campground
Cascade, ID 83611
208-382-4258

Buttercup Campground
Cascade, ID 83611
208-382-4258

Cabarton 1 Campground
Cascade, ID 83611
208-382-4258

Crown Point Campground
Cascade, ID 83611
208-382-4258

Curlew Campground
Cascade, ID 83611
208-382-4258

Herb's RV Park
P.O. Box 976
Cascade, ID 83611
208-382-3451

Huckleberry Campground
Cascade, ID 83611
208-382-4258

U.S. Campgrounds > IDAHO

Poison Creek Campground
Cascade, ID 83611
208-382-4258

Sugarloaf
Cascade, ID 83611
208-382-4258

Van Wyck Park 1
Cascade, ID 83611
208-382-4258

Van Wyck Park 2
Cascade, ID 83611
208-382-4258

Water's Edge RV Resort
P.O. Box 1018, Hwy. 55
Cascade, ID 83611
800-574-2038

West Mountain
Cascade, ID 83611
208-382-4258

Westside RV Park
P.O. Box 648
Cascade, ID 83611
208-325-4100

Bayhorse Lake
Challis, ID 83226
208-838-2201

Challis All Valley RV Park
P.O. Box 928
Challis, ID 83226
208-879-2393

Challis Hot Springs
HC 63, P.O. Box 1779
Challis, ID 83226
208-879-4442

River Delta Resort
Star Rt., Box 128
Clark Fork, ID 83811
208-266-1335

River Lake RV Resort
P.O. Box 219
Clark Fork, ID 83811
208-266-1115

Whiskey Rock Bay
Clark Fork, ID 83811
208-263-5111

Sandy Beach Resort
4405 Loop Rd.
Cocolalla, ID 83813
208-263-4328

Boulevard Motel & RV Park
2400 Seltice Way
Coeur D'Alene, ID 83814
208-664-4978

Cedar Motel & RV Park
319 Coeur d'Alene. Lake Dr.
Coeur D'Alene, ID 83814
208-664-2278

Killarney Lake
I-90 E. Hwy. 3
Coeur D'Alene, ID 83814
208-769-5000

KOA
E. 10070 Wolf Lodge Bay Rd.
Coeur d'Alene, ID 83814
208-664-4471

**Monte Vista Motel &
RV Park**
320 S. Coeur d'Alene Lake Dr.
Coeur D'Alene, ID 83814
208-664-8201

**Robin Hood
RV Park & Campground**
703 Lincoln Way
Coeur D'Alene, ID 83814
208-664-2306

**Rockford Bay Resort &
Marina**
W. 8700 Rockford Bay
Coeur D'Alene, ID 83814
208-664-6931

Shady Acres Campground
N. 3630 Government Way
Coeur D'Alene, ID 83814
208-664-3087

Wolf Lodge Campground
12425 E. I-90
Coeur D'Alene, ID 83814
208-664-2812

Cabin Creek
Council, ID 83812
208-253-4215

Evergreen
Council, ID 83812
208-253-4215

Huckleberry
Council, ID 83812
208-253-4215

Lafferty
Council, ID 83812
208-253-4215

Little Boulder Creek
Deary, ID 83823
208-875-1131

Snake River RV Park
Rt. 1. Box 33
Declo, ID 83323
208-654-2133

Lodgepole Pine Inn
P.O. Box 71
Dixie, ID 83525
208-842-2343

Kenally Creek
Donnelly, ID 83615
208-634-1453

**Southwestern Idaho Sr.
Citizens Recreation Assoc.**
P.O. Box 625
Donnelly, ID 83615
208-325-9518

Downata Hot Springs
P.O. Box 185
Downey, ID 25900
208-897-5736

Flag's West Truck Stop
Downey, ID 25900
208-897-5238

Reunion Flat
Driggs, ID 83422
208-354-2312

Reunion Flat Group Area
Driggs, ID 83422
208-354-2312

Teton Canyon
Driggs, ID 83422
208-354-2312

U.S. Campgrounds > IDAHO

Anderson Camp and RV Sales & Service
Rt 1
Eden, ID 83325
208-825-5336

Huckle Berry Heaven
P.O. Box 165
Elk River, ID 83827
208-826-3405

Capital Mobile Park
1508 E. Main
Emmett, ID 83617
208-365-3889

Bowns
Fairfield, ID 83372
208-764-2202

Canyon Transfer Camp
Fairfield, ID 83372
208-764-2202

Soldier Creek RV Park
Rt. 1, Box 1271
Fairfield, ID 83372
208-764-2684

Curry Trailer Park
21323 Hw. 30
Filer, ID 83328
208-733-3961

Neat Retreat
2701 Hwy. 95
Fruitland, ID 83619
208-452-4324

Boiling Springs
Garden Valley, ID 83622
208-365-7000

Hardscrabble
Garden Valley, ID 83622
208-365-7000

Rattlesnake
Garden Valley, ID 83622
208-365-7000

Silver Creek
Garden Valley, ID 83622
208-365-7000

Silver Creek Plunge
HC 76, Box 2377, Unit 1942
Garden Valley, ID 83622
208-344-8688

Trail Creek
Garden Valley, ID 83622
208-365-7000

Broken Arrow
P.O. Box 26
Gibbonsville, ID 83463
208-856-2241

Junction Lodge
HC 67, Box 98
Grangeville, ID 83530
208-842-2459

Sugar's 1000 Springs Resort
5 Gillhooley Ln.
Hagerman, ID 83332
208-837-4987

Albertini's Carlin Bay Resort
HCR 2, Box 45, I-97
Harrison, ID 83833
208-689-3295

Bell Bay
Harrison, ID 83833
208-769-3000

Squaw Bay Camping Resort
Rt. 2, Box 130
Harrison, ID 83833
208-664-6782

Giant White Pine
Harvard, ID 83834
208-875-1131

Laird Park
Harvard, ID 83834
208-875-1131

Pines RV Campground
4510 Hwy.
Harvard, ID 83834
208-875-0831

Alpine Country Store & RV Park
17400 N 95 Hwy.
Hayden, ID 83835
208-772-4305

Coeur D'Alene North/ Hayden Lake KOA
4850 E. Garwood Rd.
Hayden, ID 83835
208-772-4557

R&E Greenwood Store
1015 Ridgeway Rd.
Hazelton, ID 83335
208-829-5735

White Locks Marina & RV Park
3429 Hwy. 34
Henry, ID 83230
208-574-2208

Beyond Hope Resort
248 Beyond Hope Hwy. 200E
Hope, ID 83836
208-264-5251

Idaho Country Resort
141 Idaho Country Rd.
Hope, ID 83836
208-264-5505

Island View RV Park
300 Island View
Hope, ID 83836
208-264-5509

Jeb & Margaret's Trailer Haven
298 Trailer Haven
Hope, ID 83836
208-264-5406

KOA
1440 Lindsay Blvd.
Idaho Falls, ID 83402
208-523-3362

Aspen Lodge
HC 66, Box 269
Island Park, ID 83429
208-558-7406

Island Park Kampground
HC 66, Box 447
Island Park, ID 83429
208-558-7112

Pond's Lodge
P.O . Box 258
Island Park, ID 83429
208-558-7221

Redrock RV & Camping Park
HC 66, Box 256
Island Park, ID 83429
208-558-7442

U.S. Campgrounds > IDAHO

Staley Springs Lodge
HC 66, Box 102
Island Park, ID 83429
208-558-7471

Valley View General Store and RV Park
HC 66, Box 26
Island Park, ID 83429
208-558-7443

Wild Rose Ranch
340 W. 7th S, HC 66, Box140
Island Park, ID 83429
208-558-7201

KOA
5431 US 93
Jerome, ID 83338
208-324-4169

Boulder View
300 First Ave. W
Ketchum, ID 83340
208-726-7672

Apgar
Kooskia, ID 83539
208-926-4275

Three Rivers Resort
HC 75, Box 61
Kooskia, ID 83539
208-926-4430

Wild Goose
Kooskia, ID 83539
208-926-4275

Wilderness Gateway
Kooskia, ID 83539
208-926-4275

Cottonwood Family Campground
P.O. Box 307
Lava Hot Springs, ID 83246
208-776-5295

Lava Ranch Inn Motel & RV Campground
9611 Hwy. 30
Lava Hot Springs, ID 83246
208-776-9917

Mountain View Trailer Park, Inc.
P.O. Box 687
Lava Hot Springs, ID 83246
208-776-5611

Lema's Store & RV Park
P.O. Box 204
Leadore, ID 60096
208-768-2647

Hells Gate State Park
Lewiston, ID 83501
208-799-5015

Ryan's Wilderness Inn
HC 75, Box 60-A2
Lowell, ID 83539
208-926-4706

Barney's
Lowman, ID 83637
208-259-3361

Bear Valley
Lowman, ID 83637
208-259-3361

Bonneville
Lowman, ID 83637
208-259-3361

Bull Trout Lake
Lowman, ID 83637
208-259-3361

Cozy Cove
Lowman, ID 83637
208-259-3361

Helende
Lowman, ID 83637
208-259-3361

Hower's
Lowman, ID 83637
208-259-3361

Mountain View
Lowman, ID 83637
208-259-3361

New Haven Lodge
HC 77, Box 3608, Hwy. 21
Lowman, ID 83637
208-259-3344

Park Creek
Lowman, ID 83637
208-259-3361

Riverside
Lowman, ID 83637
208-259-3361

Sourdough Lodge & RV Resort
HC 77, Box 3109, Hwy. 21
Lowman, ID 83637
208-259-3326

Prospector's Gold RV & Campground
P.O. Box 313
Lucille, ID 83542
208-628-3773

River Front Gardens RV Park
HCO 1, Box 15
Lucille, ID 83542
208-628-3777

Iron Bog
Mackay, ID 83521
208-588-2224

Mackay Reservoir
Mackay, ID 83521
208-756-5400

Park Creek
Mackay, ID 83521
208-588-2224

Phi Kappa
Mackay, ID 83521
208-588-2224

River Park Golf Course & RV Campground
717 Capital Ave., P.O. Box 252
Mackay, ID 83521
208-588-2296

Star Hope
Mackay, ID 83521
208-588-2224

Timber Creek
Mackay, ID 83521
208-588-2224

Wagon Wheel Motel & RV Park
P.O. Box 22
Mackay, ID 83521
208-588-3331

White Knob Motel & RV Park
Box 180
Mackay, ID 83521
208-588-2622

U.S. Campgrounds > IDAHO

Wildhorse
Mackay, ID 83521
208-588-2224

Big Springs
Macks Inn, ID 83433
208-558-7301

Flat Rock
Macks Inn, ID 83433
208-558-7301

Mack's Inn Resort
P.O. Box 10
Macks Inn, ID 83433
208-558-7272

Upper Coffee Pot
Macks Inn, ID 83433
208-558-7301

River Haven RV Park
May, ID 83253
208-588-2224

Buckhorn Bar
McCall, ID 83638
208-634-0600

Lake Fork
McCall, ID 83638
208-634-1453

Lakeview Village
1 Pearl St., Box 8
McCall, ID 83638
208-634-5280

Ponderosa
McCall, ID 83638
208-634-1465

Upper Payette Lake
McCall, ID 83638
208-634-1453

Given's Hot Springs
HC 79, Box 103
Melba, ID 83641
208-495-2000

KOA
Box 87
Montpelier, ID 83254
208-847-0863

Rendezvous Village RV Park
577 N. 4th St.
Montpelier, ID 83254
208-847-1100

Golden Rule KOA
220 E. 10th N
Mountain Home, ID 83647
208-587-5111

The Wagon Wheel
1880 e 5th N, #3,
Mountain Home, ID 83647
208-587-5994

Twin Rivers Canyon Resort
HCR 62, Box 25
Moyle Springs, ID 83845
208-267-5932

Mason Creek RV Park
807 Franklin Rd
Nampa, ID 83653
208-465-7199

Blue Lake Campground & RV Park
HCR 01, P.O. Box 277
Naples, ID 83847
208-267-2029

Cold Springs Campground
New Meadows
New Meadows, ID 50091
208-347-2141

Goose Creek Campground
HC 75, Box 3270
New Meadows, ID 50091
208-347-2116

Grouse Creek Campground
New Meadows, ID 50091
208-347-2141

Meadows RV Park
P.O. Box 60
New Meadows, ID 50091
208-347-2325

Zim's Hot Springs
P.O. Box 314
New Meadows, ID 50091
208-347-2686

Cummings Lake Lodge
P.O. Box 8
North Fork, ID 83466
208-865-2424

Wagonhammer Springs Campground
P.O. Box 102
North Fork, ID 83466
208-865-2246

Antelope Campground
Ola, ID 83657
208-365-7000

Eastside Campground
Ola, ID 83657
208-365-7000

Hollywood Point Campground
Ola, ID 83657
208-365-7000

Sagehen Creek Campground
Ola, ID 83657
208-365-7000

Mountain View MH & RV Park
P.O. Box 25
Orangeville, ID 83530
208-983-2328

Hidden Village
14615 Hwy. 12
Orofino, ID 83544
208-476-3416

Vacation Land Motel & RV
14115 Hwy. 12
Orofino, ID 83544
208-476-4012

Blue Anchor Motel & RV
P.O. Box 645
Osburn, ID 83849
208-752-3443

Lazy River RV Park
11575 N. River Rd.
Payette, ID 83661
208-642-9667

Aquarius
Pierce, ID 83546
208-476-3775

Hidden Creek
Pierce, ID 83546
208-476-3775

Kelly Forks
Pierce, ID 83546
208-476-3775

Noe Creek
Pierce, ID 83546
208-476-3775

U.S. Campgrounds > IDAHO

Washington Creek
Pierce, ID 83546
208-476-3775

**Nester's Riverside
Campground**
HC 87, Box 210
Pine, ID 83647
208-653-2222

Pine Resort
HC 87, Box 200
Pine, ID 83647
208-653-2323

Kellogg/Silver Valley KOA
Box 949
Pinehurst, ID 83850
208-682-3612

Cowboy RV Park
845 Barton Rd.
Pocatello, ID 83201
208-232-4587

Pocatello KOA
9815 W. Pocatello Cr. Rd.
Pocatello, ID 83201
208-233-6851

Coeur D'Alene RV Resort
2600 E. Mullan Ave.
Post Falls, ID 83854
208-773-3527

Suntree RV Park
401 Idahline
Post Falls, ID 83854
208-773-9982

**Deer Cliff Store,
Cafe and RV**
1942 N. Deer Cliff Rd.
Preston, ID 30006
208-852-3320

**Twin Lakes
Mobile Home Park**
Rt. 4, Box 235
Rathdrum, ID 83858
208-687-1242

**Rainbow Lake &
Campground**
2245 S. 2000W
Rexburg, ID 83440
208-356-3681

River Village RV Park
P.O. Box 2
Riggins, ID 83549
208-628-3441

Riverside RV Park
P.O. Box 1270\
Riggins, ID 83549
208-628-3390

Seven Devils
Riggins, ID 83549
208-628-3916

Sleepy Hollow RV Park
P.O. Box 1159
Riggins, ID 83549
208-628-3401

Windy Saddle
Riggins, ID 83549
208-628-3916

7N Ranch
5156 E. Heise Rd.
Ririe, ID 83443
208-538-5097

Ririe Reservoir
Ririe, ID 83443
208-538-7871

Desert Hot Springs
Rogerson, ID 83443
208-857-2233

Murphy Hot Springs Lodge
Rogerson, ID 83443
208-857-2238

Walcott Park
Rt. 4, Box 292
Rupert, ID 83350
208-436-6117

Fox Farm RV Resort
3160 Dufort Rd.
Sagle, ID 83860
208-263-8896

Garfield Bay Resort
6890 W. Garfield Bay Rd.
Sagle, ID 83860
208-263-1078

Century II Campground
603 Hwy. 93N
Salmon, ID 83467
208-756-2063

Heald's Haven
HC 61, Box 15
Salmon, ID 83467
208-756-3929

Salmon Meadows
P.O. Box 705
Salmon, ID 83467
208-756-2640

Williams Lake Resort
P.O. Box 1150
Salmon, ID 83467
208-756-2007

Bottle Bay Resort
1360 Bottle Bay Rd.
Sandpoint, ID 83864
208-263-5916

**Sandpoint KOA
Kampground**
100 Sagle Rd.
Sandpoint, ID 83864
208-263-4824

Sandy Beach Resort
4405 Loop Rd.
Sandpoint, ID 83864
208-263-4328

Travel America Plaza
P.O. Box 199
Sandpoint, ID 83864
208-263-6522

**Silver Leaf Motel &
RV Park**
P.O. Box 151
Silverton, ID 83867
208-752-0222

White's Buffalo RV Park
Box 579
Smelterville, ID 83868
208-786-9551

Silver Beach Resort
8350 W. Spirit Lake Rd.
Spirit Lake, ID 83869
208-623-4842

**Cedars & Shade
Campground**
P.O. Box 219
St. Charles, ID 83272
208-945-2608

**Minnetonka RV &
Campground**
P.O. Box 6, 220 N. Main
St. Charles, ID 83272
208-945-2941

**Ed's R&R Shady River
RV Park**
1211 Lincoln
St. Maries, ID 83861
208-245-3549

**Misty Meadows RV Park &
Camping**
HC 03, Box 52
St. Maries, ID 83861
208-245-2639

Beaver Creek
Stanley, ID 83278
208-838-2201

Blind Creek
Stanley, ID 83278
208-838-2201

Bonanza
Stanley, ID 83278
208-838-2201

Boundary Creek
Stanley, ID 83278
208-879-5204

Chinook Bay
Stanley, ID 83278
208-726-7672

Custer #1
Stanley, ID 83278
208-838-2201

Dagger Falls #1
Stanley, ID 83278
208-879-5204

**Summer Home Trailer
Park**
HC 64, Box 9916
Stanley, ID 83278
208-774-3310

Park Creek
Sun Valley, ID 83353
208-588-2224

Phi Kappa
Sun Valley, ID 83353
208-588-2224

The Meadows RV Park
P.O. Box 1440
Sun Valley, ID 83353
208-726-5445

Wildhorse
Sun Valley, ID 83353
208-588-2224

South Fork Lodge
P.O. Box 22
Swan Valley, ID 83449
208-483-2112

Blue Lakes RV Park
1122 North Blue Lakes Blvd.
Twin Falls, ID 83301
208-734-5782

**Burren West LLC
RV/Trailer Resort**
255 Los Lagos
Twin Falls, ID 83301
208-487-2571

**Nat-Soo-Pah Hot Springs
& RV Park**
2738 E. 2400 N
Twin Falls, ID 83301
208-655-4337

**Oregon Trail Campground
& Family Fun Center**
2733 Kimberly Rd.
Twin Falls, ID 83301
208-733-0853

Mike Harris Campground
Victor, ID 83445
208-354-2321

Pine Creek Campground
Victor, ID 83445
208-354-2321

Teton Valley Campground
P.O. Box 49, 128 Hwy. 31
Victor, ID 83445
208-787-2647

Trail Creek Campground
Victor, ID 83445
208-354-2312

**Lookout RV Park and
Campground**
Lookout Pass
Wallace, ID 83873
208-744-1392

Gateway RV Park
229 E. 7th St.
Weiser, ID 83672
208-549-2539

Indian Hot Springs
914 Hot Springs Rd.
Weiser, ID 83672
208-549-0070

**Indianhead Motel &
RV Park**
747 US hwy. 95
Weiser, ID 83672
208-549-0331

Mann Creek Campground
Weiser, ID 83672
208-365-2682

**Monroe Creek
Campground**
822 US Hwy. 95
Weiser, ID 83672
208-549-2026

**Paradise/Justrite
Campground**
Weiser, ID 83672
208-549-2420

Spring Creek Campground
Weiser, ID 83672
208-549-2420

**Hammer Creek
Campground**
White Bird, ID 83554
208-962-3245

Slate Creek Campground
White Bird, ID 83554
208-962-3245

ILLINOIS

**Mendota Hills Camping
Resort**
642 US Rt. 52
Amboy, IL 61310
815-849-5930

**O'Connells Yogi Bear
Jellystone Park**
970 Green Wing Rd.
Amboy, IL 61310
815-857-3860

U.S. Campgrounds > ILLINOIS

Fox River Recreation
27884 W. Rt. 173
Antioch, IL 60001
847-395-6090

Outdoor World - Pine Country
5710 Shattuck Rd.
Belvidere, IL 61008
815-547-5517

KOA
RR 1, N. DuQuoin St.
Benton, IL 62812
618-439-4860

Lake Louise Campground
PO Box 451
Byron, IL 61010
815-234-8483

KOA
PO Box 56
Casey, IL 62420
217-932-5319

Springfield Best Holiday
9683 Palm Rd.
Chatham, IL 62629
217-483-9998

KOA
425 E. 6000 Rd.
Chebanse, IL 60922
815-939-4603

Smith's Stone House Park
3719 Suydam Rd.
Earlville, IL 60518
815-246-9732

Casino Queen RV Park
200 S. Front St.
East St. Louis, IL 62201
618-874-5000

Red Barn Rendezvous
3955 Blackburn Rd.
Edwardsville, IL 62025
618-692-9015

Gages Lake Camping
18887 W. Gages Lake Rd.
Gages Lake, IL 60030
847-223-5541

Jellystone Park of Belvidere
7050 Epworth
Garden Prarie, IL 61038
815-547-7846

Paradise RV Park
PO Box 96
Garden Prarie, IL 61038
815-597-1671

Geneseo Campground
22978 Illinois Hwy. 82
Geneseo, IL 61254
309-944-6465

Northeast/I-270/Granite City KOA
3157 W. Chain of Rocks
Granite City, IL 62040
800-562-5861

Galesburg East Best Holiday
1081 US Hwy. 150 E.
Knoxville, IL 61448
309-389-2267

Hi-Tide Recreation
4611 E. 22nd Rd.
Leland, IL 60531
815-495-9032

KOA
10982 US Hwy. 20 W.
Lena, IL 61048
815-369-2612

Tincup Camper's Park
PO Box 486
Mahomet, IL 61853
217-586-3011

Lehman's Lakeside RV Resort
19709 Harmony Rd.
Marengo, IL 60152
815-923-4533

Whispering Pines Campground
2776 E. 2625 Rd.
Marseilles, IL 61341
815-795-5720

Fitzpatrick's Yogi Bear
8574 Millbrook Rd.
Millbrook, IL 60536
630-553-5172

Quality Times RV Park
9746 E. IL Hwy. 15
Mt. Vernon, IL 62864
618-244-0399

Nauvoo RV Campground
PO Box 89
Nauvoo, IL 62354
217-453-2253

Shady Lakes Campground
3355 75th Ave.
New Windsor, IL 61465
309-667-2709

Hebron Hill Camping
14349 N. Country Rd.
Oakland, IL 61943
217-346-3385

River Road Camping & Marina
3922 River Rd.
Oregon, IL 61061
815-234-5383

Emerald Acres Campground
3351 S. Mill Grove Rd.
Pearl City, IL 61062
815-443-2550

Mt. Hawley RV Park
8327 N. Knoxville Ave.
Peoria, IL 61615
309-692-2223

Lake Camp-A-Lot
PO Box 357
Percy, IL 62272
618-497-2942

Pine Lakes Resort
RR 3, Box 3077
Pittsfield, IL 62363
217-285-6719

Condit's Ranch
RR 1, Box 13
Putnam, IL 61560
815-437-2226

Valley View Campground
2300 Bonansinga
Quincy, IL 62301
217-222-7229

U.S. Campgrounds > ILLINOIS

KOA
4320 KOA Rd.
Rochester, IL 62563
217-498-7002

Camelot Campground
2311 78th Ave. W.
Rock Island, IL 61201
309-787-0665

Blackhawk Valley Campground
6540 Valley Trail Rd.
Rockford, IL 61109
815-874-9767

Mallard Bend Campground & RV Park
2838 N. 431st Rd.
Sheridan, IL 60551
816-496-2496

Rolling Oaks Campground
Rt. 1
Sheridan, IL 60551
815-496-2334

Pearl Lake
1220 Dearborn Ave.
South Beloit, IL 61080
815-389-1479

Mr. Lincoln's Campground & RV Center
3045 Stanton Ave.
Springfield, IL 62703
217-529-8206

Bail's Timberline Lake Campground
PO Box 15
St. Elmo, IL 62458
618-829-3383

Crow Valley Campground
23807 Moline Rd.
Sterling, IL 61081
815-626-5376

Sycamore RV Resort
PO Box 15
Sycamore, IL 60178
815-895-5590

Windy City Campground
18701 S. 80th Ave.
Tinley Park, IL 60477
708-720-0030

Evening Star Camping Resort
16474 Walker Rd.
Topeka, IL 61567
309-562-7590

KOA
8404 S. Union Rd.
Union, IL 60180
815-923-4206

KOA
RR 1
Utical, IL 61373
815-667-4988

Hickory Holler Campground
9876 E. 2000th Ave.
West York, IL 62478
618-563-4779

Benton Best Holiday
12997 State Hwy. 37
Whittington, IL 62807
618-435-3401

Fossil Rock Campground
24615 W. Strip Mine Rd.
Wilmington, IL 60481
815-476-6785

INDIANA

KOA
5612 CR 11A
Auburn, IN 46706
219-925-6747

KOA
1600 Lafayette Rd.
Crawfordsville, IN 47933
765-362-4190

KOA
50707 Princess Way
Granger, IN 46530
219-277-1335

KOA
5896 W. 200 N.
Greenfield, IN 46140
317-894-1397

KOA
52867 SR 13
Middlebury, IN 46540
219-825-5932

KOA
3101 Carl Rd.
Richmond, IN 47374
765-962-1219

KOA
5995 E. Sony Dr.
Terre Haute, IN 47802
812-232-2457

IOWA

KOA
3418 L Ave.
Adel, IA 50003
515-834-2729

KOA
1961 Garfield Ave. W.
Liberty, IA 52776
319-627-2676

KOA
21788 Dogwood Ave.
Onawa, IA 51040
712-423-1633

Timberline Best Holiday Trav-L-Park
3165 Ashworth Rd.
Waukee, IA 50263
515-987-1714

KANSAS

KOA
4100 E. Hwy. 50
Garden City, KS 67846
316-276-8741

KOA
1114 E. Hwy. 24
Goodland, KS 67735
785-899-5701

KOA
3366 KOA Rd.
Grantville, KS 66429
785-246-3419

KOA
1473 Hwy. 40
Lawrence, KS 66044
913-842-3877

KOA
1109 W. Diamond Dr.
Salina, KS 67401
913-827-3182

U.S. Campgrounds > KENTUCKY

KOA
Box 235
Wakeeney, KS 67672
785-743-5612

KOA
RR 1, Box 227
Wellington, KS 67152
316-326-6114

KENTUCKY

**My Old Kentucky Home
State Park**
Bardstown, KY 40004
502-348-3502

**Dale Hollow Lake State
Resort Park**
Bow, KY 42717
502-433-7431

KOA
1960 Three Springs Rd.
Bowling Green, KY 42104
502-843-1919

**General Burnside State
Park**
Burnside, KY
42519
606-561-4104

**Lake Barkley State
Resort Park**
Cadiz, KY 42211
502-924-1131

KOA
4793 US 62
Calvert City, KY 42049
502-395-5841

**Green River Lake State
Park**
Campbellsville, KY 42718
502-465-8255

**General Butler State Resort
Park**
Carrollton, KY 41008
502-732-4384

KOA
900 Marriott Dr.
Clarksville, KY 47129
812-282-4474

**Columbus Belmont
State Park**
Columbus, KY 442032
502-677-2327

**Cumberland Falls State
Resort Park**
Corbin, KY 40701
606-528-4121

KOA
171 E. City Dam Rd.
Corbin, KY 40701
606-528-1534

Cincinnati South KOA
Box 339
Crittenden, KY 41030
800-562-9151

**Pennyrile Forest State
Resort Park**
Dawson Springs, KY 42408
502-797-3421

KOA
209 Tunnel Hill Rd.
Elizabethtown, KY 42701
502-737-7600

**Rough River Dam State
Resort Park**
Falls of Rough, KY 40119
502-257-2311

Kincaid Lake State Park
Falmouth, KY 41040
606-654-3531

KOA
PO Box 346
Franklin, KY 42135
502-586-5622

**Kentucky Dam Village
State Resort Park**
Gilbertsville, KY 42044
502-362-4271

**Greenbo Lake State
Resort Park**
Greenup, KY 41144
606-473-7324

Lake Malone State Park
Greenville, KY 42345
502-657-2111

Kenlake State Resort Park
Hardin, KY 42048
502-474-2211

**John James Audubon
State Park**
Henderson, KY 42420
502-826-2247

KOA
Box 87
Horse Cave, KY 42749
502-786-2819

**Lake Cumberland State
Resort Park**
Jamestown, KY 42629
502-343-3111

**Levi Jackson Wilderness
Road State Park**
London, KY 40741
606-878-8000

**Barren River Lake State
Resort Park**
Lucas, KY 42156
502-646-2151

**Blue Licks Battlefield
State Park**
Mount Oliver, KY 41064
606-289-5507

**Carter Caves State
Resort Park**
Olive Hill, KY 41164
606-286-4411

Grayson Lake State Park
Olive Hill, KY 41164
606-474-9727

**Pine Mountain State
Resort Park**
Pineville, KY 40977
606-337-3066

**Jenny Wiley State
Resort Park**
Prestonburg, KY 41653
606-886-2711

KOA
Red Foley Rd., Box 54
Renfro Valley, KY 40473
606-256-2474

U.S. Campgrounds > KENTUCKY

**Fort Boonesborough
State Park**
Richmond, KY 40475
606-527-3131

KOA
1440 Hwy. 1383
Russell Springs, KY 42642
502-866-5616

Carr Creek State Park
Sassafras, KY 41759
606-642-4050

KOA
2433 Hwy. 44E
Shepherdsville, KY 40165
502-543-2041

**Natural Bridge State
Resort Park**
Slade, KY 40376
606-663-2214

Taylorsville Lake State Park
Taylorsville, KY 40071
502-477-8313

Big Bone Lick State Park
Union, KY 41091
606-384-3522

LOUISIANA

Abbeville RV Park
1501 W. Port St.
Abbeville, LA 70510
318-898-4042

Chemin-A-Haut State Park
14656 State Park Rd.
Bastrop, LA 71220
318-283-0812

Night RV Park
14740 Florida Blvd.
Baton Rouge, LA 70819
225-275-0679

Maplewood RV Park
452 Maplewood Dr.
Bossier City, LA 71111
318-742-5497

KOA
64 Kisatchie Ln.
Boyce, LA 71409
318-445-5227

Maxie's Campground
PO Box 181
Broussard, LA 70518
318-837-6200

**Bayou Wilderness RV
Resort**
Carencro, LA 70520
318-896-0598

**Caney Creek Lake State
Park**
State Rd. #1209
Chatham, LA 71226
318-249-2595

Coco Marina
106 Pier 56
Chauvin, LA 70344
504-594-6626

**Land-O-Pines
Campground**
17145 Million Dollar Rd.
Covington, LA 70435
504-892-6023

KOA Baton Rouge, East
7628 Vincent Rd.
Denham Springs, LA 70726
225-664-7281

**Tranquility Lakes
Campground**
431 Tranquility Dr.
Denham Springs, LA 70706
225-664-8488

Lake Bistineau State Park
PO Box 589
Doyline, LA 71023
318-745-3503

Lake D'Arbonne
PO Box 236
Farmerville, LA 71241
318-368-2086

**Hideway Ponds
Recreational Resort**
6367 Bayou Black Dr.
Gibson, LA 70356
504-575-9928

Grand Isle State Park
PO Box 741
Grand Isle, LA 70358
504-787-2559

**Hidden Oaks Family
Campground**
669 Robert Ln.
Hammond, LA 70466
504-345-9244

**KOA New Orleans-
Hammond**
14154 Club Deluxe Rd.
Hammond, LA 70403
504-542-8094

Lake Claiborne State Park
PO Box 246
Homer, LA 71040
318-927-2976

Capri Court Campground
101 Capri Court
Houma, LA 70364
800-428-8026

**Indian Creek Campground
& RV Park**
53013 W. Fontana Rd.
Independence, LA 70443
504-878-6567

**Grand Casino Coushatta's
RV Resort**
711 Pow Wow Pkwy.
Kinder, LA 70648
888-867-8727

Quiet Oaks RV Park
18159 TV Tower Rd.
Kinder, LA 70648
888-755-2230

**Sam Houston Jones
State Park**
101 Southerland Rd.
Lake Charles, LA 70611
318-855-2665

**Fairview-Riverside
State Park**
PO Box 856
Madisonville, LA 70447
504-845-3318

Fontainebleau State Park
PO Box 8925
Mandeville, LA 70470
504-624-4443

U.S. Campgrounds > MAINE

Toldedo Bend Reservoir
15091 Texas Hwy.
Many, LA 71449
318-256-4114

Jude Travel Park & Guest House
7400 Chef Mneteur
New Orleans, LA 70126
504-241-0632

New Orleans West KOA Campground
11129 Jefferson Hwy.
New Orleans, LA 70123
504-467-1792

New Orleans-East KOA
56009 Hwy. 433
New Orleans, LA 70461
504-643-3850

Kemper Williams Park
Box 599
Patterson, LA 70392
504-395-2298

Cajun Country Campground
4667 Rebelle Ln.
Port Allen, LA 70767
225-383-8554

Bayou Teche RV Park
PO Box 219
Port Barre, LA 70577
318-585-7646

KOA New Orleans West
11129 Jefferson Hwy.
River Ridge, LA 70123
504-467-1792

Yogi Bear's Jellystone Park
PO Box 519
Robert, LA 70455
504-542-1507

KOA Lafayette
537 Apollo Rd.
Scott, LA 70583
318-235-2739

KOA Shreveport-Bossier
6510 W. 79th St.
Shreveport, LA 71129
318-687-1010

Lake Bruin State Park
Rt. 1, Box 183
St. Joseph, LA 71366
318-766-3530

Lake Fausse Pointe State Park
5400 Levee Rd.
St. Martinville, LA 70582
318-229-4764

Hidden Ponds RV Park
1201 Ravia Rd.
Sulphur, LA 70665
318-583-4709

Chicot State Park
Rt. 3, Box 494
Ville Platte, LA 70586
318-363-2403

KOA Lake Charles-Vinton
1514 Azema St.
Vinton, LA 70668
318-589-2300

St. Bernard State Park
PO Box 534
Violet, LA 70092
504-682-2101

Pavilion RV Park
309 Well Rd.
West Monroe, LA 71292
318-322-4216

Bayou Segnette State Park
7777 Westbank Expressway
Westwego, LA 70094
504-736-7140

North Toledo Bend State Park
PO Box 56
Zwolle, LA 71486
318-645-4715

MAINE

Balsam Woods Campground
112 Pond Rd.
Abbot Village, ME 04406
207-876-2731

Walnut Grove Campground
599 Gore Rd.
Alfred, ME 04002
207-324-1207

South Arm Campground
Box 310
Andover, ME 04216
207-364-5155

Sennebec Lake Campground
Rt. 131, Box 602
Appleton, ME 04862
207-785-4250

Paul Bunyan Campground
1862 Union St.
Bangor, ME 04401
207-941-1177

Pleasant Hill Campground
RFD 3, Box 180, Union St.
Bangor, ME 04401
207-848-5127

Wheeler Stream Camping Area
RR 2, Box 2800
Bangor, ME 04401
207-848-3713

Bar Harbor Campground
RFD, Box 1125
Bar Harbor, ME 04609
207-288-5185

Barcadia Campground
RR 1, Box 2165
Bar Harbor, ME 04609
207-288-3520

Hadley's Point Campground
RFD 1, Box 1790
Bar Harbor, ME 04609
207-288-4808

Mt. Desert Narrows Camping
RR 1, Box 2045
Bar Harbor, ME 04609
207-288-4782

Spruce Valley Campground
RR 1, Box 2420, Rt. 102
Bar Harbor, ME 04609
207-288-5139

Quietside Campground & Cabins
PO Box 10
Bass Harbor, ME 04653
207-244-5992

U.S. Campgrounds > MAINE

Meadowbrook Camping
33 Meadowbrook Rd.
Bath, ME 04562
800-370-CAMP

Moorings Oceanfront Campground
Rt. 1, Box 69M
Belfast, ME 04915
207-338-6860

Northport Travel Park Campground
Belfast, ME 04915
207-338-2077

Bethel Outdoor Adventures & Campground
Bethel, ME 04217
800-533-3607

Stony Brook Recreation
Rt. 2, 42 Powell Pl.
Bethel, ME 04237
207-824-2836

Shamrock RV Park, Inc.
391 West St.
Biddeford, ME 04005
207-284-4282

Camper's Cove Campground
Box 136
Boothbay, ME 04537
207-633-5013

Little Ponderosa
HC 34, Box 14
Boothbay, ME 04537
207-633-2700

Gray Homestead Oceanfront Campground
Box 334 HC66
Boothbay Harbor, ME 04576
27-633-4612

Shore Hills Campground
RR 1, Box 448M, Route 27
Boothbay Harbor, ME 04537
207-633-4782

Bridgton Pines Cabins & Campground
Bridgton, ME 04009
207-647-8227

Lakeside Pines Campground
Box 182M
Bridgton, ME 04057
207-647-3935

Vicki-Lin Camping Area
Bridgton, ME 04009
207-647-8489

River Run Canoe & Camp
Brownfield, ME 04040
207-452-2500

Woodland Acres Camp 'N' Canoe
Brownfield, ME 04040
207-935-2529

White's Beach & Campground
Brunswick, ME 04011
207-729-0415

Flying Dutchman Campground
PO Box 1639
Bucksport, ME 04416
207-469-3256

Pleasant Lake Camping Area
Calais, ME 04619
207-454-7467

Megunticook By The Sea
US Route 1, P.O. Box 375
Camden, ME 04856
207-594-2428

Skowhegan/Canaan KOA
P.O. Box 87
Canaan, ME 04924
800-562-7571

Shady Acres RV & Campground
Carmel, ME 04419
207-848-5515

Point Sebago Resort
Casco, ME 04015
800-655-1232

Lake Pemaquid
P.O. Box 967
Damariscotta, ME 04543
207-563-5202

Greenland Cove Campground
Danforth, ME 04424
207-448-2863

Sunshine Campground
Deer Isle, ME 04627
207-348-6681

Granger Pond Camping Area
Denmark, ME 04022
207-452-2342

Pleasant Mt. Camping Area
Denmark, ME 04022
207-452-2170

Mountain View Campground
208 Weld St.
Dixfield, ME 04224
207-562-8285

Birch Haven Campground
Eagle Lake, ME 04739
207-444-5102

River's Edge Campground
East Machias, ME 04630
207-255-4523

Balsam Cove Campground
PO Box C
East Orland, ME 04431
207-469-7771

Whispering Pines Campground
US Route 1
East Orland, ME 04431
207-469-3443

The Seaview
16 Norwood Rd.
Eastport, ME 04631
207-853-4471

Greenwood Acres Campground
RR 2, Box 2210, Rte. 178
Eddington, ME 04428
207-989-8898

Branch Lake Camping Area
RFD #5
Ellsworth, ME 04605
207-667-5174

U.S. Campgrounds > MAINE

Lakeside Camping & Cabins
Enfield, ME 04493
207-732-4241

Cathedral Pines Campground
Eustis, ME 04936
207-246-3491

Foggy-Bottom RV Campground
Farmingdale, ME 04344
207-582-0075

Blueberry Pond Campground
218 Poland Range Rd.
Freeport, ME 04069
207-688-4421

Cedar Haven
39 Baker Rd.
Freeport, ME 04032
207-865-6254

Desert Dunes of Main Campground
US Route 1 & 95 Desert Rd.
Freeport, ME 04032
207-865-6962

Flying Point Campground
10 Lower Flying Point Rd.
Freeport, ME 04032
207-865-4569

Recompence Shore Campsites
8 Burnett Rd.
Freeport, ME 04032
207-865-9307

Augusta/Gardiner KOA
RFD 1, Box 2410M
Gardiner, ME 04357
207-582-5086

Camp Seguin Ocean Camping
Reid State Park Rd.
Georgetown, ME 04548
207-371-2777

Sagadahoc Bay Campground
Georgetown, ME 04548
207-371-2014

Twin Brooks Camping Area
P.O. Box 194
Gray, ME 04039
207-428-3832

Casey's Spencer Bay Camps
PO Box 1190
Greenville, ME 04441
207-695-2801

Moosehead Family Campground
Greenville, ME 04441
207-695-2210

Vacationland Campsites
Harrison, ME 04040
207-583-4953

Hebron Pines Campground
Hebron, ME 04238
207-966-2179

Red Barn RV Park
Holden, ME 04429
207-843-6011

My Brothers Place
Houlton, ME 04730
207-532-6739

Birch Point
Box 120
Island Falls, ME 04747
207-463-2515

Jackman Landing Campground
Jackman, ME 04945
207-668-3301

John's Four Season Accom.
Jackman, ME 04945
207-668-7683

Loon Echo Family Campground
P.O. Box 711
Jackman, ME 04945
207-668-4829

Moose Alley Campground
Route 201, Box 298
Jackman, ME 04945
207-668-2781

The Last Resort Campground & Cabins
Jackman, ME 04945
207-668-5091

Fran Mort-Red Apple Campgound
Kennebunkport, ME 04046
207-967-4927

Kennebunkport Camping
117 Old Cape Rd.
Kennebunkport, ME 04046
207-967-2732

Salty Acres Campground
Kennebunkport, ME 04046
207-967-8623

Deer Farm Campground
Kingfield, ME 04947
207-265-4599

Kings & Queens Court Resort
Flat Rock Ridge Rd.,
RFD 1, Box 763
Lebanon, ME 04027
207-339-9465

Potter's Place Adult Park
RR 2, Box 490
Lebanon, ME 04027
207-457-1341

Riverbend Campground
Rt. 106, RR 2, Box 5050M
Leeds, ME 04263
207-524-5711

Lew/Aub No. Allen Pond Campground
Lewiston, ME 04240
207-946-7439

Old Massachusetts Homestead
Rt. 1
Lincolnville Beac, ME 04850
800-213-8142

Birches Family Campground
Litchfield, ME 04350
207-268-4330

Rol-Lin Hills
Livermore, ME 04253
207-897-6394

Littlefield Beaches Campground
RR 1, Box 4300
Locke Mills, ME 04255
207-875-3290

U.S. Campgrounds > MAINE

Kezar Lake Camping Area
RR 1, Box 246M
Lovell, ME 04051
207-925-1631

South Bay Campground
RR 1, Box 6565
Lubec, ME 04652
207-733-1037

Sunset Point Trailer Park
Rt. 189
Lubec, ME 04652
207-733-2150

Abnaki Family Camping Center
Madison, ME 04950
207-474-2070

Yonder Hill Campground
Madison, ME 04950
207-474-7353

Katahdin Shadows Campground
PO Box HM
Medway, ME 04460
800-794-5267

Pine Grove Campground & Cottages
Medway, ME 04460
207-746-5172

Frost Pond Campground
36C Minuteman Dr.
Millinocket, ME 04462
207-695-2821

Hidden Springs Campground
Millinocket, ME 04462
888-685-2288

Jo-Mary Lake Campground
Millinocket, ME 04462
800-494-0031

Nesowadnehunk Campground
Millinocket, ME 04462
207-458-1551

Wilde Pines Campground
Monticello, ME 04760
207-538-9004

Moose River Campground
P.O. Box 98
Moose River, ME 04945
207-668-3341

Somes Sound View Campground
Hall Quarry Rd.
Mount Desert, ME 04660
207-244-3890

Beaver Brook Campground
RR 1, Box 1835M
N. Monmouth, ME 04265
207-933-2108

Happy Horseshoe Campground
N. New Portland, ME 04961
207-628-3471

Papoose Pond Resort & Campground
N. Waterford, ME 04267
207-583-4470

Bay of Naples Family Camping
Route 11/114, Box 240M
Naples, ME 04055
800-348-9750

Brandy Pond Park
Naples, ME 04055
207-693-3129

Colonial Mast Campground
Kansas Rd., P.O. Box 95
Naples, ME 04055
207-693-6652

Four Seasons Camping Area
P.O. Box 927
Naples, ME 04055
207-693-6797

Loon's Haven Family Campground
P.O. Box 557
Naples, ME 04055
207-693-6881

Christies Campground
Rt. 1, Box 565
Newport, ME 04953
207-368-4645

Palmyra Gold & RV Resort
Newport, ME 04953
207-938-5677

Tent Village Travel Trailer Park
RR 2, Box 580
Newport, ME 04953
207-368-5047

Duck Puddle Campground
P.O. Box 176M
Nobleboro, ME 04555
207-563-5608

Town Line Campsites
483 E. Pond Rd.
Nobleboro, ME 04348
207-832-7055

Main Roads Camping
Norridgewock, ME 04967
207-634-4952

Pinederosa Campground
128 N. Village Rd.
Ogunquit, ME 04090
207-646-2492

Shady Oaks Campground & Cabins
32 Leaches Point
Oland, ME 04472
207-469-7739

Hid'n Pines Campground
Route 98, Cascade Rd.,
P.O. Box 647
Old Orchard Beach, ME 04064
207-934-2352

Ne're Beach Family Campground
38 Saco Ave., Route 5
Old Orchard Beach, ME 04064
207-934-7614

Old Orchard Beach Campground
Route 5/27 Ocean Park Rd.
Old Orchard Beach, ME 04064
207-934-4477

Paradise Park Resort
Old Orchard Beach, ME 04064
207-934-4633

U.S. Campgrounds > MAINE

Powder Horn Family Camping
P.O. Box 366M, Route 98
Old Orchard Beach, ME 04064
207-934-4733

Virginina Tent Trailer Park
Old Orchard Beach, ME 04064
207-934-4791

Wagon Wheel Campground & Cabins
3 Old Orchard Rd., Dept. M
Old Orchard Beach, ME 04064
207-934-2160

Wild Acres Family Camping
179M Saco Ave.
Old Orchard Beach, ME 04064
207-934-2535

Black Brook Cove Campground
P.O. Box 319
Oquossoc, ME 04964
207-486-3828

Stephen Phillips Preserve
Oquossoc, ME 04964
207-864-2003

Orr's Island Campground
Orr's Island, ME 04066
207-833-5595

Mirror Pond Campground
Oxford, ME 04270
207-539-4888

Two Lakes Camping Area
Rt. 26, Box 206
Oxford, ME 04270
207-539-4851

Ringwood Campground
Palmyra, ME 04965
207-487-3406

Matagamon Wilderness
Box 220C
Patten, ME 04765
207-446-4635

Shin Pond Village Campground
RR 1, Box 280M
Patten, ME 04765
207-528-2900

Sherwood Forest Campsite
Pemaquid Trail, P.O. Box 189
Pemaquid, ME 04554
800-274-1593

Knowlton's Campground
Perry, ME 04667
207-726-4756

Honey Run Beach & Campgrounds
456 E. Shore Rd.
Peru, ME 04290
207-562-4913

Ocean View Park Campground
Route 209
Phippsburg, ME 04562
207-389-2564

Range Pond Campground
94 Plains Rd.
Poland, ME 04274
207-998-2624

Poland Spring Campground
Route 26, P.O. Box 409M
Poland Spring, ME 04274
207-998-2151

Wassamki Springs Campground
Portland, ME 04101
207-839-4276

Arndt's Arrostook River Campground
95 Parkhurst Siding Rd.
Presque isle, ME 04769
207-764-8677

Neil E. Michaud Campground
US No. 1 Hwy.
Presque Isle, ME 04769
207-769-1951

Cupsuptic Campground
Rangeley, ME 04970
207-864-5249

Kokatosi Campground
635M Webbs Mills Rd.
Raymond, ME 04071
207-627-4642

Augusta/Gardiner KOA
Route 1, Box 2410
Richmond, ME 04357
800-562-1496

Camden Rockport Camping
P.O. Box 170, Rt. 90
Rockport, ME 04865
888-842-0592

Old Mill Campground & Cabins
Rockwood, ME 04478
207-534-7333

Woody's Campground & Cottages
Rockwood, ME 04478
207-534-7752

Silver Lake Campground
Roxbury, ME 04275
207-545-0416

Madison's Wilderness Camping
Rt. 2
Rumford, ME 04276
800-258-6234

B&B Family Camping
S. Lebanon, ME 04027
207-339-0150

Saco Portland South KOA
814A Portland Rd.
Saco, ME 04072
207-282-0502

Silver Springs Campground
705 Portland Rd.
Saco, ME 04072
207-283-3880

Apache Campground
Sanford, ME 04073
207-324-5652

Jellystone Park Camp Resort
1175 Main St., Route 109
Sanford, ME 04073
207-324-7782

Sand Pond Campground
Sanford, ME 04073
207-324-16752

U.S. Campgrounds > MAINE

Bayley's Camping Resort
Box M9, 27 Ross Rd.
Scarborough, ME 04074
207-883-6043

Wild Duck Campground
39 Dunstan Landing Rd.
Scarborough, ME 04074
207-883-4432

**Aldus Shores Lakeside
Campground**
Rt. 131, P.O. Box 38
Searsmont, ME 04973
207-342-5618

Searsport Shores Camping
Coastal US Route 1
Searsport, ME 04970
207-548-6059

**Sebago Lake Family
Campground**
1550 Richville Rd.
Sebago Lake, ME 04084
207-787-3671

**Seboomook Wilderness
Campground**
Box 560
Seboomook, ME 04478
207-534-8824

**Eaton Mountain Ski &
Campground**
Skowhegan, ME 04976
207-474-2666

Skowhegan/Canaan KOA
Skowhegan, ME 04976
207-474-2858

Two Rivers Campground
HCR 71, Box 14
Skowhegan, ME 04976
207-474-6482

**Hermit Island
Campground**
42T Front St.
Small Point, ME 04530
207-443-2101

**The Evergreens
Campground**
Route 201A
Solon, ME 04979
207-643-2324

Locklin Camping Area
South Hiram, ME 04041
207-625-8622

**Smuggler's Den
Campground**
PO Box 787, Rout 102
Southwest Harbor, ME 04679
207-244-3944

**White Birches
Campground**
Sal Cover Rd., Box 421
Southwest Harbor, ME 04679
207-244-3797

Lakeview Camping Resort
St. Agatha, ME 04772
207-543-6331

**Family -N- Friends
Campground**
140 Richville Rd., Route 114
Standish, ME 04084
207-642-2200

**Acres of Wildlife
Campground**
Route 113/11, P.O. Box 2
Steep Falls, ME 04085
207-675-CAMP

Stetson Shores Campground
Rt. 143, PO Box 86
Stetson, ME 04488
207-296-2041

Mainayr Campground
Steuben, ME 04680
207-546-2690

Greenlaw's RV Tent & Rental
Stonington, ME 04681
207-367-5049

Mountainview Campground
Sullivan, ME 04664
207-422-6215

**The Gatherings Family
Campground**
RR 1, Box 4069
Surry, ME 04684
207-667-8826

Saltwater Farm Campground
Thomaston, ME 04861
207-354-6735

Maine Wilderness Camps
HC 82, Box 1085
Topsfield, ME 04490
207-738-5052

**Narrows Too Camping
Resort**
RR 1, Box 193
Trenton, ME 04605
207-667-4300

Green Valley Campground
Vassalboro, ME 04989
207-923-3000

Loon's Cry Campground
US Route 1
Warren, ME 04864
800-493-2324

Sandy Shores RV Resort
Warren, ME 04864
207-273-2073

Blackburn's Campground
Waterboro, ME 04087
207-247-5875

**Bear Mt. Village
Cabins & Sites**
RR 2, Box 745
Waterford, ME 04088
207-583-2541

Countryside Campground
Waterville, ME 04901
207-873-4603

**Dummer's Beach
Campground**
Weld, ME 04285
207-585-2200

Bears Den RV Park
Wells, ME 04090
207-668-9227

Gregoire's Campground
Wells, ME 04090
207-646-3711

Riverside Campground
2295 Post Rd.
Wells, ME 04090
207-646-3145

Sea Breeze Campground
2073 Post Rd.
Wells, ME 04090
207-646-4301

U.S. Campgrounds > MASSACHUSETTS

Sea-vu Campground
US Route 1, P.O. Box 67
Wells, ME 04090
207-646-7732

Summer Hill RV Park
Wells, ME 04090
207-646-4032

Wells Beach Resort
1000M Post Rd., US Route 1
Wells, ME 04090
207-646-7570

Pleasant River Campground
P.O. Box 92
West Bethel, ME 04286
207-836-2000

Hemlocks Camping Area
West Poland, ME 04291
207-998-2384

Mac's Campground
West Poland, ME 04291
207-998-4238

**Glordano's Campground &
Recreation**
Winslow, ME 04901
207-873-2408

**Winterville Lakeview
Camps & Campground**
Winterville, ME 04788
207-444-4581

Augusta-West Resort
Winthrop, ME 04364
207-377-9993

Chewonki Campground
P.O. Box 261
Wiscasset, ME 04578
207-882-7426

Down East Family Camping
Wiscasset, ME 04578
207-882-5431

Sunset Acres Campground
Woodland, ME 04763
207-454-1440

Wayside Trailer Park
York Beach, ME 03910
207-363-3846

York Beach Camper Park
11 Cappy's Ln, Box 127
York Beach, ME 3910
207-363-1343

Camp Eaton
P.O. Box 626, Route 1A
York Harbor, ME 3911
207-363-3424

Libby's Oceanside Camp
Box 40, Dept. M-99, US
Route 1A
York Harbor, ME 3911
207-363-4171

MARYLAND

**Cherry Hill Park Holiday
Trav-L-Park**
9800 Cherry Hill Rd.
College Park, MD 20740
301-937-7116

**Morris Meadows
Recreation Farm**
1523 Freeland Rd.
Freeland, MD 21053
410-329-6636

Washington DC, NE KOA
768 Cecil Ave. N.
Millersville, MD 21108
800-562-0248

**Hagerstown/
Snug Harbor KOA**
11759 Snug Harbor Ln.
Williamsport, MD 21795
800-562-7607

MASSACHUSETTS

Howe's Camping
133 Sherbert Rd.
Ashburnham, MA 01430
978-827-4558

The Pines
39 Davis Rd.
Ashby, MA 01431
978-386-7702

Forge Pond Campground
62 Forge Rd.
Assonet, MA 02702
508-644-5701

Otter River State Forest
Route 202
Baldwinville, MA 01436
978-939-8962

Bass River Trailer Park
Rte. 28
Bass River, MA 02664
508-398-2011

**Circle C.G. Adult Family
Campground & RV Park**
131 N. Main St.
Bellingham, MA 02019
508-966-1136

**Circle C.G. Farm
Campground**
131 N. Main St.
Bellingham, MA 02019
508-966-1136

**Travelr's Woods of
New England**
Box 88
Bernardston, MA 01337
413-48-9105

Crystal Springs Campground
PO Box 279
Bolton, MA 01740
978-799-2711

Bay View Campgrounds
260 MacArthur Blvd.
Bourne, MA 02532
508-759-7610

Shady Knoll Campground
1709 Rte. 6A
Brewster, MA 02631
508-896-3002

Sweetwater Forest
PO Box 1797
Brewster, MA 02631
508-896-3773

Quinebaug Cover Campsite
49 E. Brimfield-Holland Rd.
Brimfield, MA 01010
413-245-9525

**Village Green Family
Campground**
228 Sturbridge Rd.
Brimfield, MA 01010
413-245-3504

U.S. Campgrounds > MASSACHUSETTS

Lakeside Resort
12 Hobbs Ave.
Brookfield, MA 01506
508-867-2737

Country Aire Campground
Box 286
Charlemont, MA 01339
413-625-2996

Mohawk Trail State Forest
PO Box 7, Route 2
Charlemont, MA 01339
413-339-5504

Bonny Rigg Camping Club
Box 14
Chester, MA 01011
413-623-5366

**Chester Blandford
State Forest**
Rte. 20
Chester, MA 01050
413-354-6347

Walker Island Camping
#27 Route 20
Chester, MA 01011
413-354-2295

Clarksburg State Forest
Middle Rd.
Clarksburg, MA 01225
413-664-8345

Lake Manchaug Camping
76 Oak St.
E. Douglas, MA 01516
508-476-2471

Cape Cod Campresort
176 Thomas Landers Rd.
E. Falmouth, MA 02536
508-548-1458

**Maple Park Family
Campground**
RFD 2
E. Wareham, MA 02538
508-295-4945

Laurel Ridge Camping Area
Box 519
East Otis, MA 01029
413-269-4804

Tolland State Forest
PO Box 342, Tolland Rd.
East Otis, MA 01029
413-269-6002

Atlantic Oaks Campground
3700 Rte. 6, RR2
Eastham, MA 02642
508-255-1437

Erving State Forest
RFD 1, Route 2A
Erving, MA 01364
978-544-3939

**Otis Trailer Village-Johns
Pond Campground**
Box 586 (Mashpee)
Falmouth, MA 02541
508-349-3007

**Savoy Mountain State
Forest**
260 Central Shaft Rd.
Florida, MA 01247
413-663-8469

**Normandy Farms
Campground**
72 West St.
Foxboro, MA 02035
508-543-7600

**Normandy Farms
Campground**
72 West St.
Foxboro, MA 02035
508-543-7600

Annisquam Campground
Stanwood Pt.
Gloucester, MA 01930
978-283-2992

D.A.R. State Forest
Route 112
Goshen, MA 01096
413-268-7098

Granville State Forest
323 W. Hartland Rd., Route 57
Granville, MA 01034
413-357-6611

Wompatuck State Park
Union St.
Hingham, MA 02043
781-749-7160

Fernwood Forest
Box 896
Hinsdale, MA 01235
413-655-2292

**Mt. Greylock State
Reservationb**
PO Box 138, Route 7
Ln.sborough, MA 01237
413-499-4262

**October Mountain State
Forest**
Woodland Rd.
Lee, MA 01238
413-243-1778

Minuteman KOA
Box 2122
Littleton, MA 01460
978-772-0042

Canoe River Campground
137 Mill St., E.
Mansfield, MA 02031
508-339-6462

John's Pond Campground
Rte. 151
Mashpee, MA 02649
508-477-0444

Otis Trailer Village
Rte. 151
Mashpee, MA 02649
508-477-0444

Plymouth Rock KOA
438 Plymouth St., Box 616
Middleboro, MA 02346
508-947-6435

Partridge Hollow
PO Box 41, Munn Rd.
Monson, MA 01057
413-267-5122

**Sunsetview Farm
Camping Area**
57 Town Farm Rd.
Monson, MA 01057
413-267-9269

Beartown State Forest
PO Box 97, Blue Hill Rd.
Monterey, MA 01245
413-528-0904

U.S. Campgrounds > MASSACHUSETTS

Prospect Lake Park
50 Prospect Lake Rd.
N. Egremont, MA 02152
413-528-4158

Pout & Trout Family Campground
94 River Rd.
N. Rutland, MA 01543
508-886-6677

Harold Parker State Forest
1951 Turnpike Rd.
North Andover, MA 01845
978-686-3391

North Truro Camping Area
Highland Rd.
North Truro, MA 02652
508-487-1847

Barton Cover Campground
99 Millers Falls Rd.
Northfield, MA 01360
413-863-9300

Pine Acres Family Camping Resort
203 Bechan Rd.
Oakham, MA 01068
508-882-9509

Camp Overflow
Box 645
Otis, MA 01253
413-269-4036

Mountain View Campground
P.O Route 8
Otis, MA 01253
413-269-8928

Lamb City Campground
85 Royalston Rd.
Phillipston, MA 01331
978-249-2049

Bonnie Brae Cabins & Campsites
108 Broadway St.
Pittsfield, MA 01201
413-442-3754

Pittsfield State Forest
Cascade St.
Pittsfield, MA 01201
413-442-8992

Peppermint Park Camping Resort
169 Grant St, Box 52
Plainfield, MA 01070
413-634-5385

Ellis Haven Family Campground
531 Federal Furnace Rd.
Plymouth, MA 02360
508-746-0803

Indianhead Resort
Rte. 3A, State Rd.
Plymouth, MA 02360
508-888-3688

Pinewood Lodge Campground
190 Pinewood Rd.
Plymouth, MA 02360
508-746-3548

Coastal Acres Camping Court
PO Box 593
Provincetown, MA 02657
508-487-1700

Dunes' Edge Campground
Box 875, 386 Rt. 6
Provincetown, MA 02657
508-487-9815

Outdoor World
90 Stevens Rd.
Rochester, MA 02770
508-763-5911

Shady Acres
PO Box 128
S. Carver, MA 02366
508-866-4040

Sandy Pond Campground
Bourne Rd.
S. Plymouth, MA 02360
508-759-9336

Black Bear Campground
54 Main St.
Salisbury, MA 01952
978-462-3183

Rusnik Campground
Box 5441
Salisbury, MA 01952
978-462-9551

Salisbury Beach State Reservation
Beach Rd., Route 1A
Salisbury, MA 01952
978-462-4481

Dunroamin' Trailer Park
5 John Ewer Rd., RR3
Sandwich, MA 02563
508-477-0541

Peters Pond Park
185 Cotuit Rd.
Sandwich, MA 02563
508-477-1775

Shady Pines Campground
547 Loop Rd.
Savoy, MA 01256
413-743-2694

Springbrook Family Camping Area
RFD 1, 32 Tower Rd.
Shelburne, MA 01370
413-625-6618

Sodom Mountain Campground
227 S. Loomis St., Box 702
Southwick, MA 01077
413-569-3930

Southwick Acres Campground
PO Box 984, College Hwy.
Southwick, MA 01077
413-569-6339

Outdoor World Resort
19 Mashapaug Rd.
Sturbridge, MA 01566
508-347-7156

Wells State Park
Rte. 39
Sturbridge, MA 01566
508-347-9257

Yogi Bear's Sturbridge Jellystone Park
Box 600
Sturbridge, MA 01566
508-347-2336

U.S. Campgrounds > MASSACHUSETTS

The Old Sawmill Campground
Box 377, Long Hill Rd.
W. Brookfield, MA 01585
508-867-2427

Cape Ann Campsite
80 Atlantic St.
W. Gloucester, MA 01930
978-283-8683

Prospect Mountain
Route 57
W. Granville, MA 01034
413-357-6494

Sutton Falls Camping Area
Manchaug Rd.
W. Sutton, MA 01590
508-865-3898

The Old Holbrook Place
114 Manchaug Rd.
W. Sutton, MA 01590
508-865-5050

Oak Haven Family Campground
Route 19
Wales, MA 01081
413-245-7148

Wagon Wheel Camping Area
909 Wendell Rd.
Warwick, MA 01378
978-544-3425

Summit Hill Campground
Summit Hill Rd.
Washington, MA 01235
413-623-5761

Indian Ranch Campground
Route 16, Box 1157
Webster, MA 01570
508-943-3871

Webster/Sturbridge KOA
Route 16, 106 Douglas Rd.
Webster, MA 01570
800-562-1895

Pearl Hill State Park
Willard Brook State Forest,
Rt. 119
West Townsend, MA 01474
978-597-2850

Willard Brook State Forest
Route 119
West Townsend, MA 01474
978-597-8802

Wyman's Beach
48 Wyman's Beach Rd.
Westford, MA 01886
978-692-6287

Windy Acres Campground
139 South St.
Westhampton, MA 01027
413-527-9862

Westport Camping Grounds
346 Old County Rd.,
Box N112
Westport, MA 02790
508-636-2555

White Birch Campground
214 North St.
Whately, MA 01093
413-665-4941

Lake Dennison State Recreational Area
Rte. 202
Winchendon, MA 01475
978-939-8962

Windsor State Forest
River Rd.
Windsor, MA 01270
413-684-0948

Berkshire Park Camping Area
Box 531, Harvey Rd.
Worthington, MA 01098
413-238-5918

Boston Hub KOA
1095 South St., Rt. 1A
Wrentham, MA 02093
508-384-8930

Boston Hum Campground
1095 South St., Box 505
Wrentham, MA 02093
508-348-8930

MICHIGAN

Traverse City KOA
9700 M 37
Buckley, MI 49620
800-562-0280

Gaylord/Michaywe KOA
5101 Campfires Prkwy
Gaylord, MI 49735
800-562-4146

Port Hurron KOA
5111 Lapeer
Kimball, MI 48074
800-562-0833

Mackinaw City KOA
Box 616
Mackinaw City, MI 49701
800-562-1738

Muskegon KOA
3500 N. Strand
Muskegon, MI 49445
800-562-3902

Newberry KOA
Route 4, Box 783
Newberry, MI 49868
800-562-5853

Oscoda KOA
3591 Forest Rd.
Oscoda, MI 48750
800-562-9667

Monroe Co/Toledo North KOA
US 23 at Exit 9
Petersburg, MI 49270
800-562-7646

Petoskey KOA
1800 N. US 31
Petoskey, MI 49770
800-562-0253

Port Austin KOA
8195 N. Van Dyke
Port Austin, MI 48467
800-562-5211

Benton Harbor/ St. Joseph KOA
3527 Coloma Rd.
Riverside, MI 49084
800-562-5341

U.S. Campgrounds > MINNESOTA

Crystal Lake Campground
1884 W. Hansen Rd.
Scottville, MI 49454
616-757-4510

St. Ignace/Mackinac Island KOA
1242 US 2 W
St. Ignace, MI 49781
800-562-0534

Cadillac KOA
23163 M-115
Tustin, MI 49688
800-562-4072

Detroit/Greenfield KOA
6680 Bunton Rd.
Ypsilanti, MI 48197
800-562-7603

MINNESOTA

Big "K" Campground
RR2, Box 965
Aitkin, MN 56431
218-927-6001

Buck's Resort
Rt. 1, Box 284
Aitkin, MN 56431
218-678-3787

Farm Island Lake Resort & Campground
Rt. 2, Box 225
Aitkin, MN 56431
218-927-3841

City of Akeley Park & Campground
P.O. Box 67
Akeley, MN 56433
218-652-2172

Greenwood Bay RV Park
754 W. Lake Cowdry Rd. NW
Alexandria, MN 56308
320-763-7391

Hillcrest RV Park & Campground
715 Birch Ave
Alexandria, MN 56308
320-763-6330

Sun Valley Resort & Campground
10045 State Hwy. 27
Alexandria, MN 56308
320-866-5417

Lazy D Campground
Rt. 1, Box 252
Altura, MN 55910
507-932-3098

Bunker Hills Campground
550 Bunker Lake Blvd.
Andover, MN 55304
612-757-3920

Schroeder County Park
9201 Ireland Ave.
Annandale, MN 55302
320-274-8870

Labanon Hills Regional Park Campground
12100 Johnny Cake Ridge Rd.
Apple Valley, MN 55124
612-454-9211

Ashby Resort & Campground
P.O. Box 57
Ashby, MN 56309
218-747-2959

Sundowner Campground & RV Park
RT. 1, Box 145
Ashby, MN 56309
218-747-2931

Beaver Trails Campground
Rt. 5, Box 71J
Austin, MN 55912
507-584-6611

Riverbend Campground
Rt. 3, Box 122-A
Austin, MN 55912
507-325-4637

Birch Lake RV Park & Campgrounds
2015 Hwy. 623
Babbitt, MN 57706
218-827-2342

Lindsey Lake Campground
RR 1, Box 383
Backus, MN 56435
218-947-4728

Pine Mountain Lake Seasonal Campground
Rt. 2, Box 51
Backus, MN 56435
218-587-4315

Bagley City Park Campground
P.O. Box 178
Bagley, MN 56621
218-694-2871

Long Lake Park & Campground
213 Main Ave. N
Bagley, MN 56621
218-657-2275

Bear Lake Park Campground
P.O. Box 101
Barnum, MN 55707
218-389-3162

Bent Trout Lake Campground
2928 Bent Trout Lake Rd.
Barnum, MN 55707
218-389-6322

Sunset Beach Resort & Campground
RR3, Box 181
Battle Lake, MN 56515
218-583-2750

Big Wolf Lake Resort & Campground
12150 Walleye Ln.
Bemidji, MN 56601
218-751-5749

Hamilton's Fox Lake Campground
2555 Island View Dr.
Bemidji, MN 56601
218-586-2231

Ambush Park
W. Hwy. 9
Benson, MN 56215
320-843-4775

Swift Falls County Park
P.O. Box 241
Benson, MN 56215
320-843-4900

U.S. Campgrounds > MINNESOTA

Big Falls Campground
410 2nd St. NW
Big Falls, MN 56627
218-276-2282

Shady River Campground
21353 Cty. Rd. 5
Big Lake, MN 55309
612-263-3705

Bunk's Territory Resort & RV Park
HC 3, Box 183A
Blackduck, MN 56630
218-335-2324

Lost Acres Resort & Campground
HC 3, Box 162D, Kitchi Lake
Blackduck, MN 56630
800-835-6414

Brookside Campground
RR 1, Box 60A
Blooming Prarie, MN 55917
507-583-2979

Fairground Campsite
Fairbault County Fairground,
N. Main & 11th
Blue Earth, MN 56013
507-526-2916

Don & Mayva's Crow Wing Lake Camp
8831 Crow Wing Camp Rd. SW
Brainerd, MN 56401
218-829-6468

Greer Lake Campground
1601 Minnesota Dr.
Brainerd, MN 56401
218-828-2565

Gull & Love Lake Marina & Campground
5617 Love Lake Rd., NW
Brainerd, MN 56401
218-829-8130

Rock Lake Campground
1601 Minnesota Dr.
Brainerd, MN 56401
218-828-2565

Shady Hollow Resort & Campground
P.O. Box 207
Brainerd, MN 56401
218-828-9308

Twin Oaks Resort
1777 Nokay Lake Rd.
Brainerd, MN 56401
218-764-2965

Welles Memorial Park & Fairgrounds
420 Nebraska Ave.
Breckenridge, MN 56520
218-643-3455

Highview Campground & RV Park
HC 83, Box 1084
Breezy Point, MN 56472
218-543-4526

Dunromin' Park Campground
Rt. 1, Box 146
Caledonia, MN 55921
800-822-2514

Stonehill Park
Stonehill Park, Box 2
Canby, MN 56220
507-223-7586

Lake Byllesby Reg'l Park Campground
7650 Echo Point Rd.
Cannon Falls, MN 55009
507-263-4447

Cass Lake Lodge Resort & RV Park
Rt. 2, Box 60
Cass Lake, MN 56633
218-335-6658

Marclay Point Campground, Inc.
Rt. 2, Box 80F
Cass Lake, MN 56633
218-335-6589

Stony Point Resort, Trailer Park & Campground
P.O. Box 518
Cass Lake, MN 56633
218-335-6311

A-J Acres Campground
1300-195th St. E
Clearwater, MN 55320
320-558-2847

St. Cloud/Clearwater KOA
2454 Cty. Rd. 143
Clearwater, MN 55320
320-558-2876

St. Cloud/Clearwater/ I-94 KOA
2454 CR 143
Clearwater, MN 55320
800-562-5025

Beaver Dam Resort
German & Jefferson Lake, RR 1, Box 202
Cleveland, MN 56017
507-931-5650

Cloquet/Duluth KOA
1479 Old Carlton Rd.
Cloquet, MN 55720
800-562-9506

Sugar Bay Campgrounds/Resort
805 N. Sugar Bay Dr.
Cohasset, MN 55721
218-326-8493

Cokato Lake Country Campground
2945 Cty. Rd. 4 SW
Cokato, MN 55321
320-286-5779

Collinwood Regional Park
17251-70th St. SW
Cokato, MN 55320
320-286-2801

Greenway Lions Beach & Campsite Area
P.O. Box 696
Coleraine, MN 55722
218-245-3382

Beddow's Campground
7516 Bayside Dr.
Crane Lake, MN 55725
218-993-2389

Island Lake Campground
1391 Middle Rd.
Cromwell, MN 55726
218-644-3543

U.S. Campgrounds > MINNESOTA

Crookston Central Park
Ash St. & MItchell Ln.
Crookston, MN 56716
218-281-1242

Schreier's On Shetek
Campground
35 Resort Rd
Currie, MN 56123
507-763-3817

Fish Trap Campground
30894 Fish Trap Lake Dr.
Cushing, MN 56443
218-575-2603

Lake Dale Campground
24473 CSAH 4
Dassel, MN 55325
612-275-3387

Backwoods Resort &
RV Park
Rt. 1, Box 299A
Deer River, MN 56636
218-246-2542

Moose Lake Campground
Box 157
Deer River, MN 56636
218-246-8343

Northern Acres Resort &
Campground
HCR 3, Box 446
Deer River, MN 56636
218-798-2845

Camp Holiday Resort &
Campground
17467 Round Lake Rd.
Deerwood, MN 56444
218-678-2495

Dalois Campground
685 Katrine Dr. NE
Deerwood, MN 56444
218-678-2203

American Legion
Campground
810 W. Lake Dr.
Detroit Lakes, MN 56501
218-847-3759

Country Campground
RR4, Box 345A
Detroit Lakes, MN 56501
218-847-9621

Forest Hills RV Resort &
Golf Course
RR 1, Box 6
Detroit Lakes, MN 56501
218-439-6033

Long Lake Campsite
Rt. 3, Box 301
Detroit Lakes, MN 56501
218-847-8920

Buffalo Valley Camping
2590 Guss Rd.
Duluth, MN 55810
218-624-9901

Indian Post Campground
75th Ave. W & Grand Ave.
(Hwy. 23)
Duluth, MN 55807
218-624-5637

Island Beach Campground
6640 Fredenberg Lake Rd.
Duluth, MN 55803
218-721-3292

River's Edge Campground
P.O. Box 295
East Grand Forks, MN 56721
218-773-7481

Larson Lake Campground
P.O. Box 95
Effie, MN 56639
218-743-3694

Lost Lake Campground
P.O. Box 95
Effie, MN 56639
218-743-3694

Owen Lake Campground
P.O. Box 95
Effie, MN 56639
218-743-3694

Tipsinah Mounds
Campground/Park
Rt. 2, Box 52A
Elbow Lake, MN 56531
218-685-5114

Canoe Country
Campground
Box 30
Ely, MN 55731
218-365-4046

Fall Lake Campground
5721A CBO Rd.
Ely, MN 55731
218-365-5638

Silver Rapids Lodge &
Campground
HC 1, Box 2992
Ely, MN 55731
800-950-9425

Superior Forest Lodge
HC 1, Box 3199
Ely, MN 55731
218-365-4870

Timber Trail Resort &
Campground
HC 1, Box 3111
Ely, MN 55731
218-365-4879

Timber Wolf Lodge
P.O. Box 147
Ely, MN 55731
218-827-3512

Valley View Campground
RR. 1, Box 111
Fairfax, MN 55322
507-426-7420

Flying Goose Campground
Rt. 2, Box 274
Fairmont, MN 56031
507-235-3458

Camp Faribo Campground/
RV Park
21851 Bagley Ave.
Faribault, MN 55021
507-332-8453

Maiden Rock Campgrounds
22661 Dodge Ct.
Faribault, MN 55021
507-685-4430

Roberds Lake Resort &
Campground
18192 Roberd Lake Blvd.
Faribault, MN 55021
800-879-5091

Wildridge Lakeside
Campground
2221 Reuben's Ln. SW
Farwell, MN 56327
320-886-5370

U.S. Lodgings > MINNESOTA

Elks Point
P.O. Box 502, Rt. 1
Fergus Falls, MN 56537
218-736-5244

Swan Lake Resort
Rt. 6, Box 426
Fergus Falls, MN 56537
218-736-4626

Fifty Lakes Campground
P.O. Box 158
Fifty Lakes, MN 56448
218-763-2616

**Wildhurst Lodge &
Campground, Inc.**
970 Hwy. 1
Finland, MN 55603
218-353-7337

Waldheim Resort
906 Waldheim Ln.
Finlayson, MN 55735
320-233-7405

**Timm's Marina &
Campground**
9080 N. Jewel Ln.
Forest Lake, MN 55025
612-464-3890

**City of Fosston
Campground**
Fosston Fairgrounds
Fosston, MN 56542
218-435-1806

**Birchmere Family Resort &
Campground**
Rt. 1, Box 159
Frazee, MN 56544
218-334-5741

Shady Oaks
340 Fairgrounds St.
Garden City, MN 56034
507-546-3986

**Alexandria Oak Park
Kampground**
9561 Cty. Rd. 8 NW
Garfield, MN 56322
320-834-2345

Wigwam Inn
18271 460th St.
Garrison, MN 56450
320-692-4579

**Gilbert Sherwood Forest
Campground**
City Hall, Box 549, 16 S.
Broadway St.
Gilbert, MN 55741
218-749-0703

Barsness Park/Chalet
137 E. Minnesota Ave.
Glenwood, MN 56334
320-634-5433

**El Reno Resort &
Campground**
Rt. 1, Box 80
Glenwood, MN 56334
320-283-5594

**Woodlawn Resort &
Campground**
2370 N. Lakeshore Dr.
Glenwood, MN 56334
320-634-3619

**Grand Marais Recreation
Area & RV Park**
P.O. Box 820
Grand Marais, MN 55604
218-387-1712

Gunflint Pines
217 S. Gunflint Lake Rd.
Grand Marais, MN 55604
218-388-4454

**Hungry Jack Lodge &
Campground**
475 Cunflint Trail
Grand Marais, MN 55604
218-388-2265

NOr'Wester Lodge
7778 Gunflint Trail
Grand Marais, MN 55604
218-388-2252

**Birch Cove Resort &
Campground**
431 Southwood Rd.
Grand Rapids, MN 55744
218-326-8754

Prairie Lake Campgrounds
400 Wabana Rd.
Grand Rapids, MN 55744
218-326-8486

Quietwoods Campground
HC 75, Box 568
Hackensack, MN 56452
218-675-6240

Ham Lake Campground
2400 Constance Blvd.
Ham Lake, MN 55304
612-434-5337

Amish Country Camping
RR 2, Box 418
Harmony, MN 55939
507-886-6731

Greenwood Campground
13797 190th St. E.
Hastings, MN 55033
612-437-5269

Old Wagon Campground
21611-132nd St. NE
Hawick, MN 56246
320-354-2165

Allanson's Park
900 S. St.
Henderson, MN 56044
507-248-3234

**Lake Hendricks
Campground**
City Hall
Henricks, MN 56136
507-275-3192

Bear Lake Campground
1208 E. Howard St.
Hibbing, MN 55746
218-262-6760

**Button Box Lake
Campground**
1208 E. Howard St
Hibbing, MN 55746
218-262-6760

**Thistledew Lake
Campground**
1208 E. Howard St.
Hibbing, MN 55746
218-262-6760

**Forest Heights
RV Park & Tenting**
2240 E. 25th St.
Hibbling, MN 55037
218-263-5782

U.S. Campgrounds > MINNESOTA

Ann Lake Campground
P.O. Box 9
Hill City, MN 55748
218-697-2476

Hay Lake Campground
P.O. Box 9
Hill City, MN 55748
218-697-2476

Boulder Campground
Rt. 2, Box 386B
Hinckley, MN 55037
612-384-6146

**Grand Casino Hinckley
RV Resort/Chalets**
Rt. 3, Box 14
Hinckley, MN 55037
800-995-4726

Pathfinder Village
Hwy. 48, Rt. 3, Box 233
Hinckley, MN 55037
320-384-7726

Snake River Campground
Rt. 2, Box 386 B
Hinckley, MN 55037
320-384-6146

**St. Croix Haven
Campground**
Rt. 3, Box 385
Hinckley, MN 55037
320-655-7989

Money Creek Haven
RR 1, Box 154
Houston, MN 55943
507-896-3544

**Fisherman's Point
Campground**
206 Kennedy Memorial Dr.
Hoyt Lakes, MN 55750
218-225-2344

Masonic/West River Park
900 Harrington
Hutchinson, MN 55350
320-587-2975

**Arnold's Campground &
RV Park**
Hwy. 53 & 21st St.
International Falls, MN 56649
218-285-9100

**Country Camping Tent &
RV Park**
750-273rd Aven. NW
Isanti, MN 55040
612-444-9626

**Breaker's Marina & RV
Park**
Lake Mille Lacs, P.O. Box 152
Isle, MN 56342
320-676-8549

Dickies Portside Resort
Mille Lacs Lake, 42089 Vista Rd.
Isle, MN 56342
320-676-8795

Eastside Marina, Inc.
HC 69, Box 150
Isle, MN 56342
320-676-8735

**South Isle Family
Campground**
Rt. 1, Box 228
Isle, MN 56342
320-676-8538

Loon Lake Campground
405-4th St.
Jackson, MN 56143
507-847-2240

Jordan-Shakopee KOA
3315 W 166th St.
Jordan, MN 55352
800-562-6317

**Cedar Cove Campsites &
Resort**
9940 Gappa Rd
Kabetogama Lake, MN 56669
218-875-3851

**Rogers' On Red Lake
Campground/RV Park**
HCR 1, Box 20
Kelliher, MN 56650
218-647-8262

Depot Campground & Cafe
P.O. Box 115,
Knife River, MN 55609
218-834-5044

Kruger Recreation Area
1801 S. Oak
Lake City, MN 55041
612-345-3216

**Lake Pepin Campground &
Trailer Court**
1818 N. High St.
Lake City, MN 55041
612-345-2909

**Eable Cliff Campground &
Lodging**
RR 1, Box 344
Ln.sboro, MN 55949
507-467-2598

**Pine Beach Resort &
Campground**
Rt. 1, Box 40
Laporte, MN 56461
218-224-2313

Peaceful Valley Campsites
213 Peaceful Valley Rd.
LeSueur, MN 56058
507-665-2297

Hillcrest RV Park
32715 N. Lakes Trail
Lindstrom, MN 55045
612-257-5352

Whispering Bay Resort
114430 291st St. N
Lindstrom, MN 55045
612-257-1784

Rice Creek Campground
7401 Main St.
Lino Lakes, MN 55038
612-757-3920

Lake Ripley Campground
East Shore/Lake Ripley, P.O.
Box 820-C
Litchfield, MN 55355
320-693-8184

Fletcher Creek Campground
Rt. 5, Box 93A
Little Falls, MN 56345
320-632-9636

Lofgren Park
413 Fourth Ave.
Littlefork, MN 56653
218-278-6710

**Holiday Haven Lakeview
Resort**
HC 2, Box 165, Mute Lake
Longville, MN 56655
218-363-2473

U.S. Campgrounds > MINNESOTA

**Longville Campground
"Austin's Swamp"**
P.O. Box 404
Longville, MN 56655
218-363-2610

Shields Lake Campground
14398 Irwin Path
Lonsdale, MN 55046
507-334-8526

Watona Park
116 W. Main
Madelia, MN 56062
507-642-3245

**Point Pleasant Resort &
Campground**
400 Sheppard Cir.
Madison Lake, MN 56063
507-243-3611

Sakatah Trail Campground
301 Main St., Box 191
Madison Lake, MN 56063
507-243-3886

**Shooting Star Lodge
Campgrounds**
P.O. Box 418, Casino Dr.
Mahnomen, MN 56557
218-935-2701

**Bray Park Blue Earth
County Park**
35 Map Dr.
Mankato, MN 56001
507-625-3281

**Daly Park Blue Earth
County Park**
35 Map Dr.
Mankato, MN 56001
507-625-3281

**Land of Memories
Campground**
P.O. Box 3368
Mankato, MN 56002
507-387-8649

Olson's Campgrounds
5669 123rd St. NW
Maple Lake, MN 55358
320-963-5175

Ponderosa Campground
RR 1, Box 209
Mazeppa, MN 55956
507-843-3611

**Menahga Memorial
Forest Park**
825 Aspen Ave.
Menahga, MN 56464
218-564-4557

Lagoon Park Campground
103 Canton Ave.
Montevideo, MN 56265
320-269-5527

Moorhead/Fargo KOA
Route 4, Box 168
Moorhead, MN 56560
800-562-0217

Gavert Campground
Rt. 2, 701 Kenwood
Moose Lake, MN 55767
218-485-5400

**Red Fox Campground &
RV Park**
P.O. Box 10
Moose Lake, MN 55767
218-485-0341

Willow River Campground
Rt. 2, 701S Kenwood
Moose Lake, MN 55767
218-485-5400

Camperville
2351-310th Ave.
Mora, MN 55051
320-679-2336

**Fish Lake Resort &
Campground**
674 Fish Lake Dr.
Mora, MN 55051
320-679-2117

Riverview Campground
764 Fish Lake Dr.
Mora, MN 55051
320-679-3275

**Pomme De Terre
Campground**
Cty. Rd. 10
Morris, MN 56267
320-589-3141

**Jackpot Junction Casino
Hotel Campground**
P.O. Box 400
Morton, MN 56270
507-644-2645

**West Two Rivers Reservoir
Campground**
Campground Rd.
Mountain Iron, MN 55768
218-735-8831

Jackson KOA
2035 Hwy. 71
N. Jackson, MN 56143
800-562-5670

Fritz's Resort
P.O. Box 803
Nisswa, MN 56468
218-568-8988

**Galle's Upper Cullen
Campground**
Upper Cullen Lake, Box 72
Nisswa, MN 56468
218-963-2249

Hilltop Family Camgpround
2186 Empire St.
Ogilvie, MN 56358
320-272-4300

Ash River Campground
P.O. Box 306, 4656 Hwy. 53
Orr, MN 55771
218-757-3274

**Cabin O'Pines Resort &
Campground**
Box CG, 4378 Pelican Rd.
Orr, MN 55771
800-757-3122

Hidden Hills Campground
10247 Ash River Trail
Orr, MN 55771
218-374-4412

**Pine Acres Resort &
Campground**
4498C Pine Acres Rd.
Orr, MN 55771
218-757-3144

U.S. Campgrounds > MINNESOTA

**Sunset Resort &
Campground**
Ash River Trail
Orr, MN 55771
218-374-3161

Woodenfrog Campground
P.O. Box 306, 4656 Hwy. 52
Orr, MN 55771
218-757-3274

**Lakeshore RV Park &
Fruit Farm**
RT. 1, Box 95
Ortonville, MN 56278
320-839-3701

**Blacks Crescent Beach
Resort/Campground**
Box 416EM, Lake Osakis
Osakis, MN 56360
320-859-2127

Hope Oak Knoll Inc.
Rt. 2, Box 71
Owatonna, MN 55060
507-451-2998

**Owatonna
Campgrounds, Inc.**
2554 SW 28th St.
Owatonna, MN 55060
507-451-8050

Big Pines Tent & RV Park
501 S. Central Ave.
Park Rapids, MN 56470
218-732-4483

Breeze Camping Resort
HC 05, Box 210
Park Rapids, MN 56470
218-732-5888

**Hungry Man Lake
Campground**
607 W. 1st St.
Park Rapids, MN 56470
218-732-3309

Mantrap Lake Campground
607 W. 1st St, Hwy. 34
Park Rapids, MN 56470
218-732-3309

**Round Bay Resort &
RV Park**
Rt. 4, Box 133C
Park Rapids, MN 56470
218-732-4880

**Sleeping Fawn Resort &
Campground**
Rt. 3, Box 271
Park Rapids, MN 56470
218-732-5356

Spruce Hill Campground
Rt. 4, Box 449
Park Rapids, MN 56470
218-732-3292

**Vagabond Village
Campground**
HC 06, Box 381-A
Park Rapids, MN 56470
218-732-5234

Koronis Regional Park
51625 CSAH 20
Paynesville, MN 56362
320-276-8843

Pelican Hills Park
Rt. 4, Box 218-B
Pelican Rapids, MN 56572
218-532-3726

Paradise Resort
HC 3, Box 204
Pennington, MN 56663
218-835-6514

**Clint Converse Memorial
Campground**
Box 27
Pequot Lakes, MN 56472
218-568-4566

Rager's Acres
Rt. 2, Box 348
Pequot Lakes, MN 56472
218-568-8752

**Pokegama Lake RV Park &
Golf Course**
RR 4, Box 54
Pine City, MN 55063
800-248-6552

Wazionia Campground
6450-120th St. NW
Pine Island, MN 55963
507-356-8594

Doty's River View RV Park
HCR 77, Box 39
Pine River, MN 56474
218-587-4112

Pipestone RV Campground
919 N. Hiawatha AVe.
Pipestone, MN 56164
507-825-2455

**Tamarac Resort &
Campground**
Rt. 1, Box 351
Ponsford, MN 56575
218-575-3262

The Old Barn Resort
Rt. 3, Box 57
Preston, MN 55965
507-467-2512

**Dakotah Meadows RV &
Park Home Campground**
2341 Park Pl.
Prior Lake, MN 55372
612-445-8800

**Fish Lake Acres
Campground**
3000-210th St. E.
Prior Lake, MN 55372
612-492-3393

**Hay Creek Valley
Campground**
31673 Hwy. 58 Blvd.
Red Wing, MN 55066
612-388-3998

Island Camping & Marina
2361 Hallquist Ave.
Red Wing, MN 55066
715-792-2502

Treasure Island RV Park
P.O. Box 75, 5734 Sturgeon
Lk. Rd.
Red Wing, MN 55066
800-222-7077

**Big Springs Resort &
Campground**
HCR 3, Box 101
Remer, MN 56672
218-566-2322

U.S. Campgrounds > MINNESOTA

Browns Lake Resort & Campground
18091 Browns Lake Rd.
Richmond, MN 56368
320-597-2611

El Rancho Manana Campground & Riding Stable
27301M Ranch Rd.
Richmond, MN 56368
320-597-2740

Yoru Haven Campground & Seasonal RV Park
18337 State Hwy. 22
Richmond, MN 56368
320-597-2450

Head Lake Camp
P.O. Box 66
Richville, MN 56576
218-346-7200

Northern Lights Resort
Rt. 1, Box 147
Richville, MN 56576
218-758-2343

Brookside RV Park
516-17th Ave. NW
Rochester, MN 55901
507-288-1413

Rochester/Marion KOA
5232 65th Ave. SE
Rochester, MN 55904
800-562-5232

Rochester/Marion KOA
5232-65th Ave. SE
Rochester, MN 55904
507-288-0785

Minneapolis NW/ Maple Grove KOA
Box 214
Rogers, MN 55374
800-562-0261

Minneapolis NW/ Maple Grove KOA
P.O. Box 214
Rogers, MN 55374
612-420-2255

Two Rivers Park
P.O. Box 137
Royalton, MN 56373
320-584-5125

Rush Lake Resort
51170 Rush Lake Trail
Rush City, MN 55069
320-358-4427

Pine River Campground
7201 Hwy. 61
Rutledge, MN 55795
320-233-7678

Town & Country Campground
12630 Boone Ave. S
Savage, MN 55378
612-445-1756

Lamb's Campgrounds & Cabins
North Shore, P.O. Box 415
Schroeder, MN 55613
218-663-7292

Huntersville Forest Campground
Rt. 2, Box 330
Sebeka, MN 56477
218-472-3262

Shell City Campground
Rt. 2, Box 320
Sebeka, MN 56477
218-472-3262

Shakopee Valley RV Park
1245 E. Bluff Ave.
Shakopee, MN 55379
612-445-7313

CC Campground 717
7595 McCarthy Beach Rd.,
P.O. Box 302
Side Lake, MN 55781
218-254-5301

Pine Beach Resort & Campground
7504 McCarthy Beach Rd.,
P.O. Box 5
Side Lake, MN 55781
218-254-3144

McKinley Park Campground
P.O. Box 382
Soudan, MN 55782
218-753-5921

Timberwoods Resort & Campground
10255 Nevens Ave. NW
South Haven, MN 55382
320-274-5140

Supersaw Valley Campground
RR 2
Spring Grove, MN 55974
507-498-5880

Edgewater 4-Season Resort & RV Park
HCR 1, Box 240C
Spring Lake, MN 56680
218-798-2620

Ghost Bay Mobile Home & RV Resort
HCR1 Box 238
Spring Lake, MN 56680
218-798-2128

Riverside Park & Campground
2 E. Central
Springfield, MN 56087
507-723-4416

Lowry Grove Campground
2501 Lowry Ave.NE
St. Anthony Villa, MN 55148
612-781-3148

Birch Lake Campground
4140 Theilman Ln., Ste. 203
St. Cloud, MN 56301
320-255-4276

St. Cloud Campground & RV Park
2491 2nd St. SE
St. Cloud, MN 56304
320-251-4463

Tiell Park
Tiell Dr.
St. James, MN 55081
507-375-3241

U.S. Campgrounds > MINNESOTA

St. Paul East KOA
568 Cottage Grove Dr.
St. Paul, MN 55129
612-436-6436

Springvale Campground
36955 Palm St. NW
Stanchfield, MN 55080
612-689-3208

Dower Lake Recreational Area
Staples, MN 56479
218-894-2550

Golden Acres RV Park & Picnic Area
15150 Square Lake Trail N.
Stillwater, MN 55082
612-439-1147

Edelweiss Resort & Campground
Rt. 2
Sturgeon Lake, MN 55783
218-372-3363

Timberline Best Holiday Trav-L-Park
Rt. 1, Box 20, Timberline Rd.
Sturgeon Lake, MN 55783
218-372-3272

Timberline Campground
Rt. 1, Box 20
Sturgeon Lake, MN 55783
218-372-3272

Camp Waub-O-Jeeg
2185 Chicago St.
Taylors Falls, MN 55084
612-465-5721

Wildwood Campground
P.O. Box 235
Taylors Falls, MN 55084
612-465-6315

Whippoorwill Ranch Kampground
RR 1, Box 145
Theilman, MN 55978
507-534-3590

Thief River Falls Tourist Park
Hw. 32 S. & Oakland Park Rd.
Thief River Falls, MN 56701
218-681-2519

Meridian East/ Toomsuba KOA
3953 KOA Campground Rd.
Toomsuba, MN 39364
800-562-4202

Hoodoo Point Campgrounds
P.O. Box 576
Tower, MN 55790
218-753-4070

Moccasin Point Resort
Box 4650 Moccasin Point
Tower, MN 55790
218-753-3309

Wakemup Bay Campground
P.O. Box 432, 609 N. Second St.
Tower, MN 55790
218-753-4500

Big Blaze Campground
Big Blaze Cir.
Two Harbors, MN 55616
218-834-2512

Burlington Bay Campground
Hwy. 61
Two Harbors, MN 55616
218-834-2021

Eckbeck Camgground
120 State Rd.
Two Harbors, MN 55616
218-834-6602

Finland Campground
120 State Rd.
Two Harbors, MN 55616
218-834-6602

Indian Lake Campground
120 State Rd.
Two Harbors, MN 55616
218-834-6602

Wagon Wheel Campground
W. Star Rt., Box 92
Two Harbors, MN 55616
218-834-4901

Pioneer Camp
130 Pioneer Dr.
Wabasha, MN 55981
612-565-2242

Sunnybrook Park Campground
P.O. Box 30
Wadena, MN 56482
218-631-2884

Anderson's Cove Campground/Resort
HC 73, Box 508
Walker, MN 56484
218-547-2999

Anderson's Northland Lodge
HCR 84, Box 376
Walker, MN 56484
800-247-1719

Bayview Resort & Campground
P.O. Box 58
Walker, MN 56484
218-547-1595

Shores of Leech Lake Campground & Marina
P.O. Box 327
Walker, MN 56484
218-547-1819

Waters Edge RV Park
HCR 73, Box 530
Walker, MN 56484
218-547-3552

Wedgewood Resort & Campground
HC 73, Box 583
Walker, MN 56484
218-547-1443

Kiesler's Campground on Clear Lake
P.O. Box 503
Waseca, MN 56093
507-835-3179

Kamp Dels
Rt. 2, Box 49
Waterville, MN 56096
507-362-8616

U.S. Campgrounds > MINNESOTA

Clear Lake Campground
36649 657th Ave.
Watkins, MN 55389
320-764-2592

**Elk Horn Resort &
Campground**
Rt 2., Box 323
Waubun, MN 56589
218-935-5437

**Oxbow Resort &
Campground**
RR 2, Box 217
Waubun, MN 56589
218-734-2244

**KC's Welcome
Campground**
RR 1, Box 127A
Welcome, MN 56181
507-728-8811

Zippel Bay Resort
HC 2, Box 51
Williams, MN 56686
218-783-6235

Wilderness Campgrounds
Long Lake Rd.
Willow River, MN 55795
218-372-3993

Winona KOA
Route 6, Box 18-I
Winona, MN 55987
800-562-0843

Winona KOA
Rt. 6
Winona, MN 55987
507-454-2851

St. Paul East KOA
568 Cottage Grove Dr.
Woodbury, MN 55129
800-562-3640

Olson Park Campground
P.O. Box 279
Worthington, MN 56187
507-372-8650

**Baylor Regional Park
Campground**
10775 Cty. Rd. 33
Young America, MN 55397
612-467-4200

Camp in the Woods
14791 289th Ave.
Zimmerman, MN 55398
612-389-2516

**Bluff Valley Campground,
Inc.**
RR 1, Box 194
Zumbro Falls, MN 55991
507-753-2955

**Shades of Sherwood
Camping Area**
14334 Sherwood Tr.
Zumbro Falls, MN 55992
507-732-5100

**Zumbro Valley Sportsman's
Park**
P.O. Box 91
Zumbro Falls, MN 55991
507-753-2568

MISSISSIPPI

**Gaywood Best Holiday
Trav-L-Park**
1100 Cowan Rd.
Gulfport, MS 39507
228-896-4840

Ocean Springs/Biloxi KOA
7501 Hwy. 57
Ocean Springs, MS 39564
800-562-7028

**Meridian East-Toomsuba
KOA**
3953 KOA Campground Rd.
Toomsuba, MS 39364
601-632-1684

MISSOURI

St. Louis South KOA
8000 Metropolitan Blvd.
Barnhart, MO 63012
800-562-3049

Branson KOA
1025 Headwaters Rd.
Branson, MO 65616
800-562-4177

Branson View Campground
2362 Hwy. 265
Branson, MO 65616
800-992-9055

Tall Pines Best Holiday
HCR 9, Box 1175
Branson, MO 65616
417-338-2445

**Paradise Cover Camping
Resort**
HC 1 Box 1067
Eagle Rock, MO 65641
417-271-4888

Forsyth KOA
11020 Hwy. 76
Forsyth, MO 65653
800-562-7560

**Trailside Campers' Inn of
Kansas City**
1000 R.D. Mize Rd.
Grain Valley, MO 64029
800-748-7729

Jonesburg/Warrenton KOA
P.O. Box H
Jonesburg, MO 63351
800-562-5634

Joplin KOA
4359 Hwy. 43
Joplin, MO 64804
800-562-5675

Kimberling City KOA
HCR 5, Box 465
Kimberling, MO 65686
800-562-5685

**Osage Beach/
Lake Ozark KOA**
498 Hwy. 42
Lake Ozark, MO 65049
800-562-7554

Menagerie Campground
RR 16, Box 1010
Lebanon, MO 65536
417-588-3353

**Kansas City East/Oak
Grove KOA**
303 NE 3rd.
Oak Grove, MO 64075
800-562-7507

**Perryville/Cape Girardeau
KOA**
89 KOA Ln.
Perryville, MO 63775
800-562-5304

U.S. Campgrounds > NEBRASKA

Lebanon KOA
18376 Campground Rd.
Phillipsburg, MO 65722
800-562-3424

**Basswood Country
RV Park**
15880 Interurban Rd.
Platte City, MO 64079
816-858-5556

Camelot RV Campground
Rt. 6, Box 1217
Poplar Bluff, MO 63901
573-785-1016

Hayti/Portageville KOA
2824 MO St. E. Outer Rd.
Portageville, MO 65873
800-562-1508

Rock Port KOA
Route 4, Box 204
Rock Port, MO 64482
800-562-5415

WAC Campground
Rt. 1, Box 1014
Sarcoxie, MO 64862
417-548-2258

Springfield KOA
5775 W. Farm Rd. 140
Springfield, MO 65802
800-562-1228

Stanton/Meramec KOA
Box 177
Stanton, MO 63079
800-562-4386

Sullivan/Meramec KOA
1451 E. Springfield
Sullivan, MO 63080
800-562-8730

MONTANA

Alder/Virginia City KOA
Box 103
Alder, MT 59710
800-562-1898

Big Timber KOA
HC 88, Box 3634
Big Timber, MT 59011
800-562-5869

Billings Metro KOA
547 Garden Ave.
Billings, MT 59101
800-562-8546

Bozeman KOA
81123 Gallatin Rd., US 191
Bozeman, MT 59715
800-562-3036

Butte KOA
1601 Kaw Ave.
Butte, MT 59701
800-562-8089

Choteau KOA
Hwy. 221
Choteau, MT 59422
800-562-4156

**Wilderness Motel, RV &
Tent Park**
308 S. Main St.
Darby, MT 59829
406-821-3405

Deer Lodge KOA
Park St.
Deer Lodge, MT 59722
800-562-1629

Dillon KOA
735 W. Park St.
Dillon, MT 59725
800-562-2751

Great Falls KOA
1500 51st St. S.
Great Falls, MT 59405
800-562-6584

Hardin KOA
RR 1
Hardin, MT 59034
800-562-1635

**Livingston/
Paradise Valley KOA**
163 Pine Creek Rd.
Livingston, MT 59047
800-562-2805

Miles City KOA
1 Palmer St.
Miles City, MT 59301
800-562-3909

Missoula KOA
3450 Tina Ave.
Missoula, MT 59808
800-562-5366

Polson/Flathead Lake KOA
200 Irvine Flats Rd.
Polson, MT 59860
800-562-2130

Red Lodge KOA
HC 50, Box 5340
Red Lodge, MT 59068
800-562-7540

St. Mary KOA
106 West Shore
St. Mary, MT 59417
800-562-1054

St. Regis KOA
105 Old Hwy. 10 E., Box187
St. Regis, MT 59866
800-562-4670

Sula KOA
7060 Hwy. 93 S.
Sula, MT 59871
800-562-9867

Three Forks KOA
15 KOA Rd.
Three Forks, MT 59752
800-562-9752

**Yellowstone Park/
West Entrance KOA**
Box 348
W. Yellowstone, MT 59758
800-562-7591

West Glacier KOA
Box 215
West Glacier, MT 59936
800-562-3313

Whitefish KOA
5121 Hwy. 93S
Whitefish, MT 59937
800-562-8734

NEBRASKA

Grand Island KOA
904 S. B Rd.
Doniphan, NE 68832
800-562-0850

U.S. Campgrounds > NEBRASKA

Gothenburg KOA
I-80 & Hwy. 47S, Box 353
Gothenburg, NE 69138
800-562-1873

West Omaha KOA
14601 Hwy. 6
Gretna, NE 68028
800-562-1632

Hastings KOA
302 E. 26th
Hastings, NE 68901
800-562-2171

Henderson/York KOA
913 Rd. B
Henderson, NE 68371
800-562-4171

Kimball KOA
RR 1, Box 128 D
Kimball, NE 69145
800-562-4785

Holiday Park
Route 4, Box 2
North Platte, NE 69101
308-534-2265

Scottsbluff/Chimney Rock KOA
180037 KOA Dr.
Scottsbluff, NE 69361
800-562-0845

Valentine KOA
HC-37, Box 3
Valentine, NE 69201
800-562-1612

NEVADA

Austin RV Park
Austin, NV 89310
702-964-1011

Baily's Hot Springs
US Hwy. 95
Beatty, NV 89003
702-553-2395

Burro Inn
US Hwy. 95
Beatty, NV 89003
702-553-2225

Death Valley National Park
State Rt. 374
Beatty, NV 89003
619-786-2331

Kay's Korral RV Park
US Hwy. 95
Beatty, NV 89003
702-553-2732

Space Station RV Park
US Hwy. 95
Beatty, NV 89003
702-533-9039

Lake Mead National Recreation Area
601 Nevada Hwy.
Boulder City, NV 89005
702-293-8906

Aqua Caliente Trailer Park
US Hwy. 93 N.
Caliente, NV 89008
702-726-3399

Beaver Dam State Park
Caliente, NV 89008
702-728-4467

Kershaw-Ryan State Park
Caliente, NV 89008
702-726-3564

Young's RV Park
US Hwy. 93
Caliente, NV 89008
702-726-3418

Camp 'N Town
2438 N. Carson St.
Carson City, NV 89706
702-883-1123

Comstock Country RV Resort
5400 s. Carson St.
Carson City, NV 89701
702-882-2445

Washoe Lake State Recreation Area
4855 E. Lake Blvd.
Carson City, NV 89704
775-687-4319

Dayton State Park
U.S. Hwy. 50 E.
Dayton, NV 89403
775-687-5678

Denio Junction
PO Box 10
Denio, NV 89404
702-941-0371

Ruby Mountain Recreation Area
Elco, NV 89801
702-752-3357

Double Dice RV Park
3730 E. Idaho
Elko, NV 89801
702-738-5642

Hidden Valley Guest & RV Resort
PO Box 1454
Elko, NV 89803
702-738-2347

Jarbidge Recreation Area
Elko, NV 89801
208-543-4129

Rydon Campground
PO Box 1656
Elko, NV 89801
702-738-3448

South Fork State Recreation Area
Elko, NV 89801
702-744-4346

Valley View RV Park
HC 34, Unit 1
Elko, NV 89801
702-753-9200

Wild Horse State Recreation Area
Elko, NV 89801
702-758-6493

Wildhorse Resort and Ranch
HC 31, Box 213
Elko, NV 89801
702-758-6471

U.S. Campgrounds > NEVADA

Cove Lake State Park
Ely, NV 89301
702-728-4467

Eldorado Service Junction
US Hwy. 50 & Strawberry
Ely, NV 89301
702-237-1002

Ely KOA
HC 10, Box 10800
Ely, NV 89301
800-562-3413

Holiday Inn-Prospector Casino RV Park
1501 Ave. F
Ely, NV 89301
702-289-8900

KOA of Ely
Pioche Hwy.
Ely, NV 89301
702-289-3413

Rainbow RV Park
1011 Pioche Hwy.
Ely, NV 89301
702-289-2622

Schelbourne Service
US Hwy. 93, Box 33620
Ely, NV 89301
702-591-0363

Valley View RV Park
HC-33, PO Box 33200
Ely, NV 89301
702-289-3303

Fallon RV Park
5787 Reno Hwy.
Fallon, NV 89406
702-867-2332

Hub Total RV & Mobile Home Park
4800 Reno Hwy.
Fallon, NV 89406
702-867-3636

Lahonton State Recreation Area
Fallon, NV 89406
702-867-3500

Fernley RV Park
1405 E. Newlands
Fernley, NV 89408
702-575-6776

Truck Inn
I-80
Fernley, NV 89408
702-575-4800

Berlin-Ichtyosaur State Park
Gabbs, NV 89409
702-964-9440

Hollbrook Station
1501 US Hwy. 395 S
Gardnerville, NV 89410
702-266-3434

Topaz Lake Park
3700 Topaz Park Rd.
Gardnerville, NV 89410
702-266-3343

Desert Lake Campground
US Hwy. 95 Walker Lake,
P.O. Box 647
Hawthorne, NV 89415
702-945-3373

Frontier RV Park
Fifth & L St.
Hawthorne, NV 89415
702-945-2733

Spanish Gardens RV Park
Corner of Gurley &
US Hwy. 93
Jackpot, NV 89825
702-755-2333

R Place
US Hwy. 93, HCR 61
Kiko, NV 89017
702-725-3545

King's Row Trailer Park
3660 Boulder Hwy.
Las Vegas, NV 89121
702-457-3606

Las Vegas KOA
4315 Boulder Hwy.
Las Vegas, NV 89121
702-451-5527

Lee Canyon Recreation Area
Las Vegas, NV 89125
702-645-2754

Spring Mountain National Recreation Area
Las Vegas, NV 89125
702-873-8800

Spring Mountain Ranch State Park
Las Vegas, NV 89125
702-875-4141

Valley of Fire State Park
Las Vegas, NV 89125
702-397-2088

Lazy K Campground & RV Park
1550 Cornell Ave., P.O. Box1661
Lovelock, NV 89419
702-273-1116

Rye Patch State Recreation Area
Lovelock, NV 89419
702-538-7321

Sunrise Valley RV Park
U.S. Hwy. 95, P.O. Box 345
Mina, NV 89422
702-573-2214

Waterhole RV Park
U.S.Hwy. 95, P.O. Box 131
Mina, NV 89422
702-573-2445

Palm Creek RV Park
3215 Warm Springs,
P.O. Box 400
Moapa, NV 89025
702-865-2777

Big 5 Trailer Park
850 S. Big 5 Rd.
Pahrump, NV 89048
702-727-6490

Seven Palms RV Park
101 S. Linda St.
Pahrump, NV 89048
702-727-6091

Cathedral Gorge State Park
Panaca, NV 89042
702-728-4467

Echo Canyon State Park
Pioche, NV 89043
702-962-5103

U.S. Campgrounds > NEVADA

Spring Valley State Park
Pioche, NV 89043
702-962-5102

Bonanza Terrace RV Park
4800 Staltz Rd.
Reno, NV 89506
702-329-9624

Chism Trailer Park
1300 W. 2nd St.
Reno, NV 89503
702-322-2281

Four Seasons RV Park
13109 S.Virginia St.
Reno, NV 89511
702-853-1423

Pyramid Lake State Park
State Rt. 445
Reno, NV 89501
775-476-1156

Fort Churchill State Historical Park
US Hwy. 95 Alt.
Silver Springs, NV 89429
702-577-2345

Lambertucci Roma
US Hwy. 95 N, P.O. Box 3347
Tonopah, NV 89049
702-482-5312

Twister Inn RV Park
Ketten Rd. & US Hwy. 6
Tonopah, NV 89049
702-482-9444

Virginia City RV Park
355 N. "F" St.
Virginia City, NV 89440
702-847-0999

I-80 Campground
I-80 Exit 43, State Rt. 447
Wadsworth, NV 89442
702-575-2181

Wellington Station Resort
2855 State Rt. 208
Wellington, NV 89444
702-465-2304

Mountain Shadows RV Park
807 Humboldt, P.O. Box 362
Wells, NV 89835
702-752-3525

Ruby Mountains Recreation Area
Wells, NV 89835
702-752-3357

Welcome Station
I-80 Exit 343, P.O. Box 340
Wells, NV 89835
702-752-3808

The Wendover KOA Campground
1250 N. Camper Dr. Exit 410
Wendover, NV 89883
702-664-2221

Wendover KOA
Box 3710
West Wendover, NV 89883
800-562-8552

Hi Desert RV Park
5575 E. Winnemucca Blvd.
Winnemucca, NV 89445
702-623-4513

Winnemucca RV Park
5255 E. Winnemucca Blvd.
Winnemucca, NV 89445
702-623-3501

Greenfield Mobile Home & RV Park
500 W. Goldfield Ave.
Yerlington, NV 89447
702-463-4912

Zephyr Cove Resort
P.O. Box 830, 760 Hwy. 50
Zephyr, NV 89448
702-588-6644

NEW HAMPSHIRE

Davies Campground
RFD 1, Box 131B, Route
Albany, NH 03818
603-447-1092

Bear Brook State Park
157 Deerfield Rd
Allenstown, NH 03275
603-485-9869

Ames Brook Campground
RFD #1, Box 102NA
Ashland, NH 03217
603-968-7998

Squam Lake Camp Resort
RFD #1, Box 42
Ashland, NH 03217
603-968-7227

Yogi Bear's Jellystone Park
RR1, Box 396
Ashland, NH 03217
603-968-9000

Ayers Lake Farm Campground
557 Route 202
Barrington, NH 03825
603-335-1110

Barrington Shores Campground
70 Hall Rd.
Barrington, NH 03825
603-664-9333

Silver Springs Campground
Box 38
Bartlett, NH 03812
603-374-2221

Twin River Campground & Cottages
P.O. Box 212
Bath, NH 03740
603-747-3640

Apple Hill Campground
P.O. Box 388
Bethlehem, NH 03574
603-869-2238

Snowy Mountain Campground & Motel
1225 Main St.
Bethlehem, NH 03574
603-869-2600

Lake Massasecum Campground
Massasecum Rd., RR1
Bradford, NH 03221
603-938-2571

Three Ponds Campground
146 North Rd.
Brentwood, NH 03803
603-679-5350

Davidson's Countryside Campground
RFD #2, Box 485, River
Bristol, NH 03222
603-744-2403

U.S. Campgrounds > NEW HAMPSHIRE

Field & Stream Park
5 Dupaw Gould Rd.
Brookline, NH 03033
603-673-4677

Branch Brook Four Season Camping
P.O. Box 390
Campton, NH 03223
603-726-7001

Goose Hollow Campground
RR2, Box 1600
Campton, NH 03223
800-204-2267

Pemi River Campground
RFD 1, Box 926
Campton, NH 03223
603-726-7015

Crescent Campsites
P.O. Box 238
Canaan, NH 03741
603-523-9910

Sun River Campground
P.O. Box 7
Center Barns, NH 03225
603-269-3333

Camp Iroquois Campground
P.O. Box 150
Center Harbor, NH 03226
603-253-4287

Long Island Bridge Campground
HCR 62, Box 455
Center Harbor, NH 03226
603-253-6053

Deer Cap Campground
P.O. Box 332
Center Ossipee, NH 03814
603-539-6030

Ossipee Lake Camping Area
Route 25
Center Ossipee, NH 03814
603-539-6631

Terrace Pines Campground
P.O. Box 98Z
Center Ossipee, NH 03814
603-539-6210

Silver Sands Campground
603 Raymond Rd.
Chester, NH 03036
603-887-3638

Hillcrest Campground
78 Dover Rd.
Chichester, NH 03234
603-798-5124

Maplewoods Scenic Camping Area
Route 1, Box 247
Colebrook, NH 03576
603-237-4237

Sandy Beach Family Campground
677 Clement Hill Rd.
Contocook, NH 03229
603-746-3591

Saco River Camping Area
P.O. Box 546N, Route 16
Conway, NH 03860
603-356-3360

The Beach Camping Area
Box 1007N
Conway, NH 03818
603-447-2723

Hidden Valley Rec. & Camping
81 Damren Rd.
Derry, NH 03038
603-887-3767

Old Stage Campground
46 Old Stage Rd.
Dover, NH 03820
603-742-4050

Forest Glen Campground
P.O. Box 676
Durham, NH 03824
603-659-3416

Oliverian Valley Campgrounds
P.O. Box 91
E. Haverhill, NH 03765
603-989-3351

Beachwood Shores Campground
HC Box 228
E. Wakefield, NH 03830
603-539-4272

Lake Forest Resort
271 N. Shore Rd.
E. Wakefield, NH 03830
603-522-3306

Lake Ivanhoe Campground
631 Action Ridge Rd.
E. Wakefield, NH 03830
603-522-8824

Tamarack Trails Camping Park
P.O. Box 24
East Lempster, NH 03605
603-863-6443

Mascoma Lake Camping Area
RR2, Box 331
Enfield, NH 03748
603-448-5076

Blake's Brook Campground
76 Mt. Rd.
Epsom, NH 03234
603-736-4793

Circle 9 Ranch Campground
P.O. Box 282
Epsom, NH 03234
603-736-9656

Epsom Valley Campground
990 Suncook Valley Hwy.
Epsom, NH 03234
603-736-9758

Lazy River Campground
427 Goboro Rd.
Epsom, NH 03234
603-798-5900

Log Haven Campground
P.O. Box 239
Errol, NH 03579
603-482-3294

Mollidgewock State Park
RFD #2, P.O. Box 29
Errol, NH 03579
603-482-3373

Umbagog Lake Campground
Box 181N
Errol, NH 03579
603-482-7795

U.S. Campgrounds > NEW HAMPSHIRE

The Exeter Elms Campground
188 Court St.
Exeter, NH 03833
603-778-7631

The Green Gate Camping Area
P.O. Box 185
Exeter, NH 03833
603-772-2100

Hunter's State Line Campground
Rt. 12, Box 132
Fitzwilliam, NH 03447
603-585-7726

Fransted Campground
P.O. Box 155
Franconia, NH 03580
603-823-5675

Pine Grove Campground
14 Timberland Dr.
Franklin, NH 03235
603-934-4582

Thousand Acres Campground
Route 3, 1079 S. Main S
Franklin, NH 03235
603-934-4440

Exeter River Camping Area
13 South Rd.
Fremont, NH 03044
603-895-3448

Glen-Ellis Family Campground
P.O. Box 397
Glen, NH 03838
603-383-4567

Green Meadow Camping Area
P.O. Box 246
Glen, NH 03838
603-383-6801

Moose Brook State Park
30 Jimtown Rd.
Gorham, NH 03581
603-466-3860

Timberland Camping Area
Box 303
Gorham, NH 03581
603-466-3872

Greenfield State Park
Box 203
Greenfield, NH 03047
603-547-3496

Emerson's Camping Area
233 Emerson Ave.
Hampstead, NH 03841
603-329-6938

Sanborn Shore Acres Campground
P.O. Box 626 Main St.
Hampstead, NH 03841
603-329-5247

Sunset Park Campground
P.O. Box 16N, 104 Emers
Hampstead, NH 03841
603-329-6941

Wakeda Campground
294 Exeter Rd.
Hampton Fall, NH 03844
603—772-527

Seven Maples Camping Area
24 Longview Rd.
Hancock, NH 03449
603-525-3321

Storrs Pond Campground
P.O. Box 106
Hanover, NH 03755
603-643-2134

Keyser Pond Campground
47 Old Concord Rd.
Henniker, NH 03242
603-428-7741

Mile Away Campground
41 Old West Hopkinton R
Henniker, NH 03242
603-428-7616

Mile-Away Best Holiday
41 Old W. Hopkinton Rd.
Henniker, NH 03242
603-428-7616

Oxbow Campground
RFD 1, Box 11
Hillsboro, NH 03244
603-464-5952

Bethel Woods Campground
Route 3, Box 201
Holderness, NH 03245
603-279-6266

Emerald Acres Campground
39 Ridgecrest Rd
Jaffrey, NH 03452
603-532-8838

Israel River Campgrounds
Box 179A
Jefferson, NH 03583
603-586-7977

Jefferson Campground
Box 112A
Jefferson, NH 03583
603-586-4510

Lantern Motor Inn & Campground
P.O. Box 97
Jefferson, NH 03583
603-586-7151

Hilltop Campground & Adventure
HCR 33, Box 186
Keene, NH 03431
603-847-3351

Gunstock Campground
P.O. Box 1307
Laconia, NH 03247
603-293-4341

Hack-Ma-Tack Campground
RFD 3, Box 90, Weir's B
Laconia, NH 03246
603-366-5977

Paugus Bay Campground
96 Hilliard Rd.
Laconia, NH 03246
603-366-4757

Beaver Trails Campground
RR #2, Box 315
Lancaster, NH 03584
603-788-3815

U.S. Campgrounds > NEW HAMPSHIRE

Mountain Lake Campground
P.O. Box 475
Lancaster, NH 03584
603-788-4509

Roger's Campground & Motel
10 Roger's Campground R
Lancaster, NH 03584
603-788-4885

Ferndale Acres Campgrounds
132 Wednesday Hill Rd.
Lee, NH 03824
603-659-5082

Country Bumbkins Campground
RR1, Box 83, Route 3
Lincoln, NH 03251
603-745-8837

Littleton KOA Kampground
2154 Route 302
Lisbon, NH 03585
603-838-5525

Littleton/Lisbon KOA
2154 Route 302
Lisbon, NH 03585
800-562-5386

Mink Brook Family Campground
Route 302, RFD 2
Lisbon, NH 03585
603-838-6658

Winnisquam Beach Resort
P.O. Box 67, 2 Grey Roc
Lochmere, NH 03252
603-524-0021

Cascade Park Camping Area
Route 106 S.
Loudon, NH 03301
603-224-3212

Clearwater Campground
26 Campground Rd.
Meredith, NH 03253
603-279-7761

Harbor Hill Camping Area
189 NH Route 25
Meredith, NH 03253
603-279-6910

Meredith Woods 4-Season Camping
26 Campground Rd.
Meredith, NH 03253
603-279-5449

Mi-Ti-Jo Campground
P.O. Box 830
Milton, NH 03851
603-652-9022

Pine Woods Campground
P.O. Box 776
Moultonbor, NH 03254
603-253-6251

Lost River Valley Campground
RD 1, Box 44
N. Woodstock, NH 03262
603-745-8321

Maple Haven Camping & Cottage
RFD 1, Box 54
N. Woodstock, NH 03626
602-745-3350

Friendly Beaver Campground
Old Coach Rd.
New Boston, NH 03070
603-487-5570

Wildwood Campgrounds
540 Old Coach Rd.
New Boston, NH 03070
603-487-3300

Twin Tamarack Family Camping
Route 104, Box 121
New Hampton, NH 03265
603-279-4387

Otter Lake Campground
55 Otterville Rd.
New London, NH 03257
603-763-5600

Great Bay Camping Village
P.O. Box 331, #56Rt/108
Newfields, NH 03856
603-778-0226

Wellington Camping Park
P.O. Box D
Newmarket, NH 03857
603-659-5065

Crow's Nest Campground
529 S. Main St.
Newport, NH 03773
603-863-6170

Loon Lake Campground
P.O. Box 345
Newport, NH 03773
603-863-8176

Northstar Campground
43 Coonbrook Rd.
Newport, NH 03773
603-863-4001

Shel-Al Camping Area
P.O. Box 700 Rt. 1
North Hampton, NH 03862
603-964-5730

Ogdensburg/ 1000 Islands KOA
4707 St. Hwy.
Ogdensburg, NH 13669
800-562-3962

Jacobs Brook Campground
P.O. Box 167, High Bridge
Orford, NH 03777
603-353-9210

The Pastures Campground
RR 1, Box 57A, Route 10
Orford, NH 03777
603-353-4579

Beaver Hollow Campground
P.O. Box 437
Ossipee, NH 03864
603-539-4800

Hidden Acres Campground
P.O. Box 94
Pittsburg, NH 03592
603-538-6919

Lake Francis State Park
285 River Rd.
Pittsburg, NH 03592
603-538-6965

U.S. Campgrounds > NEW HAMPSHIRE

**Mountain View Cabins &
Campground**
Mountain View RR1, Box
Pittsburg, NH 03592
603-538-6305

**Country Shore
Camping Area**
P.O. Box 559
Plaistow, NH 03865
603-642-5072

**Plymouth Sands
Campground**
RR1, Box 3172
Plymouth, NH 03264
603-536-2605

Pine Acres Recreation Area
74 Freetown Rd.
Raymond, NH 03077
603-895-2519

Shir-Roy Camping Area
100 Athol Rd.
Richmond, NH 03470
603-239-4768

Crown Point Campground
44 First Crown Point Rd
Rochester, NH 03867
603-332-0405

Grand View Camping Area
51 Four Rod Rd.
Rochester, NH 03867
603-332-1263

Baker River Campground
56 Campground Rd.
Rumney, NH 03266
603-786-9707

**Tuxbury Pond
Camping Area**
88 Whitehall Rd.
S. Hampton, NH 03827
603-394-7660

Autumn Hills Campground
285 S. Stark Hwy.
S. Weare, NH 03281
603-529-2425

**White Birches
Camping Park**
218 State Rt 2
Shelburne, NH 03581
603-466-2022

Coleman State Park
Diamond Pond Rd.
Stewartstown, NH 03576
603-237-4520

Twin Oaks Campground
80 Pinewood Rd.
Suncook, NH 03275
603-485-2700

Foothills Campground
506 Maple Rd
Tamworth, NH 03886
603-323-8322

Tamworth Camping Area
P.O. Box 99
Tamworth, NH 03866
603-323-8031

Ammonoosuc Campground
P.O. Box 178N
Twin Mountain, NH 03595
603-846-5527

**Beech Hill Campground &
Cabin**
P.O. Box 129
Twin Mountain, NH 03595
603-846-5521

**Dry River Campground
Crawford**
Box 177
Twin Mountain, NH 03595
603-374-2272

**Tarry-Ho Campground &
Cottage**
P.O. Box 369
Twin Mountain, NH 03595
603-846-5577

Twin Mountain KOA
Box 148
Twin Mountain, NH 03595
800-562-9117

**Twin Mountain KOA
Campground**
P.O. Box 148
Twin Mountain, NH 03595
603-846-5559

**Moose Hillcock
Campground**
RFD 1, Box 96N, Route 1
Warren, NH 03279
603-764-5294

Scenic View Campground
193AA S. Main St.
Warren, NH 03279
603-764-9380

Pillsbury STate Park
P.O. Box 1008
Washington, NH 03244
603-863-2860

**Recreational Camping at
Highland Park**
928 Valley Rd.
Washington, NH 03280
603-495-0150

Cold Springs Campground
22 Wildlife Dr.
Weare, NH 03281
603-529-2528

Cold Brook Campground
513 Battle St.
Webster, NH 03303
603-746-3390

**Pine Hollow Camping
World**
Route 3, P.O. Box 5024
Weirs Beach, NH 03247
603-366-2222

**Weirs Beach Tent &
Trailor Park**
198 Endicott St.
Weirs Beach, NH 03246
603-366-4747

Pine Haven Campground
P.O. Box 43N
Wentworth, NH 03282
603-786-9942

Swain Brook Campground
P.O. Box 157, Beech Hil
Wentworth, NH 03282
603-764-5537

**Bearcamp River
Campground**
P.O. Box 104
West Ossipee, NH 03890
603-539-3898

Chocoru Camping Village
Box 118N
West Ossipee, NH 03890
603-323-8536

U.S. Campgrounds > NEW JERSEY

**Gitchee Gumee
Campground**
Newman Drew Rd., PO
Box146
West Ossipee, NH 03890
603-539-6060

**Westward Shores
Campground**
P.O. Box 308
West Ossipee, NH 03890
603-539-6445

**Swanzey Lake Camping
Area**
P.O. Box 115
West Sawnzey, NH 03469
603-352-9880

Burns Lake Campground
R-2, Box 620A
Whitefield, NH 03598
603-837-9037

**Forest Lake Campground,
Inc.**
331 Keene Rd., Route 10
Winchester, NH 03470
603-239-4267

Robie's RV Park
139 Governor Wentworth
Wolfeboro, NH 03894
603-569-4354

Willey Brook Campground
883 Center St.
Wolfeboro, NH 03894
603-569-9493

Wolfeboro Campground
61 Haines Hill Rd.
Wolfeboro, NH 03894
603-569-9881

**Broken Branch KOA
Campground**
Box 6
Woodstock, NH 03293
603-745-8008

Woodstock KOA
Box 6, 1002 Eastside Rd.
Woodstock, NH 03293
800-562-9736

NEW JERSEY

Shady Pines Campground
443 S. 6th Ave., Dept
Absecon High, NJ 08201
609-652-1516

**Columbia Valley
Campground**
3 Ghost Pony Rd.
Andover, NJ 07821
973-691-0596

**Panther Lake Camping
Resort**
6 Panther Lake Rd.
Andover, NJ 07821
973-347-4440

**Jugtown Mountain
Campsites**
1074 State Route 173
Asbury, NJ 08802
908-735-5995

Brookville Campground
Box 169, 244 Jones Rd.
Barnegat, NJ 08005
609-698-3134

Cedar Creek Campground
1052 Route 9
Bayville, NJ 08721
732-269-1413

**Harmony Ridge Farm and
Campground**
23 Risdon Dr.
Branchville, NJ 07826
973-948-4941

Kymers' Camping Resort
69 Kymer Rd.
Branchville, NJ 07826
973-875-3167

Buena Vista Camping Park
Route 40, Box 144
Buena, NJ 08310
609-697-2004

**Beachcomber Camping
Resort**
462-G Seashore Rd
Cape May, NJ 08204
800-233-0150

Cape Island Campground
709 Route 9
Cape May, NJ 08204
609-884-5777

**Holly Shores Holiday
Trav-L-Park**
491 Route 9
Cape May, NJ 08204
609-886-1234

Lake Laurie Campground
669 Route 9
Cape May, NJ 08204
609-884-3567

Seashore Campsites
720 Seashore Rd., Dept.
Cape May, NJ 08204
609-884-4010

**Big Timber Lake Camping
Resort**
P.O. Box 366
Cape May, NJ 08210
800-542-CAMP

**Hidden Acres
Campground**
1142 Route 83, Box 354-
Cape May Court House, NJ
08210
609-624-9015

**King Nummy Trail
Campground**
205 Route 47 S., Dep
Cape May Court House, NJ
08210
609-465-4242

**North Wildwood Camping
Resort**
240 W. Shellbay Ave.
Cape May Court House, NJ
08210
609-465-4440

Ponderosa Campground
18 W. Beaver Dam Rd.
Cape May Court House, NJ
08210
609-465-7794

U.S. Campgrounds > NEW JERSEY

Shellbay Family Camping Resort
Shellbay Ave.
Cape May Court House, NJ 08210
609-465-4770

Wading Pines Campground
85 Godfrey Bridge Rd.
Chatsworth, NJ 08019
609-726-1313

Timberlane Campground
117 Timber Ln.
Clarksboro, NJ 08020
609-423-6677

Avalon Campground
1917 Route 9 N.
Clemont, NJ 08210
800-814-2267

Driftwood Camping Resort
1955 Route 9
Clemont, NJ 08210
609-624-1899

Camp Taylor Campground
85 Mt. Pleasant Rd.
Columbia, NJ 07832
908-496-4333

Delaware River Family Campground
142 Route 46
Delaware, NJ 07833
908-475-4517

Holly Lake Condo Camping Resort
P.O. Box 324
Dennisville, NJ 08214
609-861-7144

Country Mouse Campground
13 S. Jersey Ave.
Dorothy, NJ 08317
609-476-2143

Colonial Meadows Campground
1410 Somers Point Rd.
Egg Harbor, NJ 08234
609-653-8449

Union Hill Campground
163 Leektown Rd.
Egg Harbor, NJ 08215
609-296-8599

Holly Acres Best Holiday Park
218 S. Frankfurt Ave.
Egg Harbor City, NJ 08215
609-965-2287

Egg Harbor River Resort
135 Thompson Ln.
Egg Harbor Township, NJ 08234
609-927-6841

Sleepy Hollow Family Campground
132 Bevis Mill Rd.
Egg Harbor Township, NJ 08234
609-927-1969

Yogi Bear's Jellystone Park
49 Beal Rd.
Elmer, NJ 08318
609-451-7479

Pleasant Valley Family Campground
Box 73
Estell Manor, NJ 08319
609-625-1238

Fla-Net Park
Flanders-Netcong Rd.
Flanders, NJ 07836
973-347-4467

Camp Carr Campground
144 W. Woodschurch Rd.
Flemington, NJ 08822
908-782-1030

Pine Cone Campground
P.O. Box 7074, Dept. N
Freehold, NJ 07728
732-462-2230

Green Holly Campground
P.O. Box 193
Goshen, NJ 08218
609-465-9602

Acorn Campground
P.O. Box 151, Dept. N
Green Creek, NJ 08219
609-886-7119

Belhaven Lake Resort Campground
1213 Route 542
Greenbank, NJ 08215
609-965-2827

Indian Branch Park Campground
2021 Skip Morgan Dr.,
Hammonton, NJ 08037
609-561-4719

Paradise Lake Campground
500 Paradise Dr.
Hammonton, NJ 08037
609-561-7095

Butterfly Camping Resort
360 Butterfly Rd.
Jackson, NJ 08527
732-928-2107

Maple Leaf Campground
P.O. Box 1209
Jackson, NJ 08527
732-367-0177

Tip Tam Camping Resort
301 Brewers Bridge Rd.
Jackson, NJ 08527
732-363-4036

Toby's Hide-Away Campground
380 Clearstream Rd.
Jackson, NJ 08527
732-363-3662

Yogi Bear's Jellystone Park
P.O. Box 48, Reed Rd.
Jackson, NJ 08527
609-758-2235

Liberty Harbor RV Park
11 Marin Blvd.
Jersey City, NJ 07302
201-451-1000

U.S. Campgrounds > NEW JERSEY

Mountain View Campground
Box 130
Little York, NJ 08834
908-996-2953

**Bayberry Cove
Condominium Campground**
435 S. Route 9
Marmora, NJ 08233
609-390-3535

**Oak Ridge Condo
Campground**
516 S. Shore Rd., P.
Marmora, NJ 08233
609-390-0916

Whipporwill Campground
810 S. Shore Rd.
Marmora, NJ 08223
609-390-3458

River Beach Camp II
4678 Mays Landing-Somer
Mays Landing, NJ 08330
609-625-8611

Winding River Campground
6752 Weymouth Rd.
Mays Landing, NJ 08330
609-625-3191

Yogi Bear's Jellystone Park
1079 12th Ave.
Mays Landing, NJ 08330
609-476-2811

Old Cedar Campground
274 Richwood Rd.
Monroeville, NJ 08343
609-358-4881

**Oldman's Creek
Campground**
174 Laux Rd.
Monroeville, NJ 08343
609-478-4502

**Cedar Ridge Family
Campground**
205 River Rd.
Montague, NJ 07827
973-293-3512

**Shippekonk Family
Campground**
59 River Rd.
Montague, NJ 07827
973-293-3383

**Chips Folly Family
Campground**
P.O Box 56
New Gretna, NJ 08224
609-296-4434

Pilgrim Lake Campground
P.O. Box 17A
New Gretna, NJ 08224
609-296-4725

**Timberline Lake
Camping Resort**
P.O. Box 278A
New Gretna, NJ 08224
609-296-7900

Turtle Run Campground
Box 129
New Gretna, NJ 08224
609-965-5343

**Green Valley Beach
Campground**
68 Phillips Rd.
Newton, NJ 07860
973-383-4026

Rabbit Patch Campground
974 Route 619
Newton, NJ 07860
973-383-7661

**New Yorker RV Park and
Campground**
4901 Tonnelle Ave.
North Bergen, NJ 07047
800-688-5080

Echo Farm Campground
P.O. Box 610
Ocean View, NJ 08230
609-624-3589

Ocean View Campground
P.O. Box 607, Dept. S.
Ocean View, NJ 08230
609-624-1675

**Outdoor World Lake &
Shore Resort**
Corson Tavern Rd.
Ocean View, NJ 08230
609-624-1494

Pine Haven Campground
P.O. Box 606
Ocean View, NJ 08230
609-624-3437

Plantation Campground
3065 Shore Rd.
Ocean View, NJ 08230
609-624-3528

**Resort Campground
Country Club**
Box 602
Ocean View, NJ 08230
609-624-3666

Sea Grove Camping Resort
2665 Route 9, Box 603
Ocean View, NJ 08230
609-624-3529

Shady Oaks Campground
64 Route 50
Ocean View, NJ 08230
609-390-0431

Tamerlane Campground
2241 Route 9
Ocean View, NJ 08230
609-624-0767

**Baker's Acres Campground,
Inc.**
230 Willets Ave.
Parkertown, NJ 08087
609-296-2664

Four Seasons Campground
158 Woodstown-Daretown
Pilesgrove, NJ 08098
609-769-3635

Pleasantville Campgrounds
408 N. Mill Rd.
Pleasantville, NJ 08232
609-641-3176

**Evergreen Woods
Lakefront Resort**
Box 197
Pomona, NJ 08240
609-652-1577

Pomona Campground
Oak Dr., P.O. Box 675
Pomona, NJ 08240
609-965-2123

Atlantic City Blueberry Hill
Route 624, Dept., SB98,
Port Republic, NJ 08241
609-652-1644

U.S. Campgrounds > NEW JERSEY

Chestnut Lake Resort
631 Old New York Rd.
Port Republic, NJ 08241
609-652-1005

Jersey Shore Haven
728 Dennisville Rd., P.
South Seaville, NJ 08246
609-861-2293

**Pleasant Acres Farm
Campground**
61 DeWitt Rd.
Sussex, NJ 07461
973-875-4166

Beaver Hill Campground
P.O. Box 353
Sussex, NJ 07461
973-827-0670

Tall Timbers Campground
100 Tall Timbers Rd.
Sussex, NJ 07461
973-875-1991

**Outdoor World Sea Pines
Resort**
1535 US Hwy. 9
Swainton, NJ 08210
609-465-4518

Albocondo Campground
1480 Whitesville Rd.
Toms River, NJ 08755
732-349-4079

**Surf and Stream
Campground**
1801 Ridgeway Rd.
Toms River, NJ 08757
732-349-8919

**Scenic Riverview
Campground**
465 Route 49, Box 184
Tuckahoe, NJ 08250
609-628-4566

**Atlantic City North
Campground**
Stage Rd.
Tuckerton, NJ 08087
609-296-9163

Depot Travel Park
800 Broadway
West Cape May, NJ 08204
609-884-2533

Sea Pirate Campground
P.O. Box 271
West Creek, NJ 08092
609-296-7400

**Hospitality Creek
Campground**
117 Coles Mill Rd.
Williamstown, NJ 08094
609-629-5140

**Holiday Haven Family
Campground**
230 Route 50
Woodbine, NJ 08270
609-476-2963

NEW MEXICO

Albuquerque Central KOA
12400 Skyline Rd.
Albuquerque, NM 87123
505-296-2729

**Alamogordo/
White Sands KOA**
412 24th St.
Almogordo, NM 88310
800-562-3992

Great Basin National Park
State Rt. 488
Baker, NM 89311
702-234-7331

**Albuquerque N./
Bernalillo KOA**
P.O. Box 758
Bernalillo, NM 87004
800-562-3616

Bloomfield KOA
1900 E. Blanco Blvd.
Bloomfield, NM 87413
800-562-8513

**Truth or Consequences
KOA**
HC 31, Box 105
Caballo, NM 87931
800-562-2813

Clayton KOA
Box 366
Clayton, NM 88415
800-562-9507

Gallup KOA
2925 W. Hwy. 66
Gallup, NM 87301
800-562-3915

Las Vegas KOA
HCR 31, Box 16
Las Vegas, NM 87701
800-562-3423

Lordsburg KOA
1501 Lead St.
Lordsburg, NM 88045
800-562-5772

Raton KOA
1330 S. 2nd St.
Raton, NM 87740
800-562-9033

Santa Fe KOA
934 Old Las Vegas Hwy.
Santa Fe, NM 87505
800-562-1514

Santa Rosa KOA
Box 423
Santa Rosa, NM 88435
800-562-0836

Silver City KOA
11824 Hwy. 180 E.
Silver City, NM 88061
800-562-7623

Tucumcari KOA
6299 Quay Rd. AL
Tucumcari, NM 88401
800-562-1871

NEW YORK

Ausable Chasm KOA
P.O. Box 390
Ausable Chasm, NY 12911
800-562-9105

**Cooperstown Famous
Family Campground**
230 Petkewec Rd.
Cooperstown, NY 13326
607-293-7766

U.S. Campgrounds > NORTH CAROLINA

Cooperstown KOA
P.O. Box 786
Cooperstown, NY 13326
800-562-3402

Canandaigua/Rochester KOA
5374 Farmington Townline Rd.
Farmington, NY 14425
800-562-0533

**Unadilla/I-88/
Oneonta KOA**
Rd. 1, Box 186
Franklin, NY 13775
800-562-9032

Niagara Falls KOA
2570 Grand Island Blvd.
Grand Island, NY 14072
800-562-0787

Herkimer KOA
Route 28
Herkimer, NY 13350
800-562-0897

**Lake George/
Saratoga KOA**
P.O. Box 533
Lake George, NY 12845
800-562-0368

**Niagara Falls
North/Lewiston KOA**
1250 Pletcher Rd., Box 71
Lewiston, NY 14092
800-562-8715

Deer River Campsite
HCR-01, Box 101A
Malone, NY 12953
518-483-0060

Mexico KOA
291 Tubbs Rd.
Mexico, NY 13114
800-562-3967

**Natural Bridge/Watertown
KOA**
Box 71 A, Route 3
Natural Bridge, NY 13665
800-562-4780

Old Forge KOA
Box 51
Old Forge, NY 13420
800-562-3251

**Aqua Vista Valley
Campground**
82 Aemsby Rd.
Petersburg, NY 12138
518-658-3659

Syracuse KOA
7620 Plainville Rd.
Plainville, NY 13137
800-562-9107

**Newburgh/
New York City KOA**
Box 134 D
Plattekill, NY 12568
800-562-7220

**Interlake Farm
Campground**
45 Lake Dr.
Rhinebeck, NY 12572
914-266-5387

Roscoe Campsites
Roscoe, NY 12776
607-498-5264

Twin Islands Campsite
Roscoe, NY 12776
607-498-5326

Saugerties/Woodstock KOA
882 Route 212
Saugerties, NY 12477
800-562-4081

Swan Lake Camplands
Box 336, Fulton Rd.
Swan Lake, NY 12783
914-292-4781

Rome/Verona KOA
6591 Blackmans Cor Rd.
Verona, NY 13478
800-562-7218

Daggett Lake Campsites
660 Glen Athol Rd.
Warrensburg, NY 12885
518-623-2198

**Watkins Glen/Corning
KOA**
Box 228
Watkins Glen, NY 14891
800-562-7430

Westfield/Lake Erie KOA
8001 Route 5
Westfield, NY 14787
800-562-3973

NORTH CAROLINA

**Tumbling Waters
Campground & Trout
Farm**
52 Panther Creek Rd.
Almond, NC 28702
828-479-3814

**Turkey Creek
Campground**
135 Turkey Creek Rd.
Almond, NC 28702
828-488-8966

Asheville Taps RV Park
1327 Tunnel Rd.
Asheville, NC 28815
704-299-8277

**Bear Creek RV Park &
Campground**
81 S. Bear Creek Rd.
Asheville, NC 28806
704-253-0798

**French Broad River
Campground**
1030 Old Marshall Hwy.
Asheville, NC 288004
704-658-0772

**Moonshine Creek
Campground**
Dark Ridge Rd.
Balsam, NC 28707
704-586-6666

**Grandfather Mountain
Club**
Hw. 105, S. Park Rd.
Banner Elk, NC 28607
704-963-7275

Boon KOA Kampground
123 Harmony Mtn. Ln.
Boone, NC 28607
828-264-7250

U.S. Campgrounds > NORTH CAROLINA

Flintlock Campground
171 Flintlock Campground Dr.
Boone, NC 28607
704-963-5325

**Black Forest Family
Camping Resort**
Summer Rd., Cedar Mtn.
Brevard, NC 28718
704-884-2267

**Cooper Creek
Campground**
122 Cooper Creed Rd.
Bryson City, NC 28713
704-488-3922

**Deep Creek Tube Center &
Campground**
1090 W. Deep Creek Rd.
Bryson City, NC 28713
704-488-6055

Lost Mine Campground
1000 Silvermine Rd.
Bryson City, NC 28713
704-488-6445

Asheville West KOA
309 Wiggins Rd.
Candler, NC 28715
800-562-9015

**Asheville West KOA
Campground**
309 Wiggins Rd.
Candler, NC 28715
704-665-7015

Laurel Bank
350 Campers Ln..
Canton, NC 28716
704-235-8940

**Mountain Shadows
Campground**
3748 Lake Logan Rd.
Canton, NC 28716
704-648-0132

Riverhouse Acres
4744 Pisgah Dr.
Canton, NC 28716
704-646-0303

**Singing Waters Camping
Resort**
1006 Trout Creek Rd.
Cashiers, NC 28783
704-293-5872

Adventure Trail
Camp Creek Rd.
Cherokee, NC 28719
704-497-3651

**Cherokee Campground &
Cabins**
US 19 N & US 441
Cherokee, NC 28719
704-497-9838

**Cherokee/Great Smokies
KOA**
Big Cove Rd.
Cherokee, NC 28719
704-497-9711

Eljawa Campground
Old No. 4 Rd
Cherokee, NC 28719
704-497-7204

**Happy Holiday RV Park &
Campground**
Rt. 1, Box 132E, Hwy. 19F
Cherokee, NC 28719
704-497-7250

**Indian Creek Campground/
Indian Hills Cabins**
Bunches Creek Rd.
Cherokee, NC 28719
704-497-4361

Lost Cove Campground
1591 Hwy. 19
Cherokee, NC 28719
704-497-6168

Mile High Campground
Box 30, Bradley Loop Rd.
Cherokee, NC 28719
704-497-2230

River Valley Resort
Big Cove Rd.
Cherokee, NC 28719
704-497-3540

Riverside Campground
Hwy. 441 S. Bypass
Cherokee, NC 28719
701-497-9311

Twin Forks
Big Cove Rd.
Cherokee, NC 28719
704-497-4330

Wagon Train Campgrounds
US 19, Soco Rd.
Cherokee, NC 28719
704-497-9502

Welch Campground
P.O. Box 747
Cherokee, NC 28719
704-497-4716

Wolf Campground
102 Adam's Creek
Cherokee, NC 28719
704-497-9868

**Hickory Nut Falls Family
Campground**
P.O. Box 97
Chimney Rock, NC 28720
704-625-4014

**Lake Lure RV Park &
Campground**
176 Boys Camp Rd
Chimney Rock, NC 28746
704-625-9160

**Twin Lakes Camping
Resort & Yacht Basin**
1618 Memory Ln.
Chocowinity, NC 27817
252-946-5700

Riverside Campground
6 Happy Camper Dr.
Cruso, NC 28716
704-235-9128

Laurel Bush Campground
113 Fugitive Run
Dillsboro, NC 28779
704-586-8346

Enfield/Rocky Mount KOA
101 Bell Acres
Enfield, NC 27823
800-562-5894

**Smithfield Best Holiday
Trav-L-Park**
497 Hwy. 701 S.
Four Oaks, NC 27524
919-934-3181

U.S. Campgrounds > NORTH CAROLINA

Cartoogechay Creek Campground
91 No Name Rd.
Franklin, NC 28734
704-524-8553

Country Woods RV Park
2887 Georgia Rd.
Franklin, NC 28734
704-524-4339

Cullasaja River Campground
6269 Highlands Rd.
Franklin, NC 28734
704-524-2559

Downtown RV Park
160 Heritage Hollow Dr.
Franklin, NC 28734
704-369-2125

Great Smokey Mountain Fish Camp & Safaris
Hwy. 28N at The Little Tennessee River
Franklin, NC 28734
704-369-5295

Morrison Campground & Rental
29 Bates Branch Rd.
Franklin, NC 28734
704-524-4783

Mountain Springs Campground
189 Lake Ledford Rd.
Franklin, NC 28734
704-524-0469

Mt. Mountain Campground
151 Mt. Mtn. Rd.
Franklin, NC 28734
704-524-6155

Rainbow Springs Campground
7984 W. Old Murphy Rd.
Franklin, NC 28734
704-524-6376

Rose Creek Mine & Campground
115 Terrace Ridge Dr.
Franklin, NC 28734
704-524-3225

Ralph J. Andrews Park
Rt. 66, Box 132E Cullowhee
Glenville, NC 28723
704-743-3923

Hatteras Sands Camping Resort
Box 295
Hatteras, NC 27943
919-986-2422

Rivers Edge RV Park, Inc.
Hwy. 64E
Hayesville, NC 28904
704-389-6781

Sundowner RV Resort
42 Sundowner Cir.
Hayesville, NC 28904
704-389-3241

Tusquittee Campground & Cabins
9594 Tusquittee Rd.
Hayesville, NC 28904
704-389-8520

Big Willow Mountain Resort, Inc.
Rt. 13, Box 296, Willow Mt. Rd.
Hendersonville, NC 28739
704-693-0187

Blue Ridge Travel Trailer Park
3576 Chimney Rock Rd.
Hendersonville, NC 28792
704-685-9207

Lazy Boy Travel Park
110 Old Sunset Hill Rd.
Hendersonville, NC 28792
704-697-7165

Red Gates RV Park
Sugarloaf Rd.
Hendersonville, NC 28792
704-685-8787

Sassafras Gap Campground
5920 Walhalla Rd.
Highlands, NC 28741
704-526-9909

Skyline Lodge & Restaurant
Flat Mtn. Rd.
Highlands, NC 28741
704-526-2121

Hot Springs Campground & Spa
300 Bridge St.
Hot Springs, NC 28743
704-622-7676

Meadow Fork Campground
5995 Meadow Fork Rd.
Hot Springs, NC 28743
704-622-9505

Greenfield
Mt. Jefferson Rd.
Jefferson, NC 28640
704-336-9106

Pounding Branch Campground
Slick Fisher Rd.
Lake Toxaway, NC 28747
704-966-4359

Riverbend RV Park
Hwy. 281 N.
Lake Toxaway, NC 28747
704-966-4214

Miller's Camping
973 Miller Rd.. Blue Ridge Pkwy.
Laurel Springs, NC 28644
704-336-8156

Linville Falls Trailer Lodge & Camp
Gurney Franklin Rd.
Linville Falls, NC 28647
704-765-2681

Connie's Campground
68 Leisure Ln.
Maggie Valley, NC 28751
704-926-3619

Creekwood Farm RV Park
4096 Jonathan Creek Rd.
Maggie Valley, NC 28786
704-926-7977

Happy Valley RV Park
40 Happy Valley Cir.
Maggie Valley, NC 28751
704-926-0327

Hillbilly Campground & RV Park
4115 Soco Rd.
Maggie Valley, NC 28751
704-926-3353

U.S. Campgrounds > NORTH CAROLINA

Lonesome Pine Campground
887 Jonathan
Maggie Valley, NC 28786
704-926-0519

Presley Campground & RV Park
1786 Soco Rd.
Maggie Valley, NC 28751
704-926-1904

Rippling Waters Creekside RV Park
3962 Soco Rd
Maggie Valley, NC 28751
704-926-7787

Hidden Valley Campground
Rt. 1, Box 377, Deacon Dr.
Marion, NC 28752
704-652-7208

Lake James Landing
Rt. 6, Box 862
Marion, NC 28752
704-652-2907

Mountain Laurel Resort
Rt. 3, Poncheon Fork Rd.
Marion, NC 28754
704-689-5058

Mountain Paradise Campground
Rt. 3, Box 316
Marion, NC 28752
704-756-4085

Mountain Stream RV Park
1820 Buck Creek Rd.
Marion, NC 28752
704-724-9013

Daniel Boon Campground
Hwy. 181
Morgantown, NC 28638
704-396-5124

Lake James Family Campground
5786 Benefied Landing Rd.,
Morgantown, NC 28761
704-584-0190

Rose Creek Campground
3471 Rose Creed Rd.
Morgantown, NC 28655
704-438-4338

Circle "J" Family Campground
Rt. 6, Box 289
Murphy, NC 28906
704-494-7042

Mr. Piper's Campground
Rt. 6, Box 101B
Murphy, NC 28906
704-644-9130

Riverbend Campground
Hwy. 74, 19-129 N. Bypass
Murphy, NC 28906
704-837-6223

Stateline Village RV Park
Hwy. 64 W. Ducktown
Murphy, NC 28906
704-423-5006

Cape Hatteras KOA
Box 100
Nags Head, NC 27968
252-987-2307

Paddy Creek Campground
1465 Old NC 105
Nebo, NC 28761
704-584-1346

Catawba Falls Family Campground
Rt 3, Box 230
Old Fort, NC 28762
704-668-4831

Down by the River Campground
P.O. Box 428
Pineola, NC 28662
704-733-5057

RiverCamp USA, Inc.
2221 Kings Creek Rd.
Piney Creek, NC 28663
704-359-2267

Hidden Waters RV Park & Campground
Rt 3, Box 81, Tullulah Hwy.
129 S
Robbinsville, NC 28771
704-479-3509

Shook's RV Park & Trout Ponds
Rt 3., Box 120
Robbinsville, NC 28771
704-479-6930

River Creek Campground
217 River Creek Dr.
Rutherfordton, NC 28139
704-287-3915

Orchard Lake Campground
231 Orchard Lake Rd.
Saluda, NC 28773
704-749-3901

Selma/Smithfield KOA
428 Campground Rd.
Selma, NC 27576
800-562-5897

Hidden Valley Campground
Hidden Valley Rd.
Sparta, NC 28675
704-336-8911

Bear Den Family Campground
Rt.3, Box 284
Spruce Pine, NC 28777
704-765-2888

Buck Hill Campground
6401 US 19E Newland
Spruce Pine, NC 28657
704-765-7387

Midway Campground & RV Resort
114 Midway Dr.
Statesville, NC 28625
704-546-7615

Statesville KOA
162 KOA Ln.
Statesville, NC 28677
800-562-5705

Asheville East KOA
102 Hwy. 70E
Swannanoa, NC 28778
704-686-3121

U.S. Campgrounds > OHIO

Fort Tatham
175 Tatham Creek Rd.
Sylva, NC 28779
704-586-6662

**Nelson's Nantahala
Hideaway**
Hwy. 19/74
Topton, NC 28781
704-321-4407

Fayetteville/Wade KOA
P.O. Box 67
Wade, NC 28395
800-562-5350

**Winngray Family
Campground**
26 Winngray Ln.
Waynesville, NC 28786
704-926-3170

**Smokey Trails
Campground**
1385 Shoal Creek Rd.
Whittier, NC 28789
704-497-6693

Timberlake
3270 Conleys Creed Rd.
Whittier, NC 28789
704-497-7320

**Great Smokey Mountain
RV Camping Resort**
Hwy. 441
Whttier, NC 28789
704-497-2470

NORTH DAKOTA

Bismarck KOA
3720 Centennial Rd.
Bismarck, ND 58501
800-562-2636

Camp on the Heart
387 S. State Ave.
Dickinson, ND 58602
701-225-9600

Jamestown KOA
3605 80th Ave., SE
Jamestown, ND 58401
800-562-6350

Minot KOA
5261 Hwy. 52 S
Minot, ND 58701
800-562-7421

OHIO

**Bay Shore Family
Camping**
7124 Pymatuning Lake Rd.
Andover, OH 44003
440-293-7202

**Hide-A-Way Lakes
Campground**
2034 S. Ridge W., Rt. 84
Ashtabula, OH 44004
440-992-4431

**Rippling Stream
Campground**
3640 Reynoldsburg-Baltimore
Rd.
Baltimore, OH 43105
740-862-6065

**Yogi Bear's Jellystone Park
Camp Resort**
6500 Black Rd.
Bellville, OH 44813
419-886-CAMP

Twin Lakes Park
3506 TR 34
Bluffton, OH 45817
419-477-5255

Fire Lake Camper Park
13630 W. Kramer Rd.
Bowling Green, OH 43402
888-879-2267

Dayton Tall Timbers KOA
7796 Welbaum Rd.
Brookville, OH 45309
937-833-3888

Willow Lake Park
PO Box 102
Brunswick, OH 44212
330-225-6580

**Buckeye Lake/Columbus
East KOA**
4460 Walnut Rd
Buckeye Lake, OH 43008
800-562-0792

Butler/Mohican KOA
6918 Bunker Hill Rd. S.
Butler, OH 44822
800-562-8719

**Hillview Acres
Campground**
66271 Wolf's Den Rd.
Cambridge, OH 43725
740-439-3348

Camp Coonpath
4625 Coonpath Rd., NW
Carroll, OH 43112
740-756-9218

Seneca Campground
6955 S. S.R. 101
Clyde, OH 43410
419-639-2887

Evergreen Lake Park
703 Center Rd.
Conneaut, OH 44030
440-599-8802

**Windy Hill Golf and
Campground**
6231 Weaver Rd.
Conneaut, OH 44030
440-594-5251

Bob Boord Park
25067 Buffalo Rd.
E. Rochester, OH 44625
330-894-2360

**Bear Creek Resort Ranch
KOA**
3232 Downing St., S.W.
East Sparta, OH 44626
330-484-3901

Hickory Hill Lakes
7103 Rt. 66
Ft. Loramie, OH 45845
937-295-3820

U.S. Campgrounds > OHIO

Berkshire Campgrounds
1848 Alexander Rd.
Galena, OH 43021
740-965-2321

Audobon Lakes Campground
3935 N. Broadway
Geneva, OH 44041
440-466-1293

Mohican Wilderness
22462 Wally Rd.
Glenmont, OH 44628
614-599-6741

Wild Wood Lakes Campground
PO Box 26
Homerville, OH 44235
330-625-2817

Buccaneer Campsites
PO Box 352
Jefferson, OH 44047
440-576-2881

Jellystone Park at Paramount's Kings Island
Yogi Bear's Campground
Kings Island, OH 45034
513-398-2901

Long Lake Park
Rt. 3, 8974 Long Lake Dr.
Lakeville, OH 44638
419-827-2278

Logan/Hocking Hills KOA
29150 Pattor Rd.
Logan, OH 43138
800-562-4208

Campbell Cove Camping
30775 Wintergreen Rd.
Lore City, OH 43755
740-489-5837

Camp Toodik Family Campground
7700 TR 462
Loudonville, OH 44842
800-322-2663

Mohican Reservation Campgrounds
23270 Wally Rd. S.
Loudonville, OH 44842
800-766-CAMP

River Run Family Campground
3175 Wally Rd.
Loudonville, OH 44842
419-994-5257

Smith's Pleasant Valley Family Campground
Box 356
Loudonville, OH 44842
419-994-4024

Yogi Bear's Jellystone Park Camp Resort
3392 S.R. 82
Mantua, OH 44255
330-562-9100

Hickory Grove Lake Campground
805 Hoch Rd.
Marion, OH 43302
740-382-8584

Pier-Lon Park
5960 Vandemark Rd.
Medina, OH 44256
330-667-2311

Milan Travel Park Best Holiday
11404 Hwy. 250 N.
Milan, OH 44846
419-433-4277

Tri-Country Kamp Inn
17147 Gar. Hwy.
Montville, OH 44064
440-968-3400

Dogwood Valley Camp
4185 T.R. 99
Mt. Gilead, OH 43338
419-946-5230

Mt. Gilead/Columbus North KOA
5961 State Route 95
Mt. Gilead, OH 43338
800-562-3428

Rustic Knolls Campsites
8664 Keys Rd.
Mt. Vernon, OH 43050
740-397-9318

Crystal Springs
31478 Bagley Rd.
N. Ridgeville, OH 44039
440-748-3200

Happy Hills Family Campground
22245 S.R. 278
Nelsonville, OH 45764
740-385-6720

Indian Trail Campground
1400 S.R. 250
New London, OH 44851
419-929-1135

Terrace Lakes Camping
6157 St. Rt. 7
New Waterford, OH 44445
330-227-9606

Ridge Ranch Campground
5219 SR 303 N.W.
Newton Falls, OH 44444
330-898-8080

Country Stage Campground
40-C Twp. Rd. 1031
Nova, OH 44859
419-652-2267

Olive Branch Campground
6985 Wilmington Rd.
Oregonia, OH 45054
513-932-CAMP

Pines Lakes Campground
3001 Hague Rd.
Orwell, OH 44076
440-437-6218

Kool Lakes Family Camping
12990 S.R. 282, Box 673
Parkman, OH 44080
440-548-8436

Paradise Valley Campground
6690 Lawnwood Ave.
Parma Heights, OH 44130
440-888-1260

Tamsin Park Camping Resort
5000 Akron Cleveland Rd.
Peninsula, OH 44264
330-656-2859

Toledo East/Stony Ridge KOA
24787 Luckey Rd.
Perrysburgh, OH 43551
800-562-6831

U.S. Campgrounds > OKLAHOMA

Fox's Den Campground
PO Box 345
Put-in-Bay, OH 43456
419-285-5001

Top O' The Caves
26780 Chapel Ridge Rd.
S. Bloomingville, OH 43152
800-967-2434

Chaparral Family Campground
10136 Middletown Rd.
Salem, OH 44460
330-337-9381

Chippewa Valley Campground
8809 Lake Rd.
Seveille, OH 44273
330-769-2090

Wagon Wheel Campground
6787 Baker 47
Shelby, OH 44875
419-347-1392

Whispering Hill Recreation
PO Box 607
Shreve, OH 44676
330-567-2137

Sunset Lake
5566 Root Rd.
Spencer, OH 44275
330-667-2686

Enon Beach
2401 Enon Rd.
Springfield, OH 45502
937-882-6431

Rustic Lakes Campgrounds
44901 New London Eastern Rd.
Sullivan, OH 44880
440-647-3804

Toledo/Maumee KOA
4035 St. Route 295
Swanton, OH 43558
800-562-8748

Heritage Hills Campground
6445 Ledge Rd.
Thompson, OH 44086
440-298-1311

Austin Lake Park and Campground
1002 Twp Hwy. 285A
Toronto, OH 43964
740-544-LAKE

Pleasant View Recreation
Box 255
Van Buren, OH 45889
419-299-3897

Wapakoneta/Lima KOA
14719 Cemetery Rd.
Wapakoneta, OH 45895
800-562-9872

Clare-Mar Lakes Campground
PO Box 226
Wellington, OH 44090
440-647-3318

Panther Trails Campground
48081 Peck Wadsworth Rd.
Wellington, OH 44090
440-647-5453

Beck's Family Campground
8375 Friendsville Rd.
Wooster, OH 44691
330-264-9930

Meadow Lake Park
8970 Canaan Center Rd.
Wooster, OH 44691
330-435-6652

OKLAHOMA

Lake Murray Resort Park
3310 S. Lake Murray Dr. #12-A
Ardmore, OK 73401
580-223-4044

Boggy Depot State Park
PO Box 1020
Atoka, OK 74525
405-889-5625

McGee Creek State Park
HC 82, Box 572
Atoka, OK 74525
405-889-5822

Beaver State Park
PO Box 1190
Beaver, OK 73932
405-625-3373

Beavers Bend Resort Park
PO Box 10
Broken Bow, OK 74728
580-494-6300

Arrowhead State Park
HC 67, Box 57
Canadian, OK 74425
918-339-2204

Elk City/Clinton KOA
P.O. Box 137
Canute, OK 73626
800-562-4149

Tusa NE KOA
19605 E. Skelly Dr.
Catoosa, OK 74015
800-562-7657

Checotah/Henryetta KOA
HC 68, Box 750
Checotah, OK 74426
800-562-7510

Fountainhead State Park
HC 60, Box 1340
Checotah, OK 74426
918-689-5311

Oklahoma City East KOA
6200 S. Choctaw Rd.
Choctaw, OK 73020
800-562-5076

Clayton Lake State Park
Route 1, Box 33-10
Clayton, OK 74536
918-569-7981

Sherrard RV & KOA Campground
111 Sherrard Dr.
Colbert, OK 74733
800-562-2485

Wah—Sha-She
Route 1, Box 301
Copan, OK 74022
918-532-4627

Cherokee State Park
PO Box 220
Disney, OK 74340
918-435-8066

El Reno West KOA
Box 6
El Reno, OK 73036
800-562-5736

U.S. Campgrounds > OKLAHOMA

Spring River Canoe Trails
Route 1, Box 170
Fairland, OK 74343
918-540-2545

Twin Bridges State Park
14801 S. Hwy. 137
Fairland, OK 74343
918-540-2545

Fort Cobb Lake State Park
PO Box 297
Fort Cobb, OK 73038
405-643-2249

Raymond Gary State Park
HC 63, Box 1450
Fort Towson, OK 74735
405-873-2307

Foss State Park
HC 66, Box 111
Foss, OK 73647
405-592-4433

Alabaster Caverns State Park
Route 1, Box 32
Freedom, OK 73842
405-621-3381

Honey Creek State Park
Route 5, Box 209
Grove, OK 74344
918-786-9447

Red Rock Canyon State Park
PO Box 502
Hinton, OK 73047
405-542-6344

Great Salt Plains State Park
Route 1, Box 28
Jet, OK 73749
405-626-4731

Black Mesa State Park
HCR 1, Box 8
Kenton, OK 73946
405-426-2222

Lake Texoma Resort Park
Box 248
Kingston, OK 73439
405-564-2566

Quartz Mountain Resort Park
Route 1
Lone Wolf, OK 73655
405-563-2238

Lake Keystone State Park
PO Box 147
Mannford, OK 74044
918-865-4477

Ardmore/Marietta KOA
Route 1, Box 640
Marietta, OK 73448
800-562-5893

Great Plains State Park
Route 1, Box 52
Mountain Park, OK 73559
405-569-2032

Walnut Creet State Park
PO Box 26
New Prue, OK 74060
918-242-2362

Little River State Park
Route 4, Box 277
Norman, OK 73071
405-360-3572

Okmulgee-Dripping Springs State Park
210 Dripping Spring Lake Rd.
Okmulgee, OK 74447
918-756-5971

Cheokee Landing State Park
HC 73, Box 510
Park Hill, OK 74451
918-457-5716

Osage Hill State Park
HC 73, Box 84
Pawhuska, OK 74056
918-336-5635

Snowdale State Park
PO Box 6
Salina, OK 74365
918-434-2651

Sallisaw KOA
P.O. Box 88
Sallisaw, OK 74955
800-562-2797

Sallisaw State Park at Brushy Lake
PO Box 527
Sallisaw, OK 74955
918-775-6507

Adair State Park
Route 2, Box 8
Stilwell, OK 74960
918-696-6613

Talimena State Park
PO Box 318
Talihina, OK 74571
918-567-2052

Lake Tenkiller State Park
HCR 68, Box 1095
Vian, OK 74962
918-489-5643

Sequoyah Bay State Park
Route 2, Box 252
Wagoner, OK 74467
918-683-0878

Sequoyah State Park
Box 509
Wagoner, OK 74477
918-772-2046

Roman Nose Resort Park
Route 1
Watonga, OK 73772
405-623-4215

Little Sahara State Park
Route 2, Box 132
Waynoka, OK 73860
405-824-1471

Robbers Cave State Park
PO Box 9
Wilburton, OK 74578
918-465-2565

Lake Wister State Park
Route 2, Box 6B
Wister, OK 74966
918-655-7756

Boiling Springs State Park
Box 965
Woodward, OK 73802
405-256-7664

U.S. Campgrounds > PENNSYLVANIA

OREGON

Albany/Corvallis KOA
33775 Oakville Rd.
Albany, OR 97321
800-562-8526

Mountain View Holiday Trav-L-Park
2845 Hughes Ln.
Baker City, OR 97814
541-523-4824

Bend Kampground
63615 Hwy. 97 N.
Bend, OR 97701
541-382-7738

Sisters/Bend KOA
67667 Hwy. 20 W.
Bend, OR 97701
800-562-0363

Cascade Locks/Portland East KOA
841 NW Forest Ln.
Cascade, OR 97014
800-562-8698

Eugene S./Creswell KOA
298 E. Oregon Ave.,
P.O. Box 189
Creswell, OR 97426
800-562-4110

Madras/Culver KOA
2435 SW Jericho Ln.
Culver, OR 97734
800-562-1992

Sweet Home/Foster Lake KOA
6191 Hwy. 20 E.
Foster, OR 97345
800-562-0367

Medford-Gold Hill KOA
Box 320
Gold Hill, OR 97525
800-562-7608

Astoria/Seaside KOA
1100 Ridge Rd.
Hammond, OR 97121
800-562-8506

Klamath Falls KOA
3435 Shasta Way
Klamath Falls, OR 97603
800-562-9036

Bandon/Port Orford KOA
46612 Hwy. 101
Langlois, OR 97450
800-562-3298

Oregon Dunes KOA
4135 Coast Hwy.
North Bend, OR 97459
800-562-4236

Lincoln City KOA
5298 NE Park Ln.
Otis, OR 97368
800-562-2791

Salem Campground
3700 Hagers Grove Rd., S.E.
Salem, OR 97301
800-826-9605

Grants Pass/Sunny Valley KOA
140 Old Stage Rd.
Sunny Valley, OR 97497
800-562-7557

Waldport/Newport KOA
P.O. Box 397
Waldport, OR 97394
800-562-3443

Grants Pass/Redwood Hwy. KOA
13370 Redwood Hwy.
Wilderville, OR 97543
800-562-7566

PENNSYLVANIA

Bellefonte/State College KOA
2481 Jacksonville Rd.
Bellefonte, PA 16823
800-562-8127

Kinzua East KOA
Kinzua Heights
Bradford, PA 16701
800-562-3682

Carlisle Campground
1075 Harrisburg Pike
Carlisle, PA 17013
717-249-4563

Lancaster/Reading KOA
3 Denber Rd.
Denver, PA 17517
800-562-1621

Hazleton/Wilkes Barre KOA
RR 1, Box 1405
Drums, PA 18222
800-562-9751

Delaware Water Gap KOA
KOA RD 6, Box 6196
E. Stroudsburg, PA 18301
800-562-0375

Drummer Boy Camping Resort
1300 Hanover Rd.
Gettysburg, PA 17325
800-336-3269

Gettysburg/Battlefield KOA
20 Knox Rd.
Gettysburg, PA 17325
800-562-1869

Hershey KOA
P.O. Box 449
Hershey, PA 17033
800-562-4774

Jonestown/I-81 KOA
145 Old Route 22
Jonestown, PA 17038
800-562-1501

Erie KOA
6645 West Rd.
McKean, PA 16426
800-562-7610

Mercer/Grove City KOA
1337 Butler Pike
Mercer, PA 16137
800-562-2802

Allentown KOA
6750 KOA Dr.
New Tripoli, PA 18066
800-562-2138

Bear Run Campground
184 Badger Hill Rd.
Portersville, PA 16051
412-368-3564

Madison/Pittsburgh SE KOA
RR 2, Box 560
Ruffsdale, PA 15679
800-562-4034

U.S. Campgrounds > PENNSYLVANIA

Silver Valley Best Holiday
RR 4, Box 4214
Saylorsburg, PA 18353
717-992-4824

Appalachian Campsites
Box 27
Shartlesville, PA 19554
610-488-6319

Tunkhannock KOA
Box 768
Tunkhannock, PA 18657
800-562-5856

Philadelphia/West Chester KOA
P.O. Box 920D
Unionville, PA 19375
800-562-1726

Colonial Woods Campground
545 Lonely Cottage Dr.
Upper Black Eddy, PA 18972
610-847-5808

Washington KOA
7 KOA Rd.
Washington, PA 15301
800-562-0254

SOUTH CAROLINA

Anderson/Lake Hartwell KOA
200 Wham Rd.
Anderson, SC 29625
800-562-5804

Sadlers Creek State Park
940 Sadlers Creek Park Rd.
Anderson, SC 29626
864-226-8950

Lee State Park
Route 2, Box 1212
Bishopville, SC 29010
803-428-3833

Kings Mountain State Park
1277 Park Rd.
Blacksburg, SC 29702
803-222-3209

Barnwell State Park
223 State Park Rd.
Blackville, SC 29817
803-284-2212

Calhoun Falls State Park
46 Maintenance Shop Rd.
Calhoun Falls, SC 29628
864-447-8267

Colleton State Park
Canadys, SC 29433
803-538-8206

Cheraw State Park
100 State Park Rd.
Cheraw, SC 29520
800-868-9630

Chester State Park
759 State Park Dr.
Chester, SC 29706
803-385-2680

Caesars Head State Park
8155 Geer Hwy.
Cleveland, SC 29635
864-836-6115

Sesquicentennial State Park
9564 Two Notch Rd.
Columbia, SC 29223
803-788-2706

Little Pee Dee State Park
1298 State Park Rd.
Dillon, SC 29536
803-774-8872

Edisto Beach State Park
8377 State Cabin Rd.
Edisto Island, SC 29438
803-869-2156

Rivers Bridge State Park
Route 1
Ehrhardt, SC 29081
803-267-3675

Lake Hartwell State Park
19138-A S. Hwy. 11
Fair Play, SC 29643
864-972-3352

Florence KOA
1115 E. Campground Rd.
Florence, SC 29506
800-562-7807

Paris Mountain State Park
2401 State Park Rd.
Greenville, SC 29609
864-244-5565

Hunting Island State Park
2555 Sea Island Pkwy
Hunting Island, SC 29920
803-838-2011

Charleston KOA
9494 Hwy. 78
Ladson, SC 29456
800-562-5812

Andrew Jackson State Park
196 Andrew Jackson Park Rd.
Lancaster, SC 29720
803-285-3344

Jones Gap State Park
303 Jones Gap Rd.
Marietta, SC 29661
864-836-3647

Baker Creek State Park
Route 3, Box 50
McCormick, SC 29835
864-443-2457

Hickory Knob State Park
Route 1, Box 199-B
McCormick, SC 29835
800-491-1764

Oconee State Park
624 State Park Rd.
Mountain Rest, SC 29664
864-638-5353

Mt. Pleasant/Charleston KOA
P.O. Box 248
Mt. Pleasant, SC 29466
800-562-5796

Huntington Beach
Murrells Inlet, SC 29576
803-237-4440

Myrtle Beach State Park
4401 S. Kings Hwy.
Myrtle Beach, SC 29575
803-238-5325

Myrtle Beach KOA
5th Ave. S.
Myrtle Beach, SC 29577
800-562-7790

Lake Greenwood State Park
302 State Park Rd.
Ninety Six, SC 29666
864-543-3535

U.S. Campgrounds > TENNESSEE

Table Rock State Park
246 Table Rock State Park Rd.
Pickens, SC 29671
864-878-9813

Hamilton Branch State Park
Rout 1, Box 97
Plum Branch, SC 29845
864-333-2223

Dreher Island State Park
3677 State Park Rd.
Prosperity, SC 29127
803-364-4152

Givhans Ferry State Park
746 Givhans Ferry Rd.
Ridgeville, SC 29472
803-873-0692

Devils Fork State Park
161 Holcombe Cir.
Salem, SC 29676
864-944-2639

Croft State Park
450 Croft State Park Rd.
Spartanburg, SC 29302
864-585-1283

Keowee-Toxaway State Park
108 Residence Dr.
Sunset, SC 29685
864-868-2605

The Flowermill RV Park
23 Stallings Rd.
Taylors, SC 29687
864-877-5079

Poinsett State Park
6660 Poinsett Park Rd.
Wedgefield, SC 29168
803-827-1473

Aiken State Park
1145 State Park Rd.
Windsor, SC 29856
803-649-2857

Lake Wateree State Park
Route 4, Box 282 E-5
Winnsboro, SC 29180
803-482-6401

Point South KOA
P.O. Box 1760
Yemassee, SC 29945
800-562-2948

SOUTH DAKOTA

Custer/Crazy Horse KOA
Route 2, Box 3030
Custer, SD 57730
800-562-7658

Custer/Mt. Rushmore KOA
RR 1, Box 55 C
Custer, SD 57730
800-562-5828

Deadwood KOA
Box 451
Deadwood, SD 57732
800-562-0846

Mt. Rushmore/Hill City KOA
Box 295K
Hill City, SD 57745
800-562-8503

Hot Springs KOA
HCR 52, Box 112C
Hot Springs, SD 57747
800-562-0803

Badlands/White River KOA
HCR 54, Box 1
Interior, SD 57750
800-562-3897

Kennebec KOA
P.O. Box 248
Kennebec, SD 57544
800-562-6361

Belvidere East KOA
HCR 62, Box 108
Midland, SD 57552
800-562-2134

Mitchell KOA
41244 SD Hwy. 38
Mitchell, SD 57301
800-562-1236

Sioux City North KOA
Box 846
N. Sioux City, SD 57049
800-562-5439

Happy Holiday
8990 S. Hwy. 16
Rapid City, SD 57701
605-342-7635

Rapid City KOA
P.O. Box 2592
Rapid City, SD 57709
800-562-8504

Sioux Falls KOA
Box 963
Sioux Falls, SD 57101
800-562-9865

Spearfish KOA
Box 429
Spearfish, SD 57783
800-562-0805

Dakota Sioux Casino
Sioux Conifer Rd.
Watertown, SD 57201
605-882-2051

Lake Pelican Recreation
Hwy. 212
Watertown, SD 57201
605-882-5200

Memorial County Park
North Lake Dr. & Hwy. 139
Watertown, SD 57201
605-882-6290

Sandy Shores State Park
Hwy. 212
Watertown, SD 57201
605-882-5200

Stokes-Thomas Lake City Park
S. Lake Dr. & Hwy. 20
Watertown, SD 57201
605-882-6264

TENNESSEE

Hiwassee State Scenic River & Ocoee River Camping
Benton, TN 37303
423-338-4133

Rocky Top Best Holiday Trav-L-Park
496 Pearl Ln.
Blountville, TN 37617
423-323-2535

Paris Landing KOA
6290 E. Antioch Rd.
Buchanan, TN 38222
800-562-2815

U.S. Campgrounds > TENNESSEE

Paris Landing State Park
Hwy. 79
Buchanan, TN 38222
901-642-4311

Montgomery Bell State Park
Hwy. 70
Burns, TN 37029
615-797-9052

Nathan Bedford Forrest State
Hwy. 191
Camden, TN 38320
901-584-6356

Cove Lake State Park
Hwy. 25W
Caryville, TN 37714
423-566-9701

Henry Horton State Park
Hwy. 31A
Chapel Hill, TN 37034
931-364-2222

Harrison Bay State Park
Hwy. 58
Chattanooga, TN 37401
423-344-6214

Holiday Trav-L-Park
1709 Mack Smith Rd.
Chattanooga, TN 37412
706-891-9766

Chattanooga North/Cleveland KOA
Box 3232
Cleveland, TN 37320
800-562-9039

Bean Pot Holiday Trav-L-Park
23 Bean Pot Campground Loop
Crossville, TN 38558
931-484-7671

Crossville KOA
256 Werthwyle Dr.
Crossville, TN 38555
800-562-8153

Cumberland Mountain State Park
Hwy. 127
Crossville, TN 38555
931-484-6138

Bledsoe Creek State Park
Hwy. 25
Gallatin, TN 37066
615-452-3706

Crazy Horse Campground & RV Resort
4609 East Pkwy.
Gatlinburg, TN 37738
423-436-4434

Chickasaw State Park
Hwy. 100
Henderson, TN 38340
901-989-5141

Fort Pillow State Historic Park
Hwy. 51
Henning, TN 38041
901-738-5581

Buffalo/I-40/Exit 143 KOA
473 Barren Hollow Rd.
Hurricane Mills, TN 37078
800-562-0832

Pickett State Park
Hwy. 154
Jamestown, TN 37243
931-879-5821

Indian Mountain State Park
I-75
Jellico, TN 37762
423-784-7958

Bristol/Kingsport KOA
Box 5024
Kingsport, TN 37663
800-562-7640

Harpeth Scenic River and Narrows
Hwy. 70
Kingston Springs, TN 27082
615-797-9052

Knoxville East KOA
241 KOA Dr.
Kodak, TN 37764
800-562-8693

Norris Dam State Park
Hwy. 441
Lake City, TN 27769
423-426-7461

Memphis East KOA
3291 Shoehorn Dr.
Lakeland, TN 38002
800-562-8753

David Crockett State Park
Hwy. 64
Lawrenceburg, TN 28464
931-762-9408

Cedars of Lebanon State Park
Hwy. 231
Lebanon, TN 37087
615-443-2769

Davy Crockett Birthplace State Park
Hwy. 11E
Limestone, TN 37681
423-257-2167

Mousetail Landing State Park
Hwy. 50
Linden, TN 37096
901-847-0841

Standing Stone State Park
Hwy. 136
Livingston, TN 28570
931-823-6347

Manchester KOA
586 Kampground Rd.
Manchester, TN 37355
800-562-7785

Old Stone Fort Archaeological Park
Hwy. 41
Manchester, TN 37355
931-723-5073

Big Ridge State Park
Hwy. 61
Maynardville, TN 37807
423-992-5523

U.S. Campgrounds > TEXAS

Memphis/Graceland KOA
3691 Elvis Presley Blvd.
Memphis, TN 38116
800-562-9386

T.O. Fuller State Park
Hwy. 61
Memphis, TN 38133
901-543-7581

Meeman-Shelby Forest State Park
Hwy. 388
Millington, TN 38053
901-876-5215

Panther Creek State Park
Hwy. 11E
Morristown, TN 37813
423-587-7046

Holiday Nashville Travel Park
2572 Music Valley Dr.
Nashville, TN 37214
615-889-4225

Nashville/Opryland KOA
2626 Music Valley Dr.
Nashville, TN 37214
800-562-7789

Radnor State Natural Area
1160 Otter Creek Rd.
Nashville, TN 37243
615-373-3467

Johnsonville State Historic Park
Hwy. 70
New Johnsonville, TN 37134
931-535-2789

Newport/I-40/Smoky Mountains KOA
240 KOA Ln.
Newport, TN 37821
800-562-9016

Pickwick Landing State Park
Hwy. 57
Pickwick, TN 38365
901-689-3135

Pigeon Forge/Gatlinburg KOA
Box 310
Pigeon Forge, TN 37868
800-562-7703

Fall Creek Falls State Park
Hwys. 111 and 30
Pikeville, TN 37367
423-881-5241

Big Hill Pond State Park
Hwy. 57
Pocohontas, TN 38061
931-645-7967

Pulaski/I-65 Exit 14 KOA
5701 Fayettville Hwy.
Pulaski, TN 38478
800-562-4063

Roan Mountain State Park
Hwy. 143
Roan Mountain, TN 37687
423-772-3303

Rock Island State Park
Hwy. 70S
Rock Island, TN 38581
931-686-2471

Edgar Evins State Park
Hwy. 96
Silver Point, TN 38582
931-858-2446

Sweetwater/I-75/Exit 62 KOA
269 Murray's Chapel Rd.
Sweetwater, TN 37874
800-562-9224

Reelfoot Lake State Park
Hwy. 21
Tiptonville, TN 38079
901-253-7756

Tremont Hills Campground & Log Cabins
PO Box 5
Townsend, TN 37882
423-448-6363

South Cumberland Recreation Area
Hwy. 41A
Tracy City, TN 37387
931-924-2980

Frozen Head State Natural Area
Hwy. 62
Wartburg, TN 37887
423-346-3318

Natchez Trace State Park
I-40
Wildersville, TN 38388
901-968-3742

TEXAS

Abilene KOA
4851 W. Stamford St.
Abilene, TX 79603
800-562-3651

Amarillo KOA
1100 Folsom Rd.
Amarillo, TX 79108
800-562-3431

Houston East/Baytown KOA
11810 I-10 E.
Baytown, TX 77520
800-562-3418

Belton/Temple/Killeen KOA
P.O. Box 118
Belton, TX 76513
800-562-1902

Texas RV Park of Big Spring
4100 S. US 87
Big Spring, TX 79720
915-267-7900

Whip In RV Park
7000 I-20
Big Spring, TX 79720
915-393-5242

Houston West/Brookshire KOA
35303 Cooper Rd.
Brookshire, TX 77423
800-562-5417

Wichita Falls/Burkburnett KOA
1202 E 3rd St.
Burkburnett, TX 76354
800-562-2649

Dallas KOA
7100 S. Stemmons
Denton, TX 76205
800-562-1893

Fort Stockton KOA
Box 627
Fort Stockton, TX 79735
800-562-8607

Fredericksburg KOA
5681 Hwy. 290
Fredericksburg, TX 78624
800-562-0796

Traders Village RV Park Dallas
2602 Mayfield Rd.
Grand Prairie, TX 75052
972-647-8205

Houston Central KOA
1620 Peachleaf
Houston, TX 77039
800-562-2132

Traders Village RV Park Houston
7979 N. Eldridge
Houston, TX 77041
281-890-8846

Junction KOA
2145 N. Main St.
Junction, TX 76849
800-562-7506

Kerrville KOA
2950 Goat Creek Rd.
Kerrville, TX 78028
800-562-1665

Lubbock KOA
5502 County Rd. 6300
Lubbock, TX 79416
800-562-8643

Lake Corpus Christi/Mathis KOA
Route 1, Box 158B
Mathis, TX 78368
800-562-8601

Mt. Pleasant KOA
P.O. Box 387
Mt. Pleasant, TX 75456
800-562-5409

Midland/Odessa KOA
4220 S. County Rd. 1290
Odessa, TX 79765
800-562-9168

San Angelo KOA
6699 Knickerbocker Rd.
San Angelo, TX 76904
800-562-7519

San Antonio KOA
602 Gemberl Rd.
San Antonio, TX 78219
800-562-7783

Van Horn KOA
P.O. Box 265
Van Horn, TX 79855
800-562-0798

Waco North KOA
P.O. Box 157
West, TX 76691
800-562-4199

UTAH

Beaver KOA
P.O. Box 1437
Beaver, UT 84713
800-562-2912

Brigham City/Perry South KOA
Box 579
Brigham City, UT 84302
800-562-0903

Cedar City KOA
1121 N. Main
Cedar City, UT 84720
800-562-9873

Fillmore KOA
900 S. 410 W.
Fillmore, UT 84631
800-562-1516

Bear Lake/Garden City KOA
US 89
Garden City, UT 84028
800-562-3442

Glendale KOA
Box 189
Glendale, UT 84729
800-562-8635

Green River KOA
P.O. Box 14
Green River, UT 84525
800-562-3649

Cherry Hill Campground
1325 S. Main
Kaysville, UT 84037
801-451-5379

Flaming Gorge/Manila KOA
Box 157
Manila, UT 84046
800-562-3254

Moab KOA
3225 S. Hwy. 191
Moab, UT 84532
800-562-0372

Nephi KOA
Salt Creek Canyon
Nephi, UT 84648
800-562-0813

Panguitch KOA
P.O. Box 384
Panguitch, UT 84759
800-562-1625

Provo KOA
320 N. 2050 W
Provo, UT 84601
800-562-1894

Richfield KOA
600 W 600 S
Richfield, UT 84701
800-562-9382

Vernal KOA
1800 W. Sheraton Ave.
Vernal, UT 84078
800-562-7574

Redlands RV Park
650 W. Telegraph St.
Washington, UT 84780
435-673-9700

Mukuntuweep RV Park & Campground
Zion East Gate
Zion Nat'l Park, UT 84767
435-648-2154

U.S. Campgrounds > VERMONT

Zion National Park
Zion Nat'l Park, UT 84767
435-648-2154

VERMONT

Griffin's Ten Acre Campground
RD 1, Box 3560
Addison, VT 05491
802-759-2662

Alburg RV Resort
PO Box 50
Alburg, VT 05440
802-796-3733

Horeshoe Acres
RD 1, Box 206
Andover, VT 05143
802-875-2960

Camping on the Battenkill
RD 2, Box 3310
Arlington, VT 05250
802-375-6663

Running Bear Camping Area
PO Box 378
Ascutney, VT 05030
802-674-6417

Silver Lake Family Campground
Box 11
Barnard, VT 05031
802-234-9974

Silver Lake State Park
Barnard, VT 05031
802-234-9451

Belview Campground
Rt. 16 E.
Barton, VT 05822
802-525-3242

Woodford State Park
HCR 65, Box 928
Bennington, VT 05201
802-447-7169

Brandbury State Park
RR 2, Box 242
Brandon, VT 05743
802-247-5925

Fort Drummer State Park
434 Old Guilford Rd.
Brattleboro, VT 05301
802-254-2610

Moss Hollow Campground
RD 4, Box 723
Brattleboro, VT 05301
802-368-2418

Elephant Mountain Campground
RD 3, Box 850
Bristol, VT 05443
802-453-3123

Burlington's North Beach Campground
60 Institute Rd.
Burlington, VT 05401
802-862-0942

Caton Place Campground
RR 1, Box 107
Cavendish, VT 05142
802-226-7767

Mt. Philo State Park
5425 Mt. Philo Rd.
Charlotte, VT 05445
802-425-2390

Rustic Haven Campground
Rt. 2, Box 19
Concord, VT 05824
802-695-9933

Fireside Campground
Box 340
Derby, VT 05829
802-766-5109

Dorset RV Park
RR 1, Box 180
Dorset, VT 05251
802-867-5754

Emerald Lake State Park
RD Box 485
East Dorset, VT 05253
802-362-1655

Green Valley Campground
PO Box 21
East Montpelier, VT 05651
802-223-6217

Rest N' Nest
PO Box 258
East Thetford, VT 05043
802-785-2997

Brookside Campground
RD 2, Box 3300
Enosburg Falls, VT 05450
802-933-4376

Half Moon Pond
RR 1, Box 2730
Fair Haven, VT 05743
802-273-2848

Mill Pond Campground
RR 1, Box 2335
Franklin, VT 05452
802-285-2240

Champlain Adult Campground
3 Silent Cedars
Grand Isle, VT 05458
802-372-5938

Grand Isle State Park
36 E. Shore Rd, S.
Grand Isle, VT 05458
802-372-4300

Lazy Lions Campground
PO Box 56
Graniteville, VT 05654
802-479-2823

Ricker Pond State Park
Groton, VT 05046
802-584-3821

Stillwater State Park
RD 2, Box 332
Groton, VT 05046
802-584-3822

Maidstone State Park
RD Box 455
Guildhall, VT 05905
802-676-3930

Idle Hours Campground
PO Box 1053
Hardwick, VT 05843
802-472-6732

Brighton State Park
Island Pond, VT 05846
802-479-4280

U.S. Campgrounds > VERMONT

Lakeside Camping
RR 1, Box194
Island Pond, VT 05846
802-723-6649

Jamaica State Park
Box 45
Jamaica, VT 05343
802-874-4600

Gifford Woods State Park
Killington, VT 05751
802-775-5354

Killington Campground
Alphenhof Lodge, Box 2880
Killington, VT 05751
802-422-9787

Elmore State Park
Box 93
Lake Elmore, VT 05657
802-888-2982

**Hideaway "Squirrel Hill"
Campground**
PO Box 176
Ludlow, VT 05149
802-228-8800

**Groton Forest Road
Campground**
RR 1, Box 402
Marshfield, VT 05658
802-426-4122

Kettle Pond State Park
RD Box 600
Marshfield, VT 05658
802-584-3820

**Lake Dunmore
Kampersville**
Box 214
Middlebury, VT 05753
802-352-4501

**Mountain View CG &
Cabins**
Rt. 15
Morrisville, VT 05661
802-888-2178

Rivers Bend Campground
PO Box 9, Dog Team Rd. &
Rt. 7
New Haven, VT 05472
802-388-9092

Kenolie Village Campground
RR 1, Box 810
Newfane, VT 05345
802-365-7671

Carry Bay
PO Box 207
North Hero, VT 05474
802-372-8233

Kings Bay Campground
Lakeview Dr., PO Box 169
North Hero, VT 05474
802-372-3735

North Hero State Park
RD Box 259, Lakeview Rd.
North Hero, VT 05474
802-373-8389

White Caps Campground
RD 2, Box 626
Orleans, VT 05860
802-467-3345

Will-O-Wood Campground
RD 2, Box 316
Orleans, VT 05860
802-525-3575

Onion River Campground
RR 1, Box 1205
Plainfield, VT 05667
802-426-3232

Coolidge State Park
HCR 70, Box 105
Plymouth, VT 05056
802-672-3612

Lake St. Catherine State Park
RD 2, Box 1775
Poultney, VT 05764
802-287-9158

**Lake Champagne
Campground**
PO Box C, Furnace Rd.
Randloph Center, VT 05061
802-728-5293

Allis State Park
RD 2, Box 192
Randolph, VT 05060
802-276-3175

Mt. Trails Campground
RFD 1, Box 7, Quarry Rd.
Rochester, VT 05767
802-767-3352

Shelburne Camping Area
2056 Shelburne Rd.
Shelburne, VT 05482
802-985-2540

Tree Farm Campground
53 Skitchewaug Trail
Springfield, VT 05156
802-885-2889

Moose River Campground
RR 3, Box 197
St. Johnsbury, VT 05819
802-748-4334

Smugglers' Notch
7248 Mountain Rd.
Stowe, VT 05672
802-253-4014

**Champlain Valley
Campground**
RD 1, Box 4255
Swanton, VT 05448
802-524-5146

Lakewood Campground
RFD 2, Box 482
Swanton, VT 05488
802-868-7270

Thetford Hill
Box 132
Thetford, VT 05074
802-785-2266

Townshend State Park
RR 1, Box 2650
Townshend, VT 05353
802-365-7500

**South Hill Riverside
Campground**
RR 2, Box 287
Underhill, VT 05489
802-899-2232

Underhill State Park
PO Box 249
Underhill Center, VT 05490
802-899-3022

Button Bay State Park
RD 3, Box 4075
Vergennes, VT 05491
802-475-2377

U.S. Campgrounds > WASHINGTON

DAR State Park
RD 2, Box 3493
Vergennes, VT 05491
802-759-2359

Little River State Park
RD 1, Box 1150
Waterbury, VT 05676
802-244-7013

Indian Joe Court
US Rt. 2, PO Box 126
West Danville, VT 05873
802-684-3430

Barrewwod Campground
HCR 13, Box 4
Westfield, VT 05874
802-744-6340

Mill Brook Campground
PO Box 133
Westfield, VT 05874
802-744-6673

**Maple Leaf Motel &
Campground**
406 N. Harland Rd.
White River Junction, VT
05001
802-295-2817

Pine Valley RV Resort
400 Woodstock Rd.
White River Junction, VT
05001
802-296-6711

Quechee Gorge State Park
190 Dewey Mill Rd.
White River Junction, VT
05001
802-295-2990

**Limehurst Lake
Campground**
RR 1, Box 462
Williamstown, VT 05679
802-433-6662

Molly Stark State Park
705 Rt. 9 E.
Wilmington, VT 05363
802-464-5460

Ascutney State Park
Box 186, HCR 71
Windsor, VT 05089
802-886-2060

VIRGINIA

**Americamps, Richmond
North**
11322 Air Park Rd.
Ashland, VA 23005
804-798-5298

**Bowling Green/Richmond
KOA**
Box 1250
Bowling Green, VA 22427
800-562-2482

Breaks Interstate Park
Breaks, VA 24607
800-982-5122

**Harrisonburg/New Market
KOA**
12480 Mountain Valley Rd.
Broadway, VA 22815
800-562-5406

Charlottesville KOA
3825 Red Hill Rd.
Charlottesville, VA 22903
800-562-1743

**Fredericksburg/Washington
DC KOA**
7400 Brookside Ln.
Fredericksburg, VA 22408
800-562-1889

**Front Royal/Washington
DC KOA**
P.O. Box 274
Front Royal, VA 22630
800-562-9114

**Natural Bridge/Lexington
KOA**
Box 148
Natural Bridge, VA 24578
800-562-8514

Petersburg KOA
2809 Courtland Rd.
Petersburg, VA 23805
800-562-8545

**Chesapeake Bay/Smith
Island KOA**
382 Campground Rd.
Reedville, VA 22539
800-562-9795

Walnut Hills Campground
391 Walnut Hills Rd.
Staunton, VA 24401
540-337-3920

**Staunton/Verona/I-81 Exit
227 KOA**
P.O. Box 98
Verona, VA 24482
800-562-994

Best Holiday Trav-L-Park
1075 General Booth Blvd.
Virginia Beach, VA 23451
757-425-0249

Virginia Beach KOA
1240 General Booth Blvd.
Virginia Beach, VA 23451
800-562-4150

**American Heritage RV
Park**
146 Maxton Ln.
Williamsburg, VA 23188
757-566-2133

**Fair Oaks Family
Campground**
901 Lightfoot Rd.
Williamsburg, VA 23188
757-565-2101

**Williamsburg/Busch
Gardens KOA**
5210 Newman Rd
Williamsburg, VA 23188
800-562-1733

**Williamsburg/Colonial
KOA**
4000 Newman Rd.
Williamsburg, VA 23188
800-562-7609

Wytheville KOA
RR 2, Box 122
Wytheville, VA 24382
800-562-3380

WASHINGTON

**Bay Center/Willapa Bay
KOA**
P.O. Box 315
Bay Center, WA 98527
800-562-7810

U.S. Campgrounds > WASHINGTON

Burlington KOA
6397 N. Green Rd.
Burlington, WA 98233
800-562-9154

Ellensburg KOA
32 Thorp Hwy. S.
Ellensburg, WA 98926
800-562-7616

Ilwaco KOA
Box 549
Ilwaco, WA 98624
800-562-3258

Seattle/Tacoma KOA
5801 S. 212th
Kent, WA 98032
800-562-1892

Leavenworth/Wenatchee KOA
11401 Riverbend Dr.
Leavenworth, WA 98826
800-562-5709

Anderson's On the Ocean
1400 138th St.
Long Beach, WA 98631
360-642-2231

Lynden KOA
8717 Line Rd.
Lynden, WA 98264
800-562-4779

American Heritage Holiday Trav-L-Park
9610 Kimmie St., SW
Olympia, WA 98512
360-943-8778

Olympia Holiday Trav-L-Park
1441 83rd Ave., SW
Olympia, WA 98512
360-352-2551

Spokane KOA
N 3025 Barker Rd.
Otis Orchards, WA 99027
800-562-3309

Port Angeles/Sequim, KOA
80 O'Brien Rd.
Port Angeles, WA 98362
800-562-7558

Seaview Motel & RV Park
3728 Pacific Hwy.
Seaview, WA 98644
360-642-2450

Vantage KOA
Box 135
Vantage, WA 98950
800-562-7270

Winthrop/N. Cascades Nat'l Park KOA
Box 305
Winthrop, WA 98862
800-562-2158

Yakima KOA
1500 Keys Rd.
Yakima, WA 98901
800-562-5773

WEST VIRGINIA

Harpers Ferry/Washington DC NW KOA
Route 5, Box 1300
Harpers Ferry, WV 25425
800-562-9497

Pipestem KOA
HC 78, Box 37B
Pipestem, WV 25979
800-562-5418

WISCONSIN

Ahnapee River Trails Campground
E6053 W. Wilson Rd.
Algoma, WI 54201
920-487-5777

Timber Trail Campground
N8326 Co. M
Algoma, WI 54201
920-487-3707

Hixton/Alma Center KOA
N9657 State Hwy. 95f
Alma Center, WI 54611
800-562-2680

Arbor Vitae Campground
10545 Big Arbor Vitae Dr.
Arbor Vitae, WI 54568
715-356-5146

Fox Fire Campground, Inc.
11180 Fox Fire Rd
Arbor Vitae, WI 54568
715-356-6470

Mountain Jed's Camping and Canoeing
W13364 Cty., C
Athelstane, WI 54104
715-757-2406

Sandy Hill Campground
E21100 ND Rd
Augusta, WI 54722
715-286-2495

Wyalusing State Park
13342 County Hwy. C
Bagley, WI 53801
608-996-2261

Yogi Bear's Jellystone Park–Bagley
11354 County Hwy. X
Bagley, WI 53801
608-996-2201

Bailey's Bluff Campground
2701 County Rd. EE
Bailey's Harbor, WI 54202
920-839-2109

Vista Royalle Campground
8151 Co. Hwy. BB
Bancroft, WI 54921
715-335-6860

Baraboo Hills Campground
E10545 Terrytown Rd.
Baraboo, WI 53913
608-356-8505

Devil's Lake State Park
S5975 Park Rd
Baraboo, WI 53913
608-356-6618

Fox Hill RV Park
E11371 N. Reedsburg Rd
Baraboo, WI 53913
608-356-5890

U.S. Campgrounds > WISCONSIN

Mirror Lake State Park
E10320 Ferndell Rd.
Baraboo, WI 53913
608-254-2333

Rocky Arbor State Park
c/o E10320 Ferndell Rd.
Baraboo, WI 53913
608-254-8001

Big Bay State Park
P.O. Box 589
Bayfield, WI 54814
715-747-6425

Willow Mill Campsites
P.O. Box 312
Beaver Dam, WI 53916
920-887-1420

Lake Joy Campground
24192 Lake Joy Ln.
Belmont, WI 53510
608-762-5150

**Lost Falls Resort &
Campground**
436 S. Third St.
Black River Falls, WI 54615
715-284-7133

**Parkland Village
Campground**
Route 2, Box 7V
Black River Falls, WI 54615
715-284-9700

Yellowstone Lake State Park
7896 Lake Rd.
Blanchardville, WI 53516
608-523-4427

Blue Mound State Park
P.O. Box 98
Blue Mound, WI 53517
608-437-5711

Camp Holiday
Box 67 WA
Boulder Junction, WI 54512
715-385-2264

**N. Highland/American
Legion St. Forest**
4125 Co. Hwy. M
Boulder Junction, WI 54512
715-385-2704

Happy Acres Kampground
22230 45th St.
Bristol, WI 53104
414-857-7373

Crazy Horse Campground
W741 Cty F
Brodhead, WI 53520
608-897-2207

**Butternut Lake
Campground**
Route 1, Box 129A
Butternut, WI 54514
715-769-3448

**Yogi Bear's Jellystone
Camp-Resort**
8425 Hwy. 38
Caledonia, WI 53108
414-835-2565

Deer Creek Campground
N8129 Larson Rd
Cambria, WI 53923
920-348-6413

Mill Bluff State Park
Rt. 1, Box 268
Camp Douglas, WI 54618
608-427-6692

**Benson's Century Camping
Resort**
N3845 Hwy. 67
Campbellsport, WI 53010
920-533-8597

Kettle Moraine State Forest
N1765 Hwy. G.
Campbellsport, WI 53010
414-626-2115

**Hoeft's Resort &
Campground**
W9070 Crooked Lake Dr.
Cascade, WI 53011
414-626-2221

Nelson Dewey State Park
Box 658
Cassville, WI 53806
608-725-5274

Ken's Kampsites
P.O. Box 222
Chetek, WI 54822
715-859-2887

Lake Wissota State Park
18127 County Hwy. O
Chippewa Falls, WI 54729
715-382-4574

Brunet Island State Park
23125 25th St.
Cornell, WI 54732
715-239-6888

**Buckatabon Lodge &
Lighthouse Inn**
5630 Rush Rd.
Conover, WI 54519
715-479-4660

**High Falls Family
Campground**
W11594 Archer Ln.
Crivitz, WI 54114
715-757-3399

Peshtigo River Campground
Rt. 1, Box 243
Crivitz, WI 54114
715-854-2986

Grand Valley Campground
W5855 County Rd. B
Dalton, WI 53926
920-394-3643

Madison KOA
4859 CTH-V
DeForest, WI 53532
800-562-5784

**Snug Harbor Inn
Campground on Turtle Lake**
W7772-2C Wisconsin Pkwy.
Delavan, WI 53115
608-883-6999

**Happy Hollow Camping
Resort**
3831 County Rd. U
DePere, WI 54115
920-532-4386

Tom's Campground
2751 CTH BB
Dodgeville, WI 53533
608-935-5446

**Black River State Forest
Castle Mound**
910 Hwy. 54
E. Black River Falls, WI 54615
715-284-4103

U.S. Campgrounds > WISCONSIN

Kettle Moraine State Forest
S91 W39091 Hwy. 59
Eagle, WI 53119
414-594-6200

Chain-O-Lakes Resort & Camping
3165 Nine Mile Rd.
Eagle River, WI 54521
715-479-6708

Pine-Aire Resort & Campground
4443 Chain O'Lakes Rd.
Eagle River, WI 54521
715-479-9208

Hickory Hills Campground
856 Hillside Rd.
Edgerton, WI 53534
608-884-6327

Door County Kamping Resort
4906 Court Rd.
Egg Harbor, WI 54209
920-868-3151

Plymouth Rock Camping Resort
P.O. Box 445
Elkhart Lake, WI 53020
920-892-4252

Newport State Park
475 County Hwy. NP
Ellison Bay, WI 54210
920-854-2500

Wagon Trail Campground
1190 Hwy. ZZ
Ellison Bay, WI 54210
920-854-4818

Lake Hilbert Campground
N2490 Town Park Rd.
Fence, WI 54120
715-336-3013

Keyes Lake Campground
HCI Box 162
Florence, WI 54121
715-528-4907

Fond Du Lac KOA
W. 5099 Hwy. B
Fond Du Lac, WI 54935
800-562-3912

Jellystone Park of Fort Atkinson
N551 Wishing Well Dr.
Fort Atkinson, WI 53538
920-568-4100

Pilgrims Campground LLC
W7271 Cty. Hwy. C
Fort Atkinson, WI 53538
800-742-1697

Merrick State Park
Box 127
Fountain City, WI 54629
608-687-3025

Blue Top Resort & Campground
1460 Wolf River Dr.
Fremont, WI 54940
920-446-3343

Yogi Bear's Jellystone Park Camp Resort
P.O. Box 155
Fremont, WI 54940
800-258-3315

Roche-A-Cri State Park
1767 Hwy. 13
Friendship, WI 53934
608-339-6881

Pow Wow Campground
W16751 Pow Wow Ln.
Galesville, WI 54630
608-582-2995

Westward Ho Camp-Resort
N5456 Division Rd.
Glenbeulah, WI 53023
920-526-3407

James McNally Campground
416 S. Pine St.
Grantsburg, WI 54840
715-463-2405

Green Lake Campground
W2360 Hwy. 23
Green Lake, WI 54941
920-294-3543

Tomorrow Wood Campground
N3845 S. Fish Lake Rd.
Hancock, WI 54943
715-249-5954

Pike Lake State Park
3544 Kettle Moraine Rd.
Hartford, WI 53027
414-670-3400

Rice Lake-Haugen KOA
P.O. Box 3
Haugen, WI 54841
715-234-2360

Everson's Nelson Lake Lodge Resort & Campground
R 3, Box 3100
Hayward, WI 54843
715-634-3750

Hayward KOA
11544 N US Hwy. 63
Hayward, WI 54843
800-562-7631

Lake Chippewa Campground
Rt. 9, Box 9345
Hayward, WI 54843
715-462-3672

Trails End Camping Resort
Rt. 2, Box 2339 WA
Hayward, WI 54843
715-634-2423

Cedar Falls Campground
6051 Cedar Falls Rd.
Hazelhurst, WI 54531
715-356-4953

Hiles Pine Lake Campground
Rt. 2, Box 440
Hiles, WI 54511
715-649-3319

Triple R Resort
N11818 Hixton-Levis Rd., Rt. 2
Hixton, WI 54635
715-964-8777

The Playful Goose Campground
2001 S. Main St.
Horicon, WI 53032
920-485-4744

Willow River State Park
1034 County Trunk A
Hudson, WI 54016
715-386-5931

U.S. Campgrounds > WISCONSIN

Wildwood Campgrounds
Rt. 2, Box 18
Iron River, WI 54847
715-372-4072

Bong State Recreation Area
26313 Burlington Rd.
Kansasville, WI 53139
414-878-5600

Kewaunee Village Camping Resort
333 Terraqua Dr.
Kewaunee, WI 54216
920-388-4851

Mapleview Campsites
N1460 Hwy. B
Kewaunee, WI 54216
920-776-1588

Broken Bow Campground
P.O. Box 716,
14855 Deer Trail Rd.
Lac Du Flambeau, WI 54538
715-588-3844

Bluebird Springs Recreational Area
N2833 Smith Valley Rd
LaCrosse, WI 54601
608-781-2267

Pettibone RV Park & Campground
333 Park Plaza Dr.
LaCrosse, WI 54601
608-782-5858

Thornapple River Campground
N6599 Hwy. 27
Ladysmith, WI 54848
715-532-7034

Glacial Drumlin State Trail
1213 S. Main
Lake Mills, WI 53551
920-648-8774

Heaven's Up North Family Campground
18344 Lake John Rd.
Lakewood, WI 54138
715-276-6556

Maple Heights Campground
P.O. Box 201
Lakewood, WI 54138
715-276-6441

Klondyke Secluded Acres
10161 Quarry Rd.
Lancaster, WI 53813
608-723-2844

Camp Five Museum
RFD 1
Laona, WI 54541
715-674-3414

Smokey Hollow Campground, Inc.
W9935 McGowan Rd
Lodi, WI 53555
608-635-4806

Bass Lake Campground
N1497 Southern Rd.
Lyndon Station, WI 53944
608-666-2311

River Bay Resort & Campground
W1147 River Bay Rd.
Lyndon Station, WI 53944
608-254-7193

Yukon Trails Camping
N2330 Cty. Rd. HH
Lyndon Station, WI 53944
608-666-3261

Camperland
5498 Co. Rd. CV
Madison, WI 53704
608-241-1636

Bear Lake Campground
N4715 Hwy. 22-110
Manawa, WI 54949
920-596-3308

Copper Falls State Park
Rt. 1, Box 17AA
Mellen, WI 54546
715-274-5123

Menomonie KOA
2501 Broadway St. N
Menomonie, WI 54751
800-562-3417

Twin Springs Resort Campground
3010 Cedar Falls Rd.
Menomonie, WI 54751
715-235-9321

Big 6 RV Resort & Campground
P.O. Box 426
Mercer, WI 54547
715-476-2466

Council Grounds State Park
N1895 Council Grounds Dr.
Merrill, WI 54452
715-536-8773

Blackhawk Campground, Inc.
3407 E. Blackhawk Dr.
Milton, WI 53563
608-868-2586

Hidden Valley RV Resort
872 E. Hwy. 59
Milton, WI 35563
608-868-4141

Lakeland Camping Resort
2803 E. State Rd. 59
Milton, WI 53563
608-868-4700

Patricia Lake Campground
8505 Camp Pinemere Rd.
Minocqua, WI 54548
715-356-3198

Cadiz Hills Campground
W7542 Hwy. 11
Monroe, WI 53566
608-966-3310

Buffalo Lake Camping Resort
555 Lake Ave.
Montello, WI 53949
608-297-2915

Kilby Lake Campground
N4492 Fern Ave.
Montello, WI 53949
608-297-2344

U.S. Campgrounds > WISCONSIN

Lake Arrowhead Campground
W781 Fox Ct.
Montello, WI 53949
920-295-3000

Puckaway Shores Campground
N3510 E. Tomahawk
Montello, WI 53949
920-295-3389

Wilderness Campgrounds
N1499 State Hwy. 22
Montello, WI 53949
608-297-2002

Lake DuBay Campgrounds
1713 DuBay Dr.
Mosinee, WI 54455
715-457-2484

Governor Dodge State Park
4175 State Rd. 23
N. Dodgeville, WI 53533
608-935-3325

Buckhorn State Park
W8450 Buckhorn Park Ave.
Necedah, WI 54646
608-565-2789

Ken's Marina Campground & Pontoon Rental
W4240 Marina Ln.
Necedah, WI 54646
608-565-2426

St. Joseph Resort
W5630 Hwy. 21
Necedah, WI 54646
608-565-7258

Wisconsin Camping, Inc.
9042 Campers Way
Neenah, WI 54956
888-WIS-CAMP

Deer Trail Park Campground
13846 Cty. Rd. Z
Nekoosa, WI 54457
715-886-3871

New Glarus Woods State Park
P.O. Box 805
New Glarus, WI 53574
608-527-2335

Wolf River Trips and Campground
E8041 Cty. X
New London, WI 54961
920-9822458

Oakdale KOA
P.O. Box 150
Oakdale, WI 54649
608-372-5622

Circle R. Campground
1185 Old Knapp Rd.
Oshkosh, WI 54901
920-235-8909

Kalbus' Country Harbor Inc.
5309 Lake Rd.
Oshkosh, WI 54901
920-426-0062

Hickory Oaks Fly In and Campground
555 Glendale Ave.
Oshkosk, WI 54901
920-235-6694

Osseo Camping Resort
50483 Oak Grove Rd.
Osseo, WI 54758
715-597-2102

Coon's Deep Lake Campground
360 Fish Ln.
Oxford, WI 53952
608-586-5644

Circle K Campground
W1316 Island Rd.
Palmyra, WI 53156
414-495-2896

Duck Creek Campground
W6560 Co. Hwy. G
Pardeeville, WI 53954
608-429-2425

Indian Trails Campground
W6445 Haynes Rd.
Pardeeville, WI 53954
608-429-3244

Weaver's Resort & Campground
1001 Weaver Rd.
Pelican Lake, WI 54463
715-487-5217

Comfort Cove Campground & Resort
N10149 E. Solberg Lake Rd.
Phillips, WI 54555
715-339-3360

Ridgewood Campground
4800 River Ridge Rd.
Plover, WI 54467
715-344-8750

Pride of America Campground-Lake George
P.O. Box 403
Portage, WI 53901
608-742-6395

Sky High Camping
N5740 Sky High Dr.
Portage, WI 53901
608-742-2572

Flanagan's Pearl Lake Campsite
4585 Pearl Lake Rd.
Redgranite, WI 54970
920566-2758

Lighthouse Rock Campground
S2330 Co. Hwy. V
Reedsburg, WI 53959
608-524-4203

Rainbow's End Campground
18227 US Hwy. 10
Reedsville, WI 54230
920-754-4142

Lake George Campsite
4008 Bassett Rd.
Rhinelander, WI 54501
715-362-6152

U.S. Campgrounds > WISCONSIN

Rice Lake/Haugen KOA
1876 29 3/4 Ave.
Rice Lake, WI 54868
800-562-3460

Silver Springs Campsites
N5048 Ludwig Rd.
Rio, WI 53960
920-992-3537

Frontier Bar & Campground
HC 1, Box 477
Saxon, WI 54559
715-893-2461

Brady's Pine Grove Campground
N5999 Campground Rd.
Shawano, WI 54166
715-787-4555

Kohler-Andrae State Park
1520 Old Park Rd.
Sheboygan, WI 53081
920-451-4080

Red Barn Campground
W6820 Cty Rd. B
Shell Lake, WI 54871
715-468-2575

High Cliff State Park
N7630 State Park Rd.
Sherwood, WI 54169
920-989-1106

Aqualand Camp Resort
Box 538
Sister Bay, WI 54234
920-854-4573

Leon Valley Campground
9050 Jancing Ave.
Sparta, WI 54656
608-269-6400

Valley RV Park
E5016 Hwy. 14 & 23
Spring Green, WI 53588
608-588-2717

Interstate State Park
Box 703
St. Croix Falls, WI 54024
715-483-3742

Lynn Ann's Campground
P.O. Box 8
St. Germain, WI 54558
715-542-3456

Rivers Edge Campground
3368 Campsite Dr.
Stevens Point, WI 54481
715-344-8058

Kamp Kegonsa
2671 Circle Dr.
Stoughton, WI 53589
608-873-5800

Lake Kegosa State Park
2405 Door Creek Rd.
Stoughton, WI 53589
608-873-9695

Viking Village Campground & Resort
1648 County Trunk N.
Stoughton, WI 53589
608-873-6601

Potawatomi State Park
3740 Park Dr.
Sturgeon Bay, WI 54235
920-746-2891

Quietwoods North Camping Resort
3668 Grondin Rd.
Sturgeon Bay, WI 54235
920-743-7115

Yogi Bear's Jellystone Park
3677 May Rd.
Sturgeon Bay, WI 54325
920-743-9001

Travelers' Inn Motel and Campground
14017 Durand Ave.
Sturtevant, WI 53177
414-878-1415

Concord Center Campground
Q901 Concord Center Dr.
Sullivan, WI 53178
414-593-2707

Amnicon Falls State Park
6294 S. State Rd. 35
Superior, WI 54880
715-398-3000

Pattison State Park
6294 S. State Rd. 35
Superior, WI 54880
715-399-3111

Tilleda Falls Campground
P.O. Box 76
Tilleda, WI 54978
715-787-4143

Birkensee Resort & Camping
N9350 Hwy. H
Tomahawk, WI 54487
715-453-5103

Terrace View Campsites
W5220 Terrace View Rd.
Tomahawk, WI 54487
715-453-8352

Out Post
9507 Country Rd. N.
Tomahawk, WI 54487
715-453-3468

Bay Park Resort & Campground
N8347 Bay Park Rd.
Trego, WI 54888
715-635-2840

Log Cabin Resort and Campground
N7470 Log Cabin Dr.
Trego, WI 54888
715-635-2959

Perrot State Park
W26247 Sullivan Rd., P.O. Box 407
Trempealeau, WI 54661
608-534-6409

Point Beach State Forest
9400 County Trunk O
Two Rivers, WI 54241
920-794-7480

Ham Lake Campground
RR1, Box 434
Wabeno, WI 54566
715-674-2201

U.S. Campgrounds > WISCONSIN

Yogi Bear's Jellystone Park Campground Resort
P.O. Box 67
Warrens, WI 54666
608-378-4977

Rib Mountain State Park
4200 Park Rd.
Wasau, WI 54401
715-842-2522

Island Camping & Recreation
RR1, Box 144
Washington Island, WI 54246
920-847-2622

Rock Island State Park
Rt. 1, Box 1118A
Washington Island, WI 54246
920-847-2235

Hartman Creek State Park
N2480 Hartman Creek Rd.
Waupaca, WI 54981
715-258-2372

Rustic Woods
E2585 Southwood Dr.
Waupaca, WI 54981
715-258-2442

Waupaca Camping Park
E2411 Holmes Rd.
Waupaca, WI 54981
715-258-8010

Lake of the Woods
N9070 14th Ave.
Wautoma, WI 54982
920-787-3601

Lake Lenwood Beach and Campground
7053 Lenwood Dr.
West Bend, WI 53090
414-334-1335

Lazy Days Campground
1475 Lake View Rd.
West Bend, WI 53090
414-675-6511

Timber Trail Camp Resort
7590 Good Luck Ln.
West Bend, WI 53095
414-282-6394

Neshonoc Lakeside Campgrounds
N 5334 Neshonoc Rd.
West Salem, WI 54669
608-786-1792

River Forest Campground
N2755 Sunny Waters Ln.
White Lake, WI 54491
715-882-3351

Wolf River Nicolet Forest Outdoor Center
N3116 Hwy. 55
White Lake, WI 54491
715-882-4002

Scenic Ridge Campground
W7991 Town Line Rd.
Whitewater, WI 53190
608-883-2920

Tunnel Trail Campground
Route 1, Box 185
Wilton, WI 54670
608-435-6829

K & L Campground
3503 County Rd. G
Wisconsin Dell, WI 53965
608-586-4720

American World Resort & RV Park
400 Cty A & Hwy. 12
Wisconsin Dells, WI 53965
608-253-4451

Arrowhead Resort Campground
P.O. Box 285
Wisconsin Dells, WI 53965
608-254-7344

Dell Boo Campground
Box 407
Wisconsin Dells, WI 53965
608-356-5898

Dells Timberland Camping Resort
P.O. Box 72
Wisconsin Dells, WI 53965
608-254-2429

Erickson's Tepee Park Campground
E10096 Trout Rd.
Wisconsin Dells, WI 53965
608-253-3122

Holiday Shores Campground-Resort
3900 River Rd.
Wisconsin Dells, WI 53965
608-254-2717

Lake of the Dells
3879 Hwy. 13
Wisconsin Dells, WI 53965
608-254-6485

Southfork Campground, LLC
W15197 State Rd. 16
Wisconsin Dells, WI 53965
608-253-2267

Stand Rock Campground
N570 Hwy. N
Wisconsin Dells, WI 53965
608-253-2169

Wisconsin Dells KOA
S235 Stand Rock Rd.
Wisconsin Dells, WI 53965
608-254-4177

Yogi Bear's Jellystone Park Camp-Resort
P.O. Box 510
Wisconsin Dells, WI 53965
608-254-2568

Chapparal Campground
S320 Hwy. 33
Wonewoc, WI 53968
608-464-3944

Hiawatha Trailer Resort
P.O. Box 590
Woodruff, WI 54568
715-356-6111

Indian Shores
P.O. Box 12
Woodruff, WI 54568
715-356-5552

U.S. Campgrounds > WYOMING

WYOMING

Buffalo KOA
Box 189
Buffalo, WY 82834
800-562-5403

Casper KOA
2800 E. Yellowstone
Casper, WY 82609
800-562-3259

Cheyenne KOA
P.O. Box 20341
Cheyene, WY 82003
800-562-1507

Cody KOA
5561 Greybull Hwy.
Cody, WY 82414
800-562-8507

Devils Tower KOA
Box 100
Devils Tower, WY 82714
800-562-5785

Douglas KOA
Hwy. 91, Box 1190
Douglas, WY 82633
800-562-2469

Greybull KOA
Box 387
Greybull, WY 82426
800-562-7508

**Jackson South/Hoback
Junction KOA**
9705 S. Hwy. 89
Jackson, WY 83001
800-562-1878

Lyman KOA
Star Route, Box 55
Lyman, WY 82937
800-562-2762

Rawlins KOA
205 E. Hwy. 71
Rawlins, WY 82301
800-562-7559

Rock Springs KOA
P.O. Box 2910
Rock Springs, WY 82902
800-562-8699

**Sheridan/Big Horn
Mountains KOA**
63 Decker Rd., Box 35 A
Sheridan, WY 82801
800-562-7621

Laramie KOA
1271 W. Baker
St. Laramie, WY 82070
800-562-4153

**Teton Village/Jackson West
KOA**
Box 38
Teton Village, WY, 83025

4 When You Have to Leave Your Pet During a Trip

As we've mentioned, our whole philosophy at petswelcome.com is to provide a safety network for people who travel with their pets. Anyone who goes on vacation with a dog, cat or bird knows that there's much more to traveling with a pet than getting to and from a pet-friendly lodging. Most travelers use the lodging simply as a place to sleep, rest and maybe eat—a base of operations, in other words, from which to go out and enjoy and explore the environs of the particular place they are visiting.

There are, however, going to be situations when you cannot take your pet with you—on a particular day trip, for example, to a national park, museum, restaurant or show. If your hotel does not permit animals to be left unattended in the room, which is the policy of many lodgings, what are you going to do? Are you going to stay in all day, order room service and watch *Beethoven* (the St. Bernard, not the composer) movies on cable with your dog? Of course not. You're going to find a way to make it work.

Until hotels have kennel facilities or in-house (or on-call) pet sitters (and we're working on these things), we suggest that you take the bull by the horns and find a kennel or pet sitter yourself (with our help, of course). Why not? Why should you wait for the lodgings of the world to come around to being sophisticated enough to realize that you need more than a pet-friendly policy to enjoy your stay? You also need pet-friendly support services and facilities. Until that time arrives, however, we think you should take advantage of pet sitters and kennels just like you would if you were at home. It makes sense to us because you are not going to be able to spend 100% of your time with your pet. That's why we've included the following listings of pet sitters and kennels. If you need their services, give them a call and make arrangements so you can get out and enjoy yourself. It's as simple as that. In *The Portable petswelcome.com* we're concerned about addressing the reality, not the novelty, of traveling with your pet. And, most likely, you'll need more than just a pet-friendly lodging.

PET SITTERS

This book is about *not* leaving your pet behind, so why are we discussing pet sitters? In the past, pet sitters have always been thought of as a way to leave your pet at home. But we look at it differently. We think pet sitters make it easier for you to take your pet *with you*. Why just use them at home? Why not take advantage of their services in the place you are visiting?

A few years ago it would have been difficult. You would have had to call long-distance information or somehow locate the Yellow Pages of the locale you were visiting. Also, pet-friendly guides typically have not included pet sitters as a resource to use on the road. But now, the advent of the Internet enables many pet sitters to be contacted as if they were local. This opens up their valuable services to people who are traveling with their pets. Now pet sitters can assist you on your trip and help make it extremely enjoyable by allowing you peace of mind when you leave your pet behind on day trips or other excursions. Instead of worrying about your pet coping alone in a new and foreign environment, you can feel assured that he's in the hands of a professional who will take extra-special care and deliver him back to you good as new.

When you are deciding on a pet sitter, the question that will arise is the same one you should ask for any service you will use on the road: How do you know the sitter is responsible and professional, given that you've had no experience with this person? Again, we highly recommend you engage the pet sitter in a phone conversation to get a sense of who they are. In general, you should ask the same questions you would if they were pet-sitting at your home. Make sure they're bonded and insured. Ask them about their experience and training, if they have any pets of their own and if they will provide references. You should give them the specifics of your situation: Tell them that you are on vacation or a business trip and then work out the details of where they would be sitting for your pet.

When you are traveling, it's probably best that the pet sitter take your pet off the lodging premises. Ideally, you should drop your pet off with the sitter, so make sure they have the facilities to take your pet. The advantage of having them take your pet is that you are more in control of the situation. First, you don't want strangers hanging out in your room; second, you'll get a better sense of who they are since you'll see where they live or work.

Once you have decided upon a sitter, tell them your pet's history and habits. Bring along food, bowls for food and water, your pet's portable kennel and a toy or blanket for comfort. Make sure you leave the telephone number of the place you'll be visiting so the sitter can reach you in case of an emergency.

The petswelcome.com Platinum Rule (*always* call ahead) applies to pet sitters. Since they are often self-employed individuals and may be harder to get in touch with than a larger business, it makes sense to try to secure one before you leave. If you cannot reach one listed in this chapter, you can also try the National Association of Professional Pet Sitters located in Mechanicsburg, Pennsylvania. They have an on-line directory at www.petsitters.org, and their phone number is 717-691-5565.

United States

ALABAMA

Home Alone Pet Sitting
Alabaster, AL 35007
205-620-9729

TEE Pet Care Services
Decatur, AL 35602
256-301-0006

Guardian Pet Care Services
Mobile, AL 36618
334-342-1845

Martin's Home Pet Care Service
Mobile, AL 36608
334-342-5033

Kitty Kare Cat & Critter Sitters
Montgomery, AL 36109
334-279-8342

Critter Sitters
Moody, AL 35004
205-995-8006

ALASKA

Lucky Dog Enterprises
Anchorage, AK 99511
907-267-9852

Eagle River Pet Care
Chugiak, AK 99567
907-688-7387

ARIZONA

From the Heart Pet Sitting
Ahwatukee Foothills, AZ 85048
480-460-0195

Lorna Salazar
Cave Creek, AZ 85331
480-595-5165

All-Heart Pet Care
Chandler, AZ 85225
480-855-4429
allheartpet@home.com

Happy Tails
Chandler, AZ 85224
480-917-9397

No Worries Pet Sitting
Chandler, AZ 85224
480-821-5946

Pooches & Plants
Chandler, AZ 85226
480-838-8468

Canyon Pet Resort
Flagstaff, AZ 86001
520-214-9324
barover@aol.com

Bark n Play Doggie Daycare
Glendale, AZ 85304
602-334-6705

Pet's Palace
Higley, AZ 85236
480-807-0339

Our Gang Pet Sitting
Litchfield Park, AZ 85340
623-386-7654

Arizona Rainbow Pet Services
Oro Valley, AZ 85737
520-572-1467

Family Pet Sitters
Phoenix, AZ 85053
602-548-7695

Cat Feathers Pet Sitting
Prescott, AZ 86303
520-778-7895

Groom Creek Doghouse
Prescott, AZ 86302
520-771-1385

Lucky Dog
Scottsdale, AZ 85260
602-369-9787

Pet Grandma and Grandpa, LLC
Scottsdale, AZ 85260
480-502-8748

Scottsdale's Finest Feline Service
Scottsdale, AZ 85258
480-922-3993

Your Pet Sitter
Scottsdale, AZ 85260
602-809-2522

Cat's Meow Pet & House Sitting Svce.
Surprise, AZ 85374
623-544-0788

Amore Animal Care
Tucson, AZ 85730
520-270-7387

Arizona Rainbow Pet Services, Etc.
Tucson, AZ 85742
520-572-1467

Hooky Beak Hotel
Tucson, AZ 85732
520-322-9865

ARKANSAS

Super Sitter
Bentonville, AR 72712
501-855-9458

CALIFORNIA

Gloria's Kritter Korner
Anaheim, CA 92807
714-779-2684
crittersitter@gobi.com

Pet & House Sitter
Bakersfield, CA 93309
661-633-3562

Robyn the Petsitter
Berkeley, CA 94709
510-524-0793

Susie's Pet Care
Beverly Hills, CA 90046
888-525-0275

ClubMutt Pet Sitting & Dog Walking
Burbank, CA 91505
818-848-9908

Scoopergirl Pet Sitting Service
Burbank, CA 91510
818-260-0781

Walking Paws and More
Capistrano Beach, CA 92624
949-729-2779

Catnips Cat Sitting
Carlsbad, CA 92009
760-633-8445

Lovey's Quality In-Your Home Pet Care
Carona, CA 92882
909-371-7689

U.S. Pet Sitters > CALIFORNIA

You Can Count on Me
Cerritos, CA 90240
562-924-9164

Judy's Pet Sitting
Claremont, CA 91711
909-626-6243

Stanlake's Home &
Pet Sitting Service
Clovis, CA 93611
559-323-9946

Apronstrings Pet Sitting
Concord, CA 94521
925-798-7621

Love Me Tender Pet Sitting
Corona, CA 92882
909-512-5380

Home Buddies Pet Sitting
Cosa Mesa, CA 92646
714-378-5925

Purrs and Wags Service
Culver City, CA 90230
310-748-7297

Tails and Whiskers
Pet Sitting
Culver City, CA 90232
310-558-3353

Critter Care of Silicon
Valley
Cupertino, CA 95014
408-241-2416

Furry Godmother
Pet Sitting
Cupertino, CA 95015
408-322-7346

Sasha Vaz
Daly City, CA 94014
415-334-2192

Walking Paws and More
Dana Point, CA 92624
949-729-2779

While Away Prof. Pet
Sitters
Del Mar, CA 92014
619-855-7387

Creature's Comfort
El Cerrito, CA 94530
510-235-8648

Your Pet's Companion
Elk Grove, CA 95758
916-422-1355

Pets Need Walkies
Encino, CA 91316
818-458-6067

Home Buddies Pet Sitting
Fountain Valley, CA 92646
714-378-5925

Prof. Pet Sitting &
Dog Walks
Fremont, CA 94539
510-656-5095

Pet Nannies
Fresno, CA 93727
559-255-9636

Caryn's Critter Sitting
Glendora, CA 91740
626-963-2447

Virginia's Pet Care Service
Glendora, CA 91740
626-335-3247

Becky's Pet Sitting
Grass Valley, CA 95945
530-273-6215

Candy's Pampered Pets
Hayward, CA 94541
510-581-8781

Home Buddies Pet Sitting
Huntington Beach, CA 92646
714-378-5925

Pacific Paws Pet Care
Huntington Beach, CA 92647
714-841-7403

In 2 Pets
La Crescenta, CA 91214
818-559-5062

Walking Paws and More
Laguna Beach, CA 92624
949-729-2779

Daisy's Doggie Daycare
Long Beach, CA 90814
562-439-9181

Pooch Pals
Long Beach, CA 90814
562-884-6005

Tails It Is Petsitting
Long Beach, CA 90804
562-434-9302

Animal House Sitter
Service
Los Alamitos, CA 90720
562-889-3337

Bon Ami Pet Sitting
Los Angeles, CA 90039
323-665-DOGS

Dog Gone Walkies
Los Angeles, CA 90046
323-654-5545

Ecco & Sonia's Petsitting
Los Angeles, CA 90046
323-658-6496

Critter Care
Los Angeles, CA
310-372-4726

I Said Sit!
Los Angeles, CA 90034
310-839-8935

Petagree Pet Sitting
Los Angeles, CA 90065
323-225-0031

Castle Watcher Home 7
Pet Care
Los Gatos, CA 95031
408-358-4140

Kaluha's Petsitting
Mission Viejo, CA 92692
949-770-7800

Country Critters Pets
Morgan Hill, CA 8\95037
408-778-5289

Cheryl's Pet Sitting
Mountain View, CA 94040
650-428-1995

Darling Little Rascals
Newport Beach, CA 92663
949-631-6026

Home Buddies Pet Sitting
Newport Beach, CA 92646
714-378-5925

Abbie's Animal Care
Oakland, CA 94611
510-382-1214

U.S. Pet Sitters > CALIFORNIA

Marcel's Pet Care
Oakland, CA 94602
510-530-0546

Mother's Love for Your Pet
Oakland, CA 94602
510-531-1954

Red Rover Pet Care
Oakland, CA 94619
510-336-0712

Mice Will Play
Pacifica, CA 94044
650-355-1472

**Marilyn Martin TLC
Pet Sitting**
Palm Springs, CA 92263
760-416-6309

Reliable Home & Pet Care
Palm Springs, CA 92262
760-778-1933

Petagree Pet Sitting
Pasadena, CA 90065
323-225-0031

**Kristi Bluhm's Home
Sitting & Small Pet Care**
Paso Robles, CA 93446
805-237-7756

Baby Love Pet Nannies
Pleasant Hill, CA 94523
925-370-6168

Pink Parrot Pet Sitting
Poway, CA 92064
858-486-4789

TLC Petsitters
Rancho Cucamonga, CA 91739
909-899-1646

**Peace of Mind Quality
Petsitting**
Redlands, CA 92373
909-793-3084

Pet & Home Sitting
Rocklin, CA 95677
916-353-9536

Anne Williams
Sacramento, CA 95820
916-455-4167

Walking Paws and More
San Clemente, CA 92624
949-729-2779

Em's Pet Patrol
San Diego, CA 92123
858-775-PETS

Jennifer's Pet Sitting
San Diego, CA 92196
858-566-6112

No Place Like Home
San Diego, CA 92110
619-222-9644

**Pawprints In Home
Pet Sitting**
San Diego, CA 92164
619-624-0360

Allan's Animals
San Francisco, CA 94112
415-587-4679
petpaljohn@yahoo.com

Animal Day Care
San Francisco, CA 94117
415-835-4747

Happy Dogs
San Francisco, CA 94110
415-648-4388

Juliette Conde-Cruz
San Francisco, CA 94110
415-263-2715

Kasara's Kritter Sitters, Inc.
San Francisco, CA 94164
415-771-0450

Kittysitter and Birdsitter
San Francisco, CA 94112
415-333-2523

Ruff 'N Ready Pet Service
San Francisco, CA 94112
415-584-4233

**Happy Campers Pet Sitting
Service**
San Jose, CA 95120
408-997-8266

Luv-N-Care
San Jose, CA 95170
408-257-2889

Furfection Pet Service
San Lorenzo, CA 94580
877-738-9255

Inside Out Pet Sitting
San Mateo, CA 94402
650-347-8277

**Fur & Feathers,
A Pet Sitting Service**
Santa Ana, CA 92706
714-972-3188

Precious Pet & Home
Santa Ana, CA 92705
714-289-8334

Toni Kimball
Santa Ana, CA 92706
714-972-3188

Auntie M Pet Sitting
Santa Clara, CA 95051
408-472-PETS

Cathy's Pet Nannies
Sherman Oaks, CA 91423
818-783-3702

Parrotdise
Soquel, CA 95073
831-457-8285

Whiskers & Paws
Stockton, CA 95206
209-467-4619

Anamooli Pet Care
Studio City, CA 91604
818-386-2916

**Buddha's Nanny Pet Sitter
Service**
Sunnyvale, CA 94086
408-730-9687

Meg's Cat Care
Thousand Oaks, CA 91360
805-492-2877

**Top Dog Walking and
Sitting**
Tiburon, CA 94920
415-435-6477

Two Dogs Pet Sitting
Valencia, CA 91355
661-255-9667

Beth Grossman
Venice, CA 90291
310-452-7194

Pets Pampered Plus
Walnut Creek, CA 94596
925-937-3197

Home Buddies Pet Sitting
Westminster, CA 92646
714-378-5925

U.S. Pet Sitters > CALIFORNIA

Mugs & Pugs
Woodland Hills, CA 91364
818-340-0842

Keeley Kritter Kare
Yucca Valley, CA 92284
760-364-1012

COLORADO

Kathy's Critterwatch
Arvada, CO 80031
303-428-6354

Absolute Critter Comfort
Aurora, CO 80014
303-338-1702

Paramount Pet Sitters
Boulder, CO 80304
303-449-6623

**Little Paws In Home
Pet Sitting Svce.**
Colorado Springs, CO 80922
719-232-6757

Spoiled Rotten Petsitting
Colorado Springs, CO 80906
719-226-1031

TLC Pet Sitting Services
Colorado Springs, CO 80918
719-265-5455

2nd String Moms
Denver, CO 80246
303-758-8370

**Bow Wow Meow
Pet Service**
Denver, CO 80207
303-388-8652

Denver Pet Sitters
Denver, CO 80248
303-430-4858

**I'll Come Over Rover
Service**
Denver, CO 80220
303-333-9747

Wags & Wiggles
Denver, CO 80210
303-777-2564

Your Best Friend's Friend
Denver, CO 80237
303-692-1140

Absolute Critter Comfort
Ft. Collins, CO 80525
970-223-1773

**PAWSitive Petsitting
Services**
Golden, CO 80402
303-807-1408

Professional Pet Sitting
Henderson, CO 80640
303-659-1926

Kitt'n Sitt'n Pet Sitting
Lakewood, CO 80227
303-980-5752

Unique Pet Care
Lakewood, CO 80232
303-969-0569

K-9s and Kats
Vail, CO 81658
970-926-0139

A TLC Pet Service
Westminster, CO 80021
303-422-4561

CONNECTICUT

PS Train Me., Inc.
Avon, CT 06001
860-675-1822

Paws & Claws, etc.
Fairfield, CT 06430
203-255-4787

Elizabeth Marshall
Guilford, CT 06437
203-453-1044

Home-Care Petsitting LLC
Monroe, CT 06468
203-371-9207

Maxi Mode
New Haven, CT 06511
203-776-3727

Pampered Pets
New Haven, CT 06513
203-789-0660

**Have No Worries
Pet Sitting Service**
Norwalk, CT 06853
203-838-5558

P.S. Train Me
West Hartford, CT 06117
860-675-1822

Paula's Pampered Pets
West Hartford, CT 6133
860-313-0570

Kennel Alternative
West Suffield, CT 06093
860-939-9131

DELAWARE

A Pet's Companion
Dover, DE 19934
302-698-0401

Leave With Peace of Mind
Dover, DE 19904
302-678-8089

**Pawsitively Purrfect
Pet Sitting**
New Castle, DE 19720
302-324-1810

Critter Care with Kathi
Smyrna, DE 19977
302-653-1587

Precious Pet Care
Smyrna, DE 19977
302-653-7297

DISTRICT OF COLUMBIA

Capitol Area Pet Care
Washington, DC 20008
202-253-3199

FurPals
Washington, DC 20024
202-488-7387

Metro Pet Pals, LLC
Washington, DC 20016
202-895-1339

Zoolatry
Washington, DC 20003
202-547-9255

FLORIDA

Linda's Pet Sitting Co.
Astatula, FL 34705
352-343-2777

**Comfortable Critters
Pet Sitters**
Boca Raton, FL 33434
561-482-1286

U.S. Pet Sitters > FLORIDA

Critter Sitters of Bonita Springs-Naples
Bonita Springs, FL 34133
941-947-8638

Holly's Expert Loving Pet-sitting Service
Captiva, FL 33957
941-472-1176

Cozy Critters Pet Sitting Service
Cooper City, FL 33025
954-704-9145

Pawprints Pet Services
Cooper City, FL 33330
954-252-8510

Jo Ann's Pet Sitting
Coral Gables, FL 33134
305-445-5461

Safe and Secure Creature Comforts
Davie, FL 33314
954-476-0097

Creature Comforts
Deerfield Beach, FL 33442
954-428-5648

Paws-itively Affordable Pet Care
DeLand, FL 32724
904-740-8677

Harley's House Pet Sitting Svces
Delray Beach, FL 33482
561-498-9373

Regina's Pet Sitting Service
Eustis, FL 32726
352-483-3326

KD's Paws-n-Claws Pet Resort
Fort Myers, FL 33905
941-693-6767

Kathy's Critter Care
Fort Pierce, FL 34949
561-466-0971

ALL Pets Sitting Service
Fort Walton Beach, FL 32549
850-243-2882

Botelho's Critter Sitters
Ft. Myers, FL 33990
941-458-5645

Safe At Home Pet Care
Hernando, FL 34442
342-746-6230

Walk'in Paws Pet Sitters
Lehigh Acres, FL 33972
941-368-4663

La Pet Au Pair
Longboat Key, FL 34228
941-383-0049

Blue's Pet Sitting Service
Merritt Island, FL 32952
321-454-4094

Remington Canine Resorts
Merritt Island, FL 32953
321-459-0105

Fin, Fur & Feather Pet Sitting
Miami, FL 33257
305-971-6559

Rainbow Pet Sitting
Miami, FL 33196
305-388-3434

Home Alone
Naples, FL 34116
941-352-2218

Blunk's Pet Services
North Port, FL 34287
941-426-3503

The Sitter
Ocala-Marion Cnty, FL 34489
352-236-7758

Caros Critter Care
Orlando, FL 32801
407-681-2627

Cats @ Home
Orlando, FL 32808
407-491-6281

Dog Day Afternoon
Orlando, FL 32806
407-835-9200

Luv'n Care Pet Sitting Service
Orlando, FL 32819
407-290-1760

Paws and Claws Pet Sitting
Orlando, FL 32817
407-380-2430

Pet Play Care
Orlando, FL 32837
407-855-6409

Whisker Watchers Pet Sitting Svce.
Orlando, FL 32869
407-903-0621

A Cat's Best Friend
Oviedo, FL 32765
407-359-6996

Litter Sitters
Palm Coast, FL 32137
904-445-5333

Critter Crazy Pet Sitting
Palmetto, FL 34221
941-722-6885

Jennifer Winston
Pembroke Pines, FL 33024
954-435-1596

Happy Paws Pet Sitters
Pensacola, FL 32526
850-941-1193

PetCheck by Karen Hardison
Pierce, FL 34982
561-466-1287

Ask Mark Pet Sitting
Redington Shores, FL 33708
727-398-2600

Holly's Expert Loving Pet-sitting Service
Sanibel Island, FL 33957
941-472-1176

All Critters Pet Sitters
Sarasota, FL 34208
941-714-0770

Doggone Purrfect Pet Care
St,. Petersburg, FL 33734
727-522-8506

Annie the Animal Nanny, Inc.
St. Petersburg, FL 33712
727-865-0004

Creature Comfort Pet Sitting
St. Petersburg, FL 33713
813-892-3467

U.S. Pet Sitters > FLORIDA

**Fins, Feathers & Fur
Pet Sitting Service**
Tampa, FL 33612
813-931-1882

**Peace of Mind Pet Sitting
of Tampa**
Tampa, FL 33624
813-961-0609

Brevard County Petsitting
Titusville, FL 32796
321-267-5790

Easy Livin'
Vero Beach, FL 32968
561-770-3434

Angelic Pet Sitters
West Palm Beach, FL 33409
561-650-0305

Claws & Paws, Inc.
West Palm Beach, FL 33401
561-655-8232

Cari's Critter Care
Winter Park, FL 32792
407-415-1567

**Mother Hubbard's
Critter Care**
Winter Park, FL 32790
407-629-6658

GEORGIA

ManyPaws
Atlanta, GA 30307
404-378-6935

Love 'Em and Leave 'Em
Avondale Estates, GA 30002
678-469-8679

Debra Townsend-Cole
Canton, GA 30115
770-345-5740

Latch Key Pets
Decatur, GA 30030
404-373-3552

Bed & Biscuit
Duluth, GA 30096
770-232-3035

Reigning Cats & Dogs
Duluth, GA 30096
770-232-3035

**Kit-n-Kaboodle Pet Sitting
Svce.**
Hiram, GA 30141
770-656-6083

Noah's Ark Pet Sitters
Savannah, GA 31410
912-961-1725

Kathy's Critters
Smyrna, GA 30082
770-436-9998

The Pet Lady
Smyrna, GA 30082
678-596-PETS

Purrrs & Ruffs Pet Sitters
Tucker, GA 30084
770-938-7499

HAWAII

**Cuddle Time Pet Care
Services**
Honolulu, HI 96823
808-533-6069

IDAHO

**Pawswatch Professional
Pet Care**
Boise, ID 83704
208-377-2881

ILLINOIS

Expert In-Home Pet Care
Brookfield, IL 60513
708-485-8802

**All Creatures Pet Care and
the Tag Team**
Chicago, IL 60657
312-388-4155

Heaven Sent Pet Care
Chicago, IL 60201
847-332-2162

**Homebuddies Pet Sitting
Service**
Chicago, IL 60603
773-205-3835

Lucky Dog Pet Service
Chicago, IL 60613
773-327-6625

North Shore Pet Sitters
Chicago, IL 60660
773-334-3455

**Animal Angel's Professional
Pet Sitting Svce.**
East Moline, IL 61244
309-755-5510

DogMa
Highland Park, IL 60035
847-432-7957

Pet Wise
Island Lake, IL 60042
847-487-1651

Home Safe Pet Service
McHenry, IL 60050
815-363-1337

Krista Green
Skokie, IL 60076
847-674-5807

Lisa Holeton
South Holland, IL 60473
708-339-5414

INDIANA

**Bowders Buddies
Pet Visiting Service**
Boonville, IN 47601
812-897-4253

Precious Paws
Carmel, IN 46032
317-818-3489

Personal Pet Care
Cedar Lake, IN 46303
219-718-5318

At Your Service Unlimited
Fort Wayne, IN 46898
219-426-6732

Heavenly Hound
Franklin, IN 46131
317-346-6502

**Fussy Felines &
Pampered Pooches**
Indianapolis, IN 46201
317-353-8294

Stephanie Koutek
Indianapolis, IN 46219
317-890-1125

**Paws and More Pet Sitting
Service**
New Albany, IN 47150
812-941-0048

U.S. Pet Sitters > MICHIGAN

Furry Friends & Co.
Washington, IN 47501
812-254-8985

IOWA

**Cruisin' Creatures
Pet Nanny**
Clive, IA 50325
515-222-3156

**Noah's Ark: Mobile
Pet Services**
Marshalltown, IA 50158
515-752-6096

Sarah & Troy's Pet Resort
Monticello, IA 42310
319-465-6362

Aunt T's Critter Care
North Liberty, IA 52317
319-665-2910

KANSAS

Four Paws Pet Sitters
Olathe, KS 66062
913-768-1173

Pride House & Pet Sitting
Prairie Village, KS 66208
913-362-5593

Laura's Prof. Pet Sitting
Salina, KS 67401
785-827-2401

Animal Play Works
Wichita, KS 67211
316-263-6218

Guardian Angel Pet Sitting
Wichita, KS 67218
316-686-4402

Paw-Pals Pet Sitting PLUS
Wichita, KS 67206
316-258-7885

KENTUCKY

Happy Tails
Lexington, KY 40517
606-266-9815

Top Hat Pet Sitting Service
Louisville, KY
502-722-9766

LOUISIANA

Critter Care of Baton Rouge
Baron Rouge, LA 70806
225-923-2273

Carina's Critter Care
New Orleans, LA 70115
504-896-CARE

Pet's Best Friends Pet Sitters
Slidel, LA 70459
504-641-PETS

MAINE

Solitaire Care Pet Sitting
Gorham, ME 04038
207-893-2069

Pets at Home
Saco, ME 04072
207-283-2873

MARYLAND

Paw Pals Pet Sitting
Baltimore, MD 21236
410-931-7166

T.L.C. Pet Services By Kim
Baltimore, MD 21239
410-433-2351

Hooves & Paws Pet Sitting
Bel Air, MD 21014
410-838-9108

Happy Paws Pet Sitting
Germantown, MD 20874
301-515-5800

Pet Patrol, Inc.
Hunt Valley, MD 21030
410-472-0709

**Spoiled Rott'n Pet Sitting
Service**
New Market, MD 21774
301-607-6470

MASSACHUSETTS

Paladin Pets
Boston, MA 02127
617-448-7940

Ms. Paws Pet Sitting Services
Brighton, MA 02135
617-787-1386

Peterkins Pets
Brookline, MA 02135
617-739-5054

Denise
Burlington, MA 01803
781-273-3208

Mary Ann Mroz
Cambridge, MA 02140
617-492-7398

Professional Pet Care
Haverhill, MA 01832
978-373-3768

Nature's Care, Inc.
Marstons Mills, MA 2648
508-420-6050

Pawfection Pet Services
North Andover, MA 01845
978-321-5047

Marie Lillian Plasse
Springfield, MA 01104
413-731-5342

TLC Pet Haven
Sutton, MA 01590
508-865-3180

Happy Pets
Waltham, MA 02451
781-893-0719

Paws & Claws
Waltham, MA 02452
781-894-7297

Happy Paws Pet Service
Westford, MA 01886
978-970-1602

Precious Pets
Weymouth, MA 02189
781-340-5353

MICHIGAN

**Kitty Care Pet Sitting
Service**
Buchanan, MI 49107
616-695-1159

Creature Comforts
Clinton Township, MI 48036
810-463-3436

Love Your Pet Pet Sitting
Stevensville, MI 49127
616-556-0466

Love n'Care
Wyandotte, MI 48192
734-282-2454

MINNESOTA

Adventures in Animal Sitting
Hutchinson, MN 55350
320-234-5987

Hounds Cyber Lounge
Minneapolis, MN 55408
612-968-3647

B. Reeder Pet Sitter
St. Paul, MN 55104
651-645-7894

MISSISSIPPI

Happy Pets
Tupelo, MS 38804
662-842-3207

MISSOURI

Pampered Pet-Sitting
Columbia, MO 65205
573-256-PETS

Irma Yokota
Hazelwood, MO 63042
314-921-7933

Critter Sitters of K.C.
Kansas City, MO 64119
816-454-8862

Peace of Mind
Kansas City, MO 64190
816-699-0820

For Pets' Sake Prof. Pet Sitting Svces
Mexico, MO 65265
573-582-0680

PetMom, Inc.
Saint Louis, MO 63132
314-872-3632

Tucker's Friends, A Pet Sitting Service
St. Charles, MO 63304
636-978-9999

Pet Nannies
West Plains, MO 65755
417-256-6909

MONTANA

Pet Pro Pet Sitting
Billings, MT 59101
406-259-3154

NEBRASKA

Walking Four Paws
Omaha, NE 68144
402-891-1179

NEVADA

Happy at Home Pet Care Service
Las Vegas, NV 89123
702-269-9697

It's A Godsend
Las Vegas, NV 89128
702-804-7167

The Pet Guardian
Las Vegas, NV 89130
702-645-1177

The Canine Club
Sparks, NV 89431
775-331-0667

NEW HAMPSHIRE

Country Animal Tender, Ltd.
Deerfield, NH 03037
603-463-7388

Country Animal Tender, Ltd.
Portsmouth, NH 03037
603-463-7388

NEW JERSEY

Happytails Pet Sitting Svce.
Asbury, NJ 08802
908-387-9255

No Place Like Home Pet Sitters
Clifton, NJ 07012
973-458-1616

No Bones About It Pet Sitting
East Windsor, NJ 08520
609-371-4845

Kate's Kitty Jungle
Edison, NJ 08820
732-548-5599

All Creatures Great & Small
Elizabeth, NJ 07208
908-436-1381

Pampered Pets, Inc.
Hackensack, NJ 7601
201-996-1646

Jodi's Critter Sitter Service
Haddon Heights, NJ 08035
856-547-8360

4 Paws Nanny Service
Hoboken, NJ 07030
201-656-0178

Safe At Home Pet & Home Watch Services
Manahawkin, NJ 8050
609-597-6005

Pampurred Pet Care
North Bergen, NJ 07047
201-868-8610

NEW MEXICO

Ears to Rears Prof. Pet Svces.
Albuquerque, NM 87193
505-899-5390

Pet Nanny Southwest, LLC
Albuquerque, NM 87191
505-249-4108

NEW YORK

Happy Tails 2 You Pet Sitting
Albany, NY 12203
518-456-0438

Jan Tilley Pet Sitting
Astoria, NY 11106
718-728-4794

Alyssa's Pet Sitting Service
Bellmore, NY 11710
516-826-4021

Woofs 'n Whiskers, Inc
Brooklyn, NY 11231
718-237-0298

For Pet Sake
Colden, NY 14033
716-941-8965

U.S. Pet Sitters > NORTH CAROLINA

The All Pet Sitter
Dix Hills, NY 11746
516-667-0477

Sally's Kat & K-9 Kare
East Patchogue, NY 11772
631-654-3343

Kristen Gentile
Farmingdale, NY 11735
516-756-2989

The Pet Minder
Farmingdale, NY 11735
516-694-5814

Pet Sitters Club, Inc.
Great Neck, NY 11021
516-466-5617

**Mariane's Guardian Angel
Pet Sitting**
Kings Park, NY 11754
631-544-0914

Critters Choice
Latham, NY 12110
518-783-2273

Walk the Dog Services
Marcellus, NY 13108
315-673-2766

Candy's Critter Sitters
Mt. Vernon, NY 10552
914-667-MEOW

**Bed & Biscuit
Doggie Day Care**
New York, NY 10003
212-475-6064

Doggie TLC
New York, NY 10019
212-956-6767

Family Affair Pet Care
New York, NY 10028
212-249-0839

**Kasper's Friendly
Pet Sitters**
New York, NY 10028
877-966-6266

**Michelle's Pied Piper
Pet Services**
New York, NY 10036
212-245-4704

Pampered Pets, Inc.
New York, NY 10021
212-772-2181

Puddles Pet Service
New York, NY 10128
212-410-7338

The Able Pet Sitter
North Salem, NY 10560
914-669-4309

Wag'n Tail, Inc.
Poughquag, NY 12570
914-724-4294

Adventure Pet Sitting
Rochester, NY 14612
716-663-6114

Always There Pet Care
Rochester, NY 14626
716-227-2587
fluffypaw@aol.com

HomeBuddies Pet Care
Rochester, NY 14609
716-288-4044

Kritter Kare Pet Services
Rochester, NY 14625
716-889-7270

Saratoga Pet Sitters
Saratoga Springs, NY 12866
518-584-9055

Feathers n' Paws Pet Sitting
Schenectady, NY 12304
518-461-1929

Paws R Us Pet Sitters
Schenectady, NY 12306
518-346-7988

Hooves, Paws, and Claws
Smithtown, NY 11787
516-816-4398

**Safe & Sound Cat Sitting
Service**
Syracuse, NY 13215
315-498-9567

Dog & Co.
Williamsburg, NY 11211
212-982-3138

NORTH CAROLINA

**At Your Bark & Call
Pet Sitting Svce.**
Asheville, NC 28806
828-275-5345

High Country Critter Sitter
Boone, NC 28607

While You're Away
Cary, NC 27511
919-468-0832

Pet Net
Charlotte, NC 28227
704-573-7399

Tetrapods Pet Sitting
Charlotte, NC 28218
704-358-1244

JR's Pet Sitting
Cornelius, NC 28031
704-895-7703

Lakeside Sitters
Cornelius, NC 28031
704-895-0540

Custer's Critter Care
Danville, NC 27305
336-388-4498

Peace of Mind
Franklinton, NC 27525
704-867-8786

Zoo Care
Greensboro, NC 27455
336-545-0202

Lexington Area Pet Sitting
Lexington, NC 27292
336-224-2678

Pet Breaks
Matthews, NC 28105
704-849-9495

Canines, Cats, & Critters
Midland, NC 28107
704-753-4722

FurBabies Pet Care
Morrisville, NC 27560
919-649-4263

Kildaire Cat 'N Canary
Morrisville, NC 27511
919-481-6937

Barks & Bites
Raleigh, NC 27604
919-876-0385

U.S. Pet Sitters > OHIO

OHIO

Cabral's Pet Sitting
Cincinnati, OH 45238
513-451-5200

Beth Bitterman
Cleveland, OH 44121
216-381-9274

The Pet Au Pair
Cleveland Heights, OH 44121
216-291-1498

**Complete Creature
Comfort Care**
Columbus, OH 43235
614-530-7387

Debbie Strine
Conneaut, OH 44030
440-599-7469

**Tender Loving Care
Pet Companions**
Hilliard, OH 43026
614-527-TLC1

PetSitters
Mentor, OH 44060
440-289-2570

All Petz R Stars
Milford, OH 45150
513-575-2883

Pam's Pet Care
Newark, OH 43055
740-366-6838

Petz Pluz
Springfield, OH 45501
937-525-9005

**Adorable Pet Sitting
Service**
Toledo, OH 43613
419-472-7834

OKLAHOMA

Sheryl Petterson
Canadian, OK 74425
918-339-2914

**There's No Place Like
Home**
Tulsa, OK 74104
918-712-7124

OREGON

**Creature Comforts
Petsitting**
Beaverton, OR 97007
503-848-5956

Kozy Kitty
Beaverton, OR 97006
503-784-9670

All Critter Pet Sitter
Hillsboro, OR 97124
503-846-1212

Portland Pet Pampering
Lake Oswego, OR 97034
503-635-1346

Animal Nannies
Portland, OR 97006
503-439-6612

DayCare for Doggy
Portland, OR 97220
503-251-9001

**Juli Norman K-9 to 5
Pet Sitting**
Portland, OR 97225
503-244-0054

Portland Pet Pampering
Portland, OR 97206
503-788-1411

**Professional Pet &
House Sitting Svces**
Portland, OR 97207
503-224-6320

Anglin4Prfekshn
Weston, OR 97886
541-566-9412

PENNSYLVANIA

Precious Paws
Ambler, PA 19002
215-619-4676

Noah's Ark Pet Services
Bristol, PA 19007
215-781-0554

Pet Watchers
Carlisle, PA 17013
717-249-3158

**Furry Buddies In-Home
Service**
Erdenheim, PA 19038
215-836-2738

Heavenly Critters
Hanover, PA 17331
717-630-8870

Benno's Errand Services
Harrisburg, PA 17106
717-236-6480

Vicky's Treasures
Lancaster, PA 17601
717-560-0221

Janet Furler
New Freedom, PA 17349
717-2271142

Goode Times Pet Sitting
New Kensington, PA 15068
724-335-7768

C&L Pet Sitters
Oakdale, PA 15071
412-788-2661

Loving Pet Care Services
Philadelphia, PA 19111
215-342-6114

A Preferred Pet Solution
Pittsburgh, PA 15216
412-343-0133

**Marino's Suburban
Petsitters**
Port Vue, PA 15133
412-673-8748

The Country Zoo
Wayneboro, PA 17268
717-765-0583

PUERTO RICO

Exor M. Rodriguez
San Juan, PR 00926
787-765-2427

RHODE ISLAND

Pete & the Pet Sitter
Cranston, RI 02905
401-941-1866

Petscort Services
Middletown, RI 02842
401-841-5330

U.S. Pet Sitters > TEXAS

SOUTH CAROLINA

The Paddy Waggin'
Chapin, SC 29036
803-345-9491

The Animal Nannies
Charleston, SC 29407
843-573-9792

Carolina Pet Sitters
Columbia, SC 29223
803-865-6381

Pet Tender
Greenville, SC 29607
864-787-7882

Purrs and Wags Sitters
Greenville, SC 29615
864-895-7297

Mutt Palace
Summerville, SC 29485
843-875-5397

**Pawsitively Pampered
Pet Sitting**
Sumter, SC 29152
803-499-1929

TENNESSEE

**Critter's Pet &
Horse Sitting**
Collierville, TN 38027
901-877-0330

Pet Chaperone
Cordova, TN 38018
901-752-5610

**HAV-A-PET Pet Sitting
Service**
Jefferson County, TN 37820
865-475-9199

Gina's Pet Sitting Service
Knoxville, TN 37950
865-281-9745

Miranda's Petopia
Memphis, TN 38109
901-789-9363

**No Place Like Home:
Pet Sitting**
Oliver Springs, TN 37840
865-435-7328

TEXAS

The Critter Corner
Addison, TX 75001
214-497-5061

Happy Tails Pet Tending
Allen, TX 75002
972-442-5366

**Personal Pet & Home Care,
Inc.**
Allen, TX 75002
972-747-8118

Kenary Kennels
Andrews, TX 79714
915-524-9245

**Paws Prints Pet Sitting
Service**
Arlington, TX 76003
817-483-8272

Pets & Plants
Arlington, TX 76094
817-466-0441

**Second Nature Pet Care
Svcs.**
Arlington, TX 76001
817-466-2817

Your Pet's Choice
Arlington, TX 76016
817-496-0610

A La Carte Pet Sitting
Austin, TX 78746
512-327-7814

Alexander's Particular Pets
Austin, TX 78704
512-445-6507

Animaluv Pet Sitting
Austin, TX 78729
512-918-9144

**Austin Dog Adventures—
Cats Too**
Austin, TX 78731
512-467-6101

**Guardian Angel House
& Pet Sitting**
Austin, TX 78704
512-443-3907

Mary's Pet Care
Austin, TX 78651
512-255-5983

Pet Mom
Carrollton, TX 75006
972-418-1074

Pets R People 2
Carrollton, TX 75007
972-245-0606

**Town N Country
Pet Sitting**
Cedar Creek, TX 78612
512-303-4288

Rebecca Hill
Cumby, TX 75433
903-994-2565

**American Pet Sitters
'N More**
Cypress, TX 77429
281-955-6116

Just Like Mom
Dallas, TX 75229
214-357-8880

Your Professional Pet Sitter
Dallas, TX 75235
972-446-1496

Texoma Critter Sitter
Denison, TX 75021
903-465-4265

Blue Ribbon Pet Sitters
Flower Mount, TX 75028
214-513-8709

Linda Wilson
Friendswood, TX 77546
281-482-3878

Happy@Home Pet Sitting
Garland, TX 75042
972-485-1861

Murphy's Paw Petsitting
Grand Prairie, TX 75052
972-660-1579

Williams Pet Watchers
Harlingen, TX 78552
956-428-0095

Amy Vandermeer Allen
Houston, TX 77074
713-541-0325

Cat Care by Carole
Houston, TX 77062
281-480-5481

Leigh Ann's Pet Sitting
Houston, TX 77007
713-869-5559

Pampered Paws Petsitting
Houston, TX 77057
713-784-5873

Pet Pals
Houston, TX 77040
713-849-4654

Pet Sitters 'N More
Houston, TX 77065
281-955-6116

Tails Wil-Wag
Houston, TX 77088
713-702-3603

**Tender Loving Care
Pet Sitters**
Houston, TX 77027
713-828-7762

Caring Carrie's Sit-A-Pet
Kemah, TX 77565
281-559-2858

**Doggies Day Out
with Norma**
Mesquite, TX 75189
972-288-8578

Andrea's Pettenders
Plano, TX 75074
972-422-4634

Cuddle & Shuttle
Plano, TX 75024
972-202-1273

Pet Sitting, Etc.
Richardson, TX 75083
972-385-PETS

A Pet's Day In
Rockwall, TX 75032
972-771-1698

**Companion Keepers
Cat Sitting**
San Antonio, TX 78280
210-545-5333

Four Furry Feet Pet Sitting
San Antonio, TX 78247
210-834-4688

Many Paws Too, Pet Sitting
San Antonio, TX 78212
210-844-7172

**Shelley's Pet Care &
House Sitting Svce.**
San Antonio, TX 78250
210-543-1254

Cathy's Critter Care
San Antonio, TX 78148
210-945-8940

Guardian Pet Sitters
The Colony, TX 75056
972-625-5272

**Barkington Inn &
Pet Resort**
Webster, TX 77598
281-338-PAWS

UTAH

Barbara Padlo
Ogden, UT 84412
801-782-4860

VIRGINIA

Amy's Pet Care
Alexandria, VA 22315
703-786-8371

Ann Shack
Alexandria, VA 22313
703-837-1120

Extra Hours Pet Care
Alexandria, VA 22315
703-541-2129

Susan Slaughter
Arlington, VA 22201
703-527-4719

Home-Tender Pet Sitting
Chesapeake, VA 23322
757-547-2804

Ark Petsitter
Culpeper, VA 22701
540-547-3556

Fur, Feathers, and Fins
Fairfax, VA 22030
703-967-4378

Privileged Pets
Fairfax, VA 22030
703-904-7387

Petsittin' LLC
Glen Allen, VA 23060
804-261-1722

Beth's & Donna's Pet Care
Manassas, VA 20110
703-368-3782

Love Thy Pets
Spotsylvania, VA 22553
540-710-8880

Hop-N-Go Services
Virginia Beach, VA 23456
757-427-6320

VIP Pet Sitting
Virginia Beach, VA 23450
757-467-3326

WASHINGTON

DooLittle's Pet Care
Arlington, WA 98223
360-435-4601

Harbor Home Watch
Blaine, WA 98230
360-371-6259

Saye Pet Sitting
Bothell, WA 98021
425-487-1697

For Your Pet's Sake LLC
Ellensburg, WA 98926
509-925-2114

Pampurred Pet Care
Forks, WA 98331
360-374-7710

Deb's Creature Comfort
North Everett, WA 98252
360-691-5992

Southpaw Pet Sitting
Rancho Cucamonga, WA 99203
509-455-4339

Go Dog Go
Redmond, WA 98052
425-885-4340

Happy Camper Pet Service
Seattle, WA 98177
206-784-5291

Loving Care Petsitting
Seattle, WA 98122
206-275-0210

Pets Are People Too
Seattle, WA 98126
206-938-5450

U.S. Pet Sitters > WISCONSIN

Pooch Au Pair
Seattle, WA 98199
206-285-3794

Sam's Pet & Home Services
Seattle, WA 98125
206-417-2820

Seattle Pet Day Care
Seattle, WA 98145
206-529-1054

The Tail Wag
Seattle, WA 98136
206-935-3320

Confident Care
Snohomish, WA 98296
425-402-7869

Pawsitive Pet Sitting
Spokane, WA 99202
509-624-7297

Southpaw Pet Sitting
Spokane, WA 99203
509-455-4339

Whisker Watchers
Spokane, WA 99216
509-922-1900

The Pet Palace
Tacoma, WA 98404
253-474-5646
tppalace@tacomaclick.net

Pet Watch, Inc.
Vancouver, WA 98662
360-944-9519

Pets at Home
Veradale, WA 99037
509-927-1707

WISCONSIN

Pet Care Plus
Appleton, WI 54911
920-739-3082

Home Sweet Home Pet Sitting
Lake Geneva, WI 53147
262-275-0155

Auntie Ann's Pampered Pet Care
Madison, WI 53714
608-241-4514

Grandma Kitty's Kritter Kare
Muskego, WI 53150
262-679-7283

Home Alone Pet Sitting
Oregon, WI 53575
608-455-2620

Paw-fect Pet Sitters
Oregon, WI 53575
608-835-5748

Pawprints Professional Pet Sitters
Waukesha, WI 53187
262-544-0659

Mystic Pet Motel
Waupun, WI 53963
920-324-2798

Canada

ALBERTA

Hawkeye's Home Sitters
Edmonton, AB T5E 4A6
780-473-4825

It's A Dog's House
Spruce Grove, AB T7Y 1C1
780-470-0801

BRITISH COLUMBIA

Walks N Wags Pet Care
Vancouver, BC V6J 5C2
604-809-9247

Leashes
West Vancouver, BC V7S 1S2
604-723-3647

Puppy Zone Dog Day Care
Whistler, BC V0N 1B4
604-905-6705

MANITOBA

J.B. Pet Sitting
Winnipeg, MB R3M 1B4
204-791-0995

NEW BRUNSWICK

Kelly's Pet Boarding
Hampton, NB E0G 1Z0
506-832-7520

ONTARIO

KWK9 Services & Doggy Daycare
Kitchener, ON N2G 1M3
519-635-5959

T. H. Kim
Markham, ON L6C 1W3
905-887-5907

PurrBalls for Feline's Sake
Ottawa, ON K2B 6Z9
613-828-1399

The Canine Empire
Toronto, ON M1N 1T9
416-264-0741

Walkabout Services
Windsor, ON N9J 1C1
519-734-7787

QUEBEC

Kritters Kompanion
Montreal, PQ H3J 1C9
514-933-3398

Paws & Pals Professional Pet Sitters
Montreal, PQ H4A 3B3
514-481-5356

SASKATCHEWAN

Two Paws Up Pet Services
Saskatoon, SK S7T 1A2
306-477-2355

KENNELS

Obviously, the difference between using your regular kennel at home and one on the road is familiarity. Most likely you trust and are pleased with the kennel you use at home based on your numerous experiences with it. But how do you know if a kennel you've never used before is a good one? If it were local, you could visit it to experience firsthand the facilities before leaving your pet there. However, this usually isn't possible if it's a place far from your home.

If you plan on using a kennel in the place you'll be visiting, you should call the kennel ahead of time and ask to speak to the owners or operators. Ask them questions that will tell you if they are forthright and proud of their facility or if they are afraid of close scrutiny.

For example, you might inquire if you'd be allowed to tour the facility. This seems like a simple request. If they have a "no visitors" policy, you might conclude that they're trying to hide something. However, this is not always the case. It might actually mean that they are very conscientious. Many kennels don't allow visitors in with the animals because some may react badly to strangers, which could cause undue anxiety, or even injury, to the animals. Also, visitors may carry harmful bacteria or viruses into the kennel.

So if you are told that you cannot visit the facilities where the animals are housed, it's your job to determine why. At the very least, however, they should have some kind of viewing window so that you'd be able to see where your pet is staying. Also, ask them about references and check with the local Better Business Bureau to see if they've had any meaningful complaints filed against them.

You should also ask the kennel operator about the design of the kennel. Find out about drinking water and feeding procedures. Does it have indoor/outdoor runs? Are the pets kept inside, exclusively? What is the exercise routine? Do they have a veterinarian on premises? If your pet is taking medication, find our their policy: Will the kennel administer the medicine?

You will also need to inquire, directly, about many of the things that are obvious to your senses when visiting a kennel. You should be concerned about temperature control (within comfortable limits), ventilation (good with no drafts), lighting (comfortable levels with no direct sunlight), sleeping quarters (divided from other animals; clean and dry and roomy enough to stand up in and turn around). While this sounds like an overwhelming amount of information to acquire over the phone, we think that after only a few minutes of conversation you'll have what you need to make a reasonably informed decision.

Also, if you are big on accreditation, you can check to see if the kennel is a member of the American Boarding Kennels Association (ABKA). ABKA is a nonprofit association for the pet boarding industry in the United States and around the world. ABKA offers education seminars and accreditation to its members, who are supposed to follow a code of ethics and Bill of Rights for Boarded Pets that has been prescribed by ABKA. You might ask if the kennel has been awarded the Certified Kennel Operator designation, which would mean that it has been inspected and, according to the ABKA, has "met over 200 standards of excellence." It's important to understand that it isn't true that every member kennel will be fine—or that nonparticipating kennels won't be top-notch—but it's one more check on a long list that you can make.

Our Platinum Rule applies here, too: *Always* call ahead. If you are thinking about leaving your pet in a kennel while you're away, it's always smart to investigate one before you leave. If you cannot find a listing in this chapter, you can check out the website of the ABKA mentioned above (www.abka.com) to look for their member kennels. Their phone number is 719-667-1600, and they are located in Colorado Springs, Colorado.

United States

ALABAMA

Shelby Kennels
Alabaster, AL
205-664-3463

**Pet'm and Bed'm
Pet Motel**
Anniston, AL
205-238-8700

Bluefield Kennels
Bay Minette, AL
334-937-1618

Cahaba Valley Animal Inn
Birmingham, AL
205-980-0079

Pet Hotel in Rocky Ridge
Birmingham, AL
205-823-3898

Millerhof Kennels
Columbiana, AL
205-669-7174

TEE Pet Care Services
Decatur, AL
256-301-0006

Holiday Pet Resort
Dothan, AL
334-794-9248

Bud's Country Kennel
Enterprise, AL
334-393-3544

Parker's Kounty Kennel
Foley, AL
334-970-3647

**Wetonka Kennel &
Pet Motel**
Harvest, AL
205-851-9817

Kirsten's Kennels
Huntsville, AL
205-828-9006

Paws & Claws Pet Resort
Huntsville, AL
205-882-0219

Timber Run Kennel
Loxley, AL
334-964-7501

The Kennel Alternative
Montgomery, AL
334-260-8089

Harvard's K-9 Center
Opelika, AL
334-298-0414

Anna's Kennel
Piedmont, AL
205-447-2799

Canine Country Club
Theodore, AL
334-653-8926

**Kirsten's Professional
Dog Training**
Toney, AL
205-828-5397

Gunsmoke Kennels
Union Springs, AL
334-738-4642

Dog Gone Resort
Vinemont, AL
205-734-4256

ALASKA

Wuffda Kennels
Anchor Point, AK
907-235-3990

Coshoks Canine Castle
Anchorage, AK
907-345-4402

**VCA East Anchorage
Boarding Kennels**
Anchorage, AK
907-337-1562

Dog Domain Kennels
Eagle River, AK
907-694-2109

Chelsea's Kennels
Fairbanks, AK
907-457-7474

Galamar Boarding Kennel
Gakona, AK
907-822-3634

Big Dog Bed & Breakfast
Juneau, AK
907-790-2244

Lalasa Kennels
Kenai, AK
907-776-8565

**Redgate Boarding &
Training**
Kodiak, AK
907-487-2731

**Hidden Valley Ranch
& Kennels**
North Pole, AK
907-488-9414

Kathy's Boarding Kennels
North Pole, AK
907-488-6225

Ken Mar Kennels
Valdez, AK
907-835-4326

Great Land Kennels
Wasilla, AK
907-745-5380

Mounsey Mt. Idak Kennels
Wasilla, AK
907-376-9126

ARIZONA

**Mather's Sleepy Hollow
Kennels**
Casa Grande, AZ
520-836-3663

Kennel Care
Chandler, AZ
602-940-0066

Canine Country Club
Cottonwood, AZ
520-639-1624

**Cinder Hills Boarding
Kennel**
Flagstaff, AZ
602-526-3812

Critter Watch
Glendale, AZ
602-937-0075

Kelly Kennels
Golden Valley, AZ
520-565-3240

U.S. Kennels > ARIZONA

Fred Harvey Kennel
Grand Canyon, AZ
602-638-2631

**Critter Haven
Boarding Kennels**
Kingman, AZ
520-753-3620

Novak Animal Care Center
Lake Havasu City, AZ
520-855-0588

Paradise Kennels
Marana, AZ
520-682-3132

**Arizona Pet
Boarding Kennels**
Mesa, AZ
602-832-3631

Kohl's Ranch Vacation Club
Payson, AZ
520-478-5099

**A Bar A Doggie Dude
Ranch**
Phoenix, AZ
602-943-1501

All Star Kennel
Phoenix, AZ
602-276-2215

Bethany West Kennels
Phoenix, AZ
602-242-1745

Canine Country Club
Phoenix, AZ
602-244-8171

Doggie Dude Ranch
Phoenix, AZ
602-943-1501

**Homestead Training
Kennels**
Phoenix, AZ
602-992-2205

**Kennel Alternative North
Valley**
Phoenix, AZ
602-869-8881

**Rising Moon
Boarding Kennel**
Phoenix, AZ
602-788-3080

Desert Dog Rancho
Quartzsite, AZ
520-927-5528

Raintree Pet Resort
Scottsdale, AZ
602-991-3371

Scottsdale Pet Hotel
Scottsdale, AZ
602-947-9636

All American Kennel
Somerton, AZ
520-627-1467

Maroco Kennels
Somerton, AZ
520-627-8343

Sun City Pet Lodge
Sun City, AZ
602-972-4995

Animal Care Center
Tempe, AZ
602-565-8352

**University Boarding Kennel
& Veterinary Hospital**
Tempe, AZ
602-968-9275

Animal Inn
Tucson, AZ
520-797-2914

Bird Dog Kennels
Tucson, AZ
520-762-9020

Kanine Kennels
Tucson, AZ
520-750-1501

Pet Hotel Plus #1
Tucson, AZ
520-323-2275

Pet Motel
Tucson, AZ
520-887-7131

Wiseman Boarding Kennel
Tucson, AZ
520-296-2388

**King of the Mountain
Kennels**
White Mountain Lake, AZ
520-537-4988

ARKANSAS

**North Arkansas Boarding
Kennel**
Ash Flat, AR
870-994-7352

Christy Acres Kennel
Benton, AR
501-778-2781

Webb Footed Kennels
Bono, AR
870-972-0179

J Lee Kennel
Cabot, AR
501-843-9313

Bowman Kennels
Camden, AR
870-836-8754

Wee Pals Pet Inn
Fort Smith, AR
501-782-0471

Pet Haven
Gassville, AR
870-430-5151

Flying O Kennels
Heber Springs, AR
501-362-5253

Indian Mountain Kennel
Hot Springs, AR
501-321-9764

Country Manor Kennels
Hot Springs Village, AR
501-623-7961

Pet Quarters
Jonesboro, AR
870-935-7061

Bath Bed 'N Board Kennels
Little Rock, AR
501-888-9171

Fairview Kennels
Little Rock, AR
501-225-1391

Heights Country Kennel
Maumelle, AR
501-851-3647

Pine Acres Kennel
Morrilton, AR
501-354-4476

U.S. Kennels > CALIFORNIA

Premier Boarding
North Little Rock, AR
501-945-4949

New Hope
Boarding Kennel
Rogers, AR
501-936-8044

Russellville Animal Clinic
Russellville, AR
501-967-7777

Lola's Pet Motel
Shirley, AR
501-884-6600

Sunset Kennels
Springdale, AR
501-751-9659

K-9 Kennels
Stuttgart, AR
870-673-2397

Woodstock Kennels
Waldron, AR
501-637-4211

Fynmore Kennel
West Memphis, AR
870-735-5878

Southland Kennel
Compound
West Memphis, AR
870-735-9009

CALIFORNIA

Stonewall Retrievers
Acampo, CA
209-366-2816

Dark Mountain Kennel
Acton, CA
805-268-1351

Baseline Animal Resort
Alta Loma, CA
909-987-1780

Golden Glen Kennels
Anderson, CA
916-365-2151

Cats Corner
Boarding Cattery
Apple Valley, CA
760-240-3761

Pollard's Motel for
Dogs & Cats
Apple Valley, CA
760-247-7916

Grand Avenue Animal
Services Kennel
Arroyo Grande, CA
805-481-8200

Sebring Kennels
Arroyo Grande, CA
805-929-3014

A A Pet Hotel
Bakersfield, CA
805-323-5232

Bakersfield Kennels
Bakersfield, CA
805-325-9741

Cherry Avenue Kennels
Bakersfield, CA
805-589-7313

Mckay's Lazy Daze Kennels
Bakersfield, CA
805-399-2180

Four Paws Inn
Banning, CA
909-849-1462

Hi Desert Pet Motel
Barstow, CA
760-252-8200

Whispering Rivers Kennel
Beckwourth, CA
916-832-4359

The Cats Inn
Belmont, CA
650-508-9878

Camp Fox Farm
Big Bear Lake, CA
909-866-1919

Bonita Boarding Kennel
Bonita, CA
619-475-3850

Jensen's Kennel
Bonita, CA
619-479-7074

Brentwood Pet Resort
Brentwood, CA
925-634-7278

Pets Frolic Inn
Brentwood, CA
925-634-4431

Taycins Boarding Kennel
Buellton, CA
805-688-8398

K9 Kindergarten
Buellton, CA
805-693-9433

Bon Jean Kennels
Burbank, CA
818-841-5602

Rancho Pet Hotel
Burbank, CA
818-846-9674

Cat Suites of Calabasas
Calabasas, CA
818-880-1038

Cambrian Kennels
Campbell, CA
408-371-0737

Double E Ranch
Boarding Kennels
Canoga Park, CA
818-888-7613

Oaksprings Kennel
Canyon Country, CA
805-251-8204

Seacrest Kennels
Carlsbad, CA
760-438-2469

Lobos Ridge Pet Resort
Carmel, CA
408-812-2445

Melodie Lane Boarding
Kennels
Carmichael, CA
916-944-1536

K 9 Dog Ranch
Carpinteria, CA
805-684-3223

Kamp K-9
Castro Valley, CA
888-452-6759

Country Cattery
Cedar Ridge, CA
916-477-1103

U.S. Kennels > CALIFORNIA

Hideaway Kennels
Chatsworth, CA
818-341-0910

Shoestring Kennels
Chatsworth, CA
818-882-1955

Meridian Kennels
Chico, CA
916-343-4551

Clear Lake Kennels
Clearlake, CA
707-994-5241

Evergreen Kennels
Corning, CA
916-824-4766

Circle City Animal Resort
Corona, CA
909-687-0333

Little Friends Pet Hotel
Cotati, CA
707-795-6126

Danlos Kennels
Crockett, CA
510-228-6582

Carmalee Kennels
Danville, CA
510-736-5247

Glennroe Kennels
Danville, CA
510-837-4077

La Fale Cat Boarding Kennels
Davis, CA
916-753-4277

T L C Dog Boarding
Desert Hot Springs, CA
760-251-9285

Brennan's Kennels
Dixon, CA
916-678-1980

Winfield Kennels
Dixon, CA
916-678-5188

Glennroe Kennels
Dublin, CA
510-828-5355

Midway Boarding Kennel
Durham, CA
916-891-8022

Temple Dell Kennels
El Cajon, CA
619-445-2845

Green Valley Kennels
El Dorado Hills, CA
916-933-1780

Bar-Bes Kennel
El Monte, CA
626-444-2490

Duckpond Kennels
Elk Grove, CA
916-456-5683

Holiday Pet Hotel
Encinitas, CA
760-753-6754

Sholyn Kennels
Encinitas, CA
760-942-8668

Animal Care Center of Escondido
Escondido, CA
619-747-4100

Greenback Pet Resort
Fair Oaks, CA
916-726-3400

Dunnell Ranch Kennels
Fairfield, CA
707-425-3766

Fallbrook Animal Lodge
Fallbrook, CA
760-728-0892

Hughes Kismet Kennels
Fontana, CA
909-822-3898

Regency Pet Hotel
Fontana, CA
909-829-0626

Kelley's Kennels
Fresno, CA
209-255-4493

Sandcrest Kennels Boarding & Training Center
Fresno, CA
209-441-1719

Animal Friends Pet Hotel
Garden Grove, CA
714-537-4500

Animal Inns of America
Garden Grove, CA
714-636-4455

Shamrock Lane Kennels
Garden Grove, CA
714-531-7650

South Bay Pet Inn
Gardena, CA
310-515-5432

Glendale Small Animal Kennel
Glendale, CA
818-241-5181

Country Cattery Boarding Resort for Cats
Grass Valley, CA
916-477-7877

Empire Kennels
Grass Valley, CA
916-272-6971

The Kennels
Grass Valley, CA
916-272-4670

Lockleen Kennels
Grass Valley, CA
916-268-1765

Melair Kennels
Hanford, CA
209-582-0640

Harmony Kennels
Harmony, CA
805-927-8324

Country Kennels
Herald, CA
209-748-5613

Hi Desert Kennels
Hesperia, CA
760-244-4878

Country Cats Boarding
Hollister, CA
408-637-2136

All the Comforts of Home
Homeland, CA
909-926-9221

U.S. Kennels > CALIFORNIA

Valley Kennel
Indio, CA
760-342-4711

DuMoy Kennels
Inglewood, CA
310-641-2140

American River Kennels
Ione, CA
209-274-4436

Animal Lodge
Irvine, CA
714-551-8202

Jaylor Kennel
Kelseyville, CA
707-279-1624

Olive Hill Kennels
Knights Landing, CA
916-735-6217

La Jolla Pet Resort
La Jolla, CA
619-454-6155

Club Parkway Pet Resort
La Mesa, CA
619-463-5492

Walterock Kennels
Lafayette, CA
510-284-4729

Laguna Canyon Kennels
Laguna Beach, CA
714-497-1560

Cats Luv Us Boarding Hotel
Laguna Niguel, CA
714-582-1732

Dana's Pooch Palace
Lakeport, CA
707-263-3854

Carter Kennels
Lakeside, CA
619-561-1464

Kennedy's Kennels
Lakeside, CA
619-443-8687

Canine Country Club
Lancaster, CA
805-942-4251

Lemon Grove Kennels
Lemon Grove, CA
619-463-0719

Colonial Boarding Kennels
Lemoore, CA
209-584-6714

Livermore Ranch Kennels
Livermore, CA
510-447-1729

Sycamore Lane Kennels
Lodi, CA
209-334-1316

5 Star Pet Lodge
Lompoc, CA
805-736-0360

River Rock Kennels
Lompoc, CA
805-735-8108

Kennel Kare
Long Beach, CA
562-597-9587

All Pets Boarding
Loomis, CA
916-652-3687

Casita's Hotel for Cats
Los Angeles, CA
213-664-7115

Holiday Hotel for Cats
Los Angeles, CA
310-479-1440

Pacific Flyway Canine Boarding
Los Banos, CA
209-826-0618

Woodbrae Kennels
Los Gatos, CA
408-356-2889

Country View Kennels
Madera, CA
209-674-3901

Sand Piper Kennels
Malibu, CA
310-456-8982

Del Rey Kennels
Marina Del Rey, CA
310-821-5612

Farrington Kennels
Martinez, CA
510-228-6288

Woodlands Kennel
Mendocino, CA
707-937-5208

Tyson Kennels
Menlo Park, CA
650-364-3151

Ashby Boarding Kennels
Merced, CA
209-723-7822

Midway Kennels
Midway City, CA
714-893-5549

Tamalpais Pet Lodge
Mill Valley, CA
415-388-3316

Golden Retreat Kennels
Mira Loma, CA
909-681-1438

C R Ranch
Modesto, CA
209-545-1255

Country View Kennels
Modesto, CA
209-551-5070

Yosemite Boarding Kennel
Modesto, CA
209-524-1494

Dogwood Ranch Pet Resort
Monterey, CA
831-663-3647

Robalee Kennel
Mountain View, CA
650-965-9425

Sierra Vista Kennel
Mountain View, CA
650-969-1853

Crestmark Kennel
Napa, CA
707-252-7877

Silverado Boarding Center
Napa, CA
707-224-7970

U.S. Kennels > CALIFORNIA

Custom Canine
National City, CA
619-470-8639

Central Boarding Kennel
Newark, CA
510-796-7556

Calgrove Kennels
Newhall, CA
805-255-5022

Sea Breeze Kennels
Newport Beach, CA
714-756-1016

Walters Kennels
North Hills, CA
818-764-6714

Windsor House Kennels
North Hills, CA
818-765-5592

Porter Pet Hospital
Northridge, CA
818-349-8387

**Fiddler's Green
Dog Kennels**
Novato, CA
415-892-9632

Clairtone Boarding Kennels
Oakland, CA
510-632-4880

Corralitos Kennels
Ontario, CA
909-984-5154

Wallee Kennels
Ontario, CA
909-947-3901

Aiken Kennels
Orange, CA
714-639-0219

Canine Care Castle
Orange, CA
714-633-0955

Shadow Creek Kennels
Orangevale, CA
916-723-7373

Percell's Kennel
Orland, CA
916-865-9651

Pets R Inn
Oroville, CA
916-872-5727

Warcon Kennels
Oroville, CA
916-533-8951

Gaboury's Boarding Kennel
Oxnard, CA
805-485-1214

Inglis Pet Hotel
Oxnard, CA
805-647-1990

**Pacific Palisades
Veterinary Center**
Pacific Palisades, CA
310-573-7707

Linda Mar Kennels
Pacifica, CA
650-359-1627

Animal Resort High Desert
Palmdale, CA
805-274-7557

Bowsers Bed & Breakfast
Palmdale, CA
805-273-7197

Noroda Ranch Kennel
Palmdale, CA
805-270-1435

Palo Alto Kennels
Palo Alto, CA
650-323-8558

Four Paws Kennel
Paso Robles, CA
805-239-7485

Paso Robles Pet Boarding
Paso Robles, CA
805-238-4340

Bonnie Brae Kennel
Petaluma, CA
707-763-8861

Quarry House Kennels
Placerville, CA
916-624-8414

Kountry Kennels
Pleasant Grove, CA
916-991-7211

Pleasanton Pet Hotel
Pleasanton, CA
510-484-3030

Blue Ridge Kennels
Pomona, CA
909-623-2912

DMF Boarding Kennels
Quincy, CA
916-283-2833

Desert View Pet Resort
Rancho Mirage, CA
760-341-1166

**The Helen Woodward
Boarding Center**
Rancho Santa Fe, CA
619-756-3484

Trailhead Ranch Kennels
Red Bluff, CA
916-527-5215

Pachek Kennels
Redding, CA
916-223-4520

Redlands Pet Resort
Redlands, CA
909-335-1373

Alliance Dog Kennels
Redwood City, CA
650-365-8862

Fireside Kennel
Rialto, CA
909-874-3221

Rialto Kennels
Rialto, CA
909-873-9989

Cameo Kennels
Ridgecrest, CA
760-375-2319

Sea Wind Kennel
Ripon, CA
209-599-6854

Blue Hills Kennels
Riverbank, CA
209-869-0249

Esnard Kennels
Riverside, CA
909-685-1383

U.S. Kennels > CALIFORNIA

Marlou Kennels
Riverside, CA
909-687-3600

Artic-Luv Kennels
Rosemead, CA
626-350-1566

Battersea Kennels
Rosemead, CA
626-280-2223

Classic Kennels
Roseville, CA
916-771-0202

Hurstland Kennels
Rowland Heights, CA
626-913-7790

Picadilly Farms Kenne
Sacramento, CA
916-682-3229

Haustier Kennel
San Andreas, CA
209-754-3431

Sierra Kennels
San Andreas, CA
916-620-6994

Massey Boarding Kennels
San Bernardino, CA
909-885-1466

Pet Motel
San Bernardino, CA
909-884-9474

Peninsula Pet Resort
San Carlos, CA
415-592-2441

Airport Pet Resort
San Diego, CA
619-299-7388

Best Friends Pet Resort
San Diego, CA
619-565-8055

Best Friends San Diego
San Diego, CA
858-565-8455

Happy Pets Inn
San Francisco, CA
415-584-8370

Ramona Boarding Kennels
San Jacinto, CA
909-654-7127

Calero Pet Retreat
San Jose, CA
408-268-7171

Springdale Kennels
San Jose, CA
408-281-1965

Wagon Yard Kennels
San Jose, CA
408-262-5151

**Happy Tails
Boarding Kennel**
San Luis Obispo, CA
805-546-0587

San Marcos Kennels
San Marcos, CA
760-744-5171

Aspen Glen Kennels
San Martin, CA
408-6583-2163

**Terra Linda
Boarding Kennels**
San Rafael, CA
415-479-8535

Camp Canine
Santa Ana, CA
714-549-1168

Canine Country Club
Santa Ana, CA
714-549-9799

Animal Inn
Santa Barbara, CA
805-962-4790

New Star Kennel
Santa Barbara, CA
805-962-3918

Peninsula Pet Resort
Santa Clara, CA
650-592-2441

Heritage Kennel
Santa Cruz, CA
408-423-2350

Reveille Kennels
Santa Cruz, CA
408-476-3449

Rowits Kennels
Santa Cruz, CA
408-476-3449

Sea Breeze Kennels
Santa Maria, CA
805-925-2825

Santa Monica Kennels
Santa Monica, CA
310-396-2088

**Madeline's Boarding
Kennels**
Santa Paula, CA
805-525-3212

Bayside Kennels
Santa Rosa, CA
707-578-8196

Countryside Kennels
Santa Rosa, CA
707-542-3766

Shiloh Kennels
Santa Rosa, CA
707-584-9115

Springdale Kennels
Saratoga, CA
408-281-1965

Canine Country Club
Saugus, CA
805-296-0566

Bundocks Kennels
Sebastopol, CA
707-823-2342

Skansen Kennels
Sebastopol, CA
707-795-7070

Pet Resort
Sepulveda, CA
818-891-4473

Buddy Rough Kennels
Sheridan, CA
916-633-4343

Summersong Kennels
Silverado, CA
714-649-2861

Rowdy Creek Pet Motel
Smith River, CA
707-487-9645

Aberglen Kennels
Sonoma, CA
707-938-2657

U.S. Kennels > CALIFORNIA

Kamlo Boarding Kennels
Sonoma, CA
707-996-9472

Byrmar Kennels
Soquel, CA
408-475-3501

All Pets Inn
South El Monte, CA
626-443-9947

Jay Bee's Kennels
Spring Valley, CA
619-463-0207

Spartan Kennels
Spring Valley, CA
619-461-5577

Bel Canto Kennels
Stanton, CA
714-761-7144

Starline Kennels
Stanton, CA
714-826-5218

Cure the Blues Kennels
Strathmore, CA
209-568-2061

Ornbaun Ranch Kennels
Suisun City, CA
707-864-8601

All Stars Kennels
Sun Valley, CA
818-768-1158

Blue Ribbon Kennels
Sun Valley, CA
818-767-2211

Paradise Ranch
Sun Valley, CA
818-768-8708

Happiness Country Kennels
Sunol, CA
510-657-7753

Cummings Valley Kennel
Tehachapi, CA
805-822-7392

Canine Castle II
Thousand Oaks, CA
805-497-1500

Westlake Pet Motel
Thousand Oaks, CA
805-497-8669

Gretlo Kennels
Torrance, CA
310-328-1688

Jumping Jack Kennel
Torrance, CA
310-328-4742

Bittertoy Kennel
Tracy, CA
209-836-2149

Circle H Kennels
Tracy, CA
209-835-6766

Sandyland Kennels
Tulare, CA
209-686-5109

Blue Ribbon Boarding
Ukiah, CA
707-485-8454

La Boya Dog & Cat Motel
Upland, CA
909-985-1416

Dunnell Ranch Kennels
Vacaville, CA
707-448-5294

Summerwind Kennels
Vacaville, CA
707-448-1115

Jay Tee Kennels
Valley Springs, CA
209-772-1463

Van Nuys Pet Hotel
Van Nuys, CA
818-787-7232

Love'm Kennels
Victorville, CA
760-240-4321

Gail's Boarding Kennel
Visalia, CA
209-625-5490

Pet Inn
Visalia, CA
209-732-4803

Tri City Boarding
Vista, CA
760-758-2092

Camanche Kennels
Wallace, CA
209-763-2719

North Main Pet Lodge
Walnut Creek, CA
510-256-0646

R & M Kennels
Wasco, CA
805-758-0823

Weaverville Pet Motel
Weaverville, CA
530-623-0060

Almont Boarding Kennels
West Hollywood, CA
310-274-0829

Clearview Kennels
West Sacramento, CA
916-371-0313

Westlake Pet Motel
Westlake Village, CA
818-991-0606

Don O'Brien Kennels
Wilton, CA
916-687-8638

29 Palms Pet Resort
Woodland, CA
916-661-0213

Arrowpoint Kennels
Woodland, CA
916-666-5555

Country Care Pet Resort
Yorba Linda, CA
714-985-1330

Loving Care Pet Motel
Yreka, CA
916-842-5710

Donmar Farms & Kennels
Yucaipa, CA
909-795-4867

**Mahan Boarding &
Breeding Kennel**
Yucca Valley, CA
760-364-4472

COLORADO

Action Kennel Service
Arvada, CO
303-423-2243

Academy Acres Kennels
Aurora, CO
303-690-1188

U.S. Kennels > COLORADO

Broadview Kennels
Aurora, CO
303-755-0471

Dogtown Kennels
Aurora, CO
303-364-3713

Rawhide Ranch
Avondale, CO
719-948-0008

**Alpine Meadow Ranch
& Kennel**
Basalt, CO
970-927-2688

**Cottonwood Boarding
Kennels**
Boulder, CO
303-442-2602

Dog City
Boulder, CO
303-473-9963

D 'n R Kennels
Breckenridge, CO
970-453-6708

Columbine Kennels
Brighton, CO
303-659-0638

Country Kennels
Canon City, CO
719-275-5681

Skyline Ranch & Kennels
Carbondale, CO
970-963-2915

Broadmoor Bluffs Kennel
Colorado Springs, CO
719-636-3344

Clearview Animal Lodge
Colorado Springs, CO
719-392-1800

Northwest Animal Hospital
Colorado Springs, CO
719-593-8582

Rampart Kennels
Colorado Springs, CO
719-591-0066

Top Hat Kennels
Conifer, CO
303-838-4147

High Country Kennels
Cortez, CO
970-565-4910

**Cottonwood Ranch
& Kennel**
Crawford, CO
970-921-7100

**Aspenwood Animal
Hospital**
Denver, CO
303-757-5646

Elmfield Kennels
Denver, CO
303-934-2306

Evans East Animal Hospital
Denver, CO
303-757-7881

**North Washington St.
Kennels**
Denver, CO
303-288-5212

Willow Tree Kennels
Durango, CO
970-259-0018

B-G's Kennels
Englewood, CO
303-781-4577

Boarding House for Pets
Estes Park, CO
970-586-6606

All Pet Boarding
Evans, CO
970-353-2368

**Mountain Parks
Boarding Kennels**
Evergreen, CO
303-674-3156

Ashcroft Kennels
Fort Collins, CO
970-221-5689

Crystal Glen Kennel
Fort Collins, CO
970-224-3118

Hi Plains Kennels
Fountain, CO
719-382-9611

Land of Ahs Kennels
Fountain, CO
719-382-1126

**Applewood Boarding
Kennels**
Golden, CO
303-237-1254

Appleton Boarding Kennels
Grand Junction, CO
970-242-1285

West Pinyon Kennels
Grand Junction, CO
970-242-7075

Double J Pet Ranch
Greeley, CO
970-352-5330

Dog Gone Kennels
Holyoke, CO
970-854-3084

Pet Ranch Kennel
Lakewood, CO
303-238-3164

Pet Ranch Kennel
Littleton, CO
303-973-0542

Blue Hills Kennels
Longmont, CO
303-776-3907

Longmont Kennels
Longmont, CO
303-772-5335

Alpine Boarding Kennel
Monte Vista, CO
719-852-2561

Redclyffe Kennels
Montrose, CO
970-249-6395

Double J Cross Kennel
Nathrop, CO
719-539-4080

Upper Valley Kennel
Palisade, CO
970-464-5713

Enchanted Kennels
Parker, CO
303-841-5081

U.S. Kennels > COLORADO

Fox & Hounds
Peyton, CO
719-683-5544

Kamp 4 Paws
Pueblo, CO
719-545-7297

Pueblo West Boarding Kennels
Pueblo West, CO
719-547-3815

Star Boarding Kennel
Sedalia, CO
303-688-8569

Cedar Hill Kennel
Silt, CO
970-876-2451

Steamboat Boarding Kennel
Steamboat Springs, CO
970-879-1049

Pet Village Boarding Kennel
Wheat Ridge, CO
303-422-2055

CONNECTICUT

Ansonia Silver Hill Kennel & Cattery
Ansonia, CT
203-735-5454

Mountain View Kennels
Avon, CT
860-673-0555

Norwichtown Boarding Kennels
Baltic, CT
860-822-6342

Bethway Kennels
Bethany, CT
203-393-2826

Keystone Kennels
Bethany, CT
203-393-3126

Hemlock Kennels & Cattery
Bethlehem, CT
203-266-7219

Conn Trail Kennels
Bolton, CT
860-649-0079

Shoreline Pet Lodge
Branford, CT
203-488-9660

Herb Koerner Kennel
Bridgeport, CT
203-368-1670

Marta's Vineyard Canine Resort
Brookfield, CT
203-775-4404

Canterbury Kennels
Canterbury, CT
860-546-9748

Tamarack Boarding Kennels
Clinton, CT
860-669-2593

Wilcroft Kennels
Danbury, CT
203-748-1155

Oronoque Kennel
Derby, CT
203-735-3624

Westview Boarding Kennels
Durham, CT
860-349-1256

New Inn Kennels
East Haddam, CT
860-873-8149

Wes-Mar Boarding Kennels
East Hartford, CT
860-289-7585

Ellington Kennels
Ellington, CT
860-872-1950

Conlin County Kennels
Enfield, CT
860-749-4015

Highway Kennels
Fairfield, CT
203-384-2564

Tanbark Kennels
Farmington, CT
860-677-7601

Candlewick Kennels
Glastonbury, CT
860-633-6878

Lone Pine Kennels
Greenwich, CT
203-661-4358

Red Barn Kennels
Greenwich, CT
203-869-5475

Maple Ridge Kennels
Groton, CT
860-445-4999

Catnip Cat Boarding
Hamden, CT
203-281-1310

Sheridane Kennels
Hebron, CT
860-228-9089

Country Lane Boarding Kennels Dogs & Cats
Jewett City, CT
860-376-0235

Snowflake Boarding Kennels
Milford, CT
203-878-3117

Dogwood Boarding Kennels & Cattery
Monroe, CT
203-268-0788

Marryall Kennels
New Milford, CT
860-355-2732

Cassio Kennels
Newtown, CT
203-426-2881

Creater Comforts Animal Inn
North Stonington, CT
860-599-1784

Best Friends Pet Care
Norwalk, CT
203-849-1010

Best Friends Pet Resort
Norwalk, CT
203-846-6730

U.S. Kennels > FLORIDA

**Hemlock Trails
Boarding Cattery**
Old Lyme, CT
860-434-2771

The Whiskers Inn
Old Saybrook, CT
860-388-6565

Quaker Farms Kennels
Oxford, CT
203-888-2187

Scotts Kennels
Pawcatuck, CT
860-599-5172

Wayfarer Kennel
Portland, CT
860-342-1067

Best Friends Pet Resort
Rocky Hill, CT
850-721-8080

Red House Kennels
Somers, CT
860-749-4531

Valley Boarding Kennel
South Windsor, CT
860-289-1509

Lone Oak Farm Kennel
Southington, CT
860-621-6886

Bark Inn Kennels
Stafford Springs, CT
860-684-7436

Bell Starr Kennels
Stratford, CT
203-377-0134

Meadowrock Kennels
Suffield, CT
860-668-7128

**Shagg-Bark Boarding
Kennels**
Tolland, CT
860-875-7526

Holiday Pet Lodge
Wallingford, CT
203-269-4222

Pet Hotel
West Haven, CT
203-932-3320

**Winding Way Lodging
for Pets**
Westbrook, CT
860-399-7572

Town House for Dogs
Westport, CT
203-227-3276

Misty Willow Kennels
Willington, CT
860-429-1496

Sundial Liberty Kennels
Wilton, CT
203-762-7147

**Day Hill Kennels
Dog Boarding**
Windsor, CT
860-688-2370

Camelot Kennels
Wolcott, CT
203-879-4280

Barnhill Kennels
Woodbury, CT
203-263-4496

Blue & Gold Kennels
Woodbury, CT
203-263-2529

DELAWARE

Bunting Kennels
Bridgeville, DE
302-337-8003

Best Boarding Kennel
Dover, DE
302-697-2002

Home Away from Home
Lewes, DE
302-684-8576

**Never Never Land
Kennel-Cattery**
Lewes, DE
302-645-6140

Shore Boarding Kennel
Ocean View, DE
302-539-3559

Branch Oaks Kennel
Rehoboth Beach, DE
302-227-8268

Heavenly Hound Hotel
Selbyville, DE
302-227-8268

Animal Inn
Smyrna, DE
302-653-5560

Big Oak Dog Kennels
Smyrna, DE
302-653-6113

**Wilmington Animal
Hospital**
Wilmington, DE
302-762-2694

Windcrest Animal Hospital
Wilmington, DE
302-998-2995

DISTRICT OF COLUMBIA

Dogs by Day & Night
Washington, DC
202-986-6301

FLORIDA

Cherokee Country Kennel
Alford, FL
850-579-4424

Pat's K-9 Kennels
Auburndale, FL
941-965-1312

Merryfield Kennels
Boca Raton, FL
561-367-0332

A Pampered Pooch Resort
Bonita Springs, FL
941-992-4323

AAA Pet Motel
Bradenton, FL
941-746-3626

**Animal Boarding Center
of Bradenton**
Bradenton, FL
941-753-6709

Animal Acres Pet Resort
Brooksville, FL
352-796-4715

Sun Coast Kennels
Brooksville, FL
352-688-3100

U.S. Kennels > FLORIDA

Sweet 'N Lo Pet Motel
Brooksville, FL
352-796-7788

Cape Coral Kennels
Cape Coral, FL
941-574-4202

Worrell Kennels
Chattahoochee, FL
904-662-2081

Howl A Day Inn Kennel
Chipley, FL
850-638-0111

Crestview Kennels
Crestview, FL
850-682-0188

Rey Lee Kennels
Dade City, FL
352-521-0183

El Lobo Kennels
Davie, FL
954-587-7252

Alabiss Kennels & Cattery
Daytona Beach, FL
904-761-1424

Bryn Kennels
Daytona Beach, FL
904-761-3647

Craig Kennels
Daytona Beach, FL
904-253-8391

Deltona Pet Lodge
Deltona, FL
407-323-9743

Destin Animal Clinic Kennels
Destin, FL
850-837-2997

TLC Pet Care
Eau Gallie, FL
407-254-2273

Shalimar Kennels
Flagler Beach, FL
904-439-3950

Bobbi's World Kennels
Fort Lauderdale, FL
954-491-8189

Merryfield Kennels
Fort Lauderdale, FL
954-771-4030

Kings Holiday Pet Resort
Fort Myers, FL
941-543-2666

Orange River Kennels
Fort Myers, FL
941-694-6062

Friendship Kennel
Fort Walton Beach, FL
850-862-2221

Tails & Whiskers Hotel
Fruitland Park, FL
352-728-3440

Marimack Dog & Cat Boarding Kennel
Gulf Breeze, FL
850-932-5791

Creekside Kennels
Haines City, FL
941-422-4042

Park Road Pet Resort
Hallandale, FL
954-983-6748

Wolff's Kennel
Hialeah, FL
305-885-3623

Country Club Kennels
Hobe Sound, FL
561-546-5311

Holly Acres Kennel
Hollywood, FL
954-434-1535

El Saba Kennels
Homestead, FL
305-248-8013

Cypress Spring Kennel
Homosassa Springs, FL
352-628-6174

Creature Comforts Pet Resort
Jacksonville, FL
904-389-9008

Emerson Kennels
Jacksonville, FL
904-398-5786

St. Johns Beach Boarding Kennel
Jacksonville, FL
904-641-2230

Aristocat Feline Boarding
Jupiter, FL
561-744-5115

Bass Kennels
Kissimmee, FL
407-396-6031

Doggie Motel
Kissimmee, FL
407-396-6031

EPCOT Kennel
Lake Buena Vista, FL
407-939-3746

Ft. Wilderness Kennel
Lake Buena Vista, FL
407-939-3746

Magic Kingdom Kennel
Lake Buena Vista, FL
407-560-7439

MGM Studios Kennel
Lake Buena Vista, FL
407-560-7439

Country Dream Inn Boarding Kennels
Lake Placid, FL
941-465-9674

The Pet Motel
Lake Wales, FL
941-676-5736

Palm Beach Kennels & Cattery
Lake Worth, FL
561-965-1525

Lakeland Pet Motel
Lakeland, FL
941-665-2514

Parwick Kennels
Land O Lakes, FL
813-949-1687

Animal House
Lantana, FL
561-439-2246

Paradise Pet Motel
Largo, FL
813-581-6831

U.S. Kennels > FLORIDA

Driftwood Kennels
Laurel, FL
941-485-6672

JDP Kennel
Lecanto, FL
352-746-3302

Keys Animal Hospital
Marathon Key, FL
305-743-3647

Century Kennels
Melbourne, FL
407-154-1597

Pet Resort Kennels
Melbourne, FL
407-259-6224

Remington Canine Resorts
Merritt Island, FL
321-459-0105

Canine Country Club
Miami, FL
305-274-3267

Landmark Kennel
Miami, FL
305-253-1092

Merryfield Kennels of South Miami
Miami, FL
305-233-2221

Sky Lake Kennels
Miami, FL
305-931-2113

Countryside Pet Motel
Middleburg, FL
904-282-1242

Red's Kennels
Milton, FL
850-626-8331

Big Bend Kennels
Monticello, FL
850-997-5805

Tealbrook Kennels
Monticello, FL
850-997-5844

Springledge Boarding Kennel
Morriston, FL
352-629-7096

Best Friends Pet Resorts
Naples, FL
941-597-9798

Pine Ridge Kennels
Naples, FL
941-597-9219

Animal Inn
New Port Richey, FL
813-847-7480

Omy Kennels
New Smyrna Beach, FL
904-424-9750

Alpine Boarding Kennels
Newberry, FL
352-472-3592

Kritter Kennels
Niceville, FL
9004-678-6121

Juno Pet Lodge
North Palm Beach, FL
561-622-7431

Palmetto Kennels
Ocala, FL
888-453-4566

Sunridge Kennel
Ocala, FL
352-237-2086

Amigo Pet Motel
Ormond Beach, FL
904-673-1191

Eastland Boarding Kennels
Palatka, FL
904-325-9761

A K C Alternative Kennel Care
Palm Bay, FL
407-728-1245

Ponderosa Kennels
Palm City, FL
561-220-2924

Palm Harbor Pet Hotel
Palm Harbor, FL
813-784-0558

Caroldane Boarding Kennels
Palmetto, FL
941-776-1094

Milady Kennels
Panama City, FL
850-769-4192

Beaches Pet Motel
Panama City Beach, FL
850-234-2955

All Pets Boarding Kennels
Pensacola, FL
850-477-4803

Cameo Kennels
Pensacola, FL
850-438-1339

Howl A Day Inn Bed & Biscuit
Pensacola, FL
850-492-3255

Lakeview Kennels
Pierson, FL
904-749-9610

Circle L Farms & Kennel
Pomona Park, FL
904-649-8568

Dog House
Pompano Beach, FL
954-941-9391

Pompano Pet Lodge
Pompano Beach, FL
954-972-5584

North Port Kennels
Port Saint Lucie, FL
561-878-4818

Adorable Dogs Boarding
Punta Gorda, FL
941-637-9888

Cherish Farms & Kennel
Reddick, FL
352-591-2137

Mar Jo Boarding Kennels
Saint Augustine, FL
904-825-0005

Troymara Kennels
Saint Augustine, FL
904-824-2233

Collins Kennels
Saint Cloud, FL
407-892-8919

U.S. Kennels > FLORIDA

AA Kennels at Jelly Bean Junction
Saint Petersburg, FL
813-579-1136

The Dog House Pet Motel
Saint Petersburg, FL
813-526-5507

Holland Cal Kennel
Saint Petersburg, FL
813-579-1069

Kellogg's Kennel
Saint Petersburg, FL
813-526-5507

Animal Inn
Sanford, FL
407-321-3320

Pet Rest Inn Kennel
Sanford, FL
407-322-4057

The Copper Kennel
Santa Rosa Beach, FL
850-267-2101

Country Kennels
Sarasota, FL
941-921-1697

Sandy Lane Kennels
Sarasota, FL
941-371-1223

Windsong Acres Boarding Kennels and Stables
Sebring, FL
941-385-5245

Oakhurst Kennels
Seminole, FL
727-397-8844

Four Paws Boarding
Spring Hill, FL
352-596-5607

Glenwood Kennels
Spring Hill, FL
352-683-6497

Happy Dog Inn
St. Augustine, FL
904-446-8443

Top Dog Kennels
Stuart, FL
561-220-4939

ABCD Kennels
Summerfield, FL
352-245-9410

Sunrise Kennel Club
Sunrise, FL
305-748-1900

Heads or Tails Kennels
Tallahassee, FL
850-668-7296

Lafayette Boarding Kennels
Tallahassee, FL
850-656-2856

Sunshine Kennels
Tallahassee, FL
850-576-0357

White's Quality Kennels
Tallahassee, FL
850-576-2021

Tamarac Kennels
Tamarac, FL
954-733-7387

Tampa Bay Kennels
Tampa, FL
813-875-2543

The Family Kennels East
Tampa, FL
813-986-4646

Maritime Pet Kennel
Tarpon Springs, FL
813-939-1089

Westlake Animal Inn Pet Resort
Tarpon Springs, FL
727-942-3691

Canine Villa Kennels
Titusville, FL
407-269-3413

Happy Valley Boarding Kennels
Valparaiso, FL
850-678-2550

Malibu Kennels
Venice, FL
941-488-9305

Tropical Breeze Pet Resort
Venice, FL
941-488-8612

Noah's Ark Pets Motel
Vero Beach, FL
561-567-7810

Pine Run Kennel
Vero Beach, FL
561-567-6490

Animal Inn of the Palm Beaches
West Palm Beach, FL
561-833-3303

Gatorland K-9 Resort & Club
West Palm Beach, FL
561-837-9948

Winter Haven Kennels
Winter Haven, FL
941-293-5365

Winter Park Veterinary Clinic
Winter Park, FL
407-644-2676

Nassau Kennels
Yulee, FL
904-277-3889

Ga Mac Kennels
Zephyrhills, FL
813-782-3544

GEORGIA

East Albany Kennels
Albany, GA
912-432-2323

Silica Kennels & Cattery
Albany, GA
912-436-2706

Best Friends Pet Resort
Alpharetta, GA
770-475-9220

Pekay Kennels
Alpharetta, GA
770-475-3455

Mountain Pet Resort
Alto, GA
706-778-7387

Pets Retreat
Athens, GA
706-354-8944

U.S. Kennels > GEORGIA

Atlanta Pet Resort
Atlanta, GA
770-421-9001

Buckwood Pet Hotel
Atlanta, GA
404-351-3246

Berry Kennels
Augusta, GA
706-738-7168

Paradise Kennels
Augusta, GA
706-860-1977

Atlanta DogWorks
Ball Ground, GA
770-735-6200

Danville Plantation Kennels
Blackshear, GA
912-853-9413

Double J Kennels
Canton, GA
770-345-6511

Lisa's Loving Care Kennels
Carrollton, GA
770-854-5807

Sugar Valley Boarding Kennel
Cartersville, GA
770-382-3066

Windrush Kennels
Chickamauga, GA
706-375-2764

Camp Paradise Pet Resort
Conyers, GA
770-483-4738

Rockdale Kennels
Conyers, GA
770-483-3918

Smith Farms Boarding Center
Conyers, GA
770-918-9808

Indian Shoals Pet Resort
Dacula, GA
770-995-9123

North Hall Kennels
Dahlonega, GA
770-535-7829

Brenda's Boarding
Dalton, GA
706-278-1611

River Bear Design
Dawsonville, GA
706-265-1002

Best Friends Pet Resort
Duluth, GA
678-584-0999

Best Friends Pet Resort
East Cobb, GA
678-560-0880

Dandie Scottie Kennel
East Point, GA
404-762-8777

P & D Kennels
Eastman, GA
912-374-7240

Waterwood Kennel
Fayetteville, GA
770-461-9893

Gowen Kennels
Folkston, GA
912-496-2937

Professional Kennels
Fort Oglethorpe, GA
706-866-8228

Hartwell Kennels
Hartwell, GA
706-376-7327

Mountain Creek Kennel
Homer, GA
706-677-2510

Four Seasons Pet Resort
Hull, GA
706-353-7497

Mountain View Pet Lodge
Jasper, GA
705-692-6604

Big Shanty Kennels
Kennesaw, GA
770-424-6322

Kennesaw Pet Center
Kennesaw, GA
770-420-5454

Brookside Kennel
Lawrenceville, GA
770-962-1117

Mardon Kennels
Leslie, GA
912-874-8935

Sandhill Kennels
Lincolnton, GA
706-359-1991

Kings Creek Kennels
Lithonia, GA
770-0972-8787

The Pet Motel
Lyons, GA
912-526-6735

Greenwood Farm Boarding Kennels
Macon, GA
912-477-9057

Wild Wind Kennels
Madison, GA
706-342-4910

Best Friends Pet Care
Marietta, GA
678-560-0083

Cheatham Hill Kennels
Marietta, GA
770-424-0062

Montrose Pet Hotel
Marietta, GA
770-977-2000

Dog House Kennel
Newnan, GA
770-253-7234

Love Kennels
Pavo, GA
912-228-7130

Peachtree City Kennels
Peachtree City, GA
770-486-0209

Sweetwater Kennels
Pearson, GA
912-422-7962

Lime Creek Kennel
Pitts, GA
912-648-6110

Double Barrel Kennel
Register, GA
912-852-5118

U.S. Kennels > GEORGIA

H F Kennels
Rhine, GA
912-385-3841

Reeces Saint Hill Kennel
Rossville, GA
706-866-0803

Lakeview Kennels
Roswell, GA
770-993-2224

Indian Creek Kennels
Rutledge, GA
706-557-2901

Live Oak Kennels
Savannah, GA
912-352-1365

Shady Pines Kennels
Savannah, GA
912-351-0915

Hard Labor Creek Kennels
Shady Dale, GA
706-468-6532

Sleepy Hollow Kennel
Smyrna, GA
770-435-5781

Mont Royal Kennel
Social Circle, GA
770-464-4188

Just Add Love Kennels
Soperton, GA
706-745-8669

Camelot Kennels
Stone Mountain, GA
770-469-9533

Clanton-Malphus Veterinary Hospital & Pet Motel
Thomasville, GA
912-226-1914

Dekle Plantation Dog Kennel
Thomasville, GA
912-228-1411

M & M Kennels
Thomasville, GA
912-226-0631

The Pet Resort
Waycross, GA
912-287-1738

Leading Edge Kennel
Williamson, GA
770-412-0012

Winding Creek Kennels
Winder, GA
770-725-2700

Happy Hills Kennels
Winterville, GA
706-742-8852

Mountain Cove Kennels
Young Harris, GA
706-379-2021

HAWAII

Pets Are Inn
Aiea, HI
808-486-9446

Waimalu Dog & Cat Kennels
Aiea, HI
808-487-3607

Pet Express Boarding Kennel
Honolulu, HI
808-847-0058

The Honolulu Pet Clinic
Honolulu, HI
808-593-9336

The Bar King Dog Kennel
Keaau, HI
808-966-8733

Ohana Animal Inn
Kula, HI
808-878-6788

Makawao Boarding Kennel
Makawao, HI
808-573-0080

All Creature Comforts
Mountain View, HI
808-968-8497

IDAHO

Kickaboo Kennels
Athol, ID
208-683-3210

Alpine Kennels
Bellevue, ID
208-788-3520

Boise Kennels
Boise, ID
208-343-0681

Orchard Animal Clinic
Boise, ID
208-376-4433

Happy Tails Kennels
Bonners Ferry, ID
208-267-2763

Rocky Mountain Kennels
Caldwell, ID
208-459-9163

Asgard Country Kennel
Cocolalla, ID
208-265-4695

Saragold Kennels
Filer, ID
208-736-0917

Shilo Ridge Boarding Kennel
Grangeville, ID
208-983-7891

Whisper Oak Kennels
Hayden, ID
208-772-4504

AmeriPet Hotel & Pet Center
Idaho Falls, ID
208-524-3112

Teton Kennels
Idaho Falls, ID
208-524-2220

Sun Valley Animal Center
Ketchum, ID
208-726-7777

Gem Crest Kennels
Meridian, ID
208-375-4398

North Star Kennels
Meridian, ID
208-888-1388

Robertson's Kennels
Meridian, ID
208-888-4872

Lasal Kennels
Mountain Home, ID
208-587-5048

U.S. Kennels > ILLINOIS

Morning Mist Kennels
Nampa, ID
208-467-9236

Walker's Plantation & Kennels
New Plymouth, ID
208-278-5074

Pom Poso Boarding Kennels
Pocatello, ID
208-232-5228

Hatter Creek Kennels
Princeton, ID
208-875-0329

Kootenai Kennels
Rathdrum, ID
208-687-1119

Trails Inn Kennel
Rathdrum, ID
208-687-7024

Whispering Wind Kennels
Salmon, ID
208-756-3045

Green Meadow Kennels
Sandpoint, ID
208-263-2544

D & D Kennels
Star, ID
208-286-7700

North Wind Kennels
Troy, ID
208-835-6181

ILLINOIS

Heidanes Hidden Timers
Altamont, IL
618-483-5179

Kathy's Kritter Kare
Arlington Heights, IL
847-259-3545

Country Air Kennels
Assumption, IL
217-325-4202

Barrington Boarding Kennels
Barrington, IL
847-381-6009

Lawndale Kennels
Belleville, IL
618-233-1479

Scott's Boarding Kennel
Bloomington, IL
309-829-5023

Town & Country Kennel Club
Bloomington, IL
309-829-9313

Rowens Kennels
Brighton, IL
618-372-3837

River View Pet Resort
Byron, IL
815-234-2360

Indian Creek Kennel
Carbondale, IL
618-529-4700

Windy Acres Kennel
Carbondale, IL
618-964-1526

Deep Woods Kennel
Carlinville, IL
217-854-2433

Quick Kennels
Centralia, IL
618-533-4722

Cahokia Pet Resort
Charleston, IL
217-348-1080

Triple R Pet Palace
Chatham, IL
217-483-5623

7 Seas Pet Motel
Chicago, IL
773-646-3774

TLC Pet Hotel
Chrisman, IL
217-269-2050

Karolyn's Kennels
Colchester, IL
309-776-3817

Mallard Pointe Kennels
Colona, IL
309-949-2563

Bel-Kon Kennel
Darien, IL
630-968-2406

Lynnwood Kennels
Davis Junction, IL
815-645-8585

Countryside Pet Motel
DeKalb, IL
815-758-3074

Gwyaine Boarding Kennels
Decatur, IL
217-865-2504

National Dog & Cat Hotel
Des Plaines, IL
708-824-4455

Cedar Lane Kennels
Downers Grove, IL
630-969-1198

Cool Valley Boarding Kennels
Du Quoin, IL
618-542-8282

Apple Valley Boarding Kennel
East Moline, IL
309-755-0057

Denhaus Kennels
East Saint Louis, IL
618-398-3931

Stiltmore Kennels
Eldorado, IL
618-273-9278

Brewster Creek Kennels
Elgin, IL
708-697-1525

Phildon Kennels
Eureka, IL
309-467-2915

Country Lane Pet Lodge
Freeport, IL
815-232-3915

Barn Ridge Kennels
Geneseo, IL
309-944-2473

Estes Kennels
Godfrey, IL
618-466-1986

U.S. Kennels > ILLINOIS

Fantasy Kennels
Greenville, IL
618-664-1721

Jabberwok Kennels
Hammond, IL
217-262-3266

Kountry Kennels
Hampshire, IL
847-741-5434

Knob Hill Pet Lodge
Hanna City, IL
309-565-7622

Wise's Kountry Kennel
Harrisburg, IL
618-253-6886

Four Paws Pet Care
Hinsdale, IL
630-325-3647

Durbin Valley Kennels
Jacksonville, IL
217-673-3681

Oconnor's Country Kennels
Kankakee, IL
815-932-6011

Barrows Kennels
Leland, IL
815-495-9528

Lena Bed & Biscuit
Lena, IL
815-369-2552

Cha Dai Pet Motel
Lincoln, IL
217-732-1529

American Pet Motels
Lincolnshire, IL
847-634-9444

Kitty Inn
Long Grove, IL
847-634-1414

Country Lane Kennels
Loves Park, IL
815-885-3622

Sutton Boarding Kennel
Lyndon, IL
815-778-3342

Long's Kennel & Dog E Motel
Marion, IL
618-993-2043

Shoggy Kennels
Marseilles, IL
815-496-2581

Cindys Critter Camp
Maryville, IL
618-344-4096

K-9 Country Club
Mattoon, IL
217-235-5773

K 9 Estates
Mattoon, IL
217-234-2999

East Lane Kennels
Mendota, IL
815-539-5321

Innisglen Pet Lodge
Milan, IL
309-787-3627

Topono Pet Resort
Momence, IL
815-472-6836

Indian Knoll Kennel
Monec, IL
708-534-3103

Pine Lake Boarding Kennel
Morton, IL
309-263-0334

Country Acres Kennel
Mount Vernon, IL
618-244-1084

Naperville Animal Hospital
Naperville, IL
630-355-5300

Sundown Kennels
Nauvoo, IL
217-453-2568

Country Estate Kennel
O Fallon, IL
618-632-8008

Country Kennels
O Fallon, IL
618-632-4356

Green Meadow Kennels
Oak Brook, IL
708-968-3343

Almost Home Pet Motel
Oakley, IL
217-763-6333

Top Notch Kennels
Oswego, IL
630-554-9001

Park Center Kennels
Pana, IL
217-562-5123

Daisy Mae Kennels
Paxton, IL
217-379-2535

Double L Boarding Kennels
Pekin, IL
309-347-4043

Walnut Grove Boarding Kennels
Pekin, IL
309-925-5704

Greater Peoria Pet Resort
Peoria, IL
309-693-9123

American Pet Motels
Prarie View, IL
312-634-9444

K 9's Country Comforts
Reddick, IL
815-365-4228

Rock Falls Pet Hotel
Rock Falls, IL
815-626-4008

Airport Pet Lodge
Rockford, IL
815-397-4597

Tyran Kennels
Rockton, IL
815-624-6555

Stardust Kennels
Roscoe, IL
815-623-6901

Monkens Kennels
Sandoval, IL
618-247-8295

U.S. Kennels > INDIANA

Dallmann's Hi Wa Kennel
South Beloit, IL
815-389-2808

Dorr Road Kennels
South Beloit, IL
815-624-2168

Dal Acres West Kennel
Springfield, IL
217-793-3647

Tanglewood Kennels
St. Charles, IL
630-365-2388

Poochi's
Steger, IL
708-747-7074

Country Inn Kennels
Sterling, IL
815-336-2002

Lance Kennels
Tremont, IL
309-925-5125

Happy Day Kennels
Trenton, IL
618-537-4446

Pyr-Vista Kennels
Union, IL
708-923-4475

Paw Print Kennel
West Chicago, IL
630-231-1117

Brandenburg Kennels
Windsor, IL
217-459-2778

Lucky-E Kennels
Wonder Lake, IL
815-653-9016

Badlands Kennels
Woodland, IL
815-473-4256

Frisco Kennels
Zion, IL
708-746-2849

INDIANA

Spring Valley Kennels
Anderson, IN
765-643-8444

Wag Pet Village Boarding
Attica, IN
765-762-6212

Golden Post Pet Boarding
Bargersville, IN
317-422-8567

Canine Companion Training
Bloomington, IN
812-331-0665

Wayport Kennels
Bloomington, IN
812-876-2098

Country Kennels
Boonville, IN
812-897-4575

Best Friends Pet Resort
Carmel, IN
317-848-7387

Ginger Bear Kennel
Claypool, IN
219-839-3522

Deutsch's Boarding Kennels
Columbia City, IN
219-248-2415

Sanacre Kennel
Columbus, IN
812-372-6615

Land of OZ
Colwich, IN
316-796-0461

Windy Hill Pet Ranch
Crawfordsville, IN
765-362-3239

Windsong Pet Care Center
Elkhart, IN
219-262-2019

Hulsey's Wildwind Kennels
Evansville, IN
812-423-8767

Stillwater Kennel
Evansville, IN
812-867-3694

Ol' Lace Kennels
Fairmount, IN
765-948-4521

Ace Boarding Kennels
Fishers, IN
317-849-1340

Sojourn Boarding Kennels
Fishers, IN
317-849-4446

Alpine Pet Resort
Fort Wayne, IN
219-485-3512

Larkspur Richlene Kennels
Fort Wayne, IN
219-432-0013

Silvis Boarding Kennel
Fort Wayne, IN
219-489-9777

Sanbar Kennels
Frankfort, IN
765-324-2475

A & J's Country Kennel
Franklin, IN
317-736-9296

Concord Kennels
Goshen, IN
219-875-5469

Cunningham Sweet Haven Kennels
Gosport, IN
812-879-4192

Clayview Kennels
Granger, IN
219-272-6677

Parkewood Kennels
Greenfield, IN
317-894-4166

Arbor Lane Kennel
Indianapolis, IN
317-786-0773

Best Friends Pet Care
Indianapolis, IN
317-841-8182

Dog House Kennels
Indianapolis, IN
317-443-1520

Fair Meadows Kennels
Indianapolis, IN
317-291-3670

**Keystone Pet Hospital
& Boarding Kennel**
Indianapolis, IN
317-546-2476

Northwest Pet Lodge
Indianapolis, IN
317-872-4676

Dogwood Inn Kennel
Jeffersonville, IN
812-283-6960

**Timber Ridge Boarding
Kennel**
Knightstown, IN
765-345-7320

Tanner Creek Kennels
Lawrenceburg, IN
812-537-4556

The Animal Den
Lebanon, IN
317-769-5948

S R Pet Hotel
Madison, IN
812-866-5381

Country Acres Kennels
Marion, IN
765-384-5530

**Burge Kennels for Dogs
& Cats**
Martinsville, IN
765-342-9258

Country Kennels
Martinsville, IN
765-528-2587

T & J Boarding Kennels
Mooresville, IN
317-831-1180

Bannerstone Kennels
Mount Vernon, IN
812-838-3536

Sunset Boarding Kennels
Mount Vernon, IN
812-838-4567

American Pineacre Kennels
Muncie, IN
765-284-5829

Talawanda Kennels
Muncie, IN
765-284-0953

They Like Me Pet Hotel
Nashville, IN
812-988-8771

**Pleasant Run Boarding
Kennels**
New Carlisle, IN
219-654-7234

Beverly's Precious Pet Inn
Noblesville, IN
317-773-6550

Eisenberg Kennels
Noblesville, IN
317-896-2958

Hilltop Boarding Kennels
Peru, IN
765-473-9406

B & S Boarding Kennels
Plainfield, IN
317-272-2206

Shady Hill Kennel
Richmond, IN
765-962-6456

Countryside Kennel
Roanoke, IN
219-672-8272

Law's Country Kennel
Roanoke, IN
219-672-8200

Humble Acre Kennels
Rockport, IN
812-649-4010

Tatum Kennels & Training
Roselawn, IN
219-345-5540

Sundor Kennel
Saint Joe, IN
219-337-5540

**Hickory Acres Boarding
Kennels**
Sheridan, IN
317-769-4296

Catnap Inn Cat Hotel
South Bend, IN
219-288-7877

Kountry Kennels
South Bend, IN
219-233-3658

AAA Wildwood Kennels
Valparaiso, IN
219-464-4333

Cox's Kennels
Valparaiso, IN
219-464-3647

Holiday Pet Retreat II
Valparaiso, IN
219-462-5492

Wildwood Kennels
Valparaiso, IN
219-464-4333

Karefree Kennels
Van Buren, IN
765-934-3647

Shady Brook Kennel
Walkerton, IN
219-586-9306

Teegarden Kennels
Walkerton, IN
219-784-2670

The Pet Resort
Waveland, IN
765-435-2910

Klondike Kennels
West Lafayette, IN
765-463-1603

Sun Dance Kennels
Westfield, IN
317-896-2661

Pampered Pets Kennel
Westport, IN
812-591-2169

Falcroft Boarding Kennel
Yorktown, IN
765-759-5503

Zionsville Country Kennels
Zionsville, IN
317-769-6172

IOWA

Wolf Point Kennels
Ackworth, IA
515-961-3617

Docs Dog Kennel
Adel, IA
515-993-3711

U.S. Kennels > IOWA

Lockhart Freese Kennel
Amana, IA
319-846-2646

Cyclone Country Kennel Club
Ames, IA
515-233-4650

Countryside Boarding Kennels
Ankeny, IA
515-964-1180

Deboers Dog Kennels
Archer, IA
712-723-5249

Country Kennels
Audubon, IA
712-563-2696

D & S Country Kennels
Badger, IA
515-545-4515

Animal House Boarding
Bettendorf, IA
319-359-6541

Bettendorf Pleasantview Kennels
Bettendorf, IA
319-332-4555

Autumn King Kennel
Cedar Falls, IA
319-277-1744

Companion Animal Clinic
Cedar Falls, IA
319-277-2354

Hilltop Kennels
Cedar Rapids, IA
319-363-1054

Sunny Brook Kennel
Cedar Rapids, IA
319-446-7557

Tahoe Kennels
Central City, IA
319-438-1282

Griffon Point Boarding
Clear Lake, IA
515-357-8027

County Line Pet Motel Kennels
Columbus Junction, IA
319-658-3851

Darkenwald Kennels
Council Bluffs, IA
712-322-7387

Sonnie Budd Kennels
Crescent, IA
712-545-3938

Hilltop Kennels
Dallas Center, IA
515-986-3100

Dockendorff Kennels
Danville, IA
319-392-4339

Townline Pet Boarding
Decorah, IA
319-382-5194

Chanticleer Kennels & Cattery
Des Moines, IA
515-223-8196

Specks Kennel
Des Moines, IA
515-277-0666

Vista Boarding Kennels
Des Moines, IA
515-262-0309

Corner View Kennels
Donnellson, IA
319-469-3781

Green Valley Kennels
Dubuque, IA
319-588-3045

Happy Tails Kennel
Dubuque, IA
319-582-6273

Catlin Country Kennels
Eldora, IA
515-497-5721

A Plus Boarding Kennel
Eldridge, IA
319-285-9977

Ledjen Hills Kennels
Ely, IA
319-848-4171

Riverside Hills Boarding Kennels
Estherville, IA
712-362-5376

Carol's Hilltop Kennels
Forest City, IA
515-582-2368

Shiloh Kennels
Forest City, IA
515-581-4553

Kaylar Kennels
Grinnell, IA
515-236-4389

Sno Peke Kennel
Harlan, IA
712-773-5566

Puppy Heaven Kennel
Hawkeye, IA
319-427-3287

Rockaway Kennels
Hawkeye, IA
319-427-3710

Speck's Kennel
Indianola, IA
515-961-3224

Julia's Farm Kennels
Iowa City, IA
319-351-3562

Twin Lakes Puppy Ranch
Kanawha, IA
515-762-3360

Krichel Animal Hospital
Keokuk, IA
319-524-6835

Sukaro Kennels
Knoxville, IA
515-842-6621

Bohl's K-9 Kennel
Lake Mills, IA
515-592-0516

Mite-Win Kennels
Mason City, IA
515-423-4851

Heather Lane Kennels
Mediapolis, IA
319-394-3590

U.S. Kennels > IOWA

McDougall Kennels
Melvin, IA
712-736-2119

Pine Top Kennels
Montrose, IA
319-838-2203

Hidden Acre Kennels
Muscatine, IA
319-263-2497

Ehresman's K 9 Motel
Newton, IA
515-792-9909

McNair's Kennels
North Liberty, IA
319-626-2502

Pepper Hill Kennels
North Liberty, IA
319-626-2622

Willow Creek Kennel
Otley, IA
515-627-5923

**Oakview Hunting Club
& Kennels**
Prairie City, IA
515-994-2094

Northwest Kennels
Sheldon, IA
712-324-2426

Shenandoah Valley Kennels
Shenandoah, IA
712-246-1304

Eagle Bluff Kennels
Sherrill, IA
319-552-2336

Bay Kennels
Sioux City, IA
712-258-4055

Briarcreek Kennel
Solon, IA
319-644-3623

Sun Valley Kennels
Wall Lake, IA
712-664-2859

Guardian Angel Kennel
Waterloo, IA
319-236-2987

West Branch Animal Clinic
West Branch, IA
319-643-2127

Jordan Creek Kennel
West Des Moines, IA
515-224-9500

Dream On Kennel
Wever, IA
319-372-1889

KANSAS

**Turkey Creek Retriever
Kennels**
Abilene, KS
785-479-2201

**Country Meadow Boarding
Kennel**
Baldwin City, KS
785-830-0738

Kibbe's Kennels
Beloit, KS
785-738-2088

Kandue Kennels
Derby, KS
316-788-6418

La Mont Stables & Kennel
Derby, KS
316-788-3186

Kapricorn Kennel
Dodge City, KS
316-225-3668

Moon Creek Kennels
Emporia, KS
316-342-3137

Southwind Kennels
Emporia, KS
316-342-7669

Waconda Kennels
Glen Elder, KS
785-545-3437

Tannenberg Kennels
Hays, KS
785-625-8350

Shadyhill Kennel
Hiawatha, KS
785-742-7676

Circle Drive Kennels
Hill City, KS
785-421-5723

Five R Kennel
Hutchinson, KS
316-665-8711

R C Kennels
Junction City, KS
785-238-7000

Elliott Kennel
Kansas City, KS
913-334-9220

Happy Hollow Kennels
Kansas City, KS
913-721-2883

Sky's the Limit Kennel
Kansas City, KS
913-334-4184

Stewarts Lake Kennels
Kansas City, KS
913-334-0974

**Kennel Crest Country Club
for Pets**
Lawrence, KS
785-887-6920

Morning Star Kennel
Lawrence, KS
785-842-9979

Whispering Pines Kennels
Leavenworth, KS
913-682-9115

Stone Lake Kennels
Louisburg, KS
913-837-4708

H & W Kennel
Manhattan, KS
785-539-2539

**K 9 Resort Boarding
Kennel**
Mc Pherson, KS
316-241-5323

Kaufman Boarding Kennels
Mc Pherson, KS
316-241-8635

Jones Kennels
Netawaka, KS
785-933-2682

Country Kennels
Partridge, KS
316-567-3004

U.S. Kennels > KENTUCKY

All In the Family Kennel
Quinter, KS
785-754-2301

Spark's Kennels
Salina, KS
785-827-9304

Shawnee Pet Motel
Shawnee Mission, KS
913-631-0600

Trailane Kennels
Soldier, KS
785-948-2557

Final Four Kennels
Spring Hill, KS
913-592-3900

Crystal Castle for Pets
Topeka, KS
785-267-1979

Holly Lane Kennels
Topeka, KS
785-233-6612

J A Cars Kennels
Topeka, KS
785-478-4626

West Hills Kennels
Topeka, KS
785-478-4080

**Catalpa Grove Farms
Kennels**
Valley Center, KS
316-755-0720

**Wag'en Tail Ranch
Boarding Kennels**
Valley Center, KS
316-755-1461

Chisholm Creek Kennels
Wichita, KS
316-744-0191

Doggie Playground
Wichita, KS
316-652-7010

**Hallmark Boarding Kennels
& Cattery**
Wichita, KS
316-838-6683

Timber Creek Kennel
Winfield, KS
316-221-4840

KENTUCKY

Baumhaus Kennels
Battletown, KY
502-497-4189

Countryside Kennel
Bowling Green, KY
502-782-5877

Masters Boarding Kennels
Bowling Green, KY
502-842-0848

Creature Comfort Inn
Brandenburg, KY
502-422-1020

KY Kennels
Butler, KY
606-472-7387

**Country Place Boarding
Kennel**
Columbia, KY
502-384-1419

International K 9 Kennels
Corbin, KY
606-528-1112

**Alexandria Boarding
Kennels**
Covington, KY
606-635-3222

Robinwood Kennel
Covington, KY
606-781-2352

Kountry Kennel
Coxs Creek, KY
502-348-1219

Shady Grove Kennel
Danville, KY
606-236-0624

Shady Lawn Kennels
Elizabethtown, KY
502-737-5658

Tlc Pet Motel
Georgetown, KY
502-863-6781

**Bed & Biscuit Boarding
Kennel**
Goshen, KY
502-228-1887

Your Way Boarding Kennels
Henderson, KY
502-521-7943

**Zimmerman Misty Acre
Boarding Kennel**
Henderson, KY
502-826-6116

Sundance Kennels
Independence, KY
606-356-7900

Minirosa Kennels
Jeffersontown, KY
502-499-1910

Desert Fire Kennels
La Center, KY
502-665-5983

Dottidale Kennels
Liberty, KY
606-787-7585

Top Dog Kennel
Liberty, KY
606-787-5467

Bar-Ken Kennels
Louisville, KY
502-267-1526

**Bed & Biscuit Boarding
Kennels**
Louisville, KY
502-228-1887

Bow Wow Kennels
Louisville, KY
502-363-2444

Country Boarding Kennels
Louisville, KY
502-267-7444

Royalton Kennels
Louisville, KY
502-239-0827

**Shamrock Acres
Country Kennel**
Louisville, KY
502-241-7427

Rustic Roost Kennels
Morgantown, KY
502-526-2690

Waggin' Tail Kennel
Mount Sterling, KY
606-498-6463

U.S. Kennels > KENTUCKY

Paradise Kennels
Murray, KY
502-753-4106

All Creatures Inn
Nicholasville, KY
606-233-9000

Four Paws Inn
Paducah, KY
502-443-2848

Legacy Kennel
Paducah, KY
502-898-4712

Green River Kennel
Richardsville, KY
502-777-1077

Andick Kennels
Richmond, KY
606-527-3893

Pet Center Kennels
Richmond, KY
606-369-3058

TLC Pet Center
Shelbyville, KY
502-633-4442

Bar K Farm & Kennel
Simpsonville, KY
502-722-5537

Midway Kennels
Somerset, KY
606-679-5081

Woodford Veterinary Clinic Kennel
Versailles, KY
606-873-1595

Moore's Boarding Kennels
Vine Grove, KY
502-877-2294

Highland Creek Boarding Kennel
Waverly, KY
502-389-4825

Lodi Kennels
West Paducah, KY
502-488-3848

LOUISIANA

Alexandria Pet Inn
Alexandria, LA
318-445-7333

Plank Road Kennel
Baker, LA
504-778-1865

Pine-Hill Boarding Kennel
Bastrop, LA
318-281-2963

Shanon's Pleasant Acres Kennel
Baton Rouge, LA
504-753-5915

Joy's Kennels
Bayou Vista, LA
504-395-4466

Pine Tree Kennels
Blanchard, LA
318-929-7944

Puppy Love Kennel
Bossier City, LA
318-746-4821

Rainbow Kennels
Denham Springs, LA
504-664-2067

Stillwater Kennels
Denham Springs, LA
504-667-0147

Southern Comfort Kennels
Deridder, LA
318-463-7015

Spring Hill Farm & Kennels
Franklinton, LA
504-839-4477

Greenwood Kennels
Gibson, LA
504-575-8317

Ruths Country Kennel
Gonzales, LA
504-647-2220

Wild Wing Kennel
Hammond, LA
504-345-1075

Wolf's Den Kennels
Houma, LA
504-873-7828

Bonnet Carre Kennels
La Place, LA
504-651-0066

A Caring Experience Boarding Kennel
Lafayette, LA
318-988-2273

Country Kennel
Lafayette, LA
318-856-7057

Country Club Kennels
Lake Charles, LA
318-477-1460

Oxbow Kennels
Livingston, LA
504-698-3029

All Creatures Country Club
Mandeville, LA
504-626-9664

Safe Harbor Pets
Metairie, LA
504-885-3632

Hide-A-Way Boarding
Monroe, LA
318-343-6035

Good Going Pet Resort
Mooringsport, LA
318-929-2435

Southern Farms & Kennels
Natchitoches, LA
318-352-0650

Algiers Boarding Kennel
New Orleans, LA
504-362-8312

Brauner's New Orleans East Boarding Kennels
New Orleans, LA
504-254-2200

Laura Lynn Kennels
Prairieville, LA
504-673-3390

Ruston Dog & Cat Kennel
Ruston, LA
318-255-1423

Country Kennels
Shreveport, LA
318-929-3484

U.S. Kennels > MAINE

Defatta Boarding Kennels
Shreveport, LA
318-797-7583

Southside Pet Hotel
Shreveport, LA
318-797-8068

Country Inn Kennel
Thibodaux, LA
504-633-9725

MAINE

Shangri-La Kennels
Auburn, ME
207-784-4685

Carden Kennels
Bangor, ME
207-942-2161

Green Acres Kennel
Bangor, ME
207-942-2161

Acadia Woods Kennel
Bar Harbor, ME
207-288-9766

The Critter Barn
Berwick, ME
207-698-4580

Black Forest Kennels
Biddeford, ME
207-247-4426

Safe Harbor Kennel
Bremen, ME
207-529-4127

Bear Brook Kennel
Brewer, ME
207-989-7979

Atlantic Sunset Kennel
Brunswick, ME
207-725-4724

Great Lsland Kennel
Brunswick, ME
207-729-4506

Home Farm Kennels
Caribou, ME
207-498-8803

Pet Motel
Corinna, ME
207-278-2800

C P L Kennels
Eastport, ME
207-853-4484

Downeast Boarding Kennel
Ellsworth, ME
207-667-3062

Fairfield Kennels
Fairfield, ME
207-465-7801

Pleasant Hill Kennels
Freeport, ME
207-865-4279

Crosswind Kennels
Gardiner, ME
207-582-9255

Mcderry Kennels
Gray, ME
207-657-2929

Trendsetter Kennels
Hampden, ME
207-862-6093

Mariner Kennels
Jefferson, ME
207-549-7426

Mousam River Kennels
Kennebunk, ME
207-985-7826

Melodane Kennels
Kennebunkport, ME
207-282-0684

Creature Comforts
Kittery, ME
207-439-6674

Shadow Birch Kennels
Limington, ME
207-637-2671

The Cat's Inn
Manchester, ME
207-622-9915

Kaylish Kennels
Mechanic Falls, ME
207-345-3258

North Ridge Boarding Kennel
Medway, ME
207-746-9537

TLC Kennels
Mount Vernon, ME
207-778-5903

Wiley Road Kennels
Naples, ME
207-693-3394

Dew Drop Kennels
New Sharon, ME
207-778-6479

Brickyard Kennels
North Yarmouth, ME
207-829-2731

Canine Country Club
Northport, ME
207-763-3655

El Rancho Kennels
Orrington, ME
207-825-3242

The Lazy L Kennel
Oxford, ME
207-539-9188

Purbeck Isle Pet Resort
Richmond, ME
207-737-2892

Singersafe Harbor Kennel
Round Pond, ME
207-529-4127

Blackman's Kennels
Skowhegan, ME
207-474-8517

Cedarosen Kennels
Skowhegan, ME
207-474-6691

Chicopee Farm Kennels
Standish, ME
207-642-2302

Perry Greene Kennel
Waldoboro, ME
207-832-5227

Sukee Kennels
Warren, ME
207-273-3300

Clover Acres Kennel
Windham, ME
207-892-6108

Killington Kennel
Windham, ME
207-892-9649

U.S. Kennels > MAINE

The Kitty Pad
Windham, ME
207-892-8388

Gi Yan Kennel
Woolwich, ME
207-882-7470

York Country Kennels
York, ME
207-363-7950

MARYLAND

Anchors Kennels
Accokeek, MD
301-283-2626

Arnold Pet Station
Arnold, MD
410-544-1130

Deer Park Kennels
Baltimore, MD
410-655-8330

Oak Park kennels
Baltimore, MD
410-242-8735

**Kennel Loving Care
Pet Resort**
Bel Air, MD
410-420-2273

Fieldstone Kennel
Berlin, MD
301-647-6516

Linda's Dog Design
Brookville, MD
301-977-2873

**Preston Country Club
for Pets**
Columbia, MD
301-596-7387

Rainbow Bridge Kennels
Denton, MD
410-479-4811

Beechnut Kennel
Edgewater, MD
410-798-4304

Captain's Quarters for Pets
Elkton, MD
410-398-8320

Best Friends Pet Resort
Gaithersburg, MD
301-926-6005

Pets Vacationland
Hagerstown, MD
301-797-4147

**Lucky Stars Country
Kennels**
Hampstead, MD
410-0239-2100

Bed & Bones
Highland, MD
301-854-9761

Riviera Boarding Kennels
Hughesville, MD
301-274-4456

Cherry Lane Kennels
Laurel, MD
800-233-6093

Tamira Kennels
Millersville, MD
410-987-4535

Country Kennel
Mt. Airy, MD
301-831-7766

Fishing Creek Kennel
North Beach, MD
301-855-4908

Countryside Kennels
Owings, MD
410-741-5011

Fieldstone Kennels
Pasadena, MD
410-647-6516

Tiffany Kennels
Pasadena, MD
410-255-7926

Sugarland Kennels
Poolesville, MD
301-428-8300

Blue Star Kennel
Queenstown, MD
410-827-5680

Canine Country Club
Queenstown, MD
410-827-4245

**Reisterstown Boarding
Kennel**
Reisterstown, MD
410-833-2090
410-833-6767

Wonmore Kennels
Rising Sun, MD
410-658-4919

Montrose Pet Hotel
Rockville, MD
301-770-5446

Pet Dominion
Rockville, MD
301-258-0333

Doghouse
Salisbury, MD
800-644-4380

Columbia Kennels
Seabrook, MD
301-577-1090

Brocroft Kennels
Smithsburg, MD
301-824-7611

Interlude
St. Leonard, MD
410-586-1843

Country Comfort Kennels
St., MD
410-692-5055

Pinewood Kennel
Sudlersville, MD
410-758-2942

Dog & Cat Hotel
Towson, MD
410-825-8880

Camp Yuppie Puppy
Uniontown, MD
410-857-8230

Queen Anne Kennels
Upper Marlborough, MD
301-249-1210

Timber Ridge Kennel
Upperco, MD
410-239-6225

Amberlyn Kennel
Walkersville, MD
301-898-3106

Happy Hollow Kennel
Westminster, MD
410-876-1235

U.S. Kennels > MASSACHUSETTS

Shady Spring Boarding Kennels
Woodbine, MD
410-795-1957

MASSACHUSETTS

Manamooskeagin Kennels
Abington, MA
617-857-1002

Boarding Kennel of Boxboro
Acton, MA
508-263-3412

Palmer Kennels
Acton, MA
508-263-4979

Merrimac Valley Boarding Kennels
Amesbury, MA
508-388-3074

Whirl Wind Farm Kennel
Amherst, MA
413-549-3780

Doody's Animal Inn
Ashby, MA
508-386-2412

Autumn Whim Kennels
Ashland, MA
508-881-1879

Best Friends @ the Pet Quarters
Ashland, MA
508-881-7557

Mountain Top Kennel
Ashley Falls, MA
413-229-8636

Sea Master Kennel
Assonet, MA
508-763-4874

K-Nine Corner Kennels
Bedford, MA
617-861-0206

Belchertown Boarding Kennel
Belchertown, MA
413-323-7641

Coronet Kennels
Bellingham, MA
508-883-8772

Wishing Well Kennels
Bellingham, MA
508-966-7654

Petcetera Kennels
Belmont, MA
617-484-6133

Country Time Pet Retreat
Berkley, MA
508-823-1903

Sylvan Kennels
Beverly, MA
508-927-2275

Skipton Kennels
Boston, MA
617-442-0747

Weloset Kennel
Boxford, MA
508-887-5760

Straw Hollow Kennels
Boylston, MA
508-869-2803

Happy Paw Kennels
Braintree, MA
617-843-1021

Best Friends Pet Resort
Brockton, MA
508-583-8555

Animal Care Center Kennel
Brookline, MA
617-277-0401

Andora Kennels
Chelmsford, MA
508-454-8718

Animal Camp
Chelsea, MA
734-433-9089

Teakwood Kennels
Douglas, MA
508-476-7755

Shadyridge Kennels
Dunstable, MA
508-649-7020

Beresford Kennels
Duxbury, MA
617-834-9053

Greengate Farm & Kennels
Duxbury, MA
617-837-5125

Cloverleaf Kennel
East Falmouth, MA
508-540-7387

Lower Cape Kennels
Eastham, MA
508-240-2204

Nauset Kennels
Eastham, MA
508-255-0081

Creature Comforts Boarding Kennel
Easthampton, MA
413-527-6168

Berlyd Acres Boarding Kennels
Feeding Hills, MA
413-786-5633

Stacy Kennels
Fitchburg, MA
508-345-1001

Old Farm Kennels
Franklin, MA
508-528-1929

Maplewood Boarding Kennels
Granby, MA
413-467-9621

Noble House Kennels
Great Barrington, MA
413-528-9042

Town & Country Animal Hospital & Kennels
Groveland, MA
508-374-1684

Valley Vet Hospital-Inn for Pets
Hadley, MA
413-584-1223

Briarwood Kennels
Hanover, MA
617-826-9003

Heritage Kennels
Hanson, MA
617-293-7203

Harvard Kennels
Harvard, MA
508-772-4242

U.S. Kennels > MASSACHUSETTS

Golden Kennels
Harwich, MA
508-432-5649

The Good Dog:
Boarding & Daycare
Hingham, MA
781-749-8342

Bark Inn Kennel
Holbrook, MA
617-767-2200

Canine College
Holbrook, MA
617-767-3908

Nitasha D Kennels
Hopkinton, MA
508-435-5454

Puttin On the Ritz
Hubbardston, MA
508-924-4876

Country Kennel
Lee, MA
413-243-3137

Barton Brook Kennel
& Humane Shelter
Leicester, MA
508-892-0321

Malden Animal Hospital
& Kennel
Malden, MA
617-322-8795

Pine Banks Animal
Hospital & Kennels
Malden, MA
617-321-1300

Alladan Kennels
Mansfield, MA
508-339-5597

Red Dog Inn
Mansfield, MA
508-339-5912

Brigadoon Boarding
Kennels
Marshfield, MA
617-834-7675

Elja Kennels
Marshfield, MA
617-837-2644

Pet Inn
Methuen, MA
508-685-4304

Nightingale Kennel
Middleboro, MA
508-946-1870

Camelot Kennels of
Mendon
Milford, MA
508-478-6390

Cat Nap Inn
Milford, MA
508-473-0174

Camelot Kennels
Monson, MA
413-267-4036

Stirling Kennels
Monson, MA
413-267-4290

Woodland Kennels
Montague, MA
413-367-2838

Continental Kennels
Natick, MA
508-655-6188

Mardonof Kennels
North Attleboro, MA
508-699-2883

Taramanor Kennel
North Attleboro, MA
508-695-0210

Valley Inn for Pets
Northampton, MA
413-584-5252

Bedrock Kennels
Norton, MA
508-285-2221

Kalmia Kennels
Norton, MA
508-222-6970

Jan's Dog House
Oakham, MA
508-882-3838

Mt Tully Kennels
Orange, MA
508-575-0614

Lake Farm Boarding
Kennels
Orleans, MA
508-255-7214

Laughlin Kennels
Oxford, MA
508-987-7161

Palatine Kennels &
Boarding Lodge
Paxton, MA
508-757-7959

Wendell J Sammet Kennels
Pembroke, MA
617-293-7352

Pittsfield Boarding Center
Pittsfield, MA
413-499-1580

Towne Kennel
Raynham, MA
508-824-4865

Greystone Kennel
Rehoboth, MA
508-252-3948

Looks Acres Boarding
Kennel
Rochester, MA
508-763-5748

Muddy Creek Animal Care
Center
Rowley, MA
508-948-2345

Ramson Kennels
Salisbury, MA
508-388-0826

The Yankee Kennels
Sharon, MA
617-784-5397

Troutbrook Kennels
South Wellfleet, MA
508-349-3965

Wintergreen Kennels
Southampton, MA
413-562-9478

Southboro Kennels
Southboro, MA
508-485-5136

U.S. Kennels > MICHIGAN

Rama Kennels
Southbridge, MA
508-764-4417

Jordan's Boarding Kennels
Springfield, MA
413-782-2305

Blue Moon Kennel
Stockbridge, MA
413-274-6674

Great Scott Kennels
Stoughton, MA
617-344-2581

Best Friends Sudbury
Sudbury, MA
978-443-2351

TLC Pet Haven
Sutton, MA
508-865-3180

C Farm Kennels
Swansea, MA
508-678-9140

Swansea Pet Lodge
Swansea, MA
508-674-1546

Twin Beau D Kennels
Swansea, MA
508-379-0976

Bare Hill Kennels
Topsfield, MA
508-887-5216

Hickory Hill Boarding Kennels
Turners Falls, MA
413-863-9753

Best Friends Tyngsboro
Tyngsboro, MA
978-649-8585

K-Nine Corner Kennels
Tyngsboro, MA
508-649-6391

Aldrich Street Kennel
Uxbridge, MA
508-278-7790

Best Friends Wakefield
Wakefield, MA
781-245-1237

New Pond Kennels
Walpole, MA
508-668-1895

Winterhill Kennel
West Brookfield, MA
508-867-6929

Cruz Kennels
West Wareham, MA
508-295-5703

Mountain Laurel Kennels
Westminster, MA
508-874-1232

Nashoba Valley Boarding Kennel
Westord, MA
978-692-2302

Boutique Kennel
Westport, MA
508-636-8219

Van-Elger Pet Care Center
Westport, MA
508-636-8143

Weymouth Landing Cat Clinic & Hotel
Weymouth, MA
617-337-0400

Ledgebrook Kennel
Woburn, MA
617-933-0170

Witt Boarding Kennels
Worcester, MA
508-754-4530

Pinecrest Kennels
Wrentham, MA
508-883-8440

MICHIGAN

Joyce's Kitty Motel
Ada, MI
616-676-0531

Animal Inn
Adrian, MI
517-423-3800

Rosal Kennels
Albion, MI
517-857-4162

Heather Hill Kennels
Alger, MI
517-836-2327

Carrosel Boarding Kennels
Allenton, MI
810-395-4554

Mar J Kennels
Allenton, MI
810-395-2674

Tina's Boarding Kennel
Alpena, MI
517-354-6772

Wyn Dean Kennels
Alto, MI
616-868-6678

Ackley Kennels
Ann Arbor, MI
313-996-1335

Kelly Kennels
Ann Arbor, MI
313-426-4700

Arbee Kennels
Attica, MI
810-724-8436

Sher Meer Kennels
Auburn Hills, MI
248-370-0012

Wingford Kennels
Avoca, MI
810-385-5335

P B N Kennel
Bark River, MI
906-466-2867

Harper Creek Kennels
Battle Creek, MI
616-979-1622

Elken's Kennels
Belleville, MI
313-697-9183

Regency Kennels
Belleville, MI
313-699-7338

Country Kennels
Benton Harbor, MI
616-849-1071

Nagles Alternative Kennel
Boyne City, MI
616-582-2420

Tamara Kennels
Brighton, MI
810-229-4339

U.S. Kennels > MICHIGAN

Maple Valley Kennels
Brown City, MI
810-346-3395

Brigadoon Kennels
Byron Center, MI
616-878-9269

Kozy Kennels
Cadillac, MI
616-775-2903

Towne and Country Kennels
Canton, MI
313-981-4010

Pleasant Hill Boarding Kennels
Caro, MI
517-673-4796

Kintor Kennels
Central Lake, MI
616-544-6519

Donto Kennels
Charlevoix, MI
616-547-6866

Sturgeon River Kennels
Chassell, MI
906-523-4038

Copper Kennels
Cheboygan, MI
616-625-9007

Autumnwood Kennels
Clare, MI
517-386-3820

Kline Kennel
Clawson, MI
810-588-5940

Kamber Kennel
Clinton Township, MI
810-792-3000

Eko Lan Kennels
Cohoctah, MI
517-545-9352

Aradobe Kennel
Commerce Township, MI
248-669-1971

Cobb's Country Kennel
Dafter, MI
906-632-8670

Bunker Hill Kennels
Davisburg, MI
248-625-2766

Inner City Dog Kennel
Detroit, MI
313-863-5350

Blue Moon Kennels
Dowagiac, MI
616-782-7658

Sweet Talk Kennels
Dryden, MI
810-796-3357

A & M Kennels
Escanaba, MI
906-786-4753

The Dog Gone Acres
Farmington, MI
248-474-2027

Maribeau Kennels
Farmington, MI
248-626-2243

Turn A Round Kennels
Flushing, MI
810-659-8787

Brady Kennels
Fowlerville, MI
517-223-3939

Windy Acres Kennels
Freeland, MI
517-695-5994

Double "B" Kennels
Gaylord, MI
517-732-2689

Brooknelle Kennels
Grand Rapids, MI
616-363-3687

Little Farm Kennels
Grand Rapids, MI
616-453-9779

Castaway Kennels
Gregory, MI
313-498-2570

The Animal Inn
Gwinn, MI
906-346-5945

Hunters Marsh Kennels
Harrisville, MI
517-724-6430

Evergreen Kennels
Hartford, MI
616-621-2318

Rivers Edge Kennels
Hastings, MI
616-795-4852

Wolf Manor Kennels
Hesperia, MI
616-861-5527

Patterson Kennels
Higgins Lake, MI
517-821-9137

Kingsley Boarding Kennels
Holland, MI
616-399-1566

Happy Stay Boarding Kennels
Howell, MI
517-546-2900

J J's Lakeview Dog Boarding
Hubbell, MI
906-296-8701

K C Kennels
Hudson, MI
517-448-2116

A1 Dog & Cat Kennel
Irons, MI
616-266-5758

Chieftan Kennels
Ironwood, MI
906-932-3646

Hill's Kennels
Ironwood, MI
906-932-5810

Marshland Kennels
Jackson, MI
517-769-3647

Dogwood Kennels
Jones, MI
616-244-8556

Animal Inn Kennel
Kalamazoo, MI
616-381-2171

Blustrywood Kennels
Kalamazoo, MI
616-342-9649

U.S. Kennels > MICHIGAN

Lake City Kennel
Lake City, MI
616-839-5375

Orion Kennel Club
Lake Orion, MI
810-391-4200

Four Paws Pet Motel
Lansing, MI
517-327-1070

**Cairn Dale Farm
Training Kennel**
Lennon, MI
810-621-3414

Baybreeze Kennels
Linwood, MI
517-697-5222

**Belle Creek Boarding
Kennels**
Livonia, MI
313-421-1144

Anderson Creek Kennels
Ludington, MI
616-843-8397

A&M Kennels
Manistee, MI
231-723-8212

Evergreen Kennels
Marne, MI
616-677-3398

Superior Kennels
Marquette, MI
906-249-1672

Mar Creek Kennels
Marshall, MI
616-781-5439

Chapin Kennels
Merrill, MI
517-643-7032

North Twenty Kennels
Merritt, MI
616-328-4596

Whistle Lake Kennel
Metamora, MI
810-678-3159

Howl-A-Day Resort
Midland, MI
517-832-2595

Country Kennel Pet Care
Milan, MI
313-429-2375

Qualls Kennels
Milford, MI
248-887-8842

**Cedar Coast Boarding
Kennels**
Montague, MI
616-894-6617

Gunsmoke Kennels
Muskegon, MI
616-744-0259

West Highland Kennels
Muskegon, MI
616-788-3293

Northern Pine Kennels
National City, MI
517-469-3236

Chrysler Kennels
New Baltimore, MI
810-949-9705

White Oaks Pet Motel
Newaygo, MI
616-652-9372

Canine Country Club
Niles, MI
616-683-0988

Adams Kennel
North Street, MI
810-982-3267

**Leelanuau Boarding
Kennels**
Northport, MI
616-386-7340

Rolling Hills Kennels
Onsted, MI
517-467-4490

Maple Lane Kennel
Ortonville, MI
248-627-4445

**Happy Tail Boarding
Kennels**
Oshtemo, MI
616-375-2056

Round House Kennels
Otisville, MI
810-793-8962

Green Acres Kennels
Ottawa Lake, MI
313-856-5735

**Oxford Oaks Boarding
Kennel**
Oxford, MI
248-628-1776

First Class Kennels
Pinckney, MI
313-426-7866

Dawnlee Kennels
Plainwell, MI
616-629-9177

Win Ton Kennels
Plymouth, MI
313-453-0213

Pontiac Boarding Kennels
Pontiac, MI
248-332-0287

Gull Lake Kennel
Richland, MI
616-629-5249

Canine Country Club
Rochester, MI
248-852-7474

Green-In-Dale Kennels
Rockford, MI
616-866-9771

Wick Lane Kennel
Romulus, MI
313-721-0523

Heritage Kennels
Roscommon, MI
517-366-8020

Fernlee Kennels
Royal Oak, MI
248-549-5182

American Boarding Kennel
Saint Clair, MI
810-364-6301

Shores Kennel
Saint Clair Shores, MI
810-293-1429

Sunrise Kennels
Saint Ignace, MI
906-643-7726

Happy Trails Pet Hotel
Saint Louis, MI
517-463-8686

Peterson Kennels
Saline, MI
313-429-0676

Whitside Kennels
Sault Ste. Marie, MI
906-632-8614

Mason Creek Kennels
Shelby, MI
616-861-5903

Su Jo Kennels
Sherwood, MI
517-741-3452

Silver Frost Kennels
South Lyon, MI
248-437-1174

**Green Willow Boarding
Kennel**
Southfield, MI
248-356-3394

Autumn Kennels
Standish, MI
517-846-8331

Red Woof Kennel
Stevensville, MI
616-422-2555

Alert Kennel
Taylor, MI
734-287-3994

Boondocks Kennels
Three Rivers, MI
616-279-7599

Pet Hotel
Tipton, MI
517-431-2445

Classic Canine
Traverse City, MI
616-946-3646

Tulamar Kennel Boarding
Traverse City, MI
616-947-4494

Jagersbo Kennels
Troy, MI
248-644-7717

R & R Kennels
Troy, MI
248-689-7660

Oakwood Boarding Kennel
Twin Lake, MI
616-828-4337

AAA Oakridge Kennels
Union, MI
616-641-2263

Yankee Pride Kennel
Warren, MI
810-573-0997

Valley View Kennels
Watervliet, MI
616-463-4945

Caudle Boarding Kennels
Wayne, MI
313-397-2740

Brookside Kennels
West Branch, MI
517-345-7114

M & M Kennels
West Olive, MI
616-399-7333

Pine Hill Farm Boarding
West Olive, MI
616-842-7426

Companion K-9 Academy
White Lake, MI
248-887-3647

Acme Creek Kennels
Williamsburg, MI
616-938-9518

Animal Medical Center
Wyoming, MI
616-531-7387

Countryside Kennels
Zeeland, MI
616-772-2070

MINNESOTA

Armstrong Ranch Kennels
Anoka, MN
612-427-1777

Backwater Kennels
Atwater, MN
320-276-8363

**Red River Boarding
Kennels**
Baker, MN
218-789-7510

Northern Kennels
Bemidji, MN
218-751-5280

Red Oaks Pet Inn
Brainerd, MN
218-829-1902

Benson's Fairhill Kennel
Buffalo, MN
612-682-3014

**Blue Ribbon Boarding
Kennel**
Burnsville, MN
612-435-7536

Cedar Creek Kennel
Cambridge, MN
612-689-1379

Marsh Lake Kennel
Chaska, MN
612-443-2081

Oak View Kennels
Detroit Lakes, MN
218-847-1236

Clover Valley Kennel
Duluth, MN
218-525-2715

Deloia Kennels
Duluth, MN
218-729-8239

Northland Kennels
Duluth, MN
218-525-3885

C J's Tender Care Kennel
East Grand Forks, MN
218-773-9301

Elk River Kennels
Elk River, MN
612-263-6200

Canine Country Club
Elko, MN
612-461-2209

Camp Canine Kennels
Faribault, MN
507-332-8110

U.S. Kennels > MISSISSIPPI

Nan Dooley Kennels
Forest Lake, MN
612-464-7040

Country Care Boarding Kennel
Grove City, MN
507-826-3510

Woof Purr Boarding Kennel
Hibbing, MN
218-263-5818

Spruce Hill Kennels
Hoffman, MN
320-986-2939

North Oaks Kennels
Hugo, MN
612-429-1810

In the Woods Boarding Kennels
Lake City, MN
612-345-4615

Animal Inn Boarding Kennel
Lake Elmo, MN
612-777-0255

Rolling Hills Boarding Kennel
Lakeville, MN
612-461-2003

Smith's Boarding & Training Kennels
Madison Lake, MN
507-243-3372

Marshall Boarding Kennel
Marshall, MN
507-532-3616

Country Kennels
Mayer, MN
612-657-2575

Sunny Brook Kennels Too
Medford, MN
507-451-4100

Northland Kennels
Minneapolis, MN
612-786-8410

K-9 Country Club
Moorhead, MN
218-233-8050

Oak Ridge Kennels
Mound, MN
612-472-3702

Meadow Woods Kennels
New Germany, MN
320-485-2418

Kaos Kennels
New Prague, MN
612-758-5267

Dokken's Oak Ridge Kennels
Northfield, MN
507-744-2616

Silver Lake Kennel
Oakdale, MN
651-777-1051

Ideal Boarding Kennels
Pequot Lakes, MN
218-543-4215

Marise Dwire Kennels
Pequot Lakes, MN
218-568-8452

Wells Creek Kennel
Red Wing, MN
612-388-1699

K-9 Kennels
Rochester, MN
507-289-2470

Northwood Valley Kennels
Rogers, MN
612-428-4001

Autumn Brand Kennels
Saginaw, MN
218-729-9063

Del-Tone Kennels
Saint Cloud, MN
320-251-7204

Goldwood Kennels
Saint Paul, MN
612-429-0648

Lone Lake Kennels
Saint Paul, MN
612-459-2234

Quaint Country Kennel
Sherburn, MN
507-695-2334

Ring Neck Kennels
Stewart, MN
320-587-9322

Duck Pass Kennels
Stillwater, MN
612-439-9115

Meadow Brooke Kennel
Vergas, MN
218-342-3647

Magnum Retriever Kennels
Virginia, MN
218-735-8447

Camp Comfort Kennel
Wyoming, MN
612-462-4614

MISSISSIPPI

Butler's Kennel
Biloxi, MS
601-388-4093

Swan Kennels
Columbus, MS
662-328-8877

K-9 Inn
Gulfport, MS
601-896-8800

Whispering Pines Boarding Kennel
Gulfport, MS
601-831-3566

Canine Country Club
Hattiesburg, MS
601-268-1999

Twin Oak Kennel
Hernando, MS
601-429-6527

Jessieview Kennels
Independence, MS
601-233-2163

Blue Ribbon Kennels
Jackson, MS
601-981-0183

Pet Hotel
McComb, MS
601-684-6848

Pine Bark Kennels
Ocean Springs, MS
601-875-1771

U.S. Kennels > MISSISSIPPI

College Hill Kennels
Oxford, MS
601-234-3865

Animal House Kennels
Picayune, MS
601-798-7753

Southaven Boarding Kennel
Southaven, MS
601-393-2417

Gator Point Kennels
Tylertown, MS
601-876-3647

Paradise Kennels
Tylertown, MS
601-876-9040

MISSOURI

Stargate Kennel
Arnold, MO
314-296-1905

Williamsburg Kennels
Ballwin, MO
314-227-5764

Country Lane Kennel
Belton, MO
816-322-6666

Bryan's Kennel
Billings, MO
417-744-2228

Lazy K 9 Pet Ranch
Branson, MO
417-335-6045

Circle C Rock Hill Kennel
Breckenridge, MO
816-644-5167

**Buck Creek Game Farm
& Kennel**
Camdenton, MO
573-873-1201

Watson's Kennels
Camdenton, MO
573-346-7653

Busch's Kennel
Cape Girardeau, MO
573-334-1983

Bybee Quentin Kennels
Cross Timbers, MO
417-998-6360

Lebarland Kennels
Defiance, MO
314-398-5503

The Sorenson Kennels
Defiance, MO
314-828-5149

**Evergreen Boarding
Kennels**
Easton, MO
816-667-5717

Honey Dew Kennel
Elkland, MO
417-345-2721

K & J Kennels
Fair Grove, MO
417-759-2561

Legends Dog Kennels
Fenton, MO
314-343-8077

Baronwood Kennels
Florissant, MO
314-838-2021

Corywood Kennels
Foley, MO
314-662-2280

Abel Country Aire Kennel
Foristell, MO
314-327-6434

Sundowner Kennels
Goodman, MO
417-364-8597

C & B Kennels
Granby, MO
417-472-3052

Tanglewood Kennels
Greenwood, MO
816-537-6886

Hideaway Kennels
Harrisonville, MO
816-380-5387

Caraway Kennels
Haslett, MO
517-755-4178

K & L Kennels
Higginsville, MO
816-584-3647

**Dog House Boarding
Kennel**
High Ridge, MO
314-677-3131

Country Estates Kennel
House Springs, MO
314-677-7774

Thunder River Kennels
Houston, MO
417-967-5501

DJ's Kennel
Imperial, MO
314-464-1316

Honey Creek Pet Boarding
Jefferson City, MO
573-496-3138

Cool Valley Kennels
Jonesburg, MO
314-488-5901

Golden Oak Kennel
Joplin, MO
417-781-1673

Josserand Kennels
Joplin, MO
417-781-9313

Bel Air Petersham Kennels
Kansas City, MO
816-356-1180

Country Kennels
Kansas City, MO
816-353-5675

Countryside Kennels
Kansas City, MO
816-333-5050

Pet Motel
Kansas City, MO
816-942-0971

Red Bridge Kennel
Kansas City, MO
816-942-6800

Winding River Pet Motel
Kansas City, MO
816-942-0971

Kimberling Kennels
Kimberling City, MO
417-739-4905

U.S. Kennels > MONTANA

Lyons Den Kennel
Kingsville, MO
816-865-3285

Lone Pine Kennels
Kirksville, MO
816-627-3647

Pleasant Valley Kennels
Kirkwood, MO
314-822-1000

Old Drum Pet Motel
Knob Noster, MO
816-563-5111

Reedgate Kennels
Lamar, MO
417-682-5390

Foster Don Kennels
Macon, MO
816-385-3442

Stardust Kennels
Mexico, MO
573-581-3293

Doss Boarding Kennels
Monett, MO
417-235-6600

Better Kennels
Mountain Grove, MO
417-668-7731

Care-A-Lot Kennels
Nixa, MO
417-725-9342

Ozark Crest Kennels
Nixa, MO
417-725-2121

Adams Animal Inn
Ozark, MO
417-581-6946

Happy Hollow Pet Lodge
Ozark, MO
417-581-7983

Do Bo Tri Kennel
Purdy, MO
417-652-3579

Twin Oaks Kennels
Richland, MO
573-765-3757

Four Paws Country Inn Kennel
Richmond, MO
816-776-3438

Pine Tree Kennels
Rolla, MO
573-364-2492

Bluffview Kennels
Saint Charles, MO
314-441-2337

Bold Monarch Kennels
Saint Charles, MO
314-441-1350

Pet Tenders Boarding Kennel
Saint Clair, MO
314-629-3413

K-9 Boarding Kennels
Saint Louis, MO
314-846-2078

Walkers Kennels
Saint Louis, MO
314-487-4513

Allen Kennels
Salem, MO
573-729-8441

Bond Kennels
Seneca, MO
417-776-8350

American Canine Kennels
Springfield, MO
417-865-6959

Country Club Kennels
Springfield, MO
417-883-2313

Golden Rule Kennels
Stockton, MO
417-276-3843

In the Dog House
Sullivan, MO
573-860-7387

Sunburst Kennel A K C
Tuscumbia, MO
573-369-2520

Alpine Kennels
Warrensburg, MO
816-747-2413

South Point Kennel
Washington, MO
314-239-5577

Ozark Lady Kennel
West Plains, MO
417-284-3372

Fowler Boarding Kennels
Wright City, MO
314-745-3555

MONTANA

Mountain View Kennels
Arlee, MT
406-726-4006

Kota's Kennels
Billings, MT
406-656-3300

Thunder Ridge Kennels
Billings, MT
406-373-6386

F & L Pet Resort
Black Eagle, MT
406-452-6828

Kennels West Dog Boarding
Bozeman, MT
406-587-7446

Tadroh Kennel
Butte, MT
406-494-3689

Guardian Kennels
Clancy, MT
406-443-1117

Stage Stop Farm & Kennels
Columbia Falls, MT
406-892-5719

Happy Hollow Boarding Kennel
Dillon, MT
406-683-4470

Old Farm Kennels
Florence, MT
406-273-6837

Karosel Kennels
Frenchtown, MT
406-626-5280

B & J Kennels
Great Falls, MT
406-454-3900

U.S. Kennels > MONTANA

Bitterroot Kennels
Hamilton, MT
406-363-6616

Hayes Pet Boarding
Hamilton, MT
406-961-3814

A-No 1 Kennels
Kalispell, MT
406-752-9062

The Pet Palace
Laurel, MT
406-628-8760

Lazy K-Bob Boarding Kennel
Libby, MT
406-293-9825

Muir's Boarding Kennels
Missoula, MT
406-251-2540

Upland Kennel
Savage, MT
406-798-3457

Mountain View Boarding
Seeley Lake, MT
406-677-2572

Shadowalk Kennels
Stevensville, MT
406-777-5570

Madison River Kennels
Three Forks, MT
406-285-6724

Adams Kennel
Ulm, MT
406-866-3441

NEBRASKA

Heirlair Kennels
Auburn, NE
402-274-4785

Ace Kennels
Bellevue, NE
402-293-1166

Lakeshore Boarding Kennels
Bellevue, NE
402-291-2540

Royal Kennels
Fremont, NE
402-721-4160

Platte Valley Kennels
Grand Island, NE
308-382-9126

Rainwater Kennels
Grand Island, NE
308-384-1517

Patterson Kennels
Hastings, NE
402-462-4413

White's K-9 Kennels
Hastings, NE
402-463-0781

Country Care Kennels
Kearney, NE
308-234-3317

Vance Boarding Kennels
Lincoln, NE
402-467-1026

Countryside Pet Salon & Kennels
Norfolk, NE
402-379-3246

Holiday Kennels
Omaha, NE
402-453-2400

Kar Sim Kennel
Omaha, NE
402-397-6950

Sunset Pet Motel
Omaha, NE
402-571-1298

Wags Kennel
Omaha, NE
402-894-0456

Breezy Hill Kennel
Papillion, NE
402-331-3541

Prairie Grass Kennels
Reynolds, NE
402-324-3244

Cottonwood Kennels
Waterloo, NE
402-359-4155

Riverside Meadows Pet Motel
Waterloo, NE
402-779-4172

NEVADA

Canine Country Club
Carson City, NV
702-267-2251

Hound House—the Kennel
Carson City, NV
702-882-2288

Brebeau Boarding Kennels
Elko, NV
702-738-2108

Paws 'N Claws Animal Lodge
Henderson, NV
702-565-7297

Animal Inn Kennels
Las Vegas, NV
702-736-0036

A-VIP Kennels
Las Vegas, NV
702-361-8900

Dewey Boarding Kennel
Las Vegas, NV
702-362-6048

Irrenhaus Boarding Kennels
Minden, NV
702-782-3664

Sentry Kennels
Reno, NV
702-786-8161

Silver State Kennels
Reno, NV
702-677-2442

Winter Street Boarding Kennel
Reno, NV
702-322-4882

NEW HAMPSHIRE

Country Club Kennel
Amherst, NH
603-673-7710

Aftan Boarding Kennels
Bedford, NH
603-472-5001

Redgate Kennels
Belmont, NH
603-524-4263

U.S. Kennels > NEW JERSEY

Country Road Kennels
Brentwood, NH
603-772-4049

Candray Kennels
Candia, NH
603-483-8591

Royale Cocker Kennel
Chester, NH
603-483-2050

**Countryside Boarding
Kennels**
Concord, NH
603-225-0992

Trafalgar Kennels
Cornish, NH
603-542-5304

Durham Point Kennels
Durham, NH
603-659-3288

Great Bay Kennel
Durham, NH
603-868-1707

Jackson Boarding Kennel
East Swanzey, NH
603-352-8809

Grady Hill Kennels
Goffstown, NH
603-497-4823

Blue Mountain Kennel
Grantham, NH
603-863-3808

Echo Lane Kennels
Hillsboro, NH
603-464-3704

Village Sentry Kennel
Hollis, NH
603-465-7553

It's A Dog's Life Kennel
Hudson, NH
603-595-1488

Litterhof Kennel
Laconia, NH
603-524-7887

Moonlite Kennels
Lochmere, NH
603-524-0995

Little Love Kennels
Madison, NH
603-367-4545

Spruce Acre Kennels
Manchester, NH
603-622-0285

K-9 Country Club
Milford, NH
603-673-2582

Gretlyn Kennels
Moultonborough, NH
603-279-4292

Wapack Kennels
New Ipswich, NH
603-878-3784

Birch Hill Kennels
Newfields, NH
603-286-3901

Woodes Kennels
North Hampton, NH
603-964-8781

White Mountain Kennels
North Sandwich, NH
603-284-7108

Our Town Kennel
Peterborough, NH
603-924-7116

Burlshire Kennels
Pittsfield, NH
603-798-5003

North Eastern Kennels
Plainfield, NH
603-675-5901

Ebony Boarding Kennel
Plymouth, NH
603-536-4219

Abbacy Kennels
Portsmouth, NH
603-436-4922

Sea Breeze Kennel
Rye, NH
603-964-7454

Meadow Ridge Kennels
Sullivan, NH
603-847-9034

Fall Mountain Kennels
Walpole, NH
603-756-3025

Cherry Mountain Kennel
Whitefield, NH
603-837-2448

NEW JERSEY

Northcliff Kennels
Andover, NJ
973-786-5250

Lyndell Kennels
Annandale, NJ
908-730-8977

**Atlantic City Pet Care
Kennel**
Atlantic City, NJ
609-348-8660

Bed & Biscuit Inn
Belle Mead, NJ
908-874-7748

Hope's Kennels
Blairstown, NJ
908-459-5380

Best Friends Pet Resort
Cinnaminson, NJ
609-661-0707

Forest Run Kennels
Columbia, NJ
908-496-4317

Plateau Kennels
Frenchtown, NJ
908-996-4209

Willow Run Kennels
Frenchtown, NJ
908-782-7218

Carriage House Kennel
Greendell, NJ
973-383-5733

Aladdin Kennels
Hampton, NJ
908-735-4661

Arcadia Kennels
Hopewell, NJ
609-466-1476

Country Meadow Kennels
Lafayette, NJ
973-579-6010

Lake Hopatcong Kennels
Lake Hopatcong, NJ
973-663-1111

Stradbrook Kennels
Long Valley, NJ
908-850-8854

U.S. Kennels > NEW JERSEY

Koka's Kennels Dog Hotel
Mount Holly, NJ
609-267-9029

Kobesky's Kennels
Newton, NJ
973-383-9232

Mansion House Kennels
Newton, NJ
973-579-1476

Best Friends Pet Care
North Plainfield, NJ
908-822-9200

Curmat Boarding Kennel
Somerville, NJ
908-218-1939

Kerfree Kennels
Sparta, NJ
973-383-5009

Sky Run Kennels
Stewartsville, NJ
908-859-4554

Dav Jan Kennels
Stillwater, NJ
973-383-2238

Applewood Kennels
Vernon, NJ
973-764-4691

Best Friends Pet Care
West Berlin, NJ
856-719-0888

Whitehouse Kennels
Whitehouse, NJ
908-534-2444

NEW MEXICO

R & S Boarding Kennels
Alamogordo, NM
505-437-1479

Academy Boarding Kennels
Albuquerque, NM
505-884-7878

Canine Country Club
Albuquerque, NM
505-898-0725

Ford's Chaparral Kennels
Anthony, NM
505-824-4388

L & B Kennels
Artesia, NM
505-748-3842

Capitan Kennels
Capitan, NM
505-354-2509

Browning Oasis Kennel
Carlsbad, NM
505-887-2293

Diadem Kennels
Cedar Crest, NM
505-281-5939

Animals Inn
Clovis, NM
505-769-1711

Corrales Kennels
Corrales, NM
505-898-3743

Gasman Kennels
Deming, NM
505-546-4239

Black Mesa Boarding Kennels
Espanola, NM
505-753-9530

Country Club Pet Palace
Farmington, NM
505-325-2251

San-Zan Kennels & Stables
Hobbs, NM
505-392-6644

Doggie Dude Ranch & Cat Farm
Las Cruces, NM
505-647-4471

Old Mesilla Kennels
Las Cruces, NM
505-526-2213

Sunflower Kennels
Los Lunas, NM
505-865-5212

Country Canine Boarding
Moriarty, NM
505-281-3878

Coyote Kennels
Roswell, NM
505-622-0004

Mary Jo's Kennels
Roswell, NM
505-622-5133

Hondo Valley Kennels
Ruidoso Downs, NM
505-378-4047

Country Boarding Kennels
Santa Fe, NM
505-471-2444

Paw Print Kennels
Santa Fe, NM
505-471-7194

Taos Kennels & Training Center
Taos, NM
505-758-3224

NEW YORK

A Pet Station Resort
Adams Center, NY
315-232-3780

Amsel Training Kennels
Akron, NY
716-542-4411

Roszak's Kennels
Akron, NY
716-542-4710

Hollindale Kennels
Albany, NY
518-462-4103

Pine Bush Kennels
Albany, NY
518-456-0700

Starrview Kennels
Albion, NY
716-589-7311

Tri-County Kennels
Alden, NY
716-937-4717

Pinekroff Kennels
Allegany, NY
716-372-0961

Meadowdale Acres Animal Inn
Altamont, NY
518-861-6241

U.S. Kennels > NEW YORK

Honey Tree Farm & Kennels
Amsterdam, NY
518-842-3832

Double V Kennels
Athens, NY
518-945-1096

Chestnut Ridge Boarding Kennel
Auburn, NY
315-252-8087

White Shadow Ranch Kennels
Baldwin, NY
516-546-6507

Shield Crest Kennel
Ballston Spa, NY
518-885-1738

Jackpot Kennels
Batavia, NY
716-343-1122

South Main Street Kennels
Batavia, NY
716-343-5602

Northwind Kennels
Bedford Hills, NY
914-234-3771

White Birch Kennels
Binghamton, NY
607-724-3585

Snow Drift Kennels
Blue Point, NY
516-363-2226

Cicero Kennels
Bridgeport, NY
315-699-3122

Colonial Boarding Kennels
Brockport, NY
716-637-4036

Abbey Midwood Kennels
Brooklyn, NY
718-338-9600

K 9 Powerhouse Kennels
Brooklyn, NY
718-694-0600

Anderson Inner City Boarding Kennels
Buffalo, NY
716-838-5266

Connors Kennels
Buffalo, NY
716-674-0864

Old Falls Boarding Kennels
Buffalo, NY
716-695-2929

Farmhaven Boarding Kennel
Burnt Hills, NY
518-399-4989

Camillus Hills Pet Lodge
Camillus, NY
315-672-5154

Cedar Knoll Boarding Kennels
Canandaigua, NY
716-229-2392

Blue Ribbon Kennels
Canastota, NY
315-697-3100

Maple Ridge Kennels
Canton, NY
315-386-3796

Carmel Country Kennels
Carmel, NY
914-225-7717

Countryside Kennels
Castile, NY
716-493-2017

Clearwater Kennels
Cazenovia, NY
315-655-4780

Mossy Creek Kennel
Cherry Valley, NY
607-264-3933

Best Friends Pet Care
Chestnut Ridge, NY
845-371-4000

Evergreen Kennels
Churchville, NY
716-293-1920

Clayton Kennels
Clayton, NY
315-686-5141

Downey Kennels
Clinton, NY
315-853-6441

Boradaile Kennels
Cohoes, NY
518-237-2205

Windmere Kennels
Colton, NY
315-265-5935

Fonab Kennels
Commack, NY
516-543-0325

Lighthouse Kennels
Constable, NY
518-481-6730

Heritage Pet Inn
Cooperstown, NY
607-547-8488

Ancram Kennels
Copake, NY
518-329-3493

Keystone Kennels & Stables
Corning, NY
607-962-2012

Boddis Kennels
Craryville, NY
518-325-6610

Cross River Kennels
Cross River, NY
914-763-8121

Clarion Kennels
Deposit, NY
607-467-4073

Country Kennels of Dryden
Dryden, NY
607-844-9188

Shady Hill Kennels
East Amherst, NY
716-688-5445

Villanol Kennel
East Greenbush, NY
518-477-9555

Delta Pond Kennels
East Nassau, NY
518-766-5103

Sunnycrest Boarding Kennels
Eden, NY
716-992-3941

U.S. Kennels > NEW YORK

Jamison Acres Boarding & Training Kennels
Elma, NY
716-652-3353

Town and Country Kennels
Elmira, NY
607-733-1773

Valley View Kennels
Elmira, NY
607-734-8160

Sedora Kennels
Endicott, NY
607-748-8568

Touchstone Kennels
Fishkill, NY
914-831-2710

Jo Mar Dog & Cat Boarding
Floral Park, NY
516-488-2705

Mossland Kennels
Flushing, NY
718-539-0520

Brandy Keg Kennel
Frankfort, NY
315-895-7978

Malibu Pet Hotel
Freeport, NY
516-379-6040

We-Kair Kennels
Fulton, NY
315-592-9284

Ballyblue Pet Motel
Gansevoort, NY
518-793-7839

Animal Inn
Glen Cove, NY
516-759-2662

Pet Boarding
Glen Cove, NY
516-759-0833

Whispering Pines Boarding Kennel
Glenfield, NY
315-376-8349

Heatherstone Kennels
Grand Island, NY
716-773-4296

Chenango Valley Kennels
Greene, NY
607-656-7257

Malibu Kennels
Greenvale, NY
516-621-6860

Brookside Kennels
Hamburg, NY
716-649-0570

Moondance Kennels
Hamlin, NY
716-964-7930

TLC Kennels
Hannibal, NY
315-564-6485

Marjories Kennels
Harpursville, NY
607-693-2578

Balmoral Kennels
Harrison, NY
914-967-1721

Ludworth Kennels
Hastings On Hudson, NY
914-478-1633

Teakwood Kennels
Hilton, NY
716-964-2070

Woodlea Kennels
Honeoye, NY
716-229-5653

Woodland Kennels
Hopewell Junction, NY
914-221-0695

Lake Road Animal Hospital Kennels
Horseheads, NY
607-733-6509

Canine Corral Kennels
Huntington Station, NY
516-549-1544

Country Acres Kennels
Huntington Station, NY
516-427-6077

Pied Piper Kennel
Hyde Park, NY
914-229-2766

The Bed and Biscuit
Ithaca, NY
607-277-2126

TLC Kennels
Ithaca, NY
607-272-1317

Queens Boarding Kennels
Jamaica, NY
718-526-7045

Woodhaven Boarding Kennel
Jamaica, NY
718-296-8244

Sunnyside Boarding Kennel
Jamestown, NY
716-661-3430

Ritter Blackwatch Kennel
Johnson City, NY
607-798-1465

Triple H Boarding Kennel
Johnstown, NY
518-762-9059

Country Club Kennels
Lagrangeville, NY
914-223-3618

Salmon Creek Kennel
Lansing, NY
607-533-4986

Liberty Kennels
Liberty, NY
914-292-5725

Northern Pine Kennels
Lorraine, NY
315-232-3232

Stone Meadow Kennels
Mahopac Falls, NY
914-628-0200

Sportsmans Kennels
Manorville, NY
516-727-3550

Black Tie & Tail Kennel
Medford, NY
516-736-5352

Merry Lynn Kennels
Melrose, NY
518-663-5732

U.S. Kennels > NEW YORK

Malibu Kennels
Merrick, NY
516-379-6200

Wags N Tails Kennel
Middle Island, NY
516-924-7777

Cinderella's Boarding
Middletown, NY
914-344-2393

T L C Kennels
Middletown, NY
914-343-3916

Ridge Runners Kennels
Morris, NY
607-263-5547

Bihari Kennels
Nanuet, NY
914-356-1658

Hi Tor Pet Resort
Naples, NY
716-374-5741

Black Forest Kennels
New Hyde Park, NY
516-746-1547

American Kennels
New York, NY
212-838-8460

Paws Inn
New York, NY
212-645-7297

We Kare Kennels
New York, NY
212-567-2100

Pleasant Valley Kennels
Newark Valley, NY
607-642-8776

Hudson Valley Pet Resort
Newburgh, NY
914-566-0469

Niagara Kennels
Niagara Falls, NY
716-297-0696

Cedarwood Kennels
North Collins, NY
716-337-0735

Boulevard Training Kennels
North Tonawanda, NY
716-693-4965

Flanagan's Midnite Kennels
Norwich, NY
607-334-3942

Glenwood Boarding
Oneida, NY
315-363-6470

Crescent Pet Lodge
Oneonta, NY
607-432-8570

Springvale Kennels
Oneonta, NY
607-432-0797

Sunny Oaks Boarding Kennel
Ontario, NY
315-524-8626

Eagle Ridge Kennels
Orchard Park, NY
716-662-5302

Gracelane Kennels
Ossining, NY
914-762-6188

Calgary Kennels
Oswego, NY
315-342-0525

Fantasy Farm Kennels
Ovid, NY
607-869-5043

Cedar Hill Kennels
Palmyra, NY
315-597-6552

Holiday Tyme Pet Hotel
Patterson, NY
914-878-6655

Hallmark Kennels
Phelps, NY
315-548-3627

Ascot Canine Motel
Piermont, NY
914-359-8665

Fraser Kennel
Pine Plains, NY
518-398-9427

Pomona Park Kennels
Pomona, NY
914-354-2138

Ramapo Kennels
Pomona, NY
914-362-1820

AAA Almost Home Kennels
Putnam Valley, NY
914-528-3000

Woods End Kennels
Putnam Valley, NY
914-528-3211

The Country Kitty B&B
Queensbury, NY
518-792-6369

August Kennels
Rhinebeck, NY
914-876-6556

Animal Inn Pet Resort At Stony Point
Rochester, NY
716-594-7387

Central Kennels
Rochester, NY
716-342-3140

Puppy Love Hotel
Rochester, NY
716-254-2171

Jarus Hilltop Kennel
Rome, NY
315-336-3149

R & R Kennels
Rome, NY
315-337-2344

Liberty Kennel
Round Lake, NY
518-899-5098

Brookview Kennels
Rush, NY
716-624-1461

Gentle Timbers Boarding Kennel
Rushville, NY
716-554-6822

Rye Country Boarding Kennels
Rye, NY
914-967-4577

Northwest Kennels
Sag Harbor, NY
516-725-1090

U.S. Kennels > NEW YORK

A Pet Station Resort
Sandy Creek, NY
315-232-3780

**Adirondack Park
Pet Hospital**
Saranac Lake, NY
518-891-3260

**Sunnyside Veterinary
Hospital & Kennel**
Scotia, NY
518-346-1296

Dark Starr Kennels
Selden, NY
516-732-6227

Briarpatch Farm & Kennel
Sloansville, NY
518-868-2058

Aireway Dog & Cat Resort
Stanfordville, NY
914-868-7157

All Star Kennel
Staten Island, NY
718-761-1235

Country Estate Kennels
Staten Island, NY
718-356-3933

Valmark Kennel & Cattery
Stormville, NY
914-221-4707

Onondaga Hill Pet Boarding
Syracuse, NY
315-478-3161

Dater Hill Boarding Kennel
Troy, NY
518-279-3829

Applewood Kennels Tuxedo
Tuxedo Park, NY
914-351-2289

Colby Kennels
Vails Gate, NY
914-562-5275

Valley Side Kennels
Valley Stream, NY
516-561-0118

**Waggin Master Boarding
Kennel**
Vestal, NY
607-729-6677

Hilane Kennels
Victor, NY
716-924-3500

Kimbrook Kennels
Walton, NY
607-865-6266

Black Creek Kennel
Walworth, NY
315-986-4346

Orchard Kennels
Walworth, NY
315-986-1605

Supernal Pet Motel
Waterford, NY
518-235-2103

**Reigning Dogs & Cats
Boarding Kennel**
Waterloo, NY
315-539-4003

A Pet Station Resort
Watertown, NY
315-232-3780

Hillside Kennels
Watertown, NY
315-788-2844

Country Kennels of Dryden
Waterville, NY
607-844-9188

**Oshays Poodle Salon
& Boarding Kennel**
Webster, NY
716-265-0020

Groveton Kennels
West Lebanon, NY
518-794-8288

Anthony Muscarella Kennels
Westhampton, NY
516-288-3535

Dolly Marshall Kennels
Westhampton, NY
516-288-3535

Stonybrook Kennels
White Plains, NY
914-946-0961

**Dun Travlin Ranch
& Kennels**
Williamson, NY
315-589-2525

**Windrinker Farms Stable
& Kennel**
Windsor, NY
607-655-2644

Haven Valley Kennel
Wurtsboro, NY
914-888-0402

Country Club For Dogs
Yaphank, NY
516-924-3866

The Animal Inn
Yorktown Heights, NY
914-962-3129

NORTH CAROLINA

Lucky Four Kennels
Advance, NC
910-998-4402

Green Level Kennels
Apex, NC
919-362-7877

Avery Creek Kennel
Arden, NC
704-684-2161

Canine Country Club
Asheville, NC
704-255-8907

In the Valley Kennels
Black Mountain, NC
704-669-6578

**Cascade Valley Boarding
Kennels**
Brevard, NC
704-883-3030

Dog Crazy Kennel
Brevard, NC
704-877-5332

Pantheon Kennels
Brevard, NC
704-884-7304

Head On Kennels
Chapel Hill, NC
919-969-8939

Carolina Best Friends
Charlotte, NC
704-752-0504

Jordan Kennels
Charlotte, NC
704-598-7697

U.S. Kennels > NORTH CAROLINA

Woodleaf Hill Kennel
Cleveland, NC
704-278-2478

Hydelands Kennels
Climax, NC
910-674-2350

Falls Lake Kennels
Creedmoor, NC
919-528-1629

B-Con Kennels
Denver, NC
704-483-9526

Thornland Kennels
Dunn, NC
910-892-7607

Durham Boarding Kennel & Cattery
Durham, NC
919-383-4238

Shady Grove Kennel
Durham, NC
919-596-0235

Village Boarding Kennel
Durham, NC
919-688-6628

Mallard Lane Kennels
Ellerbe, NC
910-652-3359

Lake Wilson Boarding Kennels
Elm City, NC
919-291-5270

Fairview Kennels
Fairview, NC
704-628-1997

Sunny Pines Kennels
Fayetteville, NC
910-425-1713

Veterinary Kennels
Fayetteville, NC
910-822-3141

Walltop Kennels
Four Oaks, NC
919-963-4000

Battle Branch Kennels
Franklin, NC
704-369-6726

Canine Country Club
Gastonia, NC
704-864-6201

Jeric's Kennels
Goldsboro, NC
919-778-6641

Hideaway Kennels
Granite Falls, NC
704-396-8755

Battleground Pet Inn
Greensboro, NC
910-288-4940

Goldcrest Kennels
Greensboro, NC
910-668-3923

Cabarrus Kennel Club
Harrisburg, NC
704-455-5500

Wyolina Kennels
Harrisburg, NC
704-455-5500

Bacon Farm Kennels
Havelock, NC
919-447-4416

Briarwood Boarding Kennels
High Point, NC
910-886-1907

A J's Kennel
Horse Shoe, NC
704-891-7472

Bar-B's Pampered Pooch Pet Motel
Jacksonville, NC
910-577-7297

Mutt Hut Pet Hotel
Kannapolis, NC
704-932-6011

Willow Run Boarding Kennels
Kernersville, NC
910-993-3647

Tantalon Kennels
Lexington, NC
910-956-6823

Pumpkin Center Boarding Kennels
Lincolnton, NC
704-735-2711

Hillside Boarding Kennel
Marble, NC
704-837-9003

Animal Kennel Care
Matthews, NC
704-545-5192

County Line Kennels
Mebane, NC
910-421-0772

Pet Haven Kennels
Midland, NC
704-888-5393

Cedar Creek Boarding Kennel
Mocksville, NC
910-940-2552

VIP Kennels
Monroe, NC
704-289-1659

Nelson's Kennels
Morehead City, NC
919-247-2026

Animal Inn
Morganton, NC
704-437-5777

Reedy Creek Kennel
Morrisville, NC
919-469-8185

K & B Kennels
Mount Airy, NC
910-320-2219

Claws & Paws Inn
Mount Holly, NC
704-822-1966

Sheba Kennels
Mount Olive, NC
919-658-0085

Lynaire Kennels
New Bern, NC
919-633-4333

Lake Road Kennel
Newport, NC
919-223-4183

Kimoke Country Kennels
Oak Ridge, NC
910-643-9677

U.S. Kennels > NORTH CAROLINA

Dogwood Hill Kennel
Otto, NC
704-524-5353

Shrado Kennels
Pikeville, NC
919-736-3776

Oak Hill Kennel
Pinehurst, NC
910-295-6710

Armadale Farm Kennels
Raleigh, NC
919-847-0389

Fairview Kennels
Raleigh, NC
919-851-1608

Pinebrook Kennels
Raleigh, NC
919-851-1554

Rosewood Kennels
Roanoke Rapids, NC
919-537-2195

Island Creek Kennels
Rose Hill, NC
910-289-4280

Karewood Kennels
Shelby, NC
704-434-6665

Veterinary Kennels
Spring Lake, NC
910-436-4801

Wildwood Kennels
Stanley, NC
704-822-6082

Shady Rock Farm & Boarding Kennel
Sugar Grove, NC
704-297-1741

Top Dog Kennels
Swannanoa, NC
704-686-3175

Dogwood Acres Boarding Kennel
Sylva, NC
704-586-6109

Turnagain Lane Kennel
Tryon, NC
704-859-9831

Cobble Hill Kennels
Wake Forest, NC
919-556-1177

Briarwood Boarding Kennels
Wallburg, NC
910-769-2649

Sandy Ridge Kennels
Waxhaw, NC
704-843-3183

Arbor Creek Kennel
Weaverville, NC
704-645-7775

Reid J Craig Kennels
Whitakers, NC
919-443-5660

Almost Home Boarding Kennel
Winston Salem, NC
910-377-2160

Gordon Kennels
Winston Salem, NC
910-768-1302

Shady Oaks Kennel
Winston Salem, NC
910-784-0432

Winston Boarding Kennel
Winston Salem, NC
910-767-7320

Hoffman Haus Kennels
Winterville, NC
919-355-4663

Carters Country Kennel
Youngsville, NC
919-556-1029

NORTH DAKOTA

Apple Creek Kennel
Bismarck, ND
701-255-2791

Four Paws Inn
Bismarck, ND
701-222-0022

Dakota Hunting Club & Kennel
Grand Forks, ND
701-775-2074

Crown Butte Kennels
Mandan, ND
701-663-6141

Karalaite Dog & Cat Boarding Kennels
Manvel, ND
701-696-2573

Oahe Kennels Farm
Menoken, ND
701-673-3322

American Boarding Kennels
Minot, ND
701-839-5634

Dandy Kennels & Cattery
Minot, ND
701-838-8522

Morning Side Kennels Pet Boarding
Minot, ND
701-839-3299

Sterling Kennels
Minot, ND
701-852-6379

Lekota Kennels
Walhalla, ND
701-549-3868

OHIO

Doll Burt Bulldog Kennels
Akron, OH
330-688-8805

Falls Boarding Kennels
Akron, OH
330-928-9207

Marsh Run Boarding Kennel
Alger, OH
419-757-5061

High Point Kennels
Alliance, OH
330-829-0833

Guadaira Kennels
Amanda, OH
614-969-2686

Marjon Kennels
Amelia, OH
513-732-2196

U.S. Kennels > OHIO

Savannah Lake Kennels
Ashland, OH
419-962-4744

Long Run Boarding Kennel
Athens, OH
614-592-1082

Aurora Kennels
Aurora, OH
330-562-7011

Pearl's TLC Boarding Kennel
Beaver, OH
614-226-2116

Monica's Boarding Kennel
Bellevue, OH
419-483-4941

Lee-Atee's Boarding Kennels
Bethel, OH
513-734-2443

Country Oaks Boarding Kennel Belmont
Bethesda, OH
614-484-1516

Country Cousins Kennel
Brunswick, OH
330-225-2902

Animal House Boarding Kennel
Byesville, OH
614-432-4774

Canfield Boarding Kennel
Canfield, OH
330-533-7726

Gordon Kennels
Canton, OH
330-896-1400

Stock Boarding Kennels
Canton, OH
330-488-2544

Alador Kennels
Chagrin Falls, OH
440-543-9697

Western Reserve Kennel Club
Chagrin Falls, OH
440-247-1045

Chardon Country Kennels
Chardon, OH
440-285-2545

Blue Ridge Kennel
Cincinnati, OH
513-528-0382

Briarwood Pet Resort
Cincinnati, OH
513-489-6300

Country Cottage Kennels
Cincinnati, OH
513-574-7960

Eder Kennels
Cincinnati, OH
513-742-4038

Jan Rich Kennels
Cincinnati, OH
513-385-5074

Ballous North Star Pet Motel
Circleville, OH
614-474-8973

Beacon Hill Boarding Kennels
Cleveland, OH
216-524-6969

Four Gables Kennel
Cleveland, OH
216-491-9700

Wilden Woods Kennel
Cleves, OH
513-575-2572

Lorenwood Kennels
Columbia Station, OH
440-236-8847

Apples Pet Boarding
Columbus, OH
614-488-4121

Central Ohio Kennel Club
Columbus, OH
614-299-3647

Country Side Kennel
Cortland, OH
330-637-0523

A Pet Care Center
Dayton, OH
937-434-8527

Big Times Kennel
Dayton, OH
937-885-3427

Northgate Boarding Kennel
Dayton, OH
937-236-8070

Namika Kennels
Defiance, OH
419-428-3016

Oakshadows Kennel Plus
Dover, OH
330-343-7233

Arlington Dublin Kennel Boarding
Dublin, OH
614-889-2556

Pennova Kennels
East Liverpool, OH
330-385-5543

Kenilridge All Pet Boarding
Elyria, OH
440-327-8281

Brookhaven Kennels
Franklin, OH
513-746-7359

Royal Kennels
Franklin, OH
513-746-8507

Lynnwoods Kennels
Fremont, OH
419-334-2085

Town & Country Boarding Kennel
Fremont, OH
419-332-5530

Brinkman's Kennels
Goshen, OH
513-722-1082

Milford Goshen Kennel
Goshen, OH
513-722-2400

A To Z Kennels
Grafton, OH
440-748-3818

Stack Inn Boarding Kennels
Grand Rapids, OH
419-832-7387

U.S. Kennels > OHIO

All Creatures Pet Care
Hamilton, OH
513-856-8888

Colonial Acres Kennels
Hamilton, OH
513-777-2266

Nancy's Kennel
Harrisburg, OH
614-877-2304

Blue Ribbon Kennels
Hartville, OH
330-877-1937

Hayden Run Kennels
Hilliard, OH
614-876-7974

Jan Dane Kennels
Holland, OH
419-829-3641

Ridgeview Boarding Kennels
Hubbard, OH
330-568-7068

**Home Away From Home
Kennels**
Huntsville, OH
937-686-6365

Castlewood Kennels
Jefferson, OH
440-576-7387

New Holland Kennels
Jeffersonville, OH
614-426-6226

**Alexander's Boarding
Kennels**
Lebanon, OH
513-932-6909

Four Paws Inn
Leetonia, OH
330-427-2709

**Island Lake Boarding
Kennel**
Lima, OH
419-221-2988

Hart's Country Kennel
Litchfield, OH
330-648-2301

TLC Dog & Cat Boarding
Logan, OH
614-385-7808

The Dog Gone Pet Motel
Loudonville, OH
419-994-3763

Louisville Kennels
Louisville, OH
330-875-4445

Mohican Boarding Kennels
Mansfield, OH
419-884-7387

Ohio Valley Kennels
Marietta, OH
614-373-7400

Highlander Kennels
Massillon, OH
330-833-1650

Pet Nannies Kennel
Massillon, OH
330-833-9382

All Breed Kennels
Maumee, OH
419-893-7218

Stillwater Farm Kennels
Medina, OH
330-667-2170

**Pet Village Boarding
Kennels**
Mentor, OH
440-255-4013

T-Bar Kennel
Middletown, OH
513-423-3991

Rivercrest Kennel
Monroeville, OH
419-668-2875

Sunbeam Acre Kennels
Mount Vernon, OH
614-397-5009

**North Star Boarding
Kennel**
Navarre, OH
330-756-2022

New Carlisle Kennels
New Carlisle, OH
937-845-0905

Woodside Kennel
New Carlisle, OH
937-845-1951

Highview Boarding Kennel
New Vienna, OH
937-393-0340

**Cedar Hill Boarding
Kennels**
Newark, OH
614-345-4662

**Beechwood Boarding
Kennels**
North Baltimore, OH
419-257-3612

Misty Glen Kennels
North Olmsted, OH
440-871-2848

Royal York Pet Motel
North Royalton, OH
440-237-9132

Chalet Kennel
Northfield, OH
330-656-2823

**East Suburban Boarding
Service**
Northwood, OH
419-691-7201

Braemar Boarding Kennels
Norwalk, OH
419-668-4073

The Doggie Lodge
Norwalk, OH
419-668-2166

Kerry Estate Kennel
Novelty, OH
440-338-8381

**Windwood Boarding
Kennel**
Novelty, OH
440-338-6040

Olmsted Boarding Kennels
Olmsted Falls, OH
440-235-3790

A & A Kennels
Pataskala, OH
614-927-3781

**Broadway Kennels
Boarding**
Pataskala, OH
614-964-0050

Leonhaus Kennel
Perry, OH
440-259-4538

Shamrock Kennels of Dublin
Plain City, OH
614-873-3369

Country Kennel
Plymouth, OH
419-687-8880

Dynasty Kennels
Proctorville, OH
614-886-7010

Grand Valley Kennels
Rock Creek, OH
440-563-9502

Kiser Lake Kennels
Rosewood, OH
937-362-3193

Rushville Boarding Kennel
Rushville, OH
614-536-7097

M G M Boarding Kennels
Saint Clairsville, OH
614-695-3365

Cresthaven Kennels
Salem, OH
330-337-0509

Walnut Spring Kennels
Sherrodsville, OH
614-269-6265

Country Side Boarding Kennel
Sidney, OH
937-492-7199

Country Boarding & Kennel
Spring Valley, OH
937-862-4408

Country Squire Kennels
Springfield, OH
937-325-0212

Kozy Kat Motel
Springfield, OH
937-882-6518

Windsor Farms Boarding Kennels
Sterling, OH
513-724-6425

Danielle's Boarding Kennel
Strongsville, OH
440-238-7179

Chukar Hill Kennels
Swanton, OH
419-825-3349

Central Kennels
Sylvania, OH
419-829-4151

Dogwood Kennels
Thompson, OH
440-298-3696

Hopewell Boarding Kennel
Tiffin, OH
419-447-8308

A Country Vacation Kennel
Troy, OH
937-339-4363

Sanor Spread Kennels
Utica, OH
614-892-3998

Kritter Korner
Van Wert, OH
419-238-9011

Akron Road Kennel
Wadsworth, OH
330-336-8172

Champion Pet Lodge
Warren, OH
330-847-7972

Lordstown Country Kennels
Warren, OH
330-824-2127

Springhill Boarding Kennels
Wauseon, OH
419-337-5403

Santana Farm Kennel
Wellington, OH
440-647-3254

Spring Valley Kennels
Wellington, OH
440-647-4856

Blendon Kennels
Westerville, OH
614-882-2309

Westerville Boarding Kennel
Westerville, OH
614-882-1992

Cozy Kennels
Wheelersburg, OH
614-574-8936

Lone Oak Kennels
Whitehouse, OH
419-877-5094

Mentor TLC Pet Lodge
Willoughby, OH
440-975-9789

Mar Son Kennels
Windham, OH
330-527-4057

Bailey's Greenbriar Boarding Kennels
Wooster, OH
330-264-2373

Goldenbrook Kennels
Wooster, OH
330-345-5562

Oncore Kennels
Xenia, OH
937-376-9742

Briarhaven Kennels
Youngstown, OH
330-746-7574

Maplewood Dog Motel
Youngstown, OH
330-758-3162

Country Kennels
Zanesville, OH
614-454-7761

Riverside Boarding Kennels
Zanesville, OH
614-453-6071

OKLAHOMA

T C B Greyhound Kennel
Altus, OK
405-482-2333

Bartlesville Boarding Kennel
Bartlesville, OK
918-333-1125

Sunny Acres Boarding Kennels
Bartlesville, OK
918-333-2717

U.S. Kennels > OKLAHOMA

Country Club Boarding Kennels
Broken Arrow, OK
918-251-1478

Lynn Lane Boarding Kennels
Broken Arrow, OK
918-455-7721

Little Creek Kennel
Broken Bow, OK
405-420-7063

Temple Guardian Kennels
Cache, OK
405-429-8888

Risenhoover Kennels
Chelsea, OK
918-342-3764

Linbezan Boarding Kennels
Chouteau, OK
918-476-6008

Upper-Half K 9 Kennel
Claremore, OK
918-342-2540

Rocky Cor Kennels
Cordell, OK
405-832-2936

Animal Inn Boarding Kennels
Dewey, OK
918-534-1633

Delmar Smith Boarding Kennels
Edmond, OK
405-478-1171

Piney Ridge Kennels
Jay, OK
918-253-8949

Allen Kennels
Keota, OK
918-966-2330

Imokie Kennel
Keota, OK
918-966-3928

Twilite Kennels
Keota, OK
918-966-3316

Country Pleasure Kennels
Ketchum, OK
918-782-2165

Wichita Kennel
Lawton, OK
405-429-3505

Rock Creek Kennel Pet Hotel
Mcalester, OK
918-823-4600

Arrow Ridge Kennels
Norman, OK
405-321-1209

Beauregards Pet Care for Boarding
Oklahoma City, OK
405-721-6624

Best Friends Pet Care
Oklahoma City, OK
405-751-1944

Four Paws Inn
Oklahoma City, OK
405-524-9422

Misty Acres Kennel
Okmulgee, OK
918-756-5427

Appleton Marc Kennels
Piedmont, OK
405-373-2719

Cottonwood Country Club for Pets
Ponca City, OK
405-762-7790

Kountry Kennels
Seminole, OK
405-382-7300

Oklahoma K 9 Academy
Shawnee, OK
405-273-5737

Aurora Kennel
Tulsa, OK
918-250-3911

Deshane Kennels
Tulsa, OK
918-437-3343

Kastan Kennels
Yukon, OK
405-350-2345

OREGON

Cooper's Boarding Kennel
Amity, OR
503-835-3647

North Pole Ranch & Kennel
Ashland, OR
541-482-7015

Riverview Kennels
Bandon, OR
541-347-4689

Fairoaks Kennels
Beavercreek, OR
503-632-6698

Beaverton Hill Top Boarding Kennels
Beaverton, OR
503-649-5497

Cooper Mountain Kennel
Beaverton, OR
503-649-4956

Forest Glen Kennels
Beaverton, OR
503-590-2300

Bend Pet Resort
Bend, OR
541-388-0435

Ranch Kennels
Bend, OR
541-382-3634

Green Acres Kennels
Boring, OR
503-658-2434

Misty Meadow Kennels
Boring, OR
503-658-2701

White Fir Kennels
Brownsville, OR
541-466-3271

Airport Inn Pet Lodge
Canby, OR
503-263-1919

Ravenwood Kennels
Cave Junction, OR
541-592-4460

Roblen Kennels
Central Point, OR
541-664-6744

U.S. Kennels > OREGON

Pampered Pets Boarding
Coos Bay, OR
541-269-2009

North Bank Kennel
Coquille, OR
541-347-3561

Corvallis Kennels
Corvallis, OR
541-757-9089

**South Valley Boarding
Kennels**
Corvallis, OR
541-929-5476

**Brownings Dog Ranchtails
Inn**
Eugene, OR
541-688-8276

Holiday Kennels
Eugene, OR
541-747-8422

Mckenzie View Kennel
Eugene, OR
541-747-3992

Orchard Point Kennels
Eugene, OR
541-689-1685

**Applegate Country
Boarding Kennels**
Grants Pass, OR
541-479-0509

**Mountain View Boarding
Kennels**
Gresham, OR
503-666-8118

Hammond Kennel
Hammond, OR
503-861-1601

**Homestead Boarding
Kennel**
Hermiston, OR
541-567-5478

Laurel Acres Kennels
Hillsboro, OR
503-628-2169

Rock Creek Kennels
Hillsboro, OR
503-645-2912

Jay Jay's Doggie Hotel
Hubbard, OR
503-982-3906

Lin-Lee Kennels
Joseph, OR
541-432-8221

**Best Friends Boarding
Kennels**
Mcminnville, OR
503-434-5088

Bevs Kennel
Medford, OR
541-826-3504

**Rogue Boarding Kennel
& Cattery**
Medford, OR
541-773-3542

Happy Tails All Animal Inn
Merlin, OR
541-474-7714

Penrod Kennels
Milton Freewater, OR
541-938-7633

Oak Grove Kennels
Monmouth, OR
503-838-6286

J J's Dog Motel
Oregon City, OR
503-650-0023

TLC Dog Boarding Kennels
Oregon City, OR
503-631-7326

Jewel Creek Kennels
Pacific City, OR
503-965-6288

Alpha Jay Boarding Kennel
Phoenix, OR
541-535-2243

The Charlton Kennels
Portland, OR
503-621-3675

**Crestview Boarding
Kennels**
Portland, OR
503-654-0283

Fletcher's Boarding Kennels
Portland, OR
503-761-2091

Sauvie Island Kennel
Portland, OR
503-621-3204

Deschutes Pet Lodge
Redmond, OR
541-548-4066

**Rose Lodge Boarding
Kennels**
Rose Lodge, OR
541-994-8595

David's Lone Pine Kennel
Roseburg, OR
541-673-8657

Caledon Kennels
Scappoose, OR
503-543-7556

Dog & Cat Boarding
Scio, OR
503-394-3861

Jeans Boarding Kennel
Seaside, OR
503-738-6996

Windy Ridge Kennels
Sherwood, OR
503-625-6774

Hedgerow Kennels
Tangent, OR
541-967-8546

Terre Bone Kennels
Terrebonne, OR
541-548-2005

**Alsea River Boarding
Kennels**
Tidewater, OR
541-528-7785

Hidden Hill Kennels
Veneta, OR
541-935-2014

Noah's Ark Kennel
Waldport, OR
541-563-5866

Gigi's Dog Inn
Wilsonville, OR
503-638-4101

Glen Ivy Farms Kennels
Winston, OR
541-679-6288

PENNSYLVANIA

Greenview Acre Boarding Kennels
Acme, PA
412-423-7272

All Breeds Kennels
Ambler, PA
215-643-7650

Kountry Kennels
Andreas, PA
717-386-2899

Amy's Golden Touch Kennels
Apollo, PA
412-697-4040

The Kennels
Avondale, PA
610-268-8000

Bree Hill Dog School
Baden, PA
412-869-1751

Penny Meadows Farm Kennels
Bainbridge, PA
717-367-7082

Beech Hill Kennels
Bensalem, PA
215-639-5789

Bright Star Boarding Kennel
Bird In Hand, PA
717-656-6136

Amity Animal Inn
Birdsboro, PA
610-582-4252

Whispering Winds Boarding Kennel
Butler, PA
412-789-7672

Doubletree Farm Boarding Kennels
Cabot, PA
412-352-3442

Greymor Kennels
Canonsburg, PA
412-228-8566

The Animal Inn
Carlisle, PA
717-243-4250

Country Aire Kennels
Carlisle, PA
717-249-3809

The Funny Farm Kennel
Carlisle, PA
717-249-5512

Green Kennels
Carmichaels, PA
412-966-5456

Gaybird Farms
Carversville, PA
215-297-5553

Steward's Pet Resort
Chadds-Ford, PA
610-459-2724

Hickorybrook Farm
Chalfont, PA
215-348-4454

Golden Wood Kennels
Chambersburg, PA
717-263-4162

Eagle Kennel
Chester Springs, PA
610-458-5900

Waggin Tail Kennels
Clarks Summit, PA
717-586-9382

Wheeling Hill Kennel
Cochranton, PA
814-425-8328

King Kennels
Concordville, PA
610-459-3013

NV Kennels
Conneaut Lake, PA
814-382-9523

Shoalwater Kennel
Conneautville, PA
814-587-2365

Golden Hollow Kennels
Creekside, PA
412-354-4826

AR Pet Inn
Dauberville, PA
610-926-5055

Ziegler's Kennels
Dauberville, PA
610-926-4071

Tender Loving Care Kennels
Dauphin, PA
717-921-2851

Barley Croft Kennels
Dillsburg, PA
717-432-9445

Honeysuckle Kennels
Dover, PA
717-292-1408

Ridgewood Kennels
Dover, PA
717-292-4967

All Breeds Kennels
Doylestown, PA
215-348-7605

Holiday House Pet Resort
Doylestown, PA
215-345-6960

Country Pet Motel
East Berlin, PA
717-292-2160

Deer Path Kennels
East Smithfield, PA
717-596-4433

Gate House Kennels
East Stroudsburg, PA
717-424-1888

Bolingbroke Kennels
Edinboro, PA
814-734-5255

Northcountry Kennels
Elizabethtown, PA
717-533-3301

Bear Hill Kennels
Elverson, PA
610-469-6014

Valley Kennel
Emlenton, PA
412-867-8986

Hubbard's Kennels
Enola, PA
717-732-2674

Horton's Boarding Kennels
Ephrata, PA
717-733-4544

U.S. Kennels > PENNSYLVANIA

Twinbrook Veterinary Hospital & Boarding Kennel
Erie, PA
814-899-6941

Marden's Boarding & Training Kennel
Everett, PA
814-623-5145

Country Living Kennels
Fairview, PA
814-476-7202

High Wycombe Farms Kennel
Falls, PA
717-333-5307

Caledonia Kennel
Fayetteville, PA
717-352-7818

Carriage Hill Kennels
Finleyville, PA
412-833-2217

Hillcrest Kennels
Fleetwood, PA
610-944-9700

K-9 Kampus
Fogelsville, PA
610-285-6711

Shady Rest Kennels
Fogelsville, PA
610-285-4290

The Terrace
Fombell, PA
412-452-4464

Salfid Kennels
Franconia, PA
215-723-3649

Bradleys Boarding Kennels
Franklin, PA
814-432-4637

TLC Pet Resort
Franklin, PA
814-432-8854

Aberdeen Kennels
Frederick, PA
610-754-7731

Gettysburg Animal Hospital
Gettysburg, PA
717-334-2177

Maple Tree Kennel
Gettysburg, PA
717-677-6677

Cry West Kennels
Girard, PA
814-774-4993

Brookwood Kennels
Glen Rock, PA
717-227-0361

Anton Kennels
Glenmoore, PA
610-942-3676

Wyndmoor Kennels
Glenside, PA
215-836-7170

Applewood Kennel
Hanover, PA
717-633-5963

Griffins Happy Tails
Hanover, PA
717-632-1929

Laurel Hill Kennels
Hanover, PA
717-632-1440

Klos's Kennels
Harrisburg, PA
717-545-2258

South 8 Boarding Kennels
Harrisville, PA
814-786-9701

Kraus Kennels
Hazleton, PA
717-455-2700

Holzland Kennels
Hegins, PA
717-682-3654

Twin Ponds Boarding Kennel
Holtwood, PA
717-284-4006

Ability Boarding Kennel
Hummelstown, PA
717-533-7274

Alpine Boarding Kennels
Hummelstown, PA
717-566-0805

Lenape Kennels
Hummelstown, PA
717-566-2035

Baker's Boarding Kennel
Huntingdon, PA
814-643-3706

Stone Haven Kennels
Hyndman, PA
814-324-4321

Connie Winters Kennels
Indiana, PA
412-465-6120

Country Kennels
Jamison, PA
215-343-5587

Haycock Run Kennels
Kintnersville, PA
610-847-2632

Walnut Grove Boarding Kennels
Kittanning, PA
412-297-3832

Saltbox Kennels
Knox, PA
814-797-1353

Hound Hollow Farm
Kutztown, PA
610-683-5015

Country Club Pet Lodge
Lancaster, PA
717-872-5471

Marchwoods Pet Resort
Lancaster, PA
717-898-8081

Fox Meadow Farm
Landenberg, PA
610-274-8872

Roselynde Kennels
Lansdale, PA
215-855-8026

Whyte Wynd Kennels
Lebanon, PA
717-865-6055

Llewellyn Kennels
Lehighton, PA
717-386-5557

U.S. Kennels > PENNSYLVANIA

TLC Pet Lodge
Lemasters, PA
717-328-5995

Blue Rock Kennel
Lenhartsville, PA
610-756-6420

The Dog Den
Leola, PA
717-656-9744

Gochenauer Kennels
Lititz, PA
717-569-6151

McGarvey's Boarding Kennels
Lititz, PA
717-626-6961

Cloud Nine Country Kennel
Macungie, PA
610-845-7330

Solitario Kennels
Malvern, PA
610-644-3757

Canine Country Club
Manheim, PA
717-665-2710

Sun Hill Kennels
Manheim, PA
717-653-6060

Woodbine Boarding Kennels
Mansfield, PA
717-549-8102

Brickyard Kennels
Mars, PA
412-625-1475

Cedarwood Kennels
Meadville, PA
814-333-9820

Brandy Lane Kennels
Mechanicsburg, PA
717-766-9069

Glenbrooke Kennels
Mechanicsburg, PA
717-697-1200

Kinship Kennel
Mechanicsburg, PA
717-697-6508

Lambs Gap Animal Hospital
Mechanicsburg, PA
717-732-9711

Welsh Run Kennels
Mercersburg, PA
717-328-9549

Luv Kennels
Meyersdale, PA
814-634-5440

Valentine's Kennels
Mifflinburg, PA
717-922-4888

Ernest Hill Kennels
Mifflintown, PA
717-436-9267

Canine Campground
Milan, PA
717-888-0375

Sawkill Farm
Milford, PA
717-296-8246

K 9 Cuts & Kennels
Mill Hall, PA
717-726-7451

ABC Boarding Kennels
Millerton, PA
717-537-2273

Buck Hollow Kennels
Mohnton, PA
610-856-7840

Rocky Acres Kennel
Mohnton, PA
610-856-7066

Brizes Boarding Kennels
Monongahela, PA
412-384-6445

White Kennels
Montrose, PA
717-934-2294

Mackensen Kennels
Morrisville, PA
215-493-2717

Yardley Animal Kennels
Morrisville, PA
215-493-2717

Borderbrook Boarding Kennels
Murrysville, PA
412-327-7070

Murray-Valley Boarding Kennels
Murrysville, PA
412-325-2411

Belfast Kennels
Nazareth, PA
610-759-5520

Kaufman's Kennel
New Brighton, PA
412-452-6447

Great Oaks Boarding Kennels
New Castle, PA
412-924-9658

Care Time Kennels
New Cumberland, PA
717-774-2451

Lochreggand Kennels
New Milford, PA
717-278-3000

Char Will Kennels
New Ringgold, PA
717-943-2624

Country Dog Kennels
Newport, PA
717-567-6384

Laurel Lane Farm
Newtown, PA
215-968-2500

Mariner Kennels
Newville, PA
717-776-5912

Hidden Valley Kennels
Nicholson, PA
717-945-3701

Richey Kennels
North East, PA
814-725-5151

Weathervane Kennels
Northumberland, PA
717-473-8191

Whispering Pines Boarding Kennel
Oil City, PA
814-677-8802

U.S. Kennels > PENNSYLVANIA

Meadow Lane Kennels
Orangeville, PA
717-458-5908

Colanenon Kennels
Oxford, PA
610-932-2777

Allmacs Boarding Kennels
Palmyra, PA
717-469-7507

Country Club Kennels
Paoli, PA
610-648-0917

Puppy Love Kennels
Peach Bottom, PA
717-548-2743

Ridge Crest Farm
Pennsburg, PA
215-679-8606

Hickory Springs Farm
Phoenixville, PA
610-933-9584

**Birds Hill Boarding
Kennels**
Pine Grove, PA
717-345-8780

Jack's Dog Farm
Pipersville, PA
215-766-8802

**Airy Pines Boarding
Kennel**
Pittsburgh, PA
412-733-2242

Noah's Pet Farm & Motel
Pottstown, PA
610-323-2206

Windruff Kennels
Pottstown, PA
610-469-6430

**Antietam Animal Inn
Kennels**
Reading, PA
610-779-2424

Da-Mar's Acres Kennels
Reading, PA
610-777-6773

Peacock Bridge Kennels
Reading, PA
610-926-2722

Darby-Dan Kennels
Red Lion, PA
717-927-9050

Windsong Farm Kennels
Red Lion, PA
717-246-1735

Old Acres Kennels
Reedsville, PA
717-667-6004

El Nor Boarding Kennel
Reinholds, PA
610-775-2876

Crossroad Kennels
Ridgway, PA
814-776-1905

Frame's Kennels
Ridley Park, PA
610-521-1123

Fleetwood Kennels
Ringtown, PA
717-889-3047

**Angove's Farm Boarding
Kennels**
Russell, PA
814-757-4300

Winsong Kennel
Sarver, PA
412-353-2286

Country Kennels
Sayre, PA
717-888-6850

Twin Pine Kennels
Sayre, PA
717-888-4195

Buttonwood Animal Inn
Schwenksville, PA
610-287-6251

Milnerhaus Kennels
Scranton, PA
717-489-2118

**Bow Bells Blue Ribbon
Kennel**
Sellersville, PA
215-257-7243

Holly Farms Kennels
Sellersville, PA
215-723-4992

Meisterhaus Kennels
Seven Valleys, PA
717-428-2494

An Inn On Rippling Run
Sewickley, PA
412-364-4447

The Kennel
Sewickley, PA
412-741-2407

Barmyre Kennels
Shippensburg, PA
717-532-7588

Forest Kennel
Shippenville, PA
814-782-3073

Rovin Hollow Kennels
Shoemakersville, PA
610-926-4046

Country Kennels
Shohola, PA
717-559-7484

**Loyalhanna Boarding
Kennels**
Slickville, PA
412-668-8077

Candylane Kennels
Slippery Rock, PA
412-637-2420

**Chapman's Country
Kennels**
Spraggs, PA
412-435-7003

Windhaven Kennels
Spring Creek, PA
814-665-6766

Tamora Kennels
Spring Grove, PA
717-225-1928

Mount Airy Kennels
Stevens, PA
717-733-7751

Lightfoot Kennels
Sweet Valley, PA
717-477-2943

Belvedere Kennels
Towanda, PA
717-265-9549

U.S. Kennels > PENNSYLVANIA

Walters Boarding Kennels
Towanda, PA
717-265-9592

Baker's Kennel
Trout Run, PA
717-998-2614

Troy Town Kennels
Troy, PA
717-596-3220

Creature Comforts
Tunkhannock, PA
717-333-4136

Ben Jee Kennels
Tylersport, PA
215-257-1278

Sandy Hill Kennels
Valencia, PA
412-898-2895

Hillview Kennels
Wapwallopen, PA
717-379-2642

Amber Beech Kennels
Washington Crossing, PA
215-493-2201

The Golden Glow Kennel
Waterfall, PA
814-448-3792

Buckwalter Kennels
Wayne, PA
610-688-0888

Animal Inn
Wellsboro, PA
717-724-7378

Howl A Day Inn
Wellsboro, PA
717-724-2305

Rustic Ridge Boarding Kennels
Wexford, PA
412-935-1736

Tan-Zar Boarding Kennels & Cattery
Wexford, PA
412-935-0990

Penobscot Kennels
Wilkes Barre, PA
717-474-5281

Sa Lu Se Kennels
Williamson, PA
717-369-4259

Oberjoch Boarding Kennels
Williamsport, PA
717-323-2721

Happi Tee Kennels
Windsor, PA
717-246-3267

Pine Acres Kennel
Wycombe, PA
215-598-7202

Camp Canine
York, PA
717-854-3457

Locust Run Kennels
York, PA
717-252-2653

The Meadows Pet Resort
York, PA
717-266-7044

Timberlea Kennels
York Haven, PA
717-938-4040

Bamar Farm Kennels
Zelienople, PA
412-452-4714

Ingomar Kennels Boarding Kennel
Zelienople, PA
412-452-5150

RHODE ISLAND

East Bay Kennels
Bristol, RI
401-253-0082

Our House Pet Lodge
Carolina, RI
401-539-1143

Pet Resort
Chepachet, RI
401-568-7000

Colvintown Kennels
Coventry, RI
401-828-6395

Delmyra Kennels
Exeter, RI
401-294-3247

Kandy Kane Kennels
Foster, RI
401-647-2130

Rocky Knoll Boarding Kennels
Lincoln, RI
401-726-0330

Stony Lane Kennels
North Kingstown, RI
401-294-2400

Tip Top Kennel
Peace Dale, RI
401-789-1950

Aristocats Feline Hotel
Providence, RI
401-454-6835

Smithfield Kennels
Smithfield, RI
401-231-9250

Kingston Kennels
Wakefield, RI
401-789-7600

Warwick Pet Lodge
Warwick, RI
401-739-5181

Pugs-R-Us Kennels
West Warwick, RI
401-823-8090

SOUTH CAROLINA

Powderhouse Kennels
Aiken, SC
803-648-0779

Stargate Stables & Kennels
Aiken, SC
803-642-0585

Woodwynne Kennels
Aiken, SC
803-648-8443

Mason House Kennels
Bonneau, SC
803-825-6889

Buffalo Pet Center
Buffalo, SC
864-427-6535

Palos Verdes Kennels
Camden, SC
803-432-8449

U.S. Kennels > SOUTH CAROLINA

Foxridge Kennels
Campobello, SC
864-472-3002

Chapin Pet Lodge
Chapin, SC
803-345-5082

Charleston Pet Resort
Charleston, SC
803-763-0985

Dixie Kennels
Charleston, SC
803-763-1100

Gibson Kennels
Charleston, SC
803-553-1421

**Northwoods Pet Care
Center**
Charleston, SC
803-572-6635

Wil Nel Kennels
Charleston, SC
803-763-0985

Primrose Acres Kennels
Chesnee, SC
864-461-3003

Grayarlin Kennels & Farm
Chester, SC
803-581-6659

**Northeast Animal Clinic
and Kennels**
Columbia, SC
803-736-4703

Paws & Claws Kennels
Columbia, SC
803-736-8055

Pine Hill Kennels & Stables
Columbia, SC
803-735-8422

All Seasons Pet Resort
Conway, SC
803-248-2752

**Homewood Boarding
Kennels**
Conway, SC
803-365-7710

Ravencliffe Kennel
Easley, SC
864-306-1519

**Home Away From Home
Kennel**
Florence, SC
803-665-1615

Canine Country Club
Fort Mill, SC
803-548-0823

**Mt Holly Veterinary
Hospital & Boarding
Facility**
Goose Creek, SC
803-572-1707

Southern View Kennels
Graniteville, SC
803-663-6940

4 K Ranch & Kennels
Gray Court, SC
864-876-9696

**Barkingham Palace
Pet Kennels**
Greenville, SC
864-458-8550

Carolina Best Friends
Greenville, SC
864-281-7410

**Carolina Pet Boarding
& Training Center**
Greenville, SC
864-297-9141

Haywood Road Pet Motel
Greenville, SC
864-288-9492

Pet Motel
Greenville, SC
864-288-9492

Twin Creek Kennels
Hartsville, SC
803-383-0078

Evergreen Pet Lodge
Hilton Head Island, SC
803-681-8354

Low Country Kennels
Hilton Head Island, SC
803-681-3991

Pet Paradise
Hilton Head Island, SC
803-686-2275

Lakeview Kennels
Inman, SC
864-472-6317

Wag-N-Train Kennel
Irmo, SC
803-781-8825

Bridgemount Kennel
Johns Island, SC
803-768-9310

Dandie Kennel
Johns Island, SC
803-559-0769

K-9 Kastle Kennels
Johns Island, SC
803-559-0680

Low Country Kennels
Johns Island, SC
803-559-0333

Moonshadow Kennel
Johns Island, SC
803-559-0571

Da Leigh Kennel
Lake City, SC
803-389-3693

Palmetto Kennels
Lancaster, SC
803-285-1809

Lexington Pet Lodge
Lexington, SC
803-957-7297

The Red Barn Kennel
Lexington, SC
803-359-9045

Tall Pines Pet Lodge
Lexington, SC
803-794-9326

K-9 Country Club
Little River, SC
803-280-4350

Sundowner Kennels
Lyman, SC
864-439-2379

A & L Kennels
Moncks Corner, SC
803-761-3320

Best Friends Boarding
Mount Pleasant, SC
803-856-7829

U.S. Kennels > SOUTH CAROLINA

Pet Set Cat Boarding
Mount Pleasant, SC
803-881-7387

Blue Moon Kennel
Myrtle Beach, SC
803-347-9341

Pet-O-Tel
Myrtle Beach, SC
803-448-9831

Tamroc Kennels
Myrtle Beach, SC
803-236-1313

Darlene's Pet Palace
Newberry, SC
803-276-1570

Willow Pines Pet Resort
North, SC
803-247-5855

Antara Kennels
North Myrtle Beach, SC
803-249-1714

Paws Inn Kennels
North Myrtle Beach, SC
803-272-4825

Pampered Pet Motel
Orangeburg, SC
803-536-6702

Lindley's Kennel
Piedmont, SC
864-243-3583

Holly Grove Kennels
Ravenel, SC
803-889-8776

Briar Ridge Kennels
Rock Hill, SC
803-366-5706

Jet Engine Kennels
Saint George, SC
803-563-2309

Little Foot Kennels
Saint Helena Island, SC
803-838-3821

601 Self Storage
Saint Matthews, SC
803-874-3458

Foolish Heart Kennels
Seneca, SC
864-972-3678

Hi-Lo Kennel
Simpsonville, SC
864-967-4822

All Care Kennel
Spartanburg, SC
864-579-0391

**Lakeside Pet Care
& Kennels**
Spartanburg, SC
864-592-3145

Noah's Ark Kennels
Spartanburg, SC
864-576-0760

A & L Kennels
Summerville, SC
803-873-6247

Carolina Kennels
Summerville, SC
803-873-2335

Double Edge Kennels
Summerville, SC
803-821-8210

Joann Oak Glen Kennels
Summerville, SC
803-851-6387

**My Buddy Boarding Inn
for Pets**
Sumter, SC
803-773-2501

Ballentine Kennels
Swansea, SC
803-568-3810

Freedom Kennels
Taylors, SC
864-244-0177

Tallyho Kennels
Taylors, SC
864-244-0177

Deer Springs Kennels
Westville, SC
803-432-2980

Crosscreek Kennel
York, SC
803-327-4377

Four Paws Quality Kennel
York, SC
803-328-6384

SOUTH DAKOTA

Dakota Kennels
Aberdeen, SD
605-229-1126

Home Away Kennels
Brookings, SD
605-693-3264

Lone Willow Kennels
Burbank, SD
605-624-2564

Radar's Bed & Biscuit
Lennox, SD
605-368-5123

Moriah Kennels
Piedmont, SD
605-787-5431

**Black Hills Animal
Kennel**
Rapid City, SD
605-343-6067

**Happydog Boarding
Kennels**
Sioux Falls, SD
605-332-0595

Loistan Country Kennels
Sioux Falls, SD
605-334-8511

Pine Lake Kennels
Sioux Falls, SD
605-332-2151

Top Gun Kennels
Sioux Falls, SD
605-334-7116

**Dr. Doolittle Pet
Boarding**
Watertown, SD
605-882-2628

**Lake View Kennel Dog
& Cat Boarding**
Watertown, SD
605-882-3342

Riverside Kennels
Yankton, SD
605-665-7019

TENNESSEE

Country Pet Kennels
Athens, TN
423-745-7786

Thunderhawk Kennels
Baxter, TN
615-858-7435

Boone Wood Kennel
Bluff City, TN
423-538-8648

Hickory Valley Boarding Kennels
Chattanooga, TN
423-892-0412

Full Moon Kennels
Church Hill, TN
423-357-7002

Pet Motel
Clarksville, TN
615-645-9163

K 9 Country Club
Cleveland, TN
423-472-6970

Devoe Kennels
Clinton, TN
423-435-4487

Hilltop Kennels
College Grove, TN
615-368-7875

Copyright Pet Resort
Cookeville, TN
615-528-8007

Eden Kennels
Cordova, TN
901-754-2060

Perk's Boarding Kennels
Cordova, TN
901-754-5956

Appalachian Kennels
Elizabethton, TN
423-542-0830

Franklin Kennels
Franklin, TN
615-794-2333

Wildrose Kennels
Grand Junction, TN
901-764-2495

The Animal Inn
Hendersonville, TN
615-822-1450

Hermitage Pet Inn
Hermitage, TN
615-885-3033

Countryview Kennels
Jackson, TN
901-427-8585

K-Nine Kennels
Jackson, TN
901-427-6427

Dynasty Kennels
Kingsport, TN
423-288-9231

Hallmark Kennels
Kingsport, TN
423-245-4960

Catatoga Kennels
Knoxville, TN
423-693-5540

Concord Kennels
Knoxville, TN
423-966-5771

Meadowbrooke Kennel
Knoxville, TN
423-523-9282

Pinecrest Kennels
Knoxville, TN
423-577-2659

Bear Cave Kennels
Lebanon, TN
615-444-2327

Misty Mountain Kennel
Lenoir City, TN
423-988-6895

Cripple Creek Kennels
Loretto, TN
615-853-6675

Claridge Kennels
Memphis, TN
901-365-3500

Magnolia Kennels
Memphis, TN
901-363-7351

Pleasant View Kennels
Memphis, TN
901-386-3232

Southaven Boarding Kennel
Memphis, TN
901-393-2417

Hideaway Farm Canine Academy
Millington, TN
901-829-2699

Animal House Kennels
Morristown, TN
423-586-0791

Hilltop Pet Resort
Mount Juliet, TN
615-758-3842

Custom Kare Kennels
Murfreesboro, TN
615-893-8959

Green Acres Kennels
Murfreesboro, TN
615-895-6435

Belle Meade Boarding Kennels
Nashville, TN
615-352-4370

Cheekwood Animal Hospital & Kennels
Nashville, TN
615-352-9351

Critter Care
Nashville, TN
615-333-2782

Lancelot Kennels
Nashville, TN
615-832-7530

Nashville Kennel Club
Nashville, TN
615-832-1346

Smiths Critter Keepers
Nashville, TN
615-834-9063

Pet Care Kennels
Ooltewah, TN
423-238-5296

Loving Care Kennels
Pigeon Forge, TN
423-453-2028

Birchwood Kennels
Powell, TN
423-938-3201

U.S. Kennels > TENNESSEE

C & S Country Kennels
Pulaski, TN
615-363-1108

Sharaza Kennels
Rogersville, TN
423-272-4772

Mist Kennels
Sevierville, TN
423-453-6369

The Smoky Mountain Kennel
Sevierville, TN
423-429-5367

Deerwood Kennels
Signal Mountain, TN
423-886-1728

Ragland Kennels
Signal Mountain, TN
423-886-3422

P J's Farm Canine Condo
Springville, TN
901-642-8345

Two Sons Kennel
Watauga, TN
423-543-8713

TEXAS

Barr Kennels
Abilene, TX
915-677-2005

Oakridge Kennels
Abilene, TX
915-698-0518

Big Country Kennel
Albany, TX
817-762-2359

Ring Leaders Kennel
Aledo, TX
817-441-8071

Baggins Kennels
Alvarado, TX
817-790-8001

Dog Patch Boarding Kennels
Amarillo, TX
806-352-7400

Home Away From Home Kennel
Amarillo, TX
806-376-7582

Willow Creek Kennels
Amarillo, TX
806-383-6155

Oakwood Kennels
Angleton, TX
409-849-3005

Canine Country Inn
Argyle, TX
940-464-3139

Windsong Kennels
Argyle, TX
940-455-2320

Country Acres Kennels
Arlington, TX
817-467-2511

The Pet Hotel & Resort
Arlington, TX
817-261-7786

Ambassador Pet Resort
Austin, TX
512-832-1012

Bed & Biscuit Kennel
Austin, TX
512-343-0723

Blue Stone Kennel
Austin, TX
512-288-6415

Canine Hilton Kennels
Austin, TX
512-926-8905

Highmark Kennel
Austin, TX
512-288-0515

Hill Country Kennel
Austin, TX
512-288-4696

Westlake Animal Hospital Kennel
Austin, TX
512-327-3170

Bandera Kennels
Bandera, TX
830-796-4357

Arrow Valley Kennels
Bastrop, TX
512-303-1088

Metroplex Boarding Kennels
Bedford, TX
817-280-0492

Bearcreek Kennel
Belton, TX
254-933-7240

Ryckman Kennels
Boerne, TX
830-981-8883

Weimarfeld Kennels
Brandon, TX
254-632-4266

Four Paws Kennels
Brazoria, TX
409-798-1527

Windy Valley Boarding Kennels
Brenham, TX
409-836-3105

Winmore Kennels
Bridgeport, TX
940-683-4660

Pecan Hill Kennels
Brookshire, TX
281-375-6597

Valley Pet Motel
Brownsville, TX
956-428-5400

Dixieland Kennels
Bryan, TX
409-778-0288

Onion Creek Kennels
Buda, TX
512-312-0595

Lucky Dog Boarding Kennel
Burleson, TX
817-447-2543

Trails End Kennels
Burleson, TX
817-295-8681

Elley's Kennels
Cameron, TX
254-697-6943

U.S. Kennels > TEXAS

Bruce's Country Kennel
Canyon, TX
806-655-9876

Bowie Kennels
Celina, TX
972-382-3104

Cherokee Training Kennel
Chandler, TX
903-849-6183

Bear Bayou Kennels
Channelview, TX
281-452-7676

Cross Creek Kennel
Chireno, TX
409-362-2220

Ace Boarding Kennels
Cibolo, TX
210-658-1475

Pet Motel
Cleburne, TX
817-641-6179

Joda Kennels
Cleveland, TX
409-767-4969

Pecan Acre Kennels
Clute, TX
409-265-8461

Brazo's Kennels
College Station, TX
409-776-8909

Harper's Tonkawa Kennels
College Station, TX
409-776-1054

AAA Kennel
Colleyville, TX
817-283-4379

Colleyville Kennels
Colleyville, TX
817-498-6410

Schomer Kennels
Conroe, TX
409-756-9090

Country Kennels
Copperas Cove, TX
254-542-6955

Bluff Boarding Kennel
Corpus Christi, TX
512-937-5001

Country Club Kennels
Corpus Christi, TX
512-991-2685

FMC Kennel
Corpus Christi, TX
512-289-1409

London Kennels
Corpus Christi, TX
512-853-1207

Oso Creek Pet Hotel
Corpus Christi, TX
512-994-1147

Quail Run Kennels
Corsicana, TX
903-872-1767

Mesquite Flats Kennel
Crowley, TX
817-297-1566

Cypress Boarding Kennels
Cypress, TX
281-351-1823

Lakewood Forest Kennels
Cypress, TX
281-376-6744

Allen's Ra-Ra-Me Kennels
Dallas, TX
972-286-0006

Boykin Kennels
Dallas, TX
214-330-1500

Hideaway Boarding Kennel
Dallas, TX
214-350-2807

Otter Creek Pet Resort
Dallas, TX
214-521-0073

Pets Are Inn
Dallas, TX
972-407-9778

Casey's Country Kennels
Dickinson, TX
281-534-6057

Driftwood Kennels
Driftwood, TX
512-894-0003

A & L Boarding Kennels
El Paso, TX
915-855-0044

Critter Care
El Paso, TX
915-584-5298

Falkirk Kennels
El Paso, TX
915-855-1460

Goldust Kennels
Elgin, TX
512-281-2757

Hines Boarding Kennel
Farmers Branch, TX
972-247-1759

Mad River Kennels
Ferris, TX
972-544-2220

Parrie Rose Kennels
Florence, TX
254-628-8698

Smith Rick Kennels
Floresville, TX
830-216-4230

Dobson Dwight Boarding Kennels
Fort Worth, TX
817-249-1040

Happy Tails
Fort Worth, TX
817-577-2035

Meadow Hill Kennels
Fort Worth, TX
817-448-8559

Black Diamond Kennel
Friendswood, TX
281-996-9800

Camp Bow-Wow Kennels
Frisco, TX
214-287-7574

Bir Kennels
Gainesville, TX
940-668-1008

K-9 Kountry Klub
Gainesville, TX
940-665-8500

Hamilton Boarding & Breeding Kennel
Galveston, TX
409-737-2727

U.S. Kennels > TEXAS

Critter Service
Garland, TX
972-414-5957

Smith's On the Spot Kennels
Gary, TX
903-685-2311

Country Kennels
Greenville, TX
903-883-3396

Jaybar Kennels
Harlingen, TX
956-425-4060

Chaparral Kennel
Hitchcock, TX
409-986-9559

Robinson Kennel
Hitchcock, TX
409-986-9272

Aleithia's Kennels
Houston, TX
713-729-7387

Auburn Kennels
Houston, TX
713-465-6425

Best Friends Pet Resort
Houston, TX
713-664-6111

The Courtyard Kennel
Houston, TX
281-498-2773

Horlock Boarding Kennels
Houston, TX
713-686-4614

Memorial Red Oak Kennels
Houston, TX
713-467-0535

Pasadena Boarding Kennel
Houston, TX
713-472-1411

The Pet Hotel
Houston, TX
713-664-6111

Rebel Kennels
Houston, TX
713-723-6257

Sherwood Forest Kennels
Houston, TX
281-583-8000

TLC Regency Kennels
Houston, TX
713-464-9852

Tiffany Kennels
Houston, TX
713-464-9800

Windfern Kennels
Houston, TX
713-937-6229

Cedar Creek Pet Motel
Howe, TX
903-532-5300

Campbell Farm Kennels
Huffman, TX
281-324-1923

Gazebo Boarding Kennel
Huntsville, TX
409-291-7478

St Francis Kennels
Ingleside, TX
512-776-2309

Metroplex Pet Lodge
Irving, TX
972-438-7119

Nelson's Dog Ranch
Jefferson, TX
903-665-2371

Katy Kennels
Katy, TX
281-391-7387

Kennel Kare
Keller, TX
817-379-0737

Alpine Kennels
Kennedale, TX
817-478-7291

H S K Boarding Kennel
Kerrville, TX
830-895-2700

Bookers Kennel
Killeen, TX
254-699-6365

Candyland Kennels
Klein, TX
281-320-1187

Lakeview Kennels
Lake Dallas, TX
940-321-2483

T K Kennels
Lampasas, TX
512-556-2011

Connemara Kennel
Lancaster, TX
972-227-6004

Raines Paradise Kennels
Larue, TX
903-677-9507

Happy Pets Cottage
League City, TX
281-332-0130

Wagging Works Kennel
Leander, TX
830-379-7792

AAA Boarding Kennels
Longview, TX
903-758-8538

Longview Boarding Kennel
Longview, TX
903-757-0511

Brazos Valley Boarding Kennels
Lorena, TX
254-857-4104

Lollipop Farm Boarding Kennel
Lubbock, TX
806-746-6875

Lubbock Kennels
Lubbock, TX
806-745-1670

Red Iron Kennels
Manor, TX
512-276-7671

Live Oak Kennel
Mansfield, TX
817-477-1943

Lynn Manor Kennels
Manvel, TX
281-489-0315

Barkingham Palace Boarding Kennel
Marble Falls, TX
830-693-0901

U.S. Kennels > TEXAS

Patchwork Kennels
Marshall, TX
903-938-2152

Carols Kennel
Mathis, TX
512-547-9759

Camelot Kennels
Mc Kinney, TX
972-562-3000

**McQueeney Boarding
Kennel**
McQueeney, TX
830-557-6335

Animals Etc Pet Motel
Mcallen, TX
956-682-3806

Kriegsschiff Kennels
Meridian, TX
254-435-2033

Chandler Kennels
Mexia, TX
254-562-5501

Rebelee Kennels & Stables
Midland, TX
915-682-5032

Tall City Kennels
Midland, TX
915-694-6658

Shiloh Road Kennel
Midlothian, TX
972-723-3880

Brazos Boarding Kennels
Mineral Wells, TX
940-325-4390

**Cotter Key C Boarding
Kennels**
Mount Pleasant, TX
903-572-3209

K 9 Country Inn
Nacogdoches, TX
409-560-4213

Martin Kennel
Nacogdoches, TX
409-560-3643

Post Oak Kennels
Nacogdoches, TX
409-564-2816

Camp Bow Wow Kennels
Nevada, TX
972-843-4748

Willow Creek Kennels
New Braunfels, TX
830-606-5821

**Animal House Boarding
Kennel**
Odessa, TX
915-381-7387

Cozy Country Kennel
Odessa, TX
915-550-0157

Permian Basin Kennels
Odessa, TX
915-366-5516

Holiday Kennels
Orange, TX
409-886-4675

**Lakewood Boarding
Kennels**
Palestine, TX
903-729-0810

Piney Woods Kennel
Palestine, TX
903-723-0774

Golden Acres Pet Inn
Pasadena, TX
281-487-4470

Teja's Kennels
Pasadena, TX
713-941-1558

Pooch Pad Country Kennel
Pearland, TX
281-489-9727

Roka Kennel
Pearland, TX
281-489-8024

Raydane Kennels
Perrin, TX
940-798-2323

**Holiday Hideway Hotel
for Pets**
Porter, TX
281-354-3050

Hideaway Boarding Kennels
Prosper, TX
972-346-2346

Rose Creek Kennels
Red Oak, TX
972-617-6769

Cross Timbers Kennels
Rhome, TX
817-636-2200

Pecan Grove Kennels
Richmond, TX
281-342-7946

Tartan Farms Kennels
Richmond, TX
281-342-0553

**Hellmann Boarding
Kennels**
Robstown, TX
512-387-4244

Country Kennels
Rockport, TX
512-729-0446

**Best Friends Boarding
Kennel**
Rosanky, TX
512-839-4581

Black Gold Kennels
Rosenberg, TX
281-342-6590

Southaven Kennels
Rosharon, TX
281-431-0848

Lake Point Pet Resort
Rowlett, TX
972-412-7250

J D Kennels
Royse City, TX
972-636-9494

**Have A Heart Boarding
Kennels**
San Angelo, TX
915-653-1625

Pet Camp
San Angelo, TX
915-651-8867

AAA Boarding Facility
San Antonio, TX
210-271-9466

Best Friends San Antonio
San Antonio, TX
210-822-0003

U.S. Kennels > TEXAS

Double Jac Kennels
San Antonio, TX
210-655-2755

Fiesta Kennels
San Antonio, TX
210-698-2248

Holiday Boarding Kennel
San Antonio, TX
210-494-7649

Master Kennels
San Antonio, TX
210-688-3539

**Northport Boarding
Kennels**
San Antonio, TX
210-822-1425

Azure Park Kennel
San Marcos, TX
512-353-8844

Aurum Kennels
Santa Fe, TX
409-925-8591

Sylvester's Kennels
Santa Fe, TX
409-925-3654

The Creature Keeper
Seguin, TX
830-379-3073

Millercreek Kennels
Somerville, TX
409-272-8373

Foster Ranch Kennels
South Padre island, TX
956-233-5553

Best Friends Spring
Spring, TX
281-298-6500

Elkin Kennels
Spring, TX
281-353-4835

K-9 Bed & Boarding
Spring, TX
281-364-1117

Animal Inn
Sugar Land, TX
281-277-2727

Almost Home Kennel
Temple, TX
254-939-2501

Wild Goose Kennels
Terrell, TX
972-524-8549

**Boulevard Boarding
Kennels**
Texarkana, TX
903-792-2266

Foxmoor Kennels
Tomball, TX
281-351-0825

Rush Creek Kennels
Tomball, TX
281-351-4434

Bunker Kennels
Tyler, TX
903-581-6133

Double M Kennels
Tyler, TX
903-825-2829

Lanran Kennels
Tyler, TX
903-581-0686

Cibolo Creek Kennels
Universal City, TX
210-659-0914

**Acres of Animals
Boarding Kennel**
Victoria, TX
512-573-4002

Connie's Kennel
Victoria, TX
512-576-4083

Black Forest Kennel
Vidor, TX
409-769-8419

Highlander Kennels
Waco, TX
254-662-0101

Quail Creek Kennel
Waco, TX
254-662-5620

R & M Kennels
Warren, TX
409-547-3070

Clear Lake Kennels
Webster, TX
281-332-4870

Blossom Heath Kennel
Wichita Falls, TX
940-767-8821

Dog Patch
Wichita Falls, TX
940-723-0889

The Kennel
Wills Point, TX
903-873-2033

C C Kennels
Winnie, TX
409-296-4887

Jazzy Dog Bed & Breakfast
Wylie, TX
972-442-7396

UTAH

West Forest Kennels
Brigham City, UT
801-723-1184

**Von Keison Kennels
& Dog Training**
Cedar City, UT
801-865-7468

Basquay Kennels
Draper, UT
801-571-3444

D's Kennels
Draper, UT
801-571-3664

Karolyn's Pet Resort
Draper, UT
801-572-0261

Silver K Kennel
Draper, UT
801-571-2322

Goldrush Kennels
Heber City, UT
801-654-4260

South Fork Kennels
Huntsville, UT
801-745-2202

TLC Kennels
Kamas, UT
801-783-4701

U.S. Kennels > VIRGINIA

Castlecreek Kennels
Ogden, UT
801-394-4674

Miller Kennels
Ogden, UT
801-731-5034

Ikon Kennels
Orem, UT
801-224-6365

White Pine Kennels
Park City, UT
801-649-7192

Rosewood Kennels
Salem, UT
801-423-2543

Arrow Kennels
Salt Lake City, UT
801-266-4802

Brickyard Kennels
Salt Lake City, UT
801-486-6007

Dog Show Kennels
Salt Lake City, UT
801-250-2553

Tarra's Lucky Kennel
Salt Lake City, UT
801-265-2416

**Rocky Willows Kennels
& Stables**
Sandy, UT
801-571-1100

Sterling Kennels
Sandy, UT
801-566-5533

K D Kennels
Tooele, UT
801-884-3374

VERMONT

Diamond Brook Kennel
Bomoseen, VT
802-273-2941

**Puppy Acres Boarding
Kennels**
Brattleboro, VT
802-254-5496

Crangold Kennels
Charlotte, VT
802-658-6569

Mapleridge Kennels
Corinth, VT
802-439-6117

Blackdale Kennels
Cuttingsville, VT
802-773-0968

Sandy Pines Kennel
Essex Junction, VT
802-878-2636

Rotoba Farm Kennel
Hartland, VT
802-436-2974

Homike Pet Motel
Huntington, VT
802-434-3691

**Middlebury Boarding
Kennel**
Middlebury, VT
802-388-9643

Grunwald Kennel
Milton, VT
802-893-3451

Canine Bed & Boutique
Morgan, VT
802-895-4431

Lamoille Kennels
Morrisville, VT
802-888-2469

Oasis Kennels
Newport, VT
802-334-7005

Hill House Boarding Kennel
North Bennington, VT
802-442-6794

Wunderland Pet Lodge
North Clarendon, VT
802-773-8011

**Happy Tails Boarding
Kennel**
Northfield, VT
802-485-5296

**Brook Side Boarding
Kennels**
Orange, VT
802-479-0466

Hauxhurst Kennel
Orwell, VT
802-948-2892

Sykes Hollow Kennels
Pawlet, VT
802-325-3005

B & B for Dogs & Cats
Quechee, VT
802-295-3517

Royalton Hill Kennel
Royalton, VT
802-763-8131

O'Neill's Boarding Kennels
Shelburne, VT
802-985-2248

**Copperhill Boarding
Kennels**
Thetford Center, VT
802-785-2757

Bed & Board Kennels
Waitsfield, VT
802-496-3908

Doggie Daycare
Williston, VT
802-860-1144

VIRGINIA

Stonehead Dog Ranch
Aldie, VA
703-327-4660

Kingstowne Kennels
Alexandria, VA
703-971-1836

Em's Kennel
Appomattox, VA
804-352-2629

**Pet Boarding & Sitting
Services**
Ashburn, VA
703-729-3575

Yopaka Kennels
Ashland, VA
804-798-8248

**Wingmont Stables
& Kennels**
Aylett, VA
804-994-2712

**Hicks All Breed Pet Care
& Kennel**
Bassett, VA
540-629-1483

U.S. Kennels > VIRGINIA

Sta Can Kennels
Berryville, VA
540-955-0412

Fancy Pants Boarding Kennel
Big Stone Gap, VA
540-523-3352

The Animal Farm
Bristol, VA
540-466-8936

James River Boarding Kennels
Carrollton, VA
757-238-2377

Albemarles Wakefield Kennels
Charlottesville, VA
804-973-5171

The Pet Motel & Salon
Charlottesville, VA
804-295-3679

Chalquest Hilton Kennels
Chesapeake, VA
757-421-7411

Dominion Kennels
Chesapeake, VA
757-547-5922

Paws Inn
Chesapeake, VA
757-436-3973

Tsop's Kennels
Chesapeake, VA
757-421-9392

Gregory's Dog & Cat Inn
Covington, VA
540-747-5100

Montrose Pet Hotel
Fairfax, VA
703-425-5000

Fairfax Boarding Kennel
Falls Church, VA
703-820-2558

Twin Pines Kennel
Farmville, VA
804-392-5566

Wayling Hills Kennel
Fishersville, VA
540-943-7072

Calypso Boarding Kennels
Fredericksburg, VA
540-720-0050

Stonebridge Kennels
Gate City, VA
540-386-9114

AAA Woodscreek Boarding Kennels
Gloucester, VA
804-693-3389

Bethwood Kennels
Gloucester, VA
804-693-2101

Dogwood Kennels
Hartfield, VA
804-776-6309

Tidemill Boarding Kennels
Hayes, VA
804-642-6468

Burgos Kennels
King George, VA
540-775-0543

Old Mill Kennels
Leesburg, VA
703-777-4183

Brickwood Kennels
Lexington, VA
540-261-2445

Willow Run Kennels
Linden, VA
540-364-2121

Happy Critter Resort
Lyndhurst, VA
540-932-7171

Morganna Boarding Kennel
Manassas, VA
703-368-6828

Tidewater Kennels
Mathews, VA
804-725-2359

Sunny Ridge Kennel
Mount Crawford, VA
540-234-9359

Mountain Top Kennels
New Castle, VA
540-864-6828

Mountain Retreat Kennel
Roanoke, VA
540-929-4065

Dunrovin Kennels
Spotsylvania, VA
540-582-5154

Old Hickory Kennel
Spotsylvania, VA
540-895-5870

Bar Ben Kennels
Stafford, VA
540-659-5278

Thluka Boarding Kennels
Stafford, VA
540-659-4754

Just Like Home Pet Kennels
Strasburg, VA
540-465-3781

Crest Hill Animal Inn
Troutville, VA
540-992-3950

Macbeth Kennels
Troutville, VA
540-992-2800

Animal Care Center Hospital & Kennel
Virginia Beach, VA
757-468-6996

Buyrningwood Kennels
Virginia Beach, VA
757-427-1330

Hunt Club Boarding Kennel and Cattery
Virginia Beach, VA
757-427-6611

Owl Creek Pet Hotel
Virginia Beach, VA
757-425-5349

Sterling Meadows Kennel
Virginia Beach, VA
757-471-0040

My Dog Kennels
White Marsh, VA
804-693-2439

U.S. Kennels > WASHINGTON

WASHINGTON

**Sunnyhill Kennels
& Cattery**
Anacortes, WA
360-293-3434

Arlington Heights Kennels
Arlington, WA
360-435-9627

**Canine Country Club
and Cattery**
Arlington, WA
360-652-7513

Hilltop Kennels & Cattery
Arlington, WA
360-435-4118

Creature Comforts Kennels
Auburn, WA
253-833-5177

Olympic Kennels
Belfair, WA
360-275-4335

Northwest Kennels
Bellingham, WA
360-384-6578

Pets Western Inn
Bellingham, WA
360-738-1302

R & R Kennel
Bellingham, WA
360-671-8445

Penny Creek Kennels
Benton City, WA
509-588-6955

Delanda Dog Inn
Bothell, WA
425-486-4141

K-9 Kamp
Bothell, WA
425-337-7965

**Mill Creek Kennels
& Cattery**
Bothell, WA
425-743-2286

Omega Kennels
Bothell, WA
425-481-1900

Tail's-A-Waggin Dog Inn
Bothell, WA
425-481-3214

**Fairinalls Boarding
& Training Kennel**
Bremerton, WA
360-830-4427

Countryside Kennel
Brush Prairie, WA
360-253-2876

Jee Jac Kennels
Burlington, WA
360-757-0520

Wil-Ram Kennels
Centralia, WA
360-736-6471

Setter Ridge Kennels
Clinton, WA
360-341-2878

Berliner Kennels
Colbert, WA
509-238-6208

**Clarrah Kennels and
Pet Hotel**
Colbert, WA
509-466-3162

Homestead Kennels
Colville, WA
509-684-6428

Fran's Longview Kitty Inn
Coupeville, WA
360-678-4285

Eastsound Kennels
Eastsound, WA
360-376-2410

Danlyn Ranch Kennels
Ellensburg, WA
509-925-4535

Mountainview Kennels
Ellensburg, WA
509-968-3790

Pets Are Inn
Federal Way, WA
253-839-7387

Animal Inn
Friday Harbor, WA
360-378-4735

Kensington Kennels
Friday Harbor, WA
360-378-5432

Bayside Animal Lodge
Gig Harbor, WA
253-851-9170

By the Book Kennels
Gig Harbor, WA
253-851-2098

Gig Harbor Kennel
Gig Harbor, WA
253-857-2443

Vacation Pet Care
Gig Harbor, WA
253-265-8500

**Mayfield Dog & Cat
Boarding**
Graham, WA
253-847-7763

Flintlock Kennels
Greenacres, WA
509-922-8118

Cowlitz Animal Inn
Kelso, WA
360-577-1679

AA Pet Lodge
Kennewick, WA
509-582-8188

Happy Camp Kennels
Kennewick, WA
509-582-8244

**Echowood Kennel and
Cattery**
Kent, WA
253-630-5342

Holiday Kennels
Kent, WA
253-872-8015

R Way Kennels
Kettle Falls, WA
509-684-1744

Mallard Lake & Kennels
Lake Stevens, WA
425-334-5739

MSK Kennels
Lakebay, WA
253-884-9913

U.S. Kennels > WASHINGTON

The Pet Ritz of Toklat Kennels
Longview, WA
360-577-6330

Wallins Dog Motel
Lynnwood, WA
425-743-1221

Animal Inn
Manson, WA
509-687-9497

Centennial Kennels
Maple Valley, WA
425-432-0893

Hidden Valley Kennels
Maple Valley, WA
425-432-0191

McKenna Kennels
McKenna, WA
360-458-2981

Paran Tree Kennels
Mica, WA
509-924-8101

Frontier Boarding Kennel
Monroe, WA
360-794-5388

Myownly Boarding Kennel
Monroe, WA
360-794-5388

Kennel Under the Pines
Moses Lake, WA
509-766-0492

East Line Kennels
Newman Lake, WA
509-226-0288

Goldie Road Kennels
Oak Harbor, WA
360-675-6128

Sunset Kennel
Oak Harbor, WA
360-675-7288

Peninsula Pet Lodge
Olalla, WA
253-857-5990

Alderbrook Kennels
Olympia, WA
360-352-1553

Classy Canine Country Club
Olympia, WA
360-943-2275

Northwind Arabian Stables & Kennels
Olympia, WA
360-456-5631

Thistledown Kennels
Olympia, WA
360-754-4944

Cottonwood Kennels
Omak, WA
509-826-4687

Souvenir Country Kennels
Onalaska, WA
360-978-4897

Goldville Kennels
Oroville, WA
509-476-2017

Sagemoor Kennels
Pasco, WA
509-544-9682

All Animal Bed & Breakfast
Port Angeles, WA
360-452-4551

Karalanes Kennels
Port Orchard, WA
360-871-2539

Alder Creek Pet Lodge
Poulsbo, WA
360-697-6717

Viking Kennels
Poulsbo, WA
360-779-2688

Canyon Road Pet Retreat
Puyallup, WA
253-531-2220

Hearthside Kennel
Puyallup, WA
253-770-7512

Freedom Kennels
Rainier, WA
360-446-7736

May Creek Kennels
Renton, WA
425-255-5690

Badger Mountain Pet Inn
Richland, WA
509-627-5313

Campbells Town & Country Kennels
Richland, WA
509-946-0117

Waldorf Kennel
Ridgefield, WA
360-573-2421

Adorable Pet Lodge
Seattle, WA
206-242-7480

Cloverhill Kennels
Selah, WA
509-697-4405

Olympic View Kennel
Sequim, WA
360-683-2404

Burgburg Kennels
Shelton, WA
360-427-1749

Country Inn Boarding Kennels
Shelton, WA
360-943-5041

Sylvan Pet Lodge
Shelton, WA
360-426-3052

Royal Pet Motel
Spanaway, WA
253-847-0789

Tannenhaus Kennel
Spanaway, WA
253-847-2786

Animal House Kennels
Spokane, WA
509-535-2831

Blue Wing Boarding Kennels
Spokane, WA
509-624-1922

Glenacres Boarding
Spokane, WA
509-535-2279

U.S. Kennels > WISCONSIN

Glen-Mar Kennels
Spokane, WA
509-448-9311

Kingswood Kennels
Spokane, WA
509-924-3311

Marcinda Kennels
Spokane, WA
509-928-6662

Wyrequest Kennels
Spokane, WA
509-534-2939

**Cedarhome Kennels
& Cattery**
Stanwood, WA
360-652-5912

Conway Kennel
Stanwood, WA
360-445-6901

Atwood's Pet Resort
Tacoma, WA
253-531-0779

Gillshire Kennels
Tacoma, WA
253-531-5589

Ramrod Kennels
Tacoma, WA
253-475-5646

**Wilhelmsburg Boarding
Kennels**
Tacoma, WA
253-537-6398

**Scatter Creek Kennels
& Training Services**
Tenino, WA
360-273-7725

Royal Boarding Kennels
Vancouver, WA
360-892-0947

**Susie's Country Inn
for Dogs & Cats**
Vancouver, WA
360-576-5959

Top Dog Kennel
Wenatchee, WA
509-662-5457

TLC Boarding Kennels
Winlock, WA
360-262-9195

Cascade Kennels
Woodinville, WA
425-483-9333

All American Kennels
Yakima, WA
509-966-4262

Apple Valley Kennels
Yakima, WA
509-966-3870

Blackhawk Kennels
Yakima, WA
509-965-4420

R J Retriever Kennels
Yakima, WA
509-453-2558

**West Valley Boarding
Kennels**
Yakima, WA
509-966-1949

WEST VIRGINIA

Alpine Kennel
Bluefield, WV
304-589-3017

Dogwood Kennels
Bluefield, WV
304-589-3769

**Pines Hill Dog & Cat
Boarding Kennels**
Bluefield, WV
304-327-5236

**Harrison Central
Boarding Kennel**
Clarksburg, WV
304-624-9305

Pet Hut Kennels
Martinsburg, WV
304-267-6634

**Oak Ridge Boarding
Kennels**
Weirton, WV
304-748-4665

WISCONSIN

Cinnabar Kennels
Appleton, WI
920-733-0869

Windy Hills Kennel
Appleton, WI
920-731-1690

Cherry Hill Boarding Kennel
Ashland, WI
715-682-3419

Good Going Kennels
Baldwin, WI
715-796-2392

**Bed & Biscuit Boarding
Kennel**
Balsam Lake, WI
715-485-3084

Bud Loren Kennel
Baraboo, WI
608-356-5204

Ker Mor Kennels
Belgium, WI
920-994-4523

Hill Haven Kennels
Beloit, WI
608-879-2728

All Aboard Kennel
Big Bend, WI
414-662-2323

Sundance Kennels
Bristol, WI
414-857-2545

Hero's Pet Resort
Burlington, WI
414-537-2182

Hopper's Kennels
Burlington, WI
414-642-7915

Luell's Kennels
Burlington, WI
414-537-2681

Animal Motel
Butler, WI
414-781-5200

Bryerlane Pet Resort
Caledonia, WI
414-835-2444

U.S. Kennels > WISCONSIN

**Highland Hunt Club
& Kennels**
Cascade, WI
920-528-8848

Heartland Kennel
Cashton, WI
608-637-3276

Donnybrook Kennels
Cedar Grove, WI
920-668-6511

**Cozy Critter Campground
Boarding Kennel**
Chetek, WI
715-924-2823

**Black Brook Boarding
Kennel**
Clear Lake, WI
715-268-9149

Clear Lake Kennels
Clear Lake, WI
715-263-2056

Black & Ward Kennel
Delavan, WI
414-728-4553

Delavan Boarding Kennel
Delavan, WI
414-728-8354

Hollyrood Pet Camp
Eagle River, WI
715-479-2446

Ketla Kennels II
Eagle River, WI
715-479-1364

Royal Flush Kennels
Eagle River, WI
715-479-4188

Calico Kennels
Egg Harbor, WI
920-868-3804

Balsam Aire Kennels
Elcho, WI
715-275-3365

Kon Aire Boarding Kennel
Eleva, WI
715-878-4248

Stone Ridge Kennel
Eleva, WI
715-878-4920

Mecca Kennels
Elk Mound, WI
715-874-6863

Burr Oak Kennels
Endeavor, WI
608-587-2578

**Sunset Dog Boarding
Kennels**
Florence, WI
715-589-2157

Checkmates Kennels
Fort Atkinson, WI
608-423-4644

Reichland Kennels
Fort Atkinson, WI
920-563-7080

Elgersma Kennels
Fox Lake, WI
920-324-4568

Cairnshaus Kennels
Franksville, WI
414-835-2412

Meadows Kennel
Franksville, WI
414-835-4245

Windy Knoll Kennels
Franksville, WI
414-835-4858

Chesapine Kennels
Fremont, WI
920-867-2745

Countryaire Kennels
Germantown, WI
414-242-3154

Heatherwycke Kennels
Germantown, WI
414-251-2522

Shady Glen Kennels
Germantown, WI
414-251-1920

Emeran Kennels
Grafton, WI
414-377-8527

Cur Sans Kennels
Hancock, WI
715-228-5151

**Chalet Hill Kennel
& Cattery**
Hartland, WI
414-367-4111

Hickory Hill Bed & Biscuit
Hartland, WI
414-367-4111

San Lee Kennels
Hartland, WI
414-966-7578

Hayward Pet Lodge
Hayward, WI
715-634-8971

Willow Run Kennel
Hortonville, WI
920-757-6646

Free Spirit Kennels
Houlton, WI
715-549-6809

H & H Kennels
Hudson, WI
715-386-5045

Mill City Kennel
Hudson, WI
715-381-1241

Valley Boarding Kennel
Hudson, WI
715-386-1226

Cedar Creek Pet Resort
Jackson, WI
414-677-4500

Paws Inn Pet Motel
Janesville, WI
608-754-7946

Crystal Acres Kennel
Jefferson, WI
920-674-3249

Tender Touch Pet Care
Johnson Creek, WI
920-699-4596

Milbach Kennels
Kaukauna, WI
920-766-3955

The Puppy Tub & Motel
Kenosha, WI
414-654-4808

U.S. Kennels > WISCONSIN

**Country Mile Boarding
Kennel**
Kewaskum, WI
414-629-1010

**Schubert Kennels
Pet Resort**
Kiel, WI
920-894-2996

Calliope Kennels
La Crosse, WI
608-785-1516

Greenfield Boarding Kennel
La Crosse, WI
608-788-1974

**Hickory Hill Boarding
Kennel**
La Crosse, WI
608-781-2266

Kaisers Kennels
La Crosse, WI
608-788-0021

Windborne Kennels
Lake Geneva, WI
414-248-3345

Webshire Kennels
Larsen, WI
920-836-3355

River Road Kennels
Lena, WI
920-846-3939

Jutland Kennels
Luck, WI
715-472-2727

Sunshine Kennels
Luck, WI
715-857-5095

Hickory Hills Kennels
Madison, WI
608-222-9402

Park St Kennels
Madison, WI
608-256-2211

Park Ur Pooch
Madison, WI
608-249-6660

Suter's Hickory Hills Kennels
Madison, WI
608-222-9402

Clay Banks Kennels
Manitowoc, WI
920-758-2666

Kandamor Kennels
Manitowoc, WI
920-758-2777

**Marge's Small Dog
Boarding**
Manitowoc, WI
920-684-0522

Mueller's Retriever Kennels
Manitowoc, WI
920-758-2262

4 Queens Boarding Kennel
Marshfield, WI
715-676-2491

Klondike Kennels
Marshfield, WI
715-676-2504

Park View Pet Motel
Marshfield, WI
715-384-2544

Windyhill Kennel
Mc Farland, WI
608-838-9400

**Thorndale Bone & Biscuit
Kennel Inn**
Merrill, WI
715-536-8959

The Pet Lodge
Middleton, WI
608-831-8000

Astin's Animal Inn
Milton, WI
608-868-3007

Honey Lane Kennels
Milwaukee, WI
414-354-8938

Landmark Kennels
Milwaukee, WI
414-769-6685

**Noah's Ark Boarding
Kennel**
Milwaukee, WI
414-541-7250

Forest Wind Kennels
Monroe, WI
608-328-2828

Rolan Hills Kennels
Monroe, WI
608-325-7452

**Animal House Pet Care
Center**
Mosinee, WI
715-355-1117

J D Hide A Way Kennels
Muskego, WI
414-895-6271

Pine View Kennels
Muskego, WI
414-679-0288

Schultz Boarding Kennels
Neenah, WI
920-722-9696

**New Berlin Boarding
Services**
New Berlin, WI
414-782-6910

**Critter Country Boarding
Kennel**
New Richmond, WI
715-246-4734

Kodiak Kennels
New Richmond, WI
715-246-2454

B K Kennels
Oneida, WI
920-869-2523

BK Kennels
Oneida, WI
920-869-2523

Rhineskeller Kennels
Oostburg, WI
920-564-3939

Cherokee Kennels
Oregon, WI
608-835-5250

Sandhill Kennels
Oregon, WI
608-835-7600

All Pets Inn
Pewaukee, WI
414-691-2298

Rodak Kennels
Pewaukee, WI
414-542-3209

U.S. Kennels > WISCONSIN

Flambeau Kennel
Phillips, WI
715-339-4806

Bovee Farm Kennels
Plainfield, WI
715-335-6984

Banner Boarding Kennels
Platteville, WI
608-348-7690

Fountain Bluff Farms Kennel
Platteville, WI
608-348-5926

Muckamoor Boarding Kennel
Plover, WI
715-344-8533

Karryon Kennels
Plymouth, WI
920-893-8315

Sunshine Kennels
Portage, WI
608-981-2090

Country Kennel
Prescott, WI
715-262-3557

Angelcare Pet Resort
Racine, WI
414-886-8728

Berby Kennels
Racine, WI
414-639-4769

Judy's Boarding Kennel
Range, WI
715-398-5577

Countryside Kennels
Rhinelander, WI
715-369-3113

Rodak Kennels
Rubicon, WI
920-474-7714

Monday Lake Kennels
Sarona, WI
715-234-7510

Woodland Kennels
Sauk City, WI
608-544-4302

Applewood Kennels
Shawano, WI
715-526-9493

Brookdale Kennels
Sheboygan, WI
920-565-3441

Silde Kennels
Sheboygan Falls, WI
920-565-2231

Taproot Kennels
Slinger, WI
414-644-9772

Pines Boarding Kennel
Sparta, WI
608-269-8391

Castlerock Boarding Kennels
Spencer, WI
715-659-5599

Mypride Kennels
Stetsonville, WI
715-678-2828

Tartana Kennels
Stetsonville, WI
715-678-2737

The Bed & Biskit
Stevens Point, WI
715-342-1882

Cedar Valley Kennels
Stoddard, WI
608-457-2744

Appletree Kennels
Sturgeon Bay, WI
920-743-8587

Face With A View Kennel
Sturgeon Bay, WI
920-743-4324

Potowatomi Boarding Kennel
Sturgeon Bay, WI
920-743-3903

Red Wing Boarding Kennels
Sussex, WI
414-246-3850

Fancher's Kennels
Three Lakes, WI
715-546-3090

Canine Haven Boarding Kennel
Tomahawk, WI
715-453-5283

Hart O the North Kennel
Turtle Lake, WI
715-986-4688

Animal Barn Pet Boarding
Waukesha, WI
414-547-8072

Best Care Pet Motel Kennels
Waukesha, WI
414-547-7905

Deltamarsh Kennels
Waukesha, WI
414-968-2004

Stoney Acres Kennel
Waupaca, WI
715-258-5452

Mystic Pet Motel
Waupun, WI
920-324-2798

Dogwood Boarding Kennels
Wausau, WI
715-359-5476

Mountainaire Boarding Kennel
Wausau, WI
715-359-2022

Krieger's Ridge Kennels
West Bend, WI
414-334-5165

Pleasant Valley Boarding Kennel
West Bend, WI
414-677-3222

West Bend Boarding Kennels
West Bend, WI
414-334-4443

Ridgetop Kennels
West Salem, WI
608-786-0669

Country Cottage Boarding Kennels
Westfield, WI
608-296-1524

U.S. Kennels > WYOMING

Coleman Country Kennel
Whitewater, WI
414-473-8585

WYOMING

Little Goose Kennels
Big Horn, WY
307-674-6633

Norske Kennels
Casper, WY
307-234-8689

Simmons Boarding Kennels
Casper, WY
307-265-5935

Broadmoor East Boarding
Cheyenne, WY
307-632-6607

Hol-A-Pet Inn
Cheyenne, WY
307-637-4700

Chinook Boarding Kennels
Cody, WY
307-587-3379

Geyser Creek Boarding Kennels
Dubois, WY
307-455-2702

John Henry's Country Kennel
Gillette, WY
307-682-3572

Kindness Kennels
Jackson, WY
307-733-2633

Spring Creek Kennels
Jackson, WY
307-733-1606

Windy Acres Kennels
Laramie, WY
307-745-7772

Roche Jaune Kennels
Pinedale, WY
307-367-2687

Green Acres Kennels
Rawlins, WY
307-324-5393

Wind River Kennels
Riverton, WY

5

Emergency Vets

Emergency vets are just what the name implies. They handle emergency medical situations for your pet after-hours or when your regular vet is not available. According to the Veterinary Emergency and Critical Care Society, an emergency veterinary service should be staffed with at least three people, including one veterinarian and one veterinary technician. Beyond standard diagnostic procedures, they should be able to perform emergency surgery, manage cardiac and respiratory problems and administer anesthetics and whole blood transfusions. They should also be able to produce high-quality radiographs safely.

We recommend that you call ahead of time to find an emergency vet in the area you'll be staying—just in case. As we mentioned earlier, with regard to certain listings in our book, we elevate our Golden Rule (always call ahead) to the Platinum Rule. This means it's even more important that you call ahead because these businesses tend to be smaller and individually owned, which means there is a greater chance of turnover. With regard to emergency vets, if you cannot reach one listed in this chapter, you can try calling the Veterinary Emergency and Critical Care Society to see if they can help locate a member vet near your location. Located in San Antonio, Texas, their number is 210-698-5575. While they can only be reached from 8 AM to 4 PM, you can use their website (www.veccs.org) as a resource before you leave or you can call them during office hours while you're away.

If you need to use the services of an emergency vet, make sure you have the phone number of your own veterinarian so that you can contact him or her to obtain any information that might be needed in the treatment of your pet. And, as mentioned previously, it's always a good idea to have a valid health certificate with you at all times when you travel. A quick read of your pet's medical record by the attending emergency vet can greatly increase the chances of a successful diagnosis and treatment of your pet's ailment.

U.S. Emergency Vets > ALABAMA

ALABAMA

Berry Animal Hospital
Ardmore, AL
256-423-6111

Clay County Animal Hospital
Ashland, AL
205-354-2308

Emergency Animal Clinic
Birmingham, AL
205-251-5696

Emergency Pet Care
Birmingham, AL
205-988-5988

Martin Animal Hospital
Birmingham, AL
205-595-8451

Brewton Animal Hospital
Brewton, AL
334-867-4355

West Alabama Animal Hospital
Carrollton, AL
205-367-8838
205-367-8620 (emergencies)

Daphne Animal Hospital
Daphne, AL
334-626-3771

Highland Animal Hospital
Daphne, AL
334-626-2653

Turner Large Animal Hospital
Decatur, AL
256-355-0528

Animal Care Center
Dothan, AL
334-794-6333

Care Animal Center
Dothan, AL
334-794-6624

Enterprise Animal Hospital
Enterprise, AL
334-347-0086

Gardner Animal Hospital
Eufaula, AL
334-687-4722

Ellis Memorial Animal Hospital
Florence, AL
256-764-3801

Gravlee Animal Hospital
Florence, AL
256-767-0500

Smith Animal Hospital
Florence, AL
256-766-0343

Dekalb Animal Hospital
Fort Payne, AL
205-845-0046

Fyffe Animal Hospital
Fyffe, AL
205-623-3600

Gordo Animal Hospital
Gordo, AL
205-364-7565

Oakwood Animal Hospital
Guin, AL
205-468-2407

Apollo Animal Hospital
Huntsville, AL
256-881-4862

Cole Animal Hospital
Huntsville, AL
205-881-7570

Hampton Cove Animal Hospital
Huntsville, AL
205-533-3385

Linderman Animal Hospital
Huntsville, AL
205-534-7387

Animal Hospital of Montgomery
Montgomery, AL
334-272-2200

Brown-Sternenberg Animal Hospital
Montgomery, AL
334-281-0415

Cavanaugh-Bradley Animal Hospital
Montgomery, AL
334-269-9111

Goodwin Animal Hospital
Montgomery, AL
334-279-7456

Taylor Crossing Animal Hospital
Montgomery, AL
334-260-8787

Shoals Animal Hospital
Muscle Shoals, AL
205-381-2911

Andrews Avenue Animal Hospital
Ozark, AL
334-774-3737

Harrington Equine Hospital
Pelham, AL
205-663-4000

Animal Care Center
Prattville, AL
334-365-3830

Animal Medical Clinic
Prattville, AL
334-365-7543

Rainsville Animal Hospital
Rainsville, AL
256-638-7299

Main Street Animal Hospital
Roanoke, AL
334-863-7111

Critter Care
Scottsboro, AL
256-574-5278
256-218-3021 (night call)

Whitlock Animal Hospital
Sheffield, AL
256-383-2626

Town & Country Veterinary Hospital
Tuscaloosa, AL
205-345-1282

Colbert Animal Clinic
Tuscumbia, AL
256-381-6210

U.S. Emergency Vets > CALIFORNIA

ARIZONA

Casa Grande Animal Hospital
Casa Grande, AZ
520-836-5979

Chino Valley Animal Hospital
Chino Valley, AZ
520-636-4382

Kachina Animal Hospital
Dewey, AZ
520-772-8225

Green Valley Animal Hospital
Green Valley, AZ
520-625-8634

Humane Society Animal Clinic
Nogales, AZ
520-287-5654

Canada Hills Animal Hospital
Oro Valley, AZ
520-544-4734

Page Animal Hospital
Page, AZ
520-645-2816

Parker Animal Hospital
Parker, AZ
520-669-2400

Animal Care Hospital
Phoenix, AZ
602-955-5757

Mile-Hi Animal Hospital
Prescott, AZ
520-445-4581

Prescott Animal Hospital
Prescott, AZ
520-445-2190

Thumb Butte Small Animal Hospital
Prescott, AZ
520-445-2331

Sonora Animal Hospital
Tucson, AZ
520-888-8988

Foothills Animal Hospital
Yuma, AZ
520-342-0448

ARKANSAS

Atkins Animal Clinic
Atkins, AR
501-641-2244

Hatfield, Charles S. DVM
Bentonville, AR
501-273-3921

East Ash Animal Hospital
Blytheville, AR
501-762-5781

Mayflower Animal Hospital
Conway, AR
501-470-1212

Jacksonville Animal Hospital
Jacksonville, AR
501-982-2581

Nixon Animal Hospital
Mountain View, AR
870-269-4242

Ozark Animal Hospital
Ozark, AR
501-667-3652

Oak Park Animal Hospital
Pine Bluff, AR
870-534-8144

Port City Animal Hospital
Pine Bluff, AR
870-534-5435

CALIFORNIA

Acton Veterinary Clinic
Acton, CA
661-269-7060

Agoura Animal Clinic
Agoura Hills, CA
818-991-1036

Alhambra Veterinary Hospital
Alhambra, CA
626-289-9227

Mission Animal Hospital
Alhambra, CA
626-289-3643

Alpine Animal Hospital
Alpine, CA
619-445-5683

Adobe Animal Hospital
Alta Loma, CA
909-483-3535

Alta Rancho Pet & Bird Hospital
Alta Loma, CA
909-980-3575

Baseline Animal Hospital
Alta Loma, CA
909-987-4788

Victoria Animal Hospital
Alta Loma, CA
909-944-8944

Altadena Animal Hospital
Altadena, CA
818-798-0738

Lake Avenue Animal Hospital
Altadena, CA
626-798-6710

Angels Camp Veterinary Hospital
Altaville, CA
209-736-0488

VCA Ana Brook Animal Hospital
Anaheim, CA
714-772-8220

Anaheim Animal Care & Pet Hospital
Anaheim, CA
714-527-9292

Anaheim Canyon Animal Hospital
Anaheim, CA
714-637-1000

Anchor Animal Hospital
Anaheim, CA
714-635-7762

Brokhaven Animal Hospital
Anaheim, CA
714-956-5901

East Hills Animal Hospital
Anaheim, CA
714-921-2500

Las Palma Veterinary Hospital
Anaheim, CA
714-535-1141

U.S. Emergency Vets > CALIFORNIA

State College Animal
Hospital
Anaheim, CA
714-772-1611

Antioch Veterinary Clinic
Antioch, CA
925-757-4814

Antioch Veterinary Hospital
Antioch, CA
925-757-2233

East Hills Veterinary
Hospital
Antioch, CA
925-754-7960

Animal Care Hospital
Apple Valley, CA
760-247-0292

Animal Hospital
At The Narrows
Apple Valley, CA
760-242-5377

Bear Valley Bird & Animal
Hospital
Apple Valley, CA
760-240-5228

Dr. Mike's Emergency
Animal Service
Apple Valley, CA
760-240-2120

Arcadia Small Animal
Hospital
Arcadia, CA
626-447-4854

Las Tunas Animal Hospital
Arcadia, CA
626-446-7174

North Coast Veterinary
Hospital
Arcata, CA
707-822-4885

Arroyo Grande Veterinary
Clinic
Arroyo Grande, CA
805-481-9434

El Camino Veterinary
Hospital
Atascadero, CA
805-466-6677

Animal Medical Center
Auburn, CA
530-823-5166

Auburn Area Evening
Pet Clinic
Auburn, CA
530-888-7387

Companion Veterinary
Clinic
Auburn, CA
530-885-3251

Azusa Animal Hospital
Azusa, CA
626-858-0027

Azusa Hills Animal Hospital
Azusa, CA
626-969-2266

Kern Animal Emergency
Clinic
Bakersfield, CA
805-322-6019

Baldwin Park Animal
Hospital
Baldwin Park, CA
626-337-7246

Banning Veterinary
Hospital
Banning, CA
909-849-3864

Abbey Animal Hospital
Beaumont, CA
909-845-2675

Bellwood Animal Hospital
Bellflower, CA
562-633-7833

Lakewood Animal Hospital
Bellflower, CA
562-633-8126

Animal Emergency Center
Berkeley, CA
510-841-4412

Pet Emergency Treatment
Service
Berkeley, CA
510-548-6684

VCA Lakeside Animal
Hospital
Big Bear Lake, CA
909-866-2021

Brea Veterinary Hospital
Brea, CA
714-529-4988

MS Animal Hospital
Burbak, CA
323-849-3420

Camarosa Veterinary Clinic
Camarillo, CA
805-482-9823

Mother Lode Pet
Emergency Clinic
Cameron Park, CA
530-676-9044

Central Animal Hospital
Campbell, CA
408-377-4043

Emergency Animal Clinic
Campbell, CA
408-371-6252

Roswinn Pet & Hospital
Canoga Park, CA
818-718-2112

La Costa Animal Hospital
Carlsbad, CA
760-944-1266

Animal Hospital at the
Crossroads
Carmel, CA
831-624-0131

Carmel Valley Veterinary
Hospital
Carmel Valley, CA
831-659-2286

Sacramento Animal
Medical Group
Carmichael, CA
831-331-7430

Avalon Animal Hospital
& Bird Clinic
Carson, CA
310-835-0111

Torrance Animal Hospital
Carson, CA
310-328-4419

Francis Animal Hospital
Chino, CA
909-591-6581

U.S. Emergency Vets > CALIFORNIA

Canyon Hills Animal Hospital
Chino Hills, CA
909-597-4881

Kindness Pet Clinics
Chula Vista, CA
619-690-2272

A Cat & Dog Emergency
Chula Vista, CA
619-427-2881

Alta Animal Hospital
Clovis, CA
559-298-6509

Clovis Equine Clinic
Clovis, CA
559-299-1661

Animal Emergency Clinic
Colton, CA
909-825-9350

Colton Animal Hospital
Colton, CA
909-825-4335

Wilds Veterinary Clinic Grand Terrace
Colton, CA
909-783-2216

Compton Dog & Cat Hospital
Compton, CA
310-636-7233

ABC Veterinary Hospital
Concord, CA
925-674-8878

Veterinary Emergency Clinic
Concord, CA
925-798-2900

Cool Animal Hospital
Cool, CA
530-885-8322

Acacia Animal Hospital
Corona, CA
909-371-1002

Corona Community Veterinary Hospital
Corona, CA
909-279-7387

Corona Del Mar Animal Hospital
Corona Del Mar, CA
949-644-8160

Costa Mesa Animal Hospital
Costa Mesa, CA
949-548-3794

Newport Harbor Animal Hospital
Costa Mesa, CA
949-631-1030

Newport Mesa Animal Hospital
Costa Mesa, CA
949-642-2100

Cotati Small Animal Hospital
Cotati, CA
707-795-3694

Animal Hospital of the Valley
Covina, CA
626-331-0775

Citrus Animal Hospital
Covina, CA
626-332-4526

Covina Animal Hospital
Covina, CA
626-331-5374

Vetsmart Pet Hospital
Covina, CA
626-339-8546

Animal Hospital of Rancho Cucamonga
Cucamonga, CA
909-980-1788

Blair R L DVM
Cucamonga, CA
909-980-0686

A Acacia Animal Hospital
Cypress, CA
714-821-7821

ABC Animal Hospital
Cypress, CA
714-995-8033

St. Francis Square Veterinary Night Hospital
Daly City, CA
650-992-1100

Danville Veterinary Hospital
Danville, CA
925-837-4264

El Macero Veterinary Clinic
Davis, CA
530-756-6764

All Creatures Hospital
Del Mar, CA
858-481-7992

East Valley Emergency Pet Clinic
Diamond Bar, CA
909-861-5737

Village Animal Hospital
Diamond Bar, CA
909-861-7463

Dixon Veterinary Clinic
Dixon, CA
707-678-2377

Plaza Veterinary Clinic
Downey, CA
562-928-2234

Ellsworth, Kerry DVM
Duarte, CA
626-357-2251

Tri-Valley Veterinary Clinic
Dublin, CA
925-828-0654

Abbey Pet Hospital
El Cerrito, CA
510-529-0777

El Cerrito Pet Hospital
El Cerrito, CA
510-234-4582

El Segundo Pet Hospital
El Segundo, CA
310-322-6506

North Coast Veterinary Medical Group
Encinitas, CA
760-632-1072

Aark Animal Hospital
Escondido, CA
760-745-5171

Escondido Hills Animal Hospital
Escondido, CA
760-746-3647

U.S. Emergency Vets > **CALIFORNIA**

Fairfield Animal Hospital
Fairfield, CA
707-428-5300

Foothill Animal Clinic
Fontana, CA
909-350-3157

Sierra Animal Hospital
Fontana, CA
909-350-7807

Fortuna Animal Medical Center
Fortuna, CA
707-725-6114

All-Care Animal Referral Center
Fountain Valley, CA
714-963-0909

Ellis Park Animal Hospital
Fountain Valley, CA
714-963-8363

Mile Square Animal Hospital
Fountain Valley, CA
714-546-7676

Warner Avenue Animal Hospital
Fountain Valley, CA
714-540-5252

American Animal Hospital
Fremont, CA
510-791-0464

Brookvale Animal Hospital
Fremont, CA
510-796-7444

Fremont Animal Hospital
Fremont, CA
510-656-1852

Companion Animal Hospital of Woodware Park
Fresno, CA
559-432-1110

SPCA Small Animal Hospital
Fresno, CA
559-237-1125

Waterhouse Animal Hospital
Fresno, CA
559-434-4000

Airport Animal Hospital
Fullerton, CA
714-879-4531

Boulevard Animal Hospital
Garden Grove, CA
714-537-6780

Orange County Emergency Pet Clinic
Garden Grove, CA
714-537-3032

Roylyn Animal Hospital
Garden Grove, CA
714-537-0887

Alondra Animal Hospital
Gardena, CA
310-676-2255

Gavilan Animal Hospital
Gilroy, CA
408-842-0393

Angelus Pet Hospital
Glendale, CA
818-241-8333

Animal Emergency Clinic of Glendale
Glendale, CA
818-247-3973

Glen Oaks Animal Hospital
Glendale, CA
818-840-9700

Mobile Vet
Glendale, CA
818-242-5576

Alosta Animal Hospital
Glendora, CA
626-963-1674

South Glendora Animal Hospital
Glendora, CA
626-599-4813

West Foothill Animal Hospital
Glendora, CA
626-335-4912

La Concepcion Animal Hospital
Goleta, CA
805-685-4513

Balboa Veterinary Medical Clinic
Granada Hills, CA
818-368-2846

Emergency Veterinary Clinic
Granada Hills, CA
818-368-5150

Groveland Veterinary Clinic
Groveland, CA
209-962-7058

Beck, Stephen DVM
Grover Beach, CA
805-481-2595

Hacienda Heights Animal Hospital
Hacienda Heights, CA
626-961-2584

St. Francis Animal Hospital
Hacienda Heights, CA
626-968-4709

Animal Care Hospital
Hemet, CA
909-652-7387

Abbott Animal Hospital
Hemet, CA
909-845-2675

AVL Animal Hospital
Hemet, CA
909-927-2011

Hemet Animal Hospital
Hemet, CA
909-658-3119

VCA Animal Hospital
Hermosa Beach, CA
310-372-8881

Desert Care Animal Hospital
Hesperia, CA
619-949-7387

Hesperia Animal Hospital
Hesperia, CA
760-948-1553

Mobile Veterinary Service
Hesperia, CA
760-244-7722

Ausaymas Veterinary Service
Hollister, CA
831-637-0097

U.S. Emergency Vets > CALIFORNIA

Hollister Veterinary Clinic
Hollister, CA
831-637-2580

AAA Animal Hospital
Huntington Beach, CA
714-536-6537

**Animal Hospital of
Fountain Valley**
Huntington Beach, CA
714-962-6621

**Beach City Animal
Hospital**
Huntington Beach, CA
714-847-3523

Hamilton Animal Hospital
Huntington Beach, CA
714-964-4744

Valley Animal Clinic
Indio, CA
760-342-4711

Centinela Animal Hospital
Inglewood, CA
310-673-1910

Arbor Animal Hospital
Irvine, CA
949-551-2727

**Northwood Animal
Hospital**
Irvine, CA
949-559-1992

Irvine Veterinary Service
Irvine, CA
949-786-0990

**Jamestown Veterinary
Hospital**
Jamestown, CA
209-984-0232

Julian Animal Hospital
Julian, CA
760-765-0500

**Kensington Veterinary
Hospital**
Kensington, CA
510-528-0797

Kenwood Veterinary Clinic
Kenwood, CA
707-833-1000

**King City Veterinary
Hospital**
King City, CA
831-385-4878

Alpine Animal Hospital
La Habra, CA
562-694-3696

**County Line Animal
Hospital**
La Habra, CA
562-697-6725

Gregg Animal Hospital
La Habra, CA
562-691-7751

**Sunny Hills Animal
Hospital**
La Habra, CA
310-691-1698

Animal Hospital of La Jolla
La Jolla, CA
858-459-2665

Fuerte Animal Hospital
La Mesa, CA
619-440-1432

Imperial Animal Hospital
La Mirada, CA
562-941-0284

Amar Glen Animal Hospital
La Puente, CA
626-333-2282

**Industry Hill Animal
Hospital**
La Puente, CA
626-965-7521

Baldy View Animal Hospital
La Verne, CA
909-596-7771

**Crown Valley Animal
Hospital**
Laguna Niguel, CA
949-495-6744

**Laguna Niguel Animal
Hospital**
Laguna Niguel, CA
949-495-0030

Arroyo Pet Clinic
Lake Forest, CA
949-770-1808

Lake Forest Animal Clinic
Lake Forest, CA
949-837-7660

Canyon Veterinary Hospital
Lake Isabella, CA
760-379-4608

**Abo Large Animal
Veterinary Clinic**
Lancaster, CA
661-949-0569

Lancaster Pet Clinic
Lancaster, CA
661-949-9389

**North Valley Veterinary
Clinic**
Lancaster, CA
661-945-7906

**Lawndale Veterinary
Hospital**
Lawndale, CA
310-679-9522

**West Valley Veterinary
Clinic**
Lompoc, CA
805-736-1238

Evening Pet Clinic
Long Beach, CA
562-422-1223

**Mercy Animal Medical
Center**
Long Beach, CA
562-422-5458
562-423-2468 (emergencies)

**Spring Street Animal
Hospital**
Long Beach, CA
562-421-8463

**Loomis Basin Veterinary
Clinic**
Loomis, CA
916-652-5816

**Los Alamitos Animal
Hospital**
Los Alamitos, CA
562-431-6925

Animal Emergency Facility
Los Angeles, CA
310-473-1561

U.S. Emergency Vets > CALIFORNIA

California Animal Hospital
Los Angeles, CA
310-478-5915

Center Sinai Animal Hospital
Los Angeles, CA
310-559-3770

Eagle Rock Pet Clinic
Los Angeles, CA
323-254-7382

Highland Park Animal Hospital
Los Angeles, CA
323-254-6868

Southwest Animal Medical Center
Los Angeles, CA
323-752-1120

VCA West Los Angeles Animal Hospital
Los Angeles, CA
310-473-2951

Bear Valley Animal Clinic
Los Osos, CA
805-528-0693

Los Osos Pet Hospital
Los Osos, CA
805-528-4111

Malibu Animal Hospital
Malibu, CA
310-456-6441

Animal Medical Group
Manhattan Beach, CA
310-546-5731

Bay Animal Hospital
Manhattan Beach, CA
310-545-6596

Ritter Animal Hospital
Mariposa, CA
209-966-5666

Meadow Vista Veterinary Clinic
Meadow Vista, CA
530-878-2009

Atwater Veterinary Clinic
Merced, CA
209-358-4469

Merced Veterinary Clinic
Merced, CA
209-383-0555

Yosemite Veterinary Clinic
Merced, CA
209-383-4722

Middletown Animal Hospital
Middletown, CA
707-987-2000

Adobe Pet Hospital
Mill Valley, CA
415-388-4300

Alto Tiburon Veterinary Hospital
Mill Valley, CA
415-383-7700

Tamalpais Pet Hospital
Mill Valley, CA
415-388-3315

Calaveras Veterinary Clinic
Milpitas, CA
408-262-7200

Animal Urgent Care Clinic
Mission Viejo, CA
949-364-6228

Mission Viejo Animal Hospital
Mission Viejo, CA
949-582-1220

Veterinary Emergency Clinic
Modesto, CA
209-527-8844

Monrovia Animal Hospital
Monrovia, CA
626-358-1146

Santa Anita Animal Hospital
Monrovia, CA
626-359-3281

Emergency Pet Clinic of Pomona Valley
Montclair, CA
909-981-1051

Park View Veterinary Hospital
Monterey, CA
831-372-2672

Monterey Peninsula-Salinas Veterinary
Monterey, CA
831-373-7374

Atlantic Animal Hospital
Monterey Park, CA
626-576-0357

Monterey Park Animal Hospital
Monterey Park, CA
323-722-9692

San Gabriel Animal Hospital
Monterey Park, CA
626-280-4070

Moorpark Veterinary Hospital
Moorpark, CA
805-529-7003

Town Veterinary Medical Center
Moorpark, CA
805-529-7387

Alessandro Veterinary Hospital
Moreno Valley, CA
909-656-4455

Coast Veterinary Clinic
Morro Bay, CA
805-772-2228

Morro Bay Veterinary Clinic
Morro Bay, CA
805-772-4411

Alta-View Animal Hospital
Mountain View, CA
650-948-1021

Silverado Veterinary Hospital
Napa, CA
707-224-7953

Plaza Boulevard Pet Clinic
National City, CA
619-267-8200

Newport Center Animal Hospital
Newport Beach, CA
949-644-5460

U.S. Emergency Vets > CALIFORNIA

Newport Hills Animal Hospital
Newport Beach, CA
949-759-1911

Animal & Bird Hospital
Norco, CA
909-371-7120

Crossroads Animal Emergency & Referral Center
Norwalk, CA
562-863-2522

San Marin Animal Hospital
Novato, CA
415-892-8387

Bay Area Animal Hospital
Oakland, CA
510-654-8375

Oakley Veterinary Medical Center
Oakley, CA
925-625-1878

Temple Heights Animal Hospital
Oceanside, CA
760-630-3590

Euclid-Walnut Pet Clinic
Ontario, CA
909-983-2119

Mountain Avenue Animal Hospital
Ontario, CA
909-986-4548

Ontario Veterinary Hospital
Ontario, CA
909-984-2211

Animal Emergency of Orange County
Orange, CA
714-771-3870

Chapman Animal Hospital
Orange, CA
714-639-0392

Nohl Ranch Animal Hospital
Orange, CA
714-637-9730

Pet Care Centers of America
Orange, CA
714-771-7387

VCA Villa Animal Hospital
Orange, CA
714-633-9780

Pacifica Pet Hospital
Pacifica, CA
650-359-3685

Pedro Point Veterinary Clinic
Pacifica, CA
650-359-5770

Animal Medical Hospital
Palm Springs, CA
619-327-1355

Cahuilla Veterinary Clinic
Palm Springs, CA
760-324-0450

Desert Animal Hospital
Palm Springs, CA
760-323-1794

Antelope Valley Animal Hospital
Palmdale, CA
661-273-1234

High Desert Animal Care Hospital
Palmdale, CA
661-272-1616

Bayshore Animal Hospital
Palo Alto, CA
650-327-7387

Stanford Pet Clinic
Palo Alto, CA
650-493-4233

Colyer Veterinary Service
Paradise, CA
530-872-3246

Animal Emergency Clinic of Pasadena
Pasadena, CA
626-564-0704

Hastings Animal Hospital
Pasadena, CA
626-351-8863

Teresita Animal Hospital
Pasadena, CA
626-792-5143

Paso Robles Veterinary Medical Clinic
Paso Robles, CA
805-238-4622

Perris Animal Hospital
Perris, CA
909-657-3139

Petaluma Veterinary Hospital
Petaluma, CA
707-762-3511

Yolinda Animal Hospital
Placentia, CA
714-524-1156

Marin Veterinary Clinic
Point Reyes Station, CA
415-663-1940

Quartz Hill Veterinary Clinic
Quartz Hill, CA
661-943-7896

Ramona Animal Hospital
Ramona, CA
760-788-0960

Antonio Animal Hospital
Rancho Santa Margar, CA
949-858-0949

Rancho Santa Margarita Animal Hospital
Rancho Santa Margarita, CA
949-858-3181

All Cats Veterinary Hospital
Redding, CA
530-244-2287

VCA Asher Animal Hospital
Redding, CA
530-224-2200

Redlands Animal Hospital
Redlands, CA
909-793-2181

Animal Hospital of Redondo Beach
Redondo Beach, CA
310-540-9044

Animal Hospital of Riviera Village
Redondo Beach, CA
310-316-4527

Palos Verdes Animal Hospital
Redondo Beach, CA
310-540-5656

U.S. Emergency Vets > CALIFORNIA

Redwood Animal Hospital
Redondo Beach, CA
310-376-0581

Village Pet Clinic
Redondo Beach, CA
310-375-6811

McClave Veterinary Hospital
Reseda, CA
818-881-5102

Crestwood Animal Hospital
Ridgecrest, CA
760-446-7616

**Rim Forest Animal
Hospital**
Rim Forest, CA
909-337-8589

**Arlington-Arlanza Animal
Hospital**
Riverside, CA
909-354-2800

**West Riverside Veterinary
Hospital**
Riverside, CA
909-686-2242

**Animal Care Center of
Sonoma County**
Rohnert Park, CA
707-584-4343

Center Animal Hospital
Rolling Hills Estates, CA
310-377-5548

Rosemead Animal Hospital
Rosemead, CA
626-444-0565

Pet Emergency Center
Roseville, CA
916-632-9111

Colima Animal Hospital
Rowland Heights, CA
626-912-9411

**Emergency Animal Clinic
of Sacramento**
Sacramento, CA
916-362-3146

**Natomas Animal Medical
Hospital**
Sacramento, CA
916-925-6138

**Sacramento Emergency
Veterinary Clinic**
Sacramento, CA
916-922-3425

Animal Hospital of Salinas
Salinas, CA
831-424-5707

**Inland Central Animal
Hospital**
San Bernardino, CA
909-884-6126

**Loma Linda Animal
Hospital**
San Bernardino, CA
909-825-3144

**Skycrest Weekend
Veterinary Clinic**
San Bruno, CA
650-588-1151

Camino Veterinary Clinic
San Clemente, CA
949-661-1255

**San Clemente Veterinary
Hospital**
San Clemente, CA
949-492-5777

Veterinary House Calls
San Clemente, CA
949-498-9588

**ABC Veterinary Hospitals
Pacific Beach**
San Diego, CA
850-270-4120

All Care Cat Hospital
San Diego, CA
858-274-2287

**Avian & Exotic Animal
Hospital**
San Diego, CA
619-260-1412

Colina Veterinary Hospital
San Diego, CA
619-286-3360

**Emergency Animal
Hospital of San Diego**
San Diego, CA
619-299-2400

**Pacific Petcare Veterinary
of Carmel Valley**
San Diego, CA
858-481-1101

**San Carlos Veterinary
Hospital**
San Diego, CA
619-460-3100

Arrow Animal Hospital
San Dimas, CA
909-592-1931

San Fernando Pet Hospital
San Fernando, CA
818-361-8636

**All Animals Emergency
Hospital**
San Francisco, CA
415-566-0531

**Pets Unlimited Veterinary
Hospital**
San Francisco, CA
415-563-6700

**Temple City Animal
Hospital**
San Gabriel, CA
626-287-1173

Small Animal Hospital
San Jacinto, CA
909-654-7396

Akal Animal Clinic
San Jose, CA
408-254-2525

**Emergency Animal Clinic
of South San Jose**
San Jose, CA
408-578-5622

**VCA Orchard Plaza
Animal Hospital**
San Jose, CA
408-227-9110

**Capistrano Veterinary
Clinic**
San Juan Capistrano, CA
949-496-3731

**Alameda County
Emergency Pet Clinic**
San Leandro, CA
510-352-6080

U.S. Emergency Vets > CALIFORNIA

Animal Care Clinic
San Luis Obispo, CA
805-545-8212

Palomar Animal Hospital
San Marcos, CA
760-727-7622

**Northern Peninsula
Veterinary Emergency**
San Mateo, CA
650-348-2575

South Shores Pet Clinic
San Pedro, CA
310-832-5327

North Bay Animal Hospital
San Rafael, CA
415-499-8387

Terra Linda Vet Hospital
San Rafael, CA
415-479-8535

**North Canyon Animal
Hospital**
San Ramon, CA
925-743-9300

**Airport-Irvine Animal
Hospital**
Santa Ana, CA
714-754-1033

**Seventeenth Street Animal
Hospital**
Santa Ana, CA
714-542-4107

**Warner-Bristol Animal
Hospital**
Santa Ana, CA
714-540-0814

La Cumbre Animal Hospital
Santa Barbara, CA
805-967-0121

**Pacific Emergency
Pet Hospital**
Santa Barbara, CA
805-682-5120

**VCA Vets & Pets One Stop
Pet Care**
Santa Clara, CA
408-246-1893

Cat Clinic of Santa Cruz
Santa Cruz, CA
831-429-1655

Ocean Animal Clinic
Santa Cruz, CA
831-429-5100

**Santa Cruz Veterinary
Hospital**
Santa Cruz, CA
831-475-5400

**North Bay Animal
Emergency Hospital**
Santa Monica, CA
310-451-8962

**Veterinary Hospital
at Saticoy**
Santa Paula, CA
805-659-3588

**Emergency Veterinary
Clinic of Santa Rosa**
Santa Rosa, CA
707-544-1647

**Petcare Emergency
Hospital**
Santa Rosa, CA
707-573-5900

**Adler Veterinary Group
Hospital**
Sepulveda, CA
818-893-6366

**Shingle Springs Veterinary
Clinic**
Shingle Springs, CA
916-677-0390

Vet Smart Care Clinic
Signal Hill, CA
562-427-7122

Alamo Veterinary Hospital
Simi Valley, CA
805-583-8855

**Rancho Sequoia Veterinary
Hospital**
Simi Valley, CA
805-522-7476

**Los Coches Animal
Hospital**
Soledad, CA
408-678-2658

Sonoma Veterinary Clinic
Sonoma, CA
707-938-4455 (day & night)

**South Pasadena Animal
Hospital**
South Pasadena, CA
626-254-2294

**Paradise Valley Road
Pet Hospital**
Spring Valley, CA
619-475-9770

Animal Emergency Center
Studio City, CA
818-760-3882

**Solano Pet Emergency
Clinic**
Suisun City, CA
707-864-1444

Coats, David M., AVM
Sun City, CA
909-672-9632

Sun-Surf Animal Hospital
Sunset Beach, CA
562-592-1391

North Lake Veterinary Clinic
Tahoe City, CA
530-583-8587

**Animal Hospital of
Thousand Oaks**
Thousand Oaks, CA
818-493-5540

Animal Emergency Clinic
Thousand Palms, CA
760-343-3438 (day & night)

Country Hills Animal Clinic
Torrance, CA
310-539-3851

**Emergency Pet Clinic
of South Bay**
Torrance, CA
310-320-8300

Harbor Animal Hospital
Torrance, CA
310-328-3733

Truckee Veterinary Hospital
Truckee, CA
530-587-4366

**Saddleback Animal
Hospital**
Tustin, CA
714-832-8686

U.S. Emergency Vets > CALIFORNIA

**High Desert Animal
Hospital**
Twentynine Palms, CA
760-367-9511

**North State Animal
Hospital**
Ukiah, CA
707-468-5965

**Angels' Care Animal
Hospital**
Upland, CA
909-982-2888

Central Veterinary Hospital
Upland, CA
909-981-2855

Alamo Animal Hospital
Vacaville, CA
707-447-2277

AAA Pets Medical Center
Vallejo, CA
707-642-5622

Glen Cove Animal Hospital
Vallejo, CA
707-643-2571

Mesa Veterinary Care Center
Victorville, CA
760-245-0109

**Tulare-Kings Veterinary
Emergency Service**
Visalia, CA
559-739-7054

**Coastal Emergency Animal
Hospital**
Vista, CA
760-630-6343

**Animal Hospital of
Watsonville**
Watsonville, CA
831-728-1439

East Lake Animal Clinic
Watsonville, CA
831-724-6391

South Hills Animal Hospital
West Covina, CA
626-919-7661

Westside Veterinary Hospital
West Sacramento, CA
916-371-8900

**Agoura Westlake Animal
Hospital**
Westlake Village, CA
818-707-3030

Anza Animal Clinic
Westlake Village, CA
805-495-1059

Alamitos Animal Hospital
Westminster, CA
714-893-3591

Magnolia Animal Hospital
Westminster, CA
714-848-9114

**Washington Blvd Animal
Hospital**
Whittier, CA
562-693-8233

**Cache Creek Veterinary
Service**
Woodland, CA
562-666-7322

**Woodland Veterinary
Hospital**
Woodland, CA
530-666-2461

**Animal and Veterinary
Critical Care Center**
Woodland Hills, CA
818-887-2262

East Lake Animal Hospital
Yorba Linda, CA
714-777-1661

**Yucca Valley Small Animal
Hospital**
Yucca Valley, CA
760-365-3346

COLORADO

Northwest Animal Hospital
Colorado Springs, CO
719-593-8582

Aspen Animal Hospital
Aspen, CO
970-925-2611

**Valley Mobile Veterinary
Practice**
Aspen, CO
970-925-6412

**Boulder Emergency
Pet Clinic**
Boulder, CO
303-440-7722

Breckenridge Animal Clinic
Breckenridge, CO
970-453-0821

**Cortez Adobe Animal
Hospital**
Cortez, CO
970-565-9316

Animal Emergency Room
Denver, CO
303-366-3527

Durango Animal Hospital
Durango, CO
970-247-3174

Hiwan Animal Hospital
Evergreen, CO
303-670-0838

**Chappelle Small Animal
Hospital**
Fort Collins, CO
970-482-7595

Countryside Animal Hospital
Fort Collins, CO
970-223-7789

**South Mesa Veterinary
Hospital**
Fort Collins, CO
970-226-6526

Canyon Animal Hospital
Golden, CO
303-526-2652

Eldred Animal Hospital
Greeley, CO
970-352-4502

West Ridge Animal Hospital
Greeley, CO
970-330-7283

**After Hours Veterinary
Clinic**
Lakewood, CO
303-987-2026

**Northside Emergency
Pet Clinic**
Thornton, CO
303-252-7722

U.S. Emergency Vets > FLORIDA

Mountain Mobile Veterinary Service
Vail, CO
970-476-7085

CONNECTICUT

Bloomfield Animal Hospital
Bloomfield, CT
860-286-2986

Norwich Animal Hospital
Bozrah, CT
860-889-1387

Bridgeport Veterinary Hospital
Bridgeport, CT
203-334-5548

Tri-Town Animal Hospital
Ellington, CT
860-871-0826

Enfield Animal Hospital
Enfield, CT
860-745-1619

Engelberg-Kristy Animal Hospital
Fairfield, CT
203-367-4475

Greenfield Animal Hospital
Fairfield, CT
203-254-0700

Highway Animal Hospital
Fairfield, CT
203-366-6733

Greenwich Animal Hospital
Greenwich, CT
203-869-0534

Merryfield Hospital for Animals
Hamden, CT
203-281-3811

Animal Emergency Care Clinic
Hartford, CT
860-233-8387

Lebanon Animal Hospital
Lebanon, CT
860-642-7936

East Brook Animal Hospital
Mansfield, CT
860-456-1759

Milford Animal Hospital
Milford, CT
203-878-7471

Pond Point Animal Hospital
Milford, CT
203-878-4646

DMK Animal Hospital
Old Saybrook, CT
860-399-6249

Oxford Seymour Animal Hospital
Oxford, CT
203-888-9292

Preston Animal Hospital
Preston, CT
860-889-4736

Animal Hospital of Putnam
Putnam, CT
860-928-1931

Animal Hospital of Greenwich Stamford
Stamford, CT
203-967-8008

Bulls' Head Animal Hospital
Stamford, CT
203-324-5711

High Ridge Animal Hospital
Stamford, CT
203-322-0507

Rippowan Animal Hospital
Stamford, CT
203-329-8811

Stamford & Springdale Animal Hospital
Stamford, CT
203-323-9623

Torrington Animal Hospital
Torrington, CT
860-489-4231

Hartford Animal Hospital
West Hartford, CT
860-236-2610

Angel Animal Hospital
West Haven, CT
203-934-3536

Wethersfield Animal Hospital
Wethersfield, CT
860-529-9420

DELAWARE

Brenford Animal Hospital
Dover, DE
302-678-9418

Dover Animal Hospital
Dover, DE
302-674-1515

Jeter's Animal Hospital
Dover, DE
302-734-3240

Animal and Veterinary Critical Care Center
Woodland Hills, CA
818-887-2262

VCA Hockessin Animal Hospital
Hockessin, DE
302-239-4383

Pike Creek Animal Hospital
Newark, DE
302-454-7780

FLORIDA

Arcadia Animal Hospital
Arcadia, FL
941-494-5566

Matthews Animal Hospital
Arcadia, FL
941-494-2101

Best Friends Animal Hospital
Belleview, FL
904-245-2273

Camelot Animal Hospital
Belleview, FL
904-245-5181

Boca Greens Animal Hospital
Boca Raton, FL
561-482-6308

Boca Village Animal Hospital
Boca Raton, FL
561-391-2266

U.S. Emergency Vets > FLORIDA

Calusa Animal Hospital
Boca Raton, FL
561-241-7177

Clintmoore Animal Hospital
Boca Raton, FL
561-487-0226

Companion Animal Hospital at Loggersrun
Boca Raton, FL
561-488-7555

Boynton Beach Animal Hospital
Boynton Beach, FL
561-732-0777

Boynton Pet Clinic
Boynton Beach, FL
561-734-2228

Colonial Animal Hospital
Boynton Beach, FL
561-737-6448

Fountains of Boynton Animal Hospital
Boynton Beach, FL
561-737-6300

Pet-Vet
Boynton Beach, FL
561-732-2222

Bayshore Animal Hospital
Bradenton, FL
941-756-5544

Meadowrun Animal Hospital
Brandon, FL
813-685-7775

Morgan Animal Hospital
Brandon, FL
813-681-8582

All County Animal Hospital
Brooksville, FL
904-796-6788

Chipley Animal Hospital
Chipley, FL
850-638-1511

Dr. Peter's Animal Hospital
Coral Springs, FL
954-340-9904

North Springs Animal Hospital
Coral Springs, FL
954-344-8282

Crystal River Animal Hospital
Crystal River, FL
352-795-7556

All Pet Care Animal Clinic
Davie, FL
954-476-6606

Extra Care Animal Hospital
Davie, FL
954-370-0203

Animal Emergency Clinic
Daytona Beach, FL
904-252-4300

Backos Bird Clinic
Deerfield Beach, FL
954-427-0777

Deer Run Animal Hospital
Deerfield Beach, FL
954-421-2244

Mobile Vet (Johnson, Ronald DVM)
Deerfield Beach, FL
954-426-0620

Boca-Delray Animal Hospital
Delray Beach, FL
561-496-1700

Delray Beach Veterinary Hospital
Delray Beach, FL
561-276-0333

Englewood Animal Hospital
Englewood, FL
941-474-1295

Lemon Bay Animal Hospital
Englewood, FL
941-474-7711

Animal Clinic
Fort Lauderdale, FL
954-581-0710

Bayview Animal Clinic
Fort Lauderdale, FL
954-771-8520

Indian Trace Animal Hospital
Fort Lauderdale, FL
954-714-5263

Pet Emergency Center
Fort Lauderdale, FL
954-772-0420

Promenade Animal Hospital
Fort Lauderdale, FL
954-748-9600

Port St. Lucie Animal Hospital
Fort Pierce, FL
561-465-5525

River Bridge Animal Hospital
Greenacres, FL
561-966-1171

Aardvark Animal Hospital
Hialeah, FL
305-557-0531

Country Club Animal Hospitals
Hialeah, FL
305-558-8787

Panda Animal Clinic
Hialeah, FL
305-887-1018

Animal Emergency and Critical Care Center
Hollywood, FL
954-432-5611

Emerald Hills Animal Hospital
Hollywood, FL
954-983-2300

Hollywood Animal Hospital
Hollywood, FL
954-920-3556

English Plaza Animal Hospital
Homestead, FL
305-248-6536

Midway Animal Hospital
Homosassa, FL
352-795-7110

U.S. Emergency Vets > FLORIDA

Central Veterinary
Emergency Clinic
Jacksonville, FL
904-399-8800

Cornerstone Animal
Hospital
Jacksonville, FL
904-766-3089

Northside Animal Hospital
Jacksonville, FL
904-757-4610

Southside Animal Clinic
Jacksonville, FL
904-721-3500

Emergency Pet Clinic
Beaches
Jacksonville Beach, FL
904-223-8000

Cypress Animal Hospital
Jupiter, FL
407-744-7878

All Pets Clinic & House Calls
Key Largo, FL
305-453-0055

Animal Hospital of Olde
Key West & Stock Island
Key West, FL
305-296-5227

Animal Hospital
of Lady Lake
Lady Lake, FL
352-753-5333

Animal Hospital of the
Palm Beaches
Lake Worth, FL
561-965-5800

Canal Animal Hospital
Lake Worth, FL
561-582-3595

Jog Lantana Animal Clinic
Lake Worth, FL
561-964-3144

Lake Osborne Animal Clinic
Lake Worth, FL
561-586-2332

VCA Palm Beach County
Animal Medical Clinic
Lake Worth, FL
561-964-4448

Land O' Lakes Animal
Hospital
Land O' Lakes, FL
813-996-2021

Companion Animal
Hospital
Live Oak, FL
904-362-1556

Palms West Veterinary
Hospital
Loxahatchee, FL
561-793-2799

VCA Wellington Animal
Hospital
Loxahatchee, FL
561-793-4900

Wellington Animal Hospital
Emergencies & Holidays
Loxahatchee, FL
407-793-4901

All Creatures Animal
Hospital
Lutz, FL
813-949-2706

Cypress Creek Animal
Hospital
Lutz, FL
813-949-3045

Lutz Animal Hospital
Lutz, FL
904-949-3667

Animal Hospital of
The Keys
Marathon, FL
305-743-2287

Marianna Animal Hospital
Marianna, FL
850-482-3520

All Animal & Bird Hospital
Melbourne, FL
321-724-2070

Brevard Animal Emergency
Clinic
Melbourne, FL
321-725-5365

Melrose Animal Hospital
Melrose, FL
352-475-1636

All Pets Veterinary Group
Miami, FL
305-633-2402

Animal Welfare Society of
South Florida
Miami, FL
305-445-3606

Beatty Animal Clinic
Miami, FL
305-552-7922

Bird Road Animal Hospital
Miami, FL
305-264-4242

Bustillo Animal Hospital
Miami, FL
305-279-5858

Dream Lake Animal
Hospital
Miami, FL
305-225-3116

Eureka Animal Clinic
Miami, FL
305-253-6754

Hammocks Veterinary
Hospital
Miami, FL
305-388-0880

Kendale Lakes Pet Health
Care Center
Miami, FL
305-385-8000

Kendall Animal Clinic
Miami, FL
305-274-6434

Knowwes Animal Clinics
Miami, FL
305-649-1234

Miller West Animal
Hospital
Miami, FL
305-383-0421

Shaffer Central Hospital
Miami, FL
305-387-0841

South Kendall Animal
Clinic & Hospital
Miami, FL
305-238-2030

U.S. Emergency Vets > FLORIDA

West Miami Animal Clinic
Miami, FL
305-266-1825

Yarborough Animal Clinic
Miami, FL
305-634-6547

Quality Care Animal Hospital
Miramar, FL
954-964-5557

River Run Animal Clinic
Miramar, FL
954-437-6623

Humane Society Animal Hospital
Naples, FL
941-643-1555

Navarre Animal Hospital
Navarre, FL
850-939-1373

Dade Animal Hospital
North Miami Beach, FL
305-651-1421

North Port Animal Hospital
North Port, FL
941-426-0661

Animal Hospital at Merryfield
Oakland Park, FL
954-202-9840

Animal Hospital of Ft. Lauderdale
Oakland Park, FL
954-561-8777

Oakland Park Animal Hospital
Oakland Park, FL
954-731-4228

Oak Ridge Animal Hospital
Ocala, FL
352-622-4217

Skylark Animal Hospital
Ocala, FL
352-622-5055

Clay County Animal Hospital
Orange Park, FL
904-272-5111

Clay-Duval Pet Emergency Clinic
Orange Park, FL
904-264-8281

Animal Veterinary Hospital of Orlando
Orlando, FL
407-855-7387

Silver Star Animal Hospital
Orlando, FL
407-293-7297

Veterinary Emergency Clinic of Central Florida
Orlando, FL
407-438-4449

Aloma Jancy Animal Hospital
Oviedo, FL
407-671-1183

Mitchell Hammock Veterinary Clinic
Oviedo, FL
407-366-7323

Pet Emergency & Critical Care Clinic
Palm Beach Gardens, FL
407-691-9999

Gulf Winds Animal Hospital
Panama City, FL
850-233-8383

Parkway Animal Hospital
Panama City, FL
850-763-8387

Animal Care Center OFB
Panama City Beach, FL
850-235-2877

Ellenton Animal Hospital
Parrish, FL
941-776-1100

Emergency Animal Clinic
Pembroke Pines, FL
954-962-0300

Flamingo Animal Clinic
Pembroke Pines, FL
954-435-5555

Flamingo Road Animal Hospital
Pembroke Pines, FL
954-430-5200

Scenic Hills Veterinary Hospital
Pensacola, FL
850-477-6225

May Animal Hospital
Plant City, FL
813-752-1010

Plant City Animal Hospital
Plant City, FL
813-752-3073

Charlotte Animal Hospital
Port Charlotte, FL
941-625-6111

Burnt Store Animal Hospital
Punta Gorda, FL
941-637-6006

Lawrence Animal Hospital
Quincy, FL
850-627-8338

Quincy Animal Hospital
Quincy, FL
850-875-4811

Cruz Animal Hospital
Ramrod Key, FL
305-872-2559

Boyette Animal Hospital of Riverview
Riverview, FL
813-671-3400

Animal Wellness Center
Royal Palm Beach, FL
561-790-3555

Mid County Veterinary Hospital
Royal Palm Beach, FL
561-798-8000

Ruskin Animal Hospital
Ruskin, FL
813-645-6411

Sanford Veterinary Hospital
Sanford, FL
407-322-2634

Lockwood Ridge Animal Clinic
Sarasota, FL
941-359-3800

U.S. Emergency Vets > FLORIDA

Palmer Ranch Animal Clinic
Sarasota, FL
941-925-7000

Hernando Animal Hospital
Spring Hill, FL
352-683-6268

Fox & Friends Animal Hospital
Sun City Center, FL
813-633-2443

Sunset Animal Hospital
Sunrise, FL
954-749-9388

Welleby Veterinary Medical Center
Sunrise, FL
954-748-2002

Bradfordville Animal Hospital
Tallahassee, FL
850-893-3047

Animal Clinic of Woodmont
Tamarac, FL
954-726-3647

Clinic for Animals
Tamarac, FL
954-319-3323

Aba Abraam Animal Hospital
Tampa, FL
813-968-9449

Abbott Animal Hospital of Carrollwood
Tampa, FL
813-963-7297

Adventure Animal Hospital
Tampa, FL
813-885-3888

Animal Hospital at Hyde Park
Tampa, FL
813-877-2485

Animal Hospital of Tampa
Tampa, FL
813-971-7711

Avalon Animal Hospital
Tampa, FL
813-232-6261

Busch Animal Hospital
Tampa, FL
813-935-4116

Carrollwood Community Animal Hospital
Tampa, FL
813-962-1010

Connechusett Animal Hospital
Tampa, FL
813-985-1789

Dale Mabry Animal Hospital
Tampa, FL
813-839-6191

Forest Hills Animal Hospital
Tampa, FL
813-961-5810

Gandy Animal Hospital
Tampa, FL
813-839-1285

Kindness Animal Hospital
Tampa, FL
813-971-7668

Murphy Animal Hospital
Tampa, FL
813-879-6090

Northdale Animal Hospital
Tampa, FL
813-962-8862

Oak Tree Animal Hospital
Tampa, FL
813-935-2080

Pebble Creek Animal Hospital
Tampa, FL
813-973-8566

Plantation Animal Hospital Westwood Plaza
Tampa, FL
813-968-3393

Sheldon Road Animal Hospital
Tampa, FL
813-881-0600

Tampa Palms Animal Hospital
Tampa, FL
813-977-4900

Wellswood Midtown Animal Hospital
Tampa, FL
813-877-1979

Woolf Animal Hospital
Tampa, FL
813-877-8002

Garden Street Animal Hospital
Titusville, FL
321-267-4615

Sunrise Animal Hospital
Titusville, FL
321-269-0677

Bloomingdale Animal Hospital
Valrico, FL
813-681-6612

Indian River Animal Hospital
Vero Beach, FL
561-567-4324

Acacia Discount Animal Clinic
West Palm Beach, FL
561-686-9642

Animal Care Clinic of Lake Park
West Palm Beach, FL
561-848-5062

Animal Emergency Clinic of Palm Beach County
West Palm Beach, FL
561-433-2244

Belvedere Academy Animal Hospital
West Palm Beach, FL
561-833-0891

Greenacres Veterinary Clinic
West Palm Beach, FL
561-439-4309

Planco Veterinary Care
West Palm Beach, FL
561-795-9507

Prosperity Animal Clinic
West Palm Beach, FL
561-627-1261

U.S. Emergency Vets > FLORIDA

South Dixie Animal Hospital
West Palm Beach, FL
561-585-0097

Summit Boulevard Animal Hospital
West Palm Beach, FL
561-439-7900

Woodhaven Animal Clinic
West Palm Beach, FL
561-966-3399

Sumter County Animal Hospital
Wildwood, FL
352-748-5508

Mayfair Animal Hospital
Winter Park, FL
407-678-2200

Quail Hollow Animal Hospital
Zephyrhills, FL
813-973-3010

GEORGIA

Adairsville Animal Hospital
Adairsville, GA
770-773-3401

Adel Animal Hospital
Adel, GA
229-896-4517

Liberty Animal Hospital
Albany, GA
912-883-3800

Alpharetta Animal Hospital
Alpharetta, GA
770-475-7613

Atlanta Animal Hospital
Alpharetta, GA
770-475-0600

Country Place Animal Hospital
Alpharetta, GA
770-475-4159

Jones Bridge Animal Hospital
Alpharetta, GA
770-410-0044

Americus Veterinary Hospital
Americus, GA
229-924-6146

Whispering Pines Animal Hospital
Americus, GA
229-924-6054

Ambery Animal Hospital
Atlanta, GA
404-351-5960

Animal Hospital of Sandy Springs Circle
Atlanta, GA
404-255-8522

Chamblee Animal Hospital
Atlanta, GA
770-457-5245

Greenbriar Animal Hospital
Atlanta, GA
404-344-8079

Inman Animal Hospital
Atlanta, GA
404-584-8761

Lenox Animal Hospital & Bird Clinic
Atlanta, GA
404-237-0316

Pharr Road Animal Hospital
Atlanta, GA
404-237-4601

West End Animal Hospital
Atlanta, GA
404-753-1114

Aidmore Animal Clinic
Augusta, GA
706-733-7181

Animal Emergency Clinic of Greater Augusta
Augusta, GA
706-733-7458

Paradise Animal Hospital
Augusta, GA
706-860-4544

Cheek to Cheek Hospital for Animals
Brunswick, GA
912-262-6851

Daniell Veterinary Clinic
Brunswick, GA
912-264-9500

Animal Hospital of North Gwinnett
Buford, GA
770-945-9555

Buford Animal Hospital
Buford, GA
770-945-6757

Sugar Hill Animal Hospital
Buford, GA
770-271-7777

Cairo Animal Hospital
Cairo, GA
229-377-1803

Carrollton Animal Hospital
Carrollton, GA
770-834-6671

Cartersville Animal Hospital
Cartersville, GA
770-382-8570

Cedarcreek Animal Hospital
Cedartown, GA
770-748-7165

King Animal Hospital West
Cedartown, GA
770-748-0173

North Hills Animal Hospital
Chamblee, GA
770-451-6740

Peachtree Animal Hospital
Chamblee, GA
770-457-2591

Dunaire Animal Hospital
Clarkston, GA
404-292-6100

Clermont Veterinary Hospital
Clermont, GA
770-983-7851

College Park Animal Hospital
College Park, GA
404-761-9090

Red Oak Animal Hospital
College Park, GA
404-767-8513

U.S. Emergency Vets > GEORGIA

Crestview Animal Hospital
Cumming, GA
770-889-2521

East Paulding Animal Hospital
Dallas, GA
770-445-7300

Animal Hospital of Whitfield County
Dalton, GA
706-226-3710

Coral Sands Animal Hospital
Decatur, GA
404-289-3178

Columbia Belvedere Animal Hospital
Decatur, GA
404-289-5231

Country Roads Animal Hospital
Decatur, GA
404-289-6570

Dearborn Animal Hospital
Decatur, GA
404-377-6477

Emory Animal Hospital
Decatur, GA
404-633-6163

Lavista Animal Hospital
Decatur, GA
404-325-9924

Wesley Chapel Animal Hospital
Decatur, GA
404-289-0900

Whiteway Animal Hospital
Decatur, GA
404-636-6604

Lindsey & Wills Animal Hospital
Douglas, GA
912-384-8160

Bankhead Animal Hospital
Douglasville, GA
770-942-9077

Douglas County Animal Hospital
Douglasville, GA
770-949-7495

Douglas Oaks Animal Hospital
Douglasville, GA
770-949-6560

Kay Animal Hospital
Douglasville, GA
770-949-7030

Dublin Animal Hospital
Dublin, GA
478-272-7777

Shamrock Veterinary Clinic
Dublin, GA
478-272-4004

Duluth Animal Hospital
Duluth, GA
770-476-3317

Howell Ferry Animal Hospital
Duluth, GA
770-623-1399

Pleasant Hill Animal Hospital
Duluth, GA
770-476-9339

Dunwoody Animal Hospital
Dunwoody, GA
770-394-4030

Tri-City Animal Hospital
East Point, GA
404-766-3661

Calhoun County Animal Hospital
Edison, GA
912-835-2471

Columbia Veterinary Hospital
Evans, GA
706-863-0988

BrownsBridge Animal Hospital
Gainesville, GA
770-536-8831

Gainesville Veterinary Hospital
Gainesville, GA
770-532-0491

South Pointe Animal Hospital
Hephzibah, GA
706-592-2432

Hiram Animal Hospital
Hiram, GA
770-439-1117

Falcon Village Animal Hospital
Lawrenceville, GA
770-962-8326

Killian Hill Animal Hospital
Lilburn, GA
770-921-8558

Lilburn Animal Hospital
Lilburn, GA
770-921-6766

Mountain Park Animal Hospital
Lilburn, GA
770-921-2965

River Cliff Animal Hospital
Lilburn, GA
770-972-6270

AA Animal Hospital
Lithia Springs, GA
770-948-1528

Lithia Springs Animal Hospital
Lithia Springs, GA
770-948-2446

Centerville Animal Hospital
Lithonia, GA
770-979-6015

Deshon Animal Hospital
Lithonia, GA
770-482-7816

Evans Mill Animal Hospital
Lithonia, GA
770-482-5100

Lithonia Animal Hospital
Lithonia, GA
770-482-2966

Animal Emergency Care
Macon, GA
478-750-0911

Cobb Emergency Veterinary Clinic
Marietta, GA
770-424-9157

U.S. Emergency Vets > GEORGIA

Immediate Animal Service
Marietta, GA
770-578-1927

Underwood Veterinary Clinic
Marietta, GA
770-428-3381

Augusta West Veterinary Clinic
Martinez, GA
706-860-6617

Animal Hospital of Milledgeville Ltd.
Milledgeville, GA
478-452-5531

Animal Hospital of Peachtree Parkway
Norcross, GA
770-447-0033

Indian Trail Animal Hospital
Norcross, GA
770-925-4884

Medlock Bridge Animal Hospital
Norcross, GA
770-242-9272

Woods Animal Hospital
Norcross, GA
770-448-6735

Effingham Animal Hospital
Rincon, GA
912-826-5251

Atlanta Animal Emergency Center
Riverdale, GA
770-994-9291

Holcomb Bridge Animal Hospital
Roswell, GA
770-998-8865

Tyler Animal Clinic
Saint Simons Island, GA
912-638-7600

Brookwood Animal Hospital
Snellville, GA
770-979-0089

Gwinnett Animal Hospital
Snellville, GA
770-972-0447

Snellville Animal Hospital
Snellville, GA
770-972-3838

Adel Animal Hospital Emergency
Sparks, GA
229-896-4517

Statesboro Animal Hospital
Statesboro, GA
912-764-6921

Hidden Hills Animal Hospital
Stone Mountain, GA
404-296-3400

Stone Mountain Animal Hospital
Stone Mountain, GA
770-469-6111

Hannahs Mill Animal Hospital
Thomaston, GA
706-647-4164

Thomaston Animal Hospital
Thomaston, GA
706-648-2146

Quailwood Animal Hospital
Tifton, GA
229-386-8794

Currahee Veterinary Clinic
Toccoa, GA
706-886-3803

DeKalb Animal Hospital
Tucker, GA
770-938-3900

Dekalb-Gwinnett Animal Emergency Clinic
Tucker, GA
770-491-0661

Tucker Animal Hospital
Tucker, GA
770-934-5411

Shannon Parkway Animal Hospital
Union City, GA
770-964-1971

Corker's Animal Hospital
Warner Robins, GA
912-929-8287

Gibson Animal Clinic
Waycross, GA
912-285-7678

Holmes Animal Clinic
Waycross, GA
912-285-7044

Winder Animal Hospital
Winder, GA
770-867-9821

Cherokee Animal Hospital
Woodstock, GA
770-924-3720

HAWAII

Aloha Animal Hospital Association
Honolulu, HI
808-734-2242

Blue Cross Animal Hospital
Honolulu, HI
808-593-2532

Companion Animal Hospital
Kailua, HI
808-262-8141

Koolau Animal Hospital
Kaneohe, HI
808-247-3211

Lihue Veterinary Hospital
Lihue, HI
808-245-4961

Makawao Veterinary Clinic
Makawao, HI
808-572-9003

IDAHO

Animal Emergency Clinic
Boise, ID
208-376-4510

Blue Cross Animal Hospital
Burley, ID
208-678-5553

Alpine Animal Hospital
Coeur d'Alene, ID
208-664-2168

Sun Valley Animal Center
Ketchum, ID
208-726-7777

Long Valley Veterinarian Clinic
Mc Call, ID
208-634-2660

Alpine Animal Hospital
Pocatello, ID
208-237-1111

Alta Animal Hospital
Pocatello, ID
208-233-0936

Community Animal Hospital
Pocatello, ID
208-233-6840

Hawthorne Animal Hospital
Pocatello, ID
208-237-1149

Rupert Animal Hospital
Rupert, ID
208-436-9818

ILLINOIS

Berwyn Animal Hospital
Berwyn, IL
708-749-4200

Heritage Animal Hospital
Champaign, IL
217-356-2200

Meadows Animal Hospital
Champaign, IL
217-352-1446

Beverly Hills Animal Hospital
Chicago, IL
773-779-7790

Blum Animal Hospital
Chicago, IL
773-327-4446

Burnham Park Animal Hospital
Chicago, IL
312-663-9200

Family Pet Animal Hospital
Chicago, IL
773-935-2311

Mid-North Animal Hospital
Chicago, IL
773-929-0777

North Avenue Animal Hospital
Chicago, IL
773-278-1330

Fairchild Animal Hospital
Danville, IL
217-442-9009

Deerfield Animal Hospital
Deerfield, IL
847-945-4011

Hawthorne Animal Hospital Ltd.
Edwardsville, IL
618-656-4186

Berglund Animal Hospital
Evanston, IL
847-328-1440

Veterinary Associates
Galena, IL
815-777-0678

Highland Animal Hospital
Highland, IL
708-924-5050

Lincoln Animal Hospital
Lincoln, IL
217-732-1719

Mahomet Animal Hospital
Mahomet, IL
217-586-3176

Monmouth Small Animal Hospital
Monmouth, IL
309-734-5227

County Line Animal Hospital
Naperville, IL
630-983-5551

C.E. Lindley Animal Hospital
Oblong, IL
618-592-3222

Katherine Road Animal Hospital
Quincy, IL
217-222-1982

Rock Falls Animal Hospital
Rock Falls, IL
815-626-4008

St. Joseph Animal Hospital
Saint Joseph, IL
217-469-2220

Prairie Animal Hospital
Savoy, IL
217-351-5814

Brewer Animal Hospital
Springfield, IL
217-787-9730

Coble Animal Hospital
Springfield, IL
217-789-4200

Koke Mill Animal Hospital
Springfield, IL
217-793-9590

White Oaks West Animal Hospital
Springfield, IL
217-698-0280

Bethany Animal Hospital
Sycamore, IL
815-756-8926

Forest South Animal Hospital
University Park, IL
708-672-6166

A & E Animal Hospital
Urbana, IL
217-367-1137

Lipton Animal Hospital
Urbana, IL
217-344-1017

INDIANA

Brownstown Animal Hospital
Brownstown, IN
812-358-2947

Corydon Animal Hospital
Corydon, IN
812-738-8216

Four Seasons Animal Hospital
Crown Point, IN
219-663-8387

U.S. Emergency Vets > INDIANA

Aboite Animal House Call
Ft Wayne, IN
219-432-5525

Stellhorn Veterinary Hospital
Ft Wayne, IN
219-485-2888

Blue Cross Animal Hospital, The
Indianapolis, IN
317-634-3494

East Side Animal Hospital
Indianapolis, IN
317-547-3523

Shadeland Animal Hospital
Indianapolis, IN
317-547-9697

Allison Lane Animal Hospital
Jeffersonville, IN
812-283-4910

Clarksville Animal Hospital
Jeffersonville, IN
812-288-7999

La Porte Animal Hospital
La Porte, IN
219-362-2612

Lanesville Animal Hospital
Lanesville, IN
812-952-3643

Animal Hospital of Logansport
Logansport, IN
219-722-3000

Michigan City Animal Hospital
Michigan City, IN
219-872-4191

Trail Creek Animal Hospital
Michigan City, IN
219-879-8241

U. S. 12 Animal Hospital
Michigan City, IN
219-872-0661

Animal Emergency Clinic
South Bend, IN
219-272-9611

IOWA

All Pets Animal Hospital
Ames, IA
515-233-1756

Rockwood Animal Hospital
Ames, IA
515-232-2881

Highview Animal Hospital
Aplington, IA
319-346-2400

Northside Animal Hospital
Avoca, IA
712-343-2353

Clearview Animal Hospital
Bloomfield, IA
515-664-2399

Animal Hospital
Council Bluffs, IA
712-323-0598

Kimberly Crest Veterinary Hospital
Davenport, IA
319-386-1445

Avondale Animal Hospital
Des Moines, IA
515-262-7297

Bryan Animal Hospital
Des Moines, IA
515-274-3555

City South Animal Hospital
Des Moines, IA
515-285-4114

Eastown Animal Hospital
Des Moines, IA
515-262-1882

Eberle Animal Hospital
Des Moines, IA
515-262-0196

Hubbell Animal Hospital
Des Moines, IA
515-265-4239

Parkview Animal Hospital
Newton, IA
515-792-0340

Riverside Animal Hospital
Oakland, IA
712-482-5511

Ingmand Small Animal Hospital
Red Oak, IA
712-623-3890

Slater Animal Hospital
Slater, IA
515-685-3526

Westwood Animal Hospital
Sloan, IA
712-428-3177

Jordan Creek Animal Hospital
West Des Moines, IA
515-224-9500

KANSAS

Abilene Animal Hospital
Abilene, KS
785-263-2301

Animal Hospital
Columbus, KS
316-429-2902

Town & Country Animal Hospital
Frontenac, KS
316-231-5340

Girard Animal Hospital
Girard, KS
316-724-8054

Junction City Animal Hospital
Junction City, KS
785-238-5513

Welborn Pet Hospital
Kansas City, KS
913-334-6770

Animal Hospital of Old Lawrence
Lawrence, KS
785-842-0609

Bradley Animal Hospital
Lawrence, KS
785-843-9533

Clinton Parkway Animal Hospital
Lawrence, KS
785-841-3131

Liberal Animal Hospital
Liberal, KS
316-624-8461

Broadway Animal Hospital
Pittsburg, KS
316-231-5970

Countryside Animal Hospital
Pittsburg, KS
316-231-3430

Langdon Lane Animal Hospital
Pittsburg, KS
316-232-2410

Animal Hospital
Plainville, KS
785-434-7222

Shawnee Animal Hospital
Topeka, KS
785-272-3244

Bogue Animal Hospital East
Wichita, KS
316-722-1085

KENTUCKY

Berea Animal Hospital
Berea, KY
859-986-9266

Silver Creek Animal Hospital
Berea, KY
859-986-7076

Animal Hospital
Bowling Green, KY
270-781-5606

Simpson County Animal Hospital
Franklin, KY
270-586-4438

Harrodsburg Animal Hospital
Harrodsburg, KY
859-734-5171

Cook Animal Hospital
Lebanon, KY
270-692-6787

AA Small Animal Emergency Clinic
Lexington, KY
859-276-2505

Heritage Animal Hospital
Morgantown, KY
270-526-3839

Animal Hospital of Nicholasville
Nicholasville, KY
859-887-8086

Cumberland Animal Hospital
Russell Springs, KY
270-866-2207

Nashville Road Animal Hospital
Russellville, KY
270-726-2389

Russellville Small Animal Hospital
Russellville, KY
270-726-6098

Somerset Animal Hospital
Somerset, KY
606-679-1266

LOUISIANA

Bradley-Southside Veterinary Hospital
Abbeville, LA
318-893-1953

Animal Emergency Clinic of Baton Rouge
Baton Rouge, LA
225-927-8800

Helouin Veterinary Hospital
Baton Rouge, LA
225-924-2471

Old Hammond Veterinary Hospital
Baton Rouge, LA
225-275-9854

Plank Road Animal Hospital
Baton Rouge, LA
225-355-5676

Animal Hospital-Countryside
Bogalusa, LA
504-732-3131

Chalmette Animal Hospital
Chalmette, LA
504-279-1830

Animal Medical Center
Covington, LA
504-893-1616

Eunice Animal Hospital
Eunice, LA
337-457-2560

Franklin Animal Hospital
Franklin, LA
337-828-1111

Aurora Animal Hospital
Gretna, LA
504-362-8060

Gretna Animal Hospital
Gretna, LA
504-366-1371

Bellevue Road Animal Hospital
Haughton, LA
318-949-2233

Southdown Animal Hospital
Houma, LA
504-876-7138

Jennings Animal Hospital
Jennings, LA
337-824-6551

Airways Animal Hospital
Kenner, LA
504-468-9222

Metairie Small Animal Hospital
Kenner, LA
504-443-4400

Riverlands Animal Hospital
La Place, LA
504-652-6369

Lafayette Animal Emergency Clinic
Lafayette, LA
337-989-0992

Arnolds Animal Hospital
Lake Charles, LA
337-478-5555

Companion Animal Hospital
Lake Charles, LA
337-478-9144

U.S. Emergency Vets > LOUISIANA

Downtown Animal Hospital
Lake Charles, LA
337-439-2321

Lake Area Animal Hospital
Lake Charles, LA
337-479-1199

LakeShore Veterinary Hospital & Pet Lodge
Mandeville, LA
504-626-5615

Mandeville Animal Hospital
Mandeville, LA
504-626-7001

Airline Animal Hospital
Metairie, LA
504-834-4422

Lakeside Animal Hospital
Metairie, LA
504-887-0282

Metairie Small Animal Hospital
Metairie, LA
504-835-4266

Reaux Animal Hospital
New Iberia, LA
337-364-2811

Crowder Animal Hospital
New Orleans, LA
504-241-6633

Hock Animal Hospital
New Orleans, LA
504-525-2827

Animal Emergency Clinic of Shreveport-Bossier
Shreveport, LA
318-227-2345

Southern Hills Animal Hospital
Shreveport, LA
318-686-5945

Gause Boulevard Veterinary Hospital
Slidell, LA
504-641-3922

Slidell Veterinary Hospital
Slidell, LA
504-643-4822

Maplewood Animal Hospital
Sulphur, LA
337-625-2575

Expressway Animal Hospital
Westwego, LA
504-341-4603

MAINE

Bath Animal Hospital
Bath, ME
207-443-9006

Bethel Animal Hospital
Bethel, ME
207-824-2212

North Country Animal Hospital
Caribou, ME
207-492-4651

Chester Animal Hospital
Lincoln, ME
207-794-2706

Westside Animal Hospital
Cumberland Center, ME
207-829-4090

Chester Animal Hospital
Lincoln, ME
207-794-2706

Timberland Animal Hospital
Orono, ME
207-827-7177

Presque Isle Animal Hospital
Presque Isle, ME
207-764-6392

Stoneledge Animal Hospital
Westbrook, ME
207-797-4292

Westbrook Animal Hospital
Westbrook, ME
207-797-4747

Lake Region Animal Hospital
Windham, ME
207-892-7575

MARYLAND

Annapolis Animal Hospital
Annapolis, MD
410-263-4112

Bay Hills Animal Hospital
Annapolis, MD
410-757-1169

Falls Road Animal Hospital
Baltimore, MD
410-825-9100

Bethesda Animal Hospital
Bethesda, MD
301-652-3045

Brandywine Animal Hospital
Clinton, MD
301-782-4444

Indian Head Animal Hospital
Fort Washington, MD
301-899-0382

Crofton Animal Hospital
Gambrills, MD
410-721-2411

Little Seneca Animal Hospital
Germantown, MD
301-540-8670

Glen Burnie Animal Hospital
Glen Burnie, MD
410-761-1500

New Market Animal Hospital
New Market, MD
301-865-3232

Countryside Animal Hospital
Oakland, MD
301-334-9166

Seven Lock Animal Hospital
Potomac, MD
301-299-6900

Benfield Village Veterinarian
Severna Park, MD
410-987-7387

U.S. Emergency Vets > MINNESOTA

Hillandale Animal Hospital
Silver Spring, MD
301-439-9444

**New Hampshire Avenue
Animal Hospital**
Takoma Park, MD
301-270-2050

St. Charles Animal Hospital
Waldorf, MD
301-645-2550

Waldorf Animal Clinic
Waldorf, MD
301-645-2977

**Muddy Creek Animal
Hospital**
West River, MD
410-867-0770

MASSACHUSETTS

Acushnet Animal Hospital
Acushnet, MA
508-998-2148

**Burlington Veterinary
Hospital**
Burlington, MA
781-270-0044

Concord Animal Hospital
Concord, MA
978-369-3503

**Chase Road Animal
Hospital**
Dartmouth, MA
508-984-3477

Goodband Animal Hospital
Dedham, MA
781-329-5333

**Easthampton Animal
Hospital**
Easthampton, MA
413-527-0127

**Leominster Animal
Hospital**
Leominster, MA
978-534-0936

**Nantucket Animal Hospital
Medical Emergencies**
Nantucket, MA
508-228-0407

Pilgrim Animal Hospital
Plymouth, MA
508-746-5003

Plymouth Animal Hospital
Plymouth, MA
508-746-4232

Shirley Animal Clinic
Shirley, MA
978-425-4544

Associates Animal Hospital
Westborough, MA
508-870-0600

MICHIGAN

State Road Animal Hospital
Alma, MI
517-463-6807

Sharp Animal Hospital
Fraser, MI
810-296-0933

Kalamazoo Animal Hospital
Kalamazoo, MI
616-381-1570

**Howard City Animal
Hospital**
Howard City, MI
231-937-4396

**Kalamazoo Animal
Hospital**
Kalamazoo, MI
616-381-1570

Glenpark Animal Hospital
Muskegon, MI
231-755-2205

Roose Animal Hospital
Plymouth, MI
734-451-2870

Clarke Animal Hospital
Spring Lake, MI
231-798-1957

MINNESOTA

Albert Lea Animal Hospital
Albert Lea, MN
507-373-0143

Hilltop Animal Hospital
Bemidji, MN
218-751-5665

Funk Animal Hospital
Brooklyn Park, MN
763-425-3060

Brookdale Animal Hospital
Brooklyn Park, MN
763-560-6906

Elm Creek Animal Hospital
Champlin, MN
763-427-5150

Cloquet Animal Hospital
Cloquet, MN
218-879-9280

**North Cities Animal
Hospital**
Coon Rapids, MN
763-755-3931

**North Shore Veterinary
Clinic**
Duluth, MN
218-525-1937

**Pilot Knob Animal
Hospital**
Eagan, MN
651-452-8160

**Anderson Lakes Animal
Hospital**
Eden Prairie, MN
952-942-5506

Elk River Animal Hospital
Elk River, MN
763-441-5111

Excelsior Animal Hospital
Excelsior, MN
763-474-1106

Brookview Animal Hospital
Golden Valley, MN
763-546-2323

**Golden Valley Animal
Hospital**
Golden Valley, MN
763-544-4286

Southview Animal Hospital
Inver Grove Heights, MN
651-455-2258

**Maple Grove Animal
Hospital**
Maple Grove, MN
763-420-9711

U.S. Emergency Vets > MINNESOTA

Blue Cross Animal Hospital Ltd.
Minneapolis, MN
612-822-2149

Broadway Robbinsdale Animal Hospital
Minneapolis, MN
612-522-4387

Brookdale Animal Hospital
Brooklyn Park, MN
763-560-6906

Diamond Lake Animal Hospital
Minneapolis, MN
612-866-7103

Golden Valley Animal Hospital
Golden Valley, MN
763-544-4286

Lyndale Animal Hospital
Minneapolis, MN
612-872-4674

Northbrook Animal Hospital
Minneapolis, MN
612-560-5320

Glen Lake Animal Hospital
Minnetonka, MN
952-935-1232

Greenbrier Animal Hospital
Minnetonka, MN
763-542-1012

Fargo-Moorhead Animal Hospital
Moorhead, MN
218-236-9059

Westonka Animal Hospital
Mound, MN
952-472-4900

New Hope Animal Hospital
New Hope, MN
763-593-1004

North St. Paul Animal Hospital Ltd.
North Saint Paul, MN
651-777-8391

Northwest Animal Hospital
Plymouth, MN
763-475-2448

Rockford Road Animal Hospital
Plymouth, MN
763-559-7554

Ramsey Animal Hospital
Ramsey, MN
763-323-4838

Apple-Lake Animal Hospital
Rosemont, MN
952-953-4100

Roseville Animal Hospital
Roseville, MN
612-633-4884

St. Cloud Animal Hospital
Saint Cloud, MN
320-251-2494

Arcade Animal Hospital
Saint Paul, MN
651-772-3459

Capitol City Animal Hospital
Saint Paul, MN
651-489-8011

Olin Animal Hospital
Saint Paul, MN
651-774-6063

Roseville Animal Hospital
Roseville, MN
612-633-4884

Scenic Hills Animal Hospital
Saint Paul, MN
651-739-4821

South St. Paul Animal Hospital
Saint Paul, MN
651-455-5897

Shakopee Companion Animal Hospital
Shakopee, MN
952-445-4607

St. Croix Animal Hospital
Stillwater, MN
651-439-1678

Minnetonka Animal Hospital
Wayzata, MN
763-473-1239

Hudson Road Animal Hospital
Woodbury, MN
651-739-0117

Woodbury Animal Hospital
Woodbury, MN
651-738-2000

MISSISSIPPI

Columbia Animal Hospital
Columbia, MS
601-736-3041

Town & Country Animal Hospital
Hattiesburg, MS
601-261-3839

Dunkerron Animal Hospital
Natchez, MS
601-442-7002

Greenbrook Animal Hospital
Southaven, MS
601-342-6100

Southaven Animal Hospital
Southaven, MS
601-393-2417

Vicksburg Animal Hospital
Vicksburg, MS
601-636-8112

MISSOURI

Douglas County Animal Hospital
Ava, MO
417-683-4165

Cass County Animal Hospital
Belton, MO
816-331-6900

Cross Point Animal Hospital
Cape Giradeau, MO
573-334-0070

Carthage Animal Hospital
Carthage, MO
417-358-4914

Westwoods Animal Hospital
Carthage, MO
417-358-9225

U.S. Emergency Vets > NEBRASKA

Mobile Animal Hospital
Cedar Hill, MO
636-274-0410

Chillicothe Animal Hospital
Chillicothe, MO
816-646-3670

Clinton Animal Hospital
Clinton, MO
816-885-4391

Eldon Animal Hospital
Eldon, MO
314-392-1366

**Hermann Companion
Animal Hospital**
Hermann, MO
573-486-3452

Academy Animal Hospital
Joplin, MO
417-781-8681

Animal Hospital Affordable
Joplin, MO
417-782-7387

**Companion Animal
Hospital**
Joplin, MO
417-623-2032

**Cornerstone Animal
Hospital**
Joplin, MO
417-623-3080

Parkview Animal Hospital
Joplin, MO
417-781-0906

Aid Animal Hospital
Kansas City, MO
816-363-4922

**Eastwood Hills Animal
Hospital**
Kansas City, MO
816-861-9393

**Hickman Mills Animal
Hospital**
Kansas City, MO
816-761-2304

**Raytown Gregory Animal
Hospital**
Kansas City, MO
816-353-6681

Small Animal Hospital
Kansas City, MO
816-931-5989

Parkview Animal Hospital
Kirksville, MO
660-665-2719

KK Animal Hospital
Lake Ozark, MO
314-348-1356

Laurie Animal Hospital
Laurie, MO
573-374-5279

Kenbridge Animal Hospital
Lees Summit, MO
816-537-8440

Lees Summit Animal Clinic
Lees Summit, MO
816-524-0464

**Summit Park Animal
Hospital**
Lees Summit, MO
816-524-6666

Bales Animal Hospital
Liberty, MO
816-781-4595

Crossroad Animal Hospital
Liberty, MO
816-781-1510

**Liberty Animal Hospital
& Clinic**
Liberty, MO
816-781-1414

**Lake of The Ozarks Animal
Hospital**
Lin Creek, MO
573-346-5733

Animal Hospital
Neosho, MO
417-451-1556

**Countryside Animal
Hospital**
Nevada, MO
417-667-5013

**All Creatures Animal
Hospital**
O' Fallon, MO
636-240-8387

Dardenne Animal Hospital
O' Fallon, MO
314-625-1800

Osage Animal Hospital
Osage Beach, MO
314-348-1788

St. Charles Animal Hospital
Saint Charles, MO
314-946-1720

City Animal Hospital
Saint Louis, MO
314-645-2141

Hampton Animal Hospital
Saint Louis, MO
314-647-8818

Jefferson Animal Hospital
Saint Louis, MO
314-772-4438

**First Capitol Animal
Hospital**
Saint Peters, MO
314-279-2100

**Murray Lane Animal
Hospital**
Sikeston, MO
573-471-3000

Gardner Animal Hospital
Sumner, MO
816-856-6255

**Putnam County Animal
Hospital**
Unionville, MO
660-947-2015

NEBRASKA

**Beaver Valley Animal
Hospital**
Beaver City, NE
308-268-2405

Midtown Animal Hospital
Gering, NE
308-632-6888

Stanbar Animal Hospital
Imperial, NE
308-882-5234

Riverside Animal Hospital
Kearney, NE
308-234-2617

NEVADA

All Pets Mobile Clinic
Las Vegas, NV
702-382-4292

Animal Emergency Service
Las Vegas, NV
702-457-8050

Fairgrounds Animal Hospital
Reno, NV
775-329-4106

Reno Animal Hospital
Reno, NV
775-323-0100

Sierra View Animal Hospital
Reno, NV
775-825-0913

NEW HAMPSHIRE

Laconia Animal Hospital
Gilford, NH
603-524-0404

Meredith Animal Hospital
Meredith, NH
603-279-8158

Sandwich Animal Hospital
North Sandwich, NH
603-284-6206

Kindness Animal Hospital
Ossipee, NH
603-539-2272

Plymouth Animal Hospital
Plymouth, NH
603-536-1213

Rumney Animal Hospital
Rumney, NH
603-786-9040

NEW JERSEY

Bayonne Animal Hospital
Bayonne, NJ
201-339-0121

**Bernardsville Animal
Hospital**
Bernardsville, NJ
908-766-0041

Millstone Animal Hospital
Clarksburg, NJ
609-259-1955

Emergency Service
Lakewood, NJ
732-363-3200

Kingston Animal Hospital
Kingston, NJ
609-924-7415

Emergency Service
Lakewood, NJ
732-363-3200

Animerge
Raritan, NJ
908-707-9077

**Readington Animal
Hospital**
Readington, NJ
908-534-4059

**Town & Country Animal
Hospital**
Rocky Hill, NJ
609-921-1557

Andover Animal Hospital
Sparta, NJ
973-729-9145

**Quaker Bridge Animal
Hospital**
Trenton, NJ
609-586-7799

NEW MEXICO

**Albuquerque Animal
Emergency**
Albuquerque, NM
505-884-3433

**Emergency Veterinary
Clinic**
Santa Fe, NM
505-984-0625

House Calls for Pets
Santa Fe, NM
505-473-7855

Tucumcari Animal Hospital
Tucumcari, NM
505-461-3900

NEW YORK

**State Street Animal
Hospital**
Batavia, NY
716-344-4974

Paddock Animal Hospital
Bath, NY
607-776-3053

Billings Animal Hospital
Billings, NY
914-223-7054

**Briarcliff Manor Animal
Hospital**
Briarcliff Manor, NY
845-941-4040

Corning Animal Hospital
Corning, NY
607-962-5905

Broadway Animal Hospital
Elmira, NY
607-734-1272

North Shore Animal Hospital
Flushing, NY
718-423-9600

**Adirondack Park Animal
Hospital**
Gloversville, NY
518-725-8911

**East Fishkill Animal
Hospital**
Hopewell Junction, NY
845-221-0695

Hopewell Animal Hospital
Hopewell Junction, NY
845-221-7387

Lake Road Animal Hospital
Horseheads, NY
607-733-6503

**Cardinal Road Animal
Hospital**
Hyde Park, NY
914-229-2724

**Mid-Hudson Animal
Hospital**
Hyde Park, NY
845-229-7117

**Ithaca Small Animal
Hospital**
Ithaca, NY
607-273-3133

Pet Animal Hospital
Jamestown, NY
716-483-1762

U.S. Emergency Vets > NORTH CAROLINA

145th St. Animal Hospital
New York, NY
212-234-3489

Oneida Animal Hospital
Oneida, NY
315-363-1992

Pleasant Valley Animal Hospital
Pleasant Valley, NY
845-635-2110

Potsdam Animal Hospital
Potsdam, NY
315-262-2359

Arlington Animal Hospital
Poughkeepsie, NY
845-473-0301

Rhinebeck Animal Hospital
Rhinebeck, NY
845-876-6008

Glen Animal Hospital The
Watkins Glen, NY
607-535-2544

New Baltimore Animal Hospital
West Coxsackie, NY
518-731-2551

NORTH CAROLINA

Ahoskie Animal Hospital
Ahoskie, NC
252-332-6179

Carteret Animal Hospital
Beaufort, NC
252-728-7600

Animal Hospital
Carrboro, NC
910-967-9261

Veterinary Specialty Hospital
Cary, NC
919-233-4911

Emergency Veterinary Clinic
Charlotte, NC
704-376-9622

Dunn Animal Hospital
Dunn, NC
910-892-6650

St. Francis Animal Hospital
Durham, NC
919-286-2727

Triangle Pets Emergency
Durham, NC
919-489-0615

Lannons Animal Hospital
Elizabeth City, NC
252-335-7708

Veterinarian Emergency Clinic of Gaston County
Gastonia, NC
704-866-7918

Adams Farm Animal Hospital
Greensboro, NC
336-854-5980

Ambassador Animal Hospital
Greensboro, NC
336-379-1227

Americana Animal Hospital
Greensboro, NC
336-273-0555

Carolina Animal Hospital
Greensboro, NC
336-378-1003

Four Seasons Animal Hospital
Greensboro, NC
336-292-6490

Oak Ridge Animal Hospital
Greensboro, NC
336-665-0002

Southwoods Animal Hospital
Greensboro, NC
336-275-7266

Animal Hospital of Pitt County
Greenville, NC
252-756-0148

Tenth Street Animal Hospital
Greenville, NC
252-830-0881

Haywood Animal Hospital
Hendersonville, NC
828-697-0446

Onslow Animal Hospital
Jacksonville, NC
910-347-1219

Academy Animal Hospital
Laurinburg, NC
910-276-6068

Fullwood Animal Hospital
Matthews, NC
704-847-2400

Morehead Animal Hospital
Morehead City, NC
252-726-0181

Paw Creek Animal Hospital
Mount Holly, NC
704-827-7422

Nash County Animal Hospital
Nashville, NC
252-459-4001

North Wayne Animal Hospital
Pikeville, NC
919-242-6044

Brentwood Animal Hospital
Raleigh, NC
919-872-6060

Roanoke Animal Hospital
Roanoke Rapids, NC
252-535-3117

Gandy Animal Hospital
Rockingham, NC
910-997-2518

Roxboro Animal Hospital
Roxboro, NC
336-599-8303

Boulevard Animal Hospital
Shelby, NC
704-482-2508

Moss Lake Animal Hospital
Shelby, NC
704-484-0431

Brigadoon Animal Hospital
Swansboro, NC
252-393-6581

Albemarle Animal Hospital
Tarboro, NC
252-823-1177

U.S. Emergency Vets > NORTH CAROLINA

Animal Emergency Clinic
Troutman, NC
701-528-6486

Countryside Animal Hospital
Wilson, NC
252-243-6952

NORTH DAKOTA

Ellendale Animal Hospital
Ellendale, ND
701-349-3691

Airport Animal Hospital
Fargo, ND
701-293-8888

Jordahl Animal Hospital
Minot, ND
701-852-4744

Pinkerton Animal Hospital
Minot, ND
701-852-3055

West Fargo Animal Hospital
West Fargo, ND
701-282-2898

OHIO

Celina Animal Hospital
Celina, OH
419-586-3109

Lakeview Animal Hospital
Celina, OH
419-394-2464

Oak Hills Animal Hospital
Cincinnati, OH
513-451-0027

Conneaut Animal Hospital
Conneaut, OH
440-599-8142

Defiance Area Animal Hospital
Defiance, OH
419-782-0166

Horizon Animal Hospital
Galion, OH
419-468-2169

Firelands Animal Hospital
Huron, OH
419-433-6210

Ontario Animal Hospital
Mansfield, OH
419-529-5052

Harborview Animal Hospital
Port Clinton, OH
419-734-5493

Shoreway Animal Hospital
Sandusky, OH
419-626-5564

Five Points Animal Hospital
Sardinia, OH
937-446-3529

Miami Acres Animal Hospital
Troy, OH
937-335-2444

Troy Animal Hospital
Troy, OH
937-335-8387

Cedarside Animal Hospital
Wakeman, OH
440-965-4660

Cloverleaf Animal Hospital
Westfield, OH
330-948-2002

OKLAHOMA

Bethany Animal Hospital
Bethany, OK
405-787-1222

Avalon Veterinary Hospital
Broken Arrow, OK
918-258-9569

Broken Bow Animal Hospital
Broken Bow, OK
580-584-9101

Green Country Animal Hospital
Chouteau, OK
918-476-8371

Durant Animal Hospital
Durant, OK
580-924-1640

Woodland Trails Animal Hospital
Edmond, OK
405-340-9395

El Reno Animal Hospital
El Reno, OK
405-262-7728

Western Animal Hospital
Elk City, OK
405-225-0060

Southwest Animal Hospital
Geary, OK
405-884-2916

Gore West Animal Hospital
Lawton, OK
580-536-2233

Meadow Wood Animal Hospital
Lawton, OK
580-353-0344

Midtown Animal Hospital
Lawton, OK
580-353-3438

Silverleaf Animal Hospital
Moore, OK
405-794-7771

Air Depot Animal Hospital
Oklahoma City, OK
405-737-0496

Baja Metro Animal Hospital
Oklahoma City, OK
405-634-6313

Crestwood Animal Hospital
Oklahoma City, OK
405-721-9276

Grant Square Animal Hospital
Oklahoma City, OK
405-685-0131

Leighton Animal Hospital
Oklahoma City, OK
405-848-3131

Northwest Animal Hospital
Oklahoma City, OK
405-789-3644

Putnam North Animal Hospital
Oklahoma City, OK
405-722-4777

Rock Knoll Animal Hospital
Oklahoma City, OK
405-634-5700

U.S. Emergency Vets > PENNSYLVANIA

Shamrock Animal Hospital
Oklahoma City, OK
405-843-9486

Village Animal Hospital
Oklahoma City, OK
405-751-1437

Warwick Animal Hospital
Oklahoma City, OK
405-722-7717

Pryor Veterinary Hospital
Pryor, OK
918-815-1717

**Ellis County Animal
Hospital**
Shattuck, OK
580-938-2962

Animal Hospital Clinic
Sulphur, OK
580-622-2018

**Companion Animal
Hospital**
Tulsa, OK
918-747-2552

Major Animal Hospital
Watonga, OK
580-623-5703

**Animal Hospital of
Weatherford**
Weatherford, OK
580-772-2276

OREGON

Albany Animal Hospital
Albany, OR
541-926-8817

Astoria Animal Hospital
Astoria, OR
503-325-1581

Hart Road Animal Hospital
Beaverton, OR
503-591-5282

Carlton Veterinary Hospital
Carlton, OR
503-852-7009

Village Vet Animal Hospital
Clackamas, OR
503-658-4200

Hanson Animal Hospital
Coos Bay, OR
541-269-2415

Mobile Animal Hospital
Coquille, OR
541-269-1922

Coquille Animal Hospital
Coquille, OR
541-396-2226

Mobile Animal Hospital
Coquille, OR
541-269-1922

Blue Cross Animal Hospital
Eugene, OR
541-726-7821

Bush Animal Hospital
Eugene, OR
541-342-7218

Eugene Animal Hospital
Eugene, OR
541-342-1178

**West Eugene Animal
Hospital**
Eugene, OR
541-342-5858

**Westmoreland Animal
Hospital**
Eugene, OR
541-485-4595

Rockwood Animal Hospital
Portland, OR
503-665-1194

Lakeview Animal Hospital
Lakeview, OR
541-947-3383

Jackson Animal Hospital
Medford, OR
541-779-4893

Chehalem Animal Clinic
Newberg, OR
503-538-8334

Newberg Veterinary Hospital
Newberg, OR
503-538-8303

**Harbor Lights Animal
Hospital**
North Bend, OR
541-756-5156

Lombard Animal Hospital
Portland, OR
503-285-2337

Rockwood Animal Hospital
Portland, OR
503-665-1194

**S.E. Portland Animal
Hospital**
Portland, OR
503-255-8139

**Town and Country Animal
Hospital**
Portland, OR
503-761-2330

Wildwood Animal Hospital
Portland, OR
503-665-1126

Cascade Animal Hospital
Springfield, OR
541-741-1992

**Best Friends Animal
Hospital**
Talent, OR
541-535-8187

Sorrento Animal Hospital
Tigard, OR
503-524-5029

**Reigning Cats & Dogs-
Small Animal Hospital**
Tillamook, OR
503-842-2322

PENNSYLVANIA

Abington Animal Hospital
Abington, PA
215-659-0106

Alburtis Animal Hospital
Alburtis, PA
610-967-7387

**Lehigh Valley Animal
Hospital**
Allentown, PA
610-395-0328

Walberts Animal Hospital
Allentown, PA
610-434-7469

Exeter Animal Hospital
Birdsboro, PA
610-582-2593

U.S. Emergency Vets > PENNSYLVANIA

Deer Creek Animal Hospital
Butler, PA
724-282-0006

Hillmount Animal Hospital
Carlisle, PA
717-249-7272

Blue Cross Animal Hospital
Clarks Summit, PA
570-587-4025

Columbia Animal Hospital
Columbia, PA
717-684-2285

Easton Animal Hospital
Easton, PA
610-252-8276

William Penn Animal Hospital
Easton, PA
610-252-3222

Elizabethtown Area Animal Hospital
Elizabethtown, PA
717-367-7156

Emmaus Animal Hospital
Emmaus, PA
610-967-1512

Erie Animal Hospital
Erie, PA
814-838-7638

Wintergreen Animal Hospital
Erie, PA
814-825-6735

Gettysburg Animal Hospital
Gettysburg, PA
717-334-2177

All Pet Animal Hospital
Gibsonia, PA
724-444-6600

Home Town Animal Hospital
Hallstead, PA
570-879-2157

Saucon Valley Animal Hospital
Hellertown, PA
610-838-6644

Prothero Animal Hospital
Johnstown, PA
814-536-5105

Hempfield Animal Hospital
Lancaster, PA
717-285-7946

West Lancaster Animal Hospital
Lancaster, PA
717-394-7713

Landisville Animal Hospital
Landisville, PA
717-898-1721

Lebanon Valley Animal Hospital
Lebanon, PA
717-272-2515

Lehighton Animal Hospital
Lehighton, PA
610-377-5574

Manheim Animal Hospital
Manheim, PA
717-665-5465

Borderbrook Animal Hospital
Murrysville, PA
724-327-2200

Narberth Animal Hospital
Narberth, PA
610-664-4114

North East Animal Hospital
North East, PA
814-725-8836

Meadow Brook Animal Hospital
Ottsville, PA
610-847-2776

Perkiomen Animal Hospital
Palm, PA
215-679-7019

Bainbridge Animal Hospital
Philadelphia, PA
215-922-3400

Castor Animal Hospital
Philadelphia, PA
215-722-4100

Noahs Ark Animal Hospital
Philadelphia, PA
215-624-7766

Philadelphia Animal Hospital
Philadelphia, PA
215-724-5550

Queen Village Animal Hospital
Philadelphia, PA
215-925-5753

Roxborough Animal Hospital
Philadelphia, PA
215-482-3037

West Park Animal Hospital
Philadelphia, PA
215-879-8005

Schenley Park Animal Hospital
Pittsburgh, PA
412-683-3455

Pocono Lake Animal Hospital
Pocono Lake, PA
570-646-2693

Deer Creek Animal Hospital
Butler, PA
724-282-0006

Springfield Animal Hospital
Springfield, PA
610-543-5553

Metzger Animal Hospital
State College, PA
814-237-5333

Cherryville Animal Hospital
Walnutport, PA
610-767-7505

Wyomissing Animal Hospital
Wyomissing, PA
610-372-2121

RHODE ISLAND

Rhode Island Veterinary Mobile
Providence, RI
401-751-7557

West Bay Animal Hospital
Warwick, RI
401-828-5767

Turco Animal Hospital
Westerly, RI
401-596-8910

SOUTH CAROLINA

Aimant Animal Hospital
Beaufort, SC
843-525-6655

Animal Hospital of Beaufort
Beaufort, SC
843-524-2224

Holly Hall Animal Hospital
Beaufort, SC
843-524-4551

Wateree Animal Hospital
Camden, SC
803-432-9084

Clemson Animal Hospital
Clemson, SC
864-654-4204

Palmetto Animal Hospital
Conway, SC
843-347-1144

Denmark Animal Hospital
Denmark, SC
843-793-3800

Dillon Animal Hospital
Dillon, SC
843-774-8361

Westview Animal Hospital
Georgetown, SC
843-546-3821

Hutto Animal Hospital
Holly Hill, SC
803-496-5037

Johnston Animal Hospital
Johnston, SC
803-275-4652

Lancaster Animal Hospital
Lancaster, SC
803-286-4600

Greater Charleston Emergency Veterinary Clinic
North Charleston, SC
843-744-3372

Edisto Animal Hospital
Orangeburg, SC
803-533-0153

Thompson Animal Hospital
Orangeburg, SC
803-536-1284

Chappells Animal Hospital
Rock Hill, SC
803-324-4271

Lesslie Animal Hospital
Rock Hill, SC
803-328-9225

Rock Hill Animal Hospital
Rock Hill, SC
803-324-7585

Santee Animal Hospital
Santee, SC
803-854-3351

Animal Hospital
Seneca, SC
803-882-8747

TENNESSEE

Adamsville Animal Hospital
Adamsville, TN
901-632-4050

Animal Hospital
Clarksville, TN
615-484-5521

Town & Country Animal Hospital
Dandridge, TN
865-397-0200

South Water Animal Hospital
Gallatin, TN
615-452-8870

Rivergate Pet Emergency Clinic
Goodlettsville, TN
615-859-3778

Brookfield Animal Hospital
Greeneville, TN
423-639-9594

Crestview Animal Hospital
Greeneville, TN
423-639-1421

Duckworth Animal Hospital
Greeneville, TN
423-638-5382

Vet Care Animal Hospital
Greeneville, TN
423-638-2273

Lakeway Animal Hospital
Jefferson City, TN
865-475-4786

Town & Country Animal Hospital
Jefferson City, TN
865-475-2000

Mountain Empire Animal Hospital
Johnson City, TN
423-282-3771

Robinson Animal Hospital
Johnson City, TN
423-928-1616

Youngs Animal Hospital
Johnson City, TN
423-926-3878

Jonesboro Animal Hospital
Jonesborough, TN
423-753-5868

Allandale Animal Hospital
Kingsport, TN
423-246-3041

Colonial Heights Animal Hospital
Kingsport, TN
423-239-5116

Indian Ridge Animal Hospital
Kingsport, TN
423-378-4753

Loudon County Animal Hospital
Lenoir City, TN
865-986-9075

U.S. Emergency Vets > TENNESSEE

Companion Animal Hospital
Lewisburg, TN
931-359-6376

Town & Country Animal Hospital
Mc Minnville, TN
615-668-5151

All Metro Animal Hospital
Memphis, TN
901-385-0477

Berclair Animal Hospital
Memphis, TN
901-685-8204

Greene Veterinary Clinic
Memphis, TN
901-452-3171

Memphis Animal Clinic
Memphis, TN
901-272-7411

Animal Hospital
Morristown, TN
423-586-0311

Appalachian Animal Hospital
Morristown, TN
423-587-4393

Morristown Animal Hospital
Morristown, TN
423-586-2740

Ridgefield Animal Hospital
Morristown, TN
423-581-3955

Williams Animal Hospital
Murfreesboro, TN
615-895-0650

Richland Animal Clinic
Nashville, TN
615-356-6534

West Meade Veterinary Clinic
Nashville, TN
615-356-1152

Mcarthur Animal Hospital
Oak Ridge, TN
865-482-1797

Portland Animal Hospital
Portland, TN
615-325-6453

Giles County Animal Hospital
Pulaski, TN
931-363-7971

Roan Mountain Animal Hospital
Roan Mountain, TN
423-772-4124

Parkway Animal Hospital
Sevierville, TN
865-428-0190

Nisbetts Animal Hospital
Tullahoma, TN
931-455-4468

TEXAS

Silsbee Animal Hospital
Addison, TX
214-385-6588

Vogt Animal Hospital Mobile Phone
Arlington, TX
817-275-6225

East Texas Emergency Medical Service
Athens, TX
903-675-8601

Brodie Animal Hospital
Austin, TX
512-892-3486

Burnet Road Animal Hospital
Austin, TX
512-452-7606

Century Animal Hospital
Austin, TX
512-442-9518

Hill Country Animal Hospital
Austin, TX
512-329-5177

Manchaca Road Animal Hospital
Austin, TX
512-442-6744

South Lamar Animal Hospital
Austin, TX
512-441-3192

Westlake Animal Hospital
Austin, TX
512-327-1703

Baytown Animal Hospital
Baytown, TX
281-424-5575

Massey Animal Hospital
Beaumont, TX
409-866-2002

Highland Animal Hospital of Big Spring
Big Spring, TX
915-267-8291

Bridge City Animal Hospital
Bridge City, TX
409-735-8107

Southwood Valley Animal Hospital
College Station, TX
979-693-9898

Shelterwood Animal Hospital
Carthage, TX
903-693-6411

Southwood Valley Animal Hospital
College Station, TX
979-693-9898

Animal Hospital of Conroe
Conroe, TX
936-756-7761

North Loop Animal Hospital
Conroe, TX
936-756-7007

Pets Paw Animal Hospital
Conroe, TX
936-756-0304

Carroll & Harper Animal Hospital
Corsicana, TX
903-872-4686

U.S. Emergency Vets > UTAH

Rogers Animal Hospital
Corsicana, TX
936-872-6655

South Pine Animal Hospital
Crockett, TX
936-544-8788

Knox Park Animal Hospital
Dallas, TX
214-521-7660

De Soto Animal Hospital
De Soto, TX
972-223-4840

Dumas Animal Hospital
Dumas, TX
806-935-5114

Las Aguilas Animal Hospital
Eagle Pass, TX
830-773-7854

Handley Animal Hospital
Fort Worth, TX
817-451-5592

Lake Palestine Animal Hospital
Frankston, TX
903-876-4848

Arroyo Animal Hospital
Harlingen, TX
956-428-4002

183 Animal Hospital
Irving, TX
972-579-0115

Leifeste Animal Hospital
Kerrville, TX
830-896-4600

Dixie Drive Animal Hospital
Lake Jackson, TX
979-297-5299

Kimbrough Animal Hospital
Longview, TX
903-757-5543

South Green Animal Hospital
Longview, TX
903-757-8801

West Loop Animal Hospital
Longview, TX
903-759-6604

Marshall Animal Hospital
Marshall, TX
903-938-3082

McAllen Animal Hospital
McAllen, TX
956-682-4191

Bruechner Animal Hospital
Mount Pleasant, TX
903-572-8786

Lake Country Animal Hospital
Montgomery, TX
936-588-1141

Animal Hospital of Paris
Paris, TX
903-785-7606

Animal Hospital of Port Arthur
Port Arthur, TX
409-982-5213

Porter Animal Hospital
Porter, TX
281-354-8099

Ridge Road Animal Hospital
Rockwall, TX
972-771-1113

Acres North Animal Hospital
San Antonio, TX
210-494-3436

West Avenue Animal Hospital
San Antonio, TX
210-342-2611

San Benito Animal Hospital
San Benito, TX
956-399-3221

Tickle-Blagg Animal Hospital
San Marcos, TX
512-353-1871

Sanger Animal Hospital
Sanger, TX
940-458-7488

Seguin Animal Hospital
Seguin, TX
830-379-3821

Diamond W Animal Hospital
Southlake, TX
817-379-7330

Swaim Animal Hospital
Temple, TX
817-773-5195

Animal Hospital
Tulia, TX
806-995-3013

Copeland Road Animal Hospital
Tyler, TX
903-509-3454

Border Animal Hospital
Weslaco, TX
956-968-3858

Rannals Small Animal Hospital Rescue
Whitehouse, TX
903-839-7235

Stuckey Animal Hospital
Whitesboro, TX
903-564-5926

Willis Animal Hospital
Willis, TX
936-856-7387

UTAH

Blue Mountain Veterinary Services
Blanding, UT
435-678-2414

Bountiful Small Animal Hospital
Bountiful, UT
801-295-0733

Southern Utah Animal Hospital
Cedar City, UT
435-586-6216

Hurricane Animal Hospital
Hurricane, UT
435-635-7387

Moab Veterinary Clinic
Moab, UT
435-259-8710

U.S. Emergency Vets > UTAH

Johnston Animal Hospital
Ogden, UT
801-393-7387

North Ogden Animal Hospital
Ogden, UT
801-782-4401

VERMONT

Country Animal Hospital
Bethel, VT
802-234-5999

Fair Haven Animal Hospital
Fair Haven, VT
802-265-3822

Onion River Animal Hospital
Montpelier, VT
802-223-7765

Randolph Animal Hospital
Randolph, VT
802-728-3266

Rutland Small Animal Hospital
Rutland, VT
802-775-5050

Westminster Animal Hospital
Westminster, VT
802-722-4196

White River Animal Hospital
White River Junction, VT
802-295-6900

VIRGINIA

Highlands Animal Hospital
Abingdon, VA
540-628-4115

Beacon Hill Animal Hospital
Alexandria, VA
703-765-6369

Kingstowne Cat Clinic
Alexandria, VA
703-922-8228

Amelia Emergency Squad
Amelia Court House, VA
804-561-3336

Kingdom Animal Hospital
Clear Brook, VA
540-665-3030

Intervale Animal Hospital
Covington, VA
540-962-0756

Blue Ridge Animal Hospital
Culpeper, VA
540-825-8353

Dale City Animal Hospital
Dale City, VA
703-670-6181

Montclair Animal Hospital
Dumfries, VA
703-878-3442

Marion Animal Hospital
Fishersville, VA
540-949-0161

Confederate Ridge Animal Hospital
Fredericksburg, VA
540-373-6100

Fredericksburg Animal Hospital
Fredericksburg, VA
540-373-6512

Potomac Ridge Animal Hospital
King George, VA
540-775-3777

Southside Animal Hospital
Manassas, VA
703-368-8284

Hanover Animal Hospital
Mechanicsville, VA
804-746-4936

Swift Creek Animal Hospital
Midlothian, VA
804-744-7222

Baldwin Creek Animal Hospital
Moseley, VA
804-739-2933

Elam Animal Hospital
Powhatan, VA
804-794-4105

Powhatan Animal Hospital
Powhatan, VA
804-598-3168

New Kent Animal Hospital
Quinton, VA
804-932-9170

Allied Animal Hospital
Richmond, VA
804-672-7200

Ambassador Animal Hospital
Richmond, VA
804-282-4215

Bon Air Animal Hospital
Richmond, VA
804-276-5554

Courthouse Road Animal Hospital
Richmond, VA
804-745-2323

Gayton Animal Hospital
Richmond, VA
804-741-0144

Lakeside Animal Hospital
Richmond, VA
804-262-8697

Pets First Animal Hospital
Richmond, VA
804-672-3576

Salem Animal Hospital
Salem, VA
540-380-4638

Spotsylvania Animal Hospital
Spotsylvania, VA
540-582-6370

Stafford Animal Hospital
Stafford, VA
540-659-3811

Valley Animal Hospital
Staunton, VA
540-885-8985

Westwood Animal Hospital
Staunton, VA
540-337-6200

First Aid Crew Emergency
Waynesboro, VA
540-949-7118

U.S. Emergency Vets > WISCONSIN

Lake-Dale-Wood Animal Hospital
Woodbridge, VA
703-491-1600

Minnieville Animal Hospital
Woodbridge, VA
703-680-4000

Ridge Lake Animal Hospital
Woodbridge, VA
703-491-1111

WASHINGTON

Belfair Animal Hospital
Belfair, WA
360-275-6008

Northshore Veterinary Hospital
Bellingham, WA
360-738-6916

Blaine Animal Hospital
Blaine, WA
360-332-6813

Mt. Stuart Animal Hospital
Cle Elum, WA
509-674-2154

Glacierview Animal Hospital
Ferndale, WA
360-384-4482

Riverside Animal Hospital
Kelso, WA
360-577-1093

McMillin Animal Hospital
Orting, WA
253-770-7170

Sequim Animal Hospital
Sequim, WA
360-683-7286

Clearview Animal Hospital
Snohomish, WA
360-668-3005

Cascade Park Animal Hospital
Vancouver, WA
360-892-2122

Hazel Dell Animal Hospital
Vancouver, WA
360-693-8968

Camas-Washougal Animal Hospital
Washougal, WA
360-835-7240

WEST VIRGINIA

Glendale Animal Hospital
Glen Dale, WV
304-845-5454

Martinsburg Animal Hospital
Martinsburg, WV
304-267-7468

Cheat Lake Animal Hospital
Morgantown, WV
304-594-1124

Vienna Small Animal Hospital
Vienna, WV
304-295-4521

WISCONSIN

Prairie Animal Hospital
Beloit, WI
608-365-7400

Meyer Animal Hospital
Brookfield, WI
262-781-7144

Cazenovia Animal Hospital
Cazenovia, WI
608-983-2686

Animal Hospital of De Pere
De Pere, WI
920-336-5774

Denmark Animal Hospital
Denmark, WI
920-863-2184

Eagle River Animal Hospital
Eagle River, WI
715-479-7090

Animal Hospital of Howard
Green Bay, WI
920-434-1010

Downey Animal Hospital
Green Bay, WI
920-437-2756

Heritage Animal Hospital
Greenville, WI
920-757-0407

Whitnall Small Animal Hospital
Hales Corners, WI
414-425-9666

Heritage Animal Hospital
Hortonville, WI
920-779-4343

Countryside Animal Hospital
Merrill, WI
715-536-8557

Brown Deer Animal Hospital
Milwaukee, WI
414-355-2603

Capitol Drive Animal Hospital
Milwaukee, WI
414-462-2990

Crawford Animal Hospital
Milwaukee, WI
414-543-3499

Lakeside Animal Hospital
Milwaukee, WI
414-962-8040

Layton Animal Hospital
Milwaukee, WI
414-281-8270

Milwaukee Animal Hospital
Milwaukee, WI
414-545-5100

Shorewood Animal Hospital
Milwaukee, WI
414-962-6662

St. Francis Animal Hospital
Milwaukee, WI
414-744-2240

West Allis Animal Hospital
Milwaukee, WI
414-476-3544

U.S. Emergency Vets > WYOMING

Hometown Animal Hospital
Niagara, WI
715-589-2305

Brentwood Animal Hospital
Oak Creek, WI
414-762-7173

Omro Animal Hospital
Omro, WI
920-685-5516

Poynette Animal Hospital
Poynette, WI
608-635-7037

Sheboygan Animal Hospital
Sheboygan, WI
920-452-2882

Animal Hospital of Verona
Verona, WI
608-845-6700

Marathon Animal Hospital
Wausau, WI
715-845-1919

WYOMING

Alpine Animal Hospital
Laramie, WY
307-745-7341

You are more than a member...
you're family!

Members of the Super 8® V.I.P. Club family always enjoy:

- **10% discount off the regular room rate** at all Super 8 motel locations.*
- **Guaranteed express reservations** made through the Superline® reservation number (1-800-800-8000) are held until check-out time the following day without a credit card number.
- **Payment of room charges by check** for each night's lodging, **plus** the check cashing privilege of one $50 check per each night stayed.
- **Express check-in** makes checking in quick and easy.
- **Car rental discounts** good only at participating car rental locations. Not valid in conjunction with any other contracted auto rental discount.

For complete details or an application, ask at the front desk of any Super 8 or visit our website at *www.super8.com*

*Some obligations and restrictions do apply. Pets are welcome at participating locations.
Each Super 8 Motel is independently owned and operated under franchise agreement with Super 8 Motels, Inc.

"Affordable Excellence"

15% Discount

Honored at any Pet Friendly *Shilo Inn.*

One coupon per night
(Not valid with any other offer)
Offer expires December 30, 2002.

Present this form at the front desk upon registation. Offer valid 1st night only.

Toll Free (800) 222-2244 • www.shiloinns.com